Other Avon Books by
Carol McD. Wallace

20,001 NAMES FOR BABY
(revised and updated)

THE GREATEST BABY NAME BOOK EVER

Revised and updated

CAROL McD. WALLACE

AVON BOOKS
An Imprint of HarperCollinsPublishers

AVON BOOKS
An Imprint of HarperCollins*Publishers*
10 East 53rd Street
New York, New York 10022-5299

Copyright © 1992, 1998, 2004 by Carol McD. Wallace
ISBN: 0-06-056649-3
www.avonbooks.com

First Avon Books paperback printing: August 2004

Avon Trademark Reg. U.S. Pat. Off. and in Other Countries, Marca Registrada, Hecho en U.S.A.
HarperCollins® is a registered trademark of HarperCollins Publishers Inc.

Printed in the U.S.A.

10 9 8 7 6 5 4 3 2

My heartfelt thanks go to my agent, Lynn Seligman, who long ago urged me to write this book; to Rick, for his eternal patience; and to Sarah Durand at Avon Books, who sets new standards for cheerful efficiency.

I am also grateful to the researchers in this field whose work I leaned on, notably Leslie Dunkling and William Gosling, authors of *The Facts on File Dictionary of First Names*, and Connie Lockhart Ellefson, author of *The Melting Pot Book of Baby Names*. Finally, the Social Security Administration keeps fascinating records of recent fashions in American baby names which I consulted frequently in compiling this book.

ontents

bbreviations

Af	African	*Masc*	masculine
Arab	Arabian	*ME*	Middle English
Celt	Celtic	*MF*	Middle French
comb form	combining form	*Nig*	Nigerian
Czech	Czechoslovakian	*NAm Ind*	North American Indian
Dan	Danish	*Nor*	Norwegian
Dim	diminutive	*OE*	Old English
Egypt	Egyptian	*OF*	Old French
Eng	English	*OG*	Old German
Fem	feminine	*ONorse*	Old Norse
Fr	French	*OWelsh*	Old Welsh
Gael	Gaelic	*Per*	Persian
Ger	German	*Pol*	Polish
Gk	Greek	*Port*	Portuguese
Haw	Hawaiian	*Rus*	Russian
Heb	Hebrew	*Scand*	Scandinavian
Hung	Hungarian	*Scot*	Scottish
Ir	Irish	*Sp*	Spanish
It	Italian	*Swed*	Swedish
Jap	Japanese	*Teut*	Teutonic
Lat	Latin	*Var*	variant
		Viet	Vietnamese

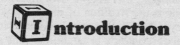

Introduction

My elder son got a hamster for his tenth birthday. Before we left the store, he insisted that somebody tell him the gender of his new pet, which was quite a production as only one member of the staff knew how to figure this out, and she was selling somebody a whole tank of goldfish. I couldn't fathom why this was so important to Will, since we had no intention of breeding hamsters, but he looked at me as if I were completely dense and said, "Mom, how can I name it unless I know if it's a boy or a girl?"

Actually, I *was* being dense. Of course he had to name it—her, actually. This was how the hamster became not just one of many squirmy furry handfuls in a cage, but his own pet: Bonnie. (Named after his assistant teacher, who claimed to be honored.) Bonnie, who has her own little rodent personality. The one and only Bonnie-the-hamster.

Names are hugely important. Every culture in the world acknowledges this with ceremonies and traditions. In China you grow through names as your circumstances change: Your "milk" name changes to your "book" name when you enter school, for instance. Some African cultures give long genealogical names, while others give names invoking certain deities. Catholic children traditionally take an additional saint's name when they are confirmed. Some Muslims believe that angels pray in houses where men named Muhammad or Ahmad live, making these names hugely popular wherever Islam predominates.

AMERICAN NAMES

Here in America, we have our own traditions. The most important one is the tradition of inventing yourself. This is the country, after all, that people come to in order to be something they couldn't be at home. American names have often reflected that freedom. Our names are full of aspiration and potential. Some cultures give names that reflect history, but Americans tend to look forward rather than back. Maybe in the old country (Greece or Italy, for instance), a baby boy is named after his paternal grandfather, but in the U.S.A. this child might be known as— Clint, for instance. You can go anywhere with a name like Clint.

Assimilation names have been the rule for a long time. This may be a melting pot, but the predominant culture is Anglo, and for generations fitting in has meant giving or choosing an English-style name: Isaac instead of Yitzhak, Joan instead of Siobhan. Times are changing, though. Yes, the names at the top of all the charts are basically English. But the names in the next tier down may not be. For girls, the Gaelic Caitlin, Scandinavian Kristen, and French Danielle are hugely popular. Not because of any huge Gaelic or Scandinavian swell in immigration, but because at this moment parents like the way these names sound.

There are two reasons for the exotic nature of many popular names. One, of course, *is* immigration, which is changing the face of parts of America that used to be homogeneous. Attitudes toward it are changing, too: Newcomers to the U.S. increasingly take pride in their background and reflect that pride when naming their children. Americans who have been here for a generation or two are also turning to their roots to find inspiration for their children's names. An Italian-American Mark may name his son Marco, for instance.

A related factor is the phenomenal pace of communications nowadays. Long ago, for most folks, the pool of names was very small. You could name a child for yourself, for your parents, for somebody you knew, maybe for some Biblical character. Those would be all the names you had ever heard. It would never occur to a farmer in eighteenth-century Massachusetts, for example, to name a child Marco. At the turn of the century, 50 percent of American children were given one of the top-ten names for their gender. I was born in 1955 and given a very fashionable name, Carol. Throughout my life I have generally been one of three or four Carols in any gathering of a few dozen people. But this kind of intense use doesn't happen as much any more, except perhaps in tightly knit communities.

Nowadays, the top-ten names account for only 25 percent of children. Another researcher put it this way: In 1990, a little more than 3 percent of American boys were named Michael, which was then the number-one name for boys. That's one in every thirty-one boys. Looking at the class lists of my sons' school, I see a few names (Dylan, Alexandra) repeated more regularly than others, but they are the exception. Startling variety is the rule.

Fashionable names also spread much more quickly now than they used to. Madison is one of the top girls' names on 2002 popularity lists; ten years ago, it wasn't even in the top fifty. As people across the country are linked by computers, as they watch TV or read magazines, notions about names spread like wildfire. A Santa Monica mom on a parenting website can suggest that Cameo is a nifty name for a baby girl, and within days babies in Kansas, Florida, and Ohio are introduced to their grandparents as Cameo.

WHAT DO PARENTS WANT?

Long ago, the meaning of a name was important: The Puritans named their daughters after virtues such as Silence and Temperance. In some cultures this is still true, but in the U.S., meaning is secondary. How else can you account for the popularity of Brendan, which seems to mean "stinking hair"? General cultural associations are more important. Names like Ethel or Seymour that remind parents of elderly relatives, for instance, are barely seen. (The name Hillary seemed to be surging toward popularity until the election of President Clinton, then dropped out of sight. Apparently few parents were willing to have it thought that they were naming a child after the controversial Hillary Clinton.)

But the majority of today's popular names haven't been used often enough to carry any real associative baggage. Parents are choosing them primarily for the sound. The hugely popular name Caitlin, for example, is one of a cluster of related names that are also frequently used: Kaylin, Kathlyn, Kayleigh, Hayleigh, Hallie, Kelly, Katie. For boys, the fashion is less clearly defined, but names that begin with "J" and names that end in "-in" are stylish. What's more, parents are very ready to simply make names up. Does anybody have a grandmother named Brianna?

Of course parents are much more conservative when it comes to boys' names. The top names for boys tend to be more familiar and certain neutral classics—like David, Michael, and Andrew—that have been steadily used for years. For girls, parents are more likely to use a noun (Diamond, Rosemary), adapt spelling (Brittney), or borrow a formerly male name (Madison, Tyler, Mackenzie). I think we're all aiming for more or less the same thing: a name that is unusual without being downright weird.

There are exceptions, of course. Many parents still choose to honor a living relative or the memory of a deceased person by naming a child for them. Chances are when you meet a kindergartner with a frankly unfashionable name like Norma, that's probably how the choice was made. There are also parents who revel in flouting convention, and they may pick retro-cool names like Buster. But most of the time, most of us would like a name that is somewhat familiar, but still individual.

SO HOW DO YOU CHOOSE?

There are a lot of possibilities out there: There are tens of thousands in this book alone. But eliminating most of them is going to be easier than you think. When my younger sister was pregnant we sat down with this manuscript and, after sifting through it, came up with only three possibilities: Simon, Mark, and Peter. (She named her son Cooper. Go figure.) There are baby name books with elaborate work sheets, but I favor a low-tech approach. You'll be able to eliminate the huge majority of candidates on the following grounds:

Leaves you cold. If a name doesn't speak to you or your partner, forget it. There are plenty of other options.

Unpleasant associations. Your old love interest, an uncle with bad breath, a character in a book you once read. These associations are strong, and you should pay attention to them.

No nickname. I would have liked to name a son after my father-in-law, but his name is Thornton. He was called "Thornt" for much of his youth. I didn't consider that beneficial, and "Thorny" was out of the question. Parents are much more inclined to use complete names than they used to be: Robert is now rarely trimmed down to Bob, for instance. But two syllables is the maximum number most people, especially school children, are likely to use.

Too trendy. If you have a feeling that a name is getting too fashionable, you are probably right. As the possessor of a once-popular name, I can sincerely urge you to look elsewhere.

Too odd. We were going to name our younger son Hugh. The hospital orderly, as he wheeled the infant and me out of the recovery room, asked me, "What's the baby's name?" I proudly answered "Hugh," and he said, "What?" I instantly realized that this was not an exchange I wanted to repeat thousands of times.

Too pretentious. Is it a name that a child can use? Think twice before naming a baby after your favorite poet or mountain peak. The famous "playground test" should weed out the duds here: If you call the name across a crowded playground, do you feel foolish? Or do heads whip around to stare at you? ("Who would name a child Everest?")

Hard to pronounce. Apparently Demi Moore has to correct everyone who tries to pronounce her name with the accent on the first syllable ("It's DeMee."). That seems like a lot of trouble. Why not just select something self-explanatory?

Hard to spell. Many parents, eager to individualize names, tinker with them phonetically. Some research suggests that unusually spelled names suggest negative qualities to many people. The more remarkable the spelling, the more difficulty it is likely to cause.

Sounds wrong with last name. Long or unusual last names seem to require simple first names, while plain last names can support more elaborate first names. If a child's last name is going to be hyphenated, take that into account. Your child could end up with a real mouthful.

The initials spell out something silly. Natasha Elizabeth Riley-Dodd will not thank you.

Once you've gotten down to a short list, mull things over. This is the point when you play with different endings, different spellings (Catherine or Katharine?), and combinations of first and middle names. It's not necessary to give a middle name, of course, but it can be a good way to use an unmanageable family name, and it can also give children more options as they get older. English actress Melissa Bell named her first son Diesel Thomas William, reasoning that if he got tired of Diesel (*if!*) he could move on to one of his more conservative middle names.

If you don't mind hearing the unvarnished truth you can try out possible names on your friends and family, but be prepared for people to say, "I've never met an Arthur I liked" or "You can't possibly call her Tootsie!" So if you are intent on using a very unusual name, you might prefer to keep your ideas secret until you have the baby. It's a little hard for even the most opinionated onlooker to gaze at an infant and say, "Why in the world did you name her Demetria?" It's also a good idea to take this book, or your short list, to the hospital. Sometimes name and baby just don't match up, and it's necessary to rethink.

The beauty of the process is that you really can't go wrong. Even if you feel you're compromising on a name, within days it will have lost all its earlier associations. It becomes, quite simply, the name of your baby. So of course it will turn out to be the perfect name.

If It's a
BOY...

Aaron Heb. "Exalted, on high." In the Old Testament, Aaron was the brother of Moses. The name was unusual until the 17th century, when so many Old Testament names first came into prominence. It has been fashionable, especially in the U.S., since the 1970s, and is very steadily used without being particularly fashionable. Currently well used in Scotland. U.S. Vice President Aaron Burr; baseball star Hank Aaron; composer Aaron Copland; actor Aaron Eckhart.

Aaran, Aaren, Aarron, Aaronas, Aeron, Aharon, Arand, Arend, Ari, Arin, Arnie, Arny, Aron, Aronne, Arran, Arron, Arun, Erin, Haroun, Ron, Ronnie, Ronny

Abbas Heb. "Father"; Arab. "Stern." One of Muhammad's uncles was named Abbas. This is one of those cases where Judaism and Islam demonstrate their common roots. Israeli statesman Abba Eban.

Ab, Abba, Abbe, Abbey, Abbie, Abo

Abbey Dim. **Abbot, Abelard, Abner.** Political activist Abbie Hoffman.

Abbie, Abby

Abbott Heb. "Father." An abbot is the head of a monastic community, so the original bearers of this name (as a surname) may have worked for an abbot. Its use as a first name occurred mostly in the 19th century. In the 1940s and early 1950s Bud Abbott served as straight man to short chubby comedian Lou Costello.

Ab, Abad, Abba, Abbe, Abe, Abbey, Abbie, Abbot, Abby, Abot, Abott

Abda Arab. "Servant."

Abdi Heb. "My servant." Old Testament name.

Abdul Arab. "Servant of." Often used in combination with another name, as in "Abdullah," or "servant of Allah." Basketball star Kareem Abdul-Jabar.

Ab, Abdal, Abdall, Abdalla, Abdallah, Abdel, Abdell, Abdella, Abdellah, Abdoul, Abdoull, Abdoulla, Abdoullah, Abdull, Abdullah, Del

Abdullah Arab. "Servant of Allah." One of the most common names in the Islamic world, and the name of Muhammad's father. A royal name in Saudi Arabia.

Abdalla, Abdallah, Abdella, Abedellah, Abdulla

Abe Dim. **Abraham**. Heb. "Father of many."

Abey, Abie

Abednego Aramaic. "Servant of Nego." One of the three Biblical unfortunates thrown in the fiery furnace by King Nebuchadnezzar, and rescued by an angel. Another form of the name is **Azariah**.

Abejundio Sp. "Like a bee."

Abejundo

Abel Heb. "Breath." Abel was the younger son of Adam and Eve, who was slain by his older brother, Cain. Abel has survived with steady use ever since the 6th century, and surprisingly enough, Cain also occurs from time to time. Abel is very well used in Spain.

Abe, Abell, Abey, Abie, Able

Abelard OG. "Highborn and steadfast." Made famous by the 12th-century French philosopher Pierre Abelard, who fell in love with and seduced his student Heloise. Her uncle and guardian had him emasculated, even though he married Heloise. She became a nun, he became a monk.

Ab, Abbey, Abby, Abe, Abel

Abiah Heb. "My father is the Lord." Another Old Testament name, used for women as well as men in the Bible. Unusual in real life.

Abia, Abija, Abijah

Abida Heb. "God knows."

Abidan

Abiel Heb. "My father is God." Old Testament name that the Puritans used in the U.S., but rare since.

Abiell, Abyel, Abyell, Ahbiel

Abimelech Heb. "My father is king." Occurred occasionally in the 19th century.

Abir Heb. "Strong."
Abeer, Abeeri, Abiri

Abisha Heb. "Gift of God."
Abidja, Abidjah, Abijah, Abishai

Abner Heb. "My father is light." Old Testament name that came to some prominence in the late 16th century. Use diminished in this century, and the name is now mostly associated with Al Capp's comic strip *Li'l Abner*. Some potential for revival, though, as the name has a masculine, uncompromising air that should be appealing to today's parents. Inventor of baseball Abner Doubleday.
Ab, Abbey, Abbie, Abby, Abna, Abnar, Abnor, Avner, Eb, Ebbie, Ebby, Ebner

Abraham Heb. "Father of many." First of the Hebrew patriarchs. In the Bible, Abraham has a son named Isaac when he is 100 and his wife Sarah is 90. The name was popular while Abraham Lincoln was president (even more so after his assassination), but has faded from use since 1900. To both Christians and Jews, the important point about Abraham is his great age, so his name may seem unfitting for an infant.
Abarran, Abe, Abey, Abie, Abrahamo, Abrahan, Abram, Abrami, Abramo, Abran, Avram, Avrom, Bram, Ibrahim

Abram Heb. "He who is high is father." Var. **Abraham**.
Abe, Abey, Abie, Abramo, Avram, Avrom, Bram

Absalom Heb. "Father is peace." The handsome son of King David who connived to steal his father's throne. He died in battle, caught by his hair in an oak tree and executed by one of his father's soldiers. King David then lamented, "Would God I had died for thee, O Absalom, my son, my son!" Also the title of a tragic novel by William Faulkner. Little used today, perhaps because of its traditional associations with terrible grief.
Absalon, Abshalom, Absolom, Absolon, Avshalom, Avsholom

Abundio Sp. from Lat. "Abundant."
Abbondio, Abondio, Aboundio, Abundo

FORMERLY KNOWN AS

You can name your child almost anything in this country, but the freedom to chose a name doesn't stop there. It's also relatively easy to change your name. Many immigrants to this country, both slaves and European newcomers, had new names arbitrarily assigned when they reached these shores. But plenty of Americans have also opted to shed, streamline, or simply rethink what they're called.

This process has been most notable in the entertainment industry, where names have been changed to add allure (Mary Pickford was originally Gladys Smith) or to present a WASP face to a xenophobic public (Judy Holliday was named Judith Tuvim by her parents). No one bothers much with this any more, unless to reverse the trend, as Martin Sheen's son Emilio Estevez did. Young actress Renee Zellwegger came to Hollywood with a name that the moguls of the 1940s and '50s would have transformed in an instant. But she stood her ground, saying, "If Arnold Schwarzenegger can keep his name, I can darn well keep mine."

Acacio Sp. from Gk. "Free of malice." **Acacia**, the feminine version, refers to a blossoming tree that symbolized, to Christians, the resurrection of Christ.
  Accacio
Ace Lat. "Unity." Connotations of superiority come from the fact that the ace is the playing card with highest face value. The term "flying ace" goes back to World War I (when planes were both novel and hazardous). Turns up occasionally for children of cool intellectual parents, but most likely as a nickname.
  Acer, Acey, Acie
Achav Heb. "Uncle." Old Testament name.
  Achiav
Achidan Heb. "My brother judged." Old Testament name.
  Abidan, Amidan, Avidan

Achilles Gk. Place name; also hero of the *Iliad,* as the greatest of the Greek heroes fighting the Trojans. He was all but invulnerable, having been dipped in the River Styx by his mother. She held him, however, by the heel, which was thus his one weak point: hence "Achilles' heel."

Achill, Achille, Achillea, Achilleus, Achillios, Achillius, Akil, Akilles, Akillios, Akillius, Aquil, Aquiles, Aquilles, Quilo

Achim Heb. "God will judge."

Acim, Ahim

Achiram Heb. "My brother is well born."

Achishar Heb. "My brother sings." Old Testament name.

Amishar, Avishar

Ackerley OE. Place name: "Oak meadow." Surname transferred to first name.

Accerly, Acklea, Ackleigh, Ackley, Acklie, Ackerlea, Ackerleigh, Ackerly

Acton OE. Place name: "Oak tree settlement." Another surname transferred to a first name: also the pseudonym used by Charlotte Brontë's sister Anne, who wrote as "Acton Bell." (The three sisters purposely chose masculine-sounding pseudonyms.)

Adael Heb. "The Lord witnesses."

Adayel

Adair Scot. Gael. Place name: "Oak tree ford." Recently becoming more popular.

Adaire, Adare, Adayre

Adalard OG. "Noble and courageous."

Adelard, Adellard

Adalfieri It. from Ger. "Noble oath."

Adelfieri, Edelfieri

Adalgiso Sp. from Ger. "Noble lance."

Adelgiso, Edelgiso

Adalric OG. "Highborn ruler." The Old German particle "-ric" is found in more common names like Frederick and Richard.

Adalrich, Adalrick, Adelric, Adelrich, Adelrick

Adam Heb. "Son of the red earth." In the Bible, God created Adam—the first man—out of the "red earth" and

breathed life into him. Steadily used from the middle
ages until the 1700's, and again beginning in the 1970's.
Fashionable in Ireland at the moment. An appropriate
name for the first boy in a family that has produced many
girls. Congressman Adam Clayton Powell, Jr.; actor
Adam Sandler.

Ad, Adamo, Adams, Adan, Adao, Addam, Addams, Addem, Addie, Addis, Addison, Addy, Ade, Adem, Adhamh, Adnet, Adnon, Adnot

Adamson OE. "Son of Adam."

Adamsson, Addamson

Adar Heb. "Noble."

Addison OE. "Son of Adam." Transferred surname. The
English poet and essayist Joseph Addison was popular
and influential through the 18th century. Addison is now
turning up more and more frequently as a girl's name.

Ad, Addeson, Addie, Addy, Adison, Adisson

Addy Teut. "Awe-inspiring; highborn." Also short for
Adam, etc.

Addie, Ade, Adi, Ado

Adel OG. "Noble, highborn." More familiar as a particle of
other names.

Adal, Edel

Adelar OG. "Noble eagle." Var. **Abelard**.

Adal, Adalar, Adalard, Adelard

Adelphe Fr. from Gk. "Brother."

Adelfo, Adelfus, Adelpho, Adelphus

Aden Possibly place name (for a region of South Yemen,
formerly a British colony) or a variation on **Aidan**.

Aiden

Adham Arab. "Black."

Adil Arab. "Righteous, fair." Currently popular in the Arabic world.

Adlai Heb. "My ornament." Used in the Old Testament,
and very rare, though brought to public notice by statesman Adlai Stevenson.

Ad, Addie, Addy, Adley

Adler OG. "Eagle." More common as a surname, especially in the U.S.

Ad, Addler, Adlar

Admon Heb. "Red." From the same root that gives us **Adam**.

Adnah Heb. "Ornamented."

Adin

Adnan Arab. Meaning unclear: possibly "to settle." Arms magnate Adnan Khashoggi.

Adney OE. Place name: "The noble's island."

Adolph OG. "Noble wolf." The Latinized form Adolphus arrived in Britain in mid-19th century, having been a German and Swedish royal name and also a saint's name. Almost unheard-of since the rise of Adolf Hitler and World War II. Filmmaker Adolph Zukor; French actor Adolphe Menjou; fashion designer Adolfo; beer magnate Adolph Coors.

Ad, Addolf, Addolph, Adolf, Adolfo, Adolfus, Adollf, Adolphe, Adolpho, Adolphus, Dolf, Dolph, Dolphus

Adonia Heb. "God is my lord." Old Testament name: one of King David's sons.

Adon, Adonias, Adonijah, Adoniya

Adonis Gk. In Greek mythology, Adonis was a young man so beautiful that Aphrodite, goddess of love, became enamored of him. The name has come to epitomize male beauty, which would make it very hard to live with.

Addonis, Adohnes, Adones

Adrian Lat. "From Adria" a north Italian city. First popular in the 1950s in Britain, and used also as a woman's name, though it seems to be holding steady as a choice for male children. Hollywood costume designer Adrian; 12th-century pope Adrian IV (the only English pope in history); actor Adrien Brody.

Ade, Adiran, Adrain, Adrean, Adreean, Adreyan, Adreeyan, Adriano, Adrien, Adrin, Adrino, Adryan, Aydrean, Aydreean, Aydrian, Aydrien, Hadrian, Hadriano, Hadrien, Haydrian, Haydrien

Aegeus Gk. "Kid, young goat." The name actually refers to a shield made of goat-skin that was the sign of Zeus, and also occurs as **Egidio** and **Giles**. In Greek myth, King Aegeus was the father of Theseus, who slew the

Cretan monster, the Minotaur. When Aegeus mistakenly thought Theseus had been killed on his venture, he threw himself into the sea near Athens, which is now known as the Aegean.

Aigeos, Aigeus

Aeneas Gk. "He who is praised." The Trojan hero of Virgil's *Aeneid*. Legend has it that he founded the Italian colony that was the origin of Rome. Football player Aeneas Williams.

Aenneas, Aineas, Aineias, Aineis. Ainneas, Eneas, Enné, Enneas, Enneis, Enneiss

Aeolus Gk. "Variable, changeable." In Greek myth Aeolus was the god of the winds. In the 19th century a brand of church organs was manufactured under the "Aeolian-Skinner" brand name.

Aeolos, Aiolos, Aiolus

Aeson Gk. Unknown meaning. In Greek mythology, the father of Jason. Since the name **Jason** has been so fashionable this name may hold considerable appeal for some.

Afif Arab. "Chaste."

Afton OE. Place name. A surname that has come into use as a first name.

Affton

Agamemnon Gk. "Working slowly." Name of one of the great heroes of Greek myth: a mighty warrior who commanded the Greeks at the siege of Troy. His proficiency in battle did not exempt him from the typical tragedy of Greek myth: his daughter Iphigenia was sacrificed before the Trojan war and when he came home from the war his wife Clytemnestra killed him.

Agamemno, Agamenon

Agapito Sp. from Gk. "Lovingkindness, charity." The root is the Greek word *agape,* and there was a Pope (later Saint) Agapetus in the 6th century.

Agapeto, Agapetus, Agapios

Agathias Gk. "Good." This can be considered the masculine version of **Agatha**.

Agathios, Agathius, Agathos

Agnolo It. "Angel." More common in the U.S. in the Spanish form, **Angelo**.

Ahab Heb. "Father's brother." Pleasant way to honor an uncle, though literary types may be reminded of the mad sea captain in Herman Melville's novel *Moby Dick*.

Ahearn Celt. "Horse-lord."
Ahearne, Aherin, Ahern, Aherne, Hearn, Hearne, Herin, Hern

Ahmed Arab. "Greatly praised." Name often used for the prophet Muhammad, and favored by Muslims in the U.S. The name is in fact commonly used throughout the Islamic world. Football player Ahmad Plummer.
Achmad, Achmed, Ahmaad, Ahmad, Ahmod, Amahd, Amed

Ahsan Arab. "Compassion."
Ehsan, Ihsan

Aidan Gael. "Fire." Saint Aidan was a 7th-century Irish monk. The name is also used for women. Actor Aidan Quinn.
Aidano, Aiden, Edan, Eden, Eidan, Eiden

Aiken OE. "Made of oak." English writer Conrad Aiken.
Aicken, Aikin, Ayken, Aykin

Aimé Fr. "Much loved." More common as **Aimée**, a girl's name, or even as **Esmé**, a variant once well used in Scotland.

Aimery Teut. "Hardworking ruler."
Aimerey, Aimeric, Amerey, Aymeric, Aymery, Imre

Aimon Fr. from Teut. "House." Also possibly phonetic variant of the Irish **Eamon**, in turn a version of **Edmund**.
Aimond, Aymon, Haimon, Heman

Ainsley Scot. Gael. Place name: "His very own meadow." A last name converted to a first name, used by both sexes.
Ainsley, Ainsleigh, Ainslie, Ansley, Aynslee, Aynsley, Aynslie

Ainsworth OE. Place name: "Ann's estate."
Answorth

Ajax Gk. "Alas." Name from Greek mythology: a hero of the Trojan war. He was King of Salamis, and a huge daring warrior, but he went mad and killed himself when his prowess as a fighter was cast into doubt.

Aias

Akbar Arab. "Great."

Akeem Var. **Hakeem** (Arab. "Judging thoughtfully"). Although it is very exotic, this name ranks above such All-American classics as **Howard** and **Nelson** in usage. Its use is probably inspired in part by basketball player Hakeem Olajuwon, who was known as Akeem when he first came to the U.S.

Ahkeem, Akhim, Akim

Akim Rus. Dim. **Joachim**. Heb. "God will judge."

Akmal Arab. "Perfect."

Aqmal

Alaire Fr. from Lat. "Joyful." Var. **Hilary**. The root is the same as "hilarious," though the meaning has shifted a bit. Alaire, unfortunately, sounds like the name of a car.

Alair, Helier, Hilaire, Hilary, Larie, Lary

Alamar Sp. from Arab. "Gilded, covered with gold." Baseball player Roberto Alomar.

Alomar

Alan Ir. Gael. Possible meanings are "rock" or "comely." Widely used in the Middle Ages, then again from the 19th century to the late 20th, with a boom around the 1950s influenced by the popularity of actor Alan Ladd. Now waning, like most fifties names. South African author Alan Paton; lyricist Alan Jay Lerner; playwright Alan Bennett; astronaut Alan Shepard; actors Alan Alda, Alan Cumming; poet Allen Ginsberg; basketball player Allen Iverson.

Ailean, Ailin, Al, Alain, Alair, Aland, Alann, Alano, Alanson, Alen, Alin, Allan, Allayne, Allen, Alley, Alleyn, Alleyne, Allie, Allin, Allon, Allyn, Alon, Alun

Alard OG. "Noble and steadfast."

Adlar, Adlard, Al, Allard

Alaric OG. "Ruler of all" or "Highborn ruler." Alaric I was the 5th-century king of the Visigoths who sacked Rome.

Al, Alarick, Alarico, Aleric, Alerick, Allaric, Allarick, Alleric, Allerick, Alric, Alrick, Ullrich, Ulrich, Ulrick

Alastair Gael. Var. **Alexander** (Gk. "Man's defender"). Generally a Scottish name, though it appears occasionally throughout the English-speaking world. Most of the variants are different phonetic spellings of the name. TV commentator Alistair Cooke; actor Alistair Sim.

Al, Alasdair, Alasteir, Alaster, Alastor, Alaisdair, Alaistair, Alaister, Aleister, Alester, Alistair, Alistar, Alister, Allaistar, Allaster, Allastir, Allistair, Allister, Allistir, Allysdair, Allysdare, Allystair, Allyster, Alysdair, Alysdare, Alystair, Alyster

Alban Lat. "From Alba," a city on a "white" hill, the oldest city in the ancient kingdom of Latium. The first Christian martyr on British soil was Saint Alban, after whom a cathedral town (which is also a pilgrimage destination) are named. Not to be confused with **Albin**, which has a different root.

Al, Albain, Alban, Albany, Albie, Albin, Albinet, Albion, Albis, Alby, Albys, Alvan, Alvin, Alvy, Auban, Auben, Aubin

Albern OG. "Noble courage."

Albert OE. "Highborn, brilliant." Most widely used during the lifetime of Queen Victoria's German prince consort, Albert. Her many children and grandchildren carried the name to most of the royal families in Europe, but her eldest son's first move as king was to drop it. Out of style since the 1920s; in fact it has a seriously quaint air. Scientist Albert Einstein; Prince Albert of Monaco; actor Albert Finney; philosopher Albert Camus; artist Albrecht Durer; baseball player Albert Belle; politician Al Gore.

Adalbert, Adalbrecht, Adelbert, Adelbrecht, Ailbert, Al, Alberto, Albie, Albrecht, Albrekt, Alvert, Alvertos, Aubert, Bert, Bertie, Berty, Dalbert, Delbert, Elbert, Elbrecht, Ulbricht

Albin Lat. "White, pale-skinned." From the root that gives us the word "albino." Common in Roman and medieval times, but not in the modern era.

Al, Alben, Albinson, Alpin, Aubin

Albion Celt. "Mountain." Used in England until the 1930s; "Albion" is a poetic name for Britain.

Alcander Gk. "Strong."
    Alcinder, Alcindor, Alkander, Alkender
Alcott OE. Place name: "The old cottage."
    Alcot, Allcot, Allcott, Alkott
Alden OE. "Old friend." Surname transferred to first name, but unusual.
    Al, Aldin, Aldwin, Aldwyn, Aldwynn, Elden, Eldin, Eldwin, Eldwyn, Eldwynn
Aldo OG. "Old." An Italian name that is occasionally used in the U.S. A Renaissance printer named Aldus Manutius designed the first italic type face.
    Aldus, Alldo
Aldous OG. "Old." Medieval name that was brought back in the 19th century to slight popularity. Proof, if proof were needed, that meaning is usually a secondary consideration when names are chosen. Made most famous by writer Aldous Huxley.
    Al, Aldis, Aldivin, Aldo, Aldon, Aldus, Alldo, Eldin, Eldis, Eldon, Eldous
Aldred OE. "Old counsel."
    Alldred, Eldred, Eldrid, Elldred
Aldrich OE. "Old leader." A name that has some prominence in America as a family related to the Rockefellers.
    Al, Aldric, Aldridge, Aldrige, Aldritch, Alldrich, Alldridge, Allric, Alrick, Audric, Eldrich, Eldridge, Eldritch, Elldrich, Rich, Richie, Richy, Ritch, Ritchey, Ritchie, Ritchy
Aldwin OE. "Old friend." See **Alden**.
    Aldwinn, Aldwinne, Aldwyn, Aldwynne, Alswynn, Elden, Eldin, Eldwin, Eldwyn, Eldwynn
Alejandro Sp. Var. Alexander.
    Alejo
Alem Arab. "Wise man."
    Alerio
Aleron Lat. "Winged one."
    Aileron
Alex Dim. Alexander. Often used independently as Alexander has become more and more popular. One of the very few names that is used with equal frequency for both gen-

ders. Russian form **Alek** is currently very popular in that country. Baseball players Alex Ochoa, Alex Rodriguez.

Alec, Aleco, Aleck, Alecko, Alek, Aleko, Aleks, Alick, Alik, Elex

Alexander Gk. "Man's defender." Given great prominence by Alexander the Great, and steadily used worldwide, as the numerous variants show. It was a royal name in Scotland, where it is still highly popular, and it is widely used in the U.S. without having attained trendy status. Offshoots like **Alec** or even **Zander** are starting to show up as given names. English poet Alexander Pope, U.S. statesman Alexander Hamilton; actors Sir Alec Guinness, Alec Baldwin; U.S. Secretary of State Alexander Haig; Soviet writer and dissident Aleksandr Solzhenitsyn; writer Alexandre Dumas.

Al, Alasdair, Alastair, Alaster, Alcander, Alcinder, Alcindor, Alec, Aleco, Alejandro, Alejo, Alek, Aleksander, Aleksandr, Alessandre, Alessandri, Alessandro, Alex, Alexandre, Alexandro, Alexandros, Alexei, Alexi, Alexio, Alexis, Alic, Alicio, Alick, Alik, Alisander, Alissander, Alissandre, Alistair, Alister, Alistir, Alix, Allistair, Allister, Allistir, Alsandair, Alsandare, Iskander, Sacha, Sander, Sandero, Sandor, Sandro, Sandros, Sandie, Sandy, Sascha, Sasha, Saunder, Saunders, Sikander, Xander, Zander, Zandro, Zandros

Alexis Gk. "Helper." Usually thought of as a diminutive of **Alexander**, though it has a different etymological root. More commonly a girl's name. Hockey player Aleksei Kovalev.

Alejo, Aleksei, Aleksi, Aleksio, Aleksios, Aleksius, Alexei, Alexey, Alexi, Alexios, Alexius, Alexy

Alfonso Sp. Var. **Alphonse** (OG. "Ready for battle"). A royal name in Spain, but little used in the U.S. in this form or as Alphonse.

Alfons, Alfonsin, Alfonsino, Alfonz, Alonso, Alonzo, Alphons, Alphonsus, Alphonzus, Alphonz, Foncho, Fonz, Fonzie, Fonzo

Alford OE. Place name: "The old river-ford."

Aldford, Allford

Alfred OE. "Counsel from the elves." After wide medieval use, the name fell out of sight until a 19th-century revival; Queen Victoria even named her second son Alfred. Out of fashion since the 1920s, and to parents who remember *Mad Magazine*'s gap-toothed Alfred E. Neuman, a highly unlikely choice. English King Alfred the Great; poet Alfred Tennyson; movie director Alfred Hitchcock.

Ahlfred, Ailfred, Ailfrid, Ailfryd, Al, Alf, Alfeo, Alfey, Alfie, Alfre, Alfredas, Alfrey, Alfredo, Alfredo, Alfy, Avery, Elfred, Fred, Freddie, Freddy, Fredo

Alger OE. "Spear from the elves." Possibly a diminutive of Algernon. Medieval name revived with the 19th-century hunger for a picturesque past, but never common. State Department Official Alger Hiss.

Al, Algar, Allgar, Allger, Elgar, Elger, Ellgar, Ellger

Algernon OF. "Wearing a mustache." A first name in several hugely powerful English aristocratic families, and given wider use in the latter half of the 19th century in Britain. Oscar Wilde used it for a brainless fop in *The Importance of Being Earnest*. All but unknown now. English poet Algernon Swinburne.

Al, Alger, Algernone, Algey, Algie, Algy, Aljernon, Allgernon

Algis OG. "Spear."

Ali Arab. "The high, exalted one." One of the ninety-nine attributes of Allah proposed by Muhammad as excellent names for boy children.

Aly

Alison OE. "Son of the highborn." More common as a girl's name, in spite of the "-son" ending.

Alisson, Allcen, Allison, Allisoun, Allson, Allyson

Allard OE. "Highborn and courageous."

Adelard, Adelhard, Alhard, Alhart, Allart

Almanzo Family name of uncertain meaning. Famous from the *Little House* books: Almanzo Wilder tells Laura that a distant English ancestor's life had been saved during the Crusades by an Arab named El Manzoor. "They changed it after a while in England, but I guess there's no way to improve it much." Which just goes to show that a hundred years ago parents also made fanciful choices for names.

Almarine OG. "Work ruler." Has nothing to do with the sea.

Almarin, Almarino

Alon Heb. "Oak tree." The feminine form, **Alona**, is more common.

Allon

Alonzo Var. **Alphonse** (OG. "Ready for battle"). This form is marginally more popular than **Alfonso**, perhaps because of the fame of basketball star Alonzo Mourning.

Alanso, Alanzo, Allonso, Allonzo, Allohnso, Allohnzo, Alohnso, Alohnzo, Alonso, Lonnie, Lonny

Aloysius OG. "Famous fighter." Latinized version of **Luigi** or **Louis**, also related to **Clovis** and **Ludwig**. The 16th-century Italian Saint Aloysius is patron saint of students.

Ahlois, Aloess, Alois, Aloisius, Aloisio, Aloys, Lewis, Louis, Ludwick, Ludwig, Lutwick

Alpha Gk. First letter of the Greek alphabet, corresponding to "A." More likely to be used for a girl, because of the "-a" ending. Still, in the Biblical Book of Revelation, Jesus says, "I am Alpha and Omega, the beginning and the end."

Alfa

Alpheus Heb. "He who follows after." Biblical, used in the 19th century, now very unusual.

Alfaeus, Alfeos, Alfeus, Alpheaus, Alphoeus

Alphonse OG. "Ready for battle." **Alfonso** is a royal name in Spain, thus very popular; this form is less used in the U.S., though even **Alonzo**, the most popular variant, is unusual. French writer Alphonse Daudet.

Affonso, Al, Alfie, Alfo, Alfons, Alfonso, Alfonsus, Alfonzo, Alfonzus, Alford, Alfy, Alonso, Alonzo, Alphonso, Alphonsus, Alphonzo, Alphonzus, Fons, Fonz, Fonzie, Phauns, Phons, Phonz

Alpin Gael. "Fair one."

Alpine, Macalpin, McAlpin, McAlpine

Alston OE. Place name: "Noble one's settlement."

Alsdon, Alsten, Alstin, Allston, Allstonn

Alta Lat. "Elevated." As in Alta, Utah, thousands of feet above sea level.

Alto, Altus

Altair Gk. from Arab. "Bird." Also the name of the brightest star in the constellation Aquila. It is about 10 times as bright as the sun.

Alltair, Altaer, Altayr

Alter Yiddish. "Old, old man." The Yiddish equivalent of **Aldous**.

Altman OG. "Old man." Last name occasionally used as a first name. Film director Robert Altman; department store magnate Bernard Altman.

Alterman, Altermann, Altmann, Eltman, Elterman, Eltermann

Alton OE. Place name: "Old town." Activist Alton Maddox.

Aldon, Allton, Alten

Alucio Sp. from Lat. "Bright, shining." The significant root here is *lux,* or light, as in "lucid."

Allucio, Alucido, Aluxio, Aluzio

Aluf Heb. "Leader, one in charge."

Alouf, Aluph

Alured Lat. Var. Alfred.

Ailured

Alva Heb. Possibly "Brilliance"; also related to Latin **Albin**. Old Testament name rarely used for men or women, in spite of Thomas Alva Edison's fame.

Alba, Alvah

Alvar OE. "Army of elves." Very rare. Architect Alvar Aalto.

Albaro, Alvaro, Alvarso, Alverio

Alvin OE. Several possible sources: the second element, "vin," means "Friend," but Al could indicate "Elf," "Noble," or "Old." Radio characters Alvin and the Chipmunks have given the name an irresistibly comical cast, however. Choreographer Alvin Ailey.

Ailwyn, Al, Aloin, Aluin, Aluino, Alva, Alvan, Alven, Alvie, Alvy, Alvyn, Alwin, Alwyn, Alwynn, Aylwin, Elvin, Elwin, Elwyn, Elwynn

Alvis Origin unclear. Possibly from an Old Norse legend

involving the dwarf Alviss; possibly a modern blend reminiscent of **Elvis**. First appeared in the mid 20th century, but never widespread.

Alviss, Alwis, Alwyss

Amadeo Sp. from Lat. "Loved by God." The Latin version is **Amadeus**, given great prominence by the 1984 film about Mozart.

Amadee, Amadei, Amadeus, Amadi, Amadieu, Amadis, Amado, Amando, Amati, Amato, Amatus, Amedeo, Amyas, Amyot

Amadour Fr. from Lat. "Lovable." A Saint Amadour, purportedly founder of a French shrine (Rocamadour), has been venerated by the Catholic church, but recent research indicates he probably never lived.

Amador, Amadore

Amahl Heb. "Labor, hard work." Familiar to Americans as the young hero of Giancarlo Menotti's often-performed opera, *Amahl and the Night Visitors.*

Amal, Amali, Amel

Amalio Sp. from OG. "Industrious." The masculine equivalent of **Amelia**.

Amelio

Amarillo Sp. "Yellow." Place name: a city in Texas. Rather a mouthful for a baby, but it has a certain rakish flair.

Amasa Heb. "Bearing a burden." Occasionally used in the 19th century, but little-known today.

Amaury Var. **Maurice** (Lat. "Dark-skinned, Moorish.")

Amory

Ambrose Gk. "Ever-living." Saint Ambrose was the 4th-century Bishop of Milan who baptized Saint Augustine. The name is more widely found on the Continent than in English-speaking countries. Writer Ambrose Bierce; Civil War General Ambrose E. Burnside.

Ambie, Ambroeus, Ambrogio, Ambroise, Ambros, Ambrosi, Ambrosio, Ambrosios, Ambrosius, Amby, Brose

Amerigo It. Var. **Emery** (OG. "Home ruler"). It's fitting that the United States, founded on the principle of home rule, should have taken its nickname of "America" from Italian explorer Amerigo Vespucci.

America, Americo, Americus, Amerika, Ameriko, Amerikus

Ames Origin unclear, but may be related to the Latin word for love, *amor*.

Aimes, Aymes

Amiel Heb. "God of my people."

Amyel

Amin Arab. "Honest, trustworthy."

Ameen, Amein

Amir Arab. "Ruler, commander." This is the term for a high-ranking and powerful official in many different capacities in the Muslim world.

Ameer, Amiran, Emeer, Emir

Amitai Heb. "Truth."

Amitay

Amjad Arab. "Full of glory."

Ammar Arab. "Long-lived."

Ammon Heb. "Teacher, builder." Biblical name: one of the sons of David, and place name: a country northeast of the Dead Sea. The Ammonites and the Israelites were frequently at war. The town of Ammam in Jordan is situated in what was Ammon.

Amon, Amnon

Amory OG. "Home ruler." Var. **Emery**. Scott Fitzgerald used this name for Amory Blaine, the hero of his first best-selling novel, *This Side of Paradise*. Writer Cleveland Amory.

Aimory, Amery, Amorey

Amos Heb. "Borne, carried." A prophet of the Old Testament. The name has been little used in this century, perhaps because of lingering negative connotations from the highly politically incorrect radio show "Amos 'n Andy" that flourished in the 1940s and 1950s. Novelist Amos Oz.

Amoss

Amram Heb. "Mighty nation." Biblical name: the father of Moses.

Amyas Lat. "Loved one." Possibly an anglicized version of **Amadeus**, though sometimes considered a masculine variant of **Amy**. Unusual.

Amias, Amyes, Amyess

Anael Biblical: the name of an archangel.

Anastasius Gk. "Resurrection." Much more common in the feminine version, **Anastasia**.

Anastas, Anastase, Anastagio, Anastasio, Anastatius, Anastice, Anastius, Anasto, Anastos, Anstas, Anstasios, Anstasius, Anstice, Stasio, Stasius

Anatole Gk. "From the east." Anatolia is a region of Turkey, which, of course, is east of Greece. French novelist Anatole France.

Anatol, Anatolio, Anatoly, Antal, Antol, Antole, Antolle, Antoly

Anchor The object as name. Most likely to be a transferred last name, possibly originating as some kind of occupational name.

Ancher, Anker

Anders Scand. Var. **Andrew**.

Ander, Anderson, Andersson

André Fr. Var. **Andrew**. Traditionally parents have chosen English-style names for boys in the U.S., but this preference seems to be changing, and names with a foreign flair are inching into acceptability, if not into trendiness. The form **Andrey** is currently very popular in Russia. Pianist André Watts; actor André Gregory; composer/conductor André Previn; tennis player Andre Agassi.

Andrae, Andras, Andrei, Andrej, Andrey, Andres, Andris, Ohndrae, Ohndre, Ondre, Ondrei, Ohnrey, Ondrey

Andrew Gk. "Masculine." In the Bible, Andrew was the first of the twelve apostles. Legend has it that after his crucifixion on an X-shaped cross, his bones were transported to Scotland, where he is patron saint. The "Saint Andrew's Cross," representing Scotland, appears on the flag of the United Kingdom. It is one of the top ten names for boys in the U.S., and is a classic example of American parents' conservatism when it comes to choosing masculine names. U.S. Presidents Andrew Jackson, Andrew Johnson; industrialist Andrew Carnegie; Prince Andrew, Duke of York; actors Andy Devine, Andy Griffith, Andy

Garcia; artists Andrew Wyeth, Andy Warhol, baseball player Andruw Jones.

Aindrea, Aindreas, Anders, Andie, Andonis, Andor, André, Andrea, Andreas, Andrei, Andrej, Andres, Andresj, Andrewes, Andrews, Andrezj, Andrey, Andrius, Andro, Andros, Andru, Andruw, Andy, Dandie, Dandy, Drew, Dru, Drud, Drugi, Ohndrae, Ohndre, Ondre, Ondrei, Ohnrey, Ondrey

Androcles Gk. "Glorious man." According to a Latin myth, Androcles was a mild-mannered slave who once removed a thorn from the paw of a lion. When Androcles, a Christian, was later tossed into an arena to face the traditional band of ravenous lions, he encountered the lion who owed him a favor, and who set him free. G.B. Shaw later used this tale as the basis for a play about Christian faith.

Androclus

Aneurin Welsh. "Honor." Mostly limited to Wales.

Aneirin, Nye

Anfernee Modern name, made famous by basketball star Anfernee Hardaway, who is generally known as "Penny." His name may be a phonetic variant of **Anthony**.

Anferney

Angel Gk. "Messenger." **Angelo** is most often used now, even in English-speaking countries, as Angel is usually considered a girl's name (although in Thomas Hardy's 1891 novel *Tess of the D'Urbervilles,* a major character is named Angel Clare). Both forms are popular in Spanish-speaking countries. Jockey Angel Cordero.

Ange, Angell, Angie, Angelmo, Angelo, Angy, Anjel, Anjelo, Anyoli, Ohngel, Ohnjel, Onjel, Onjello, Onnjel, Onnjelo

Angus Scot. Gael. "Sole or only choice." In Celtic myth Angus Og is a god of such attractive traits as humor and wisdom. The name has been more widely used in Scotland, and in the U.S. tends to be reminiscent of breeds of cattle such as the Black Angus.

Anngus, Ennis, Gus

Anicho Ger. "Ancestor, predecessor."

Aniketos Gk. "Unconquered, invincible." The name has survived in a small way in Catholic countries because of a 2nd-century martyred pope who was later canonized.
Aniceto, Anicetus, Anisio

Annan Celt. "From the brook."

Anscom OE. Place name: "Valley of the awesome one." "Combe" is an Old English term for a deep, narrow valley.
Anscomb, Anscombe, Anscoombe

Ansel OF. "Follower of a nobleman" or variant of **Anselm**. Use is very likely to refer to photographer Ansel Adams, who photographed the American wilderness so eloquently.
Ancell, Ansell

Anselm OG. "God-helmet." Saint Anselm was Archbishop of Canterbury in the 12th century, and one of the formative influences on medieval Christian thought. The name survives best as **Selma**, a variant of the feminine form. Painter Anselm Kiefer.
Anse, Ansel, Anselme, Anselmi, Anselmo, Anshelm, Anso, Elmo, Selmo

Ansley OE. Place name: "The awesome one's meadow."
Ainslea, Ainslee, Ainsleigh, Ainsley, Ainslie, Ainsly, Annslea, Annsleigh, Annsley, Anslea, Ansleigh, Anslie, Ansly

Anson Unclear origin and meaning, perhaps OG. Possibly "Son of Ann," though "Son of the divine" seems more likely. Baseball great Cap Anson.
Annson, Ansson, Hanson

Anstice Var. **Anastasius**.
Anstiss

Antaeus Greek mythology name. He was the son of the Earth and the Sea, a wrestler who was invincible while his feet touched the ground. Hercules vanquished him by lifting him in the air. *Antaeus* is the name of a literary magazine.
Antaios, Anteo, Anteus

Antenor Sp. from Gk. "Combatant, antagonist." A Trojan in the *Iliad*. The name survives in Spanish-speaking countries. South American silver magnate Antenor Patino.

Anthony Lat. Clan name of the Romans, possibly meaning "Beyond price, invaluable." The 3rd-century hermit Saint Anthony, who, according to legend, lived alone in the wilderness for over 80 of his hundred-some years, is patron saint of the poor. In England the name is usually spelled—and pronounced—without the *h*. The German version, **Anton**, is currently fashionable in that country. This form is well used in the U.S., and so, to a lesser extent, are variants **Antonio** and **Antoine**. Actors Anthony Quinn, Anthony Hopkins, Anthony Perkins, Tony Curtis, Antonio Banderas; photographer Antony Armstrong-Jones, Earl of Snowdon; composer Anton Bruckner; playwright Anton Chekhov; basketball player Anthony Mason; singer Marc Antony.

Anntoin, Antin, Antoine, Anton, Antone, Antonello, Antoney, Antoni, Antonin, Antonino, Antonio, Antonius, Antons, Antony, Antuwan, Antwahn, Antwohn, Antwon, Antwuan, Toney, Toni, Tony

Antioch Place name: city in what is now Turkey that was a center of Christianity from around 300 A.D. until the 18th century.

Antiochus

Antoine Fr. Var. **Anthony**. Popular in the U.S. in recent years. Football player Antone Davis.

Antione, Antjuan, Antuan, Antuwain, Antuwaine, Antuwayne, Antuwon, Antwahn, Antwain, Antwaine, Antwan, Antwaun, Antwohn, Antwoin, Antwoine, Antwon, Antwone

Antonio Sp. Var. **Anthony**. This form is even more popular than **Antoine**, no doubt owing to the number of Spanish-speaking immigrants to the U.S. St. Anthony of Padua is a very important saint in the Catholic church, venerated on June 13. Football player Antonio Freeman; actor Antonio Banderas.

Antolin, Antonito, Anton, Tony

Anwar Arab. "Shafts of light." Made famous by Egyptian President Anwar Sadat.

Anwell Welsh-Celt. "Loved one."

Anwel, Anwil, Anwill, Anwyl, Anwyll

Apolonio Sp. from Gk. "Follower of Apollo." The feminine form, **Apollonia**, is somewhat more familiar.
Apollonios, Apollonius

Apollo Gk. "Manly." In classical myth, Apollo is the god who drives the sun across the sky in a carriage, and also rules over healing and prophecy, speaking through the famous oracle at Delphi.
Apollon, Apollos, Apolo

Apostolos Gk. "Apostle, disciple."

Aquila Lat. "Eagle." Despite the feminine "-a" ending, used in the 19th century as a revival of an ancient Roman name.
Acquila, Acquilino, Acquilla, Akila, Akilino, Akilla, Aquilina, Aquilino, Aquilla

Aquilo Roman mythology name: the personification of the North Wind. Interesting choice for a winter baby.
Aquilino, Aquillo

Aram Assyrian. "Heights." This was an ancient place name, referring to Syria. The language spoke there in pre-Christian times was called Aramaic.
Arram

Arcadio Sp. from Gk. Ancient place name: Arkadios was a region of Greece; the name has come down to us as Arcadia, which is a kind of pastoral paradise. In Russia the name is **Arkady**, and it is a popular choice.
Alcadio, Alcado, Alcedio, Arcadios, Arcadius, Arkadi, Arkadios, Arkadius, Arkady

Arcelio Sp. from Lat. "Altar of heaven."
Arcelius, Aricelio, Aricelius

Archard Anglo-Ger. "Holy, powerful."
Archerd

Archelaus Gk. "Ruler of the people." Not uncommon in the ancient world; Herod the Great had a son of that name who is mentioned in the Bible. Rare today.
Archelaios, Arkelaos, Arkelaus

Archer OF. "Bowman." Originally surname indicating occupation (like **Miller, Smith**, or **Baker**), mildly popular in the 19th century. Philanthropist Archer Huntington.

Archibald OG. "Noteworthy and valorous." Brought to Britain with the Norman Conquest, and popular largely in Scotland, where it was in the top 20 until the 1930s. Virtually invisible in the U.S. Poet Archibald MacLeish.

Arch, Archaimbaud, Archambault, Archer, Archibaldo, Archibold, Archie, Archimbald, Archimbaldo, Archy, Arquibaldo, Arquimbaldo

Archimedes Gk. "To contemplate first." The name of a brilliant Greek mathematician in the 2d century B.C.

Arkimedes, Arquimedes

Arden Lat. "Burning with enthusiasm." The Forest of Arden in Shakespeare's *As You Like It* is a magically beautiful place.

Ard, Arda, Ardie, Ardin, Ardon, Ardy, Arrden

Ardley OE. Place name: "Home-lover's meadow."

Ardly, Ardsley, Ardsly

Ardmore Lat. "More zealous."

Ardmorr

Argento Lat. "Silvery." The country of Argentina is named for the silver its early Spanish settlers hoped to find there, but did not.

Argentio, Argentino

Argus Gk. "Vigilant guardian." In Greek mythology, a creature with 100 eyes, who was later changed into a peacock with eyes on his tail-feathers.

Argos

Argyle Scot. Place name. Also given to the indigenous knitting pattern of interlocking diamonds that occasionally surfaces in American fashion.

Argyli

Ari Heb. "Lion." This name is a particle of the more familiar **Ariel**.

Arie, Arri, Ary, Arye

Aric OG. "Ruler." Also an element of many other names, like **Alaric** and **Frederick**. Aric actually contains the elements of **Richard** in reversed order.

Arick, Arric, Arrict, Arrick, Eric, Erick, Erric, Errick, Erik, Ric, Rickie, Ricky

Ariel Heb. "Lion of God." In Shakespeare's *The Tempest,* Ariel is a sprite who can disappear at will. The name has the connotation of something otherworldly, and though

Shakespeare's Ariel is male, the name is used mostly for girls. Israeli statesman Ariel Sharon.

Aeriell, Airel, Airyel, Airyell, Arel, Arie, Ariell, Arik, Aryel, Aryell

Ares In Greek mythology, Ares was the god of war, and one of the lovers of Aphrodite, the goddess of beauty. In Roman mythology, he was known as Mars.

Aries Lat. "A ram." The name of the astrological sign for those born from March 21 to April 19.

Ares, Arese, Ariese

Arion Greek mythology name. Arion was a poet from about 700 B.C. He is sometimes erroneously identified with Orion, who was the mighty hunter and gave his name to a constellation.

Aryon

Aris Dim. **Aristeo**. A modern shortening.

Arris

Aristeo Sp. from Gk. "The best." The root is also the root of the word "aristocrat," which appears in the following names as well.

Aris, Aristio, Aristo, Aristos

Aristides Gk. "Best." Aristides was a famous Athenian general and statesman during the Golden Age of Athens.

Aristeides

Aristotle Gk. "Superior." Indelibly associated with the Greek philosopher Aristotle, though given prominence in recent years by the fame of Jacqueline Kennedy's second husband, shipping magnate Aristotle Onassis.

Ari, Arie, Aristotelis, Aristotellis, Arri, Ary

Arledge OE. Place name: "Lake with the hares." TV executive Roone Arledge.

Arlidge, Arlledge, Arrledge

Arlen Ir. Gael. "Pledge, oath."

Arlan, Arlenn, Arles, Arlin, Arlyn, Arllen, Arrlen

Arliss Old name of confused origin. Possibly goes back to a Hebrew word meaning "Pledge."

Arley OE. Place name: "Hare-meadow."

Arlea, Arleigh, Arlie, Arly

Arlo Sp. "Barberry tree." Enjoyed a spurt of popularity in the early 1970s, possibly attendant on the fame of singer Arlo Guthrie. With the current interest in artifacts of the '70s, combined with new interest in "-o" endings for boys' names, Arlo may see a spurt of use.

Arlow, Arlowe, Arrlo

Armand Fr. Var. **Herman** (OG. "Army man"). The most commonly used form in the U.S. is **Armando**, which is unusual but not as scarce as Herman itself. Actor Armand Assante.

Almando, Arman, Armande, Armando, Armani, Armin, Armon, Armond, Armonde, Armondo, Ormond, Ormonde, Ormondo

Armani Though the root of this name is probably **Herman**, in the late 20th century it most likely refers to the Italian fashion designer Giorgio Armani.

Amani, Armahni

Armin Lat. Var. **Herman** (OG. "Army man"). German actor Armin Mueller-Stahl.

Arman, Armen, Arminio, Arminius

Armon Heb. "Chestnut."

Armoni

Armstrong OE. "Strong arm."

Arnaud Fr. Var. **Arnold**.

Arnald, Arnaldo, Arnauld, Arnault

Arne OG. "Eagle." Var. **Arnold**.

Arney, Arni, Arnie

Arnett OF./Eng. "Little eagle." Broadcaster Peter Arnett.

Arnat, Arnet, Arnot, Arnott, Ornet, Ornette

Arno OG. "Eagle-wolf."

Arnoe, Arnou, Arnoux, Arnow, Arnowe

Arnold OG. "Strength of an eagle." Brought to Britain with the Norman invasion, faded out after the 13th century, and briefly revived in the late 19th century. Unusual today, perhaps because it has vaguely dorky connotations. English novelist Arnold Bennett; golfer Arnold Palmer; actor Arnold Schwarzenegger.

Arnaldo, Arnaud, Arnauld, Arnault, Arndt, Arne, Arney, Arni, Arnie, Arnoldo, Arnot, Arny

Arran Scot. Place name. The Isle of Arran is off the Atlantic coast. Also possibly a phonetic variant of **Aaron**,
even though the sources are unrelated.
Arren, Arrin, Arron

Arrigo It. Var. **Henry** (OG. "Estate ruler"). **Enrico** is the
other variation.

Arrio Sp. "Belligerent."
Ario, Arryo, Aryo

Arsenio Gk. "Masculine." A St. Arsenius was one of the
Desert Fathers of Christianity, who lived in the 4th century A.D. His most famous saying was, "I have often
been sorry for having spoken, but never for having held
my tongue." Comedian Arsenio Hall.
**Arcenio, Arcinio, Arsanio, Arseenio, Arseinio, Ar-
semio, Arsen, Arsene, Arsenios, Arsenius, Arseno, Ar-
senyo, Arsinio, Arsino**

Artemus Gk. Probably "Follower of the goddess Artemis."
New Testament name occasionally used in the 19th century. **Apollonius** and **Dennis** are the analogous "follower
of" names: it's remarkable that they have survived so
long after worship of the Greek pantheon died out. Author Artemas Ward.
**Art, Artemas, Artemis, Artie, Artimas, Artimis, Ar-
timus, Arty**

Arthur Celt. Possibly "Bear" or "Rock." Linked with King
Arthur, the legendary British hero of the Round Table,
and often used in the Middle Ages, but unfashionable until the early 19th century, when Arthur Wellesley, the
Duke of Wellington, vanquished Napoleon. The Victo-
rian enthusiasm for the romance of the past probably pro-
moted its use, and the name's popularity only began to
wane in the 1920s. It is still familiar, but not common, ex-
cept in Spain, where **Arturo** is currently fashionable.
Columnist Art Buchwald; actor Art Carney; tennis star
Arthur Ashe; writer Arthur C. Clarke; playwright Arthur
Miller.
**Arrt, Art, Artair, Arte, Arther, Arthor, Arthuro, Artie,
Artor, Artro, Artur, Arturo, Artus, Arty, Arthur**

Arundel OE. Place name: "Eagle valley."
  Arondel, Arondell, Arundale, Arundell
Arvad Heb. "Exile, voyager."
  Arpad, Arv, Arvid, Arvie
Arvin OG. "People's friend."
  Arv, Arvid, Arvie, Arvy, Arwin, Arwyn
Ary Var. Ari. Heb. "Lion."
  Arye, Aryeh
Asa Heb. "Doctor." Another Old Testament name made popular by the Puritans in the 17th century. Now unusual.
  Ase
Asad Arab. "Luckier."
  Assad
Asael Heb. "God has made." Old Testament name rarely in the 19th century in the U.S.
  Asaya, Asayel, Asahel, Asiel
Asaph Heb. "Gathered up." Old Testament name, again, scarcely used.
  Asaf, Asiph
Ascanius Latin mythology: son of Aeneas. His other name, Iulus, was the theoretical root of the name of the clan to which Julius Caesar belonged.
Ascot OE. Place name: "Eastern cottage." More specifically the name of England's famous racetrack near Windsor Castle, and also a style of tying a cravat.
  Ascott, Escot, Escott
Asgard ONorse. "Gods' courtyard." The eternal dwelling place of the Scandinavian gods. It was allegedly in the center of the universe, accessible only by a rainbow bridge.
Ash Tree name: the ash tree was common both in England and Scandinavia.
  Ashe, Asshe
Ashbel Heb. "Fire of Bel." Bel was a deity in the pre-Christian pantheon.
Ashby OE. Place name: "Ash tree farm."
  Ash, Ashbie, Ashbey, Ashburn, Ashton

Asher Heb. "Felicitous." Old Testament name brought into English use by the Puritans.

Ash, Asser

Ashford OE. Place name: "Ford near ash trees." Musician Nick Ashford.

Ash, Ashenford

Ashley OE. Place name: "Ash tree meadow." Originally a surname that migrated to first-name status, possibly helped along by Ashley Wilkes in Margaret Mitchell's *Gone With the Wind*. Though originally used for boys, it is now so hugely popular for girls that an infant named Ashley will be presumed to be feminine.

Ash, Ashely, Asheley, Ashelie, Ashlan, Ashleigh, Ashlen, Ashli, Ashlie, Ashlin, Ashling, Ashlinn, Ashly, Ashlyn, Ashlynn

Ashraf Arab. "More honorable."

Ashton OE. Place name: "Ash tree settlement." More popular in the 19th century than now, though this is the kind of name Anglophile parents of the 21st century may make more popular. Choreographer Sir Frederick Ashton; museum executive Ashton Hawkins; actor Ashton Kutcher.

Assheton, Ashtun

Ashur Semitic. "Warlike one." A name used by various Assyrian kings, who lived up to its meaning.

Asher

Asim Arab. "Guardian."

Aseem

Aslan Literary name: invented by the author C.S. Lewis for the magical lion in *The Lion, the Witch and the* ... gigantic race that walked the earth before ... round. He was the father of the winds.

Astraios

... nthology, Astraeus was one of the Ti... Martin. Famous for an En...

Aswin OE. "Spear-friend."
  Aswinn, Aswyn, Aswynn
Athanasius Gk. "Endless life."
  Atanasio, Atanasios, Atanasius, Athan, Athanasios
Athens Gk. Place name: the capital of Greece. Athens is considered the cradle of democracy, and many cities in the United States bear its name.
  Athenios
Atherton OE. Place name: "Town by the spring." The town of Atherton in Northern California is more likely to be named after early settlers named Atherton.
Athelstan OE. "Highborn rock." Used by Anglo-Saxon royalty and revived slightly by Sir Walter Scott's use of it in *Ivanhoe*. Now extremely rare.
Athol Scot. Place name, meaning unclear. The Duke of Atholl, in Scotland, is the only citizen of the United Kingdom entitled to maintain his own private army.
  Atholl
Athos Literary name: one of the Three Musketeers from Alexandre Dumas famous novel.
Atif Arab. "Compassionate."
  Ateef, Atiph
Atlas Gk. "To carry." Atlas was a mythical Titan who bore the weight of the world on his shoulders, so the name bears connotations of great strength.
  Attlas
Atley OE. Place name: "The meadow." Indicates an ancestor who, once upon a time, lived in a house near (or "at") a meadow. The same pattern is true for the following names, all based on features of a long-ago English land-
  Atne English politician Clement Attlee.
Atticus L.
  man of letters
  Roman empire.
  "publisher" because he
  temporary works like the le
  the name resounds from associat
  Attlee, Attleigh, Attley
  a famous Roman
  of the

the heroic lawyer of Harper Lee's *To Kill a Mocking-bird*.

Attila OG. "Little father." Generally remembered because of Attila the Hun, the Germanic king whose cruel invasions of the Balkans and Gaul helped hasten the end of the Roman Empire. One of his nicknames was "the scourge of God."

Atila, Atilano, Atilo, Attilia, Attilio

Atwater OE. Place name: "The water."

Attwater

Atwell OE. Place name: "The well."

Atwood OE. Place name: "The wood."

Atwoode

Atworth OE. Place name: "The farmstead."

Auberon OG. "Highborn and bearlike." Also possibly a form of **Aubrey**. Better-known, though no more common for it, as Oberon, King of the Fairies in Shakespeare's *Midsummer Night's Dream*. English writer Auberon Waugh.

Auberron, Oberon, Oberron, Oeberon

Aubrey OF. "Elf ruler." Originally a man's name that arrived in England with the Norman Conquest. Now used by girls as well, thus no doubt dooming its use as a boys' name. The 19th-century artist Aubrey Beardsley; biographer John Aubrey.

Alberic, Alberick, Alberik, Aube, Auberon, Aubry, Averey, Averie, Avery, Oberon

Audley OE. Place name of uncertain meaning.

Audric OG. "Noble ruler." Var. **Aldrich**.

August Lat. "Worthy of respect." The feminine version, **Augusta**, and the longer Latin version, **Augustus**, are more widely (though still infrequently) used in English-speaking countries. Sculptor Auguste Rodin; painter Auguste Renoir.

Agostino, Agosto, Aguistin, Agustin, Agustino, Augie, Auguste, Augustin, Augustine, Augustino, Augusto, Augustus, Augie, Augy, Austen, Austin, Gus, Guss

Augustine Lat. Dim. **August**. The 5th-century bishop Saint Augustine is famous for the frank *Confessions,* in which he says, "Oh God, make me chaste—but not yet."
Aguistin, Agustin, Augie, Augustin, Augy, Austen, Austin, Austyn

Augustus Lat. "Worthy of respect." Given historical glamor by Roman emperors and German princely families, who brought it to Britain in the 18th century, when it became very fashionable. Now little used. Sculptor Augustus Saint-Gaudens; painter Augustus John; beer magnate Augustus Busch.
Augie, Augustin, Augy, Austen, Austin, Austyn, Gus, Guss

Aurelius Lat. "Golden."
Aurelio, Aurelo, Oriel

Austin Oral form of **Augustine**, contracted by everyday speech. Now most often a family name transferred to a first name. The "Austin Powers" movies have probably disqualified it from use for a whole generation of future parents.
Austen, Austyn, Ostyn, Ostynn

Autry Var. **Audrey** (OE. "Noble strength"). Actor Gene Autry.
Autrey

Avenall OF. Place name: "Oat pasture."
Aveneil, Aveneill, Avenel, Avenell, Avenil, Avenill

Averett Var. **Everett** (OE "Board hardness").
Averet, Averit, Averitt, Averret

Averill Most likely derivation is OE. "Boar-warrior," though may also be related to French *avril* or "April." Industrialist and statesman Averell Harriman.
Ave, Averel, Averell, Averil, Averyl, Averyll, Avrel, Avrell, Avrill, Avryll, Haverell, Haverill

Avery OE. "Elf-ruler." Currently quite scarce, but a real candidate for popularity. Var. **Alfred, Aubrey**. Philanthropist Avery Fisher.
Averey

Aviel Heb. "God is my father."
Avyel

Avram Heb. Var. **Abraham**.
   Aviram
Avishai Heb. "Gift of my father."
Avital Heb. "Father of dew." Also used as a girl's name in Israel. In a dry climate like that of Israel, dew has great significance.
   Amital
Avner Heb. form of **Abner** ("My father is light").
   Abner
Axel OG. "Father of peace" and Scand. Var. **Absalom**. Rock star Axl Rose.
   Aksel, Ax, Axe, Axell, Axil, Axill, Axl
Aylmer OE. "Highborn and renowned." The homonym **Elmer** is the more common form of this very old English name.
   Aillmer, Ailmer, Allmer, Ayllmer, Elmer, Eylmer
Aylward OE. "Awesome guardian" or "Highborn guardian."
Ayman Arab. "Lucky, blessed."
Azim Arab. "Protector, defender."
   Asim, Aseem, Azeem
Aziz Arab. "Strong, mighty." Another one of Allah's ninety-nine attributes, and thus a familiar name in the Muslim world.
Azrael Biblical: the archangel who is charged with care of those born under the sign of Scorpio (Oct. 23 to Nov. 21). He appears in both Muslim and Jewish stories.
Azriel Heb. "God is my help."
   Azreel, Azryel
Azuriah Heb. "Aided by Jehovah." Although 28 different biblical characters are known by this name, it is all but obsolete today. Actor Hank Azaria.
   Azaria, Azariah, Azria, Azriah, Azuria

Babson OE. "Son of Barbara." Unusual in that it is based on a mother's rather than a father's name.
Babsen, Babsson

Bachelor MF. "Unmarried man." Usually a family name.
Bachellor, Batcheler, Batcheller, Batchelor, Batchellor

Bacchus Greek mythology name: Bacchus is the Greek god of wine, equivalent to Dionysus. He is also the god of poets, perhaps a more encouraging notion.

Bailey OF. "Bailiff." Occupational name: in the Middle Ages a bailiff was a minor officer of the law. When it appears, this is usually a transferred last name, but if its occasional use for girls takes off, parents of boys will hesitate to use it.
Bail, Bailee, Bailie, Baillee, Baillie, Baily, Baley, Baylee, Bayley, Bayly

Bainbridge Ir. Gael. "Pale bridge." Also a place name: an island in Washington state, across Puget Sound from Seattle.
Bain, Banebridge, Baynbridge, Bayne, Baynebridge

Baird Gael. "One who sings ballads." The more familiar form in English, of course, is **Bard**. This is an occupational name.
Bar, Bard, Barde, Barr, Bayerd, Bayrd

Baker OE. Occupational name transferred to surname and, in the 19th century, to a first name. Politician James Baker.

Balbo Lat. "Mutterer."
Bailby, Balbi, Balbino, Ballbo

Baldemar OG. "Bold and renowned." Like many of the more exotic names, use of this one has been prolonged by the fact that it is a saint's name. St. Baldomar was a blacksmith who became a monk, and is the patron saint of blacksmiths, a profession much less common than it used to be.

Baldomar, Baldomero, Baumar, Baumer

Balder OE. "Courageous army." In Norse myth the god Balder is called "the good," and reigns over summer, light, and innocence. Of course in Norway, "bald" may not mean "hairless."

Baldor, Baldur, Baudier

Baldric OG. "Brave ruler." *Bald,* obviously, is the particle meaning "brave" in these Old German names. *Ric,* as in **Frederick** and **Richard**, is the particle that means "ruler." In Rowan Atkinson's comic "Blackadder" series, Baldric is the buffoon sidekick.

Balderic, Balderik, Baldrick, Baudric

Baldwin OG. "Brave friend." Unusual in English-speaking countries, though **Baudoin** is a royal name in Belgium. Author James Baldwin.

Bald, Baldewin, Baldovino, Balduin, Balduino, Baldwinn, Baldwyn, Baldwynn, Balldwin, Baudoin

Balfour Gael. "Grazing land." Also the name of a town in northern Scotland. In Robert Louis Stevenson's *Kidnapped,* David Balfour is the young, idealistic hero. The Balfour Declaration of 1917 was a declaration of British support for limited Jewish settlement in Palestine. It was named for its author, British Foreign Secretary Arthur James Balfour, and Balfour was occasionally used as a first name in Israel afterward.

Balfer, Balfor, Balfore, Ballfour

Ballard OG. "Brave and strong."

Balthasar Gk. "God save the king." Along with Caspar and Melchior, one of the Three Kings who brought gifts to the baby Jesus, though they are not named in the Bible. Actor Balthazar Getty.

Baldassare, Baltasar, Baltazar, Balthasaar, Balthazaar, Balthazar, Balto, Belshazzar

Bancroft OE. Place name: "Field of beans." Many of the most common Anglo-Saxon place names that have become first names refer to simple, homely agricultural landmarks. Hubert Howe Bancroft was a prominent historian in the western United States whose collection forms the nucleus of the Bancroft Library of the University of California.

Ban, Bancrofft, Banfield, Bank, Binky

Banner OF. "Flag." This is probably an occupational name referring to someone whose job was to carry a flag or banner.

Bannerman

Banning Ir. Gael. "Small fair one" or "Son of the fair one."

Bannock Scot. Gael. "Unleavened oat bread." The name may indicate an ancestor who was a baker.

Bannoch

Baptiste Fr. from Gk. "Baptizer." Reference to John the Baptist, who baptized Jesus in the River Jordan. The Spanish form, Bautista, may be slightly more common in the U.S.

Baptist, Battista, Battiste, Bautista

Barak Heb. "Lightning." Name of an Old Testament warrior. Has a rather pugnacious sound, too.

Barber OF. "Beard." Originally an occupational name; the French word for beard is *barbe,* and long ago, men who wished to have their facial hair cut or trimmed would have it done professionally, as not everyone possessed a razor.

Barbar, Barbour

Barclay OE. Place name: "Where birches grow." This is the form most favored in Scotland; **Berkeley** is more common elsewhere. Barclays is the name of one of the biggest banks in Britain. Basketball player Charles Barkley.

Bar, Barcley, Barklay, Barkley, Barklie, Barrclay, Berk, Berkeley, Berkie, Berkley, Berklie, Berky

Bard Ir. Var. Baird.

Bar, Barde, Bardo, Barr

Barden OE. Place name: "Barley valley."

Bardon, Borden, Bordon

Bardolf OE. "Axe-wolf." A drunken fool named Bardolph figures in four of Shakespeare's plays.

Bardolph, Bardou, Bardoul, Bardulf, Bardulph

Bardrick Teut. "Axe-ruler." Just as many of the Anglo-Saxon names relate to farming, numerous Teutonic names relate to fighting.
Bardric, Bardrich

Barend OG. "Hard bear."

Barker OE. Possibly "Shepherd," though the name may also relate to birch trees, as in **Barclay**. Used more often in the 19th century. In the U.S. a barker is also someone who delivers a glib sales talk to attract customers.
Birk

Barksdale OE. "Birch valley."

Barlow OE. Place name: "The bare hillside." Joel Barlow was an early American statesman.
Barlowe, Barrlow

Barnabas Heb. "Son of comfort." In the New Testament, Barnabas is a companion of Paul's and uncle of the gospeler Mark. **Barnaby** is used more often now in Britain. One of Charles Dickens's lesser-known novels is entitled *Barnaby Rudge*. The name is used from time to time among literary parents.
Barna, Barnaba, Barnabé, Barnabee, Barnabey, Barn-abie, Barnabus, Barnaby, Barnebas, Barnebus, Barney, Barni, Barnie, Barny, Bernabé, Burnaby

Barnes OE. Place name: "Near the barns." The name's slightly rakish aura probably goes back to Jake Barnes, hero of Hemingway's novel *The Sun Also Rises*.

Barnett OE. Place name: "From the land that was burned." Or possibly a contraction of the English aristocratic title "baronet." **Duke**, **Earl**, and **Baron**, other ranks of English nobility, are used as first names from time to time.
Barnet, Barney, Barnie, Baronet, Baronett, Barrie, Barron, Barry

Barney Var. **Barnabas**. This contraction was on its way to being more often used until a large purple dinosaur hi-jacked it. Now his fame is so widespread that it will be ages before Barney could possibly be a child again.
Barny

Barnum OE. Possibly a contraction of "Baron's home." In the U.S., inseparable from Phineas T. Barnum, founder of

Barnum & Bailey's circus and one of America's great showmen.

Barnham

Baron OE. The title of nobility used as a first name. In England, a baron was the lowest rank of hereditary peerage that entitles the holder to serve in the House of Lords. Of course none of these nobility names are actually used in countries where there is still an official aristocracy.

Baronicio, Barren, Barron

Barret OG. "Bear-strength." Used as a first name mostly in the 19th century, possibly because of the fame of English poet Elizabeth Barrett Browning.

Baret, Barrat, Barratt, Barrett, Barrey, Barrie, Barry

Barrington Eng. Place name now fairly common as a first name in Britain. Perhaps a bit of a mouthful for the more democratic U.S.

Barry Gael. "Sharp, pointed." Also a place name turned into a first name used by both sexes. Possibly influenced by the fame of Sir James Barrie, author of *Peter Pan*, since it cropped up as a first name during the height of his renown. **Barry** (with the–"y") was quite popular in the 1950s. Senator Barry M. Goldwater; singer Barry Manilow; baseball player Barry Bonds.

Barree, Barrey, Bari, Barrie, Baris

Bart Dim. **Bartholomew**. Football player Bart Starr.

Barrt

Bartholomew Heb. "Farmer's son." One of the twelve apostles. The name was common in the Middle Ages but was not revived in the 19th century, as so many medieval names were. Extremely unusual today: three syllables seems to be the maximum length parents are willing to shout across a playground.

Bart, Bartel, Barth, Barthelemy, Bartho, Barthold, Bartholoma, Bartholomaus, Bartholomé, Barthlomeo, Barthol, Barthold, Bartholomeus, Bartlet, Bartlett, Bartolome, Bartolomeo, Bartolommeo, Bartome, Bartow, Bartt, Bat, Bertel

Bartlet Dim. **Bartholomew**. Literary types for generations have relied on *Familiar Quotations* compiled by

John Bartlett, first published in 1855. The liberal, scholarly President on *The West Wing* is called Josiah Bartlett, a name with old-money New England connotations.
Bartlett, Bartlitt

Barton OE. Place name: "Barley settlement," or possibly "Bart's town."
Bart, Barten, Barrton

Bartram OE. "Bright raven." See **Bertram**.
Barthram

Baruch Heb. "Blessed." Many languages have a form of this name: in English, **Benedict**; in Italian, **Benedetto**, in French, **Benoit**, in Spanish, **Benito**. American philanthropist Bernard Baruch.
Baruchi, Boruch

Basil Gk. "Royal, kingly." Brought to England by the Crusaders, having been common in the eastern Mediterranean. Unusual in the U.S., but more often used in Britain. Also the name of a common herb. As is obvious from the range of variants, the name has been widely used throughout Europe, though in the U.S. it seems a bit affected, probably because the only Basil most Americans know of is the British actor Basil Rathbone, who played Sherlock Holmes in 14 films in the 1940s. Film director Baz Lurhmann.
Basile, Basilic, Basilides, Basileios, Basilie, Basilio, Basilius, Bazeel, Bazeelius, Bazil, Bazyli, Vasilios, Vasilis, Vasilius, Vasilus, Vassilij, Vassily, Wassily

Bassett OE. "Little person." Descriptive surname transferred to first name. Also the name of a very short-legged hunting dog, the basset hound, possibly called that because its torso is so low (*bas* in French) to the ground.
Basset

Bastian Dim. **Sebastian** (Lat. "From Sebastia").
Bastien

Battista It. "Baptizer." For John the Baptist. This name survives best in countries with a strong Roman Catholic tradition. Often children are given the two-part name, "Gian Battista" or "Jean-Baptiste."
Baptist, Baptiste, Bautista

Baxter OE. Occupational name: "Baker."
Bax, Baxley

Baxley ME. "Baker's meadow."
Baxlea, Baxlee, Baxlie, Baxly

Bay Geographic name (to describe an indentation of land in a coastline) or plant name. The term "bay" is used for several different kinds of trees, including the bay laurel, whose leaves are used as an herb and were also twined into wreaths by the Greeks, to crown victors. The name is equally unusual—and equally appropriate—for boys or girls, and is usually a family name.

Bayard OE. "Russet-haired." A famous French knight of the 15th century, the Seigneur de Bayard, was known as "the irreproachable and fearless." In French medieval romance, Bayard (or Baiardo, or Bajardo) is a magical horse given to the hero Rinaldo. The horse was a bright bay color. In the U.S., three generations of Bayards were Senators from Delaware in the eighteenth and nineteenth centuries.
Baiardo, Bajardo, Bay

Bayless OF. "One who leases a bay." Perhaps refers to a fishing ancestor.
Baylless

Bayou Geography name: a slow-moving river or swamp. Used most generally in the southern United States.

Beacher OE. Place name: "Near the beech trees." Generally a last name. The 19th-century preacher Henry Ward Beecher.
Beach, Beachy, Beech, Beecher, Beechy

Beacon OE. "Signal light." Usually a bright light on a hilltop.

Beagan Ir. Gael. "Small one."
Beagen, Beagin, Beegan, Beegin

Beal OF. "Handsome." Var. **Beau**.
Beale, Beall, Bealle, Beals

Beaman OE. Occupational name: "Beekeeper." Athlete Bob Beamon.
Beamann, Beamen, Beeman, Beamon, Beemon

Beamer OE. "Trumpet player."
Beemer

Beasley OE. "Meadow of peas."
Beals, Beaslie, Beasly, Peaseley, Peasly

Beattie (masc. **Beatrice**) Ir. Gael. from Lat. "Bringer of gladness."
Beatie, Beatty, Beaty

Beau Fr. "Handsome." Dim. **Beauregard**. Used somewhat in the U.S. in the last 30 years. Nowadays the name is likely to be heard as the less formal **Bo**. English dandy Beau Brummel; actor Beau Bridges; sports star Bo Jackson.
Beal, Beale, Bo, Boe

Beauchamp OF. Place name: "The beautiful field." Pronounced by the English as "Beecham."
Beecham

Beaufort OF. Place name: "The beautiful fort."

Beaumont OF. Place name: "The beautiful mountain." More common in the 19th century than it is today. English playwright Francis Beaumont.

Beauregard Fr. "Beautiful gaze." In Patrick Dennis's novel *Auntie Mame,* Mame marries a Southerner, Beauregard Jackson Burnside, a caricature of Southern courtesy. Dennis took his name from the names of three prominent Confederate generals, Pierre Beauregard (who fired on Fort Sumter), Thomas Jackson (known as "Stonewall"), and Ambrose Burnside (better known for his whiskers, now called "sideburns"). Could also be taken to mean, in modern parlance, "easy on the eye." A lot for a boy to live up to.
Beau

Becher Heb. "Young man, first born."

Beck OE. Place name: "Small stream." The term is still in use in rural Scotland. Singer Beck.
Becker

Bede OE. "Prayer." Saint Bede was an influential 7th-century English church historian. He is also supposed to be the first documented writer of English (as opposed to Latin) prose, though his English works have been lost.
Beda

Bedell OF. "Messenger." A somewhat unusual last name.
Bedall

Beebe OE. "Bee farmer."

Belden OE./OF. Place name: "Pretty valley."
Beldene, Beldon, Bellden, Belldene, Belidon

Belindo Masc. **Belinda**. Probably intended to mean something like "Handsome," though Belinda may go back to an Old German word meaning "Dragon."
Bellindo

Belisario Sp. from Gk. "Swordsman."
Belisarios, Belisarius

Bell Dim. **Bellamy**. May also be an occupational name, for a bell-ringer.

Bellamy OF. "Handsome friend." English actor Ralph Bellamy.
Belamy, Bell, Bellamey, Bellamie, Bellemy

Bellarmine It. "Beautifully armed."

Belmont OF. "Beautiful mountain." A place name frequently found in America.
Bellmont

Belton ME. Place name: "Beautiful town." Or possibly "Town of the bells."
Bellton

Beltran Sp. Var. **Bertram** (OG. "Bright raven") or **Bertrand** (OG. "Bright shield").
Bertran

Belvedere It. "Beautiful to see." This is the name of a gallery in the Vatican that contains some of the greatest classical Greek statues, among them the *Apollo Belvedere,* which took its name from the gallery.
Bellveder, Bellvedere, Bellvidere, Belveder, Belvider, Belvidere

Bemus Gk. "Foundation."
Beamus, Bemis

Ben Heb. "Son." Dim. **Benedict, Benjamin, Benson**, etc. Now given as an independent name, especially popular in Ireland. Many Hebrew names combine Ben with another name, so that Ben-Baruch, for example, means "Son of the blessed." Playwright Ben Jonson; actors Ben Gazzara,

Ben Stiller, Ben Vereen, Ben Affleck; musician Benny Goodman.

Benn, Benny

Benedict Lat. "Blessed." Saint Benedict, founder of a monastic order, brought the name to prominence. **Bennett** is the more common form, especially in the U.S., where every schoolchild learns the tale of Revolutionary War traitor Benedict Arnold. Italian dictator Benito Mussolini; actor Benicio del Toro.

Ben, Bendick, Bendict, Benedetto, Benedick, Benedicto, Benedictos, Benedictus, Benedikt, Benedikte, Bengt, Benicio, Benito, Bennedict, Bennedikt, Bennet, Bennett, Bennie, Bennito, Bennt, Benoit, Bent, Venedictos

Benigno Lat. "Kind, well-born." From the root that gives us "benign."

Benjamin Heb. "Son of the right hand." In the Old Testament, the younger son of Jacob and Rachel. Brought into use by the Puritan fondness for Old Testament names, and persistent until the end of the 19th century. As the many variants show, it has been widely used all over Europe. After several decades of disuse, came back to great popularity by the 1970s, and is now quite standard, and positively fashionable in Spain. Diplomat and inventor Benjamin Franklin; U.S. President Benjamin Harrison; jazz musician Benny Goodman; pediatrician and oracle Benjamin Spock; British Prime Minister Benjamin Disraeli; actor Benjamin Bratt.

Ben, Benejamen, Beniamino, Benjaman, Benjamen, Benjamino, Benjamon, Benjee, Benjey, Benji, Benjie, Benjiman, Benjimen, Benjy, Benn, Bennie, Benno, Benny, Benyamin, Benyamino, Binyamin, Binyamino, Venyamin, Yamin, Yamino, Yemin

Bennett Fr. Var. **Benedict**. Choreographer Michael Bennett; humorist Bennett Cerf; author William Bennett; aviation pioneer Floyd Bennett.

Benet, Benett, Bennet, Benoit

Benoni Heb. "Son of my sorrow." In the Old Testament, Rachel, mother of Benjamin, knew she was dying after his birth and called him Benoni, but Jacob, his father, changed the name to Benjamin.

Benson "Son of Ben." Originally a surname, transferred to a first name in the 19th century.

Bensen, Benssen, Bensson

Bentley OE. "Meadow with coarse grass." Place name become surname become first name, more common for boys but used occasionally for girls. Irresistibly linked in most minds with the luxurious English cars.

Ben, Bentlea, Bentlee, Bentley, Bentlie, Bently, Lee

Benton OE. Place name. As in **Bentley**, refers to a kind of "bent" or coarse grass. Artist Thomas Hart Benton; film director Robert Benton.

Benvenuto It. "Welcome." In Italy, often refers to the joy at the birth of a long-awaited child. Goldsmith Benvenuto Cellini.

Bienvenido

Beresford OE. Place name: "Ford where barley grows." Used as a first name principally at the turn of the century. Film director Bruce Beresford.

Berg Ger. "Mountain." Often found as a suffix in German surnames like Kleinberg, ("Small mountain"), Goldberg ("Gold mountain"), or Hochberg ("High mountain").

Berger, Bergh, Burg, Burgh

Bergen Scand. "Lives on the hill." Bergen is a major port city in Norway.

Bergin, Birgin

Berger Fr. Occupational name: "Shepherd." Game show host Tom Bergeron.

Bergeron

Berilo Sp. from Gk. "Pale green gemstone." Masculine version of **Beryl**. The beryl was considered a token of good luck.

Berillo

Berkeley OE. Place name: "Where birches grow." In the U.S. probably most famous as the San Francisco suburb that is home to a branch of the University of California.

Bar, Barcley, Barklay, Barkley, Barklie, Barrclay,

Berk, Berkeley, Berkie, Berklee, Berkley, Berky, Birkeley, Birkley

Berlin Ger. "Borderline."

Berlyn

Bern OG. "Bear." Also possible nickname for **Bernard**.

Berne, Bernie, Berny, Bjorn

Bernal OG. "Strength of a bear." Occasionally used in English-speaking countries, but more common on the Continent.

Bernald, Bernhald, Bernhold, Bernold

Bernard OG. "Bear/courageous." Brought to England with the Norman Conquest. Two famous medieval saints bore the name; one was a founder of a monastic order. The other, for whom the shaggy brown and white dogs are named, is patron saint of mountain climbers. A fairly common name until the 18th century and revived a bit around 1920, but now unusual. Playwright George Bernard Shaw; statesman Bernard M. Baruch; film director Bernardo Bertolucci; art critic Bernard Berenson; comedian Bernie Mack.

Barnard, Barnardo, Barney, Barnhard, Barnhardo, Barnie, Barny, Bear, Bearnard, Bern, Bernardo, Bernarr, Bernd, Berndt, Bernhard, Bernhardo, Bernie, Bernis, Bernt, Burnard

Berry Botanical name used for both boys and girls, though the boy's name is more likely a derivative of **Bernard** or a transferred surname. Pop music impresario Berry Gordy.

Bert OE. "Shining brightly." Dim. **Albert, Egbert, Robert**, etc. Used more often as a nickname. Its popularity among show-business types of a certain age (Miss America emcee Bert Parks, actors Burt Lancaster and Burt Reynolds) suggests a jaunty, masculine connotation.

Bertie, Berty, Burt, Burty, Butch

Berthold OG. "Bright strength." Unusual in English-speaking countries, but not unheard-of. Playwright Bertolt Brecht.

Bert, Bertell, Bertil, Berthoud, Bertol, Bertoli, Bertold, Bertolde, Berton

Berton OE. Place name: "Bright settlement."
Bert, Bertie, Burt, Burton

Bertram OG. "Bright raven." Norman name revived in the Victorian era. Rare since the 1930s. Archictect Bertram Goodhue.
Bart, Bartram, Beltran, Beltrano, Berton, Bertran, Bertrand, Bertrando, Bertranno

Bertrand OG. "Bright shield." Also possibly a variation on **Bertram**. Philosopher Bertrand Russell.

Berwyn OE. "Bear friend" or "Bright friend."
Berwin, Berwynn, Berwynne

Bethel Heb. "House of God." Another biblical place name: the spot where Abraham built an altar. Unusual as a first name.
Betuel

Bevan Welsh. "Son of Evan." Mostly 20th-century use, though there may be some spillover from the popularity of soundalike **Devon**. British politician Aneurin Bevan.
Beavan, Beaven, Bev, Beven, Bevin, Bevon, Bevvan, Bevvin, Bevvon, Bivian

Beverly OE. "Of the beaver-stream." Originally an English place name transferred to a surname, then a first name for both sexes. Probably still most famous as a place name, referring to Beverly Hills. The English spelling is usually **Beverley**. In the U.S., this is more likely to be considered a girl's name.
Beverlea, Beverleigh, Beverley, Beverlie

Bevis OF. Place name: Beauvais is a town in France famous for the manufacture of tapestries. Other possible derivations are Welsh, "Son of Evan," and something related to the French word for "bull," *beuve*. This anglicized version is very unusual, and the popularity of the cartoon *Beavis and Butthead* won't do much for its eligibility as a baby name.
Beauvais, Beavess, Beavis, Beviss

Biagio It. "Stutterer." Related to **Blaise**.
Biaggio

Bickford OE. Place name: "Axe-man's ford."

Bienvenido Sp. "Welcome."
Benvenuto

Biff American slang: "To hit." The root of this expression is mysterious, and it is very unlikely to be used today.

Bill Dim. **William**. Used occasionally as an independent name. Before mid 19th century, **Will** was the more common nickname. Nowadays the many boys named William (one of the top 20 names in the U.S.) are much more likely to have their names shortened to a form with a "W." Actors Bill Cosby, Billy Crystal, Bill Bixby, Billy Crudup, Billy Bob Thornton; designer Bill Blass; singer Billy Joel.
Billie, Billy, Byll

Bing OG. Place name: "The hollow shaped like a pot." Another source claims that modern use of the name is inspired by singer Bing Crosby, who was given the nickname after a comic-strip character. His given name was actually Harry.

Bingo Origin unknown. The name of a very popular game. Usually used as a nickname.

Birch OE. Place name: "Where birch trees grow." Not uncommon in the 19th century. Senator Birch Bayh.
Birk, Burch

Birchall OE. Place name: "Birch hall."
Birchell, Burchall, Burchell

Birkett ME. Place name: "Birch coastland."
Birket, Birkit, Birkitt, Burket, Burkett, Burkitt

Birkey ME. Place name: "Island of birch trees."
Birkee, Birkie, Birky

Birley OE. Place name: "Meadow with the cow byre." Not related to the homonym **Burleigh**.
Birlie, Birly

Birney OE. Place name: "Island with the brook."
Birnie, Birny, Burney, Burnie

Birtle OE. Place name: "Hill of birds."
Bertle

Bishop OE. "Bishop." Probably originally meant "One serving the bishop," or "Bishop's man."
Bishopp

Bjorn Scan. Var. **Bernard**. The fame of tennis player Bjorn Borg is probably responsible for the use of this name in English-speaking countries.
Bjarn, Bjarne, Bjorne

Black OE. "Dark-skinned."

Blackburn OE. Place name: "Black brook." Used as a first name mostly in the 19th century. In Scotland, "burn" is still the term for a little brook.
Blackburne, Blagburn

Blackstone OE. Place name: "Black stone."

Blackwell OE. Place name: "Black well."

Blagden OE. Place name: "Dark valley."

Blaine Ir. Gael. "Slender." Surname used since the 1930s as a first name, mostly for boys but occasionally for girls. Magician David Blaine.
Blane, Blayne

Blair Scot. Gael. Place name: "Plain" or "Flat area." Surname now used as first name, again more common for boys. Like many similarly transferred names, Blair was used for girls in greater numbers starting in the early 1980s.
Blaire, Blayr, Blayre

Blaise Lat./Fr. "One who stutters." Used for both sexes, though more common for men, and popular in France. The alternate spelling of **Blaze** probably refers to fire instead. French philosopher Blaise Pascal.
Biagio, Blaize, Blas, Blase, Blasio, Blasios, Blasius, Blayse, Blayze, Blaze

Blake OE. Paradoxically, could mean either "Pale-skinned" or "Dark." Surname used as a first name for either sex, most often in the U.S. Director Blake Edwards; *Dynasty* character Blake Carrington.

Blakely OE. Place name: "Dark meadow" or "Pale meadow." See **Blake**.
Blakelee, Blakeleigh, Blakeley, Blakelie

Blakeney OE. Place name: "Dark island" or "White island."
Blakenie, Blakeny

Blanco Sp. "Fair, white."
  Bianco
Blanford OE. Place name: "Gray man's ford."
  Blandford
Blanton Lat./Fr. "Mild, bland."
  Blandon
Blaze Lat. "One who stutters." Anglicized form of **Blaise**,
  though for a child of the 21st century the name spelled
  this way is more likely to invoke flames.
  **Biaggio, Biagio, Blaise, Blaize, Blase, Blasien, Bla-
  sius, Blayse, Blayze**
Bligh OE. "Bliss." This name is related to **Bliss** and
  Blythe, but because of the fame of English sea captain
  William Bligh, whose crew on the HMS *Bounty* mutinied
  in 1789, it has taken on connotations of severity, even
  tyranny. Apparently Bligh did not learn much from the
  first mutiny, for men under his command staged rebellions twice more, in 1794 and in 1808.
  Bly
Bliss OE. "Intense happiness."
Blondell OE. "Little fair-haired one."
Blythe OE. "Happy, carefree." Made famous by the opening lines of Shelley's poem "To a Skylark" ("Hail to thee,
  blithe spirit!") and Noel Coward's play *Blithe Spirit*.
  Bligh, Blithe
Bo Dim. **Robert, Beauregard**. Rare as a given name, more
  likely to be a nickname. Swaggering macho connotations
  (possibly because of the rhyme with "Yo!"?) seem to
  limit use for babies. Football coach Bo Schembechler;
  sports star Bo Jackson.
  Boe
Boaz Heb. "Swiftness." Used for several Old Testament
  characters (including the second husband of Ruth), and
  revived with the Puritan passion for Old Testament
  names. Now very rare.
  Boas, Boase
Bob Dim. **Robert**. OE. "Bright fame." Used independently
  from time to time. The usual habit for naming, however,

is to give the full form of a name, even if the parents never intend to use anything but the nickname. And while **Bobby** was as common as **Susie** and **Linda** for children of the 1950s and '60s, that's all the more reason for today's little Roberts to be called Robbie or Rob instead of the pedestrian Bob. Comedian Bob Hope; singer Bob Dylan; chess master Bobby Fischer; actor Billy Bob Thornton.

Bobbee, Bobbey, Bobbie, Bobby

Boden OF. "One who brings news."

Bodin, Bowden, Bowdoin

Bogart OF. "Bow strength." In current use probably always refers to actor Humphrey Bogart.

Bogey, Bogie, Bogy

Bolivar Sp. from Pol. "Mighty, warlike." Use most likely reflects the fame of revolutionary Simon Bolivar who, in the early 19th century, helped to liberate much of northern South America from Spanish rule.

Bolevar, Bollivar

Bolton English surname of uncertain meaning, though the "-ton" particle probably refers to a town. Singer Michael Bolton.

Bollton, Bolten, Boltin

Bonamy Fr. "Good friend."

Bonami

Bonar OF. "Gentle, mannerly." From the French *debonnaire*. The famous line from the Sermon on the Mount, "Blessed are the meek," translates into French as *Heureux sont les debonnaires*. In English, "debonair" now means something closer to "nonchalant" or "urbane," as personified by Fred Astaire. British politician Bonar Law.

Bonnar, Bonner

Bonaventure Lat. "Blessed undertaking." The Italian St. Bonaventure was a 13th-century cardinal who, in spite of his great learning, was modest and practical. He was known as "The Seraphic Teacher."

Bonaventura, Buenaventura

Bond OE. Occupational name: "Man of the soil." Or as any moviegoer can tell you, "Bond. James Bond."

Boniface Lat. "Fortunate, of good fate." Also commonly,

though erroneously, taken to mean "doing good." Name
of a number of early popes.

Boni, Bonifacio, Bonifacius

Booker Uncertain origin; may allude to "The Book," i.e.,
the Bible. Another possibility is an Anglo-Saxon derivation from the word for "beech tree." American reformer
Booker T. Washington.

Boone OF. "Good." The French adjective is *bon* or *bonne*.
Backwoods connotations courtesy of 19th-century explorer Daniel Boone.

Booth OG. Place name: "Dwelling place." Surname whose
19th-century use as a first name was probably a tribute to
Salvation Army founder William Booth. In the U.S. made
famous also by Lincoln's assassin John Wilkes Booth,
though his precedent would hardly have promoted use.
Author Booth Tarkington.

Boot, Boote, Boothe, Both

Borden OE. Place name: "Vale of the boar."

Bordin

Boris Slavic. "Warrior." Russian playwright Pushkin and
composer Mussorgsky both based works on the career of
the bloodthirsty 16th-century czar Boris Godunov, who
became cartoon character "Boris Badenov" in *The Rocky
and Bullwinkle Show*. Consequent faint comic connotations linger. Horror-movie actor Boris Karloff; author
Boris Pasternak; tennis player Boris Becker.

Boriss, Borris, Borys

Bosley ME. Place name: "Meadow near the woods." The
French root in this and the following names is *bois*, or
"woods."

Boslea, Boslee, Bosleigh, Bosly

Boston ME. Place name: The English town for which the
capital of Massachusetts is named was originally called
"St. Botolph's town" according to some. Others suggest
the simpler derivation, "Town by the woods." Usage in
the U.S. is very likely to refer to the historic city on the
Atlantic that is home to so many institutions of higher
learning.

Boswell ME. Place name: "Well near the woods." James

Boswell was an 18th-century man of letters and the biographer of his contemporary, the lexicographer Samuel Johnson.

Bosworth ME. Place name: "Fenced farm near the woods."

Botolf OE. "Messenger wolf." An obscure 7th-century English saint who was very popular in the Middle Ages. He founded a monastery in England, which is thought to have been in the Lincolnshire town of Boston (Botolph's town).
Botolff, Botolph, Botulf, Botulph

Bourbon Place name: county in Kentucky where the liquor is made. Originally the last name of the royal family of France and Spain. Bourbon St. in New Orleans is still a famous tourist attraction for jazz fans.
Borbon

Bourne OE. Place name: "The stream." A little stream is still called a *burn* in Scotland. Or possibly OF. "Boundary, milestone." Scottish poet Robert Burns.
Born, Borne, Bourn, Burn, Burne, Byrn

Bouvier Lat./Fr. "Ox." Made famous, of course, by Jacqueline Bouvier Kennedy, so the associations may be feminine rather than masculine.

Bowen Welsh. "Son of the young one."
Bowin

Bowie Scot. Gael. "Blond." Col. James Bowie, scout and originator of the knife that bears his name. Former baseball commissioner Bowie Kuhn.
Bow, Bowen

Boyce OF. Place name: "Woods."
Boice, Boise

Boyd Scot. Gael. "Blond." Possibly also a place name, for the Scottish Isle of Bute. Actor Boyd Gaines.
Boid

Boyne Ir. Gael. "White cow." Also an historic place name in Ireland: at the 1690 Battle of the Boyne, the Protestant King William III defeated the Catholic King James II, who fled to France, thus permitting the firm establishment of the Protestant monarchy.
Boine, Boyn

Boynton Eng./Gael. "Town near the Boyne."

Bracken Plant name: a large coarse fern. Lovers of English literature are familiar with the word, if not with the plant itself.

Brad OE. "Broad." Also diminutive for **Bradley** and other "Brad-" names. Quite scarce as a given name. Actors Brad Pitt, Brad Renfro.

   Bradd

Bradburn OE. Place name: "Wide stream."

Braden OE. Place name: "Wide valley."

   Bradan, Bradin, Bradon, Braiden, Braidin, Brayden, Braydon

Bradford OE. Place name: "Wide river-crossing." Name of the first governor of the Plymouth colony, William Bradford, and a fairly common place name both in England and the U.S.

   Braddford, Bradfurd

Bradley OE. Place name: "Wide meadow." Used since the mid 19th century, more in the U.S. than in other English-speaking countries. It's hard to know why Bradley alone among this group of names became firmly entrenched as a first name: possibly the familiarity of the "-ley" ending contributed to this. The fame of actor Brad Pitt may inspire parents to use Bradley even more often, though it is quite steadily used already. Senator Bill Bradley; actor Bradley Whitford.

   Brad, Bradd, Bradlea, Bradleigh, Bradlie, Bradly, Bradney, Lee

Bradshaw OE. Place name: "Broad forest."

Brady OE. Place name: "Wide island." This name is in the air again. It has all the qualifications for a trendy name for either sex: the right combination of novelty and familiarity with an Anglo-Saxon aura.

   Bradey, Bradie, Braedy, Braidie, Braidy, Braydie

Brainard OE. "Courageous raven."

   Brainerd, Braynard

Bram Ir. Gael. "Raven." It is curious that so many names refer to the raven, a bird that historically has stood for death and destruction. Bram, of course, can also be a short-ened version of **Abraham**. *Dracula* author Bram Stoker.

Bramm, Bran, Brann

Bramwell OE. Place name: "Well where the broom grows" or "Raven well." Author Branwell Brontë.

Brammell, Bramwel, Bramwyll, Branwell, Branwill, Branwyll

Branch Lat. "Paw, extension." This word probably became a place name by referring to a branch in a river or a path.

Brand OE. "Firebrand." Also, diminutive of **Brandon**. In this country the name may have faint manly connotations of life on the rugged range.

Brander, Brandt, Brant, Brantley, Brantlie

Brandon OE. Place name: "Broom-covered hill." Also a variant of **Brendan**, which does not quite share its popu-larity: Brandon was on and off lists of the top ten baby names through the nineties, though it is fading now. Fam-ilies new to the U.S. sometimes look for a jump in assim-ilation by choosing an Anglo-Saxon name like this one. TV executive Brandon Tartikoff.

Brand, Branden, Brandin, Brandyn, Brannon, Branton

Branley OE. Place name: "Raven meadow."

Branlea, Branlee, Branlie, Branly

Brannon Ir. Gael. Elaboration of the particle ("bran" or "bram") that means "Raven." Though unusual, this name is close enough in sound to the popular **Brendan** and **Brandon** so that it may be taken up by parents looking for an uncommon yet pronounceable Gaelic name.

Brant OE. "Proud." Brant County and Brantford in south-ern Ontario are named for Joseph Brant, the Mohawk chieftain who led the Iroquois tribes into Canada after the American Revolution. Media executive Peter Brant.

Brandt, Brannt, Brantt

Branton Gael./Eng. "Raven settlement." May also be a variant of **Brandon**.

Brannton, Branten, Brantin

Braulio Sp. from Ger. "Glowing." St. Braulio was a bishop in 7th-century Spain. Jockey Braulio Baeza.

Bravilio, Bravlio

Bravo It. "Excellent, courageous." This is the exclamation that accompanies a brilliant performance, traditionally in an opera house. It is also the word that means "B" in the military alphabet: Alpha Bravo Charlie . . . A jaunty name for the 21st century.
Brahvo, Bravvo

Brawley OE. Place name: "Meadow at the slope of the hill."
Brauleigh, Braulie, Brauly, Brawlea, Brawleigh, Brawlie, Brawly

Braxton OE. "Brock's settlement." Brock is an informal word for badger.

Bray ME. "Cry out." For instance, donkeys bray. It's still a good name.
Brae

Brazier ME. Occupational name: "Works with brass."
Braiser, Braser, Brasier, Braizer, Brazer

Brazil Place name: largest country in South America. The name may come from the red dye-woods found in the country.
Brasil

Breck OE. Place name: "Gap," as in a gap in a stone wall. Breck also refers to a stretch of sandy, rolling land. A romantic character in Robert Louis Stevenson's *Kidnapped* is named Alan Breck, but the average American parent may remember instead a brand of shampoo.

Breckinridge OE. Place name: "Ridge with bracken."
Brackenridge

Breed Unclear origin. May be an occupational name having to do with the breeding of animals, or may refer to St. Brigid, also known as Bride, the Irish abbess.
Breedlove

Brendan Ir. Gael. "Smelly hair." Very few names actually mean anything as negative as this. The Irish Saint Brendan, known as "the Voyager," is supposed to have sailed as far as the Canary Islands in the sixth century. This name has usually been popular among families of Irish descent. Playwright Brendan Behan; actor Brendan Fraser.
Brendano, Brendin, Brendon, Brendyn, Brennan, Brennen, Brennon

Brennan Ir. Gael. "Teardrop." Not as common as **Brendan** or **Brandon**, but still occurrs from time to time.
Brenan, Brennen, Brennin, Brennon, Brenyn

Brent OE. Place name: "Mount, hilltop." Use as a first name dates back only 60 years or so, and has been particularly strong in Canada. Sportscaster Brent Musburger.
Brennt, Brentan, Brenten, Brentin, Brenton, Brentt, Brentyn

Brenton Possibly OE place name: "Brent's town." It is also possible that families arrive at this name by combining the popular **Brandon** with **Brent**, to end up with something a little different.
Brenten, Brentin, Brentton, Brenttyn

Brett Celt. "Man from Britain." Publicized by American writer Bret Harte. Quite popular in Australia and steadily used in the U.S. Baseball players Brett Butler, Brett Saberhagen; football player Brett Favre.
Bret, Brette, Bretton, Brit, Briton, Britt, Britte

Bretton Fr. "From Brittany." The northwest corner of France is called Brittany, and, like Cornwall across the English Channel, was home to a heavily Celtic civilization. French painter Jules Breton.
Breton

Brevard Lat. "Short, brief."

Brewster OE. Occupational name: "Brewer." Transferred to a surname, thence to a first name.
Brewer, Bruce

Brian Ir. Gael. Ancient name of obscure meaning, though many sources translate it as "Strength." Ireland's most famous King, Brian Boru, liberated the country from the Danes in 1014, and the name has been much favored in Ireland. A spell of popularity lasted from the 1920s to the 1970s, and though Brian is no longer trendy, it is still well used. Actor Brian Dennehy; film director Brian De Palma.
Briano, Briant, Brien, Brion, Bryan, Bryant, Bryen, Bryent, Bryon

Brice Var. **Bryce**. The *i* spelling was more common in the 19th century.
Bricio, Brizio

Brickell OG. "Little bridge."
Brickel

Bridgely OE. Place name: "Bridge meadow."
Bridgeley

Bridger OE. "Lives near the bridge." James Bridger was one of the 19th-century frontiersmen who explored the West. He was probably the first European-American to see the Great Salt Lake, and he built Ft. Bridger on the Oregon Trail.
Bridge

Briggs OE. "Bridges." Brigg was a term, probably influenced by German, that lingered in Scotland.

Brigham OE. Place name: "Little village near the bridge." Most uses of the name probably honor Mormon leader Brigham Young.
Brigg, Briggham, Briggs

Brinley OE. Place name: "Burnt meadow." Used mostly in England and Wales.
Brindley, Brindly, Brinlee, Brinleigh, Brinly, Brynly

Bristol Place name: an ancient and important city in England, with one of the most important ports on the west coast. Many cities in the U.S. were named after it.
Bristow

Britannicus Roman prince, son of Claudius, who was named for his father's conquests in Britain around 50 A.D. He should have become emperor of Rome but was pushed aside in favor of his younger half-brother Nero, and eventually poisoned. If parents use this name, it may be for its resemblance to the once-fashionable Brittany.

Britton OE. "From Britain."
Bretton, Briton

Brock OE. "Badger." Unusual transferred surname with mostly American use. It is used about as often as **Noah**, **Stuart**, and **Bruce**, all of which seem much more familiar.
Broc, Brocke, Brok

Brockholst OE/ONorse. "Badger's den." A family name in Old New York.

Brockley OE. Place name: "Meadow of the badger." May remind hearers of the unpopular green vegetable.

Brocklea, Brocklee, Brocklie, Brockly

Brockton OE. Place name: "Badger settlement."

Brockten, Brocktin, Brocton

Broderick ONorse. "Brother." Traveled from Ireland to Scotland as a surname. Actor Broderick Crawford.

Brod, Broddy, Broder, Broderic, Brodric, Brodrick, Ric, Rick, Rickey, Rickie, Ricky

Brody Ir. Gael. "Ditch." This name has a lot of potential. It is short, easy to say, sounds "boyish," and is extremely unusual without being in any way peculiar.

Brodee, Brodey, Brodie, Broedy

Brogan Ir. Gael. "Sturdy shoe." The root for our word "brogue," which has also come to mean the Gaelic accent.

Broggan

Bromley OE. Place name: "Meadow where broom grows." Broom is a shrub related to heather.

Bromlea, Bromlee, Bromleigh, Broomlie

Bromwell OE. Place name: "Well where broom grows."

Bromwyl

Bronco Mexican Sp. "Rough, unbroken horse." As anyone who has ever seen a cowboy movie knows, a bronco is the horse that bucks off his rider.

Bronko

Bronson OE. "Brown one's son." Actors Charles Bronson, Bronson Pinchot.

Bron, Bronnson, Bronsen, Bronsin, Bronsonn, Bronsson

Brook OE. Place name: "Near the stream or brook." Wide fame of actress Brooke Shields will probably go far to terminate use of this name for boys. Director Brooks Atkinson.

Brooke, Brookes, Brookie, Brooks

Broughton OE. Place name: "Settlement near the fortress."

Brown ME. "Russet-complected." This is such a firmly entrenched last name that it would be hard to use it as a first name.

Bruce OF. "From the brushwood thicket." Norman place name brought to fame by the Scottish king Robert Bruce,

who won Scotland's independence from England in 1327. Naturally popular as a first name in Scotland, and among Americans who cherish Scottish ancestry. Singer Bruce Springsteen; actor Bruce Willis.
Brucey, Brucie

Bruno OG. "Brown-skinned." Saint Bruno was the 11th-century founder of the Carthusian order of monks. Orchestral conductor Bruno Walter; actor Bruno Kirby.
Bruin, Bruino

Brunswick OG. "Bruno's village." The German word is *Braunschweig*. It was an independent state in pre-unification Germany.

Brutus Lat. "Meaningless, unintelligent." Shakespeare scholars know Brutus as the traitor who schemed to assassinate Julius Caesar.
Bruto

Bryan Var. **Brian**. Actor Bryan Brown; singer Bryan Ferry.
Bryen

Bryant Var. **Brian**. TV commentator Bryant Gumbel.

Bryce Unclear origin; may refer to followers of a 5th-century French bishop, Saint Brice. Bryce Canyon, in Utah, is one of the great natural splendors of the West.
Brice

Bryson OE. "Son of Brice."
Brysen, Brysin

Bubba Ger. "Boy." More commonly a nickname, usually for someone rather large.

Buck OE. "Buck deer." "Buck" was also a 19th-century term for a dandy, or a young man who cut a fine figure. It may have been used first as a nickname. Probably not related to the slang word for "dollar." Actor Buck Henry.
Buckey, Buckie, Bucky

Buckley OE. Place name: "Meadow of the deer." Author William F. Buckley.

Buckminster OE. Place name: "Monastery where deer dwell." Made famous by architect Buckminster Fuller.

Bud Modern slang, short for "Buddy." Some sources think this is a child's pronunciation of "brother." Rarely given as a first name, but fairly common as a nickname in the middle years of the 20th century. Actor Buddy Ebsen; comedians Bud Abbott, Buddy Hackett.

Budd, Buddey, Buddie, Buddy

Buell OG. Place name: "Hill."

Buel, Bueller, Buhl, Buhler

Bunyan English name of unclear meaning, though it may be related to the French *bon,* or "good." In America, it bears connotations of the mythic lumberjack Paul Bunyan and his blue ox Babe.

Burchard OE. "Castle strong."

Bucardo, Burckhardt, Burgard, Burgaud, Burkhart

Burford OE. Place name: "Ford near the castle."

Bufford, Buford

Burbank OE. Place name: "Riverbank where burrs grow." Luther Burbank was a famous turn-of-the-century plant breeder who introduced many useful strains of fruits and vegetables in the U.S.

Burdett ME. "Bird."

Burdette

Burgess OE. "Citizen." Related to the French word *bourgeois,* which has come to mean something like "middle class." Generally a transferred last name. Actor Burgess Meredith; poet Gelett Burgess.

Burges, Burgiss, Burr

Burke OF. "From the fortified settlement."

Berk, Berke, Birk, Bourke, Burk

Burl OE. "Knotty wood." Some highly prized 18th-century furniture is made with a "burled" walnut veneer. Singer Burl Ives.

Burle

Burleigh OE. Place name: "Meadow with knotty-trunk trees."

Burley, Burlie, Byrleigh, Byrley

Burnaby ONorse. "Fighter's estate."

Burne OE. Place name: "The brook." Related to **Bourne**.

Beirne, Bourn, Bourne, Burn, Burnis, Byrn, Byrne, Byrnes.

Burnell OF. "Small brown one."

Burnel, Brunel, Brunell

Burnet OE. Transferred surname of unclear origin, mostly used in the 19th century. It may have something to do with a brook ("burn"), or with brown ("brunet") coloring.
Bernet, Bernett, Burnett

Burney OE. Place name: "Island of the brook."
Beirney, Beirnie, Burnie

Burr OE. "Bristle." In the U.S., made famous by Jefferson's Vice President Aaron Burr, who is probably best known for having killed his political enemy Alexander Hamilton in a duel in 1801. Actor Raymond Burr; actor/director Burr Steers.

Burroughs OE. Place name: "In the borough or burrow." The holes in the ground that animals live in and the administrative division (similar to county) come from the same word, *burgh,* which means dwelling place or town. **Burgess** is another derivative.
Burrows

Burt Var. **Bert.** Dim. **Albert, Bertram,** etc.

Burton OE. Place name: "Fortified enclosure." Like many of the older place names, used as a first name in the 19th century. The exploits of African explorer and writer Sir Richard Burton may have influenced its use. In the 20th century, of course, the Richard Burton most people know is the one who was married to Elizabeth Taylor. Actors Burt Lancaster, Burt Reynolds.
Bert, Burt, Burtt

Busby Scot./ONorse. Place name: "Village in the thicket." A busby is also a tall military hat made of fur, such as those worn by the British soldiers who guard Buckingham Palace. Choreographer Busby Berkeley.
Busbee, Busbey, Busbie, Bussby

Buster Nickname of unknown origin, made famous by silent film star Buster Keaton. A hugely popular comic strip character of the 1930s was called Buster Brown. His pageboy haircut, sailor hat, and round collar were all dubbed "Buster Brown" after him. The name continued into the early 1960s as a brand of shoe with an advertising jingle that ended, ". . . with the boy and the dog and the foot inside." Swimmer/actor Buster Crabbe.

Butcher OE. Occupational name: "Butcher." Nickname Butch is sometimes used to address a stranger in a slightly derogatory way: "Listen, Butch . . ." The popular movie *Butch Cassidy and the Sundance Kid* did little to popularize the name.
Butch

Butler OE. Occupational name: "Bottle bearer." Originally the household servant in charge of wines and liquors. Nicholas Murray Butler was an influential turn-of-the-century president of Columbia University.
Buttler

Buzz Informal nickname of mysterious origin. Does it refer to a "buzz cut?" It is enough a name of the 1960s to be used occasionally now, with irony—if irony is appropriate in choosing children's names. Astronaut Buzz Aldrin.
Buzzey, Buzzie, Buzzy

Byford OE. Place name: "By the ford."

Byram OE. Place name. Var. **Byron**.

Byrd OE. "Birdlike."
Bird, Byrdie

Byron OE. Place name: "Barn for cows." The term "byre" is still used. Use as a first name probably in tribute to the poet Lord Byron, since it dates from the 1850s. Though a first-rate poet, he was also famous for his wildness and debauchery: he was characterized by one acquaintance as "mad, bad, and dangerous to know."
Beyren, Beyron, Biren, Biron, Buiron, Byram, Byran, Byren, Byrom

C

Caballero Sp. "Horseman." In the U.S., this comes quite close to a cowboy.

Cable OF. "Rope." Cable is generally a very thick rope, though the word is also used to describe chains (as in an anchor cable) and the insulated

wires that transmit electric messages. The first permanent telegraphic cable across the Atlantic was laid in 1866.
Cabell

Cabot Fr. Probably "To sail." The name of a 15th-century English explorer who probably made a landfall in Canada in 1497. Also, more recently, the name of a prominent Boston mercantile and shipping family.
Cabbot

Cadby OE. "Fighting man's settlement." A short, neutral, masculine-sounding name.
Cadbee, Cadbey, Cadbie

Caddis OE. "Worsted fabric." Also a kind of fly that trout like to eat, making this a potential choice for a fisherman's son.
Caddice, Caddiss

Caddock Welsh. "Eagerness for war."
Cadog

Cade OE. "Round" or "lump."
Caide, Caden, Kade, Kaden, Kayde

Cadell Welsh. "Battle." Political consultant Patrick Cadell.
Caddell, Cadel

Cadman Anglo-Welsh. "Battle man."

Cadmus Gk. "From the east." In Greek mythology, Cadmus is the founder of the city of Thebes, who ultimately turned into a serpent. He is also credited with the invention of writing in letters.
Cadmar, Cadmo, Cadmos, Cadmuss, Kadmos, Kadmus

Caduceus Gk. In Greek mythology, the caduceus was the insignia of Hermes (called Mercury by the Romans): a winged staff with two serpents twining up it. Because Hermes was the patron of doctors, it has become the symbol for medicine.

Caesar Lat. Clan name of obscure meaning, possibly "Hairy, hirsute." The term "caesarean" for a surgical delivery of a baby came about because the famous Roman emperor Julius Caesar was born that way. It has become a generic term for emperor, translated into German (*kaiser*) and Russian (*czar*). Actor César Romero.

Caezar, Casar, César, Cesare, Cesaro, Kaiser, Seasar, Sezar

Cain Heb. "Spear." Adam and Eve's elder son, who slew his brother Abel. Surprisingly enough, used with some frequency, at least in the 19th century. Homonym **Kane** has a different source. Actor Michael Caine.

Caine, Kain, Kaine

Caird Scot. Gael. Occupational name: "Traveling metalsmith." Another term would be "tinker," or "worker with tin."

Caerd, Cairde, Kaird, Kairde

Cairn Scot. Gael. Place name: "Mound of rocks." Cairns were built as long ago as the Stone Age as memorials, grave markers, and landmarks, and many of these ancient cairns can still be seen in the British Isles.

Cairne, Cairns, Kairn, Kairne, Kairns

Cairo Place name: the capital city of Egypt. The name comes from an Arabic word meaning "Victorious."

Caius Lat. "Rejoice." Var. **Gaius**. A 16th-century English physician endowed a college at Cambridge University which is called "Gonville and Caius." In the inscrutable British fashion, the name is pronounced "Keys."

Cai, Caio, Kay, Kaye, Keye, Keyes, Keys

Cajetan Var. **Gaetan** (It. "From Gaeta").

Cajetano, Kajetan, Kajetano

Cal Dim. **Calhoun, Calvin**, etc. Baseball star Cal Ripken, Jr.

Calder OE. "Stream." Little rivulets are such important features in the English landscape that regional terms for them abound, and several (**Brook, Burn**) have traced the typical path from geographical feature to place name to surname to given name. Sculptor Alexander Calder.

Caldwell OE. Place name: "Cold well."

Cale Var. **Caleb**. Another possible source is Irish Gaelic, "Thin, slender." Race driver Cale Yarborough.

Cael, Caile, Cayle, Kale

Caleb Heb. Either "Dog" or "Courageous." An Old Testament name brought to America with the Puritans, where it was fairly common until around 1920. It has shot up out of obscurity recently, moving close to the top fifty boys' names in America. Author Caleb Carr.

Cal, Cale, Cayleb, Kaleb, Kayleb, Kaylob

Caley Ir. Gael. "Lean, slight." Very similar to the trendy **Kayla/Caitlyn** group of girls' names, so that an infant named Caley would probably be taken for a girl.

Cailey, Caily, Kayley

Calhoun Ir. Gael. Place name: "The narrow woods." John Calhoun was a 19th-century American statesman, Vice President under Andrew Jackson, whose writings and ideas on states' rights contributed heavily to the Southern states' formation of the Confederacy.

Callhoun, Colhoun, Colquhoun

Callis Lat. "Chalice, goblet."

Callice, Callys, Callyx

Calogero It. "Fair old age." Name of a saint, a Sicilian hermit.

Calogeros, Kalogeros, Kalogerus

Calum Scot. Var. **Columba** (Lat. "Dove"). Saint Columba was a 6th-century Irish missionary who founded a monastery on the Scottish island of Iona. His contemporary, St. Columban, also Irish, was a missionary in France, Switzerland, and Italy. Calum and its variant **Callum** are both extremely popular in Scotland, where they may be considered variants of **Malcolm**.

Callum, Colm, Colum

Calumet Fr. from Lat. "Straw, little reed." This was the term that the French in Canada used for the Indian peace pipe, a highly ornamental pipe smoked on ceremonial occasions. One of the great horse-racing stables of the 20th century was Calumet Farms.

Callumet

Calvert OE. Occupational name: "Calf-herder." English surname. In the U.S., borne by George Calvert, founder of Maryland. The Calvert dynasty, George, Cecilius, and Charles, ruled the colony of Maryland from 1632 until 1689, though only Charles actually lived in the New World. Their proprietorship of Maryland ended when, as

Catholics, they were ousted by the newly Protestant regime in England.

Calbert

Calvin Lat. "Hairless." Roman clan name turned surname. Transferred to first name as a tribute to 16th-century Swiss religious reformer John Calvin, whose thinking deeply influenced the Presbyterian, Methodist, and Huguenot branches of Protestantism. U.S. use may have been influenced by President Calvin Coolidge, though today the name probably conjures up fashion designer Calvin Klein first and foremost. Composer Calvin Hampton; Italian author Italo Calvino.

Cal, Calvino, Kalvin, Vinnie

Camden Scot. Gael. Place name: "The twisting valley."

Camdin, Camdon

Cameron Scot. Gael. "Crooked nose." Clan name derived from the facial feature. In Scotland, the Camerons were a powerful clan. Little used as a first name until the middle of this century, but now very well established, even trendy in Scotland. The exposure given it by (female) actress Cameron Diaz may persuade parents that it is a girls' name.

Cam, Camaeron, Camedon, Camron, Camry, Kameron, Kamrey

Camillo Masc. **Camilla** (Lat. meaning unclear). Most sources trace the name to the young girls who assisted at pagan religious ceremonies. St. Camillus de Lellis was a 16th-century Italian founder of hospitals, and is patron of nurses and the sick.

Camillus, Camilo, Comillo

Campbell Scot. Gael. "Crooked mouth." Name of a very famous Scottish clan, again referring to a distinguishing feature. The hereditary heads of the Campbell clan, the Dukes of Argyll, at one time controlled vast acres of the Scottish highlands and commanded the loyalty of thousands of men. In the U.S. the primary association is probably with soup. Use as a first name dates back only to the 1930s. Actor Campbell Scott.

Campbel

Campion ME. "Champion." The name of a small wild-flower and of an English Catholic martyr (Edmund Campion). A fictional detective, Albert Campion, features in the popular murder mysteries of Margery Allingham.
Campian

Canby ME. Place name: "Settlement near the reeds." Another term for reeds is "canes."
Canbey, Canbie

Candelario Sp. "Candles." Refers to the Catholic feast of Candlemas, February 2. The feast marks the day the Holy Family took the baby Jesus to be presented at the temple. It was customary to bless all the candles for the succeeding year on the day of this feast.
Candelareo, Candelaro, Candelerio, Candelero

Candido Lat. "White, pure." Voltaire's famous novel *Candide* makes fun of the theory that "All is for the best in the best of all possible worlds." The term "candid" has come to mean "frank, without guile."
Candide, Candidio

Canfield ME. Place name: "Field of reeds." Dick Canfield was a famous gambler and casino operator in the late 19th century, and the Canfield form of solitaire was named for him.

Canning Fr. Occupational name: "Official of the church." Var. **Cannon**. Has nothing to do with preserving food in glass jars, which is what canning means to most of us.
Cannan

Cannon Fr. Occupational name: "Official of the church." Not, as might be expected by the spelling, related to firearms.
Canon, Kanon

Canute Scand. "Knot." Brought to Britain by the 11th-century King Canute of Denmark, who became King of England in 1016. Very rare, except in those of Scandinavian descent. Football coach Knute Rockne.
Cnut, Knut, Knute

Canyon Sp. "Footpath." Geography name: canyons, deep ravines, are notable features of the Western American landscape. Basketball player Rick Barry named a son Canyon.

Capp Fr. Occupational name: "Chaplain." Easily confused with the small hat attached to the head of many American boys. Still a brisk, breezy name.
Cap, Capps

Carden OE. Occupational name: "Wool carder." The production of woolen cloth, from sheep to bolt of fabric, requires many steps, and many of these steps have given last names (Shepherd, Shearer, Weaver) to the English language. Carding is the part of the process when the wool is combed to remove impurities.
Card, Cardin, Cardon

Carew Lat. "Chariot."
Carewe, Crew, Crewe

Carey Welsh. Place name: "Near the castle." Distinct from Cary, which has another source. By the 1950s, this form was usually a girl's name, often a nickname for **Caroline**. Actor Jim Carrey.
Carrey

Carl Var. **Charles** (OG. "Man"). Use in America was fairly steady 1850–1950 (probably as a result of intensive German and Scandinavian immigration), but dropped off in the 1960s. It is still steadily used, but is nothing like fashionable. Poet Carl Sandburg; journalist Carl Bernstein; astronomer/author Carl Sagan; psychologist Carl Jung.
Carel, Karel, Karl

Carleton OE. Place name: "Farmer's settlement." Only used as a first name since around 1880. In the U.S., usually spelled without the *e*.
Carl, Carlton, Charlton

Carley ME. Place name: "Farmer's meadow."
Carleigh

Carlin Ir. Gael. "Little champion." Comedian George Carlin.
Carling, Carly

Carlisle OE. Place name: "The fortified tower." Also the name of a very old city in northwest England. Historian Thomas Carlyle.
Carley, Carlile, Carly, Carlyle

Carlos Sp. Var. **Charles** (OG. "Man"). This form of

Charles is increasingly popular in the U.S. Film directors
Carlos Saura, Carlo Ponti.

Carlo, Carrlos

Carlow Irish place name: a major town and a county in inland Ireland.

Carlowe

Carlsen Scand. "Carl's son."

**Carlssen, Carlson, Carlsson, Karlsen, Karlssen, Karl-
son, Karlsson**

Carmelo It. from Heb. "Garden." Biblical place name: Mt.
Carmel is in Israel, and is often referred to in ancient
writings as a kind of paradise. Scarcely used in the U.S.

**Carmel, Carmeli, Carmello, Karmel, Karmelo,
Karmello**

Carmichael Scot. Gael. "Follower of Michael." Possibly
referring to partisans of Saint Michael.

Carmine Lat. "Song." Though carmine also means "Pur-
plish red" (from an Aramaic word meaning "crimson"),
the Latin source is more likely, since the name is almost
exclusively used by families of Italian descent.

Carman, Carmen, Carmin, Carmino, Karman, Karmen

Carney Ir. Gael. "The winner."

Carny, Kearney

Carollan Ir. Gael. "Little champion." In the U.S., likely to
be confused with a variant of **Caroline**.

Carlin, Carling, Carolan

Carpenter Lat. "Carriage maker." Another occupational
name turned last name, rarely occurring as a first name.

Charpentier

Carr Scand. "From the swampy place."

Karr, Ker, Kerr

Carrington ME. Meaning unclear: most likely a place
name, given the "-ton" ending.

Carington, Caryngton

Carroll OG. "Man." An anglicized version of **Charles**, occurring from time to time as a family name, though it is
too much like **Carol** (which was very popular in the '60s)
to be an appealing boy's name for most parents. Author

Lewis Carroll; Signer of the Declaration of Independence Charles Carroll.

Carolus, Carrol, Caroll, Cary, Caryl, Caryll

Carson OE. "Son of the marsh-dwellers." Nineteenth-century frontiersman Kit Carson was a scout and guide in the exploration of the West as well as an important factor in the Mexican War. Carson City, Nevada was named for him, and to this day an aura of rakishness and daring clings to the name. TV hosts Johnny Carson, Carson Daly.

Carswell OE. Place name: "Well where the watercress grows."

Caswell

Carter OE. Occupational name: "One who drives carts." Former President Jimmy Carter; football player Cris Carter.

Cartier

Carvell OF. "Swampy dwelling." Political strategist James Carville.

Carvel, Carvil, Carville

Carver OE. Occupational name: "One who carves wood."

Cary OE. Place name: "Pretty brook." Distinct from **Carey**. Use in the 19th century as a first name was quite rare, but when actor Archibald Leach renamed himself Cary Grant, numerous families suddenly found the name Cary appealing.

Case Fr. "Box."

Casey Ir. Gael. "Vigilant." Possibly also a short form of **Casimir**. Made famous by the song about the engineer of the Cannonball Express train, Casey Jones. Infrequently used, and though it is given to girls as well as boys, infant male Caseys predominate. Baseball personality Casey Stengel; radio disc jockey Casey Kasem; actor Casey Affleck.

Cacey, Cayce, Caycey, Kasey

Cash Dim. **Cassius** (Lat. "Vain"). Also a slang word for money, of course. Singer Johnny Cash.

Casshe

Casimir Slavic. "Bringing peace." Associated with Poland for her famous 11th-century king, who brought peace to the nation.

**Casimeer, Casimire, Casimiro, Casmir, Kasimiro, Kaz-
imierz, Kazimir**

Casper Origin unclear, though many sources suggest Per. "He who guards the treasure." Originally Jasper, Germanicized to Caspar. French is Gaspard. Traditionally one of the Three Kings (perhaps the one carrying the gold) was named Caspar. A 1960s TV series featured Casper the Friendly Ghost. Defense Secretary Casper Weinberger.

**Caspar, Cass, Gaspar, Gaspard, Gasparo, Gasper,
Jasper, Kaspar**

Caspian Place name: the Caspian Sea is the largest inland body of water in the world, lying between Russia and Asia: its southern coast is in Iran. Author C.S. Lewis named a principal character Caspian in one of his *Chronicles of Narnia*.

Cassander Sp. from Gk. "Brother of heroes." A king of Macedonia, contemporary of Alexander the Great, who married Alexander's half-sister and later murdered his widow.

Casander, Casandro, Cassandero

Cassian Lat. Clan name: "Fair, just."

Casiano, Cassio

Cassidy Ir. Gael. "Ingenious, clever." Used more often as a girl's name now.

Cassady, Cassedy, Cassidey

Cassiel The archangel who watches over Capricorns.

Cassius Lat. "Vain." Historically, Cassius was a Roman politician who was behind the plot to murder Julius Caesar. In Shakespeare's play, Caesar says, "Yon Cassius has a lean and hungry look; He thinks too much: Such men are dangerous." Boxer Cassius Clay (now Muhammad Ali).

Cash, Cass, Cassio

Castor Gk. "Beaver." In classical myth, along with Pollux, one of the heavenly twins immortalized in the constellation Gemini. They were considered the patron gods of seafarers, appearing to them in St. Elmo's fire.

Caster, Castorio, Kastor

Catlin Ir. Var. **Catherine** (Gk. "Pure"). An unusual last name. George Catlin was an American traveler and artist of the mid 19th century who is particularly famous for his penetrating portraits of Native Americans.
Cattlin, Katlin, Kattlin

Cato Lat. "All-knowing." Cato was a particularly high-minded Roman statesman of the time of Julius Caesar. The "o" ending is mildly fashionable for boys' names.
Cayto, Kaeto, Kato

Catullus Lat. Meaning obscure. One of the greatest Roman poets. A name for a family with scholarly tendencies.
Catullo

Cavan Ir. Gael. "Handsome."
Kavan

Cavanagh Ir. Gael. "Follower of Kevin." Principally an Irish last name.
Cavanaugh, Kavanagh, Kavanaugh

Cecil Lat. "Blind one," from a Roman clan name. Used in Roman times, then resurfaced in the Victorian era, possibly given a boost by the fame of industrialist (and founder of Rhodesia) Cecil Rhodes. Little used in this century. Film director Cecil B. De Mille; photographer Cecil Beaton.
Cecil, Cecilio, Cecilius, Celio

Cedric OE. "War leader." Used in two 19th-century literary landmarks (*Ivanhoe* and *Little Lord Fauntleroy*), which probably increased its popularity in Britain. Actor Sir Cedric Hardwicke; Cedric the Comedian.
Caddaric, Ced, Cedrick, Cedro, Rick, Sedric, Sedrick, Sedrik

Celesto Lat. "Heavenly." The masculine version is scarce except in Catholic countries, where the memories of Popes Celestine I and V (both saints) keep the name alive.
Célestine, Celestino, Celindo, Selestine, Selestino, Silestino

Celso It. from Lat. "High, lofty." As in "Gloria in excelsis . . ." The same particle is also found in various words for sky, like *ciel* (French) and *coelum* (Latin).
Celsius, Celsus

Cephas Heb. "Rock." New Testament name; what Jesus called his apostle Simon. **Peter** is the Latin translation by which he is more commonly known. Cephas was in steady (if infrequent) use until the 20th century.

Chad Origin cloudy; possibly OE. "Fierce." Saint Chad was a 7th-century English bishop. The name enjoyed a burst of popularity beginning in the late 1960s, reaching the top 50 names for American boys, but its popularity has declined since the mid eighties. Actors Chad Everett, Chad Lowe; football players Chad Morton, Chad Pennington.
Chadd, Chaddie

Chadwick OE. Place name: "The fighter's settlement." Has been used commercially as a generic WASP name.
Chadwyck

Chai Heb. "Living, vital."
Hai

Chaim Heb. "Life." Male version of **Eve. Hyman** is more common in English-speaking countries. Author Chaim Potok.
Chayim, Chayyim, Haim, Hayvim, Hayyim, Hy, Hyman, Hymen, Hymie, Manny

Chairo Sp. A diminutive and variant of **Jerome** (Gk. "Sacred name"), via **Hieronimo**.
Chiro, Hairo, Hiro

Chalkley OE. Place name: "Chalk meadow."
Chalklea, Chalklie

Chalmers OF. Scottish occupational name meaning "Servant of the chambers." French ties with Scotland (in league against their mutual enemy England) were very strong until the unification of Scotland with England in the early seventeenth century.
Chalmer, Chambers

Chamberlain ME. Occupational name: "Chief officer of the household." A chamberlain was an administrative post in a large royal or noble household. Actor Richard Chamberlain.
Chambellan, Chamberlin, Chambers

Champion ME. "Warrior." The word has come to mean

the supreme winner in a competition, of course. Choreographer Gower Champion.

Campion, Champ, Champeon

Chanan Heb. "He was compassionate."

Hanan

Chance ME. "Good fortune." Also var. **Chauncey.** Used more often than one might expect.

Chanse, Chantz, Chanze

Chancellor ME. Occupational name: "Chief secretary, record keeper." Rather unwieldy as a first name, and it does not provide any obvious nicknames. Broadcaster John Chancellor.

Chance, Chancelor, Chansellor, Chaunce

Chand Sanskrit. "Moon, light."

Chandak, Chandan

Chandler OF. Occupational name: "Candle merchant."

Chaney Fr. "Oak tree." Actor Lon Chaney.

Chainey, Chany, Cheney

Chang Chinese. "Smooth, free, unhindered."

Chaniel Heb. "Grace of God."

Chanyel, Haniel, Hanniel, Hanyel

Channing OF. Occupational name: "Official of the church." Related to **Cannon.** Another possibility is OF. "Canal."

Canning, Cannon, Canon

Chanoch Heb. "Dedicated." The English version is **Enoch.**

Channoch, Chanok, Hanoch, Hannoch, Hanok

Chantrey From OF. "Singing." A chantry, in the Middle Ages, was an endowment of funds to support the singing (chanting) of masses for an individual's soul. This may be an occupational name.

Chantry

Chaparral Sp. "Dwarf oak." Chaparral is the term used to describe various kinds of low-growing ground covers such as the mesquite found in the southwestern U.S. The name thus has associations with the wide-open spaces.

Chaparall

Chaplin ME. Occupational name: "Secretary." A chaplain

was usually a minor ecclesiastical position, and has come to mean something like the spiritual guide of a secular organization, like a hospital chaplain. Actors Charlie Chaplin, Ben Chaplin.
Chaplain, Chaplinn, Chappelin

Chapman OE. "Peddler." Chapmen usually sold chapbooks, pamphlets intended for a wide audience, even in the days of low literacy rates.
Chap, Chappy, Manny

Chappel OE. Occupational name: "One who works at the chapel."
Capel, Capell, Capello, Cappel, Chappell, Chaps

Charles OG. "Man." The English term "churl," meaning "serf," comes from the same root. Has been a staple ever since the era of the Emperor Charlemagne, and a royal name in many European countries, including England, where the next king will probably be Charles III. In America, it was one of the top 5 names for the first three-quarters of this century, but has since been displaced by other classics like **Nicholas, Christopher**, and **Andrew**. Naturalist Charles Darwin; French president Charles de Gaulle; author Charles Dickens; actor Charlie Chaplin; basketball player Charles Barkely.
Carel, Carl, Carlo, Carlos, Carrol, Carroll, Cary, Caryl, Chad, Charley, Charlie, Charlot, Charls, Charlton, Charly, Chas, Chay, Chaz, Chick, Chip, Chuck, Karel, Karl, Karol, Karolek, Karolik, Karoly

Charlton OE. Place name: "Charles's dwelling." Also possibly a variation on **Carlton**. Used as a given name for the last hundred years. Actor Charlton Heston.
Carleton, Carlton, Charleston, Charleton

Chase OF. "Hunter." Quite steadily used. Painter William Merritt Chase.
Chace, Chayce, Chayse

Chauncey ME. Contraction of **Chancellor**.
Chance, Chancey, Chaunsey, Chaunsy, Chawncey

Chaviv Heb. "Loved one." Closely resembles an Arabic name with the same meaning, **Habib**.
Habib, Haviv

Chaz Dim. **Charles** (OG. "Man"). This off-hand nickname is used from time to time on its own. Actor Chazz Palmintieri.
Chas, Chazz

Cherokee Native American Indian tribe. The Cherokee originally lived in the southeastern U.S., especially the mountainous areas of Tennesee, Georgia, Alabama, and the Carolinas. The tribe was deported en masse to territory west of the Mississippi in 1838 undergoing enormous hardships. The Cherokee were farmers, and one of the first tribes to produce a written language.

Cherut Heb. "Liberty."
Cheroot, Heroot, Herut

Chesley OE./Lat. "Meadow of the camp."
Cheslea, Cheslee, Chesleigh, Cheslie, Chesly

Chesney OE. Place name referring to a camp.
Cheney, Cheny, Chesnie, Chesny

Chester Lat. "Soldier's camp." Place name from Roman Britain, gradually evolved into a first name most common in the U.S. Virtually unused now, however. President Chester Arthur; newscaster Chet Huntley.
Cheston, Chet

Chetwin OE. Place name: "Little house on the twisted path."
Chetwen, Chetwyn, Chetwynd, Chetwynn

Chevalier Fr. "Knight." Comedian Chevy Chase.
Chevy

Chevron Fr. A V-shaped heraldic insignia, often used to indicate rank in the armed services.

Cheyenne Native American tribe indigenous to Minnesota, the Dakotas, and Montana. The Cheyenne were some of the fiercest opponents of European settlement in the West. The capital city of Wyoming is Cheyenne.
Chayan, Chayann, Shayan, Shayanne

Chick Dim. **Charles** (OG. "Man"). Musician Chick Corea.
Chic, Chik

Chico Sp. Dim. **Francis** (Lat. "Frenchman") via **Francisco.**

Chilton OE. Place name: "Farm near the well."
   Chelton, Chill

Chino Sp. "Chinese." Also a California place name: an agricultural area east of Los Angeles. Also a term for khaki-colored trousers.

Chip Nickname commonly used among WASP families, especially if the string of chosen surnames seems unwieldy for a small child. Also occurs as a nickname for **Charles**. Baseball player Chipper Jones.
   Chipper

Choni Heb. "Gracious."
   Honi

Chris Dim. **Christian, Christopher**. Actors Chris Cooper, Chris O'Donnell, Chris Sarandon; comedians Chris Tucker, Chris Rock: basketball player Chris Webber.
   Chriss, Kris

Christian Gk. "Anointed, Christian." A girl's name that (contrary to the usual movement) became a male name, possibly after the huge success of John Bunyan's *Pilgrim's Progress* (1684), whose hero is called Christian. In Britain and Australia, especially popular in the 1970s. Now steadily used in the U.S. French fashion designers Christian Dior, Christian Lacroix; Dr. Christiaan Barnard; actor Christian Slater.
   Chrestien, Chretien, Chris, Christer, Christiano, Christie, Christo, Christy, Cristian, Cristiano, Cristino, Cristy, Kit, Kris, Krister, Kristian, Kristo, Krystian, Krystiano

Christmas Name of the holiday, used occasionally through the 19th century for Dec. 25 babies, but now usually replaced by the French, and somewhat subtler, form, **Noel**.

Christopher Gk. "Carrier of Christ." The much-loved story of Saint Christopher is that he lived alone by a river, carrying travelers across the ford on his back. A child whom he was carrying became almost too heavy to bear, and proved afterward to be the Christ child. Actually the tale has little basis in fact, and probably springs from the literal translation of the name, which originally meant carrying Christ in one's heart. Nevertheless, Christopher is still venerated as patron saint of travelers and drivers. In the modern era the name was little used until a revival in the 1940s, possibly influenced by the popularity of A. A. Milne's *Winnie the Pooh,* whose human hero is called Christopher Robin. Hugely popular right through the 1980s and 1990s, the name is still among the top ten boys' names nationwide. As **Christophe** it is equally popular in France. Explorer Christopher Columbus; actors Christopher Plummer, Christopher Reeve; architect Christopher Wren.

Chris, Christie, Christof, Christoffer, Christoforo, Christoforus, Christoph, Christophe, Christophoros, Christos, Cris, Cristobal, Cristoforo, Cristovano, Kester, Kit, Kitt, Kris, Kriss, Kristo, Kristofel, Kristofer, Kristoffer, Kristofor, Kristoforos, Kristos, Krzysztof, Stoffel, Tobal, Topher

Chuck Dim. **Charles** (OG. "Man"). Scarce as a given name, and not even that common as a nickname these days. Cartoon director Chuck Jones; musician Chuck Mangione; aviation pioneer Colonel Chuck Yeager.

Churchill OE. Place name: "Hill of the church." Use as a first name is probably homage to English statesman Sir Winston Churchill.

Churchil

Cicero Lat. "Chickpea." Most famous for the Roman orator and statesman who lived in the 1st century B.C. Like **Cato** and **Cassius**, probably came to the U.S. as a slave name.

Cid Sp. from Arab. "Lord." El Cid was a heroic Spanish knight of the 11th century whose story is told (and embroidered) in numerous medieval epics. Easily confused with the nickname for **Sidney**.

Cyd

Cimarron Place name: a city in western Kansas and a river that runs 650 miles across the Great Plains from New Mexico to Oklahoma. It was made famous by an Edna

Ferber novel that was the basis for movies made in 1933 and 1961.

Cimeron, Simarron, Simeron

Cincinnatus Legendary consul of ancient (5th century B.C.) Rome, a statesman who, the story runs, preferred farming but performed his civic duty by leading the state.

Cipriano Sp. from Gk. "From Cyprus." St. Cyprian was a third-century bishop of Carthage.

Ciprien, Cyprian, Cyprien, Siprian, Siprien, Sipryan

Ciriaco It. from Gk. "Lord."

Ciro Sp. Var. **Cyrus** (Per. "Sun" or "Throne").

Cirrus Lat. "Lock of hair." The name of a wispy, filmy cloud formation.

Claiborne Fr./Ger. Place name: "Boundary with clover" or OE. "Boundary of clay." U.S. Senator Claiborne Pell.

Claiborn, Claibourn, Claibourne, Clayborn, Clayborne, Claybourn, Claybourne

Clair Masc. **Claire** (Lat. "Bright"). Very scarce as a masculine name.

Claire, Clare, Claro

Clancy Ir. Gael. "Red-haired fighter's child." An almost stereotypically Irish name.

Clancey, Claney

Clare Dim. **Clarence**. Very unusual for boys. In Thomas Hardy's tragic novel *Tess of the D'Urbervilles*, Tess falls in love with, and is abandoned by, a man named Angel Clare.

Clair, Claire, Clarey, Clayre

Clarence Lat. "Bright." An alternate source is the title Duke of Clarence, created for a 14th-century royal prince who married a girl from the Clare family. The bearers of the title have been ill-fated: The third, for example, was said to have drowned in a barrel of wine. In the late 19th century, prompted by the Victorian interest in the picturesque and medieval, Clarence was immensely popular, but gradually acquired the connotations of effete aristocracy and has been neglected recently. Lawyer Clarence Darrow.

Clair, Claran, Clarance, Clare, Clarens, Claron, Clarons, Claronz, Clarrance, Clarrence, Klarance, Klarenz

Clark OF. Occupational name: "Cleric, scholar." Surname transferred to first name, heavily influenced by the fame of actor Clark Gable. Also made famous by "mild-mannered" Clark Kent, alter ego of Superman in the popular comic strip. It does not, somehow, seem to be very suitable for a child, which may account for its neglect.
Clarke, Clerc, Clerk

Claude Lat. "Lame." Name of a Roman clan that produced the emperor immortalized in Robert Graves's novel (and subsequent TV dramatization) *I, Claudius*. Claud was used in the 19th century, but not in great numbers. Painter Claude Monet; composer Claude Debussy; Congressman Claude Pepper; actor Claude Rains.
Claudan, Claudell, Claudianus, Claudicio, Claudien, Claudino, Claudio, Claudius, Claudon, Clodito, Clodo, Clodomiro, Klaudio

Claus Dim. **Nicholas** (Gk. "People of victory"). Currently very popular in Germany. Actor Klaus Kinski.
Claes, Clause, Klaus

Claxton OE. Place name: "Clark's town."

Clay OE. Occupational or place name involving clay. Clay that occurs naturally in the earth was a tremendous natural resource in earlier times. Most famous modern bearer was probably Cassius Clay, later Muhammad Ali, the boxing champion; he, in turn, had originally been named for a 19th-century abolitionist, American statesman Henry Clay.
Klay

Clayborne OE. Place name: "Brook near a clay-bed" or "Border near a clay-bed."
Claiborn, Claiborne, Clay, Claybourne, Clayburn, Klaiborn, Klaibourne

Clayland OE. Place name: "Land of clay."

Clayton OE. Place name: "Settlement near the clay-bed." Given as a first name since the early 19th century.
Klayton

Cleander Combined name: possibly **Leander** (Gk. "Lion-man") and **Cleanth**.

Cleanth Gk. Derivation unknown; possibly derived from the name of a Stoic Greek philosopher, Cleanthes. The name was used occasionally in both French and English dramas of the 17th and 18th centuries. Critic Cleanth Brooks.

Cleandro, Cleanthes, Cleante, Cleanto, Cleneth, Clianth, Clianthes, Kleanth, Kleanthes

Cleary Ir. Gael. "Learned one."

Cleavant OE. Place name: "Cliff." Related to **Cleveland**. Actors Cleavant Derricks, Cleavon Little.

Cleavon, Cleevant, Cleeve, Cleevont

Clement Lat. "Mild, giving mercy." A name borne by four-teen popes as well as the author (Clement Clark Moore) of "A Visit from St. Nicholas." Nevertheless, little used in English-speaking countries. Artist Francesco Clemente; baseball player Roberto Clemente.

Clem, Clemencio, Clemens, Clemente, Clementino, Clementius, Clemmie, Clemmons, Clemmy, Klemens, Klement, Klementos, Kliment

Cleon Gk. "Renowned."

Kleon

Cleophas Gk. "Vision of glory." New Testament name: husband of one of the Marys who stood at the foot of the Cross.

Cleo, Cleofas, Cleofaso, Cleophus

Cletus Gk. "Called forth, invoked."

Anacletus, Cletis, Cletos, Kletos, Kletus

Cleveland OE. Place name: "Hilly area." During the fame of U.S. President Grover Cleveland, several towns were named after him, and the surname became a first name, though only in the U.S. Writer Cleveland Amory.

Cleavon, Cleaveland, Cleavland, Cleon, Cleve, Clevon

Cliff OE. "Steep slope." Dim. **Clifford, Clifton**. Actor Cliff Robertson; singer Cliff Richard.

Cliffe, Clyff, Clyffe

Clifford OE. Place name: "Ford near the cliff." Surname transferred to first name, most popular in the late 19th century. Older siblings of a new baby may be familiar with Clifford the Big Red Dog, the hero of many children's books. Playwright Clifford Odets.

Cliff, Clyff, Clyfford

Clifton OE. Place name: "Town near the cliff." Another transferred surname, more common in the U.S. than in Britain.

Cliff, Cliffeton, Clift, Clyffeton, Clyfton, Clyffton

Clinton OE. Place name: "Settlement near the headland." An illustrious 18th-century governor of New York, De Witt Clinton, left his name on many New York City locations. Cannot be used now without reference to President Bill Clinton. Actor Clint Eastwood; singer Clint Black.

Clint, Clintt, Klint

Clive OE. Place name: "Cliff." Given some publicity by a famous English soldier, Robert Clive, for his exploits in India. Thackeray used it as a first name in an 1855 novel, but its real popularity in England didn't come for another hundred years. Never widely used in the U.S. Critic Clive Barnes; author Clive Staples (C.S.) Lewis.

Cleve, Clyve

Clovis OG. "Renowned fighter." Early form of the name that would eventually become **Ludwig** or **Louis**. King Clovis I was the first Christian king of the Franks, and later kings' use of the name Louis probably harks back to the dynasty he founded in the 5th century. The name is rare, however, in the 20th century.

Clodoveo, Clovisito, Clovio, Clovito

Cloy Derivation unclear: may come from OF. "Nail" as an occupational name having to do with the nails in horse shoes.

Cloyce, Cloyd

Cluny Ir. Gael. "From the meadow."

Clyde Scot. Place name: The River Clyde penetrates western Scotland as far as Glasgow. This name is very scarce today, though it was somewhat familiar a hundred years ago.

Clydell

Coakley OE. Place name: "Charcoal meadow." Before coke was a drug or a soft drink, it was the flammable residue from burning coal, and a valuable source of fuel.

Coakly, Cokeley, Cokelie, Cokely

Cobb OE. The word has had many meanings, but the most likely source for the name is probably "cottage." Baseball player Ty Cobb.

Cobbett

Cobden OE. Place name: "Valley with the cottage."

Cobdenn

Cobham OE. Place name: "Village with the cottage." Cob is also an ancient term for a male swan, the head of a herring, and the seed-head of clover, any of which could actually be the source for this name.

Cobbham

Coburn Derivation unclear: "Burn" most likely refers to a small stream. One theory holds that Coburn is a variant of **Cockburn**, making it a place name: "Stream of the rooster." Actor James Coburn.

Coburne, Cockburn, Cockburne

Coby Possibly Dim. **Coburn**: possibly an invented name. Resemblance to the trendy **Cody** favors the latter notion. Basketball player Kobe Bryant; soccer player Kobi Jones.

Cobey, Cobie, Kobe, Kobey, Kobie, Koby

Cockrell OF. "Young rooster."

Cockerell, Cockrill

Cody OE. "Pillow." Some sources suggest "Son of Odo." Use as a first name was probably influenced by the fame of Buffalo Bill Cody, frontier scout and entrepreneur, who took his "Wild West Show" around the U.S. and Europe at the turn of the century. Extensively used as a first name in the 1990s.

Codey, Codie, Kody

Coffin ME. "Basket, container." The word is related to "coffer." Most likely this was an occupational name, referring to a coffin-maker. An unlikely choice, unless this is a family name.

Coffen

Colbert OE. "Renowned mariner."

Cole, Colt, Colvert, Culbert

Colburn OE. Place name: "Cold brook" or "Coal brook."
Colbourn, Colbourne, Collbourn, Collburn

Colby OE. Place name: "The dark farmstead." Surged in popularity during the '90s, probably coasting on the appeal of similar-sounding **Cody**.
Colbee, Colbey, Colbie, Collby

Colden OE. Place name: "Dark valley."
Collden, Coldin, Colldin

Cole Dim. **Nicholas** (Gk. "People of victory") and names beginning with Cole, such as **Coleman**. Monosyllabic names are out of favor now but Cole has a special appeal—is that because it sounds "cool"? Or because it sounds like trendy **Kyle**? Composer Cole Porter; outlaw Cole Younger.

Coleman OE. "Follower of Nicholas." Also contraction of the Latin word for "dove"; probably influenced by the Irish Saint Columba.
Colman

Coleridge OE. Place name: possibly "Cole's ridge" or "Dark ridge." English majors will remember English poet Samuel Taylor Coleridge, author of *The Ancient Mariner* and the famously unfinished *Kubla Khan,* written under the influence of opium.
Colerige, Colridge, Colrige

Colgate OE. Place name: "Dark gate." Associated in the U.S. with a soap-manufacturing company, and of course an Ivy League college. It was originally called Hamilton Literary and Theological Seminary, but was renamed Colgate University in 1890 for its benefactor, William Colgate of the soap fortune.
Colegate

Colin Gael. "Young creature." Also Dim. **Nicholas** (Gk. "People of victory"). Well known in the Middle Ages, and popular in Britain in the middle of this century, but didn't spread in any numbers to the U.S. until quite recently. It now hovers at the bottom of the top 100 names. Secretary of State Colin Powell; actors Colin Farrell, Colin Firth.
Colan, Cole, Collin, Colyn

(

Colley OE. "Dark-haired." Use as a first name is rare. Phil-anthropist Collis Huntington.
Collie, Collis

Collier OE. Occupation name: "Coal miner."
Colier, Colis, Collayer, Collis, Collyer

Collins Ir. Gael. "Holly." Author Wilkie Collins.

Colt OE. Occupational name. Perhaps a long-ago owner of a colt, or breeder or trainer of colts, was first given this name as a surname. In America it is reminiscent of the Colt revolving-breech pistol, or revolver, the brainchild of 19th-century inventor Samuel Colt.

Colter OE. Occupational name: "Colt-herd."

Colton OE. Place name: "Dark settlement" or possibly "Colt-settlement" or "Cole's settlement." This rather neu-tral name is used with surprising frequency.
Coleton, Collton, Colston

Colum Lat. "Dove." Short for Columba or Columban. **Calum** is the most commonly used form at the moment. Actor Colm Wilkinson.
Calum, Callum, Collumbano, Colm, Colombain, Columbano, Columbanus, Columcille

Columbus Variant of the Latin word meaning "Dove." Christopher Columbus, of course, was the Italian ex-plorer who discovered America. The name is used from time to time by parents with a taste for the exotic.
Colombe, Colombo

Colville OF. Place name of Norman origin and obscure meaning.
Colvile, Colvill

Colwyn Welsh. Place name, for a river in Wales.
Colwin, Colwynn

Comanche Name of a Native American tribe. Indigenous to the Great Plains, they were expert horsemen who op-posed European annexation of the West.

Como Lat. "Province." Place name: a province and an ex-ceptionally beautiful lake in Northern Italy.

Comstock OE. Unclear meaning. The Comstock Lode of silver in Nevada, discovered by scout and trapper Henry

Comstock, was the richest silver mine in America in the 19th century.

Comus Greek mythology name: Comus was the Greek god of mirth and hilarity. Hc is usually represented in art as a young man with a torch and a goblet.

Concord ME. "Peace." A Puritan virtue name and also a place name: the capital city of New Hampshire and the small town northwest of Boston linked with the American Revolution and later home to a bevy of 19th-century literary figures.

Conan Ir. Gael. "High, lifted up." Taken to Ireland some time after the Norman Conquest, but almost unknown til the fame of Sherlock Holmes's creator, Sir Arthur Conan Doyle. A more modern example is the movie character Conan the Barbarian, whose creators were probably unaware of the name's previous use or origin. Talk show host Conan O'Brien.

Con, Conant, Conn, Connie

Conlan Ir. Gael. "Hero."

Conlen, Conley, Conlin, Conlon, Connlyn

Connor Ir. Gael. "High longing" or possibly "lover of wolves." A name whose appeal has extended well beyond the Irish community, though it is now very fashionable in Ireland. Irish author Conor Cruise O'Brien.

Conor

Conrad OG. "Courageous advice." Despite occasional increases in its numbers, a name that has never been widely popular in English-speaking countries. In the Middle Ages, several German kings bore this name, however. Anthropologist Konrad Lorenz; hotelier Conrad Hilton; author Joseph Conrad.

Con, Connie, Conrade, Conrado, Corrado, Cort, Curt, Konrad, Kort, Kurt

Conroy Ir. Gael. "Wise man."

Constantine Lat. "Steadfast." The form **Constant** was popular among the Puritans (as a virtue name) and was revived in the 19th century to occasional modern use. Constantine, the Latin form, was the name of the first Roman emperor, eleven Byzantine emperors, and a royal name in

Greece. The Russian czars, in a bid to legitimize Russia as the new home of Orthodoxy, also used the name. Steady 19th-century use has now dwindled to neglect.

Constans, Constanz, Constant, Constantin, Constantino, Constantius, Costa, Konstantin, Konstantio, Konstanz

Consuel Sp. "Consolation."

Consuelo

Conway Welsh. "Holy river" or Ir. Gael. "Hound of the plain." Rare. Musician Conway Twitty.

Conwy

Coney ME. "Rabbit."

Cook Lat. "Cook." Occupational name, one of the 50 most common surnames in England, but an unusual first name in the 20th century.

Cooke, Cookie

Cooper OE. Occupational name: "Barrel maker." Novelist James Fenimore Cooper; actor Gary Cooper.

Coop

Cope ME. "Cape." This is probably an occupational name referring to the long cape worn by a bishop of the Catholic or Anglican church.

Corbin Lat. "Dark as a raven." Most common in the 19th century. Actor Corbin Bernsen.

Corbet, Corbett, Corbie, Corbit, Corbitt, Corby, Corbyn, Cory, Korbyn

Corcoran Ir. Gael. "Ruddy." A 19th-century financier, William Corcoran, founded a significant art gallery in Washington, D.C.

Cochran, Cork, Korcoran

Cordell OF. Occupational name: "Rope maker." Used with some regularity among African-American families. Football player Kordell Stewart.

Cord, Cordas, Cordelle, Kordell, Kordelle

Corey Ir. Gael. Place name: "The hollow." Transferred to a surname and used as a first name for either sex. Also diminutive for "Cor-" names. It is currently more popular for boys.

Correy, Corrie, Corry, Cory, Currie, Curry

Corin Lat. "Spear." The name, which refers both to a male saint and to an early Roman god of war, is more commonly given to boys. As a girl's name, it may even be a variant of **Corinne**. Actor Corin Redgrave.

Coren, Corrin, Cyran, Koren, Korin, Korrin

Cormick Gael. "Chariot driver."

Cormac, Cormack, Cormic

Cork Ir. Gael. Place name: "Swamp, marsh." A seaport, city, and county in Ireland.

Corliss OE. "Benevolent, cheery."

Corless, Corley

Cornelius Lat. "Like a horn." Comes from a famous Latin clan name, and was often used under the Roman Empire. Turns up from time to time, usually as a family name. Railroad millionaire Cornelius Vanderbilt.

Con, Connie, Cornall, Corneille, Cornelious, Cornell, Cornelus, Corney, Cornilius, Kornelious, Kornelis, Kornelius, Neal, Neel, Neil, Neely

Cornell Fr. Var. **Cornelius**. Cornell University, in Ithaca N.Y., was founded by 19th-century telegraph pioneer Ezra Cornell. He was for a while the largest stockholder in Western Union.

Cornall, Cornel, Corney

Cornwallis OE. "Man from Cornwall." Surname transferred to a first name in the 19th-century. Famous English general in the Revolutionary War George Cornwallis lost the battle of Yorktown to Washington and Lafayette, but was later more successful putting down other colonial rebellions in India and Ireland.

Corridon Ir. Gael. "Spear." An unusual Irish last name.

Cort OG. "Brave." Actor Bud Cort.

Corty, Court, Kort

Cortez Sp. last name: may mean "Court-dweller." May also refer to explorer Hernando Cortes, who conquered Mexico for Spain in the 16th century.

Cortes, Kortes, Kortez

Corwin OE. "Heart's friend or companion."

Corwan, Corwinn, Corwyn, Corwynn

Corydon Gk. "Battle-ready."
    Coridon, Coryden, Coryell

Cosgrove Ir. Gael. "Victorious champion."
    Cosgrave

Cosmo Gk. "Orderliness, organization." Saint Cosmas, a martyr, was patron saint of the Italian city of Milan, and the name was further spread there by the fame of Cosimo de' Medici, Grand Duke of Tuscany. His friend the Duke of Gordon took the name to Britain in the 17th century, but it was never widely used and is now the name of an American soccer team.
    Cosimo, Cosmé, Kosmo

Costas Gr. Var. **Constantine**. Sportscaster Bob Costas.
    Costa, Kostas, Kostis

Coster OE. "Peddler." The full word was "costermonger," which meant "seller of costards." Costards were a kind of cooking apple.

Cotton Plant name. May originally have been an occupational name from England, though the cotton plant, requiring a warm climate, was never a big source of industry in Britain. In the U.S., use may refer to the great Massachusetts clergyman Cotton Mather, whose writings contributed to the Salem witch trials. He was named for his grandfather, early American clergyman John Cotton. Actor Joseph Cotten.
    Cotten

Coty Fr. Possibly "Small hillside." More likely, however, to be a respelling of the popular **Cody**.

Coulson Surname derived from **Nicholas** (Gk. "people of victory"), mostly 19th-century use.
    Colson

Council Lat. "Group of people."
    Counsel

Courtland OE. Place name: "Land of the court."
    Cortland, Cortlandt, Court, Courtlandt

Courtney OE. "Court-dweller." Surname transferred to first name; usually feminine in U.S., though still given to boys. Immensely popular for girls in the late eighties,

which will probably limit its use as a boys' name in the future. Actors Tom Courtenay, Courtney B. Vance.
Cortney, Courtenay, Courtnay, Curt

Covert ME. Place name: "Shelter." Refers to a small area of woods that gives shelter to game.
Couvert

Covell OE. Place name: "Slope with the cave."

Covey ME. "Brood of birds." Author Stephen Covey.
Covvey

Covington OE. Place name: "Settlement near the cave."

Cowan Ir. Gael. Place name: "Hollow in the hill."
Coe

Cowrie Shell name: cowrie shells have long been used as currency in eastern Africa, and have a significant place in African American culture.
Courey, Cowrey, Cowry

Coy Unclear meaning: possibly "Woods" or "Quiet place."
Coye

Coyle Ir. Gael. "Follows the battle."

Cox ME. Occupational name: "Coxswain." A coxswain used to be in charge of the rowboats aboard large ships.
Coxe, Coxey

Craddock Welsh. "Love." Anglicization of a Welsh name, more common as a surname.
Caradoc, Caradog, Cradock

Craig Gael. "Rock." (Think "crag.") Surname that has become very popular since its introduction as a first name only 50 years ago. Though not exactly fashionable now, Craig is still steadily used.
Craig, Craigie, Craik, Kraig

Cramer OG. "Peddler." A "cram" was a peddler's pack, and our term, "to cram together" comes from that word.
Cram, Kram, Kramer

Crandall OE. Place name: "Valley of cranes." A dell is another term for a small valley, familiar to most of us from the song "The Farmer in the Dell." Yes, that's what that meant.
Crandal, Crandell

Crane OE. "Crane." This fairly common last name was probably an occupational name referring to the simple hoisting machine that resembles the long-legged bird. Cranes have been in use since early times. Actor Bob Crane.

Crain, Craine, Crayn, Crayne

Cranford OE. Place name: "Ford with the crane." This name probably refers to the water-dwelling birds.

Cranfurd

Cranley OE. Place name: "Meadow with the cranes."

Cranlee, Cranleigh, Cranly

Cranston OE. Place name: "Settlement of cranes." U.S. Senator Alan Cranston.

Craven OE. Last name, formerly place name, of unclear meaning. As an adjective, however, the usual definition is "cowardly." Mostly 19th-century use.

Crawford OE. Place name: "Ford of the crows." Particularly well used in Scotland, as both a surname and a given name.

Crawfurd

Cree Native Canadian tribe: the Cree originated in areas from Quebec to Alberta. Some of the guides for the famous Northwest explorations of North America came from Cree tribes, as they were great warriors and travelers.

Creed Lat. "I believe." A creed is a statement of belief, usually religious.

Creek Place name: "Small river." Such an important feature of any rural landscape that there are many local terms for it: brook, burn, etc.

Creik

Creighton OE. Place name: "Rocky spot."

Crayton, Crichton

Cresswell OE. Place name: "Well where watercress grows."

Carswell, Creswell, Creswill

Crisanto Sp. from Gk. "Gold flower." Usually refers to a chrysanthemum. Possibly because of the name (which sounds like "holy Christ") as many as eight minor saints of this name have been venerated, but they are no longer acknowledged by the Catholic church.

Cresento, Crisento, Crizant, Crizanto

Crispin Lat. "Curly-haired." Saint Crispin, supposedly a 3rd-century martyr (though there is some doubt about his legend), is patron of shoemakers, and Henry V fought the battle of Agincourt on his feast day, October 25. The name was somewhat popular in Britain in the 17th and 18th centuries, and was revived in the 1960s, but has not spread to the U.S. in significant numbers. Actor Crispin Glover.

Crepiñ, Crispian, Crispino, Crispo, Crispus, Crisspin

Crockett ME. "Crook." Probably an occupational name, and the crook referred to is a shepherd's crook. Author Crockett Johnson; frontiersman David Crockett.

Crock, Crocket, Croquet, Croquett, Krock

Crofton OE. "Settlement of the cottages."

Croft, Crofft, Croffton

Cromwell OE. Place name: "Winding stream." Limited use as a first name, probably out of admiration for 17th-century English reformer Oliver Cromwell. Actor James Cromwell.

Cronus Greek mythology name: the youngest Titan (predecessors of the Greek gods) and father of Zeus, Hades, Poseidon, and Demeter. He ruled over earth until he was overthrown by the Olympian gods, his children.

Cronan

Crook OE. Occupational name: "Crook." As with **Crockett**, the name probably indicates a shepherd ancestor.

Crooke, Crookes, Crooks

Crosby Scand. Place name: "At the cross." Singer Bing Crosby.

Crosbey, Crosbie

Crosley OE. Place name: "Meadow of the cross."

Croslea, Crosleigh, Crosly, Crosslee, Crossley, Crosslie

Crowell OE. Place name: "Well at the cross." The "cross" might refer to a spot where two roads cross.

Crowther OE. Occupational name: "Fiddler."

Crothers

Cruz Sp. "Cross."

Cuba Place name: the largest island in the West Indies,

since 1959 a Communist country under the control of Fidel Castro. Actor Cuba Gooding, Jr.

Cullen Ir. Gael. "Handsome." Poet William Cullen Bryant.
Cullan, Cullin, Cullinan

Culley Ir. Gael. Place name: "The woods."
Cully

Culver OE. "Dove." Related to **Colum** and **Columba**, the Latin forms.
Colver, Cully

Cunningham Ir. Gael. "Village of the milk pail." Football player Randall Cunningham.
Conyngham, Cunninghame

Curley OE. "Strong man." Related to **Charles**, via Anglo-Saxon *ceorl,* or "churl."

Curragh Ir. Gael. "Moor." Also a place name: a plain in Kildare, Ireland where the army trained, also the site of a famous race course.

Curran Ir. Gael. "Hero."
Currey, Currie, Curry

Currier ME. Occupational name: "Groom, one who curries a horse." Currying in this case means brushing. This may also be a corruption of "courier," or messenger.
Currie, Curry

Curt Dim. **Courtney, Curtis, Conrad**. Most common in the U.S., but not often a given name. Musician Kurt Cobain; actor Kurt Russell.
Kurt

Curtis OF. "Polite, courteous." Surname used as first name, notably in the U.S. since the 1950s. Used quite steadily. General Curtis Le May; golfer Curtis Strange; football player Curtis Martin.
Curcio, Curt, Curtell, Curtice, Curtiss, Kurtis

Custodio Sp. "Guardian." Refers to the guardian angels of mankind.

Cuthbert OE. "Famous, brilliant." Saint Cuthbert was a much-loved 7th-century English bishop. He was most famous in northern England and Scotland, and his name was most common there, though it fell out of favor after the 1930s. Never popular in America.

Cutler OE. Occupational name: "Knife maker."

Cyprian Gk. "From Cyprus." Steadily used in Britain until the 17th century, but never transferred to the U.S.
Cipriano, Ciprien, Cyprien

Cyrano Gk. "From Cyrene." Use is bound to recall Edmond Rostand's popular play *Cyrano de Bergerac* (1897), based on the life of the 17th-century author and swashbuckler of that name.

Cyril Gk. "The lord." Popularity confined to Britain, from the turn of the century to the 1930s. Actor Cyril Ritchard.
Ciril, Cirilio, Cyrill, Cyrille, Cirillo, Cyrillus, Cirilo, Kiril, Kyril

Cyrus Per. "Sun or throne." Famous Persian emperor who appears in the Old Testament; he allowed exiled Jews to rebuild Jerusalem. Puritan use brought it to the U.S., where it was somewhat popular, but faded in modern times. Inventor Cyrus McCormick; former Secretary of State Cyrus Vance.
Ciro, Cy

Dabney OF. Place name: "From Aubigny." This is an old Virginia name, given with pride to establish a connection with a 1649 immigrant to the New World named Cornelius d'Aubigny. It is used for both boys and girls. Actor Dabney Coleman.
Dabnee, Dabnie, Dabny

Dacey Ir. Gael. "From the south" or Lat. "From Dacia," an area that is now Romania. The form **Dacian** enjoyed a burst of popularity in the 1970s along with other "-ian" names like **Damian** and **Dorian**.
Dace, Dacian, Dacius, Dacy, Daicey, Daicy

Dack Origin unclear. The name may be considered a variant of **Dag**.

Daedalus Gk. "Craftsman." In Greek mythology, Daedalus was the designer of King Minos' labyrinth. So as not to lose the services of this master craftsman, Minos had him imprisoned in the labyrinth. To escape, Daedalus made wings from wax and feathers for himself and his son Icarus. Icarus, however, disregarding his father's instructions, flew too close to the sun. The wax in his wings melted and he fell into the sea and died.

Daidalos, Dedalus

Dag Scand. "Daylight." In Norse mythology the god Dag is the son of light. Diplomat and author Dag Hammarskjold.

Dagget, Daggett, Dagny

Dagan Heb. "Grain, the earth."

Dagon

Dagobert OG. "Bright day, shining day." Most familiar, probably, in the Spanish form **Dagoberto.** Many of these old German names (like **Adalgiso** and **Braulio**) survive in Spanish form. This may date back to the days when Spain and the German princedoms formed part of the Holy Roman Empire, although many of these names are also the names of obscure saints, long venerated in the Spanish church. This name may be the source for the racial slur "dago."

Dagbert, Dagoberto

Dagon Aramaic: meaning unknown. Old Testament name: Dagon was a god of the Canaanites.

Dagwood OE. Place name: "Shining forest." Virtually pre-empted by a character from the popular comic strip *Blondie.* Dagwood was the harassed husband of a dizzy blonde and the name is still occasionally found on menus as the name of a sandwich.

Dahy Ir. Gael. "Quick-footed."

Dahey

Dai Welsh. "To shine." Also a nickname for **David**.

Dailey Ir. Gael. "Assembly." **Daly** is another common form of this name.

Daley, Daly, Daily

Dainard OE. "Bold Dane."

Danehard, Danehardt, Daneard, Daneardt, Daine-hard, Dainhard, Daynard

Daivat Hindi. "Power, strength."

Dakota American place name: the word may be Sioux for "Allies," though another source suggests "forever smiling." Despite its "-a" ending, this name is used (perhaps because of the percussive consonants or the ruggedness it evokes) as a name for both boys and girls. Appears with some regularity. Furniture designer Dakota Jackson.

Daccota, Dakoda, Dakodah, Dakotah, Dakoeta, Dekota, Dekohta, Dekowta

Dalbert OE. "Bright-shining one."

Del, Delbert

Dale OE. Place name: "Valley." Originally a surname meaning "one who lives in the valley." The term "dale" is still used in parts of England. Most famous as a first name in the 1930s. The fame of Roy Rogers' consort Dale Evans may have made this a girl's name. Success guru Dale Carnegie.

Daile, Daley, Dallan, Dalle, Dallin, Dayle

Dallas Scot. Gael. Place name of a village in northeastern Scotland, used as a first name since the 19th century, and apparently unrelated to Dallas, Texas, which was named for a U.S. vice president. Few modern Americans, however, will fail to make the connection between the name and the city.

Dal, Dalles, Dallis, Delles

Dallin OE. Place name: "From the valley." Related to Dale.

Dallan, Dallen, Dallon

Dalton OE. Place name: "The settlement in the valley." Novelist Dalton Trumbo.

Daleton, Dallton, Dalten

Daly Ir. Gael. "Assembly." Common Irish surname, used since the 1940s as a first name. Decathlon champion Daley Thompson.

Daley, Dawley

Dalziel Scot. Gael. Place name: "The small field."

Damario Sp./Gk. "Calf." This is more familiar (though still scarce) as a girl's name, **Damaris**.

Damarios, Damarius, Damaro, Damero

Damaskenos Gk. "From Damascus." Damascus is an ancient city in what is now Syria.

Damascus, Damaskinos

Damek Slavic. Var. **Adam**. "Son of the red earth."

Adamec, Adamek, Adamik, Adamok, Adham, Damick, Damicke

Damian Gk. Meaning not clear: possibly "To tame," although the Greek root is also close to the word for "spirit." The name was revived in various forms (**Damon, Damien**) in the 1950s, having been neglected since the Middle Ages. Still quite steadily used and, as **Demyan**, extremely popular in Russia. Author Damon Runyon; ballet dancer Damien Woetzel.

Daemon, Daimen, Daimon, Daman, Damen, Dameon, Damian, Damiano, Damianos, Damianus, Damien, Damion, Damon, Damyan, Damyen, Damyon, Dayman, Daymian, Daymon, Demyan

Dan Dim. **Daniel**. Heb. "God is my judge." Used from time to time on its own. Actors Dan Ackroyd, Dan Blocker.

Dana OE. "From Denmark." Also possibly a place name referring to an English river. Surname first used as a boy's name in the 19th century, but now almost exclusively a girl's name, and a specifically American one. In 1840 Boston writer Richard Henry Dana, Jr. published the maritime classic *Two Years Before the Mast,* about his voyage in a sailing ship around Cape Horn to California. Artist Charles Dana Gibson; actor Dana Carvey.

Dane, Danie

Danar Invented name, taken from Star Trek. The character Danar is a magnificent human specimen.

Danaus Greek mythology name: a king whose fifty daughters married the fifty sons of his brother Aegiptos.

Denaus, Dinaus

Dane OE. "Dane." In the days when England was subject to regular invasions from Scandinavia, a Dane may have been an enemy. This form of the name is now more popular than **Dana** for boys. Actor Dane Clark.

Dain, Daine, Dayne

Daniel Heb. "God is my judge." In the famous Old Testament story, Daniel is thrown into a den of lions because he insists on praying to his God while a captive in Babylon; he was, of course, rescued by the same God. The name has been used with moderate frequency until a spurt of popularity in the late 1950s, which endures until today; the name is still one of the top twenty in the U.S., England, and Ireland. Novelist Daniel Defoe; entertainers Danny Thomas, Danny Kaye; Senator Daniel Patrick Moynihan; actors Daniel Day-Lewis, Danny DeVito, Danny Aiello, Daniel Radcliffe.

Dan, Danal, Dane, Daneal, Danek, Dani, Danial, Daniele, Danil, Danilo, Danko, Dannel, Dannie, Danny, Danyal, Danyel, Deiniol

Dante Lat. "Lasting, enduring." Actually a nickname, since Italian poet Dante Alighieri's full name was Durante, and modern use of the name almost always refers to him. English artist Dante Gabriel Rossetti; football player Daunte Culpepper.

Dantae, Dantay, Dontae, Dontay, Donte

Danton Fr. May mean "From Anton," a place name, or may refer to an ancestor named Anthony. *D'antan* means "long ago" in poetic French. The famous Danton this name calls to mind, though, is Georges Danton, one of the key figures in the French revolution.

Danube Geography name: the second largest river in Europe, it wanders through Germany, Austria, Hungary, and finally empties into the Black Sea.

Donau

Daphnis Greek mythology name. Daphnis (not to be confused with the female Daphne) appears in two tales as a love-struck shepherd. The more widely known story is the pastoral romance of Daphnis and Chloe.

Daquan Invented name. Parents who invent names for boys generally stop at two syllables, though girls' names often run on to three. The "qu-" sound, which occurs so rarely in English, is a popular element of invented names in the African-American community.

Daquanne, Dequan, Dequanne, Dekwan, Dekwohn, Dekwohnne

Dar Heb. "Pearl."

Darby OE. Place name: "Park with deer." Derived from **Derby**, a surname used as a first name. Darby is occasionally used for girls.
Darbey, Darbie, Derby

Darcy Ir. Gael. "Dark." Also Norman place name, "From Arcy." It was possibly this connotation of Norman aristocracy that Jane Austen sought when she named the haughty hero of *Pride and Prejudice* "Mr. Darcy." In Britain, more likely to be a boy's name, but in the U.S., more likely to be feminine.
D'Arcy, Darcey, Darsey, Darsy

Dardanos Greek mythology name: the founder of Troy and the surrounding country, Dardania. He was a son of Zeus.
Dard, Dardanio, Dardanios, Dardanus

Darian Invented name. **Adrian, Darius, Marion, Darren**: this name includes a number of familiar elements combined in a new way. This process is increasingly popular with today's parents. See **Darrien**.
Darien, Darion, Darrian, Darrien, Darrion

Darius Gk. "Rich, kingly." Darius the Great was a renowned emperor of Persia in the 5th century B. C., who permitted the Jews to rebuild the temple in Jerusalem. The name is especially popular with African-American parents.
Darias, Dariess, Dario, Darious, Darrius, Derrius, Derry

Darnell OE. Place name: "The hidden spot."
Darnall, Darnel

Darnley ME. Place name: "Grassy meadow." Darnel is a specific kind of grass. This name resonates with history beyond the mere place it commemorates, however: Henry Stewart, Lord Darnley, was the second husband of Mary, Queen of Scots, and father of James VI of Scotland and I of England.

Darold Invented name: Harold with a "D."
Darrold

Darrah Ir. Gael. "Dark oak." This was originally an Irish last name.
Darach, Darragh

Darrel Transferred surname, possibly originated as a French place name, like **Darcy**. There are many forms, of which **Darryl** is the favorite by a nose. In fact, that spelling, and the popularity of the name in the 1950s, may stem from the fame of film producer Darryl Zanuck. Baseball star Darryl Strawberry; musician Daryl Hall.

Darral, Darrell, Darrill, Darrol, Darroll, Darry, Darryl, Darryll, Daryl, Derrel, Derrell, Derril, Derrill, Deryl, Deryll

Darren Ir. Gael. "Great." Originally a surname, first used as a given name in this century. Its popularity was probably influenced by the TV series *Bewitched*, in which the rather hapless leading man was named Darren. Though hardly fashionable, it is still very steadily used.

Daren, Darin, Daron, Darran, Darrin, Darring, Darron, Darryn, Derrin, Derron

Darrien Modern combined name: possibly an elaborated form of Darren or a retooling of **Dorian**. It is possible, but unlikely, that this name is a reference to the eastern part of Panama known as Darien, which later gave its name to one of New York City's poshest suburbs. John Keats' famous sonnet "On First Looking into Chapman's Homer" ends by comparing the poet's wonder to that of Cortez, glimpsing the Pacific Ocean for the first time "Silent, upon a peak in Darien." Football player Darrien Gordon.

Darian, Darion, Darrian, Darrion, Darryan, Darryen

Darrow OE. "Spear." Use may be a tribute to the great labor lawyer Clarence Darrow.

Darro

Darshan Sanskrit. "Vision."

Dart OE. Place name: the river Dart is a small river in southern England. Dartmouth is a town at the mouth of the river. A dart, of course, is also a small arrow.

D'Artagnan OF. "From Artagnan." D'Artagnan is one of the central characters in the famous Alexandre Dumas novel *The Three Musketeers*.

Darton OE. Place name: "Settlement of the deer."

Darwin OE. "Dear friend." Naturalist Charles Darwin.
Darwon, Darwyn, Derwin, Derwynn

Dathan Heb. Meaning unclear: possibly "Spring" or "fountain." In the Old Testament, Dathan rebelled against Moses.

Davenport OF. Unknown origin. The word is occasionally used as a term for a large sofa. It is a place name and a last name in the U.S.

Davian Modern combined name: **David** plus **Ian**, or **David** plus **Dorian**.
Daivian, Daivyan, Davien, Davion, Davyan, Davyen, Davyon

David Heb. "Dear one." In the Old Testament, the young David used his slingshot to kill the mighty giant Goliath, and went on to become King of Israel and author of the Psalms. He has been a favorite subject of artists, notably sculptors of the Italian Renaissance, like Michelangelo and Donatello. Saint David is the patron saint of Wales, so the name is popular there, and in Scotland, where David was a royal name. In the U.S. the name is used by Jewish and Christian families alike, and was in the top ten boys' names from the 1950s until the 1990s. It has just recently been nudged a little farther down the charts. Explorer David Livingstone; actors David Niven, David Arquette, David Duchovny, David Schwimmer; baseball star Dave Winfield; TV host David Letterman; musician David Bowie; soccer player David Beckham.
Daffy, Daffyd, Dafydd, Dai, Dave, Davey, Davi, Davie, Davidde, Davide, Davidson, Davie, Davies, Davin, Davis, Daven, Davon, Davy, Davyd, Davydd

Davis OE. "David's son." Contraction of surname that cropped up in the Middle Ages. Confederate President Jefferson Davis; actor Brad Davis.
Dave, Davidson, Davies, Davison, Daviss, Davy

Dawson OE. "David's son." Another form of the medieval surname.
Daw, Dawe, Dawes

Day OE. "Day." Familiar as a last name but scarce as a first name. Author Clarence Day.

Daye

Dayanand Hindi. "He who loves compassion."

Daymond Modern name: Raymond with a "D." Resemblance to **Damon** makes it sound familiar.

Daimond

Dayton OE. Place name: possibly "Day's settlement" or "David's settlement." Also a city in Ohio.

Daytan, Dayten

Deacon Gk. "Messenger." A deacon is a Christian clergyman, usually lower in the hierarchy than the minister or pastor. Football player Deacon Jones.

Deakin, Deecon, Deekon, Diakonos

Dean OE. Place name: "Valley," or occupational name: "Church official." Surname used as a first name, mostly since the 1950s. Actor Dean Martin; U.S. Secretaries of State Dean Acheson, Dean Rusk.

Deane, Deen, Dene, Deyn, Dino

DeAndré Modern name: André with the prefix "De-." Names for boys are, as a rule, more conservative than names for girls. Even African-American parents, who show great invention in choosing their children's names, tend to be less adventurous, but DeAndré is common enough to be on some popularity lists.

D'André, DeAndrae, DeAndray, Diandray, Diondrae, Diondray

DeAngelo Modern name: Angelo with the prefix "De-." The least common of these "De-" names.

D'Angelo DiAngelo

Dearborn OE. Place name: "Brook of the deer."

Dearbourn, Dearburne, Deerborn

Debonair Fr. "Urbane, nonchalant." Perhaps a Norman family name: it could have meant "of good lineage." To moderns, debonair is the word you use to describe Fred Astaire.

Debonnair, Debonnaire

Decatur Last name of unclear origin. There is a process called "decating" in the manufacture of cloth. "Deca-" is

the Greek word particle meaning "ten," but it might also
mean "pure," as **Catherine** does. The name is probably
used in tribute to Stephen Decatur, an early 19th-century
naval hero. There are several U.S. towns named for him.

Deccan Place name: an area in central India.

Decimus Lat. "Tenth," as in tenth child. Opportunities for
use seem negligible today.
   Decio

Declan Ir. Unknown meaning: name of a saint, popular in
Ireland. The singer Elvis Costello was born Declan
Patrick McManus.

Dedrick Var. **Theodoric**. OG. "The people's ruler." Also
the source for the better-known Derek. Football player
Dedric Ward.
   Dedric, Diederick, Dietrich

Dee Scot. Place name: a significant river that runs into the
North Sea at Aberdeen.

Deems OE. "Judge's child."

Deepak Sanskrit. "Little lamp." Author Deepak Chopra.
   Dipak

DeForest ME. Place name: "Living near the forest."
   Defforest

DeJuan Modern name: **Juan** with the "De-" prefix.
   DaJuan, DaJuwan, DeJuwan, DeWuan, DeWonn

Dekel Heb. "Palm tree."

Delaney Ir. Gael. Meaning unclear: possibly "Offspring of
the challenger." May also have something to do with
"swarthy," or be a place name referring to the Slaney
river.
   Delaine, Delainey, Delainy, Delane, Delany

Delano OF. Surname of unclear origin: possibly "Night-
time" *(de la nuit)* or "nut tree" *(de la noix)*. It would be
merely one of those odd family names if it had not been
made famous by U.S. President Franklin Delano Roosevelt.

Delbert OE. "Day-bright." Also possibly a variant of **Albert** (Adelbert), OE. "High-born, brilliant." The title of a
very popular comic strip is the variation **Dilbert**.
   Bert, Bertie, Dalbert, Dilbert

Delius Gk. "From Delos." Delos is a tiny Greek island that was sacred to the ancient Greeks, who believed that Apollo and Artemis had been born there.
Deli, Delios, Delos

Dell OE. Place name: "Small valley." As in the old song, *The Farmer in the Dell*. May also be a diminutive of names like **Delbert** or **Odell**.

Delling ONorse. "Scintillating."

Delmore OF. "Of the sea." The more familiar form, at least as a place name, is the Spanish **Delmar**. Use is American only. Poet Delmore Schwartz.
Delmar, Delmer, Delmor

Delphin Gk. "Dolphin." This is a French form of a name with a complex origin. It alludes to the Greek town of Delphi, home of a famous oracle. The Greeks believed that Delphi was the earth's womb; the dolphin's shape resembles that of a pregnant woman. A 4th-century French bishop, later a saint, was named Delphin. The feminine version, **Delphine**, has survived much better than this form.
Delfin, Delfino, Delfinos, Delfinus, Delphino, Delphinos, Delphinus, Delvin

Delroy Fr. "The king." More common forms are **Elroy** and **Leroy**. Actor Delroy Lindo.
Delroi

Delwin OE. "Proud friend" or "Bright friend."
Dalwin, Dalwyn, Delavan, Delevan, Dellwin, Delwyn, Delwynn

DeMarcus Modern name: **Marcus** with the prefix "De-." Marcus also tends to shade into **Marquez**, which comes from an entirely different root.
Damarcus, DaMarkiss, DeMarco, Demarkess, De-Marko, Demarkus, DeMarquess, DeMarquez, DeMarquiss

Demas Biblical: a companion who forsook Paul. This may be the source for Deems, another obscure name.
Dimas

Demetrius Gk. "Follower of Demeter." It has been little used in English-speaking countries, though its Greek and

Russian forms are well-known in those countries. Lately, however, the urge toward exoticism in the U.S. (or perhaps high levels of immigration) have brought it to more frequent use. On one list, Demetrius ranks above old standbys like **Albert, Glenn**, and **Arthur**. Composer Dimitri Shostakovich.

Dametrius, Demetri, Demetrice, Demetris, Demitrios, Dhimitrios, Dimetre, Dimitri, Dimitrios, Dimitrious, Dimitry, Dmitri, Dmitrios, Dmitry

Demos Gk. "The people." Also possibly homage to Greece's most famous orator, Demosthenes. This is the word that forms the root of "democracy." Rare, even in Greece.

Demas

Dempsey Ir. Gael. "Proud." Boxer Jack Dempsey.

Dempsy

Dempster OE. "One who judges." Gossip columnist Nigel Dempster.

Denali Geography name: Mt. McKinley, over 20,000 ft. high and America's highest mountain, rises out of Denali National Park in Alaska.

Denby Scand. Place name: "The Danes' village." Film critic David Denby.

Danby, Denbey, Denney, Dennie, Denny

Denham OE. Place name: "Village in a valley."

Denholm Scot. Place name. In the public eye currently because of the English actor Denholm Elliott.

Denley OE. Place name: "Meadow near the valley."

Denlie, Denly

Denman OE. Surname derived from place name: "Man who lives in the valley."

Denmark Geography: name of one of the Scandinavian countries. Also a possibly combined name, marrying **Dennis** and **Mark**.

Dennis Gk. "Follower of Dionysius." Dionysos was the classical Greek god of wine, but the name also appears in the New Testament. Saint Denis is the patron saint of France. The name has had alternating centuries of favor and disfavor (16th out, 17th in), reaching the height of its

20th-century popularity around 1920. Actors Dennis Quaid, Dennis Christopher, Dennis Hopper, Dennis Franz, Denis Leary, Dennis Haysbert; sailor Dennis Conner.

Den, Denies, Denis, Dennes, Dennet, Denney, Dennie, Dennison, Denny, Dennys, Denys, Deon, Dion, Dionisio, Dionysius, Dionysus, Diot

Dennison OE. "Son of Dennis."

Den, Denison, Dennyson, Tennyson

Denton OE. Place name: "Settlement in the valley."

Denny, Dent, Denten, Dentin

Denver OE. Place name: "Green valley." The Colorado capital was named after the 19th-century governor of the Kansas Territory, James W. Denver. Singer John Denver.

Denzel Cornish place name, used as a first name almost exclusively in Britain. Actor Denzel Washington.

Denzell, Denziel, Denzil, Denzill, Denzyl

Deodar Sanskrit. "Divine wood." The name of an exceptionally tall species of cedar, native to India, that is also grown in California and England, where it is sometimes known as the "god tree."

Deon Var. **Dion**.

Derby OE. Place name: "Park with deer." Variant spelling of **Darby**. The English, in their confusing way, pronounce this word "Darby." This is also the name of a hat with a hard round crown, and American's most famous horse race, the Kentucky Derby. The race got its name from the English Derby, which was instituted by the Earl of Derby in 1780.

Derbey, Derbie

Derek OG. "The people's ruler." Most common of the many anglicized forms of **Theodoric**, popular starting around 1890, peaking in the 1930s, and now familiar but hardly fashionable. Basketball player Derrick Coleman; baseball player Derek Jeter.

Darrick, Darriq, Dereck, Deric, Derick, Derik, Deriq, Derk, Derreck, Derrek, Derrick, Derrik, Derryck, Derryk, Deryk, Deryke, Dirk, Dirke, Dyrk

Derland OE. "Land with deer."

Durland

Dermot Ir. Gael. "Free man." Actor Dermot Mulroney.
Dermott, Diarmid, Diarmuid

DeRon Modern name: **Ron** with the "De-" prefix. Depending on where the accent lies, this could be a variation of **Darren**.
Daron, DeRron

Derry Ir. Gael. Place name: City in Northern Ireland formerly known as Londonderry. Also short form of **Derek, Dermot**, etc. Photographer Derry Moore.
Derrie

Derward OE. "Deer keeper."
Durward

Derwent OE. Place name: there are three rivers called "Derwent" in England, possibly from the ancient word *dwr,* meaning "water."

Derwin OE. "Dear friend."
Darwin, Darwyn, Derwyn, Derwynn, Durwin

Deshan Hindi. "Of the nation."
Deshad, Deshal

DeShawn Modern name: **Shawn** with the "De-" prefix.
Dashaun, Dashawn, Desean, DeShaun, D'Shawn

Desiderio It. "Desired." Several names come from this Latin root; the girl's name **Desirée** is analogous. St. Desiderius was a 7th-century bishop and martyr in France. The name **Didier**, which is quite common in France, evolved from this root. Comedian Desi Arnaz.
Deri, Derito, Desi, Desideratus, Desiderios, Desiderius, Diderot, Didier, Dizier

Desmond Ir. Gael. "From South Munster." Munster was an ancient kingdom in Ireland. Used in England since 1900, and briefly popular around 1920, but unusual now. South African cleric and activist Bishop Desmond Tutu.
Des, Desmund, Dezmond

Detleff Germanic name of uncertain meaning and origin. Basketball player Detlef Schremp.
Detlef, Detlev

Deval Hindi. "Divine." The Sanskrit root *deva* means "god."
Deven

Deverell OE. Place name: "Bank of the river."

Devereux OF. Meaning unclear. Probably a place name having to do with water *(eau)*, or somehow related to the Old English **Everard** ("Board hardness").
Deveraux

Devin Ir. Gael. "Bard, poet," or possibly "Young deer." May also come from the French *divin,* meaning "divine." The name, spelled either this way or with an "o" instead of an "i," is also popular for girls, but is still used more often for boys. This spelling is more common.
Dev, Devinn, Devon, Devyn, Devynn

Devine Ir. Gael. "Ox" or OF. "Divine."

Devlin Ir. Gael. "Fierce courage."
Delvin, Devland, Devlen, Devlon, Devlyn

Devon English and American place name; Devon is a county in southwestern England, and several towns in the United States have been named after it. There is no clear-cut "feminine" or "masculine" spelling for this name, but the "o" spelling is somewhat more common for girls.
Deven, Devin, Devonn, Devyn

Dewey Welsh. Var. **David**. Bookish parents may remember the Dewey Decimal System, invented by Melvil Dewey in 1876 and the organizing principle for the majority of American libraries until the Libary of Congress got in on the act and changed all the numbers.
Dewi, Dewie

DeWitt Flemish. "Blond." Early American statesman De Witt Clinton.
Dewitt, Dwight, Witt

Dexter Lat. "Right-handed" or OE. "Woman dyer." Modern use, more common in Britain. Football player Dexter Carter.
Dex

Diamond OE. "Bright guardian." Also, for girls, a jewel name. Actor Lou Diamond Phillips.

Diarmid Ir. Gael. "Free man." The anglicized version is Dermot.
Diarmaid, Diarmait, Diarmi

Dice ME. "Dice." The small numbered cubes used in games.
Dyce

COOL NAMES

In this ironic age, sometimes parents give their children names that seem deliberately unfashionable, in the same way that they'd wear odd-looking glasses or drive resolutely clunky cars. The uncool thus becomes cool. Movie stars aren't immune to this trend. Check out the choices below:

- Diane Keaton: Dexter
- Tom Hanks & Rita Wilson: Chester and Truman
- Roseanne Barr & Ben Thomas: Buck
- Robin Givens: Buddy
- Melanie Griffith & Antonio Banderas: Stella
- Kate Capshaw & Steven Spielberg: Sawyer
- Nicolas Cage & Christina Fulton: Weston
- Kyra Sedgwick & Kevin Bacon: Travis
- David Duchovny & Téa Leoni: Kyd
- Justine Bateman: Duke
- Hugh Jackman & Deborra-Lee Furness: Oscar
- Richard Gere & Carey Lowell: Homer
- Anne Heche & Coley Laffoon: Homer

Dick Dim. **Richard** (OG. "Dominant ruler"). Figure skater Dick Button.

Dickinson OE. "Dick's son."

Didier Fr. "Much-desired." From **Desideratus**. Male form of **Desirée**, currently popular in France.

Diego Sp. Var. **James** (Heb. "He who supplants"). The Mexican peasant to whom the Virgin of Guadalupe appeared was named Juan Diego. Painter Diego Rivera.
Dago

Dieter OG. "Army of the people." Very fashionable in Germany.

Dietrich Ger. form of **Theodoric** (OG. "People's ruler"). See **Derek**.
Dedrick, Derek, Deke, Diederick, Dirk

Digby ONorse. "Town by the ditch." Like many English surnames adapted from place names, became a first name in the late 19th century without ever becoming very widespread.

Diggory English name of uncertain meaning, though it may be a place name, referring to a dyke.
Diggery, Diggorey, Digory

Dillon Ir. Gael. "Loyal." Often confused with its popular homonym, the Welsh **Dylan**. Actor Matt Dillon.
Dillan, Dilon, Dyllon, Dylon

Dinesh Sanskrit. "Lord of the day" or "Sun." Writer Dinesh D'Souza.

Dingo Australian. The wild dogs of Australia, similar to foxes.

Dino Usually a diminutive of **Dean** or any number of names that end in "-dino," like **Bernardino**. Movie producer Dino DeLaurentiis.

Dinsmore Ir. Gael. Place name: "The hill fortress."
Dinnsmore

Diogenes Greek philosopher, a cynic and an ascetic who believed that the simple life was the good life: taking this principle seriously, he is said to have lived in a tub.

Dion Probably short for **Dionysius**, but often used without reference to the longer name. Singer Dion (of Dion and the Belmonts); football player Deion Sanders.
Deion, Deon, Deonn, Deonys, Deyon

Dionysius Greek mythology name: Dionysius was the Greek god of wine (known to Romans as Bacchus). The name survived into the Christian era, possibly because of the man named Dionysius who was converted by St. Paul, and is traditionally considered the first bishop of Athens. **Dennis** is an offshoot of this name.
Dion, Dionio, Dionisio, Dioniso, Dionysios, Dionysos, Dionysus

Dirk Var. **Derek** (OG. "The people's ruler"). "Dirk" is also the Scottish term for a small, very sharp knife. Flemish painter Dierick Bouts.
Dierck, Dieric, Dierick, Dirck

Dixon OE. "Son of Dick." Scottish surname transferred to first name. Author Dixon Wecter.
Dickson, Dix

Doane OE. Place name: "Low, rolling hills."
Doan

Dobbs Possibly OE. Occupational name having to do with painting ("daubing"). May also be related to **Robert**.

Dodge OE. Name of unclear meaning: may be related to **Roger**. Dodge was a prominent name in American history even before the Dodge family began manufacturing cars.
Dod, Dodds, Dodgson

Doherty Ir. Gael. "Harmful." Surname common in Ireland, transferred occasionally to first-name status.
Docherty, Dougherty, Douherty

Dolan Ir. Gael. "Black-haired."

Dolph Dim. **Adolph**. Actor Dolf Lundgren.
Dolf, Dollfus, Dollfuss, Dollphus, Dolphus

Dominic Lat. "Lord." A name popular among Catholic families possibly because of the fame of Saint Dominic, founder of an important monastic order. Use has spread since the 1950s. Still more common in Britain than in the U.S. Clever for a child born on Sunday, "the Lord's day." The French version, **Dominique**, is often a girl's name in the U.S. Opera star Placido Domingo; basketball player Dominique Wilkins; hockey player Dominik Hasek.
Demenico, Demingo, Dom, Domenic, Domenico, Domenique, Domingo, Domini, Dominick, Dominie, Dominik, Dominique, Domino, Dominy, Nick

Domino Lat. "Lord, master." The rectangular game pieces marked with dots: in theory they are called dominoes because the loser of each game called out "Domino" to the winner.

Donahue Ir. Gael. "Dark fighter." TV host Phil Donahue.
Donahoe, Donohoe, Donohue

Donald Scot. Gael. "World mighty." Common in Scotland for centuries, and popular elsewhere for some 50 years, peaking in 1925. Less popular since the 1950s, perhaps because Disney preempted the name by giving it to a cartoon duck. Actors Donald Sutherland, Don Cheadle, Donal Logue; real estate tycoon Donald Trump; singer Donny Osmond.

Donal, Donaldo, Donall, Donalt, Donaugh, Donel, Donelson, Donnel, Donnell, Donnie, Donny

Donato Lat. "Given."

Donatien, Donatus

Donnelly Ir. Gael. "Brown-haired fighter."

Donnell

Donovan Ir. Gael. "Dark." Surname become first name or, in the case of the pop singer who recorded *Mellow Yellow* in the late 1960s, only name. Football player Donovan McNabb.

Donavon, Donevin, Donevon, Donoven, Donovon

Dontavius Modern name: probably combination of the quite popular **Donté**, and **Octavius**.

Dantavius, Dawntavius, Dewontavius, Dontavious

Donté It. "Lasting." This is a respelling of **Dante**: this form is popular among African-American families.

Dantae, Dantay, Dohntae, Dontae, Dontay, Dontey

Dooley Ir. Gael. "Dark hero." In the early 20th century author Finley Peter Dunne wrote more than 700 hugely popular newspaper essays that saw the world through the eyes of Martin Dooley, a fictitious Irish bartender on Chicago's West Side. Actor Paul Dooley.

Dor Heb. "Generation."

Doram, Doriel, Dorli

Doran Ir. Gael. "Fist" or "Stranger, exile."

Dore, Dorian, Doron, Dorran, Dorren

Dorian Gk. Place name: "From Doris," an area in Greece. Introduced by Oscar Wilde in *The Picture of Dorian Gray;* the hero of the tale is a beautiful young man who succumbs to a life of vice. Notwithstanding this discouraging precedent, the name has had some popularity in the U.S.

Dore, Dorien, Dorrian, Dorrien, Dorryen

Doron Heb. "Gift."

Doran, Doroni

Dorsey Probably from the French d'Orsay, meaning "From

Orsay." Band leader Tommy Dorsey; football player Dorsey Levens.
Dorsee, Dorsie

Dotson Probably a respelling of **Dodson** (and thus a variation on "Roger's son"). Author Dotson Rader.
Dotsen, Dottson

Dougal Celt. "Dark stranger." Most common in Scotland.
Doyle, Dougall, Dugal, Dugald, Dugall

Douglas Scot. Gael. Place name: "Black water." The name of a hugely powerful Scots clan. Though it was originally a girl's name, by the 19th century Douglas was used for boys. Its period of great popularity, which peaked in the 1950s, seems to have been inspired by the actors Douglas Fairbanks, father and son. Fairly steadily used, though not fashionable. Author Douglas Adams; Gen. Douglas MacArthur.
Douglass, Dugaid

Dov Heb. "Bear."

Dow Ir. Gael. "Dark-haired."
Dowan, Dowe, Dowson

Doyle Ir. Gael. "Black stranger." Var. **Dougal**. Authors Paddy Doyle, Arthur Conan Doyle.

Drake ME. This is an unusually specific name, for it derives from the word *draca,* which was the medieval term for "dragon." Originally Drake designated the man who kept the inn with the dragon trademark, or the "Sign of the Dragon." It followed the usual route of becoming a surname, and thence a first name. English explorer Sir Francis Drake.

Draper OE. Occupational name: a draper was a man who sold cloth.

Drew Welsh. "Wise." Dim. **Andrew**. Used as an independent name since the 1960s. Football player Drew Bledsoe.
Dru

Driscoll Meaning and derivation unclear: possibly Celtic "sorrowful."
Driscol

Drummond Celt. Meaning unclear. Use as a first name is concentrated in Scotland.

Drury OF. "Loved one." Drury Lane is a famous street in London's theater district, and also the home of the Muffin Man in a well-known children's song.
Drew, Drewry, Dru

Dryden OE. Place name: "Dry valley." Poet John Dryden.

Duane Ir. Gael. "Swarthy." Used primarily since the 1940s, predominantly in the U.S. **Dwayne** is the most popular spelling.
Dewain, Dewayne, Duwain, Duwaine, Duwayne, Dwain, Dwaine, Dwayne

Dudley OE. Place name: "People's field." Aristocratic family name in England, used as a first name since the 19th century. The absurd Canadian Mountie Dudley Doright was a staple character in the 1960s *Rocky and Bullwinkle Show*. Actor Dudley Moore.

Duff Gael. "Swarthy." There are many English surnames turned first names that derive from the Gaelic *dubh,* which means "dark." They may describe places (i.e., **Douglas**), or personal characteristics, as in this case.
Duffey, Duffie, Duffy

Dugan Ir. Gael. "Swarthy."
Doogan, Dougan, Douggan, Duggan

Duke Lat. "Leader." Last name transferred to first name, or possibly an abbreviation of the highly unusual **Marmaduke**. Current use is probably inspired either by John Wayne (who was nicknamed "Duke"), or the great jazz musician Duke Ellington.

Dumont Fr. Place name: "Of the mountain."

Dunbar Gael. "Castle headland."

Duncan Scot. Gael. "Brown fighter." A royal name in early Scotland: There was a King Duncan in 11th-century Scotland whose cousin Macbeth murdered him. Shakespeare later picked up the tale in his tragedy *Macbeth*. The name disappeared until a spell of 19th-century use in Scotland and a flurry of mostly English popularity in the 1950s and 1960s. Never a big hit in the U.S. Cabinetmaker Duncan Phyfe.
Dunc, Dunn

Dundee Gael. "Fort on the Tay." The Tay is a river in Scotland, and Dundee is a city there.

Dunham Gael. "Brown man."

Dunley OE. Place name: "Meadow with the hill."
Dunlea, Dunleigh, Dunlie, Dunly, Dunnlea, Dunnleigh, Dunnley

Dunlop Scot. Gael. Place name: "Muddy hill."

Dunmore Scot. Gael. Place name: "Big fortress on the hill."

Dunn Gael. "Brown." Writers Dominick and John Gregory Dunne.
Dunne

Dunstan OE. Place name: "Brown hill with stones." Name of an English saint who was Archbishop of Canterbury in the 10th century. Rarely used, even in Britain.
Dunsten, Dunstin, Dunston

Dunton OE. Place name: "Hill settlement."

Durant Lat. "Enduring." Much more common as a last name. **Dante** is an abbreviated version. The 20th-century historians Will and Ariel Durant; American painter Asher Durand; entertainer Jimmy Durante.
Dante, Durand, Durante

Durward OE. Occupational name: "Warder at the gate."
Derward

Durwin OE. "Dear friend."
Derwin, Derwyn, Durwyn

Duryea Unclear derivation: possibly related to Latin "Lasting." Since this is most often an Irish last name, a Gaelic origin seems more likely.

Dustin OG. "Brave warrior," or OE. Place name: "Dusty area." Use of the name is almost certainly influenced by the fame of actor Dustin Hoffman, and it's quite substantial.
Dustan, Dusten, Duston, Dusty, Dustyn

Duvall Fr. Place name: "Of the valley." Actor Robert Duvall.
Duval

Dwayne Ir. Gael. "Swarthy." Many English names are based on the Gaelic particle *dubh,* which means "Dark."
Duane, Duwain, Duwayne, Dwain, Dwaine

Dwight Flemish. "White or blond." Var. **DeWitt**. Some sources claim Dwight is a contraction of a surname derived from **Dionysius**. Given fame in the U.S. by two Yale University presidents, and by President Dwight Eisenhower. Its moderate use as a first name was probably inspired by him, and had trailed off by the 1970s. Baseball star Dwight Gooden.

Dwyer Ir. Gael. "Dark wise one." This was originally an Irish last name, occasionally transferred to a first name.
Dwire

Dyer OE. Occupational name: "Dyer." Curiously enough, **Dexter** refers to a female dyer.

Dylan Welsh. "Son of the sea." Welsh legend tells of a sea-god named Dylan, but modern use of the name, which has spread well beyond Wales, is probably homage to poet Dylan Thomas. Catherine Zeta-Jones, who stresses her Welsh background, chose this name for her son with Michael Douglas. Though the name is extremely popular in Ireland, it is also quite frequently used in the U.S. The best-known example of this tribute is singer Bob Dylan, whose last name was originally Zimmerman. Some of the variant spellings given below are more closely related to homonym **Dillon**. Actor Dylan McDermott.
Dillan, Dillon, Dyllan, Dylon, Dylonn

Dyson OE. Last name that is probably a contraction of **Dennison**. Transferred to first-name use in the 19th century.

Eagle Bird name. The eagle is America's national bird, of course. Since certain Native American tribes have traditionally named children after birds and animals, this name has an aura of the open spaces of the west.

Eamon Ir. Var. **Edmund** (OE. "Wealthy protector"). Irish President Eamon de Valera may have been the inspiration behind the spurt of popularity between the 1950s and the 1970s. The name is rare in America.

Amon, Aimon, Aymon, Eamonn

Earl OE. "Nobleman, leader." The most popular of the English titles of nobility to be used as a first name, though **Baron** and **Duke** also occur. In the democratic U.S. it is probably a transferred surname rather than an allusion to the hereditary aristocracy. Author Erle Stanley Gardner; actor Errol Flynn; basketball star Earl ("the Pearl") Monroe; musician Earl Scruggs; Chief Justice of the U.S. Supreme Court Earl Warren.

Earle, Earlie, Early, Erl, Erle, Errol, Erroll, Erryl, Rollo

Earland OE. Place name: "Earl's land." Earl is the oldest title in the aristocracy, which probably explains the number of words that incorporate the title. The **Erland** spelling, for linguists, comes from Old Norse and means "Foreigner." Actor Erland Josephson.

Erland

Earlham OE. Place name: "Earl's village."

Earlston OE. Place name: "Earl's settlement."

Earlton

Early ME. "Early, soon," or OE "Earl's meadow." Confederate General Jubal Early.

Earley, Earlie, Erlie, Erly

Earvin Var. **Irvin** (OE. "Sea friend"). Made famous by basketball star Earvin "Magic" Johnson.

Eastman OE. "Man from the East." Painter Eastman Johnson; photography pioneeer George Eastman.

Eaton OE. Place name: "Settlement on the river."

Eatton, Eton, Eyton

Eban Heb. "Stone, rock." Israeli statesman Abba Eban.

Eben

Ebenezer Heb. "Rock of help." In the Old Testament, Samuel created a memorial to his victory over the Philistines, and called the stone Ebenezer. The name came to America with the Puritans, and was, improbably enough, at one point almost as popular a name as John. It was fading by the 19th century, and Ebenezer Scrooge in

Charles Dickens' *A Christmas Carol* probably hastened its disappearance.

Eb, Ebbaneza, Eben, Ebeneezer, Ebeneser, Ebenezar, Eveneser, Evenezer

Eberhard OG. "Courage of a boar." Var. **Everett**. Pencil magnate Eberhard Faber.

Eberardo, Eberhardt, Eberdt, Ebert, Everard, Everhardt, Evrard, Evreux

Eberlein OG. "Small boar."

Eberle, Eberley

Ebisu In Japan, the god of hard work and also of good luck.

Eckhard OG. "Brave edge, brave point." Refers to the point of a sword. Actor Aaron Eckhart.

Eckard, Eckardt, Eckhardt, Ekkehard, Ekkehardt

Edbert OE. "Wealthy and bright."

Edel OG. "Noble." Unusual as a name in itself, but the first syllable of many combined forms such as **Adalric** and **Adelaide**. Biographer Leon Edel.

Adel, Adlin, Edelin, Edlin

Eden Heb. "Pleasure, delight." It is a short step from the Hebrew meaning of the word to its general association with Paradise. The name is used for girls as well as boys. English statesman Sir Anthony Eden.

Eaden, Eadin, Edin, Ednan, Edyn

Edgar OE. "Wealthy spearman." A royal name in Anglo-Saxon England which, like **Edmund**, endured through the Norman invasion and the resulting influx of Norman names. In Shakespeare's *King Lear,* Lear's son is called Edgar. Revived, like many Anglo-Saxon names, at the turn of the century, but the revival was short-lived. Poet Edgar Allan Poe; puppeteer Edgar Bergen; artist Edgar Dégas; author Edgar Rice Burroughs.

Eadgar, Eadger, Ed, Eddie, Edgard, Edgardo, Ned, Neddy, Ted, Teddie

Edison OE. "Son of Edward." Inventor Thomas Edison.

Eddison, Eddy, Edson

Edmar OE. "Wealthy sea."

Edmund OE. "Wealthy protector." A popular, and sainted,

king of the East Angles in the 9th century gave the name
enough popularity to survive the Norman Conquest. Astronomer Edmund Halley; poet Edmund Spenser; explorer Sir Edmund Hillary; Governor Edmund "Pat"
Brown; Senator Edmund Muskie.

**Eadmund, Eamon, Eamonn, Ed, Eddie, Edmon, Ed-
mond, Edmonde, Edmondo, Ned, Neddie, Ted, Teddy**

Edom Heb. "Red."

Edric OE. "Wealthy ruler." Anglo-Saxon name that was
pushed out of fashion by the Normans in the 11th century
but revived briefly at the end of the 19th.

Ederic, Ederick, Edrich, Edrick

Edsel OE. Place name: "Wealthy man's house." Linked in
most minds to automotive pioneer Edsel Ford, and the ill-
fated car named after him. The name is still used in the
Ford family.

Edward OE. "Wealthy defender." A name with long-
lasting popularity throughout the English-speaking
world. Used by kings of England (including the saint Edward the Confessor) since before the Norman Conquest,
and still a staple in the royal family. Though less of an
obvious choice since the 1930s, it is still popular. As a
nickname for Edward, **Eddie** has been replaced by **Ted,
Teddy**, or **Ned**. Photographer Edward Steichen; ballet
dancer Edward Villella; U.S. Senator Edward Kennedy;
poet Edward Lear; artist Edouard Manet; Edward, Duke
of Windsor; actors Edward Norton, Edward Burns.

**Eadward, Ed, Eddie, Eddy, Edik, Edouard, Eduard, Ed-
uardo, Edvard, Edvardas, Ewart, Lalo, Ned, Neddie,
Ted, Teddie**

Edwin OE. "Wealthy friend." Anglo-Saxon name revived
at the end of the 19th century, and used with some frequency since then. Astronaut Edwin "Buzz" Aldrin; Attorney General Edwin Meese III.

**Eadwinn, Ed, Eddy, Edlin, Eduino, Edwyn, Ned, Neddy,
Ted**

Efigenio Var. **Eugene** (Gk. "Noble").

Ephigenio, Ephigenios, Ephigenius, Efigenios, Efigenius

Efisio It. from Lat. "Ephesian, from Ephesus." Ephesus

was one of the early Christian communities: St. Paul addressed two of his letters to the Ephesians.

Efrat Heb. "Honored."

    Ephrat

Efrem Var. **Ephraim**. Actor Efrem Zimbalist, Jr.

    Efi, Efraim, Efrayim, Efren, Efrim

Efron Heb. "Lark."

    Efroni, Ephron

Egan Gael. "Burning." Irish use predominates.

    Eagan, Eagen, Egann, Egon

Egbert OE. "Brilliant sword." Another 19th-century Anglo-Saxon revival, now little heard.

Egerton OE. Place name: possibly "Edgar's settlement." Occurs as a surname in the English aristocracy. Transferred to first-name use mostly in Britain.

    Edgerton

Egidio It. "Kid, young goat." The anglicized version is Giles.

Egil Scand. "Edge, point." As in the point of a weapon.

    Eigil

Eginhard Ger. "Sword power."

    Eginard, Eginhardt, Einhard, Einhardt, Enno

Egmont Fr./Ger. "Fearsome protection."

    Egmond

Egon German name, having to do with the point of a sword. Prince Egon von Furstenburg.

Egor Rus. "Farmer." Currently popular in Russia, but very exotic in English-speaking countries.

    Igor, Ygor

Ehud Heb. "Love."

Eilam Heb. "Forever, eternal." In the Old Testament, the name of one of Noah's grandsons.

    Elam

Eilert Scand. "Hard point."

Eilif ONorse. "Immortal."

Eilon Heb. "Oak tree." This name is used in many different spellings, for girls and for boys.

    Eilan, Elan, Elon, Ilan, Ilon

Einar ONorse. "Battle leader." Refers to the heroes of Valhalla, in the Old Norse legends.
Ejnar, Inar

Einion Welsh. "Anvil."

Eion Ir. Var. **John** (Heb. "The Lord is gracious") by way of **Ian**.
Ean, Ion

Eilad Heb. "God is for ever."

Eladio Sp. from Gk. "Greek."

Elbert Var. **Albert** (OE. "Highborn/shining"). The long form is **Ethelbert**, but it is virtually obsolete.

Elbridge OE. Place name: "Old bridge."
Ellbridge

Elchanan Heb. "God is gracious." Old Testament name. Many of these names beginning with "El-" (Hebrew for "God") have survived because they are mentioned in the Bible. They were adopted by the American Puritans, and often survived into the 19th century without seeming the least bit exotic to a Biblically literate population.
Elchana, Elhanan, Elhannan, Elkanah

Elden Var. **Alden** (OE. "Old friend"). Also possibly "Valley of the elves." Surname changed to first name.
Eldin, Eldon, Eldwin, Eldwyn, Elton

Elder OE. Place name: "Elder trees." Also, in U.S., may denote a forebear who had high standing in one of the Protestant churches that are governed by councils of elders.
Eldor

Eldon OE. Place name: "Sacred hill." Used since the 19th century.

Eldorado Sp. "The golden man." Mythical South American country, avidly sought by Europeans like Pizarro, Coronado, and Francis Drake. The name has also been used steadily as a place name.

Eldred OE. "Old counsel." Anglo-Saxon name lost in the onslaught of Norman names, and brought back in the 19th-century craze for the picturesque remnants of the past.
Aldred, Eldrid

Eldridge Ger. "Sage ruler." **Eldrick**, a variation, is the given name of golfer Tiger Woods. Civil rights activist Eldridge Cleaver.

Eldredge, Eldrege, Eldrich, Eldrick, Eldrige

Eleazer Var. **Lazarus** (Heb. "The Lord will help"). The 19th-century fondness for obscure biblical names (Eleazer among them) tends to confirm the stereotype of the repressed religious Victorians. If nothing else, they must have read their Bibles carefully to come up with these names.

Elazar, Eleasar, Eleazaro, Eli, Elie, Eliezer, Ely

Eleodoro Sp. from Gk. "Gift from the sun."

Heliodoro, Heliodoros

Elford OE. Place name: "Old ford."

Ellford

Elger OE. "Spear from the elves." Variation of **Alger**, which is marginally more widely known.

Elgar, Ellgar, Ellger

Eli Heb. "On high." In the Old Testament, Eli was Israel's high priest. This was a very holy name to the Hebrews. The Puritans used it freely, and it persisted through the 19th century but faded after the 1930s. American inventor Eli Whitney; author Elie Wiesel; actor Eli Wallach.

Elie, Eloi, Eloy, Ely

Eliachim Heb. "The Lord will establish."

Eliakim

Eliam Heb. "God is my nation."

Elami

Elian Sp. from Lat. Based on a clan name, Aelia.

Elias Gk. Var. **Elijah**. Most common in the 17th century. Spread widely by Greek translations of the Bible, and by the King James version, in which Elijah is referred to as Elias. Currently very popular in Spain.

Elice, Ellice, Ellis, Elyas

Elihu Heb. "God, the Lord." Like **Eleazer**, occasionally used in the 19th century.

Elijah Heb. "The Lord is my God." A great prophet in the Old Testament. Felix Mendelssohn, reputedly Queen Victoria's favorite composer, wrote an oratorio about him in

1846. The name was most popular in the early 19th century. Film director Elia Kazan; actor Elijah Wood.

Eli, Elia, Elias, Elie, Elihu, Eliot, Eliyahu, Eljah, Elliot, Ellis, Ely, Elyot, Elyott

Elimelech Heb. "My God is kind." Old Testament name.

Eliron Heb. "My God is song."

Eliran

Eloi Fr. from Lat. "Elect, selected." St. Eligius, or Eloi, was a 6th-century metalworker and engraver of coins who later founded a monastery and a convent. He is patron of blacksmiths, watchmakers, and other metalworkers.

Eligio, Eligius, Eloy

Eliphalet Heb. "God delivers me." In the Old Testament, this is the name of one of David's sons. It was occasionally used in 19th-century America.

Elifalet, Elifelet, Eliphelet

Elisha Heb. "The Lord is my salvation." The successor to Elijah, as recounted in the Old Testament. Puritan name in the 17th century, a bit more widespread in the 19th, and all but obsolete now.

Eli, Elisee, Eliseo, Elisher, Eliso, Lisha

Eliyahu Heb. "The Lord is my God." This is the Hebrew form of **Elijah**.

Elkanah Heb. "God has made." A man's name in the Old Testament, but occasionally used for girls as well. A variant spelling of **Elchanah**.

Elkana

Ellard OG. "Noble and valorous."

Allard, Allerd

Ellery OE. Place name: "Island with elder trees." Some sources propose a relationship to **Hilary**. The famous fictional detective Ellery Queen is probably the best-known user of the name.

Ellary, Ellerey

Ellesmere ME. "Ellis' pond." Mere is a term related to the word "marine" that came to mean a pond, or even a swamp.

Ellington OE. Place name. Possibly "Ellistown." Used in 21st-century America, however, the name almost has to refer to the great jazz musician Duke Ellington.

Elliott Anglicization of **Elijah** or **Eli**. Surname first used as a given name in modern Scotland, quite popular in the U.S. Though the various spellings don't alter the pronunciation one whit, this is the most common form. Poet T. S. Eliot; actor Elliott Gould; Attorney General Elliot Richardson.
Eliot, Eliott, Elliot, Elyot, Elyott

Ellis Anglicization of **Elias**. Surname transferred to first name. Ellis Bell was the pseudonym used by Emily Brontë; when they first began publishing, each of the Brontë sisters chose a name that could be considered masculine. Anne was Acton Bell, and Charlotte was Currer Bell.
Elliss, Ellyce

Ellison OE. "Son of Ellis." Author Ralph Ellison.
Elison, Elisson, Ellson, Ellyson, Elson

Ellsworth OE. Place name: "Nobleman's estate" or possibly "Ellis' estate." Painter Ellsworth Kelly.
Ellswerth, Elsworth

Ellwood OE. Place name: "Nobleman's wood" or "Ellis' wood."
Elwood

Elman OE. "Noble man." A contraction of **Edelman**.

Elmer OE. "Highborn and renowned." Anglo-Saxon name that has been much more popular in the U.S. than in Britain, especially in the late 19th century. Sinclair Lewis's well-known novel *Elmer Gantry,* published in 1927, was about a compelling charlatan of a minister. It was shocking, successful, and discouraging to parents who were considering Elmer as a name for their babies. Cartoon character Elmer Fudd.
Aylmar, Aylmer, Aymer, Ellmer, Elmir

Elmo Lat. from Gk. "Amiable" or It. "Godly helmet." Var. **Anselm**. Saint Elmo is the common name for Saint Erasmus, a 4th-century bishop-martyr who is patron saint of sailors. Saint Elmo's fire (also the name of a popular movie in the early 1980s) refers to the electrical discharges occasionally sighted at the top of a ship's mast. Parents who already have children may know Elmo as a furry red toddler-monster featured on *Sesame Street*. Giving a child this name could be quite confusing right through the preschool years.

Elmore OE. Place name: "Moor with elm trees." Author Elmore Leonard.

Elof Swed. "Only heir."
 Elov, Eluf

Elois Var. **Louis** (OG. "Renowned in battle"). Nowhere near as familiar as the feminine version, Eloise, though the more elaborate **Aloysius** is another variant.
 Alois, Aloysius

Elon Heb. "Oak tree." See **Eilon**.

Elpidos Gk. "Hoping."
 Elpido

Elrad OE. "Noble counsel."
 Ellrad, Ellrod, Elrod

Elroy Var. **Leroy** (Fr. "King").
 Elroi, Elroye

Elsdon OE. Place name: "Hill of the nobleman."
 Elsden, Ellsdon

Elston OE. Place name: "Settlement of the nobleman."
 Elliston

Elton OE. Place name: "Old Settlement" or "Ella's town." Musician Elton John.
 Alton, Eldon, Ellton

Elvin OE. "Elf friend" or "Highborn friend." Var. **Alvin**.
 Elven, Elwin, Elwinn, Elwyn, Elwynne

Elvio Sp. from Lat. "Blond, fair."

Elvis Scand. "All-wise." Variants are rare, since use, as in the case of singer Elvis Costello (né Declan Patrick McManus), is almost always influenced by the fame of Elvis Presley. The prominent Elvises now reaching middle age attest to this name's popularity during the singer's heyday. Figure skater Elvis Stojko; football player Elvis Grbac.
 Alvis, Alvys, Elvio, Elviss, Elvo, Elvys

Elwell OE. Place name: "Old well."
 Elwill

Elwin Var. **Elvin**.
 Elvin, Elvis, Elvyn, Elwin, Win, Wynn

Elwyn Welsh. "Fair brow." Easily confused with **Elwin**, but more likely to be found in Wales, where it has a different meaning altogether.
Elwin, Elwynn

Elwood OE. Place name: "Old wood."
Ellwood, Woody

Ely OE. Place name (a river in South Wales and a cathedral and town in Cambridgeshire, England) turned surname. Or, more likely, a variant of **Eli**.

Emerson OG. "Emery's son." First-name use may be tribute to Ralph Waldo Emerson, the transcendentalist philosopher and "sage of Concord."

Emery OG. "Home ruler." Saw 19th-century use as a first name, predominantly American rather than British.
Amerigo, Amery, Amory, Emerey, Emeri, Emerich, Emmerich, Emmery, Emmory, Emory

Emil Lat. "Eager to please." The French form, **Emile**, took root slightly earlier in English-speaking countries. Used only since the mid 19th century, without any great period of popularity. French author Emile Zola; actor Emilio Estevez.
Aimil, Aymil, Emelen, Emile, Emilian, Emiliano, Emilianus, Emilio, Emilion, Emilyan, Emlen, Emlin, Emlyn, Emlynn

Emir Arab. "Prince, ruler."
Amir, Ameer, Emeer

Emlyn Welsh place name given some prominence by playwright and actor Emlyn Williams.

Emmanuel Heb. "God is among us." Used in both the Old and the New Testaments, and as another name for Jesus. Slight use in the 17th century grew gradually right through the 19th, then tailed off. In the U.S. **Manuel** is fairly common among Catholics of Hispanic descent, who also use **Jesus** quite freely. Fashion designer Emmanuel Ungaro; pianist Emmanuel Ax.
Eman, Emanual, Emanuel, Emanuele, Emmanual, Emmonual, Emmonuel, Emonual, Emonuel, Imanuel, Immanuel, Immanuele, Manny, Manual, Manuel, Manuelo

Emmett Various derivations are possible, including OG.

"Energetic, powerful," OE. "An ant," or even a last name relating to **Emma**. Given by Irish and Irish-American families to celebrate early 19th century Irish patriot Robert Emmet, who tried to overthrow English rule in Ireland with French help. Famous clown Emmett Kelly; football player Emmitt Smith.

Emmet, Emmit, Emmitt, Emmot, Emmott

Emmons English last name, possibly related to the Irish **Eamon**.

Emrys Welsh from Gk. "Immortal." The Welsh version of **Ambrose**.

Endicott OE. Place name: possibly "Cottage on the end." A name to reckon with in Massachusetts, where Endicotts have been prominent since 1628. Massachusetts governor Endicott Peabody.

Endecott

Endymion In Greek mythology, a youth renowned for his beauty.

Endimion

Eneas Var. **Aeneas** (Gk. "He who is praised").

Enneas, Ennes, Ennis

Engelbert OG. "Angel-bright." Entertainer Engelbert Humperdinck (whose original name, less memorable if more euphonious, was Arnold Dorsey).

Bert, Berty, Ingelbert, Inglebert

Ennis Var. **Angus** (Ir. Gael. "Sole or only choice").

Enoch Heb. "Vowed, dedicated." Old Testament name for the father of Methuselah. Briefly popular from the 1860s to 1880s, inspired by Tennyson's famous and sentimental poem "Enoch Arden." Now scarce.

Enock

Enos Heb. "Man." Old Testament name for one of Adam and Eve's great-grandsons. Mildly revived, not by the Puritans, but in the 19th century. Obscure in this century.

Enrico It. Var. **Henry**. OG. "Estate ruler." Use by English-speaking families probably reflects the fame of operatic tenor Enrico Caruso. **Enrique** is the Spanish version of the name. Singer Enrique Iglesias.

Enrique, Erico, Errico

Ensign Lat. "Badge." Possibly used in reference to the naval rank: an ensign is the most junior naval commissioned officer.

Enzo It. Var. **Henry**. OG. "Estate ruler."
Enzio

Epaminondas Gk. Meaning unknown. Epaminondas was a 4th-century B.C. military genius who invented fighting in organized units, known as "phalanxes."

Ephah Heb. "Darkness." Old Testament name.

Ephraim Heb. "Fertile, productive." Old Testament name

HARKING BACK TO
THE OLD COUNTRY

If there's one sentiment that distinguishes today's parents from those of, say, fifty years ago, it's the willingness to choose un-Anglicized names for their children. See how this plays among some celebrity parents:

- Rosanna Arquette & Paul Rossi: Enzo
- Sinead O'Connor: Brigidine
- Connie Sellecca & John Tesh: Prima
- Frank & Kathleen Stallone: Dante
- Sylvester Stallone & Jennifer Flavin: Sophia
- Quincy Jones & Nastassja Kinski: Kenya
- Mikhail Baryshnikov & Jessica Lange: Alexandra (called Shura)
- Mikhail Baryshnikov & Lisa Rinehart: Anna Katerina
- Nicole Kidman & Tom Cruise: Connor
- Frances McDormand & Joel Coen: Pedro
- Kelly Ripa & Mark Consuelos: Joaquin
- Céline Dion & René Angelil: René-Charles
- Brandy & Robert Smith: Sy'rai
- Mehki Pfeifer: Omikaye

used mostly in the 18th and 19th centuries. This spelling was most common in the U.S.

Efraim, Efrain, Efrayim, Efrem, Efren, Efrim, Efrym, Ephraem, Epbream, Ephrem, Ephrim, Ephrym

Epicurus Gk. Meaning unknown. A philosopher of great influence, who proposed that philosophy's purpose should be to make life happy. He wrote extensively on the nature of pleasure, and believed that intellectual and aesthetic pleasure, and the joys of friendship, were more important than the joys of the flesh. The word "epicure," which has its root in his name, means someone who enjoys the pleasures of the flesh, which is a misunderstanding of the philosopher's teachings.

Epifanio Sp. from Gk. "Bringing light." In English, the term is "epiphany," and in the Catholic calendar, it is the season that follows Christmas.

Epefano, Epefanio, Epephanio, Epifan, Epifano, Epiphany

Epimetheus Gk. "Afterthought." In Greek mythology, the husband of Pandora (who opened the famous box, loosing trouble on the world) and brother of Prometheus, who brought fire to mankind.

Erasmus Gk. "Loved, desired." The 16th-century Dutch humanist philosopher Geert Geerts wrote as Desiderius Erasmus. (**Desiderius** is the Latin form of Erasmus.) He may have been thinking of Saint Erasmus, who is more popularly known as Saint Elmo. Use of the name was greatest in the latter half of the 19th century, and probably refers to the philosopher rather than the saint.

Erasme, Erasmo, Ras

Erastus Gk. "Beloved." In the New Testament, Erastus was a missionary sent out by St. Paul.

Eraste, Rastus

Ercole It. "Splendid gift." This is the Italian version of **Hercules.**

Ercolo

Erhard OG. "Strong resolve."

Erhardt, Erhart

Eric Scand. "All-ruler." In spite of the renown of Viking explorer Eric the Red (who colonized Iceland around A.D. 985) and his son Leif Ericsson, who reputedly discovered North America half a millennium before Columbus, Eric was little used until the turn of the 19th century. It caught on, however, becoming fashionable in Britain in the 1920s, in the U.S. some 50 years later. It is very solidly used today, and as **Erich**, very popular in Germany. Author Erich Segal; musician Eric Clapton; skater Eric Heiden; actor Eric McCormack.

Aeric, Aerick, Aerric, Aerrick, Aerricko, Arreck, Arric, Arrick, Erek, Erich, Erick, Erik, Eriq, Errick, Eryk, Rick, Rikky

Erie American place name: one of the Great Lakes, the famous canal from Albany to Buffalo, and a tribe of Native Americans who lived in western New York State and Ohio. The Erie Canal, completed in 1825, linked America's inland waterways with the Atlantic, via the Hudson River.

Erin Ir. Gael. Name for Ireland. Mostly used by girls, and not in Ireland itself.

Erland OE. "Noble's land" or ONorse. "Foreigner, stranger." Actor Erland Josephson.

Arlan, Erlend

Erling OE. "Noble's son."

Ermin Var. **Herman** (OG. "Army man").

Erman, Ermano, Erminio, Ermino

Ernest OE. "Sincere." Its great popularity at the turn of the 20th century was only confirmed by Oscar Wilde's play, *The Importance of Being Earnest*. Fell out of use after the 1930s. It could be argued that that was the era when being earnest began to lose its desirability. Author Ernest Hemingway; actor Ernest Borgnine; entertainer Ernie Kovacs.

Earnest, Ernesto, Ernestus, Ernie, Erno, Ernst

Eros Greek mythology name: Eros was the god of love. Since, in our era, Eros generally refers to sexual love, this seems a tricky name to give a baby.

Errol Origin unclear, though most sources consider it a

variation of **Earl**. It may also derive from a Scottish place name; there have been Scottish Earls of Erroll for more than 600 years. The most famous modern Errol was dashing movie actor Errol Flynn.

Erroll, Erryl, Erryle, Eryle, Rollo

Erskine Scot. Gael. Place name: "High cliff." Transference from last name to first occurred only in this century. Novelist Erskine Caldwell.

Erv, Erve, Ervine, Ervyn, Erwin, Erwyn, Erwynn, Irvin

Ervin Scot. Gael. Place name, or "Beautiful." Var. **Irving** (OE. "Sea friend"). General Erwin Rommel.

Erving Var. **Irving** (OE. "Sea friend"). Basketball player Julius Erving.

Ervine

Esau Heb. "Hairy." In the Old Testament the story is told how Esau came out of the womb covered with hair, while his twin brother, Jacob, was hairless. The name was used somewhat in the 19th century.

Esbjorn ONorse. "Godly bear." Well used in Scandinavia.

Asbjorn, Esbern

Escott OE. Place name: "Hut near the stream."

Escot

Esias Gk. from Heb. "God is salvation." This name is a variant of the much more common **Isaiah**.

Esaias, Esiason, Esiasson

Eskel ONorse. "Divine cauldron." The name refers to a cauldron used for sacrifice to the gods.

Askel, Askell, Eskil

Esmé Fr. "Esteemed." Related to the more modern French form, *aimé* which is the root of **Amy**. Originally a male name brought to Scotland by a French cousin of James VI. Now used mostly for girls, though scace.

Esmay, Esmeling, Ismay, Ismé

Esmond OE. "Protected by grace." Survived the Norman Conquest as a last name, but was not rediscovered as a first name until the late 19th century, and was never widely used.

Essex OE. Place name: "Eastern." A county in southeastern England that gave its name to many towns in Amer-

ica. In Anglo-Saxon England, there was a kingdom of
Essex.

Esteban Sp. Var. **Stephen** (Gk. "Crowned").

Estes Place name of uncertain meaning, though some
sources relate it to the Latin *aestus* or tide, suggesting
that it means something like "by the estuary." It may also
be related to "east." Estes Park, Colorado, a popular resort high in the Rockies, was named for its first settler.

Eston OE. Place name: "Eastern town."

Ethan Heb. "Firmness, steadfastness." An Old Testament
name given fame in the U.S. by Revolutionary War leader
Ethan Allen, who captured Fort Ticonderoga with only
eighty-three men. Fairly well used now and may receive a
boost from the glamor of actor Ethan Hawke. It is very
fashionable in Wales.

Aitan, Eitan, Etan, Ethen

Etienne Fr. Var. **Stephen** (Gk. "Crowned").

Ethelbert OE. "Highborn, shining." The original form of
Albert. A 6th-century king of Kent whom Saint Augustine converted to Christianity. The name was revived in
the 19th century but is now extremely scarce.

Ethelred OE. "Noble counsel." The name of a king of the
West Saxons, and of a king of the English, around the year
1000. The latter was known as "Ethelred the Unready" in
later years, because he was such an incompetent ruler.

Aethelred

Ethelwulf OE. "Noble wolf." A king of the West Saxons in
the 9th century.

Aethelwolf, Aethelwulf, Ethelwolf

Ethelwin OE. "Highborn friend." Anglo-Saxon name that
followed the same cycle of 19th-century revival and 20th-
century disuse.

Ethelwyn, Ethelwynne

Ettore It. "Loyal." The Italian version of **Hector**. Designer
Ettore Sottsass.

Euan Ir. Gael. "Little swift one." Possibly also a variant of
Evan and thus, in a roundabout way, yet another version
of **John**.

Ewan, Ewen

Euclid Greek mathematician, generally considered the inventor of geometry.
Euclides

Eudocio Gk. "Well thought of."

Eugene Gk. "Wellborn." In use since the early Christian era, and chosen by four popes. After centuries of disuse, it was dusted off in the 19th century and became very popular in the U.S. No longer in the first rank, but still occurs. Senator Eugene McCarthy; playwrights Eugene O'Neill, Eugène Ionesco; artist Eugène Delacroix.
Efigenio, Efigenios, Efigenius, Ephigenio, Ephigenios, Ifigenio, Ifigenios, Iphigenios, Iphigenius, Eugen, Eugenio, Eugenius, Evgeny, Gene

Eulogio Gk. "Reasoning well."

Euodias Gk. "Good fortune." New Testament name; it occurs in Paul's Letter to the Philippians.

Euphemios Gk. "Well spoken." Masculine version of **Euphemia**, which was popular in the 19th century.
Eufemio, Eufemius, Eufemius, Euphemio, Euphemius

Euphrates Turkish. "Great river." Name of the river, 1,700 miles long, that flows through Asia Minor. The valley between the Tigris and the Euphrates is often known as "the cradle of civilization."
Eufrates

Euripides Gk. Meaning unknown. Greek playwright of the 5th century B.C., author of many of the classic Greek tragedies such as *Medea* and *Trojan Women*.

Eusebius Gk. "Devout." Name of a number of saints, the best-known of whom was a 4th-century Italian bishop.
Esabio, Esavio, Esavius, Esebio, Eusabio, Eusaio, Eusebio, Eusebios, Eusavio, Eusevio, Eusevios

Eustace Gk. "Fertile." Brought to Britain with the Normans, but never hugely popular there. Most common in the late 19th century, little used in the U.S. The last names **Stacey** and **Stacy** come from Eustace. (As girls' names, they are diminutives of **Anastasia**.)
Eustache, Eustachios, Eustachius, Eustachy, Eustaquio, Eustashe, Eustasius, Eustatius, Eustazio, Eustis, Eustiss

Evan Welsh. Var. **John** (Heb. "The Lord is gracious"). Most common in Wales, but well-known in all English-speaking countries ever since the mid-19th century. Quite well used among today's parents.

Euan, Euen, Evans, Even, Evin, Evyn, Ewan, Ewen, Owen

Evander Gk. "Good man." The root, *andr-*, also appears in the much more common **Andrew**. A figure in Roman mythology. Fighter Evander Holyfield.

Evangel Gk. "Good news." Masculine version of the more common **Evangline**.

Evangelin, Evangelino, Evangelo, Vangelios, Vangelis, Vangelo

Evelyn Surname transferred to first name, and more common for girls than boys. Author Evelyn Waugh's first wife was also called Evelyn; their friends referred to them as "He-Evelyn" and "She-Evelyn."

Evelin

Everard OE. "Boar hardness." Norman name more common as a surname, but revived in the 19th century. German form is **Eberhard**. Now rare.

Eberhard, Everardo, Evered, Everhart, Evrard, Evraud

Everest OE. Probably related to **Everett**. The name of the highest mountain in the world, Mt. Everest in the Himalyas, named for a 19th-century surveyor of India, Sir George Everest. Fashion designer Timothy Everest.

Everett OE. "Boar hardness." Surname deriving from **Everard**, used as a first name in the 19th century. Senator Everett Dirksen; actor Rupert Everett.

Averett, Averitt, Eberhard, Eberhardt, Everard, Evered, Everet, Everitt, Evrard, Eward, Ewart

Everild OE. "Boar battle."

Evald, Evaldo, Everald, Everhild, Everildo

Everley OE. Place name: "Boar meadow." Singing group the Everly Brothers.

Everlie, Everly

Everton OE. Place name: "Boar settlement." Used as a first name only in this century.

Evo Var. **Yves** via **Ivo** (OG. "Yew wood").

Ewald OE. "Law-powerful."
Evald, Evaldo, Euell, Ewell

Ewan Scot. Gael. Unclear origin: perhaps "Young man" or a variant of **Eugene**. Use confined to Scotland until the mid 20th century, but now spreading. Actor Ewan McGregor.
Euan, Euen, Ewen

Ewert OE. Occupational name: "Shepherd." Literally, "Ewe-herder."
Evart, Evarts, Evert, Ewart

Ewing OE. "Law-friend." Unusual, though some families may have been inspired to use it in the 1980s by the Ewing family on the popular TV series *Dallas*. Basketball player Patrick Ewing.
Ewin, Ewynn

Eyolf Norwegian. "Lucky wolf."
Eyulf

Ezekiel Heb. "Strength of God." An important Old Testament prophet. Since the end of the 19th century, very scarce.
Esequiel, Ezechiel, Eziechiele, Eziequel, Zeke

Ezer Heb. "Help, aid."
Eizer, Ezar, Ezri

Ezio It. from Lat. Possibly a clan name, possibly related to the Greek word meaning "eagle." Singer Ezio Pinza.

Ezra Heb. "Helper." Old Testament prophet. The Puritans brought the name to America, where it was most used in the 19th century. Poet Ezra Pound.
Azariah, Azur, Esdras, Esra, Ezer, Ezri

 Fabian Lat. Clan name, possibly meaning "One who grows beans." Name of a 3rd-century saint/pope, and latterly of a 1960s pop star. Not much used in the intervening 1700 years. Art director Fabien Baron.
Fabe, Fabek, Faber, Fabert, Fabianno, Fabiano, Fabi-

anus, **Fabien, Fabio, Fabion, Faebian, Faebien, Fabius, Fabiyus, Fabyan, Fabyen, Faybian, Faybien, Faybion, Faybionn**

Fabrice Fr. from Lat. "Works with the hands."
Fabriano, Fabricius, Fabritius, Fabrizio, Fabrizius

Fabron Fr. "Young blacksmith."
Fabre, Fabroni

Factor OE. Occupational name: "Businessman." A factor was the agent or steward of a large estate. The term is still sometimes used in Scotland.

Fadi Arab. "Savior."

Fagan Ir. Gael. "Little ardent one." The wily con artist Fagin in Dickens' *Oliver Twist* has probably put an indelible stamp on this name, particularly given the fame of the musical and movie versions.
Fegan, Feggan, Fagin

Fahd Arab. "Panther, leopard." This is a popular name in Arabic countries, perhaps because it is a royal name in Saudi Arabia. It bears connotations of courage and fierceness.
Fahad

Fairbairn Scot. "Fair-haired child."

Fairbanks OE. "Bank along the pathway." Also the name of a significant town in Alaska. Actor Douglas Fairbanks.

Fairchild OE. "Fair-haired child."

Fairfax OE. "Blond."

Faisal Arab. "Resolute." King Faysal of Saudi Arabia.
Faysal, Feisal

Falkner OE. Occupational name: "Falcon trainer." Author William Faulkner.
Falconer, Falconner, Faulconer, Faulconner, Faulkner, Fowler

Fallows OE. Place name: "The fallow field." Fallow means "not planted." Before the discovery of crop rotation, farmers used to let fields lie fallow to gather moisture or to kill weeds. Journalist James Fallows.
Fallow

Fane OE. "Happy, joyous."
Fain, Faine

Faolan Ir. Gael. "Little wolf."
  Felan, Phelan
Faraj Arab. "To cure."
  Farag
Faramond OE. "Traveler's protection."
  Faramund, Farrimond, Farrimund, Pharamond, Phara-mund
Fargo Origin unknown. William George Fargo was one of the original founders of Wells Fargo, a shipping company in the West, that dominated banking in the gold rush camps for a time. Fargo later became president of the American Express Company. Fargo, North Dakota, was named for him.
Farley OE. Place name: "Meadow of the sheep" or "Meadow of the bulls." Surname transferred occasionally to first name. Actor Farley Granger; author Walter Farley.
  Fairlay, Fairlee, Fairleigh, Fairlie, Farlay, Farlee, Far-leigh, Farlie, Farly, Farrleigh, Farrley, Lee, Leigh
Farmer OE. Occupational name: "Farmer." A fairly common last name.
Farnell OE. Place name: "The fern hill." Originally a surname.
  Farnall, Fernald, Furnald
Farnham OE. Place name: "Meadow with ferns." Common surname with a little spurt of late-19th-century use as a first name.
  Farnam, Farnum, Fernham
Farnley OE. Place name: "Field with ferns."
  Farnlea, Farnlee, Farnleigh, Farnly, Fernleigh, Fernley
Farold OE. "Mighty voyager."
Farouk Arab. "Discerning truth from falsehood." The last king of Egypt, deposed in 1952, was King Faruq.
  Faruq, Faruqh
Farquhar Scot. Gael. "Very dear one." First-name use is occasional, and mostly Scottish.
  Farquharson, Farquar, Farquarson
Farr OE. "Voyager." As in, someone who goes *far* away.
Farrar ME. "Blacksmith." The French term, which obviously contributes to this name, is *ferrier,* for someone

who works with iron (*fer*). Blacksmiths are sometimes called farriers.

Farrer, Farrier, Ferrar, Ferrars, Ferrer, Ferrier

Farrell Ir. Gael. "Hero, man of courage."

Farrel, Farrill, Farryll, Ferrel, Ferrell, Ferrill, Ferryl

Faunus Lat. "Animal." In Roman myth, the god of nature. He was attended by little fauns, half man and half goat.

Fawnus

Faust Lat. "Fortunate, enjoying good luck." Very rare as a first name, no doubt owing to the literary connotations, for the legendary Faust sells his soul to the devil. His story was retold by Marlowe, Goethe, and Thomas Mann, among others.

Faustino, Fausto, Faustus

Favian Lat. "Man of wisdom."

Faxon OE. "Hair."

Fay Ir. Gael. "Raven." Extremely rare as a boy's name, though somewhat familiar for girls.

Faye, Fayette

Fedor Ger. Var. **Theodore** (Gk. "Gift from God"). Author Fyodor Dostoevsky.

Faydor, Feodor, Fyodor

Feivel Yiddish form of **Phoebus** (Gk. "Brilliant one").

Feiwel

Felim Ir. Gael. "Ever good."

Feidhlim, Phelim

Felipe Sp. Var. **Philip** (Gk. "Lover of horses"). The current Crown Prince of Spain is named Felipe.

Filip, Filippo, Fillip, Flip, Lippo, Pip, Pippo

Felix Lat. "Happy, fortunate." Not common in America, possibly because of a strong association with Felix the Cat and, more recently, *The Odd Couple*'s Felix Unger. American physicist Felix Bloch.

Fee, Felic, Felice, Felicio, Felike, Feliks, Felizio, Felyx

Felton OE. Place name: "Settlement on the field."

Felten, Feltin

Fenris Scandinavian mythology name: Fenris was a giant wolf who had the power to threaten the gods.

Fenton OE. Place name: "Settlement on the marsh." First used as a given name in the 19th century, but never widespread.

Fenwick OE. "Village on the marsh."

Ferdinand OG. "Bold voyager." A name that has always been more popular in Southern Europe than in the English-speaking countries. Explorers Ferdinand Magellan, Hernando Cortez; former Philippines president Ferdinand Marcos.

Ferd, Ferdie, Ferdinando, Ferdo, Ferdynand, Fernand, Fernandas, Fernando, Hernando, Nando

Ferenc Hung. "Free man." This is a variant of Francis. Playwright Ferenc Molnar.

Fergall Ir. Gael. "Brave, manly."

Fearghall, Forgael

Fergus Ir. Gael. "Highest choice." Mostly Scottish use.

Fearghas, Fearghus, Feargus, Fergie, Ferguson, Fergusson

Fermin Sp. "Strong." The famous running of the bulls in Pamplona, Spain, takes place in honor of a bishop and saint named Fermin.

Firmin

Fernley OE. Place name: "Fern meadow." Used since the late 19th century as a first name for children of both sexes, though primarily in Britain.

Farnlea, Farnlee, Farnleigh, Farnley, Fernlea, Fernlee, Fernleigh

Ferrand OF. "Gray-haired."

Farand, Farrand, Farrant, Ferrant

Ferris Ir. Gael. Possibly derived from Fergus, or else, via **Pierce**, an Irish variant of **Peter** (Gk. "Rock"). Brought to attention in the 1980s by the movie *Ferris Bueller's Day Off*.

Farris, Farrish, Ferriss

Festus Lat. "Joyous, festive."

Fiacre Saint's name of unknown meaning: Fiacre was an Irish saint who built a hospice in France. He is patron of gardeners, and sufferers from hemorrhoids prayed to him for relief.

Fico Derivation disputed: possibly an Italian contraction of **Federico**.

Fidel Lat. "Faithful." The Puritans named boys Faithful, but Fidel is the modern form. However, since Fidel Castro's rise in Cuba, it is unlikely to be used by today's parents.

Fadelio, Fedele, Fidele, Fedelio, Fidal, Fidalio, Fidelio, Fidelis, Fidelix, Fidelo, Fido

Fielding OE. Place name: "The field." Author Henry Fielding.

Feilding, Field, Fielder

Filbert OE. "Very brilliant." Saint Philibert was a 7th-century monk who gave his name to a nut, since his feast day falls at the time when the nuts are ripe. In the U.S. filberts are more usually known as hazelnuts. The name is uncommon in any of its forms.

Bert, Filberte, Filberto, Philbert, Philibert, Phillbert

Filmore OE. "Very famous." Historically best-known under the presidency of Millard Fillmore (1850–53), but nostalgic rock fans may also remember the famous rock and roll venue in San Francisco.

Fillmore, Filmer, Fylmer

Finbarr Ir. Gael. "Fair-haired." One of the more prominent of the many abbotts and bishops who kept the Catholic Church alive in Ireland during the 7th and 8th centuries. One tale about St. Finbarr is that he crossed the Irish Sea on horseback.

Barr, Barra, Finbar, Finnbar, Finnbarr, Fionn, Fionnbharr

Finian Ir. Gael. "Fair." Perhaps familiar from the 1968 film *Finian's Rainbow* (Fred Astaire's last musical), but little used as a first name.

Finan, Finnian, Fionan, Fionn, Phinean, Phinian

Finlay Ir. Gael. "Fair-haired courageous one." Most often used in Scotland, where it is a common last name. Author Finley Peter Dunne.

Findlay, Findley, Finlea, Finlee, Finley, Finn, Finnlea, Finnley, Lee, Leigh

Finn Ir. Gael. "Fair" or OG. "From Finland." Many of the abovementioned and belowmentioned names have **Finn** as a root.
Fin, Fionn, Fingal, Fingall

Fintan Ir. Gael. "Little fair one." St. Fintan was another Irish abbot, whose monastery subsisted at a remarkable level of austerity. Fintan himself lived solely on bread and water.

Finnegan Ir. Gael. "Fair." Common Irish surname. Given some prominence by James Joyce's last novel, *Finnegan's Wake*.
Finegan

Fiorello It. "Little flower." Would be almost unknown in the U.S. without the fame of New York mayor Fiorello La Guardia.

Fisher OE. Occupational name: "Fisherman." Actor Fisher Stevens.
Fish, Fischer, Fisscher, Visscher

Fisk ME. "Fish." Probably an occupational name, indicating an ancestor who was a fishmonger.
Fiske

Fitch ME. Animal name: A fitch is a mammal related to the ferret or ermine. Use as a name probably goes back to an ancestor who hunted or kept fitches, rather than relating to the late-19th-century fashion for nature names.

Fitz OF. "Son of . . ." Usually short for one of the "Fitz-" names that follow. Derives from the Norman *filz* or "son."

Fitzgerald OF./OG. "Son of the spear-ruler." In the U.S., famous as the middle name of John F. Kennedy, and the last name of his grandfather, who was known as "Honey Fitz."

Fitzhugh OF./OG. "Son of intelligence." American painter Fitzhugh Lane.

Fitzpatrick OF./Lat. "Son of the nobleman."

Fitzroy OF. "Son of the king."

Flaminio Sp. "Roman priest."
Flamino

Flann Ir. Gael. "Ruddy, red-haired."
   Flainn, Flannan, Flannery

Flavian Lat. "Yellow hair." Originally a Latin clan name, and common enough in the Roman Empire, but never revived in an English-speaking country.
   Flavel, Flavelle, Flaviano, Flavien, Flavio, Flavius, Flawiusz

Fleetwood OE. Place name: "Woods with the stream." Very likely to refer to the band Fleetwood Mac.

Fleming OE. "Man from Flanders." Flanders is now Belgium. Author (and James Bond creator) Ian Fleming.
   Flemming, Flemmyng, Flemyng

Fletcher ME. Occupational name: "Arrow-maker."
   Flecher, Fletch

Flint OE. Place name: "Stream." Denotes an ancestor who lived near a stream. In the U.S., "flint" is a kind of stone. Publisher Larry Flynt.
   Flynt

Florent OF. "In flower." The feminine version, **Florence**, is far more popular. Impresario Florenz Ziegfeld.
   Fiorentino, Florentin, Florentino, Florentz, Florenz, Florinio, Florino, Floris, Florus

Florian Lat. "Blooming." Most common in Middle European countries, and currently very popular in Germany.
   Florien, Florrian, Floryan

Floyd Welsh. "Gray-haired." Anglicization of **Lloyd**. Boxing star Floyd Patterson.

Flynn Ir. Gael. "Son of the ruddy man."
   Flin, Flinn, Flyn

Folke Scand. "People's guardian."
   Folker, Volker, Vollker

Forbes Scot. Gael. "Field." Used mostly in Scotland. Magazine founder Malcolm Forbes.

Ford OE. Place name. "River crossing." Most Americans will automatically associate the name with the car. Author Ford Madox Ford; automotive pioneer Henry Ford.
   Forden, Fordon

Forest OF. Occupational name: "Woodsman," or place

name, "Woods." Most common in the U.S., spelled "Forrest," as in Winston Groom's novel and the popular film, *Forrest Gump*. The character Forrest is named for hardcharging Confederate General (and early member of the Ku Klux Klan) Nathan Bedford Forrest. Novelist E. M. Forster; actor/director Forrest Whittaker.

Forester, Forrest, Forrester, Forster, Foster

Fortney Lat. "Strong one." May gain usage from its familiarity, since it rhymes with the popular **Courtney**. On the other hand, the pull of Courtney may make Fortney a girl's name.

Fortenay, Forteney, Forteny, Fortny, Fourtney

Fortune OF. "Lucky."

Fortunato, Fortunatus, Fortune, Fortunio, Fortuny

Foster OE. Occupational name: "Woodsman." Var. **Forest**.

Fouad Arab. "Heart."

Fuad

Fowler OE. Occupational name: "Bird trapper."

Fox OE. "Fox." This is probably different from the numerous German names based on "Wolf," which refer to the fierce nature of the beast in a mythic way. This name probably refers either to a fox-catcher or to the location of a fox's den. Journalist Fox Butterfield; English statesman Charles James Fox.

Foxe, Foxen

Franchot Fr. Var. **Francis**. Actor Franchot Tone.

Francis Lat. "Frenchman" or "Free man." France was originally the Kingdom of the Franks. Saint Francis of Assisi gave the name its first fame; though he was named John, he had been nicknamed Francis because his father had him taught French as a boy. The name traveled to England via France, and was popular in the 17th and 19th centuries. **Frank** is more often used now probably owing to the rise of the feminine version and homonym, **Frances**. As **Francois**, this is currently a very fashionable name in France. Philosopher Sir Francis Bacon; composer Franz Josef Haydn; King Francois I of France; playwright Ferenc Molnar; French president Francois

Mitterrand; film director Francis Ford Coppola; "Star Spangled Banner" author Francis Scott Key; football players Fran Tarkenton, Franco Harris.

Chico, Ferenc, Feri, Fran, Franco, Francesco, Franche, Franchesco, Franchesko, Franchot, Francisco, Franciscus, Franciskus, Francois, Franio, Frank, Frankie, Franko, Frann, Frannie, Frans, Fransisco, Frants, Frantz, Franz, Franzel, Franzen, Franzin, Frasco, Frascuelo, Frasquito, Paco, Pacorro, Panchito, Pancho, Paquito

Frank Dim. **Francis** or **Franklin**. Used as an independent name since the 17th century, and very popular at the turn of the 20th century right through the 1930s. Now less used, though it is still more popular than such old standbys as **Philip** or **Douglas**. The durable popularity of its most famous bearer, Frank Sinatra, may do something to keep it in the public consciousness. Astronaut Frank Borman; actors Frank Langella, Franco Nero, Frankie Muniz; architect Frank Lloyd Wright; musician Frank Zappa.

Franc, Franco, Franck, Francke, Frankie

Franklin ME. "Free landholder." Surname transferred to first name, popular in the U.S., especially in the 1930s and 1940s as homage to President Franklin Delano Roosevelt. President Franklin Pierce apparently made less of an impression, as his term (1853–57) did not inspire a surge of infant Franklins.

Francklin, Francklyn, Frank, Franklinn, Franklyn, Franklynn

Frazer Derivation unclear, possibly OE. "Curly hair" or an old French place name. (Relationship to the French *fraise* {charcoal} is debated.) Used mostly in Scottish families. The popularity of the TV show *Frasier* did nothing to increase use of the name.

Fraser, Frasier, Frazier

Frayne ME. "Foreign." English playwright and novelist Michael Frayn.

Fraine, Frayn, Frean, Freen, Freyne

Frederick OG. "Peaceful ruler." Taken by the Hanoverian

kings to Britain, where it began a steady ascent to great popularity that only faded in the 1930s. No longer fashionable, but sufficiently common so that it doesn't sound outlandish. Actor Fred MacMurray; dancer Fred Astaire; cartoon character Fred Flintstone; children's TV personality Fred Rogers; composer Frédéric Chopin; abolitionist Frederick Douglass; philosopher Friedrich Nietzsche; rock musician Fred Durst; actor Freddie Prinze, Jr.

Eric, Erich, Erick, Erico, Erik, Eryk, Federico, Federigo, Fred, Fredd, Freddie, Fredek, Frederic, Frederich, Frederico, Frederigo, Frederik, Fredi, Fredric, Fredrick, Fredrik, Frido, Friedel, Friedrich, Friedrick, Fridrich, Fridrick, Fritz, Fritzchen, Fritzi, Fritzl, Fryderyk, Ric, Rich, Rick, Ricky, Rik, Rikki

Freeborn OE. Use of the descriptive term. May date back to slave days, or to the era of widespread serfdom, when to be born free was worthy of commemoration.

Freed OE. "Free" or Ger. "Peace."
Fried

Freedom Use of the word as a given name is more common than one might think.

Freeman OE. See **Freeborn**.
Free, Freedman, Freeland, Freemon, Friedman, Friedmann

Fremont OG. "Protector of freedom." Explorer John Fremont.

French ME. "From France." Transferred last name.

Frewin OE. "Free friend."
Frewen

Frey Scand. "Lord, exalted one." In Norse myth, Frey is the fertility god, and also the handsomest of all the deities.

Frick OE. "Brave man." Industrialist and philanthropist Henry Clay Frick.

Fridolf OE. "Peaceful wolf."
Freydolf, Freydulf, Friedolf, Fridulf

Friedhelm OG. "Peace helmet."
Friedelm

Fritz Ger. Dim. **Frederick**. Film director Fritz Lang.
Frits

Frode ONorse. "Wise."

Frost OE. "Freezing." Poet Robert Frost.

Fry ME. "Seedling, offspring."
Frye, Fryer

Fulbright OG. "Very bright." See **Filbert**. The name has become famous through the Fulbright Scholar program, which sends (very bright) American graduate students to study abroad.
Fulbert, Philbert, Philibert, Phillbert

Fulgentius Lat. "Brilliant, shining." Veneration of a north African bishop and saint of the 5th century keeps this elaborate name alive.
Fulgencio

Fulke OE. "Folk, people." A very old name in England, still used in families that trace their lineage back hundreds of years. A bit odd, however, in the rather newer United States.
Fulk, Fawke, Fowke

Fuller OE. Occupational name: "One who shrinks cloth." The woolen fabric that was such a staple of the medieval English economy needed to be treated by fullers before it was made into clothes. The surname was most often used as a first name in the 19th century.

Fulton OE. Place name: "Settlement of the fowl" or "People's estate." Surname used as first name: in the U.S., possibly a compliment to Robert Fulton, inventor of the steamboat. Catholic bishop Fulton J. Sheen.

Fursey Ir. Gael. Meaning unknown: the name of one of the many 7th-century Irish missionary saints who tried to convert the Angles to Christianity.

Fyfe Scot. Gael. Place name: Fifeshire is an area of Scotland. American cabinetmaker Duncan Phyfe.
Fife, Fyffe, Phyfe

Furman Ger. "Ferryman."
Fuhrman, Fuhrmann, Furmann

Fyodor Rus. from Gk. "Divine gift." Var. **Theodore**. Author Fyodor Dostoyevsky.
Fedor, Feodor, Fyodr

Gabbo ME. "Scoff, joke."

Gable OF. Dim. **Gabriel**. When used, this name is probably influenced by the fame of actor Clark Gable, who was often known by just his last name.

Gabriel Heb. "Hero of God." Gabriel is an archangel who appears in Christian, Jewish, and Muslim texts. The name was uncommon in English-speaking countries, except for a spell of use in the 18th and 19th centuries, but is now used quite steadily in the United States, perhaps because of the universality of Gabriel's story. As **Gavriel**, very popular in Russia. Musician Peter Gabriel; author Gabriel Garcia Marquez; football player Roman Gabriel; actor Gabriel Byrne.

Gab, Gabbi, Gabbie, Gabby, Gabe, Gabi, Gabie, Gabriele, Gabrielli, Gabriello, Gabrielo, Gaby, Gavriel, Gavril, Gavrilo

Gad Heb. "Fortune, luck." In the old Testament, one of Jacob's twelve sons, and founder of one of the twelve tribes of Israel.

Gadi

Gadiel Arab. "God is my fortune."

Gaddiel

Gadish Heb. "Shock of corn." Appropriate for boys born near Shavuot, the Jewish harvest festival that usually falls in October.

Gael Eng. "Speaker of Gaelic." Refers to one of the Celtic peoples of Scotland or Ireland. As a name, would be confused with **Gail**, which is traditionally female.

Gale

Gaetan It. Place name: Gaeta is a region in Southern Italy; the Gulf of Gaeta is just north of Naples.

Cajetan, Cajetano, Gaetano, Gaeton, Kajetan, Kajetano

Gage OF. "Oath." The British General Thomas Gage was

Governor of Masachusetts Bay Colony at the outbreak of the Revolutionary War.

Gaige

Gahan Possibly a Scottish variant of **John** (Heb. "The Lord is gracious"). Cartoonist Gahan Wilson.

Gehan

Gaillard ME. "Brave, cheerful, spirited." Also the name of a 16th-century dance.

Gaillhard, Gaillardet, Galliard

Gaines English last name of uncertain derivation. It may have something to do with today's meaning of "gain," that is to say, "to get."

Gains, Gayne, Gaynes

Gair Ir. Gael. "Small one."

Gaer, Geir

Gaius Lat. "Rejoice." This is probably the root of our word "gay," which used to mean "jolly." A Gaius appears in the New Testament, and another one was a Roman jurist of the 2nd century. **Caius** is a variation that occurs from time to time in England.

Cai, Caio, Kay, Kaye, Keye, Keyes, Keys

Gal Heb. "Wave, roller, swell."

Galbraith Ir. Gael. "Foreign Briton." In Ireland, the name would have been used most commonly to describe a Scot. Economist John Kenneth Galbraith.

Galbrait, Galbreath, Gallbraith, Gallbreath

Gale Ir. Gael. "Foreigner"; OE. "Cheerful, happy." Much more common now as a girl's name, when it is usually a diminutive of **Abigail**. Football player Gale Sayers.

Gael, Gaell, Gaelle, Gail, Gaill, Gaille, Gaile, Gayle

Galen Gk. "Healer" or "Tranquil." A 2nd-century Greek physician named Galen was for hundreds of years the only authority on the emergent practice of medicine. The name is seeing a flicker of trendy use among intellectuals.

Gaelan, Gaillen, Gaillen, Galeno, Galin, Gaylen, Gaylin, Gaylinn, Gaylon, Jalen, Jalin, Jalon, Jaylen, Jaylon

Galil Heb. "Hilly." This is the word that gives the name to Galilee, a hilly area in Israel.

Galileo It. "From Galilee." The name of the great 16th- and 17th-century Italian astronomer, who built the first astronomical telescope and confirmed Copernicus' theory that the planets revolve around the sun.

Gall Derivation unknown. May possibly refer to Gaelic, since St. Gall was one of the many 7th-century Irish monks who brought Christianity back to the continent of Europe after the Dark Ages.

Gallagher Ir. Gael. "Foreign helper." Actor Peter Gallagher.

Gallatin American place name: a county and river in Montana. They were probably named for Albert Gallatin, a Swiss-born American statesman of the early 19th century, but to outdoors people, the name Gallatin bears connotations of the unspoiled West.

Galloway Old Gael. "Foreign Gael." Another name for a Scot. The Irish population include a strong Scottish strain.
Gallway, Galway

Galo Sp. from Lat. "From Gaul." Gaul was the Roman name for France.
Gallo

Galt OE. Place name: "Steep wooded land." May also be derived from the Old German word particle that gives us **Walter** ("People of power").

Galton OE. "Owner of a rented land."
Galt, Galten, Gallton

Galvin Ir. Gael. "Sparrow" or "Brilliantly white."
Gallven, Gallvin, Galvan, Galven, Galvon

Galway Irish place name: a city in Western Ireland. Critic Galway Kinnell; flutist James Galway.

Gamal Arab. "Camel."
Gamali, Gamul, Gemal, Gemali, Gemul, Jamal, Jammal, Jemaal, Jemal

Gamaliel Heb. "Recompense of God." An obscure biblical name probably brought to the U.S. by the Puritans. Little used since the 19th century. President Warren Gamaliel Harding.
Gamliel, Gmali

Gamble ONorse. "Old." A household name in this country as part of the former soap-manufacturing company, Procter & Gamble.

Gamblen, Gambling, Gamel, Gammel, Gamlin

Ganesh Sanskrit. "Lord of the throngs." Ganesh is the Hindu god of wisdom, usually portrayed as a squat little man with an elephant's head.

Gannet OG. "Goose." A fish-eating web-footed sea bird related to the booby. Gannets are found in northern climates and live on cliffs and rocks.

Gannett

Gannon Ir. Gael. "Fair-skinned."

Gardner ME. Occupational name. In the eastern U.S., reminiscent of two distinguished families, known as the "blind" Gardners (the name has no *i*) or the "sighted" Gardiners. The former are famous for the Isabella Stewart Gardner Museum in Boston; the latter for Gardiner's Island on Long Island Sound.

Gardell, Gardener, Gardenner, Gardie, Gardiner, Gardnar, Gardnard

Gareth Welsh. "Gentle." The name of one of King Arthur's knights. Used in Britain since the 1930s, but rare elsewhere.

Garith, Garreth, Garret, Garyth

Garfield OE. "Spear field." Use as a first name probably honored President James Garfield, though indignation at his untimely death outweighed admiration for his skills, since his term lasted only a few months before he was assassinated in 1881. More recently the president has been upstaged by a fat orange cartoon cat who has made the name his own.

Garland OE. Place name: "Land of the spear." OF. "Wreath." Musician Garland Jeffries.

Garlan, Garlen, Garlend, Garlin, Garlind, Garllan

Garman OE. "Spearman."

Garmann, Garmen, Garmin, Garmon, Garrman

Garner ME. "To gather grain." Possibly a place name or occupational name originally, denoting an ancestor who

lived near a granary, or who helped harvest grain. Actor James Garner.
Garnar, Garnier

Garnett OE. "Spear" or OF. "Red like a pomegranate." Although the girl's name is more likely to be a jewel name in the tradition of **Pearl** or **Ruby**, for boys, Garnett is usually a transferred last name. In England, boys may have been named for a famous Victorian soldier, Sir Garnet Wolseley. Basketball player Kevin Garnett.
Garnet

Garnock OWelsh. Place name: "River of alder trees."

Garrard OE. "Spear-hard" or "Spear-brave." Related to **Gerard** via the German form, **Gerhard**.
Gerhard, Gerhardt, Gerard

Garrett Var. **Gerard** dating from the Middle Ages. Equally, it may be a variation of **Gareth/Garth**.
Gareth, Garrard, Garret, Garreth, Garretson, Garrith, Garritt, Garrot, Garrott, Garyth, Gerrit, Gerritt, Gerrity, Jared, Jarod, Jarret, Jarrett, Jarrot, Jarrott

Garrick OE. "Spear-rule." Eighteenth century English actor David Garrick did much to revive the fame of Shakespeare, and he is commemorated with street and building names in the theater district of London. Newscaster Garrick Utley.
Garek, Garreck, Garrik, Garryck, Garryk

Garrison ME. "Protection, stronghold." Author Garrison Keillor; football player Garrison Hearst.
Garrisson

Garroway OE. "Spear-fighter."
Garraway

Garson OE. "Gar's son." Gar in this case may be a diminutive of **Garrett**, **Gareth, Garland**, etc, or even a shortening of **Garrison**.

Garth Scan. Occupational name: "Keeper of the garden." Used as a first name in this century, but never widely. Illustrator Garth Williams.

Garton OE. Place name: "Triangle-shaped settlement."
Gorton

Garvey Ir. Gael. "Rough peace."

Garrvey, Garrvie, Garvie, Garvy

Garvin OE. "Spear-friend."

Garvan, Garven, Garvyn, Garwen, Garwin, Garwyn, Garwynn

Garwood OE. Place name: "Wood with fir trees."

Garrwood, Woody

Gary OE. "Spear." Popularized by film idol Gary Cooper, whose name was originally Frank. Very fashionable from the 1950s to the 1970s, and still steadily used. Cartoonists Garry Trudeau, Gary Larson; actors Gary Cooper, Gary Sinise, Gary Oldman.

Gari, Garey, Garrie, Garry

Gaspar Var. **Caspar.** Possibly Per. "He who guards the treasure."

Caspar, Casper, Gaspard, Gasparo, Gasper, Jaspar, Jasper, Kaspar, Kasper

Gaston Fr. "Man from Gascony." Gascony is a region in the south of France whose inhabitants are reputed to be hot-tempered. Since the unlucky and boorish suitor in Disney's cartoon film of *Beauty and the Beast* is named Gaston, the name has taken on new connotations of foolishness.

Gascon

Gauthier Teut. "Strong ruler." Fashion designer Jean-Paul Gaultier.

Galtero, Gaultier, Gautier, Gualterio, Gualtiero

Gavin Welsh. "White falcon" or "Little falcon." As **Gawain**, this was the name of one of King Arthur's knights. The Scottish form, Gavin, has spread from Scotland to broad acceptance in Britain, especially in the last 30 years. Still rare in the U.S. Actor Gavin MacLeod.

Gavan, Gaven, Gavyn, Gavynn, Gawain, Gawaine, Gawayn, Gawayne, Gawen, Gawaine, Gwayn

Gaylord OF. "Lively, high-spirited." This is the most familiar version of **Gaillard.** Author Gayelord Hauser.

Gaillard, Gallard, Galliard, Gay, Gayelord, Gayler, Gaylor

Gaynor Ir. Gael. "Son of the fair-skinned one." From a different root than the feminine version; for male children, this is strictly a transferred last name, and unusual at that.

Gaine, Gainer, Gainor, Gay, Gayner, Gaynnor

Geary ME. "Variable."

Gearey, Gery

Gedaliah Heb. "God is great."

Gedalia, Gedaliahu, Gedalio, Gedalya

Geddes Scottish last name of disputed meaning. It may be related to "goad," a pointed rod used to drive livestock. Author William Gaddis.

Gaddis, Geddis

Gefen Heb. "Vine." Media mogul David Geffen.

Gafni, Gefania, Gefaniah, Gefanya, Gefanyah, Gefanyahu, Geffen, Gephania, Gephaniah

Gene Dim. **Eugene** (Gk. "Well-born"). Used as an independent name since the late 19th century, especially in America. Actors Gene Kelly, Gene Wilder, Gene Hackman; jazz musician Gene Krupa.

Genio, Geno, Jeno

Genesis Gk. "Origin, beginning." Genesis is the first book in the Old Testament, and relates the story of the creation of the world.

Gennesis, Ginesis, Jenesis, Jennesis

Gennaro It. "Of Janus." Janus was an ancient Roman god with two faces, one which looked to the old year, one to the new year. He gave his name to the month of January. A Saint Januarius was martyred in the 4th century A.D. According to one source, a vial said to contain his blood, which is preserved in the cathedral at Naples, actually turns to liquid eighteen times a year. There is no scientific explanation for this.

Gennarius, Gennaros, Januario, Januarius

Gentian Flower name: the gentian was named after an ancient king of Illyria (now coastal Croatia). Gentians are brilliant blue, with fringed petals. Though flower names are usually feminine, the "-ian" ending is still masculine (**Dorian, Julian**).

Genshian, Jenshian, Jentian

Gentile Lat. "Foreigner, heathen." The term "gentile" is often used to characterize someone as non-Jewish. Italian painter Gentile da Fabriano.

Gentilo

Geoffrey Var. **Jeffrey** (OG. Meaning unclear, something to do with "Peace"). Norman name popular through the Middle Ages in Britain, and revived in the mid 19th century after a 350-year rest. The peak of its popularity was the 1970s in the U.S., and it is no longer a favorite, though the "Jeff-" spelling occurs quite often. Performer Geoffrey Holder; medieval poet Geoffrey Chaucer; fashion designer Geoffrey Beene.

Geoff, Geoffery, Geoffroy, Geoffry, Geofrey, Jefery, Jeff, Jefferey, Jefferies, Jeffery, Jeffree, Jeffrey, Jeffry, Jeffrie, Jeffries, Jefry, Jeoffroi, Jephers, Jepherson, Jephrey, Jephry

George Gk. "Farmer." The popularity of the dragon-killing Saint George (patron of Boy Scouts, soldiers, and England) is undimmed by the fact that little proof of his existence can be found. George was a royal name in England, and admiration for George Washington in the U.S. gave the name a parallel popularity in the renegade colonies from the 18th century until the middle of the 20th. Now less common but still a steady presence. Singer George Michael; fashion designer Giorgio Armani; comedians George Burns, George Carlin; baseball legend George "Babe" Ruth; U.S. Presidents George Prescott Bush, George Herbert Walker Bush; actor George Clooney.

Egor, Georas, Geordie, Georg, Georges, Georgi, Georgie, Georgios, Georgius, Georgiy, Georgy, Gheorghe, Giorgi, Giorgio, Giorgios, Giorgius, Goran, Gyorgy, Gyuri, Igor, Jerzy, Jiri, Jorgan, Jorge, Jorgen, Jurgen, Jurek, Jurik, Yorick, Yorik, Yurik, Ygor

Geraint Lat. "Old." From the same root as "geriatric." A Sir Geraint figures in certain Arthurian legends; the name is sparingly used in Britain in this century.

Gerant, Jerant, Jeraint

Gerald OG. "Spear ruler." Old name revived in the 19th century. Most popular in the middle of this century, but now less common. U.S. President Gerald Ford; TV journalist Geraldo Rivera.

Garald, Garold, Gary, Gearalt, Geralde, Geraldo, Gerard, Geraud, Gerek, Gerhard, Gerik, Gerold, Gerolld, Gerolt, Gerollt, Gerrald, Gerrard, Gerri, Gerrild, Gerrold, Gerry, Geryld, Giraldo, Giraud, Girauld, Girault, Jerald, Jerold, Jerri, Jerrold, Jerry

Gerard OE. "Spear brave." Closely related to **Gerald**, and its use follows a similar pattern, though it is increasing. Particularly popular in Ireland. Poet Gerard Manley Hopkins; painter Gerhard Richter.

Garrard, Garrat, Garratt, Garrett, Gearard, Gerardo, Geraud, Gerhard, Gerhardt, Gerhart, Gerrard, Gerri, Gerry, Girard, Girault, Giraud, Gherardo, Jarard, Jared, Jerard, Jerardo, Jerarrd, Jerrott

Geremia It. Var. **Jeremiah** (Heb. "The Lord exalts").

Gerlach Scand. "Spear sport."
Gerlaich

Germain Fr. "From Germany." There were several early saints called "Germanus" for their national origin, the most famous of whom gave his name to a church in Paris, Saint Germain-des-Prés. Singer Jermaine Jackson.

Germaine, German, Germane, Germanicus, Germano, Germanus, Germayn, Germayne, Germin, Jermain, Jermaine, Jermane, Jermayn, Jermayne

Geronimo It. Var. **Jerome** (Gk. "Sacred name") Famous as the name of an Apache Indian chief and also as the cry with which American parachutists in World War II would leap from airplanes. Nobody knows why.

Heronimo, Herinomos, Hieronimo, Hieronymus, Jeronimo, Jeronimus

Gerontius Lat. "Old man." The root of words like "geriatric" and "gerontology."

Gershom Heb. "Exile." Old Testament name, appearing, appropriately enough, in Exodus. The Puritans adopted it and brought it to the U.S., where it is rare, but like many Hebrew names, kept alive by Orthodox Jewish families.

Gersham, Gershon, Gershoom, Gerson

Gervase OG. Meaning unclear; possibly "With honor."

Because of the popularity of a Saint Gervase, the name has been steadily used by English Catholics, but is otherwise unusual.

Garvey, Gervais, Gervaise, Gervasio, Gervasius, Gervaso, Gervayse, Gerwazy, Jarvey, Jarvis, Jervis

Gethin Welsh "Dark-skinned."

Gevariah Heb. "Strength of Jehovah."

Gevaria, Gevarya, Gevaryah, Gevarayahu

Ghalib Arab. "Victorious."

Ghassan Arab. "Youth, prime of life."

Giacomo It. Var. **Jacob** (Heb. "He who supplants"). The name of one of musician Sting's sons.

Gian Italian-style respelling of **John** (Heb. "The Lord is gracious") possibly via the nickname **Gianni**. Shows up occasionally in combination, as in Gian-Carlo and Gianfranco.

Gianney, Gianni, Gianny

Gibor Heb. "Strong one."

Gibbor

Gibson OE. "Son of Gilbert." Actor Mel Gibson.

Gibb, Gibbes, Gibby, Gibbons, Gibbs, Gillson, Gilson

Gideon Heb. "Feller of trees" or "Mighty warrior." A biblical judge and hero who, with an army of only 300 men, liberated the Israelites from the Midianites. The latter-day Gideons are the group responsible for placing Bibles in hotel bedrooms. Oddly enough, Gideon did not benefit from the 1980s craze for Old Testament names that dusted off names like **Joshua** and **Jeremy**.

Gideone, Gidi, Gidon, Hedeon

Gifford OE. Either "Brave giver" or "Puffy-faced." It is astonishing how rarely the derivations of names mean anything negative; this exception to that rule is used as a first name from time to time. Sports figure Frank Gifford; U.S. conservation pioneer Gifford Pinchot.

Giffard, Gifferd, Gyfford

Gilad Arab. "Hump of a camel"; Heb. "Monument, site of testimony." Gilead is a Biblical place name, referring to the fertile region east of the Jordan.

Giladi, Gilead

Gilam Heb. "Joy of a people."

Gilbert OG. "Shining pledge." Norman name much used in the Middle Ages, but use tapered away to mostly local favor in Scotland and Northern England. Very unusual in the U.S. Author Gilbert Chesterton.

Bert, Bertie, Burt, Gib, Gibb, Gil, Gilberto, Gilburt, Gill, Giselbert, Giselberto, Giselbertus, Guilbert

Gilby ONorse. "Estate of the hostage"; Ir. Gael. "Blond boy."

Gilbey, Gillbey, Gillbie, Gillby

Gilchrist Ir. Gael. "Christ's servant."

Gillchrist

Giles Gk. "Kid, young goat." The link with a shield or shield-bearer (sometimes the translation given for Giles) probably comes from the kidskin that ancient shields were made of. In modern times the name, a particular favorite in Scotland, was popular in Britain in the 1970s.

Egide, Egidio, Egidius, Gide, Gil, Gilles, Gillis, Gilliss, Gyles, Jiles, Jyles

Gill Ir. Gael. "Servant." Also a diminutive of the many Irish names that begin with "Gil-."

Ghillie, Gilley

Gillanders Scot. Gael. "Servant of Saint Andrew." Scottish Gaelic, though not identical with the Irish language, does share the particle "Gill-," meaning servant, and it shows up in several names. In the Highlands in Victorian times, "ghillie" was a term for a kind of outdoor servant.

Gillean Ir. Gael. "Servant of Saint John." Related to **Gilchrist, Gillespie, Gilmore**, etc., which all use the "Gil-" particle, meaning "servant."

Gilean, Gilian, Gillan, Gillen, Gilleon, Gillian, Gillion, Gillon

Gillespie Ir. Gael. "Son of the bishop's servant."

Gillaspie, Gillis

Gillett OF. "Young Gilbert." Poet Gelett Burgess.

Gelett, Gelette, Gillette

Gillies Scot. Gael. "Servant of Jesus."

Ghilles, Ghillies, Gilles, Gillis, Gilliss

Gilmer OE. "Renowned hostage."

Gilman Possibly Ir. Gael. "Manservant" or OE. "Gilbert's man."
Gillman

Gilmore Ir. Gael. "Servant of the Virgin Mary."
Gillmore, Gillmour, Gilmour

Gilon Heb. "Joy."
Gil, Gili

Gilroy Ir. Gael. "Servant of the redhead."
Gilderoy, Gildray, Gildroy, Gillroy, Gillray, Gilray

Gilson OE. "Son of Gilbert."
Gillson

Gino It. Dim. **Ambrogino** (Gk. "Ever-living") or **Luigino** or possibly **Eugene** (Gk "Well-born").
Geno, Jeno, Jino

Giovanni It. Var. **John** (Heb. "The Lord is gracious"). In an indication of just how polyglot America is becoming, Giovanni is used about as often as **Abraham, Martin**, or **Damian**. The spellings of today's versions may part company with the Italian version, though. Artist Giovanni Bellini; author Giovanni Boccaccio; actor Giovanni Ribisi.
Geovanney, Geovanni, Gian, Gianni, Giannino, Giovan, Giovanno, Giovel, Giovell, Jovan, Jovanney, Jovanni, Jovanno

Girvin Ir. Gael. "Small rough one."
Girvan, Girven, Girvon

Giulio It. Var. **Julius** (Lat. "Youthful").
Giuliano

Giuseppe It. Var. **Joseph** (Heb. "The Lord increases"). Composer Giuseppe Verdi.

Giustino It. Var. **Justin** (Lat. "Just, fair").
Giustinian, Giustiniano, Giusto

Gjorn Scan. "God of peace."
Gjurd

Glade OE. "Shining." Place name, referring to a clearing in the woods.
Glades

Gladstone OE. Place name: "Kite-shaped stone." Used in the 19th century in tribute to the great British Prime Minister William Ewart Gladstone.

Gladwin OE. "Lighthearted friend."
Gladwinn, Gladwyn, Gladwynne

Glanville OF. Place name: "Settlement of oak trees."

Glen Ir. Gael. Place name: "Glen." A glen is a narrow valley between hills. As a surname, Glen would indicate an ancestor who lived in such a valley. Singer Glen Campbell; band leader Glenn Miller; pianist Glenn Gould; hockey player Glen Murray.
Gleann, Glenn, Glennard, Glennie, Glennon, Glenny, Glin, Glinn, Glyn, Glynn

Glenavon OE. Place name: "Valley near the Avon." The Avon is a river in England.
Glenavin, Glennavin, Glennavon

Glendon Scot. Gael. Place name: "Settlement in the glen."
Glenden, Glendin, Glenton

Glendower Welsh. "Valley of water."
Glin, Glyn, Glynn, Glyndwer, Glyndwr

Glenville Gael. Place name that has been used occasionally as a first name. Along with **Glendon**, it has probably gained legitimacy from the popularity of Glen as a given name.
Glanvill, Glanville, Glenvill

Glover OE. Occupational name: "Maker of gloves." Actor John Glover; tap dancer Savion Glover.

Gobind Sanskrit. "The cow finder." A prominent 17th-century guru of the Sikhs was named Guru Gobind Singh, and Govind is one of the names of Krishna, the principal Hindu deity.
Gobinda, Govind, Govinda

Goddard OG. "God-hard." Film director Jean-Luc Godard.
Godard,   Godart,   Goddart,   Godhart,   Godhardt, Gothart, Gotthard, Gotthardt, Gotthart

Godfrey OG. "God-peace." Popular medieval name that faded very gradually to its near-disuse today. The fact that it was the name of a valet in the 1936 comic film *My Man Godfrey* might indicate that there was something indefinably buffoonish about the name by that date.
Giotto, Godefroi, Godfry, Godofredo, Goffredo, Gottfrid, Gottfried

Godric OE. "God-ruler."
Goderick, Godrick, Goodrick

Godwin OE. "Friend of God" or "Good friend." Anglo-Saxon name that, though it did outlast the Norman Conquest in England, did not benefit from the 19th-century revival that resuscitated many ancient names, so it is almost unknown in the U.S.
Godden, Godding, Godewyn, Godin, Godwinn, Godwyn, Goodwin, Goodwyn, Goodwynne, Goodwynne

Golding OE. "Little golden one." *Lord of the Flies* author William Golding.
Golden, Goldman

Goldsmith OE. Occupational name: "Gold worker." Financier Sir James Goldsmith.
Goldschmidt, Goldshmidt

Goldwin OE. "Golden friend." Film pioneer Samuel Goldwyn.
Goldewin, Goldewyn, Goldwinn, Goldwyn, Goldwynn

Goliath Heb. "Exile." Though babies are frequently named for David, the Old Testament bard, very few are given the name of the giant he killed with his slingshot. Even Cain, the first assassin, has inspired more parents. Nevertheless, the name is used from time to time.
Golliath, Golyath

Gomer OE. "Famous battle" or "Good fight." Also an Old Testament name. Grown-up fans of the goofy marine depicted by Jim Nabors in the 1960s TV series *Gomer Pyle* may have trouble taking the name seriously.

Gonzalo Sp. "Wolf." Currently very popular in Spain. Tennis star Pancho Gonzales.
Consalvo, Goncalve, Gonsalve, Gonzales

Goodman OE. "Good man." This term used to be a title, like Mister. Actor John Goodman.
Goodmann, Guttman, Guttmann

Goodwin OE. "Good friend."
Goodwinn, Goodwyn, Goodwynn

Goodyear OE. "Good year." In the U.S. this name is associated with the Goodyear blimp or with tires, but even car buffs may be surprised to learn that Charles Goodyear, the inventor of vulcanized rubber, patented his process in 1844 and died in debt. What's more, the first practical use of his product was for shoes.

Gordon OE. Meaning unclear, possibly a place name meaning "Hill near meadows" or "Triangular hill." Historically associated with Scotland, but principal use has been 20th century. Balladeer Gordon Lightfoot; photographer Gordon Parks; hockey player Gordie Howe.
Gordan, Gorden, Gordie

Gore OE. "Spear" or "Wedge-shaped object." "Gore" is also an old term for a small, triangular-shaped piece of land, so this may be considered a place name, denoting an ancestor who lived on or near such a piece of land. Author Gore Vidal; politician Al Gore.
Goring

Goren Heb. "Barn floor, granary." Refers to the grain harvest.
Gorin, Gorren, Gorrin

Gorham OE. Place name: "Village near the wedge-shaped piece of land." Or possibly "Spear village." Gorham is the name of a silver company based in Rhode Island.

Gorman Ir. Gael. "Small blue-eyed one."

Gorrell OE. Place name: "Thicket in the marsh."

Gorton OE. Place name: "Settlement near the wedge-shaped piece of land." Also possibly a respelling of **Gordon**.
Gorten

Gower Old Welsh. "Pure."

Grady Ir. Gael. "Renowned." A transferred Irish last name.
Gradea, Gradee, Gradey, Graidey, Graidy

Graham OE. "Gray homestead." Mostly Scottish name that was popular in Britain in the 1950s, without ever being much used in America. Author Graham Greene; inventor Alexander Graham Bell.
Graeham, Graeme, Grahame

Granger MF. "Farmer." Grange organizations used to dot the agricultural portions of the U.S., offering services to farm communities.
Grainger, Grange

Grant Fr. "Tall, big." Another Scottish name, but one that has been more popular in the U.S. as a first name, probably inspired by President Ulysses S. Grant. Painter Grant Wood; actor Hugh Grant.
Grantham, Grantley

Grantland OE. Place name: "The large fields," or possibly "Granta's fields." Sportswriter Grantland Rice.
Grantleigh, Grantley, Grantly

Granville OF. Place name: "Big town." Though never frequent, use of the name has diminished since the 1960s, possibly because its slightly aristocratic sound has seemed too undemocratic for the age of equality.
Granvil, Granvile, Granvill, Grenville

Graves OE. Place name. Commemorates an area near a community burying ground. Fairly common as a last name in Britain. Poet Robert Graves; architect Michael Graves; actor Rupert Graves.

Gray OE. "Gray-haired." Poet Thomas Gray.
Graye, Grey

Graydon OE. Possibly "Son of the gray-haired one" or a place name: "Gray settlement." Editor Graydon Carter.
Grayton

Grayson OE. "Son of the gray-haired man."
Graydon, Greydon, Greyson

Graziano It. "Beloved, dear." Boxer Rocky Graziano.
Gracian, Graciano

Greeley OE. Place name: "Gray meadow" or perhaps "Green meadow." American use of the name (which is far from widespread) may reflect admiration for 19th-century journalist and politician Horace Greeley.
Greelea, Greeleigh, Greely

Greenwood OE. Place name: "Green wood."

Gregory Gk. "Watchful, vigilant." A staple name in the Middle Ages, used by sixteen popes and ten saints. Modern popularity dates from the 1940s, which means it is probably linked to actor Gregory Peck's rise to stardom. Like most names that were very fashionable in the 1950s, it is now a bit out of style. Cyclist Greg LeMond; musician Gregg Allman; actors Gregory Hines, Greg Wise, Greg Kinnear.

Graig, Greer, Greg, Greger, Gregg, Greggory, Gregoire, Gregoor, Gregor, Gregori, Gregorio, Gregorius, Gregos, Grigor, Grigori, Grigorios, Grygor, Grzegorz

Gresham OE. Place name: "Village surrounded by pasture."

Greville OF. Place name used occasionally in Britain.
Grevill

Gridley OE. Place name: "Level meadow."
Gridlie, Gridly

Griffin Lat. "Hooked nose." The name of a mythical beast, usually half eagle (hence the hooked nose), half lion. Use as a name may be connected to the frequent heraldic use of the animal. Actor Griffin Dunne.
Griff, Griffen, Griffon, Gryffen, Gryffin, Gryphon

Griffith Welsh. "Strong chief." Used most often as a first name in the 16th through 18th centuries. This is the kind of slightly nostalgic name that seems ripe for revival, except that it's hard to say in a hurry.

Grimaldo Ger./Sp. "Powerful protector." Grimaldi, a related name, is the last name of the royal family of Monaco.
Grimaldi

Grimshaw OE. Place name: "Dark woods."

Grimsley OE. Place name: "Dark meadow."
Grimslea, Grimsleigh, Grimslie, Grimsly

Griswold OF./Ger. Place name: "Gray woods."
Griswald

Grosvenor OF. "Great hunter." Grosvenor is the last name of one of the richest families in Britain. Their stake in London real estate is commemorated in names like Grosvenor Square.
Grosveneur

Grover OE. Place name: "Grove of trees." American use was probably inspired by President Grover Cleveland, but has faded since mid 20th century. Parents of *Sesame Street* viewers are more likely to be reminded of the self-proclaimed "cute, furry, lovable little monster" Grover.

Guerrant Fr. "Fighting, at war."

Guido It. Var. **Guy**.

Guildford OE. Place name: "Ford with yellow flowers."
Gilford, Guilford

Guillaume Fr. Var. **William** (OG. "Will-helmet") French poet Guillaume Apollinaire.
Guglielmo, Guilherme, Guillermo, Gwillym, Gwilym

Gulshan Hindi. "Garden."

Gulzar Arab. "In bloom, flourishing."

Gunther Scand. "Warrior." Author Gunter Grass.
Guenter, Guenther, Gun, Gunn, Gunnar, Gunner, Gunners, Guntar, Gunter, Guntero, Gunthar, Guntur

Gur Heb. "Cub, young lion."
Guri, Guriel, Gurion, Guryon

Gus Dim. **Augustus** (Lat. "Worthy of respect").
Guss, Gustav

Gustave Scand. "Staff of the gods." A royal name in Sweden, used elsewhere in Europe in the 17th century, and in England in the 19th century. American use (which is uncommon) tends to harken back to Scandinavian ancestry. Composer Gustav Mahler; writer Gustave Flaubert.
Gus, Guss, Gustaf, Gustaff, Gustaof, Gustav, Gustavo, Gustavus, Gustovo, Gustus, Gusztav

Guthrie Ir. Gael. Place name: "Windy spot." Folk singer Woody Guthrie.
Guthree, Guthrey, Guthry

Guy Unclear origin, though some sources make a case for French "Guide" or Old German "Warrior." Made infamous in 1605 by Guy Fawkes, scapegoat of a plot to blow up the Houses of Parliament; in Britain November 5th is still Guy Fawkes Day, when a dummy was traditionally burned in effigy. The English shunned the name for two hundred years, but it became acceptable again by the mid 19th century, and use was increasing by the 1950s. To Americans, it is still a very English-sounding name. Actor Guy Pearce; film director Guy Ritchie.
Guido

Gwalchmai Welsh. "Battle hawk."

Gwynn Old Welsh. "Fair."
  Guinn, Gwin, Gwyn, Gwynedd
Gyandev Sanskrit. "God of wisdom."
  Gyan

 Habakkuk Heb. "Embrace." One of the Minor Prophets in the Old Testament. One of the more outlandish-sounding prophet names to anglophone ears, and it has never been widely used.
  Habacuc, Habbakuk
Habib Arab. "Loved one."
  Habeeb
Hackett OF./Ger. Occupational name: "Little hewer" (of wood).
  Hacket, Hackit, Hackitt
Hackman OF./Ger. Occupational name: "Hewer, hacker" (of wood). Actor Gene Hackman.
Hadar Heb. "Splendor, ornament" or "Respect."
  Hadaram, Hadur, Heder
Hadden OE. Place name: "Hill of heather."
  Haddan, Haddon, Haddin, Haden, Hadon
Hadi Arab. "Rightly guide."
Hadley OE. Place name: "Heather meadow." Interior designer Albert Hadley.
  Hadlea, Hadlee, Hadleigh, Hadly, Leigh
Hadrian Var. **Adrian** (Lat. "From Adria"). Adria was a north Italian city. A Roman Emperor Hadrian was responsible for the building of a vast wall across northern Britain, parts of which still stand.
  Adrian, Adriano, Adrien, Hadrien
Hadriel Heb. "Splendor of Jehovah."
Hadwin OE. "Friend in war."
  Hadwinn, Hadwyn, Hadwynne, Hedwin, Hedwinn
Hafiz Arab. "One who guards."
  Hafeez, Hapheez, Haphiz

Hagen Ir. Gael. "Youthful one." Also a Germanic version of **Hakon**.
Hagan, Haggan

Hagley OE. Place name: "Enclosed meadow."
Haglea, Haglee, Hagleigh, Hagly

Haig OE. Place name: "Enclosed with hedges." Douglas Haig was a prominent English soldier in World War I.

Haidar Arab. "Lion."
Haider, Haydar, Hyder

Haim Heb. "Life." Variant spelling of **Chaim**.
Hayim, Hayyim

Hakeem Arab. "Wise, all-knowing." One of the 99 attributes of Allah, which the prophet Muhammad considered good choices for names. Basketball player Hakeem Olajuwon.
Hakim

Hakon Scand. "Of the highest race," or "Chosen son." A royal name in Norway, but little used in English-speaking countries.
Haaken, Haakin, Haakon, Hacon, Hagan, Hagen, Hakan, Hako

Hal Dim. most commonly of **Henry**. In Shakespeare's plays about Henry IV, his son (to become Henry V) is affectionately known as "Prince Hal." Actors Hal Holbrook, Hal Linden; film director Hal Hartley.

Halbert OE. "Shining hero."
Halburt

Haldan Scand. "Half-Danish." The name takes on a certain significance when you consider that in ancient Britain, the Danes were fierce and frequent invaders.
Haldane, Halden, Halfdan, Halfdane, Halvdan

Haldor ONorse. "Thor's stone."
Halldor, Halle

Hale OE. Either place name "From the hall," or "Healthy hero." Revolutionary War hero Nathan Hale was hanged by the British as a spy. His famous last words on the scaffold were "I regret that I have but one life to lose for my country."
Hal, Hayle

Haley OE. Place name "Hay meadow" or Ir. Gael. "Ingenious, clever." The widespread use of **Hayley** as a girl's name probably spells the end of its use as a boy's name. Football player Charles Haley; actor Haley Joel Osment.

Hailey, Haily, Haleigh, Halley, Hallie, Hayleigh, Hayley

Halford OE. Place name: "Valley ford" or "Hal's ford."

Hallford

Hali Gk. "The sea."

Hall OE. Occupational name: "Worker at the hall." In this case, the hall would signify a large house or manor. Musician Darryl Hall.

Hallam OE. Place name: "The valley."

Hallem

Hallberg ONorse. "Rock mountain."

Halberg, Halburg, Hallburg

Halle ONorse. "Rock." Considering the Scandinavian influence in the formation of English, it's probably impossible to sort out derivations of various "Hall-" names.

Halley OE. Place name "Meadow near the hall" or OE. "Holy." This is a different name from the homonym **Haley**, but will probably also be discarded as a boy's name as the retro-charming **Hallie** becomes more popular for girls. Astronomer Edmund Halley.

Halliwell OE. Place name: "Holy well."

Hallewell, Hallowell, Hellewell, Helliwell

Hallward OE. Occupational name: "Guardian of the hall." Like many of these Anglo-Saxon names, it is unusual as a first name.

Halward, Halwerd, Hawarden

Halsey OE. Place name: "Hal's island."

Hallsey, Hallsy, Halsy

Halstead OE. Place name: "The manor grounds."

Hallstead, Hallsted, Halsted

Halton OE. Place name: "Estate on the hill."

Halten, Hallton, Halton

Halvard ONorse. "Guardian of the rock."

Hallvard, Hallverd, Hallvor, Halvar, Halver, Halverd, Halvor

Ham Heb. "Heat." Old Testament name, one of the sons of Noah. Little used; the names of Noah's other two sons, Shem and Japheth, are even more rare.

Hamal Arab. "Lamb."
   Amahl, Amal, Hamahl
Hamar ONorse. "Hammer."
Hamid Arab. "Thankful, praising."
   Hameed
Hamilton OE. Place name of several possible meanings such as "home-lover's estate" or "hill with grass." It was the surname of several aristocratic British families, and made the transition to a first name in the early 19th century. U.S. statesman Alexander Hamilton; figure skater Scott Hamilton.
   Hamel, Hamelton, Hamil, Hamill
Hamill OE. "Scarred." May refer to the facial characteristic of a distant ancestor. Actor Mark Hamill; newspaper editor Pete Hamill.
   Hamel, Hamell, Hammill
Hamish Scot. Var. **James** (Heb. "He who supplants"). Almost unknown outside of Scotland.
Hamlet OG./Fr. "Village: home." This name, like **Hamlin**, derives from a German root that means "home." Hamlet was a common first name until the beginning of the 19th century, but now its use would inevitably recall Shakespeare's tortured Danish prince so frequently seen on screen and stage. This would not necessarily have been the case in the 17th and 18th centuries, when Shakespeare's work was not so widely performed. Author Dashiell Hammett.
   Hammet, Hammett, Hammond, Hamnet, Hamnett
Hamlin OG. "Little home-lover." Actor Harry Hamlin; Abraham Lincoln's vice-president Hannibal Hamlin.
   Hamblin, Hamelin, Hamlen, Hamlyn
Hammer OG. "Hammer maker; carpenter." An ancient occupational name.
   Hammar, Hammur
Hammond OG. "Home protector."
Hampden OE. Place name: "Home in the valley." Related to **Hampton**.
Hampton OE. Place name: "Home settlement." A name with

enormous resonance in the South. Hampton Beach, Virginia is the oldest English settlement in continuous existence in the U.S., and Hampton Roads is the channel to one of the greatest natural harbors on the eastern seaboard. South Carolina planter Wade Hampton was an important soldier in the Revolutionary War and his grandson (also Wade Hampton) was an important Confederate general and later Governor of South Carolina. Musician Lionel Hampton.

Hampten

Hancock OE. Meaning obscure, probably related to poultry in some way. Bostonian patriot John Hancock was the first man to sign the Declaration of Independence. His name lingers on in a huge insurance conglomerate and an ultra-modern glass building in downtown Boston.

Handcock

Hanford OE. Place name: "High ford."

Hani Arab. "Full of joy."

Hanif Arab. "Devout devotee of Islam." Filmmaker Hanif Kureishi.

Hank Dim. **Henry** (OE. "Estate ruler"). Usually a nickname rather than a given name. Baseball star Hank Aaron.

Hanley OE. Place name: "High meadow."

Handlea, Handleigh, Handley, Hanlea, Hanlee, Hanleigh, Hanly, Henlea, Henlee, Henleigh, Henley

Hannibal Punic. "Grace of Baal." The name of a great general of Carthage, a kingdom in North Africa. He was a great enemy of the Roman Empire and masterminded one of the military feats of all time when he crossed the Alps with a baggage train of elephants to invade Italy.

Hanoch Heb. "Vowed, dedicated." A variant of **Enoch**.

Hans Scand. Var. **John** (Heb. "The Lord is gracious"). Most familiar from the diminutive, Hansel, in the fairy tale *Hansel and Gretel*. Currently very popular in Germany. Writer Hans Christian Andersen.

Hannes, Hanns, Hansel, Hanss, Hanzel

Hanson Scand. "Son of Hans." Singing brothers Taylor, Isaac, and Zac Hanson.

Hansen, Hanssen, Hansson

Hansraj Sanskrit. "Swan king."

Harbin OF./Ger. "Little bright warrior."
  Harben

Harcourt OF. "Fortified farm."
  Harcort

Harden OE. Place name: "Valley of the hares."
  Hardin, Hardon

Harding OE. "Son of the courageous one." This name is closely related to Hardy. U.S. President Warren G. Harding.
  Hardinge

Hardwick OE. "Courageous one's settlement."
  Harwyck

Hardwin OE. "Courageous friend."
  Hardwen, Hardwinn, Hardwyn, Hardwynn

Hardy OG. "Bold, brave." Writer Thomas Hardy; fashion designer Hardy Amies.
  Hardey

Harel Heb. "God's mount."
  Harrel, Harrell

Harford OE. Place name: "Ford of the hares." Like many place names turned surnames, this was used as a first name in the nineteenth century.
  Harfurd, Harrford, Harrfurd

Hargrove OE. Place name: "Grove of the hares." In modern times it seems curious that ancient names took such close note of the whereabouts of rabbits, but they might have constituted a significant portion of the average man's diet in those days.
  Hargrave, Hargreaves

Harkin Ir. Gael. "Dark red."
  Harkan, Harken

Harlan OE. Place name: "Army land."
  Harland, Harlen, Harlenn, Harlin, Harlyn, Harlynn

Harley OE. Place name: "The long field." Familiar to most people as half of the name of a great motorcycle, the Harley-Davidson.
  Arlea, Arleigh, Arley, Harlea, Harlee, Harleigh, Harley, Harly

Harlow OE. Place name: "Army hill." Musician Arlo Guthrie.

Arlo, Harlow, Harlo, Harloe

Harmon Var. **Herman** (OG. "Army man"). Actor Mark Harmon.

Harman, Harmann, Harmonn

Harmony Lat. "Concord, joining." New Age name. Filmmaker Harmony Korine.

Harmonio

Harold Scand. "Army ruler." An Anglo-Saxon name revived to great popularity in the mid 19th century. It was greatly in vogue until the turn of the century, but is now rare. British Prime Minister Harold Macmillan; playwright Harold Pinter.

Araldo, Aralt, Aroldo, Arry, Garald, Garold, Hal, Harald, Haralds, Haroldas, Haroldo, Harry, Herold, Herrold, Herrick, Herryck

Harper OE. "Harp player."

Harpur

Harrell Heb. "God's mount."

Harrington OE. Place name: possibly "Herring town" or "Harry's town."

Harrison OE. "Son of Harry." Harrison is the more popular version of this name, but neither it nor Harris has been used much as a first name in the latter part of this century. Actor Harrison Ford.

Harris, Harriss, Harrisson

Harry Dim. **Henry** (OE. "Home ruler"). Since about 1920, Harry has been used as an independent name about as frequently as **Henry**. In the U.S. this may have something to do with admiration for President Harry S. Truman. The cultural reach of Harry Potter may dim this name's utility for a while, though in England it is currently immensely popular. English parents may be thinking of Prince Henry of Wales, widely known as Harry. Actor Harry Belafonte; U.S. Supreme Court Justice Harry A. Blackmun; magician Harry Houdini.

Harshad Hindi. "Bringer of joy."

Hart OE: "Stag." Poet Hart Crane; actor Hart Bochner.

Hartford OE. Place name: "Stag ford."

Hartley OE. Place name: "Stag meadow."
   Hartlea, Hartlee, Hartleigh, Hartly

Hartman OG. "Hard, strong man."
   Hartmann

Hartwell OE. Place name: "Well of the stags."
   Harwell, Harwill

Hartwig Ger. "Courageous in battle."

Harun Arab. "On high, exalted."
   Haroun

Harvey OF. "Burning for battle" or "Strong and ardent."
   Norman name revived in the 19th century, but now uncommon. Many people may recall the Jimmy Stewart
   movie *Harvey* in which he was upstaged by a giant invisible rabbit. Playwright Harvey Feirstein.
   Harvee, Harvie, Herve, Hervey

Harwood OE. Place name: "Wood of the hares."
   Harewood

Hashim Arab. "Crusher of evil."
   Hasheem, Hisham

Haskel Heb. "Intellect." Cinematographer Haskell Wexler.
   Haskell

Haslett OE. Place name: "Headland with the hazel trees."
   Literary critic William Hazlitt.
   Haslit, Haslitt, Hazel, Hazlett, Hazlitt

Hassan Arab. "Handsome." A very popular name in the
   Arabic world, and one of the more familiar Muslim
   names even in America.
   Hasan

Hastings OE. "Son of the austere man."
   Hastey, Hastie, Hasting, Hasty

Havelock Scand. "Sea competition." Author Havelock Ellis.

Haven OE. Place name: "Sanctuary, safe harbor."
   Hagan, Hagen, Havin, Hogan

Haward ONorse. "High guardian." Possibly related to
   Howard, which it resembles to the ear.
   Hawarden

Hawes OE. Place name: "Hedged area." May also refer to the fruit from hawthorne trees, known as "haws." They are small and resemble berries.
Haws

Hawk OE. "Falcon, bird of prey." Use of this name may be related to the perennial popularity of Alan Alda's character Hawkeye, on the long-running TV serial *M.A.S.H.*

Hawkins OE. "Little hawk."
Hawkyns

Hawley OE. Place name: "Hedged meadow."
Hawleigh, Hawly

Hawthorne OE. Place name: "Where hawthorn trees grow." Use in the U.S. may reflect admiration for the novelist Nathaniel Hawthorne.
Hawthorn

Hayden OE. Place name: "Hedged valley." Most commonly used in Wales. Actor Haden Christiansen.
Haden, Haydn, Haydon

Hayes OE. Place name: "Hedged area." U.S. President Rutherford B. Hayes; baseball player Charlie Hayes.
Hays

Hayward OE. Occupational name: "Keeper or guardian of the hedged enclosure."

Haywood OE. Place name: "Hedged forest." Writer Heywood Broun.
Heywood, Woody

Hazaiah Heb. "God decides."

Hazard OF. "Chance, luck."
Hazzard

Hazen Var. **Hayes.**
Hazin

Hazleton OE. Place name: "Settlement near hazel trees."

Hazlewood OE. Place name: "Wood of hazel trees."

Heath ME. Place name: "Heath." In Britain "heath" is the name for a large, open space that's not under cultivation. Football player Heath Shuler; actor Heath Ledger.

Heathcliff ME. Place name indicating a cliff near a heath.

Most parents today would automatically associate it with the passionate hero of Emily Bronte's *Wuthering Heights*.

Heber Heb. "Togetherness." An Old Testament name used by the Puritans but rare in this century.
Hebor

Hector Gk. "Holds fast." One of the great heroes of the Trojan war, though today the verb form "to hector" means to bully or browbeat. Designer Ettore Sottsass; composer Hector Berlioz.
Ector, Ettore

Hedley OE. Place name: "Heathered meadow." Used in Britain in the late 19th century, but rare in the U.S.
Headleigh, Headley, Headly, Hedly

Hedeon Rus. Var. **Gideon** (Heb. "Feller of trees").

Heddwyn Welsh. "Fair peace."
Hedwin, Hedwyn, Hedwynn

Heimdall ONorse mythology name. One of the sons of Odin, the principal Norse god, he was one of the founders of the human race. The name means "white god."
Heiman, Heimann

Heinrich Ger. var. **Henry.**
Heine, Heini, Heinie

Heinz Var. **Hans** (Heb. "The Lord is gracious").
Hines

Heladio Sp. "Born in Greece."
Eladio, Elado, Helado

Helgi ONorse. "Productive, successful, happy." Well used in Scandinavia. Ballet dancer Helgi Thomassen.
Helge, Helje, Helji

Heller Ger. "Bright, brilliant."

Helmut MF. "Helmet." Photographer Helmut Newton.
Hellmut, Hellmuth

Henderson OE. "Son of Henry."
Hendrie, Hendries, Hendron, Henryson

Hendrick OG. "Estate ruler." Variant form of **Henry.**
Hendrik

Henley OE. Place name: "High meadow." Variant of **Hanley,** but made famous by the English town that hosts an annual worldwide crew regatta and has given its name to a style of shirt.

Henlee, Henlie

Henry OG. "Estate ruler." Norman name that took root in Britain and became a royal name used by eight kings and, most recently, for the younger son of the Prince of Wales. This exposure may give new popularity to a name that was extremely common until the first quarter of the 20th century and is now used less than unusual names like Dakota, Tristan, or Gavin. Explorer Henry Hudson; actor Henry Fonda; author Henry James; poet Henry Wadsworth Longfellow; artists Henri Matisse, Henri de Toulouse-Lautrec, Henri Rousseau; playwright Henrik Ibsen; singer Enrique Iglesias.

Arrigo, Enrico, Enrikos, Enrique, Enzio, Hal, Hank, Harry, Heike, Heindrick, Heindrik, Heiner, Heinrich, Heinrick, Heinrik, Heinz, Hendrick, Hendrik, Henerik, Henning, Henri, Henrik, Henrique, Henryk, Heriot, Herriot, Hinrich

Herbert OG. "Bright army" or "Bright warrior." Norman name that faded in the Middle Ages, to be revived enthusiastically in the 19th century. Now unusual. U.S. President Herbert Hoover.

Bert, Bertie, Erberto, Harbert, Hebert, Herb, Herbie, Horibert, Horiberto

Hercules Gk. Meaning not quite clear: Possibly "Glorious gift" or "Glory of Hera." The legendary Greek hero who exhibited incredible strength. In modern times his physical strength might have been rivaled by the intellectual power of his namesake, Agatha Christie's fictional detective Hercule Poirot.

Ercole, Ercolo, Ercule, Herakles, Hercule, Herculie

Heribert Ger. "Renowned army."

Herman OG. "Army man." Another 19th-century revival of a Norman name, this one especially a U.S. favorite. Uncommon since the turn of the century. Authors Herman Hesse, Herman Melville.

Armand, Armando, Armin, Ermanno, Ermano, Ermin, Harman, Harmon, Hermann, Hermie, Herminio, Hermon

Hermes In Greek mythology, Hermes is the messenger god, with wings on his feet. The corresponding Roman god is Mercury. Choreographer Hermes Pan.
Ermes, Hermilo, Hermite, Hermus

Hernando Sp. Var. **Ferdinand** (OG. "Bold voyager").

Herndon OE. Place name: "Heron valley."

Herne OE. "Heron." Probably used to indicate a place where herons were to be found.
Hearne, Hern

Hernley OE. "Heron meadow."
Hernlea, Hernlee, Hernlie, Hernly

Herrick OG. "War ruler." The 17th-century poet Robert Herrick.
Herrik, Herryck

Hershel Heb. "Deer." As **Herzl**, this name is often used to commemorate Theodor Herzl, an early Zionist. Football player Herschel Walker; actor Herschel Bernardi.
Hersch, Herschel, Herschell, Hersh, Hertzel, Herzel, Herzl, Heschel, Heshel, Hirsch, Hirschel, Hirschl

Hesed Heb. "Kindness."

Hesperos Gk. "Evening or evening star." The Greeks referred to Italy as Hesperia, since the sun set and the evening star rose there.
Hesperios, Hespero, Hesperus

Hewett OF. Dim. **Hugh** (Ger. "Small intelligent one").
Hewet, Hewie, Hewitt, Hewlett, Hewlitt

Hewney Ir. Gael. "Green."
Owney

Hewson OE. "Hugh's son."

Heywood OE. Place name: "Hedged forest." Variant of **Haywood**.

Hezekiah Heb. "God gives strength." Old Testament name little used since the 19th century.
Hezeki

Hideo Jap. "Excellent man." Baseball player Hideo Nomo.

Hieremias Gk. Var. **Jeremiah** (Heb. "Jehovah lifts up").

Hieronymos Gk. Var. **Jerome** (Heb. "Sacred name"). Painter Hieronymus Bosch.
Hierome, Hieronim, Hieronimos, Hieronymus

Hilary Gk. "Cheerful, happy." The name comes from the same root as the word "hilarious." Although it was used for boys (including a pope and a saint) until the 17th century, it was revived at the turn of the 20th century as a girl's name, and after eight years with a Hillary as a highly visible First Lady, it will be hard to reclaim this name for male babies.

Helario, Hilaire, Hilar, Hilarid, Hilarie, Hilario, Hilarion, Hilarius, Hillary, Hillery, Hilliary, Hilorio, Ilario, Illario

Hildebrand OG. "Battle sword."

Hildebrandt, Hillebrand

Hill OE. Place name. Indicates a remote ancestor who lived on or near a hill.

Hillard OG. "Hard warrior."

Hilliard, Hillier, Hillyer

Hillel Heb. "Greatly praised." Sometimes used in honor of the celebrated 1st-century Jewish scholar Rabbi Hillel.

Hilliard OG. "Battle guard" or OE. Place name: "Yard on a hill." Football player Ike Hilliard.

Hiller, Hillierd, Hillyard, Hillyer, Hillyerd

Hilton OE. Place name: "Hill settlement." Hotelier Conrad Hilton.

Hylton

Himesh Hindi. "Snow king."

Hippolyte Gk. Meaning not entirely clear, but alludes to horses. The Hippolytus in Greek legend, son of Theseus, was dragged to death by his bolting chariot-horses. Extremely rare.

Hippolit, Hippolitos, Hippolytus, Ippolito

Hiram Heb. Meaning not clear, possibly "Most noble." Old Testament name little used in the 20th century, though fairly popular in the 19th. Sculptor Hiram Powers.

Hi, Hirom, Hy, Hyrum

Hiroshi Jap. "Generous."

Hitchcock OE. Meaning unclear. Film director Alfred Hitchcock.

Hjalmar ONorse. "Army helmet." Another warlike name from England's northern neighbors.

Hjalamar, Hjallmar, Hjalmer

Hobart A particularly American (though unusual) variant of **Hubert** (OG. "Bright or shining intellect").
Hobard, Hobert, Hobey, Hobie, Hoebart

Hockley OE. Place name: "High meadow."
Hocklea, Hocklee, Hocklie, Hockly

Hockney OE. Place name: "High island." Artist David Hockney.
Hockny

Hobbes OE. Variant of **Robert** (OE. "Bright fame"). Seventeenth-century English philosopher Thomas Hobbes wrote that life without government was "solitary, poor, nasty, brutish, and short." The popular cartoon character (a stuffed tiger) created by Bill Waterson was named after the philosopher.
Hob, Hobbs

Hobson OE. "Son of Robert."
Hobbson

Hodgson OE. "Son of Roger."
Hodge, Hodges

Hoffman Ger. "Courtier." *Hof* means court or castle in German. Actor Dustin Hoffman.
Hofman, Hofmann, Hoffmann

Hogan Ir. Gael. "Youth."

Holbrook OE. Place name: "Stream near the hollow." Actor Hal Holbrook.
Brook, Holbrooke

Holcomb OE. "Deep valley." "Combe" is a term, sometimes used in England, for a deep, narrow valley.
Holcombe, Holcoomb

Holden OE. Place name: "Hollow valley." The hero of J.D. Salinger's coming-of-age novel *The Catcher in the Rye* is named Holden Caulfield.

Holiday OE. "Holy day."
Holliday

Hollis OE. Place name: "Near the holly bushes" or "Holly-tree grove." Used as a girl's name with some frequency as well.
Holliss, Hollister

Holmes ME. Place name: "Islands in the river." Arthur Conan Doyle's fictional detective Sherlock Holmes.

Holt OE. Place name: "Woods, forest."

Homer Gk. "Security, pledge." The name of the classical
poet, author of the *Iliad* and the *Odyssey*. More popular in
the U.S. than elsewhere, especially in the 19th century,
but scarcely used today. Cartoon character Homer Simpson may present a discouraging example. Artist Winslow
Homer.
Homere, Homero, Homeros, Homerus, Omero

Honesto Sp. "Honest man."

Honoré Lat. "Honored one." Familiar because of a fashionable neighborhood and a shopping street in Paris
called the Faubourg Saint Honoré. French novelist Honoré de Balzac.
Honorius, Honoratus

Hooker OE. Possibly an occupational name referring to a
shepherd's hook or crook. Joseph Hooker was a prominent Union general in the Civil War.

Hooper OE. Occupational name: "Maker of hoops," the
metal circles that bound barrels.

Hopkins Welsh. "Robert's son." Hob was a long-ago nickname for Robert.
Hopkin, Hopkinson, Hopkyns, Hopper, Hoppner

Horace Lat. Clan name, possibly meaning "Timekeeper."
Late 19th-century use may have been inspired in part by
the famous Roman poet Horace. British Admiral Horatio
Nelson; journalist Horace Greeley; basketball player Ho-
race Grant.
Horacio, Horatio, Horatius, Horaz, Oratio, Orazio

Horsley OE. Place name: "Horse meadow."
Horslea, Horsleigh, Horslie, Horsly

Horst OG. "A thicket." Photographer Horst P. Horst.
Hurst

Horton OE. Place name: "Gray settlement." Dr. Seuss
character Horton of *Horton Hears a Who*.
Horten, Orton

Hosea Heb. "Salvation." Name of an Old Testament

prophet, but less popular, even in the 19th century, than other prophets' names like Joel or Amos. Unless the "-a" is pronounced clearly, Hosea is likely to be taken for **José**.

Hoshea, Hoseia, Hosheia

Houghton OE. Place name: "Settlement on the headland."

Hough

Houston OE. Place name: "Settlement on the hill" or "Hugh's town." Sam Houston was the first president of the republic of Texas, before Texas entered the United States.

Hewson, Huston, Hutcheson, Hutchinson

Hovannes Central European var. **John** (Heb. "The Lord is gracious") via **Johannes**.

Howard OE. Meaning unclear, possibly occupational name indicating a watchman of some kind. Millionaire Howard Hughes; sportscaster Howard Cosell.

Howie, Ward

Howe OG. "Lofty one" or ME. Place name: "Hill." Elias Howe patented the first sewing machine in 1845.

How

Howell Welsh. "Eminent, remarkable." The anglicized version of Hywel, a name mostly used in Wales. Author William Dean Howells.

Howel, Howells

Howland OE. Place name: "Land with hills."

Howlan, Howlen

Hoyt ONorse. "Spirit, soul."

Hoyce

Hubbard Var. **Hubert**.

Hubert OG. "Bright or shining intellect." An old European name that was popular around the turn of the century, but is now rare. U.S. Vice President Hubert Humphrey.

Bert, Hobard, Hobart, Hubbard, Hube, Huberto, Hubie, Humberto, Uberto, Ulberto

Hudson OE. "Hugh's son." Explorer Henry Hudson was the first European to visit the Hudson River, which he found while searching for a Northwest Passage to India. On a later voyage he sailed into Hudson Bay in Canada.

Hugh OG. "Mind, intellect." Popular medieval name, steadily used (though at a diminishing rate) in the modern era. Its widespread use in the Middles Ages resulted in spin-off names like Hudson, Hewson, and Houston. **Hugo** is very fashionable in Spain. Film director Hugh Hudson; *Playboy* founder Hugh Hefner; U.S. Supreme Court Justice Hugo Black; actors Hugh Grant, Hugh Jackman; football player Hugh Douglas.
   Hew, Hewe, Huey, Hughes, Hughie, Hugo, Hugues, Huw, Ugo

Hulbert OG. "Bright grace."
   Bert, Hulbard, Hulburd, Hulburt

Humbert OG. "Renowned Hun." Made famous by the narrator of Vladimir Nabokov's *Lolita,* Humbert Humbert. Italian author Umberto Eco.
   Umberto

Hume Scottish Var. **Holmes** (ME. "Islands in the river"). Scottish philosopher David Hume.
   Hulme

Humphrey OG. Meaning unclear, but alludes to peace. In the Middle Ages, the form Humfrey was used in England, but Humphrey was the usual form from 1700 on. Never immensely popular, especially since the 1960s. Actor Humphrey Bogart.
   Humfrey, Humfrid, Humfried, Humfry, Humph, Humphery, Humphry, Hunfredo, Onfre, Onfroi, Onofredo, Onofrio

Hunt OE. The word as a name, perhaps originally a shortening of **Hunter** or **Huntington**.

Hunter OE. Occupational name: "Hunter." A name that was obscure until the early 1990s, then shot into middling popularity for a brief period. Journalist Hunter Thompson.
   Hunt

Huntington OE. Place name: "Hunter's settlement." Railroad magnate and philanthropist Henry Huntington.
   Hunt, Huntingdon

Huntley OE. Place name: "Meadow of the hunter."
   Huntlea, Huntlee, Huntleigh, Huntly

Huon Var. **John** (Heb. "The Lord is gracious"), probably via **Juan**.

Hurlbert OE. "Shining army."
Hulbert, Hurlburt, Hurlbutt

Hurley Ir. Gael. "Sea tide."
Hurlee, Hurleigh, Hurly

Hurst ME. Place name: "Thicket of trees." Sometimes occurs as a place name in combination with the tree name, as in Elmhurst or Pinehurst.
Hearst, Hirst, Horst

Hussein Arab. "Small handsome one." A royal name in Jordan.
Husain, Husayn, Husein

Hutton OE. Place name: "Settlement on the bluff." Actor Timothy Hutton.
Hutten

Huxford OE. Place name: "Hugh's ford."

Huxley OE. Place name: "Hugh's meadow." Author Aldous Huxley.
Huxlea, Huxlee, Huxleigh, Huxly

Hyacinthe Fr. "Hyacinth." Owing to the English-speaking tradition of flower names for girls, unlikely to be used as a boy's name, despite its origin as a male name. French painter Hyacinthe Rigaud.
Hyacinthos, Hyacinthus, Hyakinthos

Hyatt OE. Place name: "Lofty gate."
Hayatt, Hiatt

Hyde OE. Place name referring to a "hide," a measure of land current in the early Middle Ages. It amounted to about 120 acres.

Hyman Anglicized variant of **Chaim** (Heb. "Life").
Hayim, Hayyim, Hymie, Mannie

Iago Sp. Var. **James** (Heb. "He who supplants"). The Spanish name for Saint James, Santiago, was given to a number of geographical features (rivers, lakes, mountains) in South America, as well as being the capital city of Chile. Still, most English-speaking parents will remember the treacherous villain of Shakespeare's *Othello,* and pass this name by.

Jago, Yago

Ian Scot. Var. **John** (Heb. "God is gracious"). One of the few Scottish names that has achieved really broad popularity since the beginning of this century, though John still outranks it on the charts. Ian's popularity stems from the current longing for the name that is just a little bit out of the ordinary. James Bond's creator Ian Fleming; actor Ian McKellen.

Ean, Eann, Elon, Eon, Iain, Ion

Ib Dan. "Baal's pledge." Baal was an ancient god of the Semites. Ballet dancer Ib Andersen.

Ibrahim Arab. Var. **Abraham** (Heb. "Father of many"). This form of the name is more common in Muslim countries.

Icarus Greek mythology name: Icarus was the son of Daedalus, the designer of the Labyrinth in Knossos who was held prisoner by King Minos. Daedalus made wings out of wax and feathers to facilitate his and Icarus' escape, but Icarus flew too close to the sun. The wax melted, and he fell into the sea.

Ikaros, Ikarus

Ichabod Heb. "The glory is gone." An Old Testament name brought to the U.S. by the Pilgrims and given fame by Washington Irving, who named a character Ichabod Crane in *The Legend of Sleepy Hollow.*

Ikabod, Ikavod

Idan Heb. "Era, time."

Ido Heb. "Evaporate"; Arab. "To be mighty." This is one case where a word means radically different things in Hebrew and Arabic. Frequently there is similarity between names in the two languages.
Iddo

Idris Welsh. "Eager lord." Mostly used in Wales around the turn of the century.

Ignatius Meaning unclear, though some sources suggest Latin "Ardent, burning" (from the same root as "ignite"). The most famous Ignatius is Saint Ignatius of Loyola, founder of the Society of Jesus, popularly known as the Jesuits. The name is rare in English-speaking countries.
Iggie, Ignac, Ignace, Ignacio, Ignacius, Ignatious, Ignatz, Ignaz, Ignazio, Inacio, Inigo

Igor Rus. Var. **Ingvar** (Scand. "Ing's soldier"). Composer Igor Stravinsky.
Inge, Ingemar, Ingmar, Yegor, Ygor

Ihab Arab. "Gift."

Ike Dim. **Isaac** (Heb. "Laughter"). Singer Ike Turner.

Ilan Heb. "Tree." This name is used in many forms, and is particularly popular in the feminine version, **Ilana**.
Eilon, Elam, Elan, Ilon

Ilario It. Var. **Hilary** (Gk. "Cheerful, merry").

Ilias Gk. Var. **Elijah** (Heb. "The Lord is my God").
Ilie

Ilya Rus. Var. **Elijah** (Heb. "The Lord is my God"). Nostalgic TV fans will remember the glamorous Russian Illya Kuryakin from the series *The Man from U.N.C.L.E.*
Ilia, Illya

Imad Arab. "Support, mainstay."

Immanuel Var. **Emmanuel** (Heb. "God is among us"). German philosopher Immanuel Kant.
Imanoel, Imannuel, Imanuel

Imre Hung. Possibly a variant of **Emeric** (OG. "Home ruler"). Little used outside Hungary. Another source for the same name is Heb. "My words."
Imray, Imri, Imrie

Ince Hung. "Innocent."

Indio Modern name. Possibly a masculine version of **India**, perhaps a reference to Native Americans.
Indeeo, Indeio, Indyo

Ingemar Scand. "Ing's son." Ing, in Norse mythology, was a powerful god of fertility and peace. His name is an element in several modern names. Film director Ingmar Bergman.
Ingamar, Ingemur, Ingmar

Inglebert Var. **Englebert** (OE. "Angel-bright").
Ingbert, Ingelbert

Ingo Dan. "Meadow" or Scand. "Lord."

Ingram OE. "Raven of Anglia." A first name until the 17th century, now more commonly a surname that is occasionally transferred.
Ingraham, Ingrahame, Ingrams, Ingrim, Yngraham, Yngraham

Ingvar Scand. "Ing's soldier."
Ingevar

Inigo OE. Var. **Ignatius**. In modern times, likely to be homage to the great English architect Inigo Jones.

Inman OE. Occupational name: "Innkeeper."
Innman

Innis Scot. Gael. Place name: "Island."
Ennis, Innes, Inness, Inniss

Innocenzio It. "Innocent." Thirteen Popes have chosen to be called "Innocent."
Innocent, Innocenty, Inocencio

Inver Gael. "Estuary." Most commonly combined with the names of rivers, as in Inverness, which means "Estuary of the Ness."

Ioanis Rus. Var. **John** (Heb. "The Lord is gracious").

Ioakim Rus. Var. **Joachim** (Heb. "God will judge").
Ioachim, Ioachime

Ion Pronounced with a long "I-", this is a Greek mythology name, referring to a son of Apollo who became the ancestor of the Ionians. (The western Greek islands, including Corfu, are still known as the Ionian islands.) If the name is pronounced with an initial long "E-" sound, however, it is clearly a respelling of **Ian**.

Eion

Iosef Rus. Var. **Joseph** (Heb. "Jehovah increases").

Iosif, Iosip

Ira Heb. "Watchful." Old Testament name revived in the 19th century, but never very popular. Lyricist Ira Gershwin.

Irenio Sp. from Gk. "Peace." The masculine form of **Irene**.

Irenaeus, Ireneus

Irving OE. "Sea friend." Also a Scottish place name. Used as a first name since the middle of the last century. Composer Irving Berlin, author Irving Stone.

Earvin, Erv, Ervin, Irv, Irvin, Irvine

Irwin OE. "Boar friend." Revived from roughly 1860 to 1940s, but little used since. Author Irwin Shaw, clown Bill Irwin.

Erwin, Erwinn, Erwyn, Irwinn, Irwyn

Isaac Heb. "Laughter." In the Old Testament, Abraham's son, born when his father was 100 years old. God tested Abraham's faith by ordering him to sacrifice Isaac, and when Abraham was willing to do so, God sent an angel to stop him. The scene has often been portrayed in western art, but moderns may wonder about the effect of this scene on Isaac. The Puritans used the name enthusiastically, and it remained popular through the 18th century, fading very gradually. Less fashionable in the last 50 years. Scientist Isaac Newton; angler Izaak Walton; authors Isaac Bashevis Singer, Isaac Asimov; football player Isaac Bruce; singer Isaac Hanson.

Ike, Ikey, Ikie, Isaak, Isac, Isacco, Isak, Issac, Itzak, Izaak, Izak, Izik, Izsak, Yitzhak, Zack, Zak

Isaiah Heb. "The Lord helps me" or "Salvation of God." Like so many Old Testament names, popular with the Puritans in the 17th century, brought to America, and revived by the Victorians. Now rare. Basketball player Isiah Thomas.

Isa, Isaia, Isaias, Isia, Isiah, Issiah, Izaiah, Iziah

Isam Arab. "Protection, security."

Isandro Sp. from Gk. "Man's liberator." Related to **Alexander**.

Isander, Isandero, Ysander, Ysandro

Ishaan Hindu. "The sun."

Isham OE. Place name: "Home of the iron one."

Ishmael Heb. "The Lord will hear." Old Testament name immortalized in the first line of Herman Melville's *Moby Dick*: "Call me Ishmael." The name has been used in literature to indicate an outcast, since Ishmael, son of Abraham by his servant Hagar, was cast out of Abraham's household when Isaac (the legitimate son) was born. The Arab peoples were descended from Ishmael's twelve sons. The Arabic version of this name is **Ismail**.

Ismael, Ismail, Ysmael, Ysmail

Isidore Gk. "Gift of Isis." Isis was the principal goddess of ancient Egypt, and Isidore was a popular name among the ancient Greeks. There are several saints named Isidore, but the name is probably most famous in its feminine form, **Isadora**.

Dore, Dorian, Dory, Isador, Isadore, Isidor, Isidoro, Isidorus, Isidro, Issy, Izidor, Izydor, Izzy, Ysidro

Iskander Arab. var. **Alexander** (Gk. "Man's defender").

Ismail Arab. A variant of **Ishmael**, who built the temple of Kaaba at Mecca. Film director Ismail Merchant; football playing brothers Raghib and Qadry Ismail.

Ishmael, Ismaal, Ismael, Ismal, Ismayl, Izmail, Ysmal, Ysmail

Ismat Arab. "Protecting." Related to **Isam**.

Israel Heb. Meaning unclear, though some sources suggest "Wrestling with the Lord," for this was the name given Jacob in the Old Testament after his three-day bout with his Lord. Came to be synonymous with the Jewish people, and was consequently used as the name for the new Jewish state founded in 1948. Author Israel Shenker.

Yisrael

Issachar Heb. "His reward will come." Old Testament name: one of the twelve sons of Jacob who founded the Twelve Tribes of Israel.

Isachar, Yisachar, Yissachar

Istvan Hung. Var. **Stephen** (Gk. "Crowned"). Film director Istvan Szabo.

Itai Heb. "The Lord is at my side."
Ittai, Itiel

Italo It. "From Italy." Novelist Italo Calvino.

Itamar Heb. "Palm island."
Ithamar, Ittamar

Ivan Rus. Var. **John** (Heb. "God is gracious"). Used in English-speaking countries for the last hundred-odd years. Tennis star Ivan Lendl.
Ifan, Iwan

Ivo OG. "Yew wood." Since yew wood was used for bows, the name may have been an occupational one meaning "archer." The most famous form is probably **Ives** from the old nursery rhyme "As I was going to St. Ives/I met a man with seven wives . . ." Uncommon nevertheless.
Ivair, Ivar, Iven, Iver, Ives, Ivon, Yves, Yvo

Ivor Norse, meaning unclear. Possibly related to **Ivo** or to **Ingvar**. Used now and then in Britain, scarce in the U.S. Songwriter Ivor Novello.
Ifor, Ivar, Iver, Yvor

Iyar Heb. "Light."
Iyyar

Jabbar Arab. "Consoler."
Jabar

Jabez Heb. "Borne in pain." Old Testament name that lasted until around 1930.
Jabes, Jabesh

Jabir Arab. "Consolation."

Jace Dim. **Jason** (Heb. "The Lord is my salvation"). Far from common, but nevertheless well-established for a name that didn't even exist twenty years ago.
Jacey, Jacian, Jaice, Jayce

Jacinto Sp. from Gk. **Hyacinth** (flower name). There was a 3rd-century Saint Hyacinth, and the name has been used for both sexes. In Greek legend, Apollo loved a beautiful youth of the name; the hyacinth flower sprang up from his blood when he died.

Giacintho, Giacinto, Jacindo

Jack Familiar form of **John** (Heb. "The Lord is gracious") or, less often, **Jacob** (Heb. "He who supplants"). Used as an independent name from the 1850s to the 1920s, then subsided. Currently experiencing quite a little renaissance, possibly because of its slightly rugged, down-home aura. Also very fashionable in England, Scotland, and Ireland. Actors Jackie Gleason, Jack Nicholson, Jack Black; comedian Jack Benny; exercise guru Jack LaLanne.

Jackie, Jackman, Jacko, Jacky, Jacq, Jacqin, Jak, Jaq

Jackson OE. "Son of Jack." May indicate an ancestor's admiration for U.S. President Andrew Jackson or, in Southern families, Civil War General Stonewall Jackson. Possibly driven by **Jack**'s popularity (or the current fashion for *J*- names), Jackson is quite well used. Artist Jackson Pollock; singer Jackson Browne.

Jack, Jackie, Jacksen, Jacky, Jakson, Jaxen

Jacob Heb. "He who supplants." In the Old Testament, Jacob, Esau's brother, impersonates his brother at his blind father Isaac's deathbed by covering his hands with a goatskin ("for Esau was a hairy man"), securing the blessing meant for the elder son. His ten sons and two grandsons were the founders of the twelve tribes of Israel, the name Jacob himself received after wrestling with an angel. One of the top five names in the U.S. for several years, though most boys officially named Jacob will probably be called **Jake**. Senator Jacob Javits; actor Jake Gyllenhall.

Cob, Cobb, Cobby, Giacamo, Giacobo, Giacomo, Giacopo, Hamish, Iacopo, Iacovo, Iago, Iakob, Iakobos, Iakov, Jaco, Jacobo, Jacobi, Jacoby, Jack, Jackie, Jacko, Jacky, Jacques, Jacquet, Jago, Jaime, Jake, Jakie, Jakob, Jakov, Jakub, James, Jamesie, Jamey, Jamie, Jamsey, Jay, Jayme, Jim, Jimmie, Seamus, Shamus, Yakov

---

YIKES, IT'S A BOY!

Over and over again I've heard parents say that it's much harder to choose a name for a boy. With all the possibilities out there, why should this be true?

There are a couple of reasons. One is that parents choose more conservative boys' names. Fashions in girls' names change much faster, and parents are more likely to make an unusual selection for a girl baby. For instance Olivia, currently in the top ten, is a Latin name that was virtually unheard-of as recently as the mid-1990s. Meanwhile the top boy's name was Michael, for nearly forty years. It has only just been dislodged by Jacob—but only as far as the number two spot. So the pool of boy's names that people hear in daily life is probably smaller, and certainly less inventive.

What's more, that pool shrinks every time parents use what was a boy's name for a girl. Ashley, Leslie, Hilary, and Kelsey are a few formerly masculine names that are rapidly becoming feminine. And Taylor and Madison, once obscure last names occasionally used as first names for boys, are now wildly popular for girls. Once a name is perceived as feminine, it very rarely crosses back over to become a boy's name. No wonder parents of boys stick with the tried and true Michael, Matthew, and Daniel!

Jacques Fr. Var. **James** via **Jacob**. Familiar from the well-known song *Frère Jacques*. Undersea explorer Jacques Cousteau.
   Jacot, Jacque, Jaq, Jaques

Jade Sp. Jewel name, for the semiprecious green stone. Jewel names are commonly used for girls, but the brisk monosyllable of this name (and the fact that it has not been widely used) makes it an appealing choice for a boy.
   Jaide, Jayde

Jaden Modern invented name. Will Smith and Jada Pinkett have a son named Jaden, probably formed from **Jada**.

Something about the ever-popular "J-"sound and the two-syllable cadence (as well as the celebrity provenance?) has made other parents choose this name as well.

Jael Heb. "Mountain goat." Also used for girls, although rare in either case.
Yael

Jafar Arab. "Stream." It will be quite some time before Jafar loses its villainous connotations, courtesy of Disney's *Aladdin*.
Jaffar

Jagger OE. Occupational name. Possibly "One who cuts" as in jagged edges of cloth: also possibly a peddler. Modern parents who choose this name will no doubt be thinking of musician Mick Jagger instead, making this name incredibly cool instead of merely obscure.

Jago Variant of **Jacob** or **James**, similar to **Iago**.

Jahan Sanskrit. "The world."
Jehan

Jaime Sp. Var. **James**. Quite well used in the polyglot U.S.
Jaimey, Jaimie, Jayme, Jaymie

Jaimini Sanskrit. "Victory."

Jair Heb. "He enlightens." Jairus, in the New Testament, is the man whose daughter Jesus raised from the dead.

Jake Dim. **Jacob**. Used independently since the 1960s, and quite steadily chosen by today's parents.

Jaladhi Hindi. "Ocean."
Jaladi, Jeladhi, Jeladi

Jalal Arab. "Greatness, superiority, renown."
Jallal, Jalil, Jaliyl, Jelal, Jellal

Jalen Modern name, probably **Galen** (Gk. "Healer" or "Tranquil") with a *J*. Since there is no standard spelling for many of these modern names, phonetic spellings abound, each one more imaginative than the last.
Jaelan, Jaelin, Jaelon, Jailin, Jaillen, Jaillin, Jailon, Jalan Jalin, Jalon, Jayelan, Jayelen, Jaylan Jaylen, Jaylon, Jaylonn

Jamal Arab. "Handsome." Very popular in the U.S. among black or Muslim families. Jamaal, Jamahl, Jamall, Jamaul, Jameel, Jamel, Jamell, Jamil, Jamill, Jammal, Jemaal, Jemahl, Jemall, Jimal, Jimahl, Jomal, Jomahl, Jomall

Jamar Modern name, a variant of **Jamal**.

Jamarr, Jemar, Jemarr, Jimar, Jimarr

James English variant of **Jacob** (Heb. "He who supplants"). In the New Testament there are two apostles known as James, though the Old Testament version of the name is always **Jacob**. The apostles are known a bit unfairly as James the Greater and James the Less. The name was popularized by the Stuart kings James I and II, and has been a stable favorite ever since, especially in the British Isles. Like **John**, this is a tremendously popular old standby. Writer James Joyce; actors James Mason, James Caviezel, James Gandolfini, Jimmy Stewart; entertainer Jimmy Durante; five U.S. presidents: James Buchanan, James Garfield, James Madison, James Polk, Jimmy Carter.

Diego, Giacomo, Giamo, Hamish, Iago, Jacques, Jago, Jaime, Jaimes, Jaimey, Jaimie, Jameson, Jamesie, Jamesy, Jamey, Jamie, Jamison, Jaymes, Jaymie, Jaymz, Jim, Jimmie, Jimmy, Seamus, Seumas, Seumus, Shamus

Jameson OE. "Son of James."

Jaimison, Jamieson, Jamison

Jamie Dim. **James**. Traditionally mostly Scottish, but currently quite steadily used as an independent name. However, since it is very popular as a girl's name, this phenomenon may fade.

Jaime, Jaimie, Jamee, Jamey, Jayme

Jan Dutch. Var. **John** (Heb. "The Lord is gracious"). According to records maintained by the Social Security Administration, in 2001 Jan was the 483rd most popular name for boys. This is probably a testament to the polyglot nature of America; parents born abroad are unlikely to perceive this as a girl's name and probably even pronounce it with a "Y" rather than a "J." Painters Jan Van Eyck, Jan Vermeer.

Hans, Janek, Janos

Janesh Hindi. "Leader of the people."

Janson Scand. "Jan's son." Used as a first name only in the 20th century.
Jansen, Janssen, Jansson, Jantzen, Janzen, Jenson, Jensen

Janus Lat. "Gateway." Janus was the Roman guardian of doors as well as of beginnings and endings. He had two faces, one of which looked forward and the other backward, and gave his name to the first month of the year, January.
Gennadi, Gennaro, Janan, Janiusz, Januarius, Janusz, Jenaro, Jenarius, Jennaro

Japheth Heb. "He expands." Along with Ham and Shem, one of Noah's sons. Little used, except by the Puritans.

Jardine Fr. "Garden." The name of a significant financial concern based in Hong Kong.

Jareb Heb. "He will struggle."

Jared Heb. "He descends." Related to **Jordan**. Old Testament name used by the Puritans, and suddenly, inexplicably popular in the 1960s. Widely used now as well.
Jarad, Jarid, Jarod, Jarrad, Jarrard, Jarred, Jarrid, Jarrod, Jerad, Jerod, Jerrad, Jerred, Jerrod

Jarek Slavic. Dim. of the many Slavic names that begin with "Jaro-," a word particle that means "spring."

Jarlath Ir. Gael. Ancient name of unclear origin.
Jarleath, Jarlaith

Jarman OG. "German." Film director Derek Jarman.
Jarmann, Jerman

Jaromir Slav. "Famous spring." Hockey player Jaromir Jagr.

Jaron Modern name. Possibly Darren with the fashionable initial *J*. Invented names are chosen for their sound and for their novelty; their source doesn't really matter at all.
Jaran, Jaren, Jarin, Jarran, Jarren, Jarrin, Jarron

Jaroslav Slavic. "Beauty of spring." A popular name in Czechoslovakia. Historian Jaroslav Pelikan.
Jarek, Jaroslaw

Jarrell Var. **Gerald** (OG. "Spear ruler"). Poet Randall Jarrell.
Jarrall

Jarrett Var. **Garrett** (OE. "Spear-brave").

Jarett, Jarret, Jarrot, Jarrott, Jerrett, Jerrot, Jerrott

Jarvis Var. **Gervase** (OG. Meaning unclear: possibly "With honor"). This version is used much more often than the somewhat effete-seeming source. Musician Jarvis Cocker.

Jarvey, Jary, Jervey, Jervis

Jascha Slavic Var. **James** (Heb. "He who supplants"). Violinist Jascha Heifetz.

Jasha

Jason Heb. "The Lord is salvation." The name is actually a variation of **Joshua**, formed by biblical translators. Jason was a legendary Greek hero who, after many adventures, recovered the Golden Fleece from an enemy kingdom. The name was phenomenally popular in the 1970s after centuries of sporadic use, and is still very well used, as its variety of phonetic variations attests. Now on the wane. Actors Jason Robards, Jason Lee, Jason Priestley, Jason Patric, Jason Biggs.

Jace, Jacen, Jaisen, Jaison, Jase, Jasen, Jasin, Jasun, Jay, Jayce, Jaysen, Jayson

Jasper Eng. Var. **Caspar**. Possibly Persian "He who guards the treasure." Jasper is also a strikingly colorful variety of quartz. Painter Jasper Johns.

Gaspar, Gasper, Jaspar, Jesper

Javier Sp. Var. **Xavier**. Meaning obscure, but refers to Saint Francis Xavier.

Havier, Haviero, Javi, Javiero

Jay Lat. "Jaybird." A medieval name that has survived especially in the U.S., where it is given to boys and girls alike. Its use may be inspired by the first Chief Justice of the U.S. Supreme Court, John Jay. Financier Jay Gould; comedian Jay Leno; author Jay McInerney; actors Jaye Davidson, Jay Mohr.

Jae, Jaye, Jeh

Jazz Improvisational modern music. The origin of the word is unknown, and it is only occasionally adopted as a proper name.

Jean Fr. Var. **John** (Heb. "The Lord is gracious"). In France it is frequently combined with other names, as in Jean-Claude, Jean-Paul, Jean-Philippe. Author and artist Jean Cocteau; playwright Jean Molière; author Jean-Paul Sartre; actor Jean-Claude Van Damme.

Jeb Nickname of dashing Confederate general James Ewell Brown Stuart. He was a wily commander of the cavalry, and died during the war. The name is occasionally carried on in a Southern family. Politician Jeb Bush.

Jed Dim. **Jedidiah**. Lent a certain rustic aura by Jed Clampitt, a character on the popular 1960s TV show *The Beverly Hillbillies*.
Jedd, Jedediah

Jedidiah Heb. "Beloved of the Lord." Old Testament name that was used by the Puritans in the 17th century.
Jedd, Jedediah

Jeff Dim. **Jefferson, Jeffrey**. Used as an independent name in this century. Actors Jeff Daniels, Jeff Goldblum, Jeff Bridges.

Jefferson OE. "Son of Jeffrey." Surname used as a first name. A sterling example of this use is president of the Confederacy Jefferson Davis, who was born in 1808, during the presidency of Thomas Jefferson.
Jeff, Jeffers, Jeffersson, Jeffey, Jeffie

Jeffrey OG. Meaning unclear, but refers to "peace." Norman name popular through the Middle Ages in Britain and revived in the mid-19th century after a 350-year rest. The peak of its popularity was the 1970s in the U.S., with this form preferred to **Geoffrey**. Still steadily used, however. Race-car driver Jeff Gordon.
Geoff, Geoffrey, Geoffroi, Geoffroy, Geoffry, Geofrey, Geofry, Godfrey, Godfry, Gottfried, Jefery, Jeff, Jefferey, Jefferies, Jeffery, Jeffree, Jeffries, Jeffry, Jeffy, Jefry, Jeoffroi, Joffre, Joffrey

Jehoiakim Heb. "God will judge." A longer version of **Joachim**.
Akim, Jehoioachim, Jehoiakin, Joachim, Joachim, Joaquin, Josquin, Yachim, Yakim

Jehu Heb. "He is God."

Jem Dim. **James** or **Jeremiah**. Rare as nickname or independent name.

Jenkin Flemish. "Little John." A name as popular and well used as **John** has naturally produced numerous last names as well, some of which find their way back to first-name status.
Jenkins, Jenkyn, Jenkyns, Jennings

Jens Scand. Var. **John**.
Jensen, Jenson, Jensson

Jeremiah Heb. "The Lord exalts." Old Testament prophet who lived in Jerusalem when it fell to the Babylonians. The Book of Jeremiah is so relentlessly gloomy in outlook that "jeremiad" has become the term for a lengthy denunciatory complaint. The Puritans used Jeremiah somewhat, but **Jeremy** has eclipsed it in modern times.
Dermot, Dermott, Diarmid, Geremia, Jem, Jemmie, Jereme, Jeremia, Jeremias, Jeremija, Jeremiya, Jeremy, Jermyn, Jerry, Yeremia, Yeremiya, Yeremiyah

Jeremy Modern form of **Jeremiah**. One source suggests that the modern penchant for Jeremy was sparked by a 1960s TV series called *Here Come the Brides*. This may be true, since the Jeremy on the show had brothers named **Jason** and **Joshua**, names that were simultaneously fashionable. The vogue for Jeremy and **Jason** is fading, though Joshua remains is one of the top names in the U.S. Actor Jeremy Irons; football player Jeremy Shockey.
Jem, Jemmie, Jemmy, Jeramee, Jeramey, Jeramie, Jere, Jereme, Jeremie, Jeromy, Jerry

Jericho Biblical place name: one of the oldest cities in Palestine, and the first one that Joshua conquered when he brought the Israelites back into the promised land. An old spiritual relates how "Joshua fit the battle of Jericho. . . . and the walls came tumbling down." Though not historically a proper name, Jericho has the familiar *Jer-* particle and the trendy "-o" ending that may bring it to popularity.
Jerico, Jericko, Jerrico, Jherico

Jerick Modern name: **Derek** (OG. "The people's ruler") with a *J.* Six of the top twenty boy's names through the 1990s began with *J,* and many parents like to update names by substituting the fashionable *J* for a different initial consonant.

Jerack, Jereck, Jerek, Jerrick, Jerrik, Jerriq

Jermaine Var. **Jarman** (OG. "German") or **Germain** (Fr. "From Germany"). Made famous by Michael Jackson's older brother, Jermaine. Basketball player Jermaine O'Neal.

Germain, Germaine, Jermane, Jermin, Jermyn

Jeroboam Old Testament name: a king of the Israelites who permitted the worship of idols. Because he was a big man, a very large bottle of champagne is known as a jeroboam.

Jerome Gk. "Sacred name." The 5th-century Saint Jerome was responsible for a Latin translation of the Bible. He is often portrayed with a lion, from the legend that he removed a thorn from the lion's pad and the beast rewarded him with lifelong fidelity. The name has been best used in the 16th and 19th centuries. Songwriter Jerome Kern; choreographer Jerome Robbins; football player Jerome Bettis.

Gerome, Geronimo, Gerrie, Gerry, Hierome, Hieronim, Hieronimo, Hieronimos, Hieronimus, Hieronymos, Hieronymus, Jairo, Jairome, Jeroen, Jeromo, Jeronimo, Jerrome, Jerron, Jerrone, Jerry

Jerrell Modern name: probably a variant of **Gerald**, perhaps influenced by Darrell.

Gerall, Gerrall, Jerall, Jerel, Jeril, Jeroll, Jerrill, Jerroll, Jerryll

Jerry Dim. **Jeremy, Gerald,** etc. Scarce as a given name. Actor Jerry Orbach.

Gerrey, Gerry, Jerre, Jerrey, Jerrie

Jerzy Pol. Var. **George** (Gk. "Farmer"). Writer Jerzy Kozinski.

Jesimiel Heb. "The Lord establishes."

Jessimiel

Jessamine English var. **Jesse**. Very unusual, and likely,

these days, to be confused with the fashionable girl's name **Jasmine**. Author Jessamyn West.
Jessamyn

Jesse Heb. "The Lord exists." The biblical father of King David. In America the formidable athlete Jesse Owens (whose success at the 1936 Olympics chagrined the Nazis) has given the name great resonance for black families; the fame of politician Jesse Jackson may continue to do so. Outlaw Jesse James.
Jess, Jessie, Yishai

Jesus Heb. "The Lord is salvation." Used mostly by families of Latin American origin, but **Joshua**, from the same Hebrew derivation, is tremendously popular across the U.S.
Jesous

Jethro Heb. "Preeminence." Old Testament name that occurred from time to time until the late 19th century. A flicker of modern use may have been inspired by the rock group Jethro Tull.
Jeth, Jethroe

Jett Mineral name: jet is a shiny black substance used for making jewelry. Jette is a girl's name in Scandinavia. In the U.S. this name is more likely to conjure up aircraft.
Jette

Jevon Modern name. Possibly Devon with a *J,* though the accent is sometimes placed on the last syllable. Football player Jevon Kearse.
Jeavan, Jeaven, Jeavin, Jevan, Jeven, Jevin, Jevvan, Jevven, Jevvin, Jevvyn

Jim Dim. **James** (Heb. "He who supplants"). Used occasionally as an independent name. Actors Jim Broadbent, Jim Carrey.
Jimi, Jimmee, Jimmey, Jimmie, Jimmy, Jimson

Jivan Hindi. "Life."

Joab Heb. "Praise Jehovah."

Joachim Heb. "God will judge." Composer Josquin Des Pres; actor Joaquin Phoenix.
Akim, Ioakim, Jachim, Jakim, Joacheim, Joaquim, Joaquin, Josquin, Yachim, Yakim

Joash Heb. "Given by the Lord."

Job Heb. "The afflicted." In the Old Testament, the Book of Job recounts the trials of an innocent man who was sorely tried by his God but remained faithful: hence "the patience of Job." Revived by the Puritans and used fairly steadily since the 17th century.

Joab, Jobe

Jock Familiar var. **Jacob** (Heb. "He who supplants") or **John** (Heb. "The Lord is gracious"). A slang term for a Scotsman, probably because the local accent turns **Jack** into Jock. Not actually used in Scotland, and in the U.S. avoided because it is a slightly derogatory term for an athlete. Sportsman Jock Whitney.

Jocko

Jody Familiar var. **Joseph** (Heb. "Jehovah increases"). In Marjorie Kinnan Rawlings' Pulitzer Prize-winning novel *The Yearling,* the young hero is called Jody, but the name is more likely to be used for a girl.

Jodey, Jodi, Jodie

Joe Dim. **Joseph**. Sometimes given as an independent name. Baseball player Joe diMaggio; boxer Joe Louis; hockey player Joe Thornton.

Joel Heb. "Jehovah is the Lord." Along with **Amos**, the most common of the Old Testament prophets' names, though **Hosea** also occurs. Joel is currently very popular in Spain. For some reason the parents of the late 20th century who have scoured the Old Testament for names have had a strong predilection for those beginning with *J.* Actors Joel McCrea, Joel Grey.

Yoel

Joffrey Var. **Jeffrey** (OG. meaning unclear).

Jophrey

Johar Hindi. "Jewel."

John Heb. "The Lord is gracious." Given a sound foundation by two crucial saints, John the Baptist and John the Evangelist. (There are another thirty-odd significant saints named John.) The name has been used by 25 popes, an English king, and endless numbers of parents all over the world. In the English-speaking countries it was the most popular boy's name for over 400 years, losing ground only in the 1950s. Now some of its variants, like **Ian** and **Sean**, are gaining. Almost every country that was dominantly Christian has a version of the name, some of which—**Hans, Giovanni**, or **Evan**, for instance—barely resemble this English form. Actors John Gielgud, John Barrymore, John Wayne, John Cusack, John Leguizamo, Johnny Depp; four U.S. presidents: John F. Kennedy, John Tyler, John Adams, John Quincy Adams; poet John Donne; Beatle John Lennon; composer Johannes Bach; football player John Elway; lawyer Johnnie Cochrane.

Anno, Ean, Eian, Eion, Euan, Evan, Ewan, Ewen, Gian, Giannes, Gianni, Giannis; Giannos, Giovanni, Hannes, Hanno, Hans, Hanschen, Hansel, Hansl, Iain, Ian, Ioannes, Ioannis, Ivan, Ivann, Iwan, Jack, Jackie, Jacky, Jan, Jancsi, Janek, Janko, Janne, Janos, Jean, Jeanno, Jeannot, Jehan, Jenkin, Jenkins, Jens, Jian, Jianni, Joannes, Joao, Jock, Jocko, Johan, Johanan, Johann, Johannes, Johon, Johnie, Johnnie, Johnny, Jon, Jona, Jonnie, Jovan, Jovanney, Jovanni, Jovonni, Juan, Juanito, Juwan, Sean, Seann, Shane, Shaughn, Shaun, Shawn, Vanek, Vanko, Vanya, Yanni, Yanno, Zane

Johnson OE. "Son of John." Mostly 19th-century use. Playwright Ben Jonson; track star Michael Johnson; President Lyndon B. Johnson.

Jonson, Johnston

Jolyon Var. **Julian** (Lat. "Young"). Jolyon Forsyte is a major character in John Galsworthy's series of novels, *The Forsyte Saga*.

Jonas Gk. var. **Jonah** (Heb. "Dove"). Jonah is the biblical hero who was swallowed alive by a whale, in whose belly he lived for three days. He had been thrown overboard by sailors from the ship he was traveling on in order to calm a stormy sea; by extension, the term "Jonah" means someone who brings bad luck. The name, nevertheless, has been used with some frequency, though never immense popularity. Medical pioneer Jonas Salk.

Jonah, Jonaso

Jonathan Heb. "Gift of Jehovah." Related to **Nathan**, rather than to **John**, though the alternate **Johnathan** spelling clouds this issue. In the Old Testament, the great friend of King David. Used in the 17th century, then neglected from the 18th until the 1940s. Some of its current extensive use probably comes about because it resembles John. Today's parents seem a bit reluctant to give a child a name of just one syllable, so Jonathan may be used instead. English author Jonathan Swift; actors Jon Voight, Jonathan Lipnicki.

Johnathan, Johnathon, Jon, Jonathon

Jones Surname derived from John. Particularly popular in Wales.

Jordan Heb. "Descend." Named after the River Jordan. First used in the Middle Ages by Crusaders returning from the Holy Land. Revived slightly in the 19th century. Unusual in that it is quite popular for both boys and girls. Male use has the edge at the moment. Possibly the fame of basketball star Michael Jordan, and Nike's extensive line of Air Jordan athletic shoes, maintains the perception that this is a masculine name.

Giordano, Jared, Jarred, Jarod, Jarrod, Jarrot, Jarrott, Jerad, Jerred, Jerrod, Jerrot, Jerrott, Jordaan, Jordao, Jordon, Jori, Jory, Jourdain, Jourdan, Jud, Judd

Jorge Sp. Var. **George** (Gk. "Farmer"). Baseball player Jorge Posada.

Jorgen Dan. Var. **George** (Gk. "Farmer").

Jeorg, Jerzy, Jorg, Jori, Joris, Jurgen, Juri

Jory Dim. **Jordan**.

Jorey, Jorie

José Sp. Var. **Joseph**. The most popular of the Latino names in the U.S. Baseball player José Canseco; opera singer José Carreras.

Joseito, Pepe, Pepito

Joseph Heb. "Jehovah increases." Name that occurs for principal figures in both the Old and the New Testaments of the Bible. It has been less widely used than **John** and has fewer international variants, probably because of the relative prominence of these figures. The Old Testament Joseph, though significant, was not a saint. For hundreds of years, Catholic parents named their children exclusively after saints, and the two Biblical Johns (as well as dozens of St. Johns) were far more important than the New Testament Saint Joseph, whose role in Jesus' life is small. Currently a top-ten name in England. Actors Josef Sommer, Joseph Fiennes; writers Joseph Conrad, Joseph Wambaugh; revolutionary Che Guevara; painter Joseph M.W. Turner.

Che, Giuseppe, Giuseppino, Iosep, Iosef, Iosif, Iosip, Jessop, Jessup, Jo, Jodi, Jodie, Jody, Joey, Joop, Joos, Jose, Josef, Joseito, Josep, Josip, Josif, Josephe, Josephus, Joss, Josue, Joszef, Jozef, Osip, Pepe, Pepito, Peppi, Pino, Pipo, Sepp, Seppi, Yousef, Yusif, Yussuf, Yusuf, Yusup, Yuszef

Joshua Heb. "The Lord is salvation." An Old Testament hero, Moses' successor. Passed over by the Puritans, revived somewhat in the 18th century, and currently immensely fashionable in the U.S. and Britain alike. It may be cherished by parents precisely because it has no history, and therefore no connotations, positive or negative. Painter Joshua Reynolds; director Joshua Logan; actors Josh Lucas, Josh Hartnett.

Josh, Joshuah, Josua, Josue, Joushua, Jozua, Yehoshua

Josiah Heb. "The Lord supports." An Old Testament king of Judah. Most common in the 18th century, now rather rare. Why is **Joshua** one of the top five names in the U.S. while **Josiah**, so apparently similar, is rare? Ask a parent with a son named **Josh**. Porcelain entrepreneur Josiah Wedgwood.

Josia, Josias

Joss English name that may be a variant of **Joseph** or a surviving morsel of **Jocelyn**, which was a masculine name until early in this century. Actor Joss Ackland.

Joslin, Josslin

Jotham Heb. "The Lord is upright." Old Testament name.

Jove Roman mythology name: the Roman name for the sky god whom the Greeks knew as Zeus. He was also called Jupiter.

Joyner OE. Occupational name: "Carpenter."
Joiner

Juan Sp. Var. **John** (Heb. "The Lord is gracious"). Basketball player Juwan Howard; baseball player Juan Gonzales; King Juan Carlos of Spain.
Juwan

Jubal Heb. Meaning uncertain, though it may come from the Hebrew term for a ram's horn, like the word Jubilee. Jubal is said to have invented musical instruments. Confederate general Jubal Early.

Judah Heb. "Praise." In the Old Testament Judah is the ancestor of one of the Twelve Tribes of Israel. **Jude** is the more common form.
Jud, Judas, Judd, Jude

Judd Variant of **Jordan** (Heb. "Descending"), used as a last name and transferred to first name use. Given exposure by two actors, Judd Hirsh and Judd Nelson.
Jud

Jude Lat. Var. **Judah**. Very unusual, probably because of the traitorous apostle Judas Iscariot. There was, however, another apostle named Jude who now enjoys some popularity as the patron saint of lost causes. The literary-minded will associate this name with Thomas Hardy's novel *Jude the Obscure*. Actor Jude Law.
Jud, Judah, Judas, Judd, Judsen, Judson

Jules Fr. Var. **Julius**. Author Jules Verne; playwright Jules Feiffer.

Julian Lat. Var. **Julius**. First took hold in the 18th century, and became fashionable in the 1950s through 1970s. The French form, **Julien**, is currently popular in France. Steadily used today. Musician Julian Lennon; activist Julian Bond.
Jolyon, Julyan, Julianus, Julien

Julius Lat. Clan name: "Youthful." Common in Christian Rome and revived in the 19th century. This form and the

---

THE LETTER J

Names starting with *J-* have been stylish for boys for the last 25 years. The trend began when Jason appeared on the charts in 1970, joining perennials John, James, Joseph, and Jeffrey. By 1980, Jason was extremely fashionable. Joshua and Justin, apparently riding on its coattails, were on some top-ten lists. By 1990 Jason had skidded, Joshua was hot, and Jonathan and Jacob were starting to climb. In 2002, Jacob, Joseph, and Joshua were three of the ten most popular boys' names in the United States, keeping that *J-* fashion going.

Spanish form, **Julio**, are used about the same amount. Singers Julio Iglesias, Julius La Rosa; basketball player Julius Erving.
Giulio, Jolyon, Jule, Jules, Julio

July Dim. **Julius**. Or possibly the month name. If it's pronounced like the month, it is less likely to be taken for the girl's name **Julie**.
Julee, Juley, Juli

Juniper Plant name: evergreen shrub with berries from which gin (known as *genever* in Dutch) is traditionally distilled.

Junius Lat. "Young." Rare. Financier Junius Spencer Morgan; football coach June Jones; author Junot Diaz.
June, Juneau, Junio, Junot

Jupiter Roman mythology name: the sky god, supreme Roman deity, corresponding to the Greek god Zeus. Lightning bolts were thought to be messages from Jupiter to mortals on earth.
Juppiter

Jurgen Scand. Var. **George** (Gk. "Farmer"). Well used in Germany. Photographer Jurgen Teller; actor Jurgen Prochnow.
Jorgen

Juri Slavic. Var. **George** (Gk. "Farmer").

Jaris, Yuri

Justin Lat. "Fair, righteous." Another name well used by Roman Christians, but unusual elsewhere until very recently. It is now extremely fashionable, right up there with **Joshua**, **James**, and **John**. Actor Justin Henry; singer Justin Timberlake.

Giustino, Giusto, Joos, Joost, Just, Juste, Justen, Justinas, Justinian, Justinius, Justino, Justinus, Justis, Justo, Justus, Justyn

Juvenal Lat. "Young." The name of a Roman satiric poet of the 1st century A.D.

Kaden Modern name, probably formed in response to the popularity of **Kayla**, **Kaitlin**, etc. for girls. The "-en" ending is perceived as masculine (**Damien, Julien**) in the way that "-ie" endings are considered feminine. Though meanings are almost irrelevant when it comes to a name like this, parents could extract an Old German refence to a swamp or an Old English word meaning "round" from Kaden.

Caden, Caidan, Caiden, Caidin, Caidon, Caydan, Cayden, Caydin, Caydon, Kadan, Kadin, Kadon, Kaidan, Kaiden, Kaidin, Kaidon, Kaydan, Kayden, Kaydin, Kaydon

Kadir Arab. "Capable, competent." As Al-Qadir, this is one of the 99 attributes of Allah.

Kadeer, Qadeer, Qadir

Kadmiel Heb. "Who stands before God." Old Testament name.

Kahn Heb. from Ger. "Priest."

Kai Possibly variant spelling of **Kay**: some sources suggest South African, "Beautiful."

Keh, Kye

Kaiser Var. **Caesar** (Lat. Possibly "hairy"). The connotations, of course, are of imperial rule, as in Germany's Kaiser Wilhelm.

Kaleb Heb. "Dog." Anglicized as Caleb. Old Testament name.

Caleb

Kalil Arab. "Friend." Writer Kahlil Gibran.

Kahil, Kahleel, Kahlil, Kaleel, Khaleel, Khalil

Kalogeros Gk. "Lovely old age." A concept to be wished for, but an unwieldy name for a small child.

Kamal Arab. "Perfection, perfect."

Kameel, Kamil

Kane Welsh. "Beautiful" or Ir. Gael. "Warrior's son." Surname transferred occasionally to first name in this century.

Cahan, Cahane, Cain, Kahan, Kahane, Kain, Kaine, Kayne, Keane

Kaniel Heb. "The Lord supports me."

Kari ONorse. "Puff of wind" or "Curly hair." Mythology name, but also long used as an attribute name for someone with curls.

Kareem Arab. "Highborn, generous." This is the name of the current Aga Khan. Basketball star Kareem Abdul-Jabbar.

Karam, Karim

Karl OG. "Man." Var. **Charles**. The Germanic form of the name; as **Carl**, it was fairly well used in the U.S. 1850–1950. *K* spellings are not as readily adopted for boys' names as they are for girls'. Fashion designers Karl Lagerfeld, Karl Kani; economist Karl Marx; basketball player Karl Malone.

Carl, Kale, Karel, Karlan, Karlens, Karli, Karrel, Karol, Karoly

Karmel Heb. "Garden." Biblical place name: Mt. Carmel is in Israel, and is often referred to in ancient writings as a kind of paradise. This name is most often seen as **Carmelo** in the U.S.

Carmel, Carmeli, Carmelo, Karmeli, Karmelli, Karmelo, Karmello, Karmi

Karr Var. **Carr** (Scand. "From the swampy place").

Kasi Sanskrit. "Shining." Also possibly a respelling of **Casey**, which used to be primarily a boy's name.
Kasee, Kasey, Kasie

Kaspar Var. **Caspar** (Possibly Per. "He who guards the treasure"). Originally **Jasper**. Traditionally one of the Three Kings (perhaps the one carrying the gold) was named **Caspar**.
Kasper

Katzir Heb. "Harvesting."
Katzeer

Kauai Hawaiian place name: the "Garden Island," considered by some to be the most beautiful in the Hawaiian archipelago.
Kawai

Kaufman Ger. "Merchant." Comedian Andy Kaufman.
Kaufmann

Kavan Ir. Gael. "Handsome."
Cavan, Kayvan, Kayven

Kavanagh Ir. Gael. "Follower of Kevin." Principally an Irish surname.
Cavanagh, Cavanaugh, Kavanaugh

Kay Old Welsh. "Rejoicing." Ancient name borne, in legend, by one of the knights of the Round Table. Now all but obliterated as a male name by the women's name **Kay**, which is a diminutive of **Katherine**.
Kai, Keh

Kazimierz Var. **Casimir** (Slavic. "Bringing peace"). Associated with Poland for her famous 11th-century king who brought peace to the nation.
Kaz, Kazimir, Kazmer

Keane OE. "Sharp." As in a "keen wit" or a "keen eye." Actor Edmund Kean.
Kean, Keen, Keene

Kearney Var. **Carney** (Ir. Gael. "The winner").
Karney, Karny, Kearny

Keaton English place name, meaning unknown. Used as a first name in the U.S. in recent years. May be influenced by actors Michael Keaton and Buster Keaton.

Keats English last name: meaning unknown. John Keats was one of the great English romantic poets, who, despite his death at the age of 26, left a large body of unmatched verse.

Kedar Arab. "Powerful."
   Kadar, Keder

Keefe Ir. Gael. "Handsome; lovable, loved." Actor Michael Keefe.
   Keeffe

Keegan Ir. Gael. "Small and ardent." Historian John Keegan.
   Keagan, Keagen, Keegen, Keeghan, Kegan

Keelan Ir. Gael. "Small and slim."
   Kealan, Keallan, Keallin, Keilan, Keillan, Kelan

Keeley Ir. Gael. "Handsome." Also possibly a variant of **Kelly** (Ir. Gael. "Eager for battle").
   Kealey, Kealy, Keelie, Keely

Keenan Ir. Gael. "Small and ancient." Two actors, Keenan Ivory Wayans and Keenan Wynn, have brought this name to the attention of the public, and it is the most common of these Irish names (with the exception of **Keith** and **Kevin**). Football player Keenan McCardell.
   Keen, Keenen, Kienan, Kienen

Kefir Heb. "Young lion."

Keir Gael. "Dark-skinned, swarthy." Actor Keir Dullea.

Keith Scot. Gael. "Forest." Originally a place name, adopted as a first name for non-Scots in the 19th century. Peaked in the 1960s in the U.S., but still fairly steadily used. Baseball player Keith Hernandez; Rolling Stone Keith Richard; actor Keith Carradine.

Kelby ONorse. Place name: "The farm near the spring."
   Kelbey, Kelbie, Kellby

Kell ONorse. Place name: "Spring."

Kellagh Ir. Gael. "Battle, strife, warfare."
   Kellach

Kellen May be related to **Kell**, or to an Old German word that means "swamp."
   Kellan, Kellin

Keller Possibly Ir. Gael. "Dear friend" or OG. "Cellar-keeper," which probably referred to someone whose cellar was stored with ales or wines.

Kelly Ir. Gael. "Warrior." Originally a very common Irish last name, and very popular as a girl's first name from the 1950s. Use for boy babies has diminished accordingly. TV producer David Kelley.
Kelley, Kellie

Kelsey OE. Place name, incorporating a word particle that means "island." Until ten years ago this was a boy's name, but by 1995, it was one of the top twenty girl's names in the U.S., often with the more "feminine" spelling of **Kelsie** or **Kelcie.** Actor Kelsey Grammer.
Kelsie, Kelsy

Kelton OE. Place name: "Town of the keels." Probably originally referred to a town where ships were built.
Keldon, Kelltin, Kellton, Kelten, Keltin, Keltonn

Kelvin Meaning and origin unclear: possibly OE. "Keel friend" (keel, in this case, standing in for ship) or a place name alluding to a river. Brief spurt of use in the 1920s was mostly British, but there has been a recent resurgence in America.
Kelvan, Kelven, Kellven, Kelvon, Kelvyn, Kelwin, Kelwinn, Kelwyn

Kelvis Modern name: Elvis with the popular "K-" initial consonant.
Kellvis, Kelviss, Kelvys

Kemp ME. "Fighter, champion." Basketball player Shawn Kemp.

Kempton ME. Place name: "From the warrior's settlement."

Kemuel Heb. "Helper of God." Considered as **Samuel** with a consonant shift, the name has potential for popularity, though most of currently the hot "K-" names seem to be based on Gaelic sources.

Ken Dim. **Kenneth** and other "Ken-" names. Used independently, but parents who played with Barbie dolls may be hard put to name a baby after Barbie's boyfriend Ken. Baseball player Ken Griffey, Jr.; singers Kenny Rogers, Kenny Loggins; saxophone player Kenny G; writer Ken Kesey.
Kenney, Kennie, Kenny

Kendall OE. Place name: "The valley of the Kent," a river

in western England. Some sources also suggest "the bright river valley." In either case, a transferred surname used as a first name since the 19th century. There is a real vogue for "Ke-" names and **Kendall, Kelvin, Kendrick, Keaton, Keegan,** and the like are surprisingly well used.
Kendal, Kendel, Kendell, Kendill, Kendle, Kendyl, Kendyll, Kenny

Kendrick OE. "Royal ruler." Revived as a first name in the 19th century, and benefitting from the fashion for "Ke-" names. It is the sound, rather than the meaning, that makes these names popular.
Kendricks, Kendrik, Kendryck, Kenric, Kenrick, Kenricks, Kenricks, Kenrik

Kenelm OE. "Brave helmet." The name of a 9th-century king of Mercia (one of the kingdoms that predated a united England) who was later canonized.
Kenhelm, Kennelm

Kenley OE. Place name: "The king's meadow."
Kenlea, Kenlee, Kenleigh, Kenlie, Kenly

Kenn Welsh. "Bright water." Also a variant of **Kenneth**.

Kennard OE. "Brave and strong."
Kennaird

Kennedy Ir. Gael. Some sources suggest "Helmet/head," while "Ugly/head" is also offered, which would make this one of the rare names to refer to negative characteristics or habits possessed by ancestors. Use of Kennedy as a first name may be inspired by President John F. Kennedy. In that case "ugly/head" seems inaccurate. Violinist Nigel Kennedy.
Canaday, Canady, Kennedey

Kenneth Ir. Gael. "Handsome" or "Sprung from fire." Originally a favorite Scottish name that spread starting in the late 19th century. Very popular in the U.S. in the 1950s and 1960s, and one of the most widely used of the "Ke-" names. Art historian Kenneth Clark; actor Kenneth Branagh.
Ken, Kennet, Kennett, Kennith, Kenny

Kent OE. Place name: a county in England. Familiar as a

surname, and used in the U.S. as a first name. In the 1930s and 1940s monosyllabic names (**Clark, Burt, Kirk**) seemed to project a manly aura and enjoyed a consequent burst of popularity. Football player Kent Graham; artist Rockwell Kent.

Kennt, Kentt

Kenton OE. Place name: "The royal settlement." In use as a first name since the 1950s.

Kentan, Kentin, Kenton

Kenward OE. "Brave or royal guardian."

Kenway OE. "Brave or royal fighter."

Kenyatta Used in recognition of Jomo Kenyatta, first president of Kenya as an independent country.

Kenyon Ir. Gael. "Blond."

Keon Modern name, possibly related to the girl's name **Kiana**, or an adaptation of the popular **Deon**.

Keion, Keioni, Keyawn, Keyon, Kion, Kiohn, Kionn

Kepler Ger. "Hatter, cap maker." Astronomer Johannes Kepler.

Kappler, Keppel, Keppeler, Keppler

Kerem Heb. "Vineyard."

Kermit Ir. Gael. "Without envy." A variant of **Dermot**, made famous (and virtually unusable) by the popular green Muppet Kermit the Frog.

Kern Ir. Gael. "Small swarthy one." Kern was also a term, used especially in Scotland or Ireland, for a lightly armed footsoldier.

Curran, Kearn, Kearne, Kearns

Kernaghan Ir. Gael. "Victorious."

Carnahan, Kernohan

Kerr Scand. Place name: "The swampy place." Used basically in Scotland as a first name.

Carr, Karr

Kerry Irish place name: Kerry is a county in southwestern Ireland. Also, according to some sources, "dark-haired." Used more often for girls. Football player Kerry Collins; basketball player Kerry Kittles.

Kearie, Keary, Kerrey, Kerrie

Kerwin Possibly OE. "Swamp friend" or Ir. Gael. "Little dark one."

Kervin, Kervyn, Kerwinn, Kirwan, Kirwen

Keshet Heb. "Rainbow."

Kester Gaelic diminutive of **Christopher** (Gk. "Bearing Christ").

Kettil Swed. "Cauldron." Huge kettles for sacrifices played a part in the old Scandinavian religion.

Keld, Kjeld, Ketil, Ketti

Kevin Ir. Gael. "Handsome" (a meaning that certainly applies to two famous Kevins, actors Kline and Costner). Originally an Irish name that spread to wider use in the 20th century. Most popular in the 1960s, but still fairly standard. Makeup artist Kevyn Aucoin; basketball player Kevin Garnett.

Kevan, Keven, Kevon, Kevyn

Keyes OE. Probably an occupational name having to do with possession of keys. In the Middle Ages, locks would have been quite novel, and the man in charge of their keys would bear quite a responsibility. Francis Scott Key, author of *The Star-Spangled Banner.*

Key, Keys

Keyshawn Modern name combining two popular elements, Shawn and the voguish "Ke-" particle. Football player Keyshawn Johnson has given this name exposure.

Khadim Arab. "Servant." Used in the U.S. as **Kadeem**.

Kadeem, Kadeen, Khadeem, Khadim

Khalid Arab. "Never-ending."

Khalil Arab. "Friend." See **Kalil**.

Kibo African place name: the highest summit in Africa, atop Mt. Kilimanjaro. The peak is at 19,710 feet.

Kieran Ir. Gael. "Dark, swarthy." Becoming popular in Ireland, and showing some signs of spreading further afield. Actor Kieran Culkin.

Ciaran, Keiran, Keiron, Kernan, Kieren, Kiernan, Kieron, Kierren, Kierrin, Kierron

Kidd Middle English. "Kid, young goat." Probably an occupational name, possibly indicating an ancestor who kept goats. Pirate Captain William Kidd.

Kidder

Kiefer Ger. "Barrel maker." Actor Kiefer Sutherland; painter Anselm Kiefer.

Keefer, Kieffer, Kiefner, Kieffner, Kiefert, Kuefer, Kueffner

Killian Ir. Gael. "Small and fierce." From the same root as **Kelly**. Mysteriously enough, this name is currently very popular in France.

Kilean, Kilian, Killean

Kim Dim. "Kim-" names like Kimball and Kimberly. Also the title of a famous Kipling novel, but the days when children were named for Kipling characters is long since past, and Kim is almost always a girl's name now.

Kimball OE. "Bold war-leader."

Kimbal, Kimbel, Kimbell, Kimble

Kimberly OE. Place name: The "-ly" suffix indicates a meadow. *The Facts on File Dictionary of First Names* traces the masculine use of the name to the Boer War, when many English soldiers were fighting in the South African town of Kimberley. It has been virtually taken over by girls, however, and was a great favorite in the 1960s.

Kim, Kimbo, Kimberleigh, Kimberlev

Kincaid Celt. "Battle leader." Artist Thomas Kinkade.

Kinkade

King OE. "King." A last name since the Middle Ages. Modern use may be homage to Martin Luther King.

Kingman OE. "King's man." U.S. Ambassador Kingman Brewster.

Kingsley OE. Place name: "King's meadow." Surname transferred to first name, particularly in Britain. Novelist Kingsley Amis; actor Ben Kingsley.

Kingslea, Kingslie, Kingsly, Kinsey, Kinslea, Kinslee, Kinsley, Kinslie, Kinsly

Kingston OE. Place name: "King's settlement."

Kingswell OE. Place name: "King's well."

Kinnard Ir. Gael. Place name: "The tall hill."
  Kinnaird
Kinnell Ir. Gael. Place name: "Top of the cliff."
Kipling Origin unclear. Possibly related to **Kipp**: may even mean "small pointed hill." Usage is likely to reflect admiration for the great English poet and storyteller Rudyard Kipling, who gave the world *Kim, The Jungle Book,* and the *Just So Stories.*
  Kippling
Kipp OE. Place name: "Pointed hill."
  Kip, Kyp
Kiran Sanskrit. "A ray of light."
Kirby OE. Place name: "Church village." Mostly 19th-century use. Baseball player Kirby Puckett.
  Kerbie, Kerbey, Kirbey, Kirbie, Kirkby
Kiril Gk. "The Lord." As **Cyril**, used in Britain around the turn of the century.
  Cyril, Cyrill, Kirill, Kirillos, Kyril, Kyrill
Kirk ONorse. "Church." Some 19th-century use in Britain, but it was really brought into circulation by actor Kirk Douglas. Unusual today, but not unheard-of.
  Kerk, Kirke
Kirkland OE. Place name: "Church land." In the era when last names were being formed in England, everyone was Catholic and the church played a central role in everyday life.
  Kirtland
Kirkley OE. Place name: "Church meadow." Like **Kirkwell** and **Kirkwood**, this became a last name after being a place name, and is only occasionally used as a first name.
  Kirklea, Kirklee, Kirklie, Kirkly
Kirkwell OE. Place name: "Church spring."
Kirkwood OE. Place name: "Church forest." Author James Kirkwood.
Kit Dim. **Christopher** (Gk. "Bearer of Christ"). A nickname for Christopher long before **Chris** was thought of. Christopher Columbus named the Caribbean island of Saint Kitts for himself and Saint Christopher, the patron of travelers.
  Kitt

Klaus Var. **Claus** (dim. **Nicholas**; Gk. "Victorious people"). Even spelled with the more anglicized "C," unusual in English-speaking countries. Actor Klaus Maria Brandauer.
Klaas, Klaes

Klein Ger. "Small." German last names are not transferred as often to first names as often as their English counterparts.
Kleiner, Kleinert, Kline

Klemens Var. **Clement** (Lat. "Mild, giving mercy").
Klemenis, Klement, Kliment

Knightley OE. Place name: "Knight's meadow."
Knight, Knightlea, Knightlee, Knightlie, Knightly, Knights

Knoll OE. Place name: "Little hill." Conspiracy theorists will remember the "grassy knoll" at the scene of John F. Kennedy's assassination. The word is scarcely used otherwise.
Knolles, Knollys, Knowles

Knox OE. Place name. May be a variant of **Knoll**. Religious reformer John Knox founded the Scottish Presbyterian church in the mid-16th century.

Knud Dan. "Kind."

Knut Scand. "Knot." Brought to Britain by the 11th-century King Canute of Denmark, who became the King of England in 1016. Very rare, except in those of Scandinavian descent. Football coach Knute Rockne; author Knut Hamsun.
Canute, Cnut, Knute

Kobi Hung. Variant **Jacob** (Heb. "He who supplants"). A couple of young athletes (basketball player Kobe Bryant, soccer player Cobi Jones) have brought this unusual name to the notice of the public. Did their parents know they were choosing a Hungarian nickname for Jacob? Probably not: the name has other sources as well, just as it has numerous spellings. Kobe Bryant was named for a special Japanese brand of beef.
Cobe, Cobey, Cobi, Cobie, Coby, Kobe, Kobey, Kobie, Koby

Kodiak Place name: island group at the western end of the Strait of Alaska. Settled in the 18th century by Russians.

Kody Var. **Cody** (OE. "Pillow"). The "C" spelling for this popular name is standard, but today's parents seek departure from the standard, so this spelling may become more common.
Kodey, Kodi, Kodie

Kofi Ghanaian. "Born on Friday." Some African names that are pronounceable to English-speakers are becoming more visible in America. Statesman Kofi Annan.

Kojo Ghanaian. "Born on Monday."

Kolya Rus. dim. **Nicholas** (Gk. "People of victory"). Currently a popular first name in Russia.

Konrad Var. **Conrad** (OG. "Courageous advice"). Despite occasional increases in numbers, a name that has never been widely popular in English-speaking countries. Anthropologist Konrad Lorenz.
Kord, Kort, Kunz

Konstantin Var. **Constantine** (Lat. "Steadfast"). The form Constant was popular among the Puritans (as a virtue name) and was revived in the 19th century to occasional modern use. Constantine, the Latin form, was the name of the first Christian Roman emperor, and a royal name in Greece.
Konstant, Konstantio, Konstanty, Konstanz, Kostas

Kornel Var. **Cornelius** (Lat. "Like a horn"). Comes from a Latin clan name and, as Cornelius, was often used under the Roman Empire. Painter Kees Van Dongen.
Kees, Kornelisz, Kornelius, Kornell

Koren Heb. "Gleaming."

Koresh Heb. "Cultivator, digger, farmer."
Choresh

Krispin Var. **Crispin** (Lat. "Curly-haired"). Saint Crispin, supposedly a 3rd-century martyr, is patron of shoemakers. The name was somewhat popular in Britain in the 17th and 18th centuries, and was revived in the 1960s, but has not spread to the U.S. in any significant numbers.

Kristian Var. **Christian** (Gk. "Anointed, Christian"). A girl's name that (contrary to the usual movement) became a male name, possibly after the huge success of John Bunyan's *Pilgrim's Progress* (1684), whose hero is called Christian.

Krist

Kristofer Var. **Christopher** (Gk. "Carrier of Christ"). The much-loved story of Saint Christopher is that he lived alone by a river, carrying travelers across the ford on his back. A child whom he was carrying became almost too heavy to bear, and proved afterward to be the Christ child. Actually the tale has little basis in fact, and probably springs from the literal translation of the name, which originally alluded to carrying Christ in one's heart. Actor Kris Kristofferson.

Kristoffer, Kristofor, Kristopher, Kristophor, Krzysztof

Kumar Sanskrit. "Male child."

Kurt Ger. Var. **Conrad** (OG. "Courageous advice"). Actor Kurt Russell; author Kurt Vonnegut; musician Kurt Cobain; football player Kurt Warner.

Kwame Ghanaian. "Born on Saturday." The most widely used of these names from the Akan people of Ghana.

Kwasi Ghanaian. "Born on Sunday." Activist Kwasi Mfume.

Kwesi

Kyle Scot. Place name: "Narrow spit of land." Well traveled parents may have crossed the Kyle of Lochalsh to reach the Isle of Skye, and indeed the name is very well used in Scotland. Kyle is one of the two dozen most popular names in the U.S. for boys, and a "feminine" version of the name, **Kylie**, is almost as hot for girls. This seems to be the result of the craze for "K-" names rather than the significance of the name itself. Actor Kyle MacLachlan.

Kyler Dutch. "Bowman, archer." Moderately popular in the last six years.

Cuyler, Kylor

Kynaston OE. Place name: "Royal peace settlement."

Kyrone Modern name: **Tyrone** (Ir. Gael. "Land of Owen") with a "K-."

Keirohn, Keiron, Keirone, Keirown, Kirone, Kyron

Laban Heb. "White." Old Testament name revived by the Puritans. Has appeared sporadically since.

Lavan

Lachlan Scot. Gael. Either "Belligerent" or "From the fjord-land," which would refer to Norway, thus indicating a Viking ancestor. The name is unusual, even in Scotland. Media magnate Lachlan Murdoch.

Lachman Ger. Place name: "Man from the lake."

Lachmann

Lacrosse Fr. "The cross." Lacrosse is a game played with a long racquet with a netted pocket: its name comes from the French term for a crozier, or bishop's crook. This is also the place name for a city and county in Wisconsin that was originally a fur trading post.

Lacy OF. Place name of obscure meaning, used as a boy's name in the 19th century more commonly for girls today, probably owing to the double whammy of the "feminine" "-y" ending and the connotations of one fabric that even the dressiest guys don't wear.

Lacey, Lacie

Ladd ME. "Manservant or young man." Most likely to be a transferred surname. Actor Alan Ladd.

Lad, Laddey, Laddie, Laddy

Ladislas Slavic. "Glorious rule." Related to **Vladislav**. The variants like **Laszlo** are more common. This was a royal name in medieval Hungary.

Lacko, Ladislaus, Laslo, Laszlo, Lazlo

Lafayette French name of uncertain meaning, though it may refer to faith (*foi*). First used in this country in homage to the French general the Marquis de Lafayette whose participation in the American Revolution included both military action and solicitation of French help for the cause. When Lafayette returned to the U.S. in 1824–25, he was welcomed as a hero.

Laird Scot. "Lord of the land."

Lake Geography name: a small, contained body of water. Names of this sort gained some popularity in the late 1990s and early 2000s as parents search for ever more unusual choices.

Laike, Laiken, Laikin, Laken, Lakon

Lakshman Hindi. "Auspicious, foreseeing good fortune."

Lalo Lat. "To sing a lullaby." Musician Lalo Schiffren.

Lale, Lallo

Lamar OG. "Land famous." Plutocrat Lamar Hunt.

Lamarr, Lemar, Lemarr

Lambert OG. "Land brilliant." Medieval and Renaissance use was encouraged by veneration for the Belgian martyr Saint Lambert, but in the more secular times since, nothing has occurred to save it from neglect. Actor Christopher Lambert.

Lambart, Bert, Lamberto, Lambirt, Landbert

Lamont Scand. "Man of law." Mostly U.S. use around the 1940s. Bicycle racer Greg LeMond.

Lammond, Lamond, Lemond

Lance Var. **Lancelot.** Mildly popular on its own in the middle of this century. Parents may have erroneously thought it referred to the medieval jousting weapon. It is fairly widely used, misunderstood or not. Bicycle racer Lance Armstrong; singer Lance Bass.

Lantz, Lanz, Launce

Lancaster OE. Place name: a city and county that probably took its name from the river Lune, in western England. It was the center of much industry in the 19th century, and several cities in the U.S. also bear this name.

Lancashire, Lancester, Lanchester, Lankester

Lancelot OF. "Servant." Most famous, of course, for the knight of the Round Table who seduced King Arthur's wife, Guinevere. Used as a first name in the romantic 19th century, rare since the middle of this century.

Launcelot

Lander ME. Occupational name: Possibly "Laundry-man" or "Landowner." More probably the latter, since the laundering trade, in medieval Britain, was unlikely to provide

much of a career. Another, possibly more credible derivation is German, "Picket fence," which would make this a
place name. Lander, Wyoming was named after explorer
and Civil War general Frederick W. Lander.

Land, Landers, Landis, Landiss, Landor, Landry

Landon OE. Place name: "Grassy plain."

Land, Landan, Landen, Landin

Lane ME. Place name. More common for boys than for
girls, though still unusual for both. This is the kind of
name that is likely to be a mother's maiden name transferred to a first name.

Laine, Layne

Lang ONorse. "Tall one."

Lange

Langdon OE. Place name: "Long hill."

Landon, Langden

Langford OE. Place name: "Long ford." Many English
place names are just compounds of familiar elements that
still exist in our spoken language.

Langhorne OE. "Long horn." May refer to ancient possession of a cow with this distinguishing characteristic. This
is an old Virginia name, borne by the illustrious Nancy
Langhorne Astor, the first woman ever to serve as a member of Britain's House of Commons.

Langhorn

Langley OE. Place name: "Long meadow." As fans of adventure novels and films know, Langley, Virginia is home
to the Central Intelligence Agency.

Langlea, Langlee, Langleigh, Langly

Langston OE. Place name: "Long town" or "Tall man's
town." The "Lang-" element could have two meanings in
this instance. Author Langston Hughes.

Langsden, Langsdon, Langton

Langward OE. Descriptive/occupational name: "Tall
guardian."

Langworth OE. Place name: "Long paddock."

Lanier OF. Occupational name: "Woolworker."

Lanny Dim. **Roland**. OF. "Famous land." More common
as a nickname.

Lansing Possibly related to **Lancelot**. Also a place name: the capital of Michigan was named for an early American statesman named John Lansing.

Laramie Place name: a city in southern Wyoming, named for 19th-century fur trapper Jacques Laramie. The original spelling of his name is not entirely certain; it may have been Lorimier or LaRamee.

Larch Nature name: a kind of deciduous evergreen. The eastern larch is also known as a tamarack; the western larch is grown commercially as a lumber tree. The word "larch" comes from its Latin name, *Larix*.

Laredo Place name: a city in southern Texas, on the Rio Grande. It was founded by Spaniards in 1755. The plaintive folk song, "As I walked through the streets of Laredo" may be familiar to some parents.

Largo Sp. "Tall, long." As in Key Largo, Florida. In musical terms, "Largo" indicates a very slow tempo.

Lark ME. Nature name, used since the 1950s, mostly in the U.S. and predominantly for girls. Larks are usually thought of as playful, lighthearted songbirds.

Larkin Ir. Gael. "Rough, fierce." Poet Philip Larkin.

Larrimore OF. "Armorer."
Larimore, Larmer, Larmor, Lorimer

Larron Modern name: possibly **Darron** with an "L," or a variant of **Lawrence.**
Laren, Larin, Laron, Larran, Larren, Larrin

Larry Dim. **Lawrence.** Given as an independent name in this century, and with some regularity today. In fact this form is used more often that Lawrence, in spite of modern parent's reluctance to use nicknames. Basketball player Larry Bird; actor/comedian Larry David.

Lars Scand. Var. **Lawrence.** Artist Carl Larsson.
Larsen, Larson, Larsson

Laszlo Hung. "Famous ruler." A variant of the more unwieldy **Ladislas.**
Laslo, Lazlo

Latham Scand. Place name: "The barn."
Lathom

Lathrop OE. Place name: "Farmstead with barns."

Latif Arab. "Gentle, kind."
Lateef, Lateeph, Latiph

Latimer ME. Occupational name: "Interpreter." Possibly one who could translate into Latin.
Lattemore, Lattimore, Latymer

Laud Lat. "Praise." Archbishop of Canterbury William Laud.

Laughlin Ir. Gael. "Dweller at the fjord-land." This was the Irish term for invaders from Scandinavia.
Loughlin

Lauriston OE. Place name: "Lawrence's settlement."

LaVerne This is actually the name of a classical goddess—of minor criminals, no less. The name has been used widely as a girl's name, but does sometimes occur for boys. It sounds enough like the romance languages' word for green (*vert, verde*) to have acquired misplaced connotations of green trees or springtime. Football player Laveranues Coles.
Lavern, Levern, Leverne, Luvern, Luverne

Lawford OE. Place name: "The hill-ford." Actor Peter Lawford.

Lawler Ir. Gael. "Mutterer."
Lawlor, Loller, Lollar

Lawrence Lat. "From Laurentium." Laurentium was a city south of Rome known for its numerous laurel trees. Though the place no longer exists, the name endures, at first given staying power by the popularity of Saint Lawrence (who was martyred by being grilled alive). Brought to Britain with the Norman Conquest, and after an eventual 19th-century decline, was soundly revived in the U.S. in this century. Popularity began to tail off after the 1970s. Actors Laurence Olivier, Laurence Fishburne; band leader Lawrence Welk; football player Lawrence Taylor; author Laurens Van Der Post; opera singer Lauritz Melchior; impresario Lorenz Ziegfeld.
Larance, Laranz, Larenz, Larrance, Larrence, Larrens, Larrey, Larry, Lars, Laurance, Lauren, Laurence, Laurens, Laurent, Laurentios, Laurentius, Laurenz, Laurie, Laurits, Lauritz, Lavrans, Lavrens, Lawrance,

Lawrey, Lawrie, Lawry, Lenci, Lon, Lonny, Lorant, Loren, Lorenc, Lorencz, Lorens, Lorentz, Lorenz, Lorenzen, Lorenzo, Lorin, Loritz, Lorrence, Lorrenz, Lorry, Lowrance

Lawson OE. "Son of Lawrence." Used as a first name mostly since 1850. Author Robert Lawson.

Lawton OE. Place name: "Hill-town." Actor Charles Laughton.

Laughton, Loughton

Lawyer Modern occupational name. Perhaps the mother who first used this name hope that her son would become an attorney. Football player Lawyer Milloy.

Lazarus Heb. "The Lord will help." Biblical name: Lazarus was the man whom Jesus raised from the dead. Little used, perhaps since in the Middle Ages it became a synonym for "leper."

Eleazer, Lazar, Lazare, Lazarillo, Lazaro, Lazear, Lazer, Lazzaro

Leander Gk. "Lion-man." The mythical Greek Leander swam across the Hellespont to visit his beloved, Hero. This was a saint's name as well, but has never been very widely used.

Ander, Leandre, Leandro, Leandros, Leanther, Lee, Leiandros, Leo, Liander, Liandro

Leary Ir. Gael. Anglicization of *laoghaire,* which means "herder." Comedian Denis Leary.

Lebrun Fr. "Brown-haired one." The most common version of this descriptive name is **Bruno**, but **Brunel** and **Burnett** also come from the same source. Basketball player LeBron James.

Labron, Labrun, Lebron

Lech Polish "A Pole." An old name from the myth of the origins of the Slavic peoples. Three brothers, Czech, Rus, and Lech, were the ancestors of the Czechs, the Russians, and the Poles. Polish president Lech Walesa.

Lee OE. Place name: "Pasture or meadow." One of the few truly unisex names. Usually a name becomes exclusively feminine once it is used for girls (**Ashley, Leslie**). The tenacious masculine hold on Lee may have been helped by tough-guy actor Lee Marvin. U.S. use seems to have been sparked by admiration for Confederate General Robert E. Lee. Peaked in the 1950s. Chrysler chairman Lee Iacocca; actor Lee Majors.

Lea, Leigh

Leggett OF. "One who is sent; delegate."

Legate, Leggitt, Liggett

Lehman Ger. "Tenant, renter." This name indicates a long-ago ancestor who was a tenant as opposed to an owner, probably of farmland.

Lehmann

Leif Scand. "Loved." Explorer Leif Ericsson.

Lief

Leighton OE. Place name: "Meadow settlement." Used as a first name starting in the 19th century. Artist Frederick Leighton.

Layton, Leyton

Leith Scot. Gael. "Broad river."

Leland OE. Place name: "Meadow land." Philanthropist Leland Stanford; dramatic agent Leland Hayward.

Le, Leeland, Leighland, Leyland

Lemuel Heb. "Devoted to God." Old Testament name passed over in the wholesale Puritan revival of biblical names, but given new life from around 1840 into the 1930s. Currently extremely rare.

Lem, Lemmie

Lenis Lat. "Mild."

Lennon Ir. Gael. "Small cloak or cape." Admiration for John Lennon has not inspired much use of this name, though some pop stars (Bob Dylan, Elvis Presley) have numerous namesakes.

Lennox Scot. Gael. "With many elm trees." This is the name of an aristocratic landowning family in Scotland that had huge influence in the 16th century.

Lenox

Leo Lat. "Lion." Common in Roman times, and the name of 13 popes, but little used in the 18th and early 19th centuries. Perhaps it was the historical appeal of the name that made it more popular at the turn of the century. Astrological appeal notwithstanding, it is only moderately used today. Author Leo Tolstoy; actor Leo G. Carroll.

Lee, Leon, Leoncio, Leonel, Leonello, Leontios, Lev, Lion, Lyon

Leomaris Lat. "Lion of the sea." An elaboration of **Leo**.

Leon Gk. Var. **Leo**. Very popular in the U.S. 1870–1890, and currently more familiar than Leo, but still very unusual. Author Leon Uris.

Leoncio, Leone, Lioni, Lionisio, Lionni

Leonard OG. "Lion-bold." Name of a saint who was much venerated in the Middle Ages (as patron of prisoners, among others), but did not inspire many parents until the 18th century. Use grew gradually to 1930, has diminished since. Artist Leonardo Da Vinci; composer Leonard Bernstein; actors Leonard Nimoy, Leonardo DiCaprio.

Lee, Len, Lenard, Lenn, Lennard, Lennart, Lennerd, Lennie, Lenny, Leo, Leon, Leonardo, Leondaus, Leone, Leonerd, Leonhard, Leonid, Leonidas, Leonides, Leonis, Lonnard, Lonny

Leonzio It. var. **Leo**.

Leonce, Leontios, Leontius

Leopold OG. "People brave." Use mainly British and European. The fact that it has been a royal or aristocratic name in Belgium, Austria, and Britain has not increased its sparse use.

Leo, Leupold

Leroy OF. "The king." Occupational name: one of the servants or pages of a king. Revived in the late 19th century, especially in America, but use today is minimal. Poet Amiri Baraka was originally named Everett LeRoi Jones.

Elroi, Elroy, Lee, Leeroy, Leroi, Roy

Leslie Scot. Gael. Place name: Some sources suggest "The gray castle." Became a last name, then (in the 18th century) a first name used for boys and girls. Boys' use has been tied to admiration for actor Leslie Howard, and is more common in Britain. Infrequent for boys babies in the U.S., as Leslie has become a girl's name. Actor Leslie Nielsen.

Leslea, Leslee, Lesley, Lesly, Lezly

Lester OE. Place name: "From Leicester," an area in central England. First-name use dates from the mid 19th century, and its popularity lasted about 100 years.

Leicester, Les

Lev Rus. Var. **Leo**.

Levander Several sources are possible. May mean "From the Levant," i.e. the eastern Mediterranean. Equally possibly, the name is a variant of **Leander**, or **Evander** with an initial *L* added.

Levant Fr. "Rising." This is a place name, referring to the eastern Mediterranean where the sun rises, if you are in Italy, for instance.

Leverett OF. "Baby rabbit." May indicate an ancestor who hunted or trapped rabbits.

Leveret, Leverit, Leveritt

Leverton OE. "From the rush-farm."

Levi Heb. "Joined, attached." In the Old Testament, one of Jacob's sons, whose descendants (known as the Levites) were Israel's tribe of priests. After its revival by the Puritans, the name has been steadily used.

Levey, Levin, Levon, Levy

Leviticus Gk. "Beloning to the Levites." The name of the third book of the Old Testament, which contains religious and ethical laws that regulated the behavior of priests and believers.

Lewis Anglicization of **Louis** (OG./OF. "Renowned warrior"). Briefly popular in the late 19th century, but now takes a back seat to **Louis**, which is not particularly fashionable. In Britain, though, this version is very much in style. Author Lewis Carroll.

Lew, Lewes, Lou, Louis

Lexer Ger. Dim. **Alexander** (Gk. "Man's defender"). May also come from **Alexis**.

Lex, Lexo, Lexus

Lexus Lat. "Law." To most people, this is now the name of a car.

Liam Ir. Var. **William** (OG. "Will-helmet"). This name has grown steadily more fashionable in the last ten years, and has reached the top ten in Scotland. Actor Liam Neeson.

Liberio Port. "Freedom." Other versions of this name, like the Spanish **Liberato**, are actually based on the Latin word that means "released" or "set free."

Liberato, Liberatus, Liberto

Lidio Port. "From Lydia." Lydia was an area of Asia famous for its two rich kings, Midas and Croesus. The female form, **Lydia**, is more common than the male.

Licio, Lydio

Lidon Heb. "Judgment is mine."

Ledon, Leedon

Lincoln OE. Place name: "Town by the pool." Surname transferred occasionally to a first name. The fame of Abraham Lincoln did not, surprisingly enough, encourage parents to use the name widely, and it is not a favorite today. Football player Lincoln Kennedy.

Linc, Link

Lindberg OG. Place name: "Linden tree mountain." Would probably be unknown as a first name without the career of flier Charles Lindbergh. Very scarce.

Lindbergh, Lindburg, Lindy

Lindell OE. Place name: "Linden tree valley."

Lindal, Lindall, Lindel, Lyndall, Lyndell

Lindeman Ger. "Dweller near the lindens."

Lindemann, Linder

Linden Nature name: a tall, handsome deciduous tree, also known as a lime tree or basswood. Its wood is particularly easy to carve.

Lindo, Lindon, Lynden, Lyndon

Lindhurst OE. "Linden village."

Lindenhurst, Lyndenhurst, Lyndhurst

Lindley OE. "Linden tree meadow."

Lindlea, Lindlee, Lindleigh, Lindly

Lindsay OE. Place name: "Island of linden trees." Originally a surname, used for boys until the middle of this century, but now quite popular as a girl's name. Film director Lindsay Anderson; New York mayor John Lindsay.

Lind, Lindesay, Lindsee, Lindsey, Lindsy, Lindy, Linsay, Linsey, Linzy, Lyndsay, Lyndsey, Lyndsie

Linford OE. Place name: "Linden tree ford" or "Flax ford." The elements meaning flax ("Lin-") and linden tree

("Lind-") are so similar that they have probably been confused over the years. Track star Linford Christie.
Lindford, Lynford

Link Possibly a diminutive of **Lincoln**. May also mean "an enclosure, paddock."

Linley OE. Place name: "Flax meadow."
Linlea, Linlee, Linleigh, Linly

Linn OE. May refer either to flax, as in **Linus**, or to linden trees, as in **Lindsay**. Rare, whatever its derivation, and will be greatly confused with the girl's name **Lynn**.
Lin, Linnie, Lyn, Lynn

Linton OE. Place name: "Flax settlement."
Lintonn, Lynton, Lyntonn

Linus Gk. "Flax." May have originated as a descriptive name, applied to someone with flaxen or extremely pale hair. This description does not apply to today's best-known Linus, the famous *Peanuts* character who is lost without his blanket. In Greek myth, Linus is a son of Apollo, and a musician, who taught music to both Hercules and Orpheus. Actor Linus Roache.
Lino

Lionel Lat. "Young lion." Used in the Middle Ages and never resoundingly revived beyond a twinge of popularity in the 1920s and 1930s. Actor Lionel Barrymore; pop star Lionel Richie.
Leonel, Leonello, Lionell, Lionelo, Lionello, Lionnel, Lionnell, Lionnello, Lyonel, Lyinell, Lyonelo, Lyonnel, Lyonnell, Lyonnello

Liron Heb. "My song."
Leeron, Lyron

Lisle Place name: Lille, France, center of the French textile industry. Lisle thread, a strong cotton used for gloves and stockings, was originally made there. This name may also be related to **Lyle**, which means "the island."
Lyall, Lyell, Lyle, Lysle

Litton OE. Place name: "Settlement on the hill." Author Lytton Strachey.
Litten, Littonn, Lytten, Lytton

Livingston OE. Place name: "Leif's settlement." The Livingston family were prominent Hudson River landowners in the 18th and 19th centuries.

Livingsten, Livingstin, Livingstone

Llewellyn Welsh. "Resembling a lion." This is the generally accepted meaning, though some scholars think the origin relates to an element meaning "leader." Rare outside of Wales in any case.

Lew, Lewellen, Lewellyn, Llewellen, Llwewellin

Lloyd Welsh. "Gray" or "Sacred." One of the most common Welsh names in general use, perhaps because it is one of the simplest. Particularly widespread in the 1940s. Actor Lloyd Bridges; Senator Lloyd Bentsen.

Floyd, Loyd

Lobo Sp. "Wolf." A well-known Latino pop group is called "Los Lobos."

Lochner OG. Place name: "Dweller by the pond."

Lockner

Locke OE. Place name: "Woods" or "Fortified place," or OG. "Pond." Possibly an occupational name for locksmiths, though locks were not in general use when English last names came into use. Philosopher John Locke.

Lock, Lockwood

Lockhart OE. Possibly "Deer from the forest."

Lockwood OE. Place name: "Forest near the fortified place."

Lodge ME. "Shelter." U.S. Senator Henry Cabot Lodge.

Lodur Scand. Mythology name: Lodur was one of Odin's brothers.

Loeb Ger. "Lion." Seen as a last name, or occasionally a middle name.

Loeber, Loew, Loewe, Loewy

Logan Ir. Gael. Place name: "Small hollow." For a name with no connections to a celebrity who might have brought it into public view, this name has become quite popular over the last ten years. Author Logan Pearsall Smith; playwright/director Joshua Logan.

Logen

Loki Norse mythology name: Loki was the mischief-maker in the Norse pantheon.

Loman Ir. Gael. "Small bare one."

Lombard Lat. "Long-bearded." May also have origins as a place name: Lombardy is an area in northern Italy. Very rare as a first name. Football coach Vince Lombardi; bandleader Guy Lombardo.
Lombardi, Lombardo

Lon Dim. **Alonso** (OG. "Ready for battle"). Mostly associated with sinister film actor Lon Chaney. Lonnie is actually the more popular form.
Lonn, Lonnie, Lonny

London Place name: the capital of Great Britain (the name was originally Londinium). The name may be used by anglophiles or admirers of American novelist (*Call of the Wild, White Fang*) Jack London.

Long OE. "Tall." Rare as a first name.
Lang

Longfellow OE. "Tall one." Used in admiration of poet Henry Wadsworth Longfellow, who wrote *Evangeline, The Song of Hiawatha,* and "Paul Revere's Ride" among other poems. His technical skill and his romantic view of early American history made him the best-loved—and best-selling—American poet of the 19th century.

Lonzo Dim. **Alonzo** (OG. "Ready for battle").

Lorcan Ir. Gael. "Small fierce one."

Lord OE. "Loaf-keeper," or, in more modern terms, someone with power and authority. Less common in the U.S. than **Earl** or **Duke**, which are higher ranks in England's aristocracy. Actor Jack Lord.

Loren Var. **Lawrence** via **Lorenzo**. A purely modern form, in use since the 1940s but not common, possibly because of potential confusion with the girl's name Lauren.
Lorin, Lorren, Lorrin, Loron

Lorenzo It. Var. **Lawrence** (Lat. "From Laurentium"). Substantially used in the U.S., most likely in Latino communities. Actor Lorenzo Lamas.
Laurencio, Loreno, Lorent, Lorento, Lorentz, Lorenzino, Nenzo

Lorimer Lat. Occupational name: "Harness maker." Probably related to **Larrimore**.
Lorrimer, Lorymer

Loring OG. "Renowned warrior's son." Related to **Louis**.
  Lorring

Lorne Var. **Lawrence** (Lat. "From Laurentium"). Also a Scottish place name, and more common in Scotland. Actor Lorne Green; TV producer Lorne Michaels.
  Lorn

Lot Heb. "Veil, covering." In the Old Testament, as Lot and his wife fled the destruction of Sodom, his wife looked back and turned into a pillar of salt.

Lothar OG. "Famous army." A character called Lothario in an early 18th-century English play made this name synonomous for a while with a libertine or a careless seducer of women.
  Lother, Lothair, Lothario, Lothur

Loukas Gk. "From Lucania," an area of southern Italy. This name and its variants are almost indistinguishable from various forms of **Luke, Lucas**, and **Lucian**.
  Loukanos, Loukas, Loukianos

Louis OG./Fr. "Renowned warrior." The German form is **Ludwig**, and an early French variant was **Clovis**, a name borne by several Frankish kings. The later French kings (18 of them) who chose Louis as their name were no doubt harking back to those early monarchs, one of whom included the 13th-century saint. **Lewis** was the more common form in Britain until a mid 19th-century revival of Louis, which was very popular in the U.S. until the depression era. The name is still quite steadily used. Musician Louis Armstrong; scientist Louis Pasteur; archaeologist Louis Leakey; authors Louis L'Amour, Robert Louis Stevenson; actor Lou Gossett, Jr.
  Aloysius, Lew, Lewes, Lewis, Lodewick, Lodovico, Lou, Louie, Lucho, Ludovic, Ludovicus, Ludvig, Ludvik, Ludwig, Luigi, Luis

Lowell OF. "Young wolf." Mostly 19th-century use. The Lowell family of Massachusetts has produced poets, academics, and textile magnates. Lowell, Mass. was named for an early 19th-century member of the family. Poet Robert Lowell.
  Lovel, Lovell, Lowe, Lowel

Lubomir Polish "Great love."

Lucan Lat. "From Lucania." Lucania was an area in southern Italy. It can be very difficult to sort out **Lucan, Lucas, Luke** and their variants.
Loucan, Louccan, Lukan

Lucas Var. **Luke**. Generally a transferred last name, but gaining popularity in Britain as a first name, and quite popular in the U.S. as well. In Germany, this is a top-ten name. Actor Lukas Haas.
Loucas, Loukas, Lukas

Luce Lat. "Light." Scarce as a first name. Magazine publisher Henry Luce.

Lucian Lat. "Light." More unusual form of **Lucius**, which itself is quite rare. Artist Lucian Freud; opera star Luciano Pavarotti.
Luciano, Lucianus, Lucien, Lucio, Lucjan, Lukianos, Lukyan

Lucius Lat. "Light." Used by the Romans, but extremely scarce in the 20th century.
Luca, Lucas, Luccheus, Luce, Lucias, Lucio, Lukas, Luke, Lukeus

Lucky Modern name: descriptive. Lucky has usually been used as a nickname but some parents, perhaps full of hope, use it as a given name.

Lucretius Lat. Clan name of uncertain meaning, though some sources suggest "wealth." Lucretius was the name of a Roman philosophical poet.

Ludlow OE. Place name: "Ruler's hill."
Ludlowe

Ludoslaw Pol. "Glorious people."

Ludwig Ger. "Renowned in battle." Very unusual in English-speaking countries, where **Louis** or **Lewis** are used instead. Composer Ludwig van Beethoven.
Ludo, Ludovic, Ludovico

Luis Sp. var. **Louis** (Ger. "Renowned in battle"). More popular than the English spelling.
Luiz

Luke Gk. "From Lucanus," a region of southern Italy. Not, strictly speaking, a nickname for **Lucius** and **Lucian**, though it may be used that way. The most famous Luke is, of course, the author of the Gospel and of Acts. He was a physician, and is patron saint of doctors and artists. After medieval use, rather neglected, but the name is turning up quite frequently in preschools and hospital nurseries. The character of Luke Skywalker from the Star Wars movies keeps it in front of audiences in an appealing form—as for that matter, do actors Luke Perry and Luke Wilson.

Loukas, Luc, Lucas, Lucian, Lucien, Lucio, Lucius, Luck, Lucky, Lukacs, Lukas

Lundy Scot. Place name "Grove near the island," or possibly Fr. "Monday's child." Generally a transferred surname.

Lunn Ir. Gael. "Strong, warlike."

Lon, Lonn

Luther OG. "Army people." Generally homage to Martin Luther, the German religious reformer, or to Martin Luther King, Jr., the civil rights activist. Botanist Luther Burbank; singer Luther Vandross.

Lotario, Lothair, Lothar, Lothario, Louther, Lutero

Lyle OF. Place name: "The island." First-name use was mostly in the middle of this century. May also come from **Lisle**, the name of a city in northeast France.

Lisle, Lyall, Lyell, Lysle

Lyman OE. "Meadow-dweller."

Leaman, Leyman

Lynch Ir. Gael. "Mariner." One of the most common Irish last names, occasionally transferred for first-name use. Film director David Lynch; actor John Lynch.

Lyndell OE. Place name: "Linden tree valley."

Lindall, Lindell, Lyndall

Lyndon OE. Place name: "Linden tree hill." First-name use coincides with the 19th-century fondness for transferred surnames, but has been given extra renown by President Lyndon Baines Johnson.

Lin, Linden, Lindon, Lindy, Lyn, Lynden

Lynford OE. Place name: "Linden tree ford."
Linford, Linnford

Lynley OE. Place name: "Flax field."

Lyon Fr. "Lion." May be a place name, referring to the city of Lyons, in southern France.
Lyons

Lysander Gk. "Liberator." In Greek history, Lysander was a Spartan naval and military commander some 400 years before Christ. A character in Shakespeare's *A Midsummer Night's Dream* also bears this name.
Lesandro, Lisandro, Lizandro

Lytton OE. Place name: "Settlement on the hill." Author and critic Lytton Strachey.

Mabon Welsh "Son."

Mabry Origin unclear; probably an Old English place name, however: the "-bry" ending is likely to be a contraction of "-bury," which ultimately comes from a Germanic word meaning "fortified place." The first syllable could be reference to the month of May, or even a contraction of "Mary."
Mabrey, Maybery, Mayberry, Maybrey, Maybury

Mac Scot. Gael. "Son of." Also used as a nickname for given names that begin with "Mac-," many of which are transferred last names.
Mack, Mackey, Mackie

Macadam Scot. Gael. "Son of Adam." The 19th-century engineer John McAdam gave his name to a method of paving roads that became very widespread.
MacAdam, McAdam

Macallister Scot. Gael. "Son of Alistair." Alistair is the Scottish version of **Alexander**.
MacAlister, McAlister, McAllister

Macardle Scot. Gael. "Son of great courage."
MacArdell, McCardell

Macarios Gk. "Blessed." The name of some 73 Catholic saints.
Macario, Macarius, Makar, Makari, Makario, Makarios, Makary

MacArthur Scot. Gael. "Son of Arthur." Some parents used this name in admiration of World War II General Douglas MacArthur.
McArthur

Macbride Ir. Gael. "Son of the follower of Saint Brigid,"who was an influential 5th-century Irish nun.
Macbryde, McBride

Maccabee Arab. "Hammer." Other sources suggest the derivation comes from a Hebrew acrostic reading "Who is like unto thee among the gods, oh Lord!" Refers to a group of Jewish patriots who overthrew Syrian rule in the century before Christ; this was their battle cry. The Hannukah story took place during this struggle, making this an appropriate name for boys born during the holiday.
Macabee, Makabee

Maccoy Ir. Gael. "Son of Hugh." The phrase "the real Mc-Coy" came from Scotland, where it referred to something of the highest quality.
MacCoy, McCoy

Maccrea Ir. Gael. "Son of grace." Actor Joel McCrea.
MacCrae, MacCray, MacCrea, Macrae, McCrea

Macdonald Scot. Gael. "Son of Donald." The McDonalds were a powerful Scottish clan. One of their members, Flora McDonald, smuggled Bonnie Prince Charlie to the Isle of Skye when he was fleeing from the British who had defeated him in his bid for the English throne.
MacDonald, McDonald

Macdougal Scot. Gael. "Son of Dougal." Since Dougal means "dark foreigner," this may refer to an ancestor who was a Viking invader (not all of whom were blond).
MacDougal, MacDowell, McDougal, McDowell

Mace ME. "Heavy staff or club." In the Middle Ages, maces were often spiked, and used to break armor. May also be a nickname for **Mason**.
Maceo, Macey

Macedonio Sp. from Gk. "From Macedonia." Macedonia is a mountainous area to the north of Greece.

Macgowan Ir. Gael. "Son of the blacksmith."
MacCowan, MacCowen, MacGowan, Magowan, McGowan, McGowen, McGown

MacHenry Scot. Gael. "Son of Henry." Fort McHenry was part of the defenses of Baltimore in the War of 1812, and it was the bombardment of this fort in 1814 that inspired Francis Scott Key to write *The Star-Spangled Banner*.
McHenry

Mackenzie Ir. Gael. "Son of the wise ruler." Currently enjoying a considerable vogue as a girl's name.
MacKensie, McKenzie, McKensie

Mackinac Place name: the strait between the peninsula of Upper and Lower Michigan, and the name of the highly picturesque resort island located there. The name is a shortening of the Iroquois word Michilimackinac.

Mackinley Ir. Gael. "Learned ruler." The highest peak in the U.S. is Mt. McKinley, 20,300 feet high. In 1896 an Alaskan prospector dubbed it Mt. McKinley after the Republican Presidential candidate. It is also known as Denali, its Athabaskan Indian name, which means "the big one." William McKinley, incidentally, was assassinated early in his second term. Vice-President Theodore Roosevelt thus became president.
MacKinlay, McKinlay, McKinley

Macmahon Ir. Gael. "Son of the bear." TV host Ed McMahon.
MacMahon, McMahon

Macmurray Ir. Gael. "Son of the seafarer." Actor Fred McMurray.
MacMurray, McMurray

MacNeil Scot. Gael. "Son of Neil."
MacNeal, MacNeill, McNeal, McNeil, McNeill

Macon Place name: city in central France, in the center of the Burgundy wine district. Also a significant city in Georgia.

Macy OF. Place name: "Matthew's estate." This name, like Mackenzie, is also enjoying popularity among parents looking for an unusual girl's name. Department store founder R.H. Macy; actor William Macy.

Macey

Maddock Old Welsh. "Benevolent, charitable."

Madoc, Madock, Madog

Maddox Anglo-Welsh. "Benefactor's son." A contracted form of "Maddock's son." Novelist Ford Madox Ford.

Madocks, Maddocks, Madox

Madison OE. "Son of the mighty warrior." More common than many of these "son of" names, possibly because of admiration for U.S. President James Madison. There are towns or cities named Madison in at least fourteen states. However, since this name has been in the top ten girls' names since 1997, parents of boys are unlikely to use it. Novelist Madison Smartt Bell.

Maddison, Maddy, Madisson

Magal Heb. "Scythe."

Magee Ir. Gael. "Son of Hugh."

MacGee, MacGhee, McGee

Magni ONorse. "Tremendous might." In Norse myth, Magni was the son of Thor.

Magnus Lat. "Great." Appropriately enough, a royal name in Norway and Denmark. It was transferred from Scandinavia to Scotland, where it is used somewhat.

Magnes, Magnusson, Manus

Maguire Ir. Gael. "Son of the beige one."

MacGuire, McGuire, McGwire

Magus Lat. "Sorcerer." The three kings, or wise men, who visited the baby Jesus, are supposed to have belonged to a tribe of priests from ancient Iran, who were thought to have power of demons. The name is the root of the word "magic."

Mahatma Sanskrit. "Great-souled." This was the title given to Mohandas Gandhi; it is used for those of great spiritual development.

Mahavira Hindi. "The great hero."

Mahavir

Mahesh Hindi. "Great ruler."

Mahir Arab. "Skillful."

Mahlon Heb. "Sickness." Old Testament name.

Mahmoud Arab. "Praiseworthy." Though it comes from the same root, this is not the same name as **Muhammad**. It is, however, popular in the Arab world.
Mahmood, Mehmood, Mehmud

Maimon Arab. "Dependable, faithful." Other sources suggest "Good fortune." This word is the root of Maimonides, the name of a great Jewish philosopher and scholar who lived in 12th-century Spain.
Maimun

Maitland OE. Place name: may refer to a meadow, or possibly to "Matthew's land."
Maytland

Majid Arab. "Glorious."
Majeed

Major Lat. "Greater." Use (which is sparing) probably harks back to the military title used in the British and American armies.
Majer, Mayer, Mayor

Makarios Gk. "Blessed."
Macario, Macarios, Macarius, Maccario, Maccarios, Mackario, Mackarios, Makar, Makkarios

Maks Var. **Max** (Lat. "Greatest").

Malachi Heb. "Angel, messenger." Name of one of the minor prophets in the Old Testament, but not widely used. Author Malachi Martin.
Malachie, Malachy, Malaki, Malakie, Malaquias, Malechy, Maleki, Makequi

Malcolm Scot. Gael. "Devotee of St. Columba." The name of the prince of Scotland who became king after Macbeth murdered his father, Duncan. Shakespeare's play was based on historical fact. The name has been used primarily in Scotland, but spread more widely in the middle of the 20th century. Black families may use it in honor of Malcolm X who, upon his conversion to Islam, took the name El-Hajj Malik El-Shabazz. Publisher Malcolm Forbes.
Malcolum, Malkolm

Malden OE. Place name: possibly "Strong warrior's valley." Actor Karl Malden.

Maldon

Malik Arab. "Master." Malcolm X's Islamic name was El-Hajj Malik El-Shabazz. Actor Art Malik.

Maleek, Maleeq, Mallik, Maliq

Malin OE. "Little strong warrior."

Mallen, Mallin, Mallon

Malki Heb. "My king." Many variations of this name exist, with slightly different meanings in Hebrew; it is also the root of **Melchior**, one of the three kings' names. It is also used as a girl's name.

Malcam, Malkam, Malkiel, Malkior, Malkiya, Mehlech

Mallory OF. "Unhappy, unlucky." Literally, *malheureux*. Originally a nickname, transferred to a last name and thus to a first name. Used quite often for girls now, though it was originally a man's name. Poet Sir Thomas Malory.

Mallery, Mallorie, Malory

Maloney Ir. Gael. "Pious, disciple of Sunday worship."

Malone, Malonee, Malonie, Malony

Malvin Var. **Melvin**. Could come from a number of sources: possibly Ir. Gael. "Polished chief," OE. "Council-friend," or an adaptation of **Melville**.

Malvinn, Malvyn

Mamun Arab. "Worthy of trust."

Mamoun

Manasseh Heb. "Making forgetfulness." This is the anglicized version, and is popular in Israel, while Hispanic variants also thrive. The Civil War battle of Bull Run was fought near the town of Manassas in Virginia.

Manassas, Manases, Manasio, Menashe, Menashi

Manchester OE. Place name: an important city in northern England. Its Latin name was Mancunium. In the 19th century Manchester was the foremost city in the world for the manufacture of cotton fabric.

Mandan Native American: the name of a tribe indigenous to the upper Missouri River. The Mandan had developed high levels of material culture but were nearly wiped out by smallpox in 1837. A city in North Dakota is named after them.

Mandel Ger. "Almond."
Mandell, Mandelson

Manfred OE. "Man of peace." Seldom found in real life, but used by Byron for an antihero in an eponymous epic poem.
Manfredo, Manfrid, Manfried, Mannfred, Mannfryd

Mankato Native American place name: "Blue earth." A city in north central Kansas.

Mannheim Ger. Place name: "Swamp hamlet."
Manheim

Manley OE. Place name: "Man's meadow." Or originally a descriptive term meaning "masculine." Poet Gerard Manley Hopkins.
Manlea, Manleigh, Manly

Mann Ger. "Man." Author Thomas Mann.

Manning OE. "Son of the man." Football player Peyton Manning.
Mannyng

Mannix Ir. Gael. "Little monk." An anglicized version of Munchin or Mainchin. Under English rule, many Gaelic names were very roughly anglicized, and often the correspondences are just approximate.

Manoach Heb. "Place of rest." Old Testament name: the father of Samson.
Manoa, Manoah

Manolo Var. **Manuel**. Shoe designer Manolo Blahnik.
Mano, Manollo

Mansel OE. "From the manse." A manse is a house occupied by a clergyman.
Mansell

Mansfield OE. Place name: "Field by the little river."

Mansur Arab. "Victorious."
Mansoor, Mansour

Manton OE. Place name: "Man's or hero's town."
Manten, Mannton

Manuel Dim. **Emanuel** (Heb. "God be with us"). Most

LAW AND ORDER

In this country, you can name your child almost anything. Numbers are forbidden, as are obscene names, but from the very beginning, when Oceanus Hopkins was born on board the *Mayflower,* Americans have had great latitude in choosing names. Mister, Aladdin, even Messiah would be perfectly legal (if unwise) selections. Not so in many countries, though. There's a law on Argentina's books that forbids names "contrary to our customs." "Foreign" names have to be "Hispanicized." Aristobulo would be acceptable; Jack would not. France has also been historically concerned with maintaining Frenchness, and under Napoleon the government created a list of French names with French spellings for parents to choose from. The list has been updated, but when you go to register the birth of your child in France, your name choice can be refused if it isn't considered correct. Saints' names are fine; names of American soap opera characters are not. Germany has a similarly strict approach: In 1900 their civil code embraced guidelines governing name choice. German parents have to choose names that are, well, *names.* Not descriptions (forget Precious) and not last names (goodbye Madison). Most startling to American parents would be the ruling that a first name should indicate the child's gender. (So long Ashley, Leslie, Mackenzie, Taylor. . . .)

widely used in Spanish-speaking countries, but it has a considerable presence in the U.S. as well. Shoe designer Manolo Blahnik; artist Manuel Ocampo; baseball player Manny Ramirez.

Mano, Manolo, Manny

Manville OF. Place name: "Great town."

Mandeville, Manvel, Manvile, Manvill

Marcel Fr. Dim. **Marcellus** (Lat. "Little warrior"). One of the less common of a group of names that all have their root in the Roman god of war, Mars. Author Marcel Proust; pantomime artist Marcel Marceau; football player Marcellus Wiley.

Marceau, Marcelin, Marcellin, Marcellino, Marcello, Marcellus, Marcelo, Marcely

March OF. Place name: "Borderland, frontier." The Marches of western England border Wales: similarly, in Italy, *le marche* was a territory between two ancient kingdoms. The verb "march," meaning "to walk" comes from a slightly different root. The name may also, of course, be used to commemorate the month of birth. Actor Frederic March.

Marcio, Marzo

Marco It. var. **Mark**. Italian explorer Marco Polo.

Marcos

Marcus Lat. "Warlike." The root of such names as **Mark** and **Marcel**, and based on the name of the Roman war god, Mars. Common enough in Roman times, but unknown in English-speaking countries until the 19th century. When Mark was hugely popular in the 1970s, **Marcus** also crept up the charts possibly boosted by the hit TV series *Marcus Welby, M.D.* It may also be used in memory of civil rights activist Marcus Garvey. Retailer Stanley Marcus; hockey player Markus Naslund.

Marc, Marco, Marko, Markus

Marden OE. Place name: "The valley with the pool." Painter Brice Marden.

Mariano Sp./Lat. "Of Marius." Possibly an old Roman clan name referring to Mars, possibly a reference to the Latin word for "manly." It is most likely used, however, as a reference to the Virgin Mary. Baseball players Mariano Duncan, Mariano Rivera.

Marianos, Marianus, Marimo

Mario It. Var. **Mark**. New York governor Mario Cuomo; chef Mario Batali.

Marianus, Marius, Meirion

Marion Fr. Var. **Mary** (Heb. "Bitter or rebellious"). Almost always a girl's name, and likely to cause some confusion if given to a boy. The most famous male Marion, Marion

Morrison, chose the unmistakably masculine "John Wayne" when he changed his name. Revolutionary war soldier Francis "Swamp Fox" Marion.

Mariano

Marino Gk./Lat. "The sea." A third-century Roman martyr named Marinus was canonized; another St. Marinus, for whom the Italian republic of San Marino is named, seems to be legendary.

Marinos, Marinus

Mark Lat. "Warlike." The anglicized version of **Marcus**, and the most popular in this country. In spite of the automatic exposure given the name by the evangelist Saint Mark, it was not widely used in the Middle Ages, nor indeed was it really common until a sudden inexplicable flurry of use in the 1950s. The popular author Mark Twain (whose real name was Samuel Clemens) took his pseudonym from the call of Mississippi River boatmen: "Mark twain!" meant that the water they were navigating was two fathoms deep. Explorer Marco Polo; choreographer Mark Morris; New York governor Mario Cuomo; swimmer Mark Spitz; baseball player Mark McGwire; fashion designer Marc Jacobs; actors Mark Harmon, Mark Wahlberg.

Marc, Marco, Marcos, Marcus, Marek, Mario, Marius, Marko, Markos, Markus, Marq, Marquus

Markham OE. Place name: "Mark's village."

Marland OE. Place name: "Land near the lake." Some sources suggest that the name means "famous land" and is the source of **Marlon** as well.

Marlin, Marlon, Marlond, Marlondo

Marley OE. Place name: "Meadow near the lake." Musician Bob Marley.

Marlea, Marleigh, Marly

Marlon OF. "Little hawk," or possibly a variation of **Merlin**. Current use, which is scanty, is inspired by the career of actor Marlon Brando.

Marlen, Marlin, Marlinn, Marlonn

Marlow OE. Place name: "Hill near the lake." Rare as a first name, though classic film lovers might be reminded of Humphrey Bogart as Philip Marlowe in *The Big Sleep*. English playwright Christopher Marlowe.

Marloe, Marlowe

Marmaduke Old English name of uncertain derivation. It may be an adaptation of a Gaelic name. Has almost comical English upper-class connotations.

Duke, Marmeduke

Marmion OF. "Tiny one." Extremely rare, though used by Sir Walter Scott in a popular narrative poem of that title.

Marmeon, Marmionn, Marmyon

Marom Heb. "Height, peak."

Merom

Marquez Sp. "Nobleman." In the European nobility, Marquis is a lower rank than Duke, but higher than Earl (or Count), Viscount, or Baron, and means "lord of the marches" or "frontier." Of all these titles, Viscount alone has never made the transition to a first name, and **Earl** is the most common. Football player Marquez Pope; baseball player Marquis Grissom.

Markese, Markess, Markise, Markiss, Markize, Markwees, Markwess, Marques, Marquess, Marquis, Marquise, Marquiz

Marr OG. Place name: "Swamp."

Mar

Marriner Eng. "Mariner, sailor, seaman." This is not one of the old-style occupational names because, at the time when last names came into formation, being a mariner simply was not a possible career. Musician Neville Marriner.

Mariner, Marinor, Marrinor

Mars Mythology name: the classical god of war. Politically incorrect.

Marsden OE. Place name: "Swampy valley." Painter Marsden Hartley.

Marsdin, Marsdon

Marsh OE. Place name: "Swamp or marsh." Like **Marsden** and **Marston**, more generally a last name, occasionally used as a first name. Nineteenth-century parents were particularly fond of transferring surnames as given names. Painter Reginald Marsh.

Marshall OF. Occupational name: "Horse-keeper." Also a military title of great honor, as in "field marshal." As a last name, common in Scotland, and used rather widely as a first name since the early 19th century. Department store founder Marshall Field; media theorist Marshall McLuhan; actor David Marshall Grant; Supreme Court Justice Thurgood Marshall; football player Marshall Faulk; pop singer Marshall Mathers.

Marchall, Marischal, Marischall, Marschal, Marsh, Marshal, Marshell

Marston OE. Place name: "Town by the marsh."

Martell Fr. dim. **Martin**.

Martin Lat. "Warlike." Like **Marcus** and its variants, Martin originates with the Roman war god, Mars. The 4th-century Saint Martin (most famous for dividing his cloak in two and giving half to a beggar) was much venerated, making his name popular in the Middle Ages. The influence of Protestant reformer Martin Luther may have added to the name's appeal, since it was used very steadily right into the 19th century, though there are comparatively few variants. The pattern since then has been of moderate use, except for a spurt of popularity in the 1950s. Even the eminence of civil rights activist Martin Luther King, Jr. has not drawn parents to this name in great numbers. U.S. President Martin Van Buren; film director Martin Scorsese; actors Martin Short, Martin Lawrence.

Marinos, Mart, Martel, Martell, Marten, Martenn, Martie, Martijn, Martinien, Martino, Martinos, Martinus, Marton, Marty, Martyn

Marvell OE. Derivation unclear: may be a diminutive of **Marvin**, formed as **Martell** was. Also possibly related to the verb, "to marvel." Poet Andrew Marvell.

Marvel

Marvin Origin obscure, though many sources suggest OE. "Sea lover," while others claim that it is Welsh. Popular in America starting in the 19th century, peaking in the

1920s, and now unusual. Actor Lee Marvin; songwriter Marvin Hamlisch; singer Marvin Gaye; football player Marvin Harrison.

Marve, Marven, Marwin, Marwynn, Mervin, Mervyn, Merwin, Merwyn, Murvin, Murvynn

Marwood OE. Place name: "Lake near the woods."

Maryland Place name: the state of Maryland, which was named for English Queen Henrietta Maria, the wife of King Charles I, who was on the throne when the vast tract of land that now includes much of Pennsylvania, as well as Delaware and Maryland, was granted to Lord Baltimore.

Mariland, Marilland, Marriland, Marryland

Masefield Eng. Place name: "Corn field." This name could not have developed with many of the English place names because corn (or maize) is not native to England. It was not imported to Europe until after 15th-century exploration of the New World had begun. Poet John Masefield.

Maslin OF. "Little Thomas."

Maslen, Masling, Maslon, Masslen, Masslin, Masslon

Mason OF. Occupational name: "Stoneworker." Transferred from surname status starting in the mid 19th century, and used today quite steadily. Actor James Mason.

Masos Heb. "Gladness, happiness."

Massey Origin unclear. May go back to the German *masse* which means "mass, measure," or it may be related to the Catholic Mass. Actor Raymond Massey; author Robert K. Massie.

Massie

Mataniah Heb. "Gift of God."

Matanya, Matanyahu, Mattania, Mattaniah

Mather OE. "Powerful army." The surname of a dynasty of 17th- and 18th-century Massachusetts theologians, Richard, Increase, and Cotton Mather.

Maither, Matther

Matthew Heb. "Gift of the Lord." Like **Mark, Luke**, and **John**, given great exposure by the author of one of the four Gospels. In more religious eras, parents would hear these names over and over again in the course of a year.

Matthew began to be neglected in the 19th century and was little used early in the 20th until an enthusiastic revival at midcentury. It is still one of the top ten boys' names in the United States and in Britain as well. Actors Matthew Broderick, Matthew Modine, Matthew Perry, Matthew McConaughey, Matt Leblanc, Matt Damon; photographer Mathew Brady; poet Matthew Arnold; tennis star Mats Wilander.

Madteo, Madteos, Madtheos, Mat, Mata, Mateo, Mateusz, Mathé, Matheu, Mathew, Mathian, Mathias, Mathieu, Matias, Matico, Mats, Matt, Mattaeus, Mattaus, Matteo, Matthaus, Mattheus, Matthias, Matthiew, Mattias, Mattie, Mattieu, Matty, Matvey, Matyas, Matz

Matthias Ger. Var. **Matthew**. German painter Matthias Grunewald.

Mathias, Mattias

Maurice Lat. "Dark-skinned, Moorish." Roman name brought to Britain by the Normans and widely used into the 17th century. A 19th-century revival faded around 1900, the name still occurs. Actor Maurice Chevalier; writer Maurice Sendak; composer Maurice Ravel.

Mauricio, Maurids, Maurie, Maurise, Maurits, Mauritius, Mauritz, Maurizio, Maury, Maurycy, Morey, Morice, Moricz, Moris, Moritz, Moriz, Morrel, Morrey, Morrice, Morrill, Morris, Morriss, Moss

Max Dim. **Maxwell, Maximilian**. Appeared at the turn of the 20th century, fashionable by the 1930s, then faded, but today's parents are showing interest in it again. Writer Max Beerbohm; actor Max von Sydow.

Maks, Maxence, Maxson

Maximilian Lat. "Greatest." Appropriately enough, used by the emperor of Mexico and the Holy Roman emperor, though a bit of a mouthful for a child. German parents apparently don't see it that way, for the name is extremely popular there. Actor Maximilian Schell.

Mac, Mack, Maks, Maksim, Maksym, Maksymilian, Massimiliano, Massimo, Max, Maxey, Maxemilian, Maxemilion, Maxie, Maxim, Maxime, Maximiliano,

Maximilianus, Maximilien, Maximillian, Maximino, Maximo, Maximos, Maxy, Maxymilian, Maxymillian

Maxwell OE. Place name: Maybe "Maccus' well," though some sources also suggest "large well" or "important man's well." Mostly Scottish last name, fairly common as a first name. Parents who wish to call a son **Max** but want to give him something a little more important-sounding as a first name may turn to Maxwell. Editor Maxwell Perkins; playwright Maxwell Anderson.

Maxwelle

IT'S A PUPPY, IT'S A KITTEN, IT'S A BABY!

Every now and then parents go a little too far in choosing inventive names for their children, and it seems that the name they've picked would really be more suited to a pet. Could this be some cosmic confusion? Some of the hottest names for pets right now have been borrowed from the human world: Max is the top choice for four-legged family members, with Jake, Molly, and Sam right up there. Parents are even using the hypherfashionable Samantha for their pets. When the ASPCA polled vets to arrive at this list, though, some of the favorites were traditional choices like Lady, Bear, and Muffin. Cat owners won't be the least bit surprised to know that the seventh most popular name for American pets is that unavoidable old standby, Kitty.

Mayer Lat. "Larger." Var. **Major**. Also Ger. "Farmer," Heb. "Bright, shining." Banker Mayer Rothschild.

Maier, Meir, Meyer

Mayes Eng. Origin unclear; may be related to the month of

May, or to the cultivation of corn ("maize") or even to veneration of the Virgin Mary. Baseball player Willie Mays.

Mays

Mayfield OE. Place name: "Strong one's field."

Mayhew OF. Var. **Matthew** (Heb. "Gift of the Lord").

Maynard OE. "Hard strength." See **Meinhard**. Economist John Maynard Keynes.

Mayne, Maynhard, Meinhard, Meinhardt, Menard

Mayo Ir. Gael. Place name: "Yew tree plain." Mayo is a county in western Ireland. It is also most commonly the short name for a condiment used in sandwiches, a fact parents should bear in mind.

Mazor Heb. "Bandage."

Mead OE. Place name: "Meadow." General George Meade was in charge of the Army of the Potomac in the Civil War, and played a crucial part in the Union victory at Gettysburg. Architect William Rutherford Mead.

Meade, Meed

Medad Heb. "Friend."

Meydad

Medford OE. Place name: "Ford at the meadow."

Meadford

Medwin OG. "Strong friend."

Medvin, Medwinn, Medwyn

Meged Heb. "Blessing, goodness."

Meilyr Welsh "Chief ruler."

Meinhard Ger. "Hard strength." **Maynard** is the anglicized form.

Mainard, Maynard, Meinhardt, Meino

Meinrad Ger. "Strong counsel."

Meir Heb. "Bright, shining." This name is currently popular in Israel, possibly in remembrance of Prime Minister Golda Meir. More common forms in the U.S. include some of the variant spellings.

Meiri, Mayer, Meyer, Myer

Mel Dim. **Melvin** and other "Mel-" names. Actor Mel Gibson; filmmaker Mel Brooks.

Melbourne OE. Place name: "Mill stream." Also the name

of a prominent city in Australia, which was called Melbourne after the man who was Prime Minister of England in 1837, when Queen Victoria came to the throne. Occasional use.

Mel, Melborn, Melburn, Milbourn, Milbourne, Milburn, Millburn, Millburne

Melchior Pol. "King." The root of the name is actually the Hebrew **Malki**, which means King. One Hebrew version is **Malkior**. Traditionally the name of one of the Three Kings, along with **Caspar** and **Balthasar**. Opera singer Lauritz Melchior.

Malchior, Malkior, Melker, Melkior

Melchisedek Heb. "My king is righteousness." Old Testament name.

Melchisadak, Melchisadeck, Melchizadek

Meldon OE. Place name: "Mill hill."

Melden

Meldrick OE. "Mill ruler."

Melderick, Meldric

Melesio Sp. from Gk. "Careful, meticulous."

Melacio, Melasio, Melecio, Melicio, Meliseo, Milesio

Mellen Ir. Gael. "Small pleasant one."

Meldan, Mellan, Mellin, Mellon

Melville OE./OF. Place name: "Industrious one's town." Author Herman Melville.

Melvin Could come from a number of sources: possibly Ir. Gael. "Polished chief," OE. "Sword friend," or an adaptation of **Melville**.

Malvin, Malvyn, Malvynn, Mel, Melvyn, Melwin, Melwyn, Melwynn, Vinnie

Menachem Heb. "Comforter." Israeli statesman Menachem Begin.

Menahem, Nachum, Nahum

Mendel Semitic. "Wisdom, learning." The father of modern genetics, Gregor Mendel, was a 19th-century Austrian priest, abbot of an order of monks.

Mendell, Mendeley

Mentor Greek mythology name: in the *Odyssey,* Mentor was the name of a friend of Odysseus', who became his son Telemachus' tutor. To speak to Odysseus the goddess Athena assumed Mentor's guise. The name has been adapted as the current noun, meaning a wise and trusted guide.

Mercer ME. Occupational name: "Storekeeper." Choreographer Merce Cunningham; musician Johnny Mercer.

Merce

Mercury Mythology name: the messenger of the gods. He corresponds to the Greek Hermes, and was usually depicted as a young man with winged sandals. He was the god of science and commerce, as well as the patron of travelers and thieves! A sixth-century priest named Mercury changed his name to John when he was elected to the papacy, since he felt that it was inappropriate for a pope to have the name of a pagan god. Football player Mercury Morris.

Mercure, Mercuree, Mercurey

Mercator Lat. "Merchant." The Latinate name of Gerardus Kremer, the 16th-century cartographer whose projection for a map of the world was extremely useful to navigators.

Meredith Welsh. "Great ruler." More commonly a girl's name, but still clung to for boys in Wales. Composer Meredith Willson.

Meredyth, Merideth, Meridith

Merle Fr. "Blackbird." Very rare for boys. Singer Merle Haggard.

Merlin ME. "Small falcon." Also the name (via a mistranslation: see **Mervin**) of the wizard of the Arthurian legends. Use dates from the 20th century. Football player Merlin Olsen.

Marlin, Marlon, Merle, Merlen, Merlinn, Merlyn, Merlynn

Merrick Anglicization of a Welsh variant of **Maurice**. Used from time to time in this century. Theater producer David Merrick.

Merrik, Meyrick

Merrill Origin disputed, perhaps OF. "Famous" or a phonetic variation of the girl's name **Meryl**. Its status as a surname probably depends on the medieval use of its antecedent, **Muriel**. Poet James Merrill.

Meril, Merill, Merrel, Merrell, Merril, Meryl

Merritt OE. "Little renowned one."

Merrett, Merit, Meritt

Mersey OE. Place name, meaning unclear. A river in Western England that runs into the Irish sea, and connects the industrial cities of Liverpool and Manchester.

Merton OE. Place name: "Town by the lake." Theologian Thomas Merton.

Merwyn, Murton

Mervin Old Welsh. "Sea hill." **Mervyn** is more common in Britain. Merlin the wizard of Arthurian legend was known in Welsh as Myrddin, translated into Latin as **Merlin**. The name was mildly popular around the turn of the century.

Merven, Mervyn, Mervynn, Merwin, Merwinn, Merwyn, Murvin, Murvyn

Meshach Heb. Meaning unknown. Old Testament name: one of three Hebrew men (along with the now scarce Shadrach and Abednego) thrown into a fiery furnace by King Nebuchadnezzar and rescued by an angel. Used sparingly in the 19th century, even more rare today. Actor Meshach Taylor.

Methodios Gk. "Fellow traveler." St. Methodius, a bishop of Constantinople, is venerated in the Orthodox church for his support of sacred images such as icons, which came under attack in the 9th century. Ironically the term "fellow traveler" came to be used of communists, especially in England, in the 20th century.

Methodius

Methuselah Heb. Possibly "One who was sent." Biblical character Methuselah lived to be 969 years old. A name that would sit oddly on a baby.

Mathusela

Meyer Ger. "Farmer"; Heb. "Bringer of light." Architect Richard Meier; financier Mayer Rothschild.

Mayeer, Mayer, Mayor, Meier, Meir, Myer

Micah Heb. Var. **Michael**. Very easily confused with

Michael when it is spoken. And though Michael is a perennial favorite among names and parents sometimes tinker with its spelling, they do not turn to this alternative in great numbers.

Mike, Mikey, Mikal, Mycah

Michael Heb. "Who is like the Lord?" In the New Testament, Michael is the name of the archangel who defeats the dragon. Usage was steady until a period of neglect that lasted from the early 19th to the early 20th century. The subsequent revival was immense, and Michael was, according to many listings, the most popular name for American boys from the 1970s right through to 1997 when it was displaced by **Jacob**. Even as we move into the 21st century, this continues to be a favorite. In France, as **Michel**, and in Russia as **Mikhail**, it is also on the top-ten list. Baseball star Mickey Mantle; actors Mickey Rooney, Michael Caine, Michael J. Fox, Michel Chiklis, Michael Gambon, Michael Imperioli, Mike Meyers; singers Michael Jackson, Mick Jagger; cartoon star Mickey Mouse; Soviet statesman Mikhail Gorbachev; hockey player Mike Modano; fashion designer Michael Kors.

Micael, Mical, Michal, Micheal, Michel, Michele, Michiel, Mickey, Micky, Miguel, Mihail, Mihaly, Mikael, Mike, Mikel, Mikey, Mikhail, Mikhalis, Mikhos, Mikkel, Miko, Mikol, Miky, Mischa, Misha, Mitch, Mitchell, Mychal, Mykal, Mykell

Michelangelo Comb. form **Michael** (Heb. "Who is like the Lord?") and **Angelo** (Gk. "Messenger"). Use, mostly Italian, probably refers to the great Italian Renaissance artist, Michelangelo Buonarroti.

Middleton OE. Place name: "Settlement in the middle" or possibly "Settlement near the meadow."

Midian Old Testament name: a son of Abraham who founded the tribe of Midianites, who continually oppressed the Israelites until their decisive defeat by Gideon.

Migdal Heb. "Tower."

Migdahl, Migdoll

Miguel Sp. var. **Michael** (Heb. "Who is like the Lord?").
Migelly

Milbank OE. Place name: "Mill on the bank."
Millbank

Milan Possibly a variant of **Miles**; also possibly reference to the northern Italian city of Milan (or Milano), which takes its name from a Celtic word meaning "mid-plain."
Milano

Miles Several possible origins, including Lat. "Soldier," OG. "Merciful," or variant of **Emil** (Lat. "Eager to please"). Since the end of the 18th century, it has been quite unusual. Pilgrim leader Miles Standish; musician Miles Davis.
Milan, Milo, Myles

Milburn OE. Place name: "Mill near the stream."
Milborn, Milborne, Milbourne, Millborn, Millborne, Millbourne, Millburne

Milford OE. Place name: "Mill-ford."
Millford

Millard OE. "Guardian of the mill." U.S. President Millard Fillmore.
Millerd, Millward, Milward

Millbrook OE. Place name: "Mill by the brook."
Milbrook, Milbrooke, Millbrooke

Miller OE. Occupational name. Use as a first name began in the late 19th century, is now sparing. Playwright Arthur Miller.
Millar, Myller

Mills OE. Place name "Near the mills," or possibly a contraction of "Miles' son."

Milo Ger. Var. **Miles**. Very unusual. Actor Milo O'Shea.

Milton OE. Place name: "Mill town" or perhaps "Middle town." One of the more commonplace names transferred to a first name, dating from the early 19th century. Now it sounds like a name for a man of a previous generation. Poet John Milton; comedian Milton Berle.
Milt, Millton, Milten, Miltin, Mylton

Miner Occupational name: "Miner."

Minor Lat. "Younger." It used to be the practice in English boarding schools, where boys were known by their last names, to call younger brothers Churchill and Churchill Minor, for instance. Photographer Minor White.

Menor, Miner, Meinor, Mynor

Minos Greek mythology name: the king of Crete who built the labyrinth. According to legend, Cretan civilization reached a peak under his reign.

Minster OE. Place name: "Church." It originally meant a church belonging to a monastery.

Miroslaw Slavic "Great glory."

Mirek, Miroslav, Miroslawy

Misha Rus. Var. **Michael**. Given some modern exposure as the nickname of superstar dancer Mikhail Baryshnikov. Musician Misha Dichter.

Mischa

Mistral Provencal. "Masterful." The name of a cold, violent wind that blows seasonally in the South of France.

Mitchell ME. Var. **Michael**. The last name evolved in the Middle Ages, when surnames began to be regularly used, and it was transferred back to a first name in the 19th century. It was popular in the middle of the 20th century, and is now steadily used without being fashionable. Band leader Mitch Miller.

Mitch, Mitchel, Mitchill, Mytch

Mitford OE. Place name: probably "Middle ford."

Moab Old Testament name of uncertain meaning: Moab was one of the sons of Lot, and the tribe of Moabites was consistently in conflict with the Israelites.

Modesto Sp. from Lat. "Modest, humble."

Madesto, Medesto, Modestus

Modred OE. "Brave counselor." In the Arthurian legend, Modred is Arthur's illegitimate son who tries to claim his father's throne, and engineers his ultimate downfall.

Mordred

Mohajit Sanskrit. "Alluring, bewitching."

Mohammed Arab. "Highly praised." The name of the prophet and founder of Islam. There are many different forms of this name as it has been spelled in many different languages, many of which had little in common with

Arabic. The Islamic population of England is so large that this is now one of the top thirty names in that country. Boxer Mohammed Ali.

Mahmood, Mahmoud, Mahmud, Mahomet, Mehmood, Mehmoud, Mehmud, Mohammad, Muhammad, Muhammed

Mohandas Sanskrit. "Servant of Mohan." Mohan, which means "alluring," is one of the names of Krishna, one of the great Hindu gods. Mohandas was the first name of the Indian leader Ghandi, also known as Mahatma Ghandi. His use of passive resistance and civil disobedience were instrumental in gaining Indian independence from Britain.

Mohave American place name: the Mohave desert covers about 15,000 miles in southern California. It takes its name from the Mohave Indians, related to the Yumans.

Mojave

Mohawk Native American name: the Mohawk Indians were a tribe of the Iroquois confederacy. Their name has been given to a river and also to a roadway, the Mohawk Trail, by which many settlers traveled from the eastern seaboard to the area of the Great Lakes.

Mohegan Native American name: a tribe related to the Algonquins, indigenous to eastern Connecticut. They have also been known as Mahicans and Mohicans, and as such were subjects of the James Fenimore Cooper novel (made into a film in the 1990s), *The Last of the Mohicans*. They have been considered a division of the Pequot tribe, which has been so successful in pioneering gambling in Connecticut.

Mahican, Mohican

Monahan Ir. Gael. "Monk."

Monaghan, Monoghan

Monckton OE. Place name: "Monk's settlement."

Monkton

Monroe Ir. Gael. Place name: May mean "Mouth of the Roe River" or possibly "The red marsh." U.S. President James Monroe; novelist H.H. Munro.

Monro, Munro, Munroe

Montague Fr. Place name: "Sharply pointed mount." More common as first name in the 19th century.

Montagew, Montagu

Montana Latinate place name: "Mountainous." The name is not true Latin, but is understood as if it were. This kind of pretentious naming was common in the 19th century, when to call a state simply "Mountain State" would have seemed undignified. Though the "-a" ending usually signifies a female name, the state itself is so rugged and the legend of the West so masculine that Montana, like **Dakota** (but significantly less often), is sometimes used for boys.

Montgomery OE. Place name: "Mount of the rich man." Unusual as a first name, and very likely to be shortened to "Monty." Actor Montgomery Clift.

Monte, Montie, Montgomerie, Monty

Monty Dim. "Mont-" names like **Montague** and **Montgomery**, used rarely as a given name. Given slightly ridiculous connotations by TV master of ceremonies Monty Hall and British comedy troupe Monty Python.

Moore OE. Place name: "The moors" or OE. "Dark-skinned" (as in "Moorish"). Clement Clarke Moore was the author of the much-loved poem " 'Twas the night before Christmas."

More

Mordecai Heb. Meaning not clear, but possibly "Follower of Marduk" (who was a god of the Babylonians). An Old Testament name revived by the Puritans and neglected since the 19th century.

Mordechai, Mordy, Mort

Moreland OE. Place name: "Moor-land." Moor is a British term referring to a large, rolling expanse of scrubby, infertile wild land.

Moorland, Morland

Morgan Different sources give several meanings, including Welsh. "Great and bright" and OE. "Bright or white sea dweller." The name is most common in Wales as both a first and a last name. It occurs infrequently in the U.S.

for boy babies but quite often for girls. Actor Morgan Freeman; financier J.P. Morgan.

Morgen, Morgun, Morrgan

Moriel Heb. "God is my teacher."

Mori

Morley OE. Place name: "Meadow on the moor." TV commentator Morley Safer.

Moorley, Moorly, Morlee, Morleigh, Morly, Morrley

Morris Anglicization of **Maurice** (Lat. "Dark-skinned, Moorish"). Now more common as a surname. Choreographer Mark Morris.

Morey, Morice, Moris, Morrey, Morrie, Morrison, Morrisson, Morry

Morse OE. "Son of Maurice." Contracted from Morrison. Inventor Samuel F.B. Morse.

Morrison

Mortimer OF. Place name: "Still water." Literally, "dead sea," *mort mer.* First-name use, as with so many of these place names, dates from the 19th century. Entrepreneur Mortimer Zuckerman.

Mort, Morty, Mortymer

Morton OE. Place name: "Moor town." Like **Mortimer**, used as a first name since the 19th century, though probably more common.

Morten

Morven Scot. Gael. "Huge mountain." First-name use is mostly Scottish, and generally confined to girls.

Morfin, Morfinn, Morfyn, Morvyn

Moses History unclear. Some sources suggest Heb. "Savior," while others claim it means "Taken from the water." The latter definition clearly comes from the biblical story of the infant Moses afloat in the bulrushes, whence he was rescued by Pharaoh's daughter, later to become the great leader of the exiled Israelites. Always current in Jewish families, adopted by the Puritans in the 17th century, now uncommon. The fashion for Old Testament names that brought **Jeremy** and **Joshua** to popularity bypassed Moses completely, possibly because we tend to think of Moses as a great leader, the one who received the tablet of the Ten Commandments. It may seem like too big a name for a child. Israeli defense minister Moshe Dayan.

Mioshe, Mioshye, Mo, Moe, Moise, Moises, Mose, Moshe, Mosheh, Mosie, Moss, Moyses, Mozes

Moss Possibly OE. place name describing a locale covered with moss, or perhaps an adaptation of **Moses**. Director and playwright Moss Hart.

Mostyn Welsh. Place name: "Mossy settlement."

Muhammad Arab. "Greatly praised." Name of the prophet and founder of Islam. There are some 500 variants of this name, and if they were all counted as one name, it would be the most popular name in the world. Many Muslims believe that angels pray with families which have a member named Muhammad. Converts to Islam (Cassius Clay being a notable example) often take a holy name when they convert: the boxer, of course, became Muhammad Ali.

Hamid, Hammad, Mahomet, Mehmet, Mihammad, Mohamet, Mohammad, Mohammed, Muhamet, Muhammed

Muir Scot. Gael. Place name: "Moor." Naturalist John Muir.

Muller Ger. Occupational name: "Miller."

Mueller

Munchin Ir. Gael. "Little monk." This is the anglicized version of Mainchin. **Mannix** is another form.

Mungo Scot. Gael. Some sources suggest "Most dear," while others dispute this meaning. Mungo (from *Munghu*) is a nickname for the ancient name Kentigern, and the 7th-century Scottish Saint Kentigern is sometimes referred to as Saint Mungo. The name appears from time to time in Scotland.

Munir Arab. "Shining, glowing."

Mouneer, Mouneir, Mounir, Muneer, Muneir

Munroe See **Monroe**.

Murdock Scot. Gael. "Sea fighter" or "Sailor." Generally Scottish usage; in the U.S., occurs mainly as a transferred surname. Media magnate Rupert Murdoch.

Murdo, Murdoch, Murtagh, Murtaugh

Muriel Ir. Gael. "Sea bright." Usually a female name.

Murphy Ir. Gael. "Sea fighter." A quintessentially Irish last name, in occasional use as a first name.

Murfee, Murfey, Murfie, Murphee, Murphey, Murphie

Murray Scot. Gael. Place name, or possibly "Mariner." Somewhat common as a first name in the 1930s and 1940s, but now little used.

Moray, Murrey, Murry

Murrow Celt. "Sea warrior." Journalist Edward R. Murrow.

Morrow, Morrowe, Murough, Murrough

Mustafa Arab. "Chosen." This is one of the names of Muhammad. It is also the name of the Turkish general who helped found modern Turkey.

Mustapha

Myron Gk. "Fragrant oil." Not, despite its sound, related to myrrh (as carried by the Three Kings). Like **Murray**, most common in the middle third of the 20th century.

Miron

Nabil Arab. "Highborn."
   Nabeel
Nachman Heb. "Comforter."
   Menachem, Menahem, Nacham, Nachmann, Nahum

Nachson Heb. "Adventurous person."

Nachum Heb. "Comfort."

Nahum, Nechum, Nehum

Nadim Arab. "Friend."

Nadeem

Nadir Arab. "Precious, scarce." Parents should bear in mind that in English the nadir of something is its lowest point, so this name may have negative connotations.

Nadeer, Nadeir

Naftali Heb. "Wrestle, struggle, fight." Old Testament name: a son of Jacob and one of the ancestors of the Twelve Tribes of Israel.

Naphtali, Naphthali, Neftali, Nefthali, Nephtali, Nephthali

Nagel Ger. Occupational name: "Maker of nails."

Naegel, Nageler, Nagelle, Nagle, Nagler

Nagid Heb. "Ruler, leader."

Nahir Heb. "Clear, bright."

Naheer

Naim Heb. "Sweet," Arab. "Contented."

Naeem

Nairn Scot. Gael. Place name: "River with alder trees."

Nairne

Nairobi African place name: the capital of Kenya.

Najib Arab. "Of highborn parentage."

Nageeb, Nagib, Najeeb

Naldo Sp. Dim. **Reginald** (OG. "Powerful advice").

Nalin Hindi. "Lotus." The name signifies different plants in several different cultures: The Egyptians consider it a kind of water lily, while to the Greeks it is a shrub. It also has great significance in both Buddhism and the Hindu religion, in which the lotus, as a beautiful flower that flourishes in muddy waters, symbolizes enlightenment found in the most unpromising circumstances. Buddha is frequently depicted sitting on a lotus blossom. In Homeric legend, by contrast, eating the lotus causes people to forget their homes and families and long for a life of idleness.

Naleen

Napier Scottish place name. Sixteenth-century Scottish mathematician Sir John Napier was very influential.

Neper

Napoleon OG. Meaning unclear, though tradition says it means "Lion of Naples." Another possibility is Greek "New town." Napoleon Bonaparte (who obviously inspired its use) came not from Naples, but from Corsica.

Leon, Leone, Nap, Napoleone

Narcisse Fr. "Daffodil." Not, as it would be in English, a flower name, but the name of a beautiful Greek youth who became enamored of his own reflection—hence "narcissism."

Narciso, Narcissus, Narkissos, Narses

Naren Sanskrit. "Superior man."

Nash OE. Meaning obscure but "Headland, cliff" is one possibility. Poet Ogden Nash; architect Sir John Nash.

Nashua Place name: a city in New Hampshire at the conjunction of the Nashua and Merrimack rivers. This is also the name of a famous race horse who won the Kentucky Derby in 1955. Despite its sound, this is not a Hebrew or Old Testament name.

Nasser Arab. "The winner."
Nasir, Naser, Nasr

Nat Dim. **Nathan, Nathaniel**.

Natal Sp. "Birthday." Referring, of course, to the birthday of Jesus, or Christmas. This is also a place name, a province in South Africa. It is called Natal because explorer Vasco da Gama caught sight of the shore on Christmas Day 1497. Durban is its principal port.
Natale, Natalino, Natalio, Nataly

Nathan Heb. "Given." Old Testament name, revived in the 18th century and quite popular in the last 40 years. It has been in the top fifty boys' names in the U.S. for a dozen years. Nathan Hale was the American spy who declared, just before he was hanged by the British in 1776, "I regret that I have but one life to lose for my country." Critic George Jean Nathan; actor Nathan Lane.
Nat, Natan, Nate, Nathen, Nathon

Nathaniel Heb. "Given by God." New Testament name of one of the apostles (who was also called Bartholomew). Used by the Puritans, and a steady presence ever since, though quite a bit less popular than **Nathan**. Author Nathaniel Hawthorne; musician Nat "King" Cole; slave insurrectionist Nat Turner.
Nat, Natanael, Nataniel, Nate, Nathan, Nathaneal, Nathanial, Nathanyal, Nathanyel, Natty, Nethanel, Nethaniel, Nethanyel, Thaniel

Naylor OE. Meaning obscure. This may come from an Old English name meaning "sea," or it may be an occupational name referring to a carpenter or "nailer."
Nailer, Nailor

Naveed Per. "Auspicious news."
   Navid
Nazaire Latin version of Nazareth, the town where Jesus grew up. St. Nazarius was an obscure 4th-century Italian martyr. This is also the name of a town on the northwest coast of France.
   Nasareo, Nasarrio, Nazario, Nazarius, Nazaro, Nazor
Neal Ir. Var. Neil.
   Neale, Neall, Nealle, Neel
Neander Gk. "New man." In 16th century Germany, many educated Germans or scholars changed their names by Latinizing them, substituting Faber ("maker") for Schmidt ("smith"), for instance. Neander is a translation of the German Neumann, a little bit of old-fashioned pretentiousness. Johann Neander, a 19th-century German theologian, was born the Jewish David Mendel, and changed his name when he converted to Christianity.
Nebo Mythological name: a Babylonian god of wisdom who invented writing.
Nectarios Gk. "Of nectar." Nectar is the drink of the gods, in classical myth. Nektarios is the name of a Greek saint, canonized in 1961, who devoted his life to the restoration and organization of a convent on the Greek island of Aegina. He died in 1920.
   Nectaire, Nectarius, Nektario, Nektarios, Nektarius
Ned Dim. **Edward** (OE. "Wealthy defender"); **Edmund** (OE. "Wealthy protector").
Negasi Amharic. "He will wear a crown." Amharic is the language spoken in Ethiopia.
Nehemiah Heb. "The Lord's comfort." Old Testament prophet, Puritan name, rare in this century.
   Nechemia, Nechemiah, Nechemya
Neil Gael. "Champion." Although the name of the most famous Celtic king of Ireland (Niall of the Nine Hostages), it has been used mostly in Scotland until the middle of this century. Astronaut Neil Armstrong; singers Neil Diamond and Neil Young; playwright Neil Simon; actor Sam Neill.
   Neal, Neale, Neall, Nealle, Nealon, Neel, Neile, Neill, Neille, Neils, Nels, Nial, Niall, Niel, Niles

Nels Scand. Var. **Nicholas** (Gk. "People of victory").

Nelson Eng. "Son of Neil." Established by parents who admired the exploits of English Admiral Nelson at the Battle of Trafalgar. Used consistently, if never widely, since then. Actor Nelson Eddy; New York Governor and U.S. Vice President Nelson Rockefeller; South African activist Nelson Mandela.
Nealson, Neils, Neilson, Neillson, Nels, Nelsen, Niles, Nils, Nilson, Nilsson

Nemesio Sp. "Justice."

Nemo Literary name: the captain in Jules Verne's adventure novel *20,000 Leagues Under the Sea*. In Latin, *nemo* can also mean "nobody," which Verne (who enjoyed giving punning names to his characters) probably knew.

Neptune Roman god of the sea, and a fanciful name for sea-loving parents.

Ner Heb. "Light, flame, candle." Appropriate name for boys with Hannukah birthdays.

Nereus Greek mythology name: Nereus was the old man of the sea, father of the sea-nymphs, the nereids.
Nereo

Nesbit OE. Place name: "Bend shaped like a nose." Refers to a bend in a road, or else to a plot of land.
Naisbit, Naisbitt, Nesbitt, Nisbet, Nisbett

Nestor Gk. "Traveler, voyager." In Greek legend, Nestor was the wise ruler of the kingdom of Pylos who, when he went to fight in the Trojan wars, was constantly called on for advice. Cinematographer Nestor Almendros.
Nester, Nesterio, Nestore, Nestorio

Neville OF. Place name: "New town." More common in Britain, but very rare in the U.S. Musical conductor Neville Marriner.
Nev, Nevil, Nevile, Nevyle

Nevin Anglicization of Gaelic names that mean "Holy, sacred," or "Little bone" or "Servant of the saint's disciple." Not very widely used, though it may profit from **Kevin**'s popularity, since it has the same sound.
Nev, Nevan, Neven, Nevins, Nevon, Niven

Newbury ME. "New borough, new settlement."
> **Newbery, Newberry**

Newcomb OE. Place name: "New valley." Combe is an old British term for a valley or the flank of a hill.
> **Newcombe**

Newell OE. Place name: "New hall." The "hall" was often a term for the local manor in early England.
> **Newall, Newel, Newhall**

Newland OE. Place name: "New land."

Newlin OWelsh. Place name: "New pond."

Newman OE. "Newcomer." Began to be used as a first name in England in the 19th century, perhaps influenced by the fame of reforming cleric John Henry (Cardinal) Newman. Now scarce. Actor Paul Newman.
> **Neuman, Neumann, Newmann**

Newport OE. Place name: "New port." In the U.S. the name has been given "cool" connotations by the Newport Jazz Festival and a brand of mentholated cigarettes. The resort of Newport, Rhode Island is only one of ten cities or towns named Newport in America.

Newton OE. Place name: "New town." Like many place names turned last names, made the move to a first name in the 19th century, and has now drifted back to last-name status. Entertainer Wayne Newton; English mathematician Isaac Newton.

Nezer Heb. "Diadem, crown."

Niall Ir. Gael. "Champion." A less common variant of **Neil**, used chiefly in Ireland.
> **Nial**

Niaz Per. "A presentation, a present."

Nicandro Sp. from Gk. "Man of victory."
> **Nicandreo, Nicandrios, Nicandros, Nikander, Nikandreo, Nikandrios**

Nicholas Gk. "People of victory." A New Testament name given even greater fame by the 4th-century Saint Nicholas, patron saint of children and (via his Dutch name, Sinte Klaas) the original Santa Claus. The name was widespread in the Middle Ages through the 17th century, then had a long period of disuse which ended in the middle of the 20th century. This is now one of the top ten names for boys in the nation and is also extremely well used in Germany, Russia, and France. Theater director Nikos Psacharapolous; Dickens' novel *Nicholas Nickleby;* actors Nicholas Cage, Nickolas Grace, Nicol Williamson; composer Nicolai Rimsky-Korsakov; political philosopher Niccolo Machiavelli.

Claas, Claes, Claus, Colas, Cole, Colet, Colin, Collin, Klaas, Klaes, Klaus, Nic, Nicanor, Niccolo, Nichol, Nichole, Nicholl, Nichols, Nick, Nickey, Nickie, Nicklas, Nickolas, Nickolaus, Nicky, Nicol, Nicola, Nicolaas, Nicolai, Nicolas, Nicolao, Nicolay, Nicolet, Nicollet, Nicolis, Nicoll, Nicolls, Nicolo, Nik, Niki, Nikita, Nikki, Nikkolas, Nikkolay, Nikky, Niklaas, Niklas, Nikolai, Nikolas, Nikolaus, Nikolay, Nikolos, Nikos, Nilos

Nickleby OE. Place name: "Nicholas' village." Made famous by the Charles Dickens' novel *Nicholas Nickleby*.

Nico Gk. Diminutive of any of the "Nico-" names.

Nicos, Niko, Nikos

Nicodemus Gk. "Victory of the people." New Testament name, very scarce.

Nicodemo, Nikodema

Nicomedes Gk. "Pondering victory." It is the mark of a fierce people that so many names should feature the word particle meaning "victory."

Nicomedo, Nikomedes

Niels Dan. Var. **Neil** (Gael. "Champion").

Niel, Niles, Nils

Nigel Ir. Gael. "Champion." Related not, as many sources claim, to the Latin *niger* ("black"), but to the Latin form of **Neil**, Nigellus. Almost exclusively a British name, popular in this century. Actor Nigel Havers.

Nikostratos Gk. "Army of victory."

Nicostrato, Nicostratos, Nicostratus

Niles Scand. "Son of Neil." Not common, but cool.

Nyles

Nimrod Heb. "We shall rise up, we shall rebel." Nimrod "the mighty hunter" is mentioned in Genesis.

Ninian Meaning unknown. An Irish saint of the 5th century A.D. Little used, possibly because it sounds so much like "ninny."

Nissan Heb. "Miracle." This is the name of the first month in the Jewish year, when Passover falls. The accent falls on the second syllable, differentiating this name from the Japanese car company.
Nisan

Nissim Heb. "Wondrous things."

Nixon OE. "Son of Nicholas." A contraction of "Nicolas's son," or "Nick's son." After the disgrace of President Nixon in the early 1970s, unlikely to be used as a first name.

Njord Scand. "North." In Norse myth, the god of the sea, patron of fishermen and seafarers.
Njorth

Noah Heb. Meaning unclear, possibly "rest" or "wandering." The latter would be appropriate for the patriarch who drifted in the ark for 40 days. Steadily but not widely used since the 17th century. Lexicographer Noah Webster; actor Noah Wyle.
Noach, Noak, Noé

Noam Heb. "Pleasantness, charm, tenderness." Critic Noam Chomsky. Related to **Naim**.

Noble Lat. "Aristocratic." Use as a first name may derive from surnames, or from the use of the adjective as a name. Mostly 19th century.

Noel Fr. "Christmas." Used since the Middle Ages, but not very widespread. More likely to be chosen for girls. Playwright and actor Noel Coward.
Nata, Natal, Natale, Nowel, Nowell

Nolan Ir. Gael. "Renowned." A last name transferred to first name. Baseball star Nolan Ryan.
Noland, Nolen, Nolin, Nollan

Noor Arab. "Light, brilliance."
Nour, Nur

Norbert OG. "Renowned northerner." Saint's name that was mildly popular in the middle of the 20th century.
Bert, Bertie, Berty, Norberto

Norman OE. "Northerner." The Normans of France were originally from Scandinavia, or the North, but the name was also used in England even before the Norman Conquest. After medieval use, it was neglected until a substantial 19th-century revival, which has long since faded. Artist Norman Rockwell; authors Norman Vincent Peale, Norman Mailer; TV producer Norman Lear.
Norm, Normand, Normen, Normie

Norris OF. "Northerner." May also derive from the French word for "nurse." Modern use dates from the 19th century. Novelist Frank Norris.

Northcliff OE. Place name: "Northern cliff."
Northcliffe, Northclyff, Northclyffe

Northrop OE. Place name: "Northern farm." Critic Northrop Frye.
Northrup

Norton OE. Place name: "Northern town." Revived as a first name in the mid 19th century. The comical Norton on the TV show *The Honeymooners* made this name impossible for older baby boomers to use.

Norville Old Anglo/Fr. Place name: "Northern town."
Norval, Norvel, Norvell, Norvil, Norvill, Norvylle

Norvin OE. "Northern friend."
Norvyn, Norwin, Norwinn, Norwyn, Norwynn

Norward OE. "Warden of the north."
Norwerd

Norwell OE. "Northern well."

Norwood OE. "Woods in the north."

Nuncio It. "Messenger." Comes from the same root that gives us the word "announce."
Nunzio

Nuri Arab. "Light."
Noori, Nur, Nuriel, Nuris

Nuriel Heb. "Light of God, fire of God." Obviously related to the Arab *nur*.
Nooriel, Nuriya, Nuriyah, Nurya

Oakes OE. Place name: "Near the oak trees." Transferred surname. This is also sometimes an anglicization of the German *Ochs,* which means "ox."

Oak, Oaks, Ochs

Oakley OE. Place name: "Oak-tree meadow." The equally unusual **Ackerley** and **Acton** also refer to landmark oak trees.

Oak, Oakes, Oakleigh, Oaklee, Oakly

Obadiah Heb. "Servant of God." One of the lesser Old Testament prophets. The name has faded gradually from sight after its revival by the Puritans in the 17th century.

Obadias, Obadya, Obed, Obediah, Obie, Ovadiah, Ovadiach, Oved

Oberon OG. "Highborn and bearlike." This is its more famous (though little-used) form, as used by Shakespeare for the King of the Fairies in *A Midsummer Night's Dream.* It also occurs (very rarely) as **Auberon.** Author Auberon Waugh.

Auberon, Auberron, Oberron

Obert OG. "Wealthy and bright."

Obi Ibo (Nigerian) "Heart."

Octavius Lat. "Eighth child." In English-speaking countries the name had its heyday in the Victorian era of large families. It has survived slightly better in Latin countries, but it is used in America. Probably very few of today's Octaviuses, though, have seven elder sibliings. Mexican poet Octavio Paz.

Octave, Octavian, Octavien, Octavio, Octavious, Octavo, Octavus, Ottavio

Odell Derivation disputed. Some sources relate it to either German "Rich" or Greek "Song," but *The Facts on File Dictionary of First Names* claims that it derives from an Old English place name: "Woad hill." Woad is a blue dye reputedly used by the ancient Druids in their religious rites.

Dell, Odall, Odie

Odilo OG. "Prospers in battle." The root name is **Otthild**, and the feminine form **Odile** is more common. St. Odilo was an 11th-century monk who instituted the observation of All Souls' day on November 2. Like St. Odo, he was abbott of the influential monastery at Cluny. French painter Odilon Redon.

Odilio, Odilon, Otildo, Ottild, Ottildo

Odin Norse mythology name. The meaning is unknown, but Odin was the principal god in the Norse pantheon. He ruled over culture as well as giving life and souls to people. Finally, he reigned over the dead.

Odolf OG. "Prosperous wolf." In the Middle Ages, to allude to a man as a "wolf" was to compliment his fierceness and courage.

Odolff, Odulf

Odo Var. **Otto** (OG. "Prosperous"). The "-o" ending is most often found in Germanic and Scandinavian names. St. Odo was a French saint of the 9th century who was abbott at the famous monastery of Cluny.

Odran Ir. Gael. "Little pale green one." It's hard to imagine what this name refers to: eye color? A greenish complexion?

Odhran, Oran

Odysseus Greek mythology name: the word particle *dys* means "hate." Odysseus is the wanderer in Homer's great epic poem *The Odyssey*. The Latin version of the name, **Ulysses**, is a little better known in America, because of the fame of President Ulysses S. Grant.

Odysse

Ofir Heb. "Gold." **Ophir** is an Old Testament place name. It is frequently mentioned as an exceptionally rich source of gold, sandalwood, precious stones, and other luxuries. Its actual location is a moot point: scholars can narrow it down no further than India, Africa, or Arabia. In the late 19th century one of the most productive mines in California's Comstock Lode was called "Ophir."

Ofeer, Ophir

Ogden OE. Place name: "Oak valley." Launched as a first name in the 19th century, but never widely used. Poet Ogden Nash.

Ogdan, Ogdon

Ohad Heb. "Loved one."

Ohed

Oisin Gael. "Little deer." In Irish history this was the name of the son of a legendary Gaelic poet, Fionn MacCumhail. Oisin MacCumhail was a warrior and a bard in his own right. In its English form, **Ossian**, it is also the name of a famous literary hoax. A mid 18th century Scottish poet, James MacPherson, published a group of poems that he claimed he had translated from ancient sources. The purported author was Ossian, who was supposed to have lived late in the 3rd century. But after initial acclaim and great popularity, skeptics began to perceive the truth: that MacPherson had written much of the poetry himself.

Ossian, Ossin

Olaf Scand. "Ancestor." A royal name in Norway, as well as a saint's name, but when it came to the British Isles with Norse invaders, it did not catch on. There was a King Olaf of Dublin in the 10th century, but when the Irish finally succeeded in expelling the Norse from Ireland, this name did not stay behind. Novelist Ole Edvart Rolvaag.

Olaff, Olav, Olave, Ole, Olin, Olle, Olof, Olov

Oleg Rus. "Holy." Fashion designer Oleg Cassini.

Olexei Var. **Alexei**, Rus. Var. **Alexander** (Gk. "Defender of mankind").

Oleksei, Oleksey, Oleksi, Oleksiy, Olexey, Olexi, Olexiy

Olimpio "From Mt. Olympus." Olympus was the legendary home of the Greek gods.

Olimpo, Olympios, Olympus

Olin Eng. Var. **Olaf**. Actor Ken Olin.

Olen, Olyn

Olindo Lat. "Scented."

Oliver Lat. "Olive tree" is the most common meaning assigned, but some scholars suggest ON. "Kindly" or "ancestor," among other possibilities. It came to Britain from France, and the controversial Lord Protector Oliver Cromwell made it unpopular for generations. A mild revival occurred in the late 19th century, and the name is infrequently used in the U.S. today. It is very fashionable in England, though. Charles Dickens' *Oliver Twist;* director Oliver Stone; actor Oliver Platt.

Noll, Oliverio, Olivero, Olivier, Oliviero, Olivio, Olivor, Olley, Ollie, Olliver, Ollivor

Omar Arab. "Elevated; follower of the Prophet." Heb. "Expressive." Currently popular in Arab countries and among Muslims in the U.S. This is in fact the most popular of all the "O-" names for boys. Poet Omar Khayyam; actor Omar Sharif; General Omar Bradley.

Omer

Omri Heb. "My sheaf" (of grain, etc.) Another possible meaning is "Jehovah's servant."

Ondré Var. **André** (Gk. "Man").

Ohndrae, Ohndray, Ohndre, Ohndrei, Ohndrey, Ondrae, Ondray, Ondrei, Onndrae, Onndrai, Onndray, Onndre

Onofrio It. from Ger. "Peace defender." Actor Vincent D'Onofrio.

Onofre, Onofrius, Onophrio

Onslow OE. Place name: "Enthusiast's hill."

Onslowe, Ounslow

Ophir Heb. "Gold." See **Ofir**.

Or Heb. "Light, brilliance." Related to **Oran**. This name is often used in combination with other names as in Or-Chaim ("Light of life") and Or-Zion ("Light of Zion").

Oran Ir. Gael. "Green." Also Aramaic, "Light."

Oren, Orin, Orran, Orren, Orrin

Orazio It. "Prayer." May also be a variant of **Horace**, an ancient Latin clan name of uncertain meaning.

Oratio

Oren Heb. "Pine tree"; Ir. Gael. "Fair, pale-skinned." Very unusual. U.S. Senator Orrin Hatch.

Orin, Orren, Orrin

Orestes Gk. "Man of the mountain." An important figure

in Greek myth, the son of Agamemnon and the brother of Electra, with whose help he murdered his mother (to avenge his father, whom *she* had murdered). Orestes appears in eight of the classic Greek tragedies. Not a cheerful heritage, overall.

Aoresty, Aresty, Oreste

Orford OE. Place name: "Ford of cattle."

Orion Gk. "Son of fire or light." In Greek myth, Orion was a mighty hunter who was turned into the constellation of the same name.

Oryon

Orlando Sp. Var. **Roland** (OG. "Famous land"). Mostly literary and minor late19th-century use. Virginia Woolf's novel *Orlando* is a gender-bending fantasy inspired by Woolf's friend Vita Sackville-West. Composer Orlando Gibbons; football player Orlando Pace; actor Orlando Bloom.

Arlando, Land, Lanny, Orlan, Orland, Roland, Rolando

Orman OG. "Sea-man" or OE. "Spear-man."

Ormand

Ormond OE. Place name "Mountain of bears," or "Spear or ship protector"; Ir. Gael. "Red." Irish last name, occasionally transferred.

Ormand, Ormonde

Oro Sp. "Golden."

Orpheus Greek mythology name. Orpheus' music gave him spellbinding power over all living things. He married a nymph, Eurydice, and went to the Underworld to find her. The gods, enchanted by his music, permitted him to take her back to earth on the condition that he not look at her as he led her upward to the lands of open sky. He could not resist glancing at her, and she vanished back into Hades. The story of Orpehus and Eurydice has been made into several operas.

Orfeo

Orrick OE. Place name: "Old oak tree." Poet Orric Johns.

Orric

Orson Lat. "Like a bear." In an old French story, a child named Orson is reared in the forest by a bear. The name is very unusual, though it may be used by ardent fans of director Orson Welles. Actor Orson Bean.

Orsen, Orsin, Orsini, Orsino, Orsis, Orsonio, Sonny, Urson

Orton OE. Place name: "Shore settlement." Playwright Joe Orton.

Orval OE. "Strength of a spear." Also variant of **Orville**.

Orville OF. Place name: "Town of gold." Though the name translates this way, it may actually have been coined by an 18th-century novelist. Never widespread. Flight pioneer Orville Wright.

Orv, Orval, Orvell, Orvil

Orvin OE. "Spear-friend."

Orwin, Orwynn

Osage Name for a Native American tribe of the Plains. This name is probably a French version of their own name for themselves. They were displaced from Missouri and Arkansas into smaller land holdings in Oklahoma.

Osbert OE. "Divine and bright." Anglo-Saxon name revived mildly with the antiquarian craze of the 19th century, but now extremely rare. Poet Osbert Sitwell.

Osborn OE. "Divine bear." The 19th-century revival of this Anglo-Saxon name was followed by another small spurt of use in the middle of the 20th century. Rock star Ozzy Osbourne.

Osborne, Osbourn, Osbourne, Osburn, Osburne, Ozzie

Oscar Scand. "Divine spear." Anglo-Saxon name revived by 18th-century literary use, reaching substantial popularity by the late 19th century. Fans of *Sesame Street* might hesitate to name a baby for the curmudgeonly Oscar the Grouch, but some parents bravely persist. Lyricist Oscar Hammerstein II; playwright Oscar Wilde; fashion designer Oscar de la Renta.

Oskar, Osker, Ossie, Ozzy

Osei Ghanaian. "Honorable, worthy of respect."

Osgood OE. "Divine Goth." The Goths were a Germanic ethnic group that took over various parts of Europe after the fall of the Roman Empire. Since the Goths were not

Christian until well into the sixth century, the meaning of this name is puzzling.

Osher Heb. "Happiness, good fortune."

Osier OE. Place name: "By the willows." Osier twigs or shoots have long been used to make baskets and wicker.

Osmar OE. "Divine and wonderful."

Osmond OE. "Divine protector." Anglo-Saxon name revived in the 19th century, but scarcely found now. Henry James named one of his most sinister characters (Isabel Archer's suitor in *The Portrait of a Lady*) Gilbert Osmond. Singer Michael Osmond; actor Haley Joel Osment.
Osman, Osment, Osmonde, Osmont, Osmund, Osmunde

Osred OE. "Divine counsel."

Osric OE. "Divine ruler."
Osrick

Osten Var. Austin (Lat. "Worthy of respect").
Austen, Austin, Ostin, Ostyn

Oswald OE. "Divine power." Another Anglo-Saxon name that endured partially because of the fame of two saints of the name. Use has been mostly 19th century, though actor Ozzie Nelson's real name was Oswald. After President Kennedy's assasination was pinned on Lee Harvey Oswald, this name became unusable in America until memories faded. Fashion designer Ossie Clark.
Ossie, Osvald, Osvaldo, Oswaldo, Oswell, Ozzie, Waldo

Oswin OE. "Divine friend."
Osvin, Oswinn, Oswyn, Oswynn

Othman OG. "Wealthy man."

Othniel Heb. "God's strength, God's lion."
Otniel

Otis OE. "Son of Otto." Use is mostly American. Maybe because of associations with composer Otis Redding, this name is currently quite cool, a rock-star's child kind of name. Actor Otis Skinner.
Oates, Otess

Ottfried OG. "Prosperous peace."
Ottfrid

Otto OG. "Prosperous." German name that was fairly common in English-speaking countries until Otto von Bismarck's German armies became threateningly powerful at the turn of the 20th century. The Second World War against Germany further limited the name's use. The slight vogue for names ending with "-o" may bring it back to favor.
Odo, Othello, Otho

Oved Heb. "Worshiper, follower." Related to **Obadiah**.
Obed

Ovid Meaning disputed: some sources suggest "Shepherd," others offer "Egg" or "Obedient." This may be a Latin clan name: it was the middle name of Publius Obidius Naso, a Roman poet of the first century A.D. whose *Metamorphoses* has been a staple of the Western literary canon.

Owen Welsh. Var. Eugene. Gk. "Wellborn." Fairly common outside Wales since the 18th century. Owen Glendower was a 14th-century Welsh chieftain who battled unsuccessfully for Welsh independence from England. Now steadily used in the U.S. Author Owen Wister; actor Owen Wilson.
Ewan, Ewen, Owain, Owin

Oxford OE. Place name: "Ford of the oxen." Once upon a time this was either a kind of laced shoe (generally detested by children) or possibly a famous English university. Now also a health-care company.
Oxxford

Oz Heb. "Power, force, courage."

Pablo Sp. Var. **Paul** (Lat. "Little"). Spanish names have now reached considerable popularity in the U.S. and in some cases the Spanish version of a name may be more popular than its English cognate. This is not true with Pablo, however. Paul is somewhere in the top 75 percent of names in the U.S., while Pablo ranks with oddities like **Fabian, Brock**, and **Gustavo**. Artist Pablo Picasso; cellist Pablo Casals; poet Pablo Neruda.

Pablos

Pace Possibly a variation of **Pascal** (Fr. "Easter"). Connotations of efficiency and speed may make this name appealing.

Paice, Payce

Paciano Sp. from Lat. "Peaceful."

Pacifico Sp. from Lat. "Calmed, tranquil." Obviously the root is the same as it is for **Paciano**: the Latin *pax*. This is, of course, where the (rather deceptive) name of the Pacific Ocean comes from.

Pacificus

Packard Origin disputed. Some sources give German, "Dweller at the brook," while others refer to a peddler's pack. Packard was a brand of car earlier in the 20th century. Author Vance Packard.

Packer, Packert

Paco Sp. Var. **Francis** (Lat. "From France"). A diminutive of **Francisco**. Fashion designer Paco Rabanne.

Pacorro

Paddy Ir. Var. **Patrick** (Lat. "Noble, patrician"). Unusual as a given name, though so common as a nickname that it used to be used as a generic term for Irishmen. Author Paddy Chayefsky.

Paddey, Paddie, Padraic, Padraig

Pagan Lat. "From the country, countryman." Pagan has come to mean heathen, someone not initiated into the true religion (which true religion depends on who is calling whom a pagan). The name Paine comes from this term.

Page Fr. A young boy in training as a personal assistant to a knight. Usually a transferred surname, possibly indicating an ancestor who was a page. In the U.S., this has become almost exclusively a girl's name, but some of the diminutives and variations, like Padgett, are still used for boys.

Padget, Padgett, Paget, Pagett, Paige, Payge

Pagiel Heb. "God disposes." Old Testament name.

Paine Lat. "Countryman." Thomas Paine, a political theorist of the 18th century, wrote many political pamphlets that were influential during the American Revolution, and his *The Rights of Man* supported the French Revolution.
Pain, Payne

Paisley Scottish place name: an industrial town west of Glasgow. The name "paisley" referring to a pattern on fabric comes from this town, since shawls with that pattern were made here in the 18th century. The characteristic elongated comma shape, however, is actually Indian, and based on a pine cone.

Paladio Sp. from Gk. "Follower of Pallas" which was another name for the Greek goddess Athena. St. Palladius was the first bishop of the Christians in Ireland, in the middle of the fifth century A.D.
Palladius

Paley OE. Origin unclear: may relate to **Paul**, or may be a place name, with the "-ley" ending indicating a meadow. CBS founder William Paley.

Palmer OE. "One who holds a palm." Usually indicates a pilgrim, who would have carried a palm branch on his pilgrimage.
Pallmer, Palmar, Palmerston

Palomo Sp. "Dove." More popular in the feminine form, Paloma.

Paltiel Heb. "God is my deliverance."
Platya, Platyahu

Paquito Sp. Dim. **Francis** (Lat. "From France").
Paco

Paris OE. Place name: "From Paris," the city. Also a key figure in Greek myth. Paris was a young man of staggering beauty, son of King Priam of Troy. He was chosen to judge a beauty contest of the goddesses by awarding to one of them a golden apple which bore the legend, "For the fairest." Hera, the wife of Zeus, promised Paris greatness if he chose her. Athene offered him greatness in war, and Aphrodite the love of the world's most beautiful woman. He chose Aphrodite, who caused Helen of Troy to fall in love with him. The Trojan War was the outcome:

Paris died an ignoble death in it. The Judgment of Paris has frequently been portrayed in European painting, probably as a good excuse to depict three scantily clad beauties. Use of the name is predominantly American and is beginning to cross over to use for girls.

Parris

Parker OE. "Park keeper." Occupational name turned surname, popular in the 19th century as a given name but now more unusual. Also occasionally used for girls. Actor Parker Stevenson; musician Charlie Parker; historian Francis Parkman.

Parke, Parkes, Parkman, Parks

Parkin OE. "Little Peter."

Parken

Parmenio Sp. "Intelligent, studious."

Parmenios, Parmenius

Parnell OF. "Little Peter." Made famous by the 19th-century Irish politician Charles Parnell, who campaigned for home rule in Ireland.

Parrnell, Pernell

Parr OE. Place name: "Castle park."

Parrish OF. "Ecclesiastical locality." A parish is the area under the care of one pastor or priest. The name would originally have been a last name based on a place name.

Parish, Parris, Parriss

Parry OWelsh. "Son of Harry." Composer Hubert Parry.

Parrey, Parrie

Parsons OE. Occupational name: "Clergyman." This word originally mean "Man in charge of a parish," and it's the source of our word "person."

Parson, Person, Persons

Parthenios Gk. "Virginal." Difficult to use unless there are compelling familial reasons to do so. A very hard name for a child to explain to his peers!

Parthenius

Parton OE. Place name: possibly "Peter's settlement" or "Castle park settlement."

Parvaiz Per. "Lucky, happy."

Parvez, Parviz, Parwiz

Pascal Fr. "Child of Easter." Used as a first name in English-speaking countries only since the 1960s, and very scarce. The little boy in *The Red Balloon* is called Pascal, which gives the name faintly poignant associations. Philosopher Blaise Pascal.

Pascale, Pascalle, Paschal, Paschalis, Pascuale, Pasquale

Patrick Lat. "Noble, patrician." A Roman name made famous by the 5th-century missionary (and patron of Ireland) Saint Patrick, whose feast day on March 17 is celebrated with parades in the United States, an honor accorded to no other saint. The name spread outside of Ireland in the 18th century and was widely used by the middle of the 20th century. It is now steadily used and has lost its firm associations with Ireland. U.S. statesman Patrick Henry; actors Patrick Fugit, Patrick Swayze, Patrick Dempsey, Jason Patric; playwright John Patrick Shanley; basketball player Patrick Ewing.

Paddey, Paddie, Paddy, Padhraig, Padraic, Padraig, Padriac, Pat, Patrece, Patric, Patrice, Patricio, Patrik, Patrizio, Patrizius, Patryk, Pats, Patten, Patton, Patty

Patterson OE. "Son of Peter."

Paterson, Pattison

Patton OE. Place name: "Fighter's town." Almost too appropriate a meaning for the name of General George Patton. Author Alan Paton.

Paten, Patin, Paton, Patten, Pattin

Paul Lat. "Small." Popular Roman and medieval name whose tremendously widespread modern use dates from the 18th century. Paul is the name of the resilient Sir Paul McCartney, as well of the pope who spearheaded Vatican II. It is not fashionable in the current vogue for original names, but steadily used by parents seeking a familiar name that everybody knows how to spell. In Russia, as **Pavel**, currently very popular. Artists Paul Cézanne, Paul Gauguin; actors Paul Newman, Paul Bettany; Revolutionary War hero Paul Revere; musician Paul Simon; hockey player Pavel Bure.

Paavo, Pablo, Paolo, Pauel, Paulie, Paulin, Paulinus, Paulus, Pauly, Pavel, Pawel, Pol, Poll, Poul

Pawnee Native American tribal name. The Pawnee were a Plains tribe, excellent horsemen, who by 1859 were already settled onto a reservation on the Platte river. Their chief enemies were the Sioux and Wichita tribes rather than European settlers.

Paxton Lat./OE. Place name: "Peace town." This kind of name that combines a Latin word with an Old English word is rare: usually compounds put together particles of the same language. Actors Paxton Whitehead, Bill Paxton.

Packston, Paxon, Paxten, Paxtun

Payne Lat. "Countryman." See **Paine**.

Paine

Pazel Heb. "God's gold." The simpler form, **Paz**, is also used for boys and girls alike. In Spanish the same word means "peace."

Paz

Peabody OE. Origin unclear. It may be related to a bird name (the pea bird, for instance) or to the familiar vegetable. It is a name to reckon with in Massachusetts, the home of 19th-century financier and philanthropist George Peabody and his numerous descendants, many of whom have been educators.

Peak Geography name: the top of a mountain. Good name for a climber's son.

Peale OE. Possibly occupational name referring to a bellringer: a "peal" is a bellringing pattern that dates from the Middle Ages. May also be a variant spelling of **Peel**. Painter Charles Willson Peale, Raphaelle Peale, Rembrandt Peale.

Peal, Peall, Pealle

Pedro Sp. Var. **Peter** (Gk. "Rock"). Filmmaker Pedro Almodovar.

Pedrio, Pepe, Petrolino, Piero

Pedahel Heb. "Redeemed by God."

Pedael, Pedayel

Peel OE. Probably a place name. A peel tower was a small fortified tower common in northern England that permitted a family and its livestock to shelter together in a massive building with limited access to enemies. The humans would live upstairs and withdraw all ladders when they were attacked. English statesman Sir Robert Peel.
Peele

Pelagios Gk. "Of the sea, from the sea."
Pelagius, Pelayo

Peleh Heb. "Miracle."

Pelham OE. Place name: possiby "Tanner's settlement" or "Clerk's settlement."
Pellam

Pell ME. "Skin, parchment." As in parchment that legal documents would be written on; this may be an occupational name, indicating an ancestor who was a clerk.
Pall

Pembroke Celt. Place name: "Bluff, headland."
Pembrook

Pendleton OE. Place name: "Overhanging settlement." May refer to an ancient town on a clifftop. Actor Austin Pendleton.

Penley OE. Place name: "Enclosed meadow."
Penlea, Penleigh, Penly, Pennlea, Pennleigh, Pennley

Penn OE. "Enclosure." In the U.S., tied to the eminent Quaker and founder of Pennsylvania, William Penn.
Pen

Pepper Plant name. Of course the black pellets come from a different kind of plant entirely than the jalapenos or serranos that season Latin and Indian food. This name has probably been used more generally as a nickname, to describe someone of a peppery temperament. Football player Pepper Johnson.

Percival OF. "Pierce the vale." Invented by a medieval poet for one of King Arthur's knights, and its meaning is not completely clear. Adopted with some enthusiasm, however, and was particularly well used in the late 19th century, along with more genuinely ancient names. It may have become popular because Percival was the one

Knight of the Round Table who actually caught a glimpse of the Holy Grail, the famously evasive chalice from Christ's Last Supper. Wagner's opera *Parsifal* is based on one version of this knight's story. The name is now scarce.

Parsafal, Parsefal, Parsifal, Perce, Perceval, Percevall, Percey, Percivall, Percy, Purcell

Percy Fr. "From Percy." A Norman place name that became associated with an immensely powerful aristocratic family in the North of England. Its greatest popularity coincided with that of **Percival**, and like that name, Percy is now widely neglected. Author Walker Percy; poet Percy Bysshe Shelley.

Pearcy, Percey, Percie

Perdido Sp. "Lost." The feminine version, **Perdita**, is occasionally used in English literature. This form is scarce.

Peregrine Lat. "Traveler, pilgrim." "Peregrinations" is a synonym for "wanderings." Peregrine is also the name of a kind of falcon. The name persists in a small way in Britain. English writer Peregrine Worsthorne.

Peregrin, Peregrino, Peregryn

Peretz Heb. "Breach, breakthrough." (As in a wall.)

Perez

Perfecto Sp. "Perfect." Refers to Jesus Christ, the only perfect man.

Peri Heb. "Fruit, result."

Pericles Gk. name of uncertain meaning. Athenian statesman of Greece's golden age, the 4th century B.C. He promoted systematic democracy on the one hand, and the dominance of Athens on the other. In the 19th century South, slave owners sometimes gave slaves classical names like Pericles or Aeneas, and they have been handed down in Southern families since then.

Perkin OE. "Little Peter."

Perkins, Perkyn, Perrin

Perry Dim. **Peregrine**; or OE. Place name: "Pear tree." Modern use seems mostly to be inspired by fictional detective Perry Mason. Matthew Calbraith Perry was the American naval officer who established American trade relations with Japan in 1854, which for almost 200 years had been closed to Western trade or contact. Singer Perry Como; designer Perry Ellis.

Parry, Perrie

Perseus Greek mythology name: the son of Zeus and Danae (whom Zeus visited in the guise of a shower of gold). He killed the Medusa, a monster with snakes for hair who turned all who looked at her into stone. Then he rescued Andromeda from a sea monster, and later married her.

Pesach Heb. "Spared." The Hebrew name for the great holiday of Passover, which commemorates the fact that Jehovah spared the Israelites in a plague that killed many Egyptians.

Pessach

Peter Gk. "Rock." New Testament name; the saint who, tradition has it, guards the gates to Heaven. The name's greatest popularity came in the first three-quarters of the 20th century, prompted, some sources suggest, by the play *Peter Pan*. The numerous variants suggest how widespread this name has been. In the U.S. it is still a standby, though nowhere near fashionable. In France, though, **Pierre** is a real favorite. Artists Piero della Francesca, Peter Paul Rubens; Russian emperor Peter the Great; actors Peter O'Toole, Peter Krause; Peter Rabbit; film directors Peter Jackson, Peter Bogdanovich; tennis player Pete Sampras.

Peadar, Pearce, Peder, Pedro, Peerus, Peirce, Per, Perkin, Pero, Perrin, Perry, Pete, Petey, Peto, Petr, Pierce, Piero, Pierre, Pierson, Piet, Pieter, Pietrek, Pietro, Piotr, Pjotr, Pyotr

Petuel Aramaic. "Vision of the Lord." Old Testament name.

Peverell OF. "Piper."

Peverall, Peverel, Peveril

Peyton OE. Place name: "Fighting-man's estate." Probably related to **Patton**. Primarily American use, probably as a transferred last name, i.e., a mother's maiden name. Football players Walter Payton, Peyton Manning; basketball player Gary Payton.

Payton

Phelan Ir. Gael. "Wolf." Mostly Irish use.
Felan, Phelim, Felim

Phelps OE. "Son of Philip."

Philander Gk. "Loving mankind." This word has come to mean "flirt" in English, but it still occurs as a name, especially in the South.

Philemon Gk. "Affectionate." Old Testament name: one of St. Paul's epistles is addressed to Philemon.

Philip Gk. "Lover of horses." The name of one of the twelve apostles, and a staple since early Christian times, though it receded somewhat in the 19th century. A 20th-century resurgence peaked in the 1960s and like **Peter**, Philip is familiar but not common. The French use **Philippe** very often, though. Britain's Prince Philip; Crown Prince Felipe of Spain; painter Filippo Lippi; playwright Philip Barry; talk show host Phil Donahue; actor Philip Seymour Hoffman; author Philip Roth; football player Phil Simms.
Felipe, Filip, Filippo, Fillip, Fyllip, Phil, Philipp, Philippe, Philippos, Philippus, Phillip, Phillips, Phyllip, Pip, Pippo

Philo Gk. "Loving." Regrettably similar in sound to phyllo pastry. This is the same root that we use in words like bibliophile and philanthropist (which, strictly translated from Greek, means "loving others").

Phineas Derivation and meaning unknown, though many sources offer Heb. "Oracle." Another possible meaning is "mouth of brass," which would be appropriate for showman Phineas T. Barnum. Violinist Pinchas Zuckerman.
Fineas, Phinehas, Pincas, Pinchas, Pinchos, Pincus, Pinhas, Pinkus

Phipps OE. "Son of Philip."
Philips, Philipson, Phips

Phoebus Gk. "Shining, brilliant." One of the epithets of Apollo, the sun god, was Phoebus Apollo, referring to the fact that he brought light. The feminine version, **Phoebe**, has always been much better established as a common name, perhaps because there is a Phoebe in the New Testament.
Phoibos

Phoenix Gk. "Dark red." In myth, the phoenix is an Arabian bird that periodically sets itself aflame and rises alive from the ashes. It is often considered a symbol of immortality. In our era, this is the last name of a family of actors, Leaf, Joaquin, and the late River Phoenix.
Fenix, Phenix

Pickford OE. "From the ford at the peak."

Pierce Var. **Peter** (Gk. "Rock"). One of a group of **Peter**-derived names along with **Piers, Pearson**, etc. Actor Pierce Brosnan.
Pearce, Pears, Pearson, Pearsson, Peerce, Peirce, Piers, Pierson, Piersson

Pierre Fr. Var. **Peter**. Canadian Prime Minister Pierre Trudeau.

Piers Gk. "Rock." **Peter** is actually the Latin form of the name that the Normans took to Britain as Piers. This form, along with **Pierce**, has been an alternate form more popular in Britain than in America.
Pearce, Pears, Pearson, Pierce, Pierson, Piersson

Pike OE. Possibly a place name referring to a turnpike road where fees for use are collected at toll-gates. May also refer to a large freshwater fish. Zebulon Pike, for whom Pike's Peak in Colorado was named, was an early 18th-century soldier and explorer who first sighted Pike's Peak in his search for the source of the Mississippi River.
Pyke

Pio Lat. "Pious." A name used by twelve popes, but not found much among English-speaking children.
Pius

Piper Occupational name; one who plays the pipes.

Pitney OE. Place name: "Island of the stubborn one."
Pittney

Pitt OE. Place name: "Pit or ditch." Actor Brad Pitt.

Placido Sp. "Serene." Made famous currently by opera star Placido Domingo.
Placedo, Placidus, Placijo, Placyd, Placydo, Plasedo

Plantagenet OF. "Sprig of broom." Broom is an English flower. The Plantagenet family ruled England in the 13th and 14th centuries, and the name resonates, in England, with connotations of ancient high rank. Victorian novelist Anthony Trollope named his powerful English duke "Plantagenet Palliser."

Plato Gk. "Broad-shouldered." Its occasional use in English-speaking countries may be inspired by admiration for the famous Greek philosopher.

Platon

Platt OF. Place name: "Flat land."

Platte

Pluto Gk. "Rich." In Roman mythology, the god of the underworld. In Disney myth, a dog who walks on his hind legs. Unlikely name for a child.

Pocano Pueblo Indian. "Arrival of the spirits."

Pollard ME. "Shorn head." "Poll" was originally a term for head, hence our expression "take a poll." A pollard tree's branches have been cut back to the trunk to promote a bushy growth at the top. Thus the name may either be a place name (for someone who lived near a pollard tree) or a descriptive name (for someone whose head had been closely cropped).

Poll, Pollerd, Pollyrd

Pollock OE. Var. **Pollux**. Also the name of a large fish. In German, *pollak* is the term for someone from neighboring Poland. Artist Jackson Pollock.

Pollack, Polloch

Pollux Gk. "Crown." Along with Castor, one of the Heavenly Twins, the constellation also known as Gemini.

Pomeroy OF. Place name: "Apple orchard." The French word for apple is *pomme*.

Pommeray, Pommeroy

Pompey Lat. Meaning unclear. Pompey was a Roman statesman and military man, and Caesar's chief rival. This name was occasionally used as a slave name in the South, and also survived in Latin culture because of a saint whose feast day is April 10.

Pompeyo, Pompi, Pompilio, Pomponio

Ponce Sp. "Fifth." Made famous by Spanish explorer Ponce de Leon, but no more common than **Quintus**, its Latin equivalent.

Pope Gk. "Father." A transferred last name, and extremely unusual. English poet Alexander Pope.

Porat Heb. "Fruitful, productive."

Poriel Heb. "Fruit of God."

Porfirio Gk. "Purple stone." The English term is "porphyry." Very rare, but borne by one of the 20th century's great playboys, Porfirio Rubirosa, as well as a saint of the 4th century.
Porphirios, Prophyrios

Porter Lat. "Gatekeeper." Occupational name.

Porthos Literary name: along with Athos and Aramis, one of the three musketeers from Alexandre Dumas' novel of the same name. Dumas may have invented the name for the way it sounded with the two others.

Portland OE. Place name: "Land near the port."

Poseidon Greek mythology name: the sea god, corresponding to the Roman Neptune. He is usually depicted with a trident, with which he caused storms and earthquakes.

Potter OE. Occupational name: "Maker of pots."

Powell OE. Surname related to **Paul**. Author Anthony Powell.
Powel

Powhatan Algonquin Indian. "Powwow hill." The name of the father of Pocahontas, who in history was a powerful chieftain in Virginia.

Pradeep Hindi. "Light."

Pratap Hindi. "Majesty, magnificence."

Pratt OE. Fairly common last name whose origin is cloudy. One early meaning of "prat" was the buttocks, as in the comedy term "a pratfall." Another similar word, "prate," meant to babble or talk without meaning. Pratt may come from one of these two terms.

Prentice ME. "Apprentice."
Prentis, Prentiss

Prescott OE. Place name: "Priest's cottage." One of the middle names of former President George H.P. Bush, but not widespread.
Prescot, Prestcot, Prestcott

Presley OE. Place name: "Priest's meadow." In the Middle Ages, when these names came into use, the priest was a very important figure in any community. Of course, in the late 20th century the name is associated with another important figure, Elvis Presley.

Presleigh, Presly, Presslee, Pressley, Prestley, Priestley, Priestly

Preston OE. Place name: "Priest's estate." Actor Robert Preston; film director Preston Sturges.

Prewitt OF. "Brave little one."

Prewet, Prewett, Prewit, Pruitt

Price Welsh. "Son of Rhys." **Rhys** is a common Welsh name meaning "ardent."

Brice, Bryce, Pryce

Priestley OE. Place name: "Priest's meadow."

Priestly

Primo It. "First; firstborn." Number names usually refer to children born with quite a number of older siblings (**Quintus, Octavian**), and tend to indicate exhaustion of the imagination, but Primo may allude to great pride in the firstborn, especially a son. Author Primo Levi.

Preemo, Premo, Prime

Prince Lat. "Prince." As a last name, it may have indicated someone who worked in a prince's household, and occasional first-name use is generally transferred from the last name. There are, of course, exceptions, like the musician formerly known as Prince, who undoubtedly cherished the name for its royal connotations. Comedian Freddie Prinze and actor Freddie Prinze Jr.; theatrical producer Harold Prince.

Printz, Printze, Prinz, Prinze

Prior See Pryor.

Procopius Gk. "Forward-looking." Procopius was a saint who was beheaded in the early fourth century for refusing to worship pagan gods. The oldest restaurant in Paris, still in business on a picturesque street of the Left Bank, is called "Le Procope."

Procopio, Procopius

Proctor Lat. "Official, administrator." Occupational last name.
Prockter, Procter

Prosper Lat. "Fortunate," as in "prosperous." Poet Prosper Mérimée.
Prospero

Proverb English: "A short, pithy saying." The name usually comes from one of the books of the Old Testament, Proverbs. Unusual. Football player Proverb Jacobs.

Prudencio Sp. from Lat. "Caution, discretion." As **Prudence**, this was one of the more popular and durable virtue names. The male version is rare.
Prudentius

Pryor Lat. "Monastic leader." A prior is the monk in charge of a monastery, so this might be an occupational name. On the other hand, the tradition of monastic chastity would seem to prevent such a name's being handed down to children.
Prior

Purvis Eng./Fr. "Purveyor." Originally indicated someone who provided food, or provisions.
Purves, Purviss

 Qadir Arab. "Capable, competent." This is one of the ninety-nine attribute names of Allah. Football player Qadry Ismail.
Qadar, Qadry

Qasim Arab. "Charitable, generous; one who gives to the people."

Quanah Native American: "Fragrant, sweet-smelling."

Quennell OF. Place name: "Small oak."
Quennel

Quentin Lat. "Fifth." Probably used without any consideration of its meaning since so few families extend to five children any more. Author Quentin Crisp.

Quent, Quenten, Quenton, Quint, Quintin, Quinton, Quintus

Quigley Ir. Gael. Meaning disputed: possibly "Distaff," or "One with messy hair."

Quillan Ir. Gael. "Cub."
Quillen

Quiller OE. Possibly an occupational name: a "quiller" could have been a scribe, or someone who wrote with a quill pen.

Quimby ONorse. Place name: "Estate of the woman." A woman's estate would have been quite a rarity in the Old Norse era.
Quinby

Quincy OF. Place name: "Estate of the fifth son." Last name of a prominent Massachusetts family whose name is borne by a town and by the 6th U.S. President, John Quincy Adams. Musician Quincy Jones.
Quin, Quincey, Quinsy

Quinlan Ir. Gael. "Fit, shapely, strong."
Quindlen

Quinn Ir. Gael. Meaning unknown, though some speculate that it means "descendant of Con," which in turn means something like "intelligence." Very common Irish last name, occasionally transferred to first-name status, especially in the U.S. Actor Aidan Quinn.

Quinton OE. Place name: "Queen's settlement." This spelling may be perceived as a variation of **Quentin**.
Quinntan, Quinnten, Quinntin, Quinnton, Quintain, Quintan, Quintyn, Quintynn

Rabi Arab. "Gentle wind."
   Rabbi, Rabee
Racham Heb. "Mercy, compassion."
   Rachim, Raham, Rahim
Rad OE. "Adviser." This word particle, which comes from

Scandinavian and Slavic sources, occurs in many other names.

Radbert OE. "Bright adviser."

Radburn OE. Place name: "Red brook."
Radborn, Radborne, Radbourn, Radbourne, Radburne

Radcliff OE. Place name: "Red cliff." In America, most likely to be associated with the renowned women's college that is now part of Harvard. Actor Daniel Radcliffe.
Radcliffe, Radclyffe, Ratcliff, Ratcliffe

Radek Slavic. Var. **Roderick** (OG. "Famous ruler").

Radford OE. Place name: "Red ford" or "Ford with reeds."
Radferd, Radfurd

Radimir Slavic. "Famous joy."

Radley OE. Place name: "Red meadow." As in **Radford**, the first element could also refer to reeds.
Radlea, Radlee, Radleigh, Radly

Radnor OE. Place name: "Red shore" or "Reedy shore."

Radwan Arab. "Pleasure, satisfaction."

Rafael Var. **Raphael** (Heb. "God has healed"). This is the form most often used in the United States. Use appears to have peaked in the early nineties and has steadily declined since. Baseball player Rafael Palmiero.
Rafe, Rafel, Rafello, Rafer, Raffaelo, Raffaello, Raphael

Rafferty Ir. Gael. "Prosperity wielder." Irish last name occasionally used as a first name.
Raferty, Raffarty, Raffertey

Rafi Arab. "Holding high."
Rafee, Raffi, Raffy

Rafiq Arab. "Friend" or possibly "gentle."
Rafi, Rafik

Ragnar Nor. "Powerful army" or "Warrior of judgment." Though this ancient Scandinavian form is very rare in the U.S., it is related to Germanic names like **Reginald** and **Rainier**.
Ragnor, Rainer, Rainier, Rayner, Raynor, Regner, Reiner

Raiden Mythology name: the Japanese god of thunder.

Rahim Arab. "Empathetic, merciful." This is one of the ninety-nine attributes of Allah which are considered by Muslims to be particularly auspicious names.

Raheem, Rahiem

Rainart Ger. "Mighty judgment."

Rainhard, Rainhardt, Reinart, Reinhard, Reinhardt, Reinhart, Renke

Raines English name of uncertain derivation. It may be yet another spinoff from **Reginald/Reynold/Rainier**, or come from a different English root that means "lord." Actor Claud Rains.

Rain, Raine, Rains, Rayne, Raynes

Rainier Fr. Var. **Reginald** (OE. "Counsel power"). A famous place name in the Pacific Northwest, where the peak of Mt. Rainier, at 14,408 feet, is an important landmark. The peak was named for a British naval officer, but the Indian name was Tacoma or Tahoma, meaning "snowy peak." The nearby city took that name. Today's most famous Rainier is the late Grace Kelly's husband, Prince Rainier of Monaco. Poet Rainer Maria Rilke.

Rainer, Rayner, Raynier

Rajiv Sanskrit. "Striped." Familiar to non-Indians because of Rajiv Gandhi, son of Indira Gandhi and a prominent Indian politician in his own right, who was assassinated in 1991.

Raleigh OE. Place name: "Meadow of roe deer." Commemorates Sir Walter Raleigh, explorer and court favorite of Queen Elizabeth I, who is supposed to have spread his cape over a puddle so she could cross with dry feet. The city in North Carolina was named for him. Usually a boy's name, but the two-syllable "-leigh" form, based on the popularity of **Ashley**, is increasingly being considered appropriate for girls as well.

Ralegh, Rawleigh, Rawley, Rawly

Ralph OE. "Wolf-counsel." A name that has been steadily, if not enormously, popular for the last thousand years (though today's parents might not recognize it immediately in older forms like Rathulf or Radolphus). Its greatest vogue in the U.S. occurred at the turn of the 20th century. Traditional Englishmen (actor Ralph Fiennes among them) pronounce it "Rafe," to the confusion of most Americans. Now uncommon. Poet Ralph Waldo Emerson; consumer activist Ralph Nader; actor Ralph Macchio.

Rafe, Raff, Ralf, Raoul, Raul, Rolf, Rolph

Ralston OE. Place name: "Ralph's settlement."

Ram Sanskrit. "Pleasing."

Rahm

Ramiro Port. "Great judge." Baseball player Manny Ramirez.

Ramirez

Ramon Sp. Var. **Raymond** (OG. "Counselor-protector"). Given its greatest exposure by the silent-movie star of the 1920s, Ramon Novarro. Baseball player Ramon Martinez.

Ramsay OE. Place name: "Raven island" or "Ram island." Originally a last name common in Scotland. English statesman Ramsay McDonald; U.S. Attorney General Ramsey Clark.

Ramsey

Ramsden OE. Place name: "Ram valley." Like most of these place names turned last names, this was transferred to a first name in the 19th century.

Ramses The name of several of the most prominent kings of ancient Egpyt.

Rameses, Ramesses

Rance Unusual name of uncertain derivation. It may come from an old Scottish term for a tool used to make holes, akin to a reamer; so perhaps it is an occupational name.

Rancel, Rancell

Rand OE. "Shield, fighter." Generally a diminutive of **Randolph** and related names.

Randall OE. "Shield-wolf." This is the medieval spoken form of **Randolph**. Enjoyed some popularity with parents in the baby boom era, and is steadily used today, without being particularly popular. Actor Tony Randall; football player Randall Cunningham; poet Randall Jarrell.

Rand, Randal, Randel, Randell, Randey, Randie, Randi, Randle, Randy

Randolph OE. "Shield-wolf." From the same root as **Randall**, which has been more popular in the U.S. English politician Lord Randolph Churchill.

Randal, Randall, Randell, Randolf, Randy

Randy Dim. **Randall, Randolph**. More popular now than either Randall or Randolph, which makes this name an exception to the trend of parents overlooking nicknames in favor of longer, more formal names. In British slang, "randy" means "amorous," so this name is barely used there.

Randey, Randi, Randie

Ranger OF. "Forest guardian."

Rainger, Range

Ranjit Sanskrit. "Charmed, beguiled." Ranjit Singh was an important maharajah of the Punjab area of India in the late 18th and early 19th centuries.

Ranjeet

Rankin OE. "Little shield" or Celt. "Son of Francis." A last name found in Scotland and Ireland, rarely transferred as a first name.

Rankine, Rankinn

Ransford OE. Place name: "Raven ford."

Ransley OE. Place name: "Raven meadow."

Ransleigh, Ransly

Ransom Opinions differ: possibly OE. "Shield's son," possibly a diminutive of **Randolph**. It seems unlikely that the casual meaning of money paid to redeem a captive has anything to do with the name. First-name use is mostly a late-Victorian phenomenon.

Ransome

Raoul Fr. Var. **Ralph** (OE. "Wolf-counsel"). Uncommon among English-speaking parents. Actor Raul Julia.

Raul, Roul, Rowl

Raphael Heb. "God has healed." The name of one of the archangels, possibly (because of his name) the one who stirred the waters at the pool of Bethesda to give it healing powers. Most common in very religious eras (16th and 17th centuries) and the 19th century, which cherished the picturesque. May become more popular (as **Gabriel** has) in the current quest for the unique. Painter Raphael Sanzio; author Rafe Yglesias.

Falito, Rafal, Rafael, Rafaelle, Rafaelo, Rafaello, Rafe, Rafel, Rafello, Raffael, Raffaello, Raphaello, Raphello, Ravel

Rashad Arab. "Having good judgment." Related to **Rashid**, but much more popular in the U.S.
Rashaad, Rashod

Rashid Arab. "Righteous, rightly advised." **Rashida** is also used for girls.
Rasheed, Rasheid, Rasheyd

Rasmus Dim. **Erasmus** (Gk. "Loved, desired"). Used occasionally in German-speaking countries.

Rastus Dim. **Erasmus** (Gk. "Loved, desired").

Raven Name of the large black bird that is closely related to the crow. A fanciful name for a black-haired or dark-skinned baby. Probably more common for girls, owing to the fame of actress Raven Symone of *The Cosby Show.*
Ravinn, Rayven, Rayvin

Ravi Hindi. "Sun." Made familiar to today's parents by the eminent sitar player Ravi Shankar.
Ravee

Rawlins OF. Ultimately a diminutive of **Roland**. A name like this was originally an oral contraction (**Rolandson** to **Rawlinson** to **Rawlins**), then became a last name, and was revived in the late 19th century as a first name.
Rawlinson, Rawson

Ray Dim. **Raymond**. Quite firmly rooted as an independent name, used mostly in the 20th century. Singer Ray Charles; boxer Sugar Ray Leonard; author Ray Bradbury; actors Ray Liotta, Ray Romano.
Rae, Rai, Raye, Reigh

Rayburn OE. Place name: "Roe-deer brook." Painter Henry Raeburn.
Raeborn, Raeborne, Raebourn, Raeburn, Rayborn, Raybourne, Rayburne

Raymond OG. "Counselor-protector." Old Teutonic name

that was used in the Middle Ages, then forgotten until a very strong 19th-century revival, especially in America. Though far from fashionable, it is steadily used in a quiet way. Author Raymond Chandler; actors Raymond Massey, Raymond Burr.

Raemond, Raemondo, Raimond, Raimondo, Raimund, Raimundo, Rajmund, Ramon, Ramond, Ramonde, Ramone, Ray, Rayment, Raymondo, Raymund, Raymunde, Raymundo

Raynor Nor. "Mighty army." An anglicized version of **Ragnar**, and a version of the better-known **Rainier**.

Ragnar, Rainer, Rainier, Rainor, Ranieri, Raynar, Rayner

Raziel Aramaic. "The Lord is my secret."

Read OE. "Red-haired." Descriptive name that long ago became a last name, and thence a first name, especially in the U.S.

Reade, Reed, Reid, Reide

Reading OE. "Son of the red-haired." Also a place name.

Redding, Reeding, Reiding

Redford OE. Place name: "Red ford." Hard to use today without invoking the ultrafamous blond actor, Robert Redford.

Radford, Radfurd, Redfurd

Redley OE. Place name: "Red meadow."

Radley, Redlea, Redleigh, Redly

Redman OE. Obscure: could mean either "Man of counsel" or "Man who rides." Never a common choice for parents.

Redmond Ir. Var. **Raymond**.

Radmond, Radmund, Redmund

Reece Welsh. "Fiery, zealous." The native Welsh form is **Rhys**, and it is very popular in Wales. Actor Roger Rees.

Rees, Reese, Rhys, Rice

Reed OE. "Red-haired." It is also perfectly possible that Reed comes from a place name referring to the reeds in a swampy place. This spelling of the name had a mild flourish of popularity in the baby boom era.

Read, Reade, Reid, Reyd

Reeve ME. Occupational name: "Bailiff." A reeve was an administrator for the king or someone of high position, who collected rents and maintained order on the lord's estates. Actor Christopher Reeve.

Reave, Reeves

Regan Ir. Gael. "Little king." Mostly 20th-century use.

Reagan, Reagen, Regen

Reginald OE. "Counsel power." **Ronald** and **Reynolds** are just two of the names that come from the same source; Reginald's popularity was mainly British and 19th century. But the name has clearly been used across Europe, to judge from the variety of spellings and pronunciations. Actor Judge Reinhold; baseball star Reggie Jackson; theologian Reinhold Niebuhr.

Naldo, Raghnall, Rainault, Rainhold, Raonull, Raynald, Rayniero, Reg, Reggie, Regin, Reginalt, Reginauld, Reginault, Reginvald, Reginvalt, Regnauld, Regnault, Reinald, Reinaldo, Reinaldos, Reinhold, Reinold, Reinwald, Renaud, Renault, Rene, Reynaldo, Reynaldos, Reynold, Reynolds, Rheinallt, Rinaldo, Ronald

Regino Unusual name that may be a variation of **Reginald** or may be a way of making **Regina** (Latin for "queen") masculine. In the languages most closely related to Latin, the words for "king," like the French *roi* or the Spanish *rey,* are much shorter.

Regis Fr. "Kingly." This was a French last name transferred to a first name: literally, it is the Latin word for "of the king" and there are Catholic schools all over the country called "Regis" (the king, in this case, being Jesus). This is a very unusual name made familiar by talk show host Regis Philbin.

Reid OE. Place name: "Near the reeds" or descriptive name: "Red-haired." This is the most popular spelling at the moment.

Read, Reade, Reed

Remedio Sp. "Help, remedy." The name refers to help from a divine source. The feminine version, **Remedios,** is well used in South America.

Remington OE. Place name: "Raven-family settlement." Familiar to Americans as a brand of razors. Artist Frederick Remington.

Remy Fr. "From Rheims." Champagne, and the fine brandies made from champagne, are the principal product of Rheims, a town in central France. The name is used—albeit rarely—for both boys and girls. Author Remy Charlip.

Remee, Remi, Remie, Remmey, Remmy

Remus Lat. "Swift." The name of one of the legendary twins (the other was Romulus) who founded Rome. At the turn of the century Joel Chandler Harris' "Uncle Remus" stories (including the famous one about the Tar Baby) were very popular.

Remo

Ren Probably a nickname for **Reginald** or any of the "Ren-" names, or else a variant of **René**. It was used occasionally before the success of the cartoon "Ren and Stimpy."

Renne, Renny

René Fr. "Reborn." The modern form of **Renatus**, which did not survive as a male name. Unlike the female version, René has not really spread beyond French-speaking families, probably because it is well entrenched as a girl's name. Actor René Auberjonois.

Renat, Renato, Renatus

Renfred OE. "Powerful peace."

Renfrew OWelsh. Place name: "Calm river."

Renny Ir. Gael. "Small and mighty."

Reno Place name: the largest city in Nevada. It was named for a Confederate general, Jesse Lee Reno, and became prosperous as the silver mines of Nevada were exploited. It later became the divorce capital of the United States; Nevada had lenient divorce laws and required a short residency. Because it is now something of a gambling center the name still has an aura of the rough-and-ready about it.

Renshaw OE. Place name: "Raven woods."

Renishaw

Renton OE. Place name: "Settlement of the roe deer."

Renwick OE. Place name: "Roe deer village" or "Raven village."
Renwyck

Renzo Dim. **Lorenzo** (Lat. "Laurel"). Interior designer Renzo Mongiardino.

Reuben Heb. "Behold, a son." Old Testament name that came into general use in the 18th century. Also a sandwich that features corned beef, sauerkraut, and Swiss cheese. Singer Ruben Blades.
Reuban, Reubin, Reuven, Rouvin, Rube, Ruben, Rubin, Rubino, Ruby

Reuel Heb. "Friend of the Lord."
Ruel

Rex Lat. "King." Mostly 20th-century use, possibly influenced by actor Rex Harrison. Probably most common as a name for a dog.

Rexford OE. Place name: "King's ford."

Rey Sp. "King." The Hispanic equivalent of **Rex** or **Leroy**. Not in general use.
Reyes, Reyni

Reynard OF. "Fox" or OG. "Powerful and courageous." Some of the variations (like **Renaud**) come close to variations of the **Reynold/Reginald** names, but are not as common. The French word for fox (*renard*) actually comes from a set of medieval European animal stories in which the cunning fox is known as "Reynard," no doubt to emphasize his cleverness.
Raynard, Reinhard, Reinhardt, Renard, Renaud, Renauld, Rennard

Reynold Var. **Reginald** (OE. "Counsel power"). Probably most familiar in America as a surname, though in the Middle Ages this was the most common form of **Reginald**. Painter Joshua Reynolds.
Reinaldo, Renado, Renaldo, Renato, Renauld, Renault, Reynaldo, Reynolds, Rinaldo

Rhett Var. **Rhys**. Modern parents can hardly use it without thinking of Margaret Mitchell's immortal Rhett Butler, and his great line, "Frankly, my dear, I don't give a damn!"

Rhinebeck Ger. Place name: "Brook of the Rhine." The Rhine is a major European river that serves as the boundary between France and Germany. The name of a picturesque town on the Hudson River.
Rheinbeck

Rhinelander Ger. Place name: "Dweller at the Rhineland."
Rheinlander

Rhodes Gk. "Where roses grow." The name of an important Greek island and an important British philanthropist, Cecil Rhodes. He gave his name to both a country (Rhodesia) and a scholarship fund that would allow outstanding students from England's former colonies to study at Oxford in England. Some famous former Rhodes scholars are Senator Bill Bradley and President Bill Clinton.
Rhoads, Rhodas, Rodas

Rhys Welsh. "Fiery, zealous." This is the native Welsh form of the name that appears more often in English-speaking countries as **Reece**. It is currently very popular in Wales. Actor Roger Rhys.

Rice Either an anglicization of **Rhys** or a respelling of a German name, Reis, that has many meanings. The most appealing for descendants is "Knight on horseback," a far more attractive prospect as an ancestor than "Gatherer of twigs," "Wood carver," or "Dweller in the brush." This is generally a last name, and could cause quite a few giggles among preschool children. Football player Jerry Rice.

Richard OG. "Dominant ruler." Norman name that went on to be a steady favorite for the last 900 years, with one century (the 19th) of neglect. In the current hunger for the unusual, it is somewhat overlooked, but plenty of parents still choose it. It is unfortunately short of nicknames at the moment, given the slang meaning of **Dick**. **Ricardo** is very popular in Spain. English Kings Richard I-III; rock star Little Richard; composer Richard Rodgers; actors Richard Burton, Richard Kiley, Richard Gere, Richard Chamberlain; photographer Richard Avedon; U.S. President Richard Nixon; football player Rich Gannon.

Dick, Dickie, Dicky, Raechard, Ric, Richard, Ricardo, Riccardo, Rich, Richardo, Richart, Richerd, Richie, Rick, Rickard, Rickert, Rickey, Ricki, Rickie, Ricky, Rico, Rikard, Riki, Rikki, Riocard, Ritchard, Ritcherd, Ritchie, Ritchy, Ritchyrd, Ritshard, Ritsherd, Ryszard

Richmond OG. "Powerful protector." Most frequently encountered in the U.S. as a place name, like the capital city of Virginia.

Rick Dim. **Richard, Frederick**. Used independently, though more common as a nickname, and one that isn't often used today. Humphrey Bogart's character in *Casablanca* was named Rick. Actors Rick Moranis, Rick Nelson.

Ric, Ricci, Rickey, Rickie, Ricky, Rik, Rikki, Rikky

Ricky Dim. **Richard, Frederick**. More common than **Rick** as an independent name. Baseball player Rickey Henderson.

Ricci, Rickey, Ricki

Rickward OE. "Mighty guardian."

Rickwerd, Rickwood

Rico It. Dim. **Henry** (OE. "Home ruler") via **Enrico**, or dim. **Ricardo**.

Rider OE. "Horseman." Likely to be a transferred last name, for instance a mother's maiden name. Author Rider Haggard; painter Albert Pinkham Ryder.

Ridder, Ryder

Ridge OE. Place name: "Ridge." Referring to a geographical feature in a landscape, as do **Ridgeway** and **Ridgeley**.

Rigg

Ridgeway OE. Place name: "Road on the ridge."

Ridgeley OE. Place name: "Ridge meadow."

Ridgeleigh, Ridgeley, Ridglea, Ridglee, Ridgleigh

Ridley OE. Place name: "Red meadow." Film director Ridley Scott.

Riddley, Ridlea, Ridleigh, Ridly

Rigoberto Sp. from Ger. "Brilliant and mighty." A number of German names survive only in Spanish forms. They may date back to the days when Spain and Germany formed part of the Holy Roman Empire, or even further

back to when the Goths began to overrun Europe in the fifth century A.D., before dividing into tribes that occupied Germany and Spain.
Rigobert

Riley Ir. Gael. "Courageous." Irish last name used as a first name for the last 150 years. Actor John C. Reilly.
Reilly, Ryley

Ring OE. "Ring." Very unusual, though given exposure by author Ring Lardner. Beatles fans will remember that Ringo Starr took his name from the jewelry he favored.
Ringo

Rio Sp. "River." Unusual place name. The Brazilian capital is Rio de Janeiro, which means "January river" in Portuguese. The Rio Grande is the boundary river between Texas and Mexico; its name means "big river" in Spanish.
Reo

Riordan Ir. Gael. "Bard, minstrel."
Rearden, Reardon

Rip Invented name: made famous by actor Rip Torn, who was actually named Elmore. Before his fame, the best-known American Rip was Rip van Winkle, the man who slept for twenty years in Washington Irving's tale.

Ripley OE. Place name: "Shouting man's meadow."
Ripleigh, Riply

Rishon Heb. "The first."

Risley OE. Place name: "Meadow with shrubs."
Rislea, Rislee, Risleigh, Risly, Wrisley

Riston OE. Place name: "Settlement near the shrubs." Financier Walter Wriston.
Wriston

Ritter Ger. "Knight." Actor John Ritter.

River Place name. As a last name, **Rivers** is more common, but this name was given a lot of exposure by the late actor River Phoenix. Born in 1970, he and one of his brothers (actor Leaf Phoenix) were given nature names. The third brother, also an actor, got away with Joaquin.
Rivers

Rives OF. Place name: "Dweller by the riverbank." Sounds the same as **Reeves**, but with a completely different history.

Riyad Arab. Place name: "Gardens." The name of the capital of Saudi Arabia.

Riyadh

Roald OG. "Famous and powerful" or "Famous ruler." Rare in English-speaking countries, though the immense popularity of author Roald Dahl keeps this name in the public eye. Polar explorer Roald Amundsen.

Roark Ir. Gael. "Illustrious and mighty." Usually occurs as a last name. This spelling recalls Howard Roark, the protagonist of Ayn Rand's influential novel *The Fountainhead*. Actor Mickey Rourke.

Roarke, Rorke, Rourke, Ruark

Rob Dim. **Robert**. The most common nickname for Robert is probably **Bob**, but Rob may be given more often as an independent name. Actor Rob Lowe.

Robb, Robbie, Robby

Robert OE. "Bright fame." Another staple male name, common for the last millennium and still in the American top fifty. It has steadily drifted out of top-twenty status in the last dozen years. Parents tend to be more conservative with boys' names, which explains why **Michael, James, David, Andrew** and, yes, **Robert** are still favorites. Senator Robert Kennedy; poet Robert Burns; actors Robert DeNiro, Robert Duvall, Rob Schneider; author Robert Lawson; General Robert E. Lee; author Robert Ludlum; baseball players Roberto Alomar, Roberto Clemente.

Bert, Bertie, Bob, Bobbie, Bobby, Rab, Rabbie, Riobard, Rip, Rob, Roban, Robb, Robben, Robbin, Robbins, Robbinson, Robby, Robers, Roberto, Robertson, Robi, Robin, Robinson, Robson, Robyn, Robynson, Rupert, Ruperto, Ruprecht

Robin Dim. **Robert**. Usually a girl's name in America, though A.A. Milne immortalized his son as Christopher Robin in the *Winnie the Pooh* stories. Actor Robin Williams; TV personality Robin Leach.

Roban, Robben, Robbin, Robbyn, Robyn

Robinson OE. "Son of Robert." More commonly a last name. Singer Smokey Robinson; poet Robinson Jeffers; actor Paul Robeson.

Robbinson, Robeson, Robynson, Robson

Rocco Ger./It. "Rest." The most common form (in America, at least) of the name of a popular saint who cured plague victims. He was especially venerated in Italy, which may be why this version of the name is the most common. **Rocky** is usually a nickname.

Roch, Roche, Rochus, Rock, Rocko, Rocky, Roque

Rochester OE. Place name: "Stone camp or fortress."

Chester, Chet, Rock

Rocio Sp. "Dew." Alludes to the dew of Heaven.

Rock Var. **Rocco.** Actor Rock Hudson is the most important precedent for using this name. His original name was Roy Scherer.

Rocky

Rockley OE. Place name: "Rock meadow."

Rocklee, Rockleigh, Rockly

Rocklin Possibly OE. Place name: A contraction of **Rockland** for instance. May also be a continental name, something like "Little Rocco."

Rockwell OE. Place name: "Rock spring." Illustrators Norman Rockwell, Rockwell Kent.

Rocky Var. **Rocco.** Impossible to use today without invoking Sylvester Stallone's *Rocky* movies.

Rod Dim. **Roderick.** Used sparingly as an independent name. Actors Rod Steiger, Roddy McDowall.

Rodd, Roddie, Roddy

Rodeo Sp. "Roundup." A show of the skills used by cowboys in rounding up cattle: roping, riding bucking horses, and so forth. A name redolent of the Wild West.

Roderick OG. "Renowned rule." Most commonly used in Scotland and other parts of Britain; never a great favorite in America.

Broderick, Brodrick, Brodryck, Rhoderick, Rhodric, Rod, Rodd, Rodderick, Roddie, Roddrick, Roddy, Roderic, Roderich, Roderigo, Roderyck, Rodrick, Ro-

drik, **Rodrigo, Rodrigue, Rodrigues, Rodriguez, Rodrique, Rodriquez, Rodryck, Rodryk, Roric, Rorick, Rory, Rurek, Rurik, Ruy**

Rodman OG. "Renowned man." Basketball player Dennis Rodman.

Rodmann

Rodney OE. Place name: "Island near the clearing." Like many last names, this one began intensive use as a first name in the mid 19th century. This mild popularity has endured for some 150 years. Comedian Rodney Dangerfield.

Rodnee, Rodnie

Rodolfo Var. **Rudolph** (OG. "Famous wolf"). This was the original version of Rudolph Valentino's given name: the rest of the impressive string was Alfonzo Raffaelo Pierre Filibert Guglielmi.

Rodolf, Rodolphe, Rodolpho

Roe ME. "Roe deer." May originally have been an occupational name indicating an ancestor who hunted or trapped such deer.

Row, Rowe

Rogan Ir. Gael. "Red-head." Irish Gaelic has several names to indicate red hair; but then, the Irish people produce many redheads.

Roger OG. "Renowned spearman." At its most popular in the Middle Ages and the 19th and 20th centuries, but on the wane since the 1950s. Actors Rutger Hauer, Roger Moore; opera singer Ruggiero Raimondi.

Dodge, Hodge, Rodge, Rodger, Rog, Rogelio, Rogerio, Rogers, Rogiero, Rudiger, Ruggero, Ruggiero, Rutger, Ruttger

Roland OG. "Renowned land." **Orlando** is a more common variant in several European languages. **Rowland** was, for a long time, the preferred version in English. The name dates from the Dark Ages, and the most famous Roland was the valorous nephew of Charlemagne, about whom many romantic tales were written.

Lannie, Lanny, Orlando, Roeland, Rolando, Roldan, Roley, Rolland, Rollie, Rollin, Rollins, Rollo, Rolly, Rowe, Rowland

Rolf Var. **Rudolph** (OG. "Famous wolf"). Most common in Scandinavian countries.

Rolfe, Rolle, Rollo, Rolph, Rowland

Rollo Var. **Roland**. Used occasionally in continental Europe, where the "-o" ending for first names is more common. Author Rollo May.

Roman Lat. "From Rome." The name of several obscure saints and one short-lived pope. The significance of the name no doubt comes from the fact that Rome is the center of the Roman Catholic faith. Film director Roman Polanski; author Romain Gary.

Romain, Romaine, Romanes, Romano, Romanos, Romanus

Romeo It. "Pilgrim to Rome." Cannot be used without reference to the famous romance, and sure to engender a lot of teasing.

Romney OWelsh. Place name: "Winding river." Painter George Romney.

Romulus Lat. "Man of Rome." Along with Remus, the legendary founder of Rome, though Romulus actually murdered his twin brother in a quarrel over where to situate the city, which he then ruled for 37 years. A rare name. Playwright Romulus Linney.

Romolo

Ronald OE. "Counsel power." Also from the same source as **Reginald** and **Reynold**. Though it was fairly common in the 1940s and 1950s, most parents will associate Ronald with two-term President Ronald Reagan and with clown Ronald McDonald.

Ranald, Renaldo, Ron, Ronaldo, Roneld, Ronell, Ronello, Ronnie, Ronny

Ronan Ir. Gael. "Little seal." Mostly Irish use.

Ronson OE. "Son of Ronald."

Rooney Ir. Gael. "Red-haired." Yet another Irish name indicating the traditional Irish coloring. Actor Mickey Rooney.

Roone, Rowan, Rowen, Rowney

Roosevelt Old Dutch. Place name: "Rose field." A name that would be simply an ethnic curiosity if it hadn't been borne by two 20th-century presidents, Theodore and Franklin Delano Roosevelt (who were second cousins).

Roper OE. Occupational name: "Rope maker."

Rory Ir. Gael. "Red." Also occurs as a nickname for **Roderick**. Mostly Scottish use, but the name seems highly eligible for 21st-century popularity, since it is unusual without being weird

Rosario Port. "The rosary." Most common, for obvious reasons, among Catholic families.

Roscoe ONorse. Place name: "Woods of the female deer." This is a place name from northern England, where Norse influence may be more likely to have lingered in the language. Tennis star Roscoe Tanner.

Ross, Rosscoe

Roshan Per. "Daybreak, dawn."

Roslin Scot. Gael. "Little redhead."

Roslyn, Rosselin, Rosslyn

Ross Scot. Gael. "Headland." A place name in Scotland, and very popular as a first name there, as well. The name (like so many of the *R* names) may also come from the Gaelic word for "red." Presidential candidate Ross Perot.

Rosse, Rossell

Roswell OE. Place name: "Rose spring."

Roth OG. "Red." Could apply to hair or complexion, though England's flaxen-haired Teutonic invaders might have used it more for the former, in sheer surprise. Actor Tim Roth.

Rothe

Rothwell ONorse. Place name: "Red spring."

Rousseau OF. "Little red-haired one." A relative of **Russell**. May be given to honor Jean-Jacques Rousseau, the 18th-century French philosopher whose writings influenced the French and American Revolutions.

Roussell, Russo

Rover ME. "Traveler, wanderer." The term "roving" turns up most often in poetry and songs (as in Byron's poem

"So, We'll Go No More A-Roving"), and the name is most commonly given to dogs.

Rowan OE. Place name: "Rowan tree." The rowan is a flowering tree that later produces red berries. Also possibly another Gaelic name meaning "red." Presumably, since the term applied to so many people, variations in the name were necessary to tell them apart.

Roan, Rohan, Rowe

Rowdy Eng. "Boisterous." In England making a row (rhymes with how) means making a lot of noise. Probably used most often as a nicnkame. Diver Rowdy Gaines.

Rowell OE. Place name: "Roe deer well."

Rowley OE. Place name: "Roughly cleared meadow."

Rowlea, Rowlee, Rowleigh, Rowly

Roxbert OE. "Bright raven."

Roxbury OE. Place name: "Rook's town or fortress." "Rook" may have referred to a large population of rooks or crows.

Roxburghe

Roy Gael. "Red" or Fr. "King." Most popular earlier in the 20th century, but hard to use because of the Roy Rogers chain of fast-food restaurants. Cowboy Roy Rogers; actor Roy Scheider.

Rey, Roi, Ruy

Royal OF. "Royal." Scarce as a name, though the merely aristocratic names like **Earl** and **Marquez** occur much more often.

Royall

Royce Meaning and origin unclear: Some sources offer OF./OE. "Son of the king"; others suggest OG. "Kind fame." The most famous Royce is the man who, along with Mr. Rolls, began turning out England's foremost luxury car.

Roice

Royden OE. Place name: "Rye hill."

Roydan, Roydon

Royston OE. Place name: Not related to **Roy** at all, but a name whose original meaning varied geographically.

Rozen Heb. "Ruler."

Ruben Sp. Var. **Reuben** (Heb. "Behold, a son"). This form occurs more often than the anglicized **Reuben** or the original Hebrew, **Reuven**. Singer Ruben Blades.

Rube, Rubi, Rubin, Rubino

Rubio Sp. "Ruby."

Rudd OE. "Ruddy-skinned." Student leader Mark Rudd.

Rudiger Ger. "Spear fame." May refer to an ancestor's skill with a weapon.

Rudolph OG. "Famous wolf." Parents would have to have very strong feelings about the name to use it, given the enormous fame of Rudolph the red-nosed reindeer. Actor Rudolph Valentino; ballet star Rudolf Nureyev.

Dolph, Raoul, Rodolfo, Rodolph, Rodolphe, Rolf, Rolfe, Rollo, Rolph, Rolphe, Rudey, Rudi, Rudie, Rudolf, Rudolfo, Rudolphus, Rudy

Rudy Dim. "Rud-" names. Well-established by singer Rudy Vallee, and more common than **Rudolph**, perhaps because of that pesky reindeer. Fashion designer Rudi Gernreich; New York City mayor Rudy Giuliani.

Rudee, Rudi

Rudyard OE. Place name: "Red paddock." Preempted by English poet and novelist Rudyard Kipling, though fans of the *Just So Stories* or the *Jungle Book* might want to use it.

Rufaro Shona (Zimbabwe). "Happiness, elation."

Rufino Lat. var. **Rufus**.

Ruffino

Ruford OE. Place name: "Red ford" or "Rough ford."

Rufford

Rufus Lat. "Red-haired." Another redhead name, though this one comes from Latin rather than Gaelic. Most common in the 19th century.

Ruffus, Rufous

Rugby OE. "Rook fortress." The name of a famous British school, which in turn gave its name to a famous game.

Rune ONorse. "Secret, whisper." Runes were the alphabet of the ancient Germanic peoples, dating from about the

LAST NAME FIRST

Last names aren't necessary unless tracking a lot of people is important. In self-contained societies, a first name suffices. If you refer to Rufus ("red-haired" in Latin), everybody knows who you're talking about. As populations grow, last names get added on to avoid confusion: Rufus Miller grinds the flour while Rufus Ford lives by the river ford.

The big change comes when last names are fixed. If Rufus Miller's son became a shepherd in 9th-century England, he would have been called Rufus Shepherd. But some time after the Norman Conquest in 1066, all of Rufus Miller's children would have shared his last name, and his grandchildren as well. In 1267, last names became officially hereditary.

This turning point arrived in different cultures at different times. The Irish reached it in the tenth century, before any other country in post-Roman Europe. The Chinese were way ahead of Europeans and adopted hereditary last names around the time of Christ. But the Ashkenazy Jews of Northern Europe didn't use hereditary last names until the 18th and 19th centuries, when they were required to do so by law.

third century A.D. They carry the aura of mystery because they could not be translated until comparatively recently. Not related to **Roone**, despite the sound.

Rumford OE. Place name: "Wide river-crossing."

Rupert Var. **Robert**. Well-established in Britain since the 18th century, but less used here, possibly because to Americans, it has a very English flavor. Actor Rupert Everett; publisher Rupert Murdoch.

Ruprecht

Rurik Rus. Var. **Roderick** (OG. "Famous king").

Rush OE. Place name: "Dweller by the rushes." Given great exposure by commentator Rush Limbaugh, but par-

ents don't necessarily name their children after their favorite radio star.

Rushford OE. Place name: "Ford with rushes."

Ruskin OF. "Little red-haired one." Author John Ruskin.

Russell Fr. "Red-head; red-skinned." Originally a last
name, but popular as a first name in the middle of the
20th century. Like most fashions of that era, the name is
now somewhat neglected. Philosopher Bertrand Russell;
author Russell Baker; actor Russell Crowe.
Roussell, Russ, Russel

Ruston OE. Place name: "Rust's estate," referring, once
again, to that red-haired ancestor.
Rustin, Russton

Rusty Fr. "Red-haired." Most commonly a nickname,
given when the fact of red hair is well established (which
may occur long after a bald baby is given a proper name).

Rutherford OE. "Cattle crossing." Most commonly a family name transferred to first-name use, since passionate
admiration for U.S. President Rutherford Hayes seems
unlikely to influence parental choice. Use may also be
limited by the fact that there is no handy nickname.
Rutherfurd

Rutland ONorse. Place name: "Land of roots" or "Red
land."

Rutledge OE./ONorse. Place name: "Root ledge" or "Red
ledge."
Routledge

Rutley OE. Place name: "Root meadow" or "Red meadow."

Ryan Ir. last name. Meaning is unclear, though some
sources connect it with "king." Has been very popular in
recent years, to the extent that boys named Ryan are numerous in elementary schools. Highly popular in Scotland and Ireland. Actors Ryan O'Neal, Ryan Philippe;
baseball player Ryne Sandberg.
Rian, Rien, Ryen, Ryon, Ryun

Rycroft OE. Place name: "Rye field."
Ryecroft

Rye The name of a grain that is widely grown in northern

Europe and the United States. It is used as a basis for bread and also for whiskey.

Ryland OE. Place name: "Land where rye is grown."
 Ryeland

 Saad Aramaic. "Aid, help."
 Saahdia Aramaic. "The help of the Lord."
  Saadya, Seadya
  Saarik Hindi. Nature name: a kind of thrush, a small, drably feathered songbird.
 Saariq, Sareek, Sareeq, Sariq

Saber Fr. "Sword." The kind of curved sword traditionally used by cavalrymen; also a weapon used in modern-day fencing. Slightly bloodthirsty as a first name.
 Sabr, Sabre

Sabin Lat. "Sabine." The Sabines were a tribe living in central Italy around the time Romulus and Remus established the city of Rome. In an effort to provide wives for the citizens of Rome, Romulus arranged the mass kidnapping of the Sabine women, which came to be known (and frequently portrayed in art and literature) as the "Rape of the Sabines." The name is more common in the feminine form, **Sabina**.
 Sabeeno, Sabino, Savin, Savino

Sable OF. Animal name. In ancient heraldic terms, sable is black, even though the furry little creatures are actually golden-brown to brown.

Sacha Rus. Dim. **Alexander** (Gk. "Defender of mankind"). Cropped up in English-speaking countries in the last 20 years. The "-a" ending in Russian is not necessarily feminine, and in fact this name is used for boys as well as girls in the U.S. French singer Sacha Guitry.
 Sascha, Sasha

Sachar Heb. Var. **Yisachar** ("Reward").
 Sacar

Sacheverell OE. Possibly of Norman origins, meaning lost to time. Poet Sir Sacheverell Sitwell was known to his family as "Sachie."

Sachiel Heb. The name of the archangel whose job it is to watch out for people born under the sign of Sagittarius.
Sachiell

Sackville OE. "Saxon's town." Saxony is an area in Northern Germany that sent many invaders to England. (Hence Anglo-Saxon.)

Sadiki Swahili. "Faithful, loyal."
Sadeeki

Sadler OE. Occupational name: "Harness maker." Like most last names turned first names, this one was first transferred in the 19th century.
Saddler

Safford OE. Place name: "Willow river crossing."

Saffron Plant name: Saffron refers to a substance (the dried stamens of saffron crocuses) used as a spice in Mediterranean and other Southern cuisines. It produces a bright orange-yellow color, and is sometimes used as a dye. Monks of some Eastern religions wear saffron robes, which may explain why the name was used occasionally in the 1960s, an era when saffron robes and Eastern religions went mainstream.
Saffran, Saffren, Saphron

Sage Plant name: a shrubby herb that grows widely in the West, and is also used for seasoning in cooking. It is considered to have healing properties, too. "Sage" is also sometimes used as to mean a wise man. Actor Sage Stallone; philanthropist Russell Sage.
Saige, Sayge

Sagiv Heb. "Great, sublime, mighty."
Segev

Saguaro The variety of tall, branched cactus that has become an icon for the American Southwest. They may grow as tall as 70 feet. Saguaro National Monument in Arizona is a wild area of almost 80,000 acres.
Seguaro

Sahil Hindi. "Leader."
Sahel

Said Arab. "Happy." Currently popular in Arabic countries and also used in Northern and Eastern Africa. Actor Saeed Jaffrey.
Saeed, Saiyid, Sayeed, Sayid, Syed

Sail Noun used as name. Appealing for parents who like its quintessentially outdoorsy connotations.

Sainsbury OE. "Saint's settlement." The name of a huge grocery store chain in the United Kingdom.
Sainsberry

Saint Lat. "Holy." This name is more readily used as a first name in Latin (and Catholic) cultures.

Sajan Hindi. "Loved one."

Saladin Arab. "The righteous faith." The name of an important Muslim sultan of the 12th century who captured Jerusalem from the Crusaders.
Saladdin

Salem Heb. "Peace." Related to **Shalom, Solomon**, etc. Used in the Psalms as an abbreviation for Jerusalem. In the U.S., this name has been used for some dozen cities and towns including the capital of Oregon and the historic coastal town in Massachusetts, site of the Salem witch trials and setting of Nathaniel Hawthorne's tale, *The House of the Seven Gables*.

Salim Arab. "Tranquility."
Saleem, Salem, Selim

Salisbury ME. Place name: probably "Willow settlement." *Saule* is the French word for willow. In England, Salisbury is a picturesque and important cathedral town. This is also an American place name.
Salisbery, Salisberry, Saulsberry, Saulsbery, Saulsbury, Saulisbury

Salman Arab. "Safety." Author Salman Rusdie.

Salton OE. Place name: "Manor settlement" or "Willow settlement." The Salton Sea, in southern California, is a body of water 287 feet below sea level.

Salvatore It. "Savior." Used mostly by families of Latinate descent. Salvador is an important place name in Latin America. Artist Salvador Dali.

Sal, Salvador, Salvator, Salvidor, Sauveur, Xavier, Xaviero, Zavier, Zaviero

Salvio Lat. "Saved." The feminine term is **Salvia**, which is the Latin word for the herb sage.

Salvian, Salviano, Salviatus

Sam Dim. **Samuel** or **Samson**. Occasionally used on its own, more commonly a nickname. Playwright Sam Shepard; actor Sam Waterston; singer Sammy Davis, Jr.

Samm, Sammey, Sammie, Samy

Sami Arab. "On high, exalted." Pronounced "Sahmi."

Samson Heb. "Sun." In the Old Testament, Samson was the warrior whose strength ebbed away when his hair was cut by Delilah. The name was used in the Middle Ages, and the Puritans kept it current with their fondness for Old Testament names, but it has not been fashionable for several hundred years.

Sam, Sampson, Sansom, Sanson, Sansone, Shem

Samuel Heb. "Told by God." A judge and prophet in early Israel; two Old Testament books are named for him. The name was used, predictably, by the Puritans and has never really faded since then, though it peaked in the 19th century. In contrast to lukewarm U.S. use, this is a top-ten name in England. Opera singer Samuel Ramey; lexicographer Samuel Johnson; playwright Samuel Beckett; author Samuel Clemens (Mark Twain); actor Samuel L. Jackson.

Sam, Sammie, Sammy, Samuele, Samuello, Samwell, Shem

Sanborn OE. Place name: "Sandy stream."

Sanborne, Sanbourn, Sanburn, Sanburne, Sandborn, Sandbourne

Sancho Lat. "Sacred." Don Quixote's sidekick was called Sancho Panza, which is a little joke, since "Panza" is Spanish slang for "belly." When French-born journalist Sanche de Gramont took American citizenship, he changed his name to Ted Morgan. This name is very popular in Spain.

Sanche, Sanctio, Sancos, Sanzio, Sauncho

Sandberg OE. Place name: "Sand village." Poet Carl Sandburg.
Sandbergh, Sandburg, Sandburgh

Sander Ger. Var. **Alexander** (Gk. "Defender of mankind"). Used in Europe.
Sandino, Sandor, Sender, Xan, Xander, Zander

Sanders ME. "Son of Alexander." (Gk. "Defender of mankind").
Sanderson, Sandor, Saunders, Saunderson, Sandros

Sandor Hung. Var. **Alexander** (Gk. "Defender of mankind"). Novelist Sandor Marai.
Sandros, Xandros

Sanditon OE. "Sandy settlement."

Sandhurst OE. Place name: "Sandy thicket of trees." In England, the premier military academy is known as Sandhurst, for the village where it is located.
Sandhirst

Sandy Dim. **Alexander** (Gk. "Defender of mankind"). Sometimes also given as a nickname based on a person's coloring, like **Rusty**. Apparently red or reddish hair is unusual enough to warrant this kind of name, but corresponding names for blonds or brunets don't seem to exist.
Sandey, Sandie, Sandino

Sanford OE. Place name: "Sandy ford." Acting teacher Sanford Meisner.
Sandford, Sandfurd

Sanjay Sanskrit. "Conquering, triumphant."

Satchel Lat. "Sack, small bag." Made famous by baseball player Satchel Paige.
Satchell

Santiago Sp. "Saint James." Catholics are traditionally less reluctant to use religious names than Protestants, routinely naming children **Salvatore, Socorro**, and even **Jesus**, as well as choosing the names of individual saints.
Sandiago, Sandiego, Santeago, Santiaco, Santigo

Santo It./Sp. "Holy." Also a nickname for full saints' names.
Santos

Sapir Heb. "Sapphire."
Safir, Saphir, Saphiros

Sargent OF. Occupational name: "Officer." Painter John Singer Sargent; politician Sargent Shriver.
Sarge, Sergeant, Sergent, Serjeant

Sassacus Native American: "Wild man" in the Massachuset language. This was the name of the last chief of the Pequot tribe of Connecticut. Though virtually exterminated in 1637, the Pequots have had the last laugh by building immensely successful casinos on their tribal lands in eastern Connecticut.

Saturnin Sp. "Saturn." A "saturnine" temperament is moody or sullen, and people born under the sign of Saturn (Capricorns) are generally considered painstaking, reliable, and reserved.
Saturnino

Saul Heb. "Asked for." The name of the first king of Israel, and also the name of the apostle Paul before his conversion to Christianity. Overlooked in the 16th-century revival of Old Testament names, at its peak in the late 19th century. Author Saul Bellow.
Saulo, Shaul, Sol, Sollie

Saville Fr. "Willow town." Savile Row, in London, is the worldwide source for fine men's tailoring.
Savil, Savile, Savill, Savylle

Saviero Sp. Var. **Xavier** (Basque "New house"). The wide use of Xavier and its variations is partly the result of veneration of St. Francis Xavier, but it may also be influenced by the fact that Xavier and "savior" sound so much alike that parents may take them to be related.

Savion Modern name, possibly derived from **Xavier** (Basque, "New house"). Brought to the public's eye by the fame of tapdance genius Savion Glover.
Xavion, Savionn

Savoy Place name: an area of southeastern France bordering Switzerland. There used to be a kingdom of Savoy, whose descendants ruled Italy into this century. The name's connotations of luxury go back to a splendid palace in London built by Peter of Savoy in the 13th century. A famously lavish hotel was later built on its site.

Savyon Heb. Plant name: a low-growing shrubby groundcover.

Sawyer ME. Occupational name: "Wood-worker." Most familiar as the name of Mark Twain's boy hero, *Tom Sawyer.*

Saxe OE. "From Saxony." Saxony was the area of northern German where the Saxon tribe originated.
Sachs, Sachsen

Saxon OE. "Knife, sword." Used for one of the Germanic tribes that fought with short-bladed weapons. The name may also refer to origin in the German area of Saxony, which probably took its name from those effective daggers.
Saxe, Saxen

Sayer Welsh. "Woodworker." Football star Gale Sayers.
Sayers, Sayre, Sayres

Scanlon Ir. Gael. "Little trapper."
Scanlan, Scanlen

Schubert Ger. "Shoemaker." Made famous by 19th-century German composer Franz Schubert.
Shubert

Schultz Ger. "Village magistrate or administrator." A German occupational name.

Schuyler Dutch. "Shield, protection" or "Scholar." Harks back to the Dutch settlers who brought the name to America in the 17th century. A homonym, **Skyler**, is steadily used. For some reason **Skylar** is the preferred spelling for girls.
Schuylar, Skuyler, Skylar, Skyler, Skylor

Scipio Ancient Roman name of uncertain meaning. Scipio Africanus was the Roman general who, in the Punic War (around 200 B.C.), defeated the Carthaginian general Hannibal. Western European culture has identified so strongly with Greco-Roman culture that for generations this was seen as the good guys defeating the bad guys, making Scipio a hero. Scipio was used in the south as a slave name (with an unpleasant note of irony) and has survived in some southern families.

Scirocco It. from Arab. "Warm wind." The word originally described the wind that blew over Italy from the Libyan deserts.

Cirocco, Sirocco

Scorpio Lat. "Scorpion." Zodiac sign, for people born between Oct. 21 and Nov. 21. Scorpions carry a vicious sting in their tails, making this a startling name for a child.

Skorpios

Scott OE. "Scotsman." Use is emphatically 20th century, and while the name is not fashionable it certainly is familiar to parents and nursery school teachers in our era. Actors Scott Glenn, Scott Caan; authors Scott Peck, F. Scott Fitzgerald, Scott Turow; musician Scott Joplin; basketball player Scottie Pippen.

Scot, Scottie, Scotto, Scotty

Scout OF. "To listen." (French-speakers will recognize the word *écouter*.) Occupational name: someone who scouts, gathers information quietly. When Bruce Willis and Demi Moore named their daughter Scout after a character in *To Kill a Mockingbird*, they gave the name a new credibility. It is so unusual, though, that its gender is still up for grabs.

Scribner OE. Occupational name: "Scribe, copier." Or "scrivener," to use the old term. Charles Scribner & Son was a prominent American publishing firm.

Seabert OE. "Shining sea."

Seabright, Sebert, Seibert

Seabrook OE. Place name: "Stream near the sea."

Seabrooke

Seabury OE. Place name: "Settlement near the sea." Samuel Seabury was the first Episcopal bishop of the United States, appointed in 1789.

Seaberry, Seabry

Seal Animal name. Brought to prominence by a rock musician who uses only this name.

Seaman OE. Occupational name: "Mariner."

Seamus Ir. Var. **James** (Heb. "He who supplants").

"Shamus" is old-fashioned American slang for a detective, possibly because the urban police force has traditionally been heavily Irish. Poet Seamus Heaney.

Seumas, Seumus, Shamus

Sean Ir. Var. **John** (Heb. "God is gracious"). Spread outside of Ireland only in the 20th century. Quite heavily used now, perhaps influenced by the popularity of actors Sean Connery and Sean Penn. A top-ten name in Ireland. Basketball player Shawn Kemp; actors Sean Hayes, Sean Astin, Sean Bean; musician and entrepreneur Sean ("Puffy" or "P. Diddy") Combs.

Shane, Shaughn, Shaun, Shawn

Searle OE. "Armor." Cartoonist Ronald Searle.

Seaton OE. Place name: "Town near the sea."

Seeton, Seton

Sebastian Lat. "From Sebastia" (an ancient city). Saint Sebastian, an early Christian martyr, was killed in a hail of arrows, and was a favorite subject for Old Master painters. (He is now patron of soldiers.) The name has never been common, though the British have used it somewhat since the 1940s, possibly influenced by a character in Evelyn Waugh's popular *Brideshead Revisited*. In the last dozen years, it has become quite fashionable in the U.S. as well, breaking into the top 100 names for boys. In France **Sebastien** is very popular. Track star Sebastian Coe.

Bastian, Bastien, Seb, Sebastiano, Sebastien, Sebestyen, Sebo

Secondo It. "Second son." For parents who simply cannot agree on anything else?

Segundo

Sedgley OE. Place name: "Sword meadow." Could indicate a kind of coarse, sharp reedlike grass growing in a meadow, or that the meadow belonged to (or was frequented by) a swordsman. In all cases, refers to a long-ago meadow.

Sedgeley, Sedgely

Sedgwick OE. Place name: "Sword place." As with Sedgley, the sword could refer to grass or an actual weapon.

Sedgewick, Sedgewyck, Sedgwyck

Seeley OE. "Blessed." From the same Germanic root as Selig.

Sealey, Seely, Seelye

Seferino Sp. from Gk. "A soft, gentle wind." Another version of **Zephyr**, or **Zefirino**. Before he was the monkey in the Babar stories, Zephyr was the West Wind personified in Greek myth. He was married to Iris, the rainbow.

Cefirino, Sebarino, Sephirio, Zefarin, Zefirino, Zephir, Zephyr

Sefton OE. Place name: "Town in the rushes."

Seger OE. "Sea fighter." Musician Pete Seeger.

Seager, Segar, Seeger

Segundo Sp. "Second." Not common: parents usually have enough imagination to come up with at least two proper names.

Secondo

Sela Heb. "Boulder, cliff." This is also a word that occurs frequently in the Psalms, though its meaning is unknown. It may be an ancient musical notation.

Selah

Selby OE. Place name: "Manor village." As **Shelby** is appropriated by girls, Selby may lose its maleness.

Selbey, Shelbey, Shelbie, Shelby

Seldon OE. Place name: "Willow valley."

Selden, Sellden, Shelden

Selig OG. "Blessed."

Seligman, Seligmann, Zelig

Selkirk Scot. Gael. Place name: its meaning is unclear, though "kirk" means church. It is an area in Scotland. Scottish sailor Alexander Selkirk is thought to have been Daniel Defoe's inspiration for the novel *Robinson Crusoe*.

Sellers OE. "Marshland dweller." Actor Peter Sellers.

Sellars

Selwyn OE. "Manor-friend." Alternatively, an offshoot of **Silvanus**. Mostly 19th-century use.

Selwin, Selwinn, Selwynn, Selwynne

Seminole Native American name: the tribe, related to the Creeks, who settled in Florida and resisted European-American attempts to annex their land in the ten-year

Seminole War. The football team of Florida State University is known as "the Seminoles."

Seneca Both the name of a Native American tribe (part of the Iroquois confederacy) and several New York State place names, and the name of a Roman philosopher and statesman around the time of Christ. He was Nero's tutor.

Senior OF. "Lord." Hard to use in these days when it has come to mean any individual older than 65.

Sennett Fr. "Elderly." Related to **Senior**. Comedian Mack Sennett.
Sennet

Septimus Lat. "Seventh." Most common in the 19th century, when very large families were the norm.

Sequoia Cherokee: "Sparrow." The 19th-century Cherokee scholar who developed a form of written language for his tribe was named Sequoia. This is also the name of a kind of redwood tree, called after him.
Sequoya, Sequoyah

Seraphim Heb. "Ardent." The seraphim are the highest-ranking angels in Heaven (above angels, archangels, cherubim, etc.). They have six wings and are noted for their zealous love. There have been two Saints Seraphim, one a 17th-century Italian, one an 18th-century Russian mystic.
Sarafino, Saraph, Serafin, Serafino, Seraph, Seraphimus

Sereno Lat. "Tranquil." Though the feminine form, **Serena**, is somewhat popular, the masculine version is very rare.
Cereno

Sergio Lat. "Servant, attendant." Strongly associated with Russia, perhaps because of composers Rachmaninoff and Prokofiev, yet it comes from a Latin name and was used by an early pope. This Spanish form is the most common one in the U.S. Impresario Serge Diaghilev; film director Sergio Leone.
Seargeoh, Sergei, Sergey, Sergi, Sergio, Sergios, Sergiu, Sergiusz, Serguei, Sirgio, Sirgios

Servas Lat. "Redeemed." Used in northern Europe.
Servaas, Servacio, Servatus

Sesame The seed and flavoring agent.
Sesamey, Sessame, Sessamee
Seth Heb. "Set, appointed." In the Old Testament, Adam and Eve's third son (after Cain and Abel). Passed over in the Puritan revival of biblical names, but included to some extent in the late 20th-century revival of the same. Actor Seth Green.
Seton OE. Place name: "Sea settlement."
Severin Lat. "Severe."
Severino, Severinus, Seweryn
Severn OE. "Boundary." The Severn is an important river running through southern England.
Seward OE. "Sea guardian" or "Victory guardian." An 11th-century Earl of Northumberland (in England), born in Denmark, was named Siward. Largely 19th century. Secretary of State under Lincoln and Johnson, William Henry Seward was responsible for the U.S. purchase of Alaska from Russia.
Sewerd, Siward
Sewell OE. "Sea strong."
Sewald, Sewall
Sexton ME. Occupational name: "Church custodian." The sexton (or sacristan) is charged with the upkeep of a church building.
Sextus Lat. "Sixth." Less common than Septimus or Octavius, though five popes have used it. The first one, oddly enough, was actually Christendom's seventh pope.
Sesto, Sixto, Sixtus
Seymour OF. "From Saint Maur." Indicates an ancestor who came from a village called Saint Maur, most probably in Normandy. Quite a popular name in the 19th century, but virtually invisible today.
Seamore, Seamor, Seamour, Seymore
Shabat Heb. "To finish, to stop." Related to the term Sabbath, for the end of the week.
Shabbat
Shachar Heb. "Dawn, sunrise."
Shadow OE. "Shade."
Shadoe

Shad Possibly dim. **Shadrach**. Also a nature name: the shad is a common food fish in both Europe and America.

Shadrach Heb. Meaning unknown. Old Testament name: one of three Hebrew men (along with Meshach and Abednego) thrown into a fiery furnace by King Nebuchadnezzar and rescued by an angel. Used steadily in the 16th-19th centuries, but now rare.
Shad, Shadrack

Shafiq Arab. "Empathetic, merciful."
Shafeek, Shafik

Shafir Heb. "Handsome."
Shafeer, Shafer, Shefer

Shahzad Per. "Son of the king." *Shah* is Persian for king.

Shai Heb. "Present, gift."

Shakil Arab. "Good-looking, well-developed." The root of Shaquille O'Neal's name, and more accurate than his parents could ever have predicted.
Shakeel, Shakill, Shakille, Shaqueel, Shaquil, Shaquille

Shakir Arab. "Gratitude, thanksgiving."
Shakeer, Shaqueer

Shalom Heb. "Peace." Related to **Solomon**. Not just a name but also a common greeting to speakers of Hebrew.
Sholom, Solomon

Shamir Heb. "Flint, thorn." Shamir is a legendary material capable of cutting stone; Solomon used it in the building of the Temple. Israeli statesman Yitzhak Shamir.
Shameer

Shamus Var. **Seamus** (Ir. Var. **James**: Heb. "The supplanter").

Shanahan Ir. Gael. "Wise, clever." Football coach Mike Shanahan.

Shandy Possibly OE. "Boisterous, high-spirited." Name of a drink popular in Britain, half beer and half lemonade or ginger ale. Also used for girls, possibly because it sounds like the familiar **Sandy** or **Mandy**.
Shandey

Shane Var. **Sean** (Ir. Var. **John**: Heb. "The Lord is gracious"). Popularity in the 1950s and 1960s probably de-

pended on the film *Shane*. Now losing ground to **Sean**, as those now-grown Shanes watch their children grow up. Screenwriter Shane Black.
Shaine, Shayn, Shayne

Shani Heb. "Crimson, bright red." Also used for girls.

Shanley Ir. Gael. "Small and ancient." Playwright John Patrick Shanley.
Shannley

Shannon Ir. Gael. "Old, ancient." The name of an important river, county, and airport in Ireland, used as a first name in this century. Most popular among families with Irish roots, and more common for girls. Football player Shannon Sharpe.
Shanan, Shanen, Shannan, Shannen, Shanon

Shaquille Modern respelling of **Shakil** (Arab. "Well-developed, good-looking"). Known the world over as the name of basketball megastar Shaquille O'Neal.
Shaq, Shaqeell, Shaqueel, Shaquil

Sharif Arab. "Honest." Actor Omar Sharif.
Shareef

Shashi Hindi. "Moonbeam." Indian movie star Shashi Kapoor.

Shasta Oregon mountain of some 14,000 feet that rises from nearly sea level. It is at the southernmost end of the Cascade Mountain range. Also the name of a brand of soda, though parents using this name are more likely to be evoking America's natural beauty. The "-a" ending may make Shasta more appealing to parents of girl babies.

Shavon Phonetic spelling of the Irish name **Siobhan**, which corresponds to the English **Joan**. Used as a boy's name in this context.
Shavonne, Shivaun, Shovon

Shaw OE. Place name: "Copse, grove of trees."

Shawn Var. **Sean**. This version is not as common as the Irish spelling, **Sean**. Basketball player Shawn Kemp.
Shawnel, Shawnell

Shawnee Name of a Native American tribe that originated in the eastern forests of the U.S. and gradually migrated westward. Shawnee Mission is the name of a town in Kansas. Also, possibly, a variant of **Shawn**.

Shawney, Shawnie

Shayan Phonetic spelling of **Cheyenne**, the name of a Native American tribe.

Shea Ir. Gael. "From the fairy fort." More commonly an Irish last name.

Shae, Shay, Shaye, Shays

Sheehan Ir. Gael. "Small and tranquil."

Sheffield OE. Place name: "Crooked meadow." Sheffield is the name of a city in England that was famous for manufacture of cutlery, and "Sheffield plate" is a term for silverplating copper, a process that originated there.

Shelby OE. Place name: "Village on the ledge." Author Shelby Foote.

Shelbey, Shelbie

Sheldon OE. Place name: "Steep valley," or possibly "Flat-topped hill." Most common in the middle of the 20th century. This is one of a group of Old English names (along with **Seymour, Marvin, Irving**) that were enthusiastically used by Jewish immigrants eager to assimilate to the U.S. Author Sidney Sheldon.

Shelden, Sheldin

Shelley OE. Place name: "Ledge meadow." Last name made famous by the poet Percy Bysshe Shelley. Much more commonly used for girls at the moment.

Shelly

Shelton OE. Place name: "Ledge village."

Shem Heb. "Fame." The name of Noah's eldest son in the Old Testament. (Ham and Japheth were the other two.) None of the sons' names are as popular as that of their father, and though the entire human race descends, according to the Bible, from these three men and their wives, the wives are never named at all.

Shenandoah Place name: a city in Iowa and a town in Pennsylvania, but most famously, a long, fertile, beautiful valley between the Allegehenies and the Blue Ridge Mountains in Virginia. There is a famous, wistful folk song that begins "Oh, Shenandoah, I long to hear you. . . ." The name may be related to the Iroquois word for deer.

Shepherd OE. Occupational name: "Shepherd." Mostly 19th-century use, very uncommon now. *Pooh* illustrator Ernest Shepard.

Shep, Shepard, Shephard, Shepp, Sheppard, Shepperd

Shepley OE. Place name: "Sheep meadow."

Sheplea, Shepleigh, Shepply, Shipley

Sherborn OE. Place name: "Bright stream."

Sherborne, Sherbourn, Sherburn, Sherburne

Sheridan Ir. Gael. Unclear meaning, possibly "Wild man." Used mostly in Britain. Critic Sheridan Morley; playwright Richard Brinsley Sheridan; Civil War General Philip Sheridan.

Sheredan, Sheridon, Sherridan

Sherill OE. Place name: possibly "Bright hill." A common enough last name, but easily confused with **Cheryl** as a first name. Opera singer Sherrill Milnes.

Sherrill

Sherlock OE. "Bright hair." Irresistibly reminiscent of Arthur Conan Doyle's fictional detective, Sherlock Holmes.

Sherlocke, Shurlock

Sherman OE. Occupational name: "Shear man." Around the time when last names were coming into being, England's great export was wool. The wool business has given the modern world a number of occupational names, like Sherman, **Shepherd, Fuller,** and **Weaver.** Civil War general William Tecumseh Sherman.

Scherman, Schermann, Shearman, Shermann

Sherrerd Unknown origin. Possibly related to **Sheridan.** Familiar-sounding enough, owing to the "Sher" component, to be used occasionally as a name, more often for girls. There is no definitive spelling.

Sherard, Sherrard, Sherrod

Sherwin ME. "Bright friend."

Sherwind, Sherwinn, Sherwyn, Sherwynne

Sherwood OE. Place name: "Shining forest." Sherwood

Forest, a real forest in central England, was the home of the legendary bandit/hero Robin Hood. Playwright Robert Sherwood; author Sherwood Anderson.
Sherwoode, Shurwood

Shiloh Heb. Meaning disputed: possibly "His gift" or "He who was sent." Biblical place name used for a small town in Tennessee, the site of the bloodiest Civil War battle, where both Confederate and Union armies had casualties (men wounded and killed) of over 10,000 men.
Shilo, Shylo, Shyloh

Shipton OE. Place name: "Sheep village" or "Ship village."

Shiva Sanskrit. "Benign, bringing good fortune." This is the name of one of the preeminent Hindu gods who takes many forms with many different characteristics. His name is used as part of many other names in India.

Shlomo Var. **Solomon** (Heb. "Peaceable").
Shelomi, Shelomo, Shlomi

Shomer Heb. "Watchman."

Shoshone Native American tribe, indigenous to eastern Nevada, southern Idaho, and western Utah. These nomads were also known as the "Snake" Indians. Sacajawea, Lewis and Clark's guide on their Western explorations, was a Shoshone.
Shoshoni

Shoval Heb. "Path." Old Testament name.

Shura Rus. Dim. **Alexander** (Gk. "Man's defender"). Used in Russia as a nickname for a man.
Schura, Shoura

Sicily Place name: large island off the tip of Italy's "boot." Many Italian immigrants to the United States have roots in Sicily.
Sicilly

Sidney OE. "From Saint Denis." Famous English last name turned first name in the 18th century, very fashionable in the late 19th century, now little used for boys. It is getting a new lease on life as a girl's name, though. Author Sidney Sheldon; film director Sydney Pollack; actor Sidney Poitier.
Sid, Sydney

Sidonio Lat. "From Sidonia." Sidon was an area in the Middle East. Most often used as a girls' name in France.

Siegfried OG. "Victory peace." The hero of the last two of Wagner's *Ring* cycle of operas, son of Siegmund, husband of Brunhilde.
Sigfred, Sigfrid, Sigfried, Sigfryd, Sigvard, Sygfried

Sigbjorn ONorse. "Victory bear."
Siegbjorn

Sigmund OG. "Victorious protector." Another character from the *Ring* cycle, son of the god Wotan. He fathers Siegfried on his own sister, Sieglinde. The other famous Sigmund is the father of psychoanalysis, Sigmund Freud. A name with many weighty connotations.
Seigmond, Segismond, Siegmund, Sigismond, Sigismondo, Sigismund, Sigismundo, Sigismundus, Sigmond, Szygmond

Signe Unknown Scandinavian meaning, though the word particle meaning "victory" may give us a clue.
Signy

Sigwald OG. "Victorious leader."
Siegwald

Sigurd ONorse. "Guardian of victory."

Silas A contraction of **Silvanus**. New Testament name used in the Puritan era and occurring since then. Has an old-fashioned air that may appeal to parents of the 21st century.
Silvan, Silvano, Silvaon, Silvanus, Silvio, Sylas, Sylvan

Sill OE. "Beam, threshold."
Sills

Silvanus Lat. "Wood dweller." Also a New Testament name, but never as widely adopted as its spinoff, Silas.
Silvain, Silvano, Silvio, Sylvanus, Sylvio

Silver Noun as name, or possibly a contraction of **Silvester**. Scarce.
Sylver

Silverman OG. Occupational name: "Silver worker."
Silberman, Silbermann

Silverton OE. Place name: "Silver settlement."
Silvertown

Silvester Lat. "Wooded." Original form of the name we know as **Sylvester**.
Silvestre, Silvestro, Sylvester

Simba Swahili. "Lion." It's reassuring to find that the Walt Disney Company does its research thoroughly, and that *The Lion King*'s lion hero is actually named "lion."

Simcha Heb. "Joy."
Simha

Simeon Heb. "Listening intently." In the New Testament, Simeon is a holy old man who has been promised that he would see the Messiah before he died; when the infant Jesus was presented at the Temple, Simeon recognized him instantly. **Simon** is the more common anglicized form.
Shimon, Simyon

Simmons OE. "Son of Simon." Music producer Russell Simmons.
Semmes, Sim, Simms, Syms, Simmonds, Symonds

Simon Heb. "Listening intently." Prominent New Testament name, one of the twelve apostles. A common name from the Middle Ages through the 18th century, then revived early in the 20th century. To Americans, it has a rather English air. **Simeon**, the Old Testament version, has never been as common. Orchestra conductor Simon Rattle; Latin American freedom fighter Simon Bolivar.
Shimon, Si, Sim, Simen, Simeon, Simmonds, Simmons, Simms, Simone, Simonson, Simpson, Symms, Symon, Syms, Szymon

Simpson OE. "Son of Simon."

Sinbad A character in the *Arabian Nights* stories, a merchant from Baghdad who goes on seven adventurous voyages and, through wit and ingenuity, comes home rich.
Sindbad

Sinclair OF. Place name: "From Saint Clair." Still much more familiar as a last name. Authors Sinclair Lewis, Upton Sinclair.
Sinclare, Synclair

Sinjin Phonetic spelling of the English pronunciation of St. John, an unusual name in a widely Protestant culture.

Sion Heb. "Highest point." In the Christian religion, Sion is a symbolic name for heaven, and is used often in hymns and even the names of some churches.

Zion

Siraj Arab. "Light, beam."

Sirius Star name: the brightest star seen from earth.

Sixtus Lat. "Sixth." See **Sextus**.

Sivney Ir. Gael. "Well-going." Rare Irish last name.

Sivneigh, Sivnie

Skeet ONorse. "To shoot." Skeet shooting consists of shooting with a rifle at a clay "pigeon," or target tossed into the air mechanically to simulate the flight of a bird. A very rarefied sport. Actor Skeet Ulrich.

Skelly Ir. Gael. "Bard."

Scully

Skerry ONorse. Place name: "Stony isle."

Skinner OE. Occupational name: "Skinner of hides." Actor Otis Skinner; psychologist B.F. Skinner.

Skip "Ship boss." The term that has come down to us is "skipper," for the captain of a ship or boat. Skip occurs more commonly as a nickname.

Skipp, Skipper

Skiriki Pawnee. "Coyote." Nature name with Native American credibility.

Skye Scot. Place name: the name of a spectacular island off the west coast of Scotland. With the current trend toward nature and geography names, it may also refer to the big blue bowl overhead.

Skie, Sky

Skyler Dutch. "Giving shelter." Most probably an adaptation of the Dutch last name **Schuyler**, which was brought to New York by 17th-century settlers. Used for both boys and girls, in widely variant spellings.

Schuyler, Schyler, Skielar, Skielor, Skylar, Skylen, Skyller

Slade OE. Place name: "Valley." Art collector Felix Slade.

Slaide, Slayde

Slater OE. Occupational name: "Hewer of slates." Actor Christian Slater.

Slavin Ir. Gael. "Mountain man."
Slawin, Slavin, Sleven

Slavomir Czech. "Renowned glory."

Slim Eng. "Slender." Most often, given as a nickname to someone who is notably thin.

Sloan Ir. Gael. "Man of arms." An Irish last name that has become well entrenched in Britain and the U.S. Sometimes makes the leap to first-name status, perhaps as a maternal maiden name. Given extra prominence by the fact that Britain's version of preppies are known as "Sloane Rangers," for the area in London where they congregate. Novelist Sloan Wilson.
Sloane

Smedley OE. Place name: "Flat meadow."
Smedleigh, Smedly

Smith OE. Occupational name: "Blacksmith." This extremely common last name occurs as a first name, but parents would be unlikely to use it unless it was a family name. Economist Adam Smith; Mormon leader Joseph Smith; Smithsonian founder James Smithson.
Smithson, Smitty, Smyth, Smythe, Smythson

Smokey Descriptive name. Made famous by singer Smokey Robinson, which gives this name a very cool aura.
Smoky

Snowden OE. Place name: "Snowy peak." The name of a mountain in Wales, and the title (Earl of Snowdon) of the late Princess Margaret's ex-husband.
Snowdon

Snyder OG. Occupational name: "Tailor."
Schneider, Snider

Socorro Sp. "Aid, help." Most likely refers to the aid or help provided by the Almighty.

Socrates Gk. Meaning unknown. The name of the great Greek philosopher, used mostly by Greek families.
Sokrates

Sofus Gk. "Wisdom." The highly unusual masculine version of **Sophie**.
Sophus

Sohan Hindi. "Charming, handsome."
  Sohil
Solomon Heb. "Peaceable." In the Old Testament, the wise king of Israel. Used in the Middle Ages and the 18th century, but currently a far from common choice.
  Salmon, Salomo, Salomon, Salomone, Shalmon, Sol, Solaman, Sollie, Soloman
Somerby ME. Place name: "Summer village."
  Somerbie, Somersby, Sommersby
Somerley Ir. Gael. "Summer sailors" or Vikings, who made their invading voyages in the summer.
  Somerled, Sorley
Somers Probably short for an Old English place name having to do with summer, like **Somerset**. Actor Josef Sommer.
  Sommers
Somerset OE. Place name: "Summer settlement." A county in England, and a last name given prominence as a first name by author and playwright Somerset Maugham.
  Sommerset, Summerset
Somerton OE. Place name: "Summer town."
  Somervile, Somerville
Somerville ME. "Summer town." Probably refers to settlements where grazing was particularly good in summer, not what we think of as summer resorts.
  Somervil, Sommerville
Sonny Word as name, sometimes friendly and sometimes a little condescending. Sonny Bono, entertainer turned politician, seems to have lived down any disparaging connotations to the name.
  Sunny
Sophocles Gk. Meaning unknown. Name of one of the greatest classical Greek playwrights, author of *Oedipus the King*.
Soren Meaning unclear: may be related to **Severin** (Lat. "Severe"). This is a Danish form, known to literati as the first name of philosopher Soren Kierkegaard.
Sorrell OF. "Red-brown." A term now used to describe the

color of a horse, perhaps applied long ago to the color of an ancestor's hair.

Sorel, Sorrel

Sothern OE. Place name: "From the south."

Southern

Southwell OE. Place name: "South well."

Spalding OE. Place name: "Divided field." More commonly a last name, rarely transferred to first-name use. Sports-minded families already know this name as the manufacturer of sports equipment. Performance artist Spalding Gray.

Spaulding

Spark Lat. "To scatter." Noun used as name: a scattered bit of fire. Has probably been used most often as a nickname. Baseball player Sparky Lyle.

Sparky

Spear OE. Occupational name: "Spear-man." Names are sometimes a window into the concerns of a former era, and a number of names from the war-torn Anglo-Saxon age have to do with weapons.

Speare, Spears, Speer, Speers, Spiers

Speed OE. "Good fortune." Long ago, the phrase "God speed" meant, "God bring you good fortune." Speed has come to mean swiftness.

Spencer ME. Occupational name: "Provisioner." Used for the person in a large household who dispensed food and drink. Usually a last name, but occurs as a first name, more commonly in Britain. Actors Spencer Tracy, John Spencer; poet Edmund Spenser.

Spence, Spenser

Spider Noun as name. Usually used as a nickname because of the slightly creepy connotations. Skier Spider Sabich.

Spyder

Spike Noun as name. Possibly because of sports connotations ("spiking" a ball means slamming it to the ground), Spike is a very cool name, though a big hard-edged for a small child. Filmmakers Spike Lee, Spike Jonze.

Spiridon Gk. "Basket." The name of a 4th-century Cypriot sheep farmer who became a bishop and a popular Greek saint. The name is little used outside Greek communities. U.S. Vice President Spiro Agnew.
Speero, Spero, Spiridion, Spiro, Spiros, Spyridon, Spyros

Spud Derivation unclear, possibly related to the Middle English word for a spade (as in a shovel). In slang terms, a spud is a potato. The name occurs as a nickname, most often in sporting contexts.

Squire ME. Occupational name: "Knight's companion." In more modern terms, perhaps, an aide-de-camp. First-name use mostly 19th century.
Squier, Squiers, Squires, Squyre, Squyres

Stacy Dim. **Eustace** (Gk. "Fertile"). More common as a female name. Actor Stacy Keach.
Stacey, Stacie

Stafford OE. Place name: "Landing place ford." As with many of these place/last names, used mostly in the 19th century.
Stafforde, Staford

Stanbury OE. Place name: "Stone fortification."
Stanberry, Stanbery, Stanburghe, Stansberry, Stans-burghe, Stansbury

Stancliff OE. Place name: "Stony cliff."
Stancliffe, Stanclyffe, Stanscliff, Stanscliffe

Standish OE. Place name: "Stony parkland." The Pilgrims' military leader was Miles Standish, whose courtship Longfellow immortalized in a poem.

Stanfield OE. Place name: "Stony field."
Stansfield

Stanford OE. Place name: "Stony ford." Familiar as the name of the great California railroad magnate Leland Stanford, who founded the university that bears his name. Probably because Stanford is thought of as California's answer to the Ivy League, the name has Waspy connotations. Composer Charles Stanford.
Stamford, Standford

Stanislaus Slavic. Possibly "Glorious camp or stand." The patron saint of Poland, Saint Stanislaus, was an 11th-century bishop and martyr.
Stana, Stanek, Stanicek, Stanislas, Stanislav, Stanislaw, Stannes, Stanousek, Stasio

Stanley OE. Place name: "Stony field." It is not clear why some place names, like **Sidney** and Stanley, became popular enough so that they made the transition to common first names, while others, like **Stanford** or **Sinclair**, remain primarily last names. As with Sidney, Stanley's transformation to a first name was the result of great popularity at the turn of the century. Filmmaker Stanley Kubrick; actor Stanley Tucci.
Stan, Stanlea, Stanlee, Stanly

Stanmore OE. Place name: "Stony lake." On the evidence of this group of "Stan-" names, stones seem to have occupied a great deal of Anglo-Saxon man's attention, perhaps because they had to be cleared from the earth before it could be farmed effectively.
Stanmere

Stanton OE. Place name: "Stony village."
Stanten, Staunton

Stanway OE. Place name: "Stony roadway."
Stanaway, Stannaway, Stannway

Stanwick OE. "Dweller at the rocky village."
Stanwicke, Stanwyck

Stanwood OE. Place name: "Stony woods."

Stark Ger. "Strong."
Starck, Starke

Starling Bird name. The starling is a fairly common bird with drab plumage, so the name's appeal may reside in its resemblance to the word "star."

Starr ME. "Star." Beatle Ringo Starr; football player Bart Starr.

Stavros Gk. "Crowned." Related to **Stephen**, and currently popular in Greece. Greek plutocrat Stavros Niarchos.

Steadman OE. Occupational name: "Farmstead occupant."
Steadmann, Stedman

Steed OE. "Stallion, spirited horse." As in, "the hero's trusty steed."

Steel OE. "Like steel." In the rough times when the name was coined, this would have been quite a compliment. TV character Remington Steele.

Steele

Stefan Ger. and Scand. variant of **Stephen**, quite widely used in the U.S. by parents who have no Northern European ties whatever. Sometimes variations on a very popular name will become popular themselves, as parents seek something just a little bit different from the hot name of the moment. Tennis star Stefan Edberg; basketball player Stephon Marbury.

Staffan, Stefanos, Steffen, Steffon, Stefonn, Stephonn

Stein Ger. "Stone." Skiing champion Stein Erickson.

Steen, Sten, Steno, Stensen, Stenssen

Steinar ONorse. "Stone fighter."

Steinard, Steinart, Steinhardt

Stennis Scottish place name: a spot in the Orkneys, to the north of Scotland, where there are a set of standing stones, a prehistoric monument akin to Stonehenge.

Stephanus Gk. "Garland." Obviously related to **Stephen**, but a slightly different name. The popular blossom stephanotis (the name in Greek means "fit for a crown") is often used in bridal headpieces.

Stefanas, Stefanos, Stefanus, Stephanas, Stephanos

Stephen Gk. "Crowned." As the name of Christianity's first martyr (Saint Stephen, who was stoned to death), common until the late 18th century. A slow decline was reversed in the middle of the 20th century, and **Steven** is still going very strong after a long period of great popularity. Though the "ph-" spelling is traditional, the "v-" is much more common. Actors Stephen Collins, Steve Martin, Steve McQueen, Steve Buscemi; songwriter Stephen Foster; physicist Stephen Hawking; author Stephen King; filmmaker Steven Spielberg; musician Stevie Wonder; computer entrepreneur Steven Jobs; film director Stephen Daldry.

Esteban, Estefan, Estevan, Etienne, Staffan, Steban,

Steben, Stefan, Stefano, Steffen, Steffon, Stephan, Stephanus, Stephens, Stephenson, Stephon, Stevan, Steve, Steven, Stevenson, Stevie, Stevy

Stepney OE. Place name: "Stephen's island."
Stepny

Sterling OE. "Genuine, first-rate." As in sterling silver. The derivation is not clear, but might come from stars engraved on early pennies. Since then it has come to refer to either the legal proportion of silver to alloy in sterling silver, or to the British currency, known as pounds sterling. Not common, but has potential for 21st-century popularity. Race-car driver Stirling Moss; sports commentator Sterling Sharpe.
Stirling

Sterne ME. "Stern, unbending"; Ger. "Star." Authors Laurence Sterne, Thomas Stearns Eliot; violinist Isaac Stern.
Stearn, Stearne, Stearns, Stern

Stetson Probably Old English surname meaning "Stephen's son." It has a certain rakish air, probably conveyed by the associations of the famous Stetson "ten gallon" hat, worn by cowboys in the late 19th century.
Stetcyn, Stettson

Stewart OE. Occupational name: "Steward." An early variant of **Stuart**, which finally became the more popular form of the name. It is more common as a first name than many occupational names (**Baker, Shepherd, Carpenter**), but has never really become a standard first name either. Actors Jimmy Stewart, Patrick Stewart, Steward Townsend.
Steward, Stuart

Stian ONorse. "Voyager, pilgrim." Used quite often in Scandinavia. **Stig**, though it sounds quite different, comes from the same source.
Stig, Styg, Stygge

Stiles See **Styles**.

Stillman OE. "Silent man." This name may also have to do with the process of distillation, or brewing liquor from grain, which is performed in a still. Filmmaker Whit Stillman.

Stockard Probably an Old English place name referring to a tree stump (the "stock-" particle). Used as a first name occasionally.
Stocker, Stockerd

Stockley OE. Place name: "Tree-stump field." Like the stones in the "Stan-" names, tree stumps would be a hindrance to efficient farming, and thus worthy of note and commemorated in last names.

Stockton OE. Place name: "Tree-stump settlement."

Stockwell OE. Place name: "Tree-stump well."

Stoddard OE. "Horse guard" or "Horse herder." Occupational name.
Stoddart

Stone Noun as name. It is a fairly common last name, very occasionally transferred to a first name. The connotations are a little harsh for a child, and might well invite teasing.
Stoner, Stones, Stoney

Storey OE. "Level of a house or building." Transferred last name. Sculptor William Wetmore Story.
Story

Storm OE. "Tempest; storm." The almost too appropriate name of meteorologist Storm Field.

Strahan Ir. Gael. "Minstrel, sage." Football player Michael Strahan.
Strachan

Stratford OE. Place name: "Street river-crossing."
Strafford

Straus Ger. "Ostrich" or "Bouquet" or "Fight." Strange though it may seem, "ostrich" may be the most usual meaning for this common last name, because long-ago inns or taverns might have been named after an ostrich. Composers Johann and Richard Strauss; retailer Isidor Straus.
Strauss

Strickland OE. Place name: "Flax field."

Strom Ger. Place name: "Stream, brook." Politician Strom Thurmond.

Strong OE. "Powerful." Originally a name that would characterize its bearer. In the last name, the meaning is lost.

Struthers Ir. Gael. Place name: "Near the brook."
Struther

Stuart OE. Occupational name: "Steward." The steward would administer a large feudal household. This was the name of kings of Scotland and England, often considered the most romantic ruling family. (Long curls, a taste for luxury, a reputation for womanizing, and a couple of beheadings all added to the romance.) Most popular in the middle of the 20th century. Though not often used, this form is more popular than **Stewart**. Portrait painter Gilbert Stuart.
Steward, Stewart

Styles OE. Place name: "Stile." A stile is a set of stairs placed over a wall so it can be crossed easily on foot—an important feature in a rural landscape.
Stiles

Sudbury ME. Place name: "Southern settlement." In this case, unlike Suffield, the French form of "Sud-" has survived.
Sudbery, Sudberry, Sudborough

Suffield OE. Place name: "Southern field."

Suffolk OE. "People from the south." As opposed to Norfolk, people from the north. The name of a region (formerly a county) in England, south of London.

Sujay Hindi. "Good victory."
Sujit

Sulaiman Arab. "Peaceable." The Arabic version of **Solomon**. The Turkish sultan Suleiman the Magnificent brought civilization in his country to new heights, but contemporaneous Western rulers would never have characterized him as living up to his name.
Suleiman, Suleyman

Sullivan Ir. Gael. "Black-eyed." Composer Arthur Sullivan; TV host Ed Sullivan; architect Louis Sullivan.
Sullavan, Sullevan, Sully

Sully OE. Place name: "South meadow." Painter Thomas Sully.
Sulleigh, Sulley

Suman Hindi. "Clever, wise."

Sumner OE. Occupational name: "One who serves a summons." A medieval legal official. In Geoffrey Chaucer's famous *Canterbury Tales,* a summoner is one of the pilgrims headed to Canterbury. Entrepreneur Sumner Redstone.

Sunil Hindi. "Navy blue."

Sunny Word as name: most likely to be a nickname characterizing a child's temperament, or a respelling of Sonny.
Sunney, Sunnie

Sutcliff OE. Place name: "Southern cliff."
Sutcliffe

Sutherland "Southern land." Sutherland is the name of a county in northern Scotland, which was nevertheless to the south of the Nordic people who called it that.
Southerland

Sutton OE. Place name: "Southern settlement."

Svatomir Czech. "Renowned and holy."

Svatoslav Czech. "Holy glory." Sometimes these names reveal a great deal about the countries they come from: in the Slavic languages, the word particle "Slav-" means "glory."

Sven "Youth." Currently popular in Sweden, but not much used in English-speaking countries.
Svein, Sveinn, Svend, Swain, Swen, Swensen, Swenson

Swahili Arab. "Coast people." Language spoken in much of east Africa.

Swaine OE. Occupational name: "Swineherd." Swine is an old term for pigs. **Swain** may also be related to **Sven**, though: the first Danish king of England (1013 A.D.) was named Swain.
Swain, Swayn, Swayne

Swanton OE. Place name: "Swan settlement." Swans were considered a great delicacy in the Middle Ages.

Sweeney Ir. Gael. "Small hero."
Sweeny

Swinburne OE. Place name: "Swine stream." Swine, or pigs, were also an important feature of life in the days when last names were being formed. Poet Algernon Swinburne.

Swinborn, Swinbourne, Swinburn, Swinbyrn, Swynborne

Swinford OE. Place name: "Swine ford."

Swynford

Swinton OE. Place name: "Swine settlement."

Swithin OE. "Quick, strong." Saint's name: St. Swithin was a 9th-century bishop of Winchester in England, whose feast day, July 15, was a notable fixture on the calendar. It was said that whatever the weather was like on St. Swithin's day, it would remain the same for the next forty days. Given England's changeable climate, this is hard to believe.

Swithinn, Swithun

Sylvester Lat. "Wooded." In spite of a distinguished past, the name is now associated with a cartoon cat and an extremely muscular actor, Sylvester Stallone.

Silvester, Sly

Syon Sanskrit. "Happy, fortunate."

 Tab Several origins are proposed, including OG. "Shining, brilliant" and ME. "Drummer." But the name would be merely a curiosity without the career of fifties teen idol Tab Hunter, whose given name was Arthur.

Tabb, Taber, Tabor

Tabasco Place name: a state in southeastern Mexico. Also the name of a fiery pepper condiment. A jaunty choice.

Tabor Hung. "Encampment" or Heb. "Misfortune, bad luck." The name of a mountain in Israel.

Taber, Taibor, Tavor, Taybor, Tayber

Tabib Turkish. "Doctor."

Tabeeb

Tacitus Meaning unclear. The name of a celebrated Roman historian of about 100 A.D.

Tad Dim. **Thaddeus** (meaning unknown). Also OWelsh. "Father." Also used as a nickname in the U.S., where "tad" is slang for "small," probably from "tadpole."
Tadd, Thad

Tadeo Sp. Var. **Thaddeus** (meaning unknown).
Taddeo, Tadzio

Tadi Native American: Omaha. "Breeze, wind."

Taft Meaning unknown, though some sources offer OE. "Marsh" or "River." William Howard Taft was 26th President of the United States and was also appointed Chief Justice of the Supreme Court after he had retired from politics.

Taggart Ir. Gael. "Son of the priest."
Taggert

Tahir Arab. "Pure, unsullied."
Taheer

Tahoe Native American. "Big water." A remarkably beautiful lake in Nevada and northern California, at some 6,000 feet above sea level. Good choice for the outdoorsy.

Tahoma Navajo. "Coast, edge of the water" or Pacific Northwest Indian. "Snowy mountain peak." The name is familiar in the latter form as the Native American name of the peak later renamed Mt. Rainier, and also as the name of a city in Washington state.
Tacoma, Tekoma, Tocoma

Tait ONorse. "Cheerful, gay."
Tate, Tayte

Taj Sanskrit. "Crown." As in the Taj Mahal, the famous pleasure palace/mausoleum built in 17th-century India by Shah Jehan for his favorite wife, Mumtaz Mahal.

Takoda Sioux. "Considered friends." The basis for **Dakota**.

Tal Heb. "Rain, dew."
Tahl, Talor

Talbot Meaning unknown. An aristocratic last name in England, used as a first name since the 19th century. Tennis star Billy Talbert.
Talbert, Talbott, Tallbot, Tallbott

Talfryn Welsh. "High hill."
Talfrin, Talfrynn, Tallfryn

Talib Arab. "One who seeks wisdom."
    Taleeb

Taliesin Welsh. Meaning unknown, but this was the name of a Welsh poet of around 550 A.D. The name has persisted into the 20th century because architect Frank Lloyd Wright named his two residences Taliesin (in Wisconsin) and Taliesin West (in Arizona).

Tallis OE. Meaning unknown. This was the name of a great 16th-century English composer of church music, Thomas Tallis, some of whose tunes (notably "Tallis's Canon") are still familiar.
    Tallys, Talys

Talmai Aramaic. "Hillock, mound."

Talmon Heb. "Oppressed, downtrodden." An Old Testament name.

Talon Noun as a name: the large claw of a bird of prey such as a hawk or an eagle. This name's meaning is probably less important than its sound, though, in recommending it to parents.
    Talen, Talin, Tallan, Tallen, Tallin, Tallon

Tamarack Nature name: a common name for a tree also known as a larch.

Tamarisk Nature name: small shrubby tree with blossoms that flourishes in a great range of climates.

Tamerlane Possibly "Timur the Lame." This was the name of a Mongol warrior descended from Genghis Khan, who conquered huge tracts of Asia, from Russia to India. His tale was retold by 16th-century English poet Christopher Marlowe as a romantic tragedy. Edgar Allan Poe also wrote about Tamerlane in an early poem.
    Tamarlain, Tamarlayn, Tamberlain, Tamberlaine, Tamberlane, Tamburlaine, Tamburlane, Tamurlaine, Tamurlayn

Tamir Heb. "Erect, tall," or Arab. "One who owns many palm trees." Related to the girl's name **Tamar**, which means "Date palm."

Tammany Native American: Delaware. "Friendly, cheerful." The name of a Native American chief who was friendly to William Penn. After the American Revolution

"Tammany Societies" sprang up. They were patriotic and social in nature at first, but by 1850 the members of New York's Tammany Society controlled New York politics.

Tamson OE. "Son of Thomas." The girl's form, **Tamsin** and **Thomasina**, are more common, but still scarce.
Tamsen

Tancred OG. "Well-considered counsel or advice." Tancred was a Norman knight who played a prominent part in the First Crusade, at the end of the 11th century. An epic poem by Tasso (*Gerusalemme Liberato*) and operas by Rossini and Monteverdi were based on his story and keep the name alive today, especially in Italy.
Tancredi, Tancredo

Tandie Modern name, possibly derived from a Scottish nickname for **Andrew** or from the Zulu name **Thandiwe**. It may also be adapted from the name of an Irish patriot, James Napper Tandy, whose exploits are immortalized in the ballad, "The Wearing of the Green."
Tandey, Tandy

Tanner OE. Occupational name: "Leather tanner." Hides need to be tanned, or treated with a substance containing tannin, before they become leather. Fairly well used, though its popularity has been waning since the late 1990s. Artist Henry Ossawa Tanner.
Tan, Tanier, Tannen, Tanney, Tannie, Tannis, Tannon

Tannon Invented name, possibly based on **Tanner** or on **Shannon**, or on the German word for "fir tree," *tanne* (as in the famous Christmas carol, "O Tannenbaum.")
Tannan, Tannen, Tannin, Tansen, Tanson

Tanton OE. Place name: "Still river settlement."

Taos Place name: city and county in New Mexico. Located at 7,000 feet above sea level, it has long attracted artists for the quality of the light. There are also a famous Indian pueblo and a ski resort in Taos. Very hip.

Tarik Arab. "The one who knocks to enter."
Tareek, Tariq

Tarleton OE. "Thor's settlement." Margaret Mitchell fans will remember the Tarleton twins, admirers of Scarlett O'Hara, in the early pages of *Gone With the Wind*.

Tarquin Roman clan name of uncertain meaning. The Tarquins were early Etruscan kings of Rome, dating from around the 5th century B.C. The son of the last king was the perpetrator of the famous Rape of Lucretia, the Roman matron who killed herself rather than live with her shame. This unlovely episode led to the dethronement of the Tarquins and the installation of elected consuls to rule Rome instead. It has also been turned into poetry and drama in many languages.

Tarquinius, Tarquino

Tarrant OWelsh. "Thunder."

Tarrent

Tarun Sanskrit. "Youthful."

Taroon, Taroun

Tasso It. "Cup." The name of a great Italian epic poet of the 16th century, Torquato Tasso.

Tate ME. "Happy, cheerful." Related to Norwegian **Tait**.

Tait, Taitt, Tayte

Tau Tswana (from Botswana). "Lion."

Taurus Lat. "Bull." Sign of the zodiac; the sun enters Taurus on April 20. Taurus is also the name of a constellation.

Tavaris Modern name, meaning and derivation unclear. The use of the name may be inspired by a 1970s band called Tavares. The band may have taken its name in turn from a town in Central Florida. Another possible source is a Spanish last name that may mean "Hermit's place."

Tavaress, Tavarious, Tavariss, Tavarous, Tevarus

Taverner OE. Occupational name: "Tavern-keeper."

Tavener, Tavenner, Tavernier

Tavi Aramaic. "Good."

Tavee

Tavish Ir. Gael. "Twin."

Tavis, Tevis

Tay Scottish place name: the largest river in Scotland, renowned for salmon fishing.

Taylor ME. Occupational name: "Tailor." Twelfth U.S. President Zachary Taylor served only one year of his term and died of typhus in 1850. Like many occupational names, this was first used as a given name in the 19th century. It has recently become much more popular. In the mid-1990s it was a top-ten girls' name, which may have disqualified it as a choice for boys. Film director Taylor Hackford; football player Lawrence Taylor; singers James and Livingston Taylor.

Tailer, Tailor, Tayler

Tayton Modern name, possibly a variant on **Taylor** or **Peyton**.

Tayten, Taytin, Teytan, Teyten, Teytin, Teyton

Taz Modern name. Probably promoted by the use of **Chaz**, and possibly also by a cartoon character, the Tasmanian Devil, known as Taz. The Australian state of Tasmania was named for 17th-century Dutch explorer Abel Tasman, who discovered it.

Tasman, Tazman, Tazz

Teague Ir. Gael. "Bard, poet." This name and its variants are experiencing a little flicker of popularity among parents who want to be adventurous in their choice of names.

Teagan, Tegan, Teger, Teigan, Teige, Teigen, Teigue

Tecumseh Shawnee. "Traveling, moving." Tecumseh was a prominent Shawnee chief of the 18th-19th centuries who tried to unite various tribes to negotiate with the U.S. government. His name appeared again as the middle name of Union Army General William Tecumseh Sherman.

Ted Dim. **Theodore** (Gk. "Gift of God") or **Edward** (OE. "Wealthy defender"). Rarely used as an independent name. Parents tend to give the longer rather than the shorter version of a name, even if they have decided ahead of time to use the diminutive form. Newscaster Ted Koppel; actor Ted Danson.

Tedd, Teddey, Teddie, Teddy

Tedmund OE. "Protector of the land."

Tedmond

Teilo Welsh. Meaning unknown. The name of a prominent Welsh saint of the 6th century. There is a cathedral named after him (and three other saints) in the Welsh town of Llandaff.

Telford OF. "Iron-piercer."
Telfer, Telfor, Telfour, Tellfer, Tellfour

Temani Heb. "From the south." This is the Hebrew term for someone from Yemen, which is south of Israel. The word literally means "on the right side," which is, of course, to the south when you are facing east. Old Testament name.
Teman, Temeni

Tempest Fr. "Storm." Occurs as an aristocratic English last name, and occasionally as a first name, though few parents could wish for a baby's personality to fit the name.
Tempestt

Temple Lat. "Sacred place." Probably a place name transferred to first name.
Templar, Templer

Templeton OE. Place name: "Temple settlement." Also the name of the rat in *Charlotte's Web*, a point that the young are sure to seize on.
Temp, Temple, Templeten

Tempo It. "Time." In musical terms, how fast a piece of music is supposed to be performed.

Tennant OE. "Tenant, renter." Last name used as first name.
Tenant, Tennent

Tennessee Cherokee place name, used for the state. Made famous by playwright Tennessee Williams (whose given name was Thomas) and likely to be used by parents in homage, or perhaps in nostalgia for a childhood home.

Tennyson ME. "Son of Dennis." Used by 19th-century parents in homage to British Poet Laureate Alfred, Lord Tennyson.
Tenny

Teom Heb. "Twin." The basis of the name **Thomas**.

Terach Heb. "Old fool" or "Wild goat." A Biblical name: the father of Abraham.
Terah

Terence Lat. Clan name of unknown meaning, though some sources propose "Smooth" or "Polished." Early Christian name that was never widely adopted until the late 19th century, and even then did not become a standard choice. The most common spelling today is **Terrance**. Actor Terence Stamp; playwright Terence McNally; priest Terence Cardinal Cooke.

Tarrants, Tarrance, Tarrenz, Terencio, Terrance, Terrence, Terrey, Terri, Terris, Terrious, Terrius, Terron, Terronce, Terry

Tern Nature name: a marine bird smaller than a seagull. The Arctic tern migrates 11,000 miles twice yearly, from Arctic to Antarctic and back. Clearly a creature with tremendous stamina.

Terrell OG. "Following Thor." Thor, the god of thunder, was a crucial figure in Norse mythology. The son of Odin, the chief god, Thor was the benevolent intercessor for mankind. His name is an element in many names that have come down to us, the most notable being "Thursday." Parents may think of this name as a variant of **Terence**, though it hardly matters. Football players Terrell Davis, Terrell Owens.

Tarrall, Terrall, Terrel, Terrill, Terryal, Terryl, Terryll, Tirrell, Tyrrell

Terron Modern name. Possibly a respelling of **Darren**, or a variation of **Terence**. Spellings are almost infinite in number.

Taran, Tarin, Taron, Tarran, Tarren, Tarrin, Tarron, Tarryn, Teran, Teron, Terrin, Terryn, Teryn

Terry Dim. **Terence**. Lat. Clan name. Used for both boys and girls, almost as frequently as Terence itself. Football player Terry Bradshaw; filmmaker Terry Gilliam.

Terrey, Terri, Terrie

Teton Western American place name: a river and, more famously, a range of mountains on the border between Idaho and Wyoming. Grand Teton National Park is a favorite destination for hikers and climbers.

Tevon Modern name, **Kevin** or **Devon** with a "T-."

Tevan, Teven, Tevin, Tevinn, Tevonn

Tex Modern name of the Lone Star state, used occasionally as a first name. It has a rakish aura, no doubt from association with cowboys and the Wild West.

Thaddeus Aramaic. Meaning unclear, though "Courageous" and "Praise" have been suggested. He was one of the more obscure of the twelve apostles, but even this distinction has not popularized the name. **Jude** is another form of the name.

Tad, Tadd, Taddeo, Taddeusz, Tadeo, Tadio, Tadzio, Thad, Thaddaios, Thaddaos, Thaddaeus, Thaddaus, Thadeus, Thady

Thandiwe Zulu. "Loved one."

Tandie, Tandy, Thandey, Thandie, Thandy

Thane OE. "Landholder." In Old England a thane fit, socially, between the serfs and the nobility. He held his own land, but owed service to his lord. Rare even as a last name.

Thaine, Thayne

Thatcher OE. Occupational name: "Roof thatcher." Very soon this name will be free of any associations with British Prime Minister, Margaret Thatcher. It will be interesting to see if it is taken up by parents as other occupational names (**Hunter, Taylor, Tanner**) have been.

Thacher, Thatch, Thaxter

Thaw OE. "Melt." Found more often as a last name.

Thayer Old English name of uncertain meaning: may be related to **Thatcher**.

Theobald OG. "Courageous people." Unusual, though some of its foreign variants like **Thibault** are more common in their countries of origin. **Tybalt**, another version of the name, is an important character in Shakespeare's *Romeo and Juliet*.

Dietbald, Dietbold, Ted, Teddy, Teobaldo, Thebault, Theo, Thibaud, Thibault, Thibaut, Tibold, Tiebold, Tiebout, Tybald, Tybalt, Tybault

Theodore Gk. "Gift of God." Early Christian name and saint's name, but only mildly popular until President Theodore Roosevelt brought it to prominence. (The teddy bear, of course, is named for him.) The name is now neither popular nor unpopular; a good choice for parents who want an unusual but not fashionable name. Authors Theodore Dreiser, Theodore Sturgeon; painter Théodore Rousseau.

Fedor, Feodor, Fyodor, Teador, Ted, Teddie, Teddy, Tedor, Teodoor, Teodor, Teodoro, Theo, Theodor, Theodorus, Theodosios, Theodosius, Todor, Tudor

Theodoric OG. "People's ruler." This is the original form of **Dietrich** and the more common **Derek** or **Dirk**. In this version it is extremely rare.

Derek, Derrick, Dieter, Dietrich, Dirck, Dirk, Rick, Ted, Teodorico, Thedric, Thedrick

Theophilus Gk. "Loved by God." A New Testament name that is very rare, though Thornton Wilder entitled one of his most popular novels *Theophilus North*. French author Théophile Gautier.

Teofil, Teofilo, Théophile

Theron Possibly derived from a Greek word meaning "hunter," but just as likely this is a modern name combining the popular "-on" ending with unusual "Ther-."

Tharon

Theseus In Greek mythology, the young hero who slew the Cretan Minotaur, among many other exploits. He was the son of King Aegeus, for whom the Aegean Sea around Greece is named. He figures in several of the classic Greek tragedies as well as in Chaucer's *Canterbury Tales* and Shakespeare's *Midsummer Night's Dream*.

Thierry Fr. Var. **Theodoric**. Not, as one might suppose, the French version of **Terry**. Fashion designer Thierry Mugler.

Thomas Aramaic. "Twin." One of the apostles was known as Doubting Thomas because he refused to recognize the risen Christ unless he could see and feel the marks of the crucifixion. In spite of this skeptical example, the name has been hugely popular since the 12th-century martyrdom of Thomas à Becket. Other Saints Thomas include Thomas Aquinas and Thomas More, but the name has been so widely used that it has no religious aura to it. The recent vogue for unusual names has somewhat eclipsed this old standard but it is still one of the basic names for boys born in America, and a top-ten name in England. President Thomas Jefferson; inventor Thomas Edison; actors Tom Cruise, Tom Hanks; dancer Tommy Tune; fashion designer Tom Ford

Tam, Tamas, Tamhas, Thom, Thoma, Thomason, Thomson, Thompson, Tom, Tomas, Tomaso, Tomasso, Tomasz, Tome, Tomek, Tomey, Tomie, Tomislaw, Tomkin, Tomlin, Tommaso, Tommey, Tommie, Tommy

Thor ONorse. "Thunder." The Norse god of thunder, Thor, holds an important place in the Norse pantheon, but in the Anglo-Saxon world the name appears more often in derivative forms, as in **Terrell**. Explorer Thor Heyerdahl.

Thorin, Thorvald, Tor, Tore, Torre, Tyrus

Thorald ONorse. "Follower of Thor."

Terrell, Terrill, Thorold, Torald, Tyrell

Thorbert ONorse. "Thor's brightness."

Torbert

Thorburn ONorse. "Thor's bear."

Thorbern, Thorbjorn

Thoreau Possibly a Frenchified version of **Thorald**, but parents using this name would be invoking the 19th-century naturalist and author of *Walden* Henry David Thoreau.

Thorley OE. Place name: "Thor's meadow" or "Thorn meadow."

Thorlea, Thorlee, Thorleigh, Thorly, Torley

Thormond OE. "Defended by Thor." Senator Strom Thurmond.

Thurman, Thurmond, Thurmund

Thorndike OE. Place name: "Thorny bank."

Thorndyck, Thorndyke

Thorne OE. Place name: "Thorn thicket."

Thorn

Thornley OE. Place name: "Thorny meadow."

Thornlea, Thornleigh, Thornly

Thornton OE. Place name: "Thorny village or town." Used as a first name since the 19th century. Writer Thornton Wilder.

Thornycroft OE. Place name: "Thorny field." "Croft" is an old British term for a small farm of five to ten acres, usually farmed by a tenant farmer.

Thorneycroft

Thorpe OE. Place name: "Hamlet, village." Athlete Jim Thorpe.
Thorp

Thurgood Puritan virtue name. Supreme Court Justice Thurgood Marshall's name was probably originally "Thoroughgood," quite a mouthful and a lot to live up to.

Thurlow OE. Place name: "Thor's hill."
Thurloe

Thurman ONorse. "Defended by Thor." Probably the most common variant of **Thormond**. Baseball player Thurman Munson.
Thurmon

Thurston Scand. "Thor's stone." Parents who have watched a lot of old sitcoms might shy away from a name that recalled Thurston Howell, the effete millionaire castaway on *Gilligan's Island*. Social critic Thorstein Veblen.
Thorstan, Thorstein, Thorsten, Thurstain, Thurstan, Thursten, Torsten, Torston

Tibor Slavic. "Sacred place."

Tiburon Sp. "Shark." California place name: a town on San Francisco Bay where presumably someone once saw a you-know-what in the water.

Tiernan Ir. Gael. "Lord."
Tiarnan, Tiarney, Tierney

Tiger Nature name. Given immense exposure recently by young golf phenomenon Tiger Woods, whose given name is actually Eldrick (see **Eldridge**).
Tige, Tigre, Tigris

Tilden OE. Place name: "Fertile valley." Statesman Samuel Tilden; tennis champion William Tilden.
Tillden, Tildon

Tilford OE. Place name: "Fertile ford."

Till Ger. "People's ruler." Another form of **Theodoric**, vaguely familiar to American ears from the German legends about Till Eulenspiegel, inspiration for a tone poem by Richard Strauss.
Thilo, Tillman, Tilmann

Tillman OE. Occupational name: "One who plows the earth." Tilling the soil meant turning and lightening it before it was planted. An important process in an agricultural economy.
Tilghman, Tilman

Tilton OE. Place name: "Fertile estate." All of these "Til-" names were last names, used occasionally as first names starting in the 19th century.

Timon Greek name of uncertain meaning. Shakespeare wrote a play, *Timon of Athens*, about a misanthropic Greek of the 4th century B.C., but most parents are more likely to be familiar with the meerkat Timon from Disney's movie of *The Lion King*.

Timothy Gk. "Honoring God." New Testament name, correspondent with Saint Paul. Scanty use until the 18th century, then increased gradually to the middle of the 20th. After a baby boom peak, it has faded to steady but unspectacular use. Radical thinker Timothy Leary; actors Timothy Hutton, Tim Allen, Tim Roth; hockey player Teemu Selanne; basketball player Tim Duncan.
Tim, Timmo, Timmy, Timmothy, Timo, Timofei, Timofeo, Timofey, Timon, Timoteo, Timothé, Timotheo, Timothey, Timotheus, Tymmothy, Tymon, Tymoteusz, Tymothy

Tino Sp. Dim. **Agostino** and other "-tin" names. Baseball player Tino Martinez.
Teeno, Teino, Tyno

Tipu Hindi. "Tiger."
Tippoo

Titus Lat. Unknown meaning. New Testament character. Use is mostly 18th and 19th centuries. Has nothing to do, in spite of its sound, with titans or giants.
Tito, Titos

Tobias Heb. "The Lord is good." Old Testament name that faded after the Puritans used it, and was revived in the 19th century. The diminutive, **Toby**, is slightly more common now, though still very unusual. Author Tobias Wolff.

Thobey, Thobie, Thoby, Tobe, Tobee, Tobey, Tobi, Tobia, Tobiah, Tobie, Tobin, Tobit, Toby, Tobyn

Toby Dim. **Tobias**. Actor Tobey Maguire.

Thobey, Thobie, Thoby, Tobe, Tobee, Tobey, Tobi, Tobie

Todd ME. "Fox." Used mostly in this century, and fashionable for a spell in the 1970s. Still quite steadily used; much more popular that **Tobias**, for instance. Hockey player Todd Bertuzzi.

Tod

Todhunter OE. Occupational name: "Foxhunter." Ralph Lauren should know about this name!

Togo Place name: a country on the Gulf of Guinea in western Africa, between Benin and Ghana.

Tom Dim. **Thomas** (Aramaic. "Twin"). Most common in the 19th century as an independent name. Actors Tom Cruise, Tom Hanks.

Thom, Tomm, Tommy

Tomlin OE. "Little Tom."

Tomalin, Tomlinson

Tommy Dim. **Thomas**. Given with some regularity as a first name. Baseball player Tommy John; actor Tommy Lee Jones; fashion designer Tommy Hilfiger; musician Tommy Lee.

Tompkins OE. "Little Thomas."

Tompkinson

Tony Dim. **Anthony** (Lat. "Beyond price"). Used independently only since the middle of the 20th century. Actors Tony Curtis, Tony Danza; singer Tony Bennett.

Toney, Tonie

Tor Nor. "Thunder." Var. **Thor**. Also, Hebrew for "Turtledove."

Thor

Torger ONorse. "Thor's spear."

Toril Hindi. "Character, temperament."

Torquil ONorse. "Thor's kettle." Refers to a cauldron used in sacrifice. Used in Scandinavian countries and a tiny bit in Britain.

Thirkell, Thorkel, Torkel, Torkill

Torr OE. Place name: "Tower."
Tor

Torrance Ir. Gael. Place name: "Little hills."
Tore, Torin, Torr, Torrence, Torrens, Torrey, Torrin, Torry

Torry ONorse "Thor." With this spelling, a boy's name, though the same name spelled **Tori** is a girl's name derived from Victoria. Football player Torry Holt.
Torrey

Toussaint Fr. "All saints." Used with some frequency in Haiti, in honor of Haitian leader Toussaint L'Ouverture, a former slave who helped Haiti gain independence from France in the early 19th century. Also appropriate for babies born on November 1, All Saints' Day.

Tower OE. Place name. While nature names, even those of fierce animals or mountain peaks, are used as children's names, architectural features somehow seem a little too inanimate to be appropriate. Yet as a transferred last name, Tower may make sense.
Towers

Townley OE. Place name: "Town meadow."
Townlea, Townlee, Townleigh, Townlie, Townly

Townsend OE. Place name: "End of town."
Townshend

Trace Possibly the noun as name, equally possibly a variation of **Tracy.**

Tracy OF. Place name. Almost always a girl's name now. Author Tracy Kidder; basketball player Tracy McGrady.
Trace, Tracey, Treacy

Trahern Welsh. "Strength of iron." Poet Thomas Traherne.
Trahearn, Trahearne, Traherne

Trail Noun as name. Connotations of the outdoors, nature, mountains, and general ruggedness.
Traill

Traugott Ger. "Faith in God."

Travis OF. Occupational name: "Toll taker." Most common in the U.S., and quite steadily used without being trendy. Fictional detective Travis Magee.
Traver, Travers, Traviss, Travys

Tremain Celt. Place name: "Stone house." Popular among African-American families.
Tramain, Tramaine, Tramayne, Tremaine, Tremayne

Tremont Fr. Place name: "Three mountains."

Trent Lat. "Gushing waters." Name of an important river in England, thus a place name. U.S. Senator Trent Lott; football player Trent Dilfer.
Trenten, Trentin, Trenton

Trenton OE. Place name. "Trent's town." Or an elaboration of **Trent**, with the fashionable "-on" ending. Probably not used much around Trenton, New Jersey.
Trenten, Trentin

Trevor Welsh. "Large homestead." Use expanded outside of Wales in the mid-Victorian era, but the name was most popular in the middle of the 20th century. Actor Trevor Howard.
Trefor, Trevar, Trever

Trey ME. "Three." Related to the French *trois* for "three." Unusual, but more often found that old standards like **Arthur** or **Gerald**. Actor Trey Hunt.
Trai, Traye, Tre

Tristan Welsh. The name's Welsh meaning is unclear, but since *triste* is French for "sad," that explanation is often given. Tristan, in the medieval legends, is the knight who is in love with Isolde, wife of his uncle. The tale has been told in many forms, including an epic poem by Tennyson and an opera by Wagner. Currently very popular in Spain.
Tris, Tristam, Tristram

Trowbridge OE. Place name: "Bridge by the tree."

Troy Ir. Gael. "Foot-soldier." The name of the famous Greek city where the Trojan wars were fought, and a fairly common place name in America (as in Troy, NY). Actor Troy Donahue may have been behind the name's surge of popularity in the 1960s and 1970s. Jane Fonda named one of her children Troy. Football player Troy Aikman.
Troi, Troye

True OE. "True." May be used for its emotional qualities.

Truesdale OE. Place name: "Honest man's valley."

Truman OE. "Loyal one." Unusual as a last name or a first name, in spite of the greatly admired author Truman Capote or U.S. President Harry S. Truman.
Trueman, Trumaine, Trumann

Trumble OE. "Powerful."
Trumball, Trumbell, Trumbo, Trumbull

Tucker OE. Occupational name: "Fabric pleater." Another occupational name relating to one of medieval Britain's principal industries, the woolen trade.
Tuck, Tuckerman

Tudor Welsh. Var. **Theodore** (Gk. "Gift of God"). Famous as the name of the English dynasty of kings.

Tully Ir. Gael. "Mighty people."
Tulley, Tullie, Tullis

Tune Eng. "A melody." Dancer Tommy Tune.

Tupper OE. "Ram, male sheep." Tupper Lake is a resort in the Adirondack Mountains.

Turbo Lat. "Spinning object." Usually used to indicate the presence of a turbine engine in combination with something else, as in a turbopropellor. Connotations are of speed and great energy, making this a likely nickname for an extremely energetic child.

Turk Eng. "From Turkey."
Turck

Turner ME. Occupational name: "Wood-worker." "Turning" referred to use of a lathe, which provided the decorative elements on much furniture in the 16th and 17th centuries. Painter J.M.W. Turner.

Tuvyah Heb. "Goodness of the Lord." Related to **Tobias, Toby,** etc.
Tov, Toviach, Tovyah, Toviah, Tuviyahu

Twain ME. "Divided in two." The most famous bearer of this name, the American writer Mark Twain, took it from the calls of riverboatmen. His original name was Samuel Clemens.
Twaine, Twayn

Twyford OE. Place name: "Double river crossing."

Ty Diminutive or variant of the "Ty-" names that follow, but used much more frequently than **Tyrone**. Baseball player Ty Cobb; football player Ty Law.

Tychon Gk. "Accurate."

Tyler OE. Occupational name: "Maker of tiles." The name of one of the country's less memorable presidents (John Tyler, 1841-1845). Still, the name rocketed up popularity charts in the 1990s, with no clear prompting from popular culture. It seems likely that thousands and thousands of parents just liked the way it sounds. After a spell in the top ten it is beginning to drift out of fashion.

Tilar, Ty, Tylar, Tylor

Tynan Ir. Gael. "Dark, dusky."

Tienan, Tynell, Tynen, Tynin, Tynnen, Tynnin, Tynon

Typhoon Chinese. "Great wind." The name of the tropical storms of the Asian coasts. Not predictive of a toddler's behavior, with any luck.

Tyquan Modern name composed of two fashionable elements.

Tyquahn, Tyquann, Tyquohn, Tyquonne

Tyr Ancient Norse god, the bravest and boldest of a warlike bunch.

Tyree Modern name. Possibly an elaboration of the fashionable "Ty-" sounds.

Tyrell Modern name. Could be related to **Terrell**, or may be another elaboration of "Ty-." The "-el" ending is fashionable with African-American families.

Tirell, Tyrel, Tyrrel, Tyrrell

Tyrone Ir. Gael. "Land of Owen." Given prominence almost entirely by the actors Tyrone Power, Sr., and Jr., around the middle of the 20th century. Football player Tyrone Wheatley.

Tirone, Tirohn, Tirown, Tyron

Tyson OF. Meaning unclear, though "spark, firebrand" has been suggested. Parents may use it in admiration of the boxing star (and firebrand) Mike Tyson.

Thyssen, Tiesen, Tycen, Tyssen

Ubadah Arab. "Serves God."

Uberto It. Var. **Hubert** (OG. "Bright or shining intellect").

Udayan Hindi. "Rising, showing up."

Udi Heb. "My torch, burning stick."

Udell OE. Place name: "Valley of yew trees." Politician Morris Udall.

Dell, Eudel, Udel, Udall, Yudale, Yudell

Udo Dim. Ulric.

Udolf OE. "Wolf-wealth."

Udolfo, Udolph

Ugo It. Var. **Hugh** (OG. "Mind, intellect").

Ukiah North American Indian. "Deep valley." Place name: a town in Mendocino County in Northern California.

Ulf OG. "Wolf." More common in the Scandinavian countries.

Ulick Ir. Gael. "Little Willliam." This is the anglicized version: the Gaelic, very hard for English-speakers to pronounce or spell, is Uilleog.

Ull Norse. "Glory." One of the gods in the ancient Norse pantheon, whose special responsibility was winter. He was thought to have created the aurora borealis, the northern lights.

Ulmer OE. "Fame of the wolf."

Ullmar, Ulmar

Ulric OG. "Power of the wolf" or "Power of the home." Used in Britain before the Norman invasion, but barely known in the last 900-odd years. Actor Skeet Ulrich.

Rick, Udo, Ullric, Ulrich, Ulrick, Ulrik

Ulysses Lat. Var. **Odysseus**, which may mean "wrathful." American use was spurred by the presidency of Civil War hero Ulysses S. Grant. Now rare.

Ulises, Ulisse

Umar Arab. "Prospering, thriving." A popular name in the

Arab world. In the U.S., as **Omar**, it is quite steadily used.
Omar, Omer, Umer

Umber Fr. "Shade." A brown color derived from minerals that is a staple of the artist's palette. The word "umbrella" comes from the same source.
Umbro

Umberto It. Var. **Humbert** (OG. "Renowned Hun"). A royal name in Italy, though very scarce in English-speaking countries. Author Umberto Eco.

Umed Hindi. "Desire, goal."

Umi African: (Yao.) "Life."
Umee

Uncas Native American: Mohegan. "The fox." In James Fenimore Cooper's novel *The Last of the Mohicans*, Uncas is the noble Mohican who rescues and falls in love with English Cora Munro. In the filmed version it is Hawkeye, the Englishman raised by the Indians (and played by heart-throb Daniel Day-Lewis) who gets the girl and Uncas is demoted to sidekick.

Unwin OE. "Nonfriend."
Unwinn, Unwyn

Updike OE. Place name: "Upper bank." Author John Updike.
Updyke

Upshaw OE. Place name: "Upper thicket."

Upton OE. Place name: "Upper settlement." Mostly last-name use. Author Upton Sinclair.

Upwood OE. Place name: "Upper forest."

Urban Lat. "From the city." We have a modern word, "urbane," from the same root. Apparently in ancient times city-dwellers had better manners than their rural contemporaries. Though the name was used by eight popes, it is scarce today in English-speaking countries.
Urbain, Urbaine, Urbane, Urbano, Urbanus

Uri Heb. "My light, my flame." Related to **Uriah** and **Uriel**.

Uriah Heb. "The Lord is my light." Prominent Old Testament name at its most popular in the 19th century, though literary parents will be reminded of the smarmy, hand-wringing Uriah Heep in Dickens' *David Copperfield*.

Dickens may have killed off the name, in fact; it is very scarce today.

Uri, Uria, Urias, Urija, Urijah, Uriyah, Yuri, Yuria

Uriel Heb. "Flame of God." The Muslim version of the name is Israfil; he is the Muslim angel of music and appears in the Koran along with Gabriel and Michael. In Christian terms he is one of seven named archangels.

Usamah Arab. "Like a lion."

Urso It. "Bear."

Ursel, Ursino, Ursins, Ursinus

Usher Lat. "River mouth." By extension, a doorkeeper. This is also an anglicization of an Irish place name that occurs occasionally as Ussery or Ossory. A famous Edgar Allan Poe tale is entitled *The Fall of the House of Usher*. Musician Usher Raymond.

Ussher

Uther Ancient English name of uncertain meaning. In legend, Uther Pendragon was the father of King Arthur.

Uziah Heb. "The Lord is my strength." Old Testament name; a King of Judah around 700 years before Christ. He was on the throne when Isaiah was prophesying.

Uzziah

Uziel Heb. "Strength, power."

Uzziah, Uzziel

Vachel OF. "Small cow." Something of a curiosity, brought to public notice by the poet Vachel Lindsay.

Vachell

Vail OE. Place name: "Valley." Famous now as a ski resort in Colorado. Generally a transferred last name.

Bail, Bale, Vaile, Vaill, Vale

Val Dim. **Valentine**. Perhaps because **Valerie** was such a popular name a number of years ago, Val still seems more like a girl's name, despite the fame and macho appeal of actor Val Kilmer.

Valdemar OG. "Renowned leader." A royal name in early Denmark.
Waldemar

Valentine Lat. "Strong." This name and **Valerian** come from the same root. Valentine is used for both boys and girls, although the early Christian martyr for whom the holiday is named was male. It seems likely that the hearts-and-flowers observations of this day actually belonged to a pagan feast day celebrating spring and fertility and all that stuff. Canny early churchmen probably combined the two feasts. St. Valentine himself had nothing to do with romantic love.
Val, Valentijn, Valentin, Valentinian, Valentino, Valentinus, Valentyn

Valerian Lat. "Strong, healthy." Far less common than the feminine version, **Valerie**. Designer Valerian Rybar; conductor Valery Gergiev.
Valerien, Valerio, Valerius, Valery, Valeryan

Vali Old Norse mythology name; another warlike son of Odin.

Van Dutch. "Of." A particle of many Dutch names, as in **Vandyke**. Also possibly a nickname for **Evan**. Originally may have been used as a nickname for children with transferred Dutch last names, but it became generally popular in the middle of the 20th century. Neglected now. Pianist Van Cliburn; actor Van Johnson.
Vann, Von, Vonn

Vance OE. Place name: "Marshland." Author Vance Packard; diplomat Cyrus Vance.

Vandan Hindi. "Salvation."

Vander Possibly a particle of a Dutch place name meaning "from the," as in Van der Meer or Van der Velt. Also possibly a shortening of **Evander** (Gk. "Good man"). An unusual name with a certain individualistic air.

Vandyke Dutch. Place name: "Of the dyke." The New York area was originally settled by Dutch colonists, and a few Dutch names survive, though not many are used as first names. A "Vandyke" is also the name of a small beard or goatee, from the beards portrayed in portraits by the 17th-century Flemish painter Anthony Van Dyck. Actor Dick Van Dyke.

Vane OE. "Banner." A device usually attached to a mast or flagpole to indicate the direction of the wind. An aristocratic family name in England.

Vanya Rus. Dim. **John** (Heb. "The Lord is gracious") via **Ivan**. Rare outside of Russia.

Vardon OF. Place name: "Green knoll." The second half of the name comes from the French word that gives us "dune."
Varden, Verdon, Verdun

Varick OG. "Leader who defends."
Varrick, Warick, Warrick

Varun Hindi. "Water god."
Varoun

Vasilis Gk. "Royal, kingly." More familiar in its anglicized form, **Basil**. Painer Wassily Kandinsky.
Vasileios, Vasilij, Vasily, Vaso, Vasos, Vassilij, Vassily, Vasya, Wassily

Vaughn Welsh. "Small." Appeared as a first name at the turn of the 20th century, at its peak popularity in the baby boom era. Never especially common, though. Actors Robert Vaughn, Vince Vaughn; composer Ralph Vaughan Williams.
Vaughan

Veltry Modern name, coined for euphony.

Venezio It. "Venice." The feminine forms like **Venetia** are more common, though still rare.
Venetziano, Veneziano

Venturo Sp. "Good fortune, good luck."
Venturio

Vere Fr. Place name of unknown meaning. It was an upper-class last name in England, and took on near-caricature connotations of nobility, especially after Tennyson published "Lady Clara Vere de Vere," a poem praising the simple values of simple folk. (It contains the famous line "Kind hearts are more than coronets.") Vere has not been used much in the self-consciously democratic U.S.

Verlyn Modern name. Derivation not entirely clear. It may depend on **Vernon**, or else on the syllable "Ver-" which is often taken to mean "green." As with most modern names, the sound seems to be more important to parents than the meaning. Writer Verlyn Klinkenborg.

Verle, Verlin, Verllin, Verlon, Verlyn, Virle, Vyrle

Vermont Fr. "Green mountain." Mountainous New England state, much loved by skiers and hikers for the recreational opportunities it provides. Author Vermont Royster.

Vernon OF. Place name: "Alder grove." A Norman name that took root as an English last name and, by the 19th century, a first name. Statesman Vernon Jordan.

Lavern, Vern, Vernal, Verne, Vernen, Vernin, Verney

Verrier Fr. Occupational name: "Glassblower." Or possibly a variation on **Farrier**, which means "blacksmith."

Verrill OF. "Loyal" or OG. "Masculine."

Verill, Verrall, Verrell, Verroll, Veryl

Vester Dim. **Sylvester** (Lat. "Wooded").

Vesuvio It. Place name: a large, active volcano near Naples.

Victor Lat. "Conqueror." Extremely common in Christian Rome, as was its female form, **Victoria**. Revived during the reign of Queen Victoria, but not very popular (except among her numerous descendants and godchildren). It was used most during the baby boom era, but not very widely. Cinematographer Vittorio Storaro; film director Vittorio de Sica; actor Victor Mature; author Victor Hugo.

Vic, Vick, Victorien, Victorin, Vidor, Viktor, Vitorio, Vittorio, Vittorios

Vidal Sp. from Lat. "Vigorous, lively." Related to **Vito**. Author Gore Vidal; hairdresser Vidal Sassoon.

Bidal, Videl, Videlio

Vidar ONorse. Mythology name: a son of Odin, immensely strong, who did not speak.

Vijay Sanskrit. "Victory."

Bijay, Vijun

Villard Nineteenth-century invented name. Henry Hilgard of Bavaria changed his name to Villard when he came to the U.S. Since he later became a financier and railroad magnate, it has some connotations of wealth and grandeur, especially in New York where he lived. Perhaps he chose this name with those aspirations in mind.

Villiers Fr. "Town-dweller." Aristocratic Franco-English name.

Vilmos Hung. "Determined fighter." Cinematographer Vilmos Szigmond.

Vincent Lat. "Conquering." From the same root as **Victor**, but used much more steadily since early Christian days. It has not suffered neglect, but neither has it ever been truly popular. Saint Vincent de Paul, a 17th-century priest, founded an order of missionary brothers, and the Saint Vincent de Paul Society, an international charitable organization, was founded in his honor in the 19th century. Painter Vincent Van Gogh; film director Vincente Minnelli; actors Vincent Gardenia, Vince Vaughn, Vin Diesel, Vincent D'Onofrio, Vinnie Jones; football coach Vince Lombardi; basketball player Vince Carter.

Vicente, Vicenzio, Vincenzo, Vin, Vince, Vincens, Vincentius, Vincents, Vincenty, Vincenz, Vincenzio, Vincenzo, Vincien, Vinicent, Vinnie, Vinny, Vinzenz, Wincenty

Vine OE. Occupational name: "Vineyard worker."

Vinson OE. "Son of Vincent."

Vinton OE. Place name: "Vine settlement" or "Vincent's settlement."

Vireo Nature name: a small, migratory, insect-eating bird with green plumage and a melodious song.

Virgil Lat. Clan name: possibly meaning "staff bearer." (The staff would have been part of official insignia in ancient Rome.) The name is usually homage to the Roman author of *The Aeneid*. Composer Virgil Thomson.

Verge, Vergil, Vergilio, Virgilio

Virginius Lat. "Chaste." Masculine version of **Virginia**. Much less common, perhaps because chastity has, historically, been less prized for males. It occasionally occurs in old Virginia families, in which case it refers to the state known as the Old Dominion rather than to sexual experience or the lack of it.

Virginio

Vischer Ger. "Fisherman." Probably an occupational name.

Visscher

Vito Lat. "Alive." Generally used by Italian families. St. Vitus was an early martyr whose legend held that he could cure epilepsy and another disorder known as "St. Vitus' dance."

Vital, Vitale, Vitalis, Vitaly, Vitas, Vitus, Witold

Vivek Sanskrit. "Discernment, wisdom."

Vivian Lat. "Full of life." Used occasionally for boys in Britain, but an American infant named Vivian would be assumed to be a girl.

Viviani, Vivien, Vivyan, Vyvian, Vyvyan

Vladimir Slavic. "Renowned prince." Popular in Russia. Pianist Vladimir Horowitz.

Vladamir, Vladimeer, Wladimir, Wladimyr

Vladislav Old Slavic. "Splendid rule."

Volker Ger. "People's defender." From the German word that gives us "folk."

Volney OG. "Spirit of the folk."

Von ONorse. "Hope." Also a respelling of the Dutch-derived **Van**.

Vonn

Wade OE. Place name: "River ford." Transferred last name with a certain popularity in old southern families, after Confederate General Wade Hampton.

Waddell, Wadell, Wayde

Wadham OE. Place name: "Ford village." At a river ford, of course, it was possible to wade across the water, hence all these names.

Wadley OE. Place name: "Ford meadow."
Wadleigh, Wadly

Wadsworth OE. Place name: "Village near the ford." Transferred last name of a family that has long been prominent on the American cultural scene. Poet Henry Wadsworth Longfellow.
Waddsworth

Wagner Ger. Occupational name: "Wagon-builder." New York City Mayor Robert Wagner; composer Richard Wagner.
Waggoner, Wagoner

Wahib Arab. "Giver, donor." One of Allah's ninety-nine attributes.
Waheeb

Wainwright OE. Occupational name: "Wagon-builder." Quite a mouthful as a first name, and most likely to be used when it's a family name, such as a mother's maiden name.
Wainright, Wainewright, Wayneright, Waynewright, Waynright

Waite ME. Occupational name: "Guard, watchman." In other words, one who waited for something to happen. Christmas carolers used to be known as "waits" because the custom of singing carols originated with bands of watchmen who would sing a tune to mark the passing hours of the night. Actor/musician Tom Waits.
Waights, Waits, Wayte

Wakefield OE. Place name: "Damp field."

Wakeley OE. Place name: "Damp meadow."
Wakelea, Wakeleigh, Wakely

Wakeman OE. Occupational name: "Watchman." Or one who was awake when others slept. All too appropriate for most babies.
Wake

Walcott OE. Place name: "Cottage by the wall." Could originally have referred to the great Roman wall that still stands in the north of England.
Wallcot, Wallcott, Wolcott

Wald Ger. Place name: "Woods, forest." Vast tracts of Europe were originally covered with dense, impenetrable forest.

Waldemar OG. "Renowned ruler." Many of these Old German names (**William** is another) are actually made up of two particles that are both nouns: in this case they are "fame" and "power." In German, two nouns are often joined to make a new word, but translations of some of these names into English are awkward and approximate.
Valdemar

Walden OE. Place name: "Wooded valley." Could also be another variant of one of the Old German names that include the "Wald-" ("power") element, like **Walter**. Many literature-loving parents may think of Thoreau's book and the pond *Walden*.
Waldenn, Waldi, Waldon

Waldo Dim. **Waldemar**, etc. The "-o" ending is a particularly Germanic diminutive. Possibly also a German place name: "Forest meadow." Though more common than some of the longer forms like Waldemar, it's still unusual and may retain a slightly comical aura from the "Where's Waldo" books that were popular among children in the 1990s. Poet Ralph Waldo Emerson.

Waldorf Ger. Place name: "Village in the woods."
Waldorp

Waldron OG. "Powerful raven."

Waldwick Ger/OE. Place name: "Village in the forest."
Waldwyck

Walford OE. Place name: "Brook ford." Composer Walford Davies.

Walfred OG. "Ruler of peace."
Walfried

Walid Arab. "Just born."
Waleed

Walker OE. Occupational name: "Cloth-walker." The era that saw the rise of last names was also the great English era of the wool trade, giving us such cloth-manufacturing names as **Fuller, Dyer,** and **Weaver**. In that medieval era, workers trod on the wool to cleanse it of impurities. Author Walker Percy; photographer Walker Evans.

Wallace OE. "Welshman." Originally a Scottish name, used to identify foreigners from the south. Like many last names, it was most popular as a first name in the 19th century. In this case the popularity could have been sparked by the Victorian passion for the past; Sir William Wallace was a Scottish patriot of the 13th century who struggled (in vain) against the English King Edward I. Poet Wallace Stevens; actor Wallace Beery.

Wallach, Wallas, Wallie, Wallis, Wally, Walsh, Welch, Welsh

Waller OE. Occupational name: "Wall maker" or OG. "Powerful one."

Wally Dim. **Walter, Wallace**, etc. Actors Wally Shawn, Wally Cox.

Walsh OE. "Welsh." Also related to **Wallace**.

Walter OG. "People of power" or "Army of power." Norman name that took root strongly in Britain and has been used quite steadily for the last 900 years (with the occasional century of neglect). Not particularly fashionable now. Cartoonist Walt Disney; poet Walt Whitman; journalist Walter Cronkite; actors Walter Brennan, Walter Matthau.

Gaultier, Gauthier, Gautier, Gualterio, Gualtiero, Valter, Valther, Walder, Wally, Walt, Walther, Wat, Watkins

Waltham OE. Place name: "Walt's village."

Walton OE. Place name: "Walled town." Composer William Walton; entrepreneur Sam Walton.

Walworth OE. Place name: "Walled farm."

Walwyn OE. "Welsh friend."

Walwin, Walwinn, Walwynn, Walwynne, Welwyn

Wanamaker Ger. Occupational name: "Basket maker." John Wanamaker was a merchant in 19th-century Philadelphia who founded one of the first American department stores.

Wannamaker

Wapiti Native American: "White, whitish." The name refers to the pale rump and tail of the American elk, a majestic member of the deer family usually seen in sizable herds in national parks.

Warburton OE. Place name: "Long-standing fortress town."

Ward OE. Occupational name: "Watchman." Like many of these occupational or place names turned last names, Ward was revived as a first name in the 19th century. It is still somewhat more common as a first name than most other occupational names (**Smith, Baker, Turner**, etc.). Author Ward Just.
Warde, Warden, Worden

Wardell OE. Place name: "Watchman's hill."

Wardley OE. Place name: "Watchman's meadow."
Wardlea, Wardleigh

Ware OE. "Watchful, aware."

Warfield ME. Place name: "Field by the weir." A weir is a kind of enclosure built into a stream to trap fish.

Warford ME. "Ford near the weir."

Warley ME. "Meadow near the weir."

Warner OG. "Fighting defender." Philosopher Wernher Erhardt; U.S. Senator John Warner.
Werner, Wernher

Warren OE. "Watchman" or ME. "Park warden." A warren was originally an area devoted to breeding game, especially rabbits. By extension, the word is now used to describe human dwellings that resemble the haphazard and overcrowded rabbits' tunnels. As a name, Warren was used in the late 19th century and given a boost by the career of President Warren G. Harding. Actor Warren Beatty; U.S. Supreme Court Chief Justice Warren Burger; football player Warren Sapp.
Ware, Waring, Warrin, Warriner

Warton OE. Place name: "Town near the weir."
Wharton

Warwick OE. Place name: "Buildings near the weir." The town of Warwick in England was home for centuries to the very powerful Earls of Warwick.
Warick, Warrick

Washburn OE. Place name: "Flooding stream."
Washborn, Washbourne, Washburne

Washington OE. Place name: Possibly "Clever man's settlement." Author Washington Irving, born in 1783, was in all likelihood named for the first U.S. president, but the name has not been used as much as one might think, possibly because of its length. Educator Booker T. Washington.

Wasim Arab. "Good-looking, beautiful."

Waterford OE. Place name: "Ford over the water." Irish place name: a county in southern Ireland with two notable harbors.

Watkins OE. "Son of Walter, little Walter."

Watson OE. "Son of Walter." Last name used as a first name primarily in the 19th century. Most famous as the name of the sidekick to whom Sherlock Holmes perpetually condescended: "Elementary, my dear Watson." IBM founder Thomas Watson.

Watt Dim. **Walter**. The watt, a unit of electrical power (as in the 60-watt bulb) was named after Scottish inventor James Watt who refined and marketed the steam engine early in the 19th century.
Watts, Watts

Waunakee NAm. Ind. (Algonquin.) "Peaceful one."

Waverley OE. Place name: "Meadow of quivering aspens." Sir Walter Scott's series of 32 historical novels, written in the mid 19th century, was known as the "Waverley novels" after the title of the first one.
Waverlee, Waverley

Wayland OE. Place name: "Land by the path." Singer Waylon Jennings.
Way, Waylan, Waylen, Waylin, Waylon, Weylin

Wayne OE. Occupational name: "Wagon builder or driver," as in **Wainwright**. Its period of greatest popularity coincided with the popularity of the actor Marion Morrison, better known as John Wayne. Still used from time to time, but uncommon. Performer Wayne Newton; hockey player Wayne Gretzky.
Wain, Wayn

Weaver OE. Occupational name: "Weaver." Most familiar as a last name.

Webb OE. Occupational name: "Weaver." Mostly 19th-century use. Actors Clifton Webb, Jack Webb.
Web, Weber, Webster

Webley OE. Place name: "Weaver's meadow."
Webbley, Webbly, Webly

Webster OE. Occupational name: "Weaver." As in, weaving a web. Lexicographer Noah Webster produced America's first dictionary in 1828, and students today still depend on various editions of Webster's dictionaries. Statesman Daniel Webster.
Web, Webb, Webbster

Wedgwood OE. Place name: "Triangular woodland." The name of a famous English potter who produced a specific style of blue and white china beginning in the 18th century. The company is still in existence.
Wedgewood

Weissman Ger. "White-haired man."
Weissmann

Welborne OE. Place name: "Spring-fed stream." Not, alas, indicative of patrician origins.
Welborn, Welbourne, Welburn, Wellborn, Wellbourn, Wellburn

Welby OG. Place name: "Well-farm." A television series about an avuncular doctor named Marcus Welby was very popular in the early 1970s.
Welbey, Welbie, Wellbey, Wellby

Weldon OE. Place name: "Well-hill."
Welden, Welldon

Welford OE. Place name: "Well-ford."
Wellford

Wellington OE. Place name of unclear meaning. Has aristocratic connotations, no doubt from the famous Duke of Wellington, who defeated Napoleon and gave his name to tall, waterproof boots and filet of beef wrapped in pastry.

Wells OE. Place name: "Wells." The name of a famous cathedral town in western England. First-name use was mostly 19th century. Baseball player David Wells.

Welton OE. Place name: "Well-town."

Wenceslaus Old Slavic. "Glorious garland." King Wenceslas, the patron saint of the Czech Republic, was a 10th-century monarch of Bohemia and a martyr for the faith. The famous Christmas carol (written in the 19th century) refers to an entirely imaginary episode, but the name would be unknown to us without it.
Wenceslas, Wenzel, Wiencyslaw

Wendell OG. "Wanderer." Quite rare. Attorney Wendell Willkie.
Wendall, Wendel

Wentworth OE. Place name: "Pale man's settlement."

Werner OG. "Defense army." Closely related to **Warner**. Use is mostly confined to the U.S.
Verner, Warner, Wernhar, Wernher

Wesley OE. Place name: "Western meadow." Used in honor of John and Charles Wesley, who founded the Methodist church in the 18th century. The name is quite steadily used, and despite the "-ley" ending that is so fashionable for girls, Wesley is still solidly masculine. Actors Wesley Snipes, Wes Bentley.
Wesly, Wessley, Westleigh, Westley

Westbrook OE. Place name: "Western stream." This group of place names illustrates one way last names came into use: They described the location of someone's dwelling. Fencer Peter Westbrook.
Brook, Brooke, Wesbrook, West, Westbrooke

Westby OE. Place name: "Western farmstead."
Westbey, Westbie

Westcott OE. Place name: "Western cottage."
Wescot, Wescott, Westcot

Westerly OE. "From the west, toward the west."
Westerley

Weston OE. Place name: "Western settlement." Photographer Edward Weston.
Westen, Westin

Wetherby OE. Place name: "Wether-sheep farm." A wether is a male sheep that has been castrated; a bellwether is a wether who wears a bell and leads a flock. Again, the importance of the wool trade in England when last names were formed gives these "Wether-" names unusual prominence.

Weatherbey, Weatherbie, Weatharby, Wetherbey, Wetherbie

Wetherell OE. Place name: "Wether-sheep corner."

Weatherell, Weatherill, Wetherill, Wethrill

Wetherly OE. Place name: "Wether-sheep meadow."

Weatherley, Weatherly, Wetherleigh, Wetherley

Wharton OE. Place name: "Shore or bank settlement." Author William Wharton.

Warton

Wheatley OE. Place name: "Wheat field." Football player Tyrone Wheatley.

Wheatlea, Wheatleigh, Wheatly

Wheaton OE. Place name: "Wheat settlement."

Wheeler OE. Occupational name: "Wheel maker."

Wheelwright OE. Occupational name: "Wheel maker." Corresponds to **Wainwright**.

Whistler OE. Occupational name: "Whistler or piper." Artist James Whistler.

Whitbeck OE. Place name: "White stream."

Whitby OE. Place name: "White farm." All of these "Whit-" names are more commonly last names, though some were used more regularly as first names in the 19th century.

Whitbey, Whitbie

Whitcomb OE. Place name: "White valley." Poet James Whitcomb Riley.

Whitcombe, Whitcumb

White OE. Descriptive name: "White or fair." Probably referred to complexion or hair color of an ancestor. Extremely unlikely to be used as a first name today. Architect Stanford White; baseball player Whitey Ford.

Whitey

Whitehead OE. Descriptive name: "Fair-headed."

Whitelaw OE. Place name: "White hill." Diplomat Whitelaw Reid.

Whitlaw

Whitfield OE. Place name: "White field."

Whitford OE. Place name: "White ford."

Whitley OE. Place name: "White meadow." Author Whitley Streiber.

Whitlock OE. "White lock of hair."

Whitman OE. "White man." The description would refer to hair or complexion. Poet Walt Whitman.

Whitmore OE. Place name: "White moor."
Whitmoor, Whittemore, Witmore, Wittemore

Whitney OE. Place name: "White island." Last name that was annexed as a girl's name in the 1980s. It became much more popular for girls than it ever was for boys. Even though the vogue for female Whitneys is fading, the name is almost never used for boys now. Railroad millionaire William Collins Whitney; inventor Eli Whitney.

Whittaker OE. Place name: "White field." The last part of the name may refer to an acre of land. Actor Forrest Whittaker.
Whitacker, Whitaker

Wickham OE. Place name: "Village paddock."

Wickley OE. Place name: "Village meadow."

Wilbert OG. "Brilliant and resolute." Not the same as **Wilbur**, despite the similar sound. Used sporadically in the 19th and 20th centuries.
Wilburt

Wilbur OG. Last name of obscure meaning. Probably confused with **Wilbert** over the years. E.B. White fans will associate it with the protagonist of *Charlotte's Web*, Wilbur the Pig. Aviator Wilbur Wright.
Wilber, Willbur

Wilder Ger. Occupational name: "Hunter." In other words, someone who traps or kills wild animals. A nonconformist choice for the heavily civilized 21st century. Playwrights Thornton Wilder, Oscar Wilde.
Wild, Wilde

Wiley OE. Place name: "Water meadow." Indicates a meadow that would be flooded from time to time.
Willey, Wylie

Wilford OE. Place name: "Willow-ford." Actor Wilford Brimley.

Wilfred OE. "Purposeful peace." Like **Waldemar**, another name whose two elements are both nouns (in this case "will" and "peace"), to the confusion of the translator. Neglected after the Norman invasion, but revived in the 19th century to some popularity, which never spread as far as the U.S. author Wilfred Sheed.

Wilfredo, Wilfrid, Wilfried, Wilfryd, Will, Willfred, Willfredo, Willfrid, Willfried, Willfryd

Wilkes OE. Probably a contraction of **Wilkins**. Presidential assassin John Wilkes Booth.

Wilkie, Willkes, Willkie

Wilkinson OE. "Son of little Will."

Wilkins, Willkins, Willkinson

Willard OG. "Bold will." Most common in the U.S., though far from a household word. TV weatherman Willard Scott.

Willerd

Willet OE. "Little Will."

Willets, Willett

William OG. "Will-helmet." Another two-noun name, more often translated as "resolute protection" or the like. Given a great boost in Norman England by William the Conqueror and succeeding English kings. Between the 17th and 20th centuries, one of the top handful of boy's names. Its popularity faded somewhat in the middle of the 20th century but by the end, it was one of the top two dozen boys' names in America. Its popularity may have been partially prompted by the example of Prince William of Wales. Just as boys named **Robert** are no longer called **Bobby**, boys named William are not nicknamed **Billy**. The currently popular diminutive is **Will**. Playwright William Shakespeare; actors William Hurt, Willem Dafoe, Billy Crudup, Bill Pullman; film director Wim Wenders; poet William Blake; author William Faulkner; U.S. Presidents William H. Harrison, William H. Taft, William McKinley, Bill Clinton.

Bill, Bille, Billie, Billy, Guglielmo, Guillaume, Guillermo, Liam, Vilhelm, Villem, Wilek, Wiley, Wilhelm, Wilhelmus, Wilkes, Wilkie, Wilkinson, Will,

Willem, Willhelmus, Willi, Williamson, Willie, Willis, Willkie, Wills, Willson, Willy, Wilmar, Wilmot, Wilmott, Wilson, Wim

Willis OE. Dim. **William**. Basketball player Willis Reed.

Willes, Willess, Williss, Williston

Willoughby OE. Place name: "Willow farm." In the early English agricultural economy willows were important because their pliable branches could be woven into baskets.

Willoughbey, Willoughbie, Willughby

Wilmer OG. "Determined fame."

Wilmar, Willmar, Willmer, Wylmer

Wilson OE. "Son of Will." Last name turned first name, possibly in compliment to President Woodrow Wilson. Composer Robert Wilson; Beach Boy Brian Wilson.

Willson

Wilton OE. Place name: "Well settlement."

Windsor OE. Place name: "Riverbank with a winch." Famous from the town and castle of that name in England, and above all from the fact that it is the British royal family's last name. Until 1917 it had been Wettin, but during World War I emotions ran so high against Germany that it seemed more patriotic to adopt a staunch English name. Also the name of a standard way to tie a necktie, invented by the Duke of Windsor, who was a great dandy.

Winsor, Wyndsor

Winfield OE. "Friend's field." Baseball player Dave Winfield; Civil War general Winfield Scott.

Winnfield, Wynfield, Wynnfield

Wingate OE. Place name: "Winding gate." May refer to a gate like a turnstile.

Winslow OE. Place name: "Friend's hill." Painter Winslow Homer.

Winsted OE. Place name: "Friend's farm."

Winstead

Winston OE. Place name: "Friend's town" or "Wine's town." For modern parents, recalls both English statesman Winston Churchill and a popular brand of cigarettes.

Winsten, Winstonn, Wynstan, Wynston

Winter OE. Season name. Musician Paul Winter.
    Winters
Winthrop OE. Place name: "Friend's village." In the U.S., it hearkens back to the Puritan governor of Massachusetts, John Winthrop, and his numerous Bostonian descendants.
Winton OE. Place name: "Friend's settlement." Closely related to **Winston**. Musician Wynton Marsalis.
    Wynton
Winwood OE. Place name: "Friend's woods." Musician Steve Winwood.
Wistar Ger. Last name of uncertain meaning. Used with pride among Philadelphia families: Caspar Wistar was a very prominent doctor in late 18th century Philadelphia, and taught at what became the University of Pennsylvania. An earlier Caspar Wistar (in all likelihood the doctor's father) founded a thriving glass factory in southern New Jersey in the 1740's. The flower wisteria was named after the doctor. Author Owen Wister.
    Wister
Wolcott OE. Place name: "Wolf's cottage." Wolf, in this case, would be a first name. Oliver Wolcott of Connecticut signed the Declaration of Independence.
Wolfe OG. "Wolf." From the evidence of names and Grimm's fairy tales, it's obvious that wolves occupied a big part in the medieval German imagination. They obviously posed a threat (remember *Little Red Riding Hood*?) but at the same time their qualities of fierceness and tenacity must have seemed admirable. It's an interesting window on the life of the times: would we name a son "Shark?" Irish patriot Wolfe Tone.
    Wolf, Wolff, Wolfhart, Woolf, Wulf, Wulfe
Wolfert OG. "Wolf army."
Wolfgang OG. "Wolf gait." A very Germanic name that would not be considered by English-speaking parents without the fame of composer Wolfgang Amadeus Mozart.
Wolfram OG. "Wolf raven."
    Wulfram

Woodrow OE. "Row by the woods." "Row" could refer to a row of houses or trees or bushes (as in a hedgerow). The name has been given prominence beyond the usual place name by admirers of U.S. President Woodrow Wilson.
Woody

Woodson OE. "Wood's son." Football players Rod Woodson, Darren Woodson.

Woodstock OE. "Wooden fence." As in stockade fencing. Also as in the rock festival of the 1970s, which still echoes in popular culture.

Woodward OE. Place name: "Woods warden." Actor Edward Woodward.
Woodard

Woody Dim. **Woodrow**, etc. A particularly American name adopted by actor Allen Konigsberg, now better known as Woody Allen. Folk singer Woody Guthrie.

Woolworth OE. "Wool farm." Famous as the name of a chain of stores.

Worth OE. Place name: "Fenced farm." Used since the 19th century.
Worthey, Worthing, Worthington, Worthy

Woyzeck Slavic. "Comforting soldier." Opera fans will recognize the variation **Wozzeck** as the name of an opera by Alban Berg.
Wojtek, Wozzeck

Wray ONorse. Place name: "Dweller in the corner."

Wright OE. Occupational name: "Carpenter." This word occurs in names like **Wainwright** and **Wheelwright**. Again, mostly 19th-century use. The astounding feats of aviators Orville and Wilbur Wright apparently did not inspire parents to use their name in homage. Painter Joseph Wright of Derby; architect Frank Lloyd Wright.

Wyandanch Native American: Montauk. "Speaks with wisdom." The name of a town on Long Island in New York State.

Wyatt OF. "Small fighter." Last name occasionally used as a first name, notably by Wild West Sheriff Wyatt Earp.
Wiatt, Wye, Wyeth

Wyck OE. Place name: "Village." Occurs more often in combination with other names, like **Wickham**.
Wick, Wyche

Wycliff OE. Place name: "White cliff."
Wycliffe

Wyckoff OG. "Wine seller."
Wykoff

Wycombe OE. Place name: "White valley."
Wycomb

Wylie OE. "Clever, charming, full of wiles." Literary agent Andrew Wylie.
Wiley, Wye

Wyman OE. "Fair-haired man."

Wyndham OE. Place name: Either "Wyman's hamlet" or "Hamlet near the winding way." Used as a first name in the 19th century and into the 20th, but very unusual today. Author Wyndham Lewis.
Windham, Wynndham

Wynn Welsh. "Fair, white" or OE. "Friend." Used more frequently for girls in the past few years, but still uncommon. Gambling entrepreneur Steve Wynn.
Win, Winn, Wynne

Wystan OE. "Battle stone." The first name of poet Wystan Hughes Auden. Otherwise obscure.
Wystann

Xan Dim. **Alexander** (Gk. "Defender of mankind").

Xanthus Gk. "Golden-haired."
Xanthos

Xavier Basque. "New house." Most often found as a middle name following **Francis**, in honor of Saint Francis Xavier, a 16th-century Jesuit missionary who took Christianity to the East Indies and Japan. Some of its popularity may be explained by the fact that it sounds a lot like the word "savior," a synonym for Jesus to Christians. Band leader Xavier Cugat; baseball player Javier Lopez.

Javier, Saviero, Savion, Savyon, Xaviell, Xayvion, Xever, Zavier

Xenophon Gk. "Foreign voice." Xenophon was a Greek historian of the 4th century B.C.

Xeno

Xenos Gk. "Hospitality."

Zeno, Zenos

Xerxes Per. "Monarch." Xerxes was the title of several Persian rulers. One (in the 5th century B.C.) made war on the Greeks and also appears in the biblical Apocrypha as Ahasuerus, husband of Esther.

Ximenes Sp. Var. **Simon** (Heb. "Listening intently").

Jimenes, Jimenez, Ximenez

Yaakov Heb. Var. **Jacob** ("He who supplants"). Comedian Yakov Smirnov.

Iago, Yaacob, Yachov, Yacov, Yago, Yakob, Yakov

Yaar Heb. "Forest."

Yakar Heb. "Precious."

Yakim Heb. Var. **Joachim** ("The Lord will set up").

Jachim, Jakim, Yacheem, Yachim

Yaholo North American: Creek. "He who yells." Highly appropriate for most children.

Yale OE. Place name: "Fertile moor." Familiar as the name of one of the Ivy League universities, founded by Elihu Yale.

Yael

Yanai Aramaic. "He will answer." Old Testament name.

Yancy Origin unclear. Several sources suggest this was an Indian word for "Englishman," and propose that this was the origin of the word "Yankee." But the *Facts File Dictionary of First Names* claims the name is used to honor

a Southern proslavery politician of the 19th century. Rare, in any case. Football player Yancey Thigpen.
Yance, Yancey, Yantsey

Yann Fr. Var. **John** (Heb. "The Lord is gracious"). Comparable to the Dutch **Jan**. Tennis player Yannick Noah.
Yannic, Yannick

Yannis Gk. Var. **John** (Heb. "The Lord is gracious").
Ioannis, Yanni, Yannakis

Yaphet Heb. "Comely." Actor Yaphet Koto.
Japhet, Japheth, Yapheth

Yardley OE. Place name: "Fenced meadow."
Yardlee, Yardlea, Yardleigh, Yardly, Yarley, Yeardley

Yarrow Plant name: a strongly scented herb. Musician Peter Yarrow.

Yasahiro Jap. "Serene."

Yasir Arab. "Well to do." Palestinian leader Yasser Arafat.
Yaseer, Yasr, Yasser

Yates ME. Place name: "The gates." Poet W.B. Yeats.
Yeats

Yazid Arab./Swahili. "Becoming greater."
Yazeed

Yehudi Heb. "Praise." Related to the feminine **Judith**, as well as to **Jude**. Violinist Yehudi Menuhin.
Judah, Yechudi, Yechudit, Yehuda, Yehudah, Yehudit

Yeoman ME. "Attendant, servant."
Youman

Yevgeny Rus. Var. **Eugene** (Gk. "Wellborn"). Musician Yevgeny Kissin.
Yevgeniy

Yishachar Heb. "Reward will come."
Issachar, Yisachar

Yitzhak Heb. Var. **Isaac** ("Laughter"). Violinist Itzhak Perlman.
Itzak, Izaak, Yitzchak

Ymir ONorse. Mythology name: the giant from whose body the earth was created.

Yochanan Heb. "The Lord is gracious." A form of **John**.
Johanan, Yohannan

Yoelvis Modern name: possibly, in Spanish, "I, Elvis." Or a variation of **Elvis** (Scand. "All-wise"). Olympic track athlete Yoelvis Quesada.

Yonas Heb. "Dove." The English form is **Jonas**.

Yorath Welsh. "Handsome lord."

Yorick OE. "Farmer." Related to **George** and **Yuri**. Most people have only heard this name in the context of Shakespeare's play *Hamlet*, in which Hamlet mutters to a skull, "Alas! poor Yorick."

York OE. Place name: "Boar settlement" or "yew settlement." Used as a title (Duke of York) in the English royal family for several hundred years. Also familiar as an American place name, which makes it a bit difficult to use as a first name.

Yorick, Yorrick, Yorke

Yosemite Place name: a national park in Eastern California on the western slope of the Sierra Nevada. The name may be a Native American term for grizzly bear.

Young Eng. Adjective as name: usually a transferred last name.

Yovanny Phonetic variant on **Giovanni**, the Italian form of **John** (Heb. "The Lord is gracious").

Yovanney, Yovanni

Yucatan Mexican place name: the peninsula that separates the Caribbean from the Gulf of Mexico, and is a very popular vacation spot.

Yukon Canadian place name: territory between Alaska and the Northwest Territories, famous for its gold and its cold.

Yule OE. "Winter solstice." The time of year around Dec. 21, the pagan winter feast. Now, of course, it means Christmas. Rarely used, even for Christmas babies.

Euell, Ewell

Yuri Rus. Var. **George** (Lat. "Farmer").

Yurii, Yury

Yusuf Var. **Joseph** (Heb. "The Lord increases"). Currently very popular in Arabic-speaking countries. The "-uf" ending is more typically Arab, the "-ef" ending more often Hebrew.

Yosef, Yoseff, Yusef, Yusuff

Yves Fr. Var. **Ivo** (OG. "Yew wood"). Since yew wood was used for bows, the name may have been an occupational one meaning "archer." This form is almost exclusively found in France; its closest cognate in America is the feminine **Yvonne**. Singer Yves Montand; fashion designer Yves Saint Laurent.
Evo, Ives, Ivo, Yvo, Yvon

Zachariah Heb. "The Lord has remembered." Biblical name occurring in both Old and New Testaments. As might be expected, it was revived by the Puritans and found fairly constantly through the 19th century. The numerous phonetic variations hint at its current popularity.
Zacaria, Zacarias, Zacary, Zaccaria, Zaccariah, Zaccheus, Zach, Zachaios, Zacharia, Zacharias, Zacharie, Zachary, Zacheriah, Zachery, Zacheus, Zack, Zackariah, Zackerias, Zackery, Zak, Zakarias, Zakarie, Zakariyyah, Zakery, Zecheriah, Zekariah, Zekeriah, Zeke

Zachary Heb. "The Lord has remembered." The most popular form of **Zachariah**, one of the top two dozen names for boys in the country. Probably brought to fashion by the Old Testament names **Jeremy, Jason,** and **Joshua.** Parents tend to look for names similar to—but not exactly the same as—what's stylish. President Zachary Taylor.
Zaccary, Zaccery, Zacharie, Zachery, Zackarey, Zackary, Zackery

Zaccheus Heb. "The Lord has remembered." A variation of **Zechariah**. The name was borne by a tax collector in the New Testament who, being short, climbed into a tree to see Jesus in a crowd. Jesus spotted him in his perch, called to him by name, and visited his house. This is a story that has immense appeal to children.
Zachaios, Zacchaeus

Zadok Heb. "Fair, righteous."
  Zadoc, Zaydok

Zafar Arab. "Victory."
  Zaphar

Zahavi Heb. "Gold."

Zahir Arab. "Flourishing, brilliant"; Heb. "Shining." Currently popular in Arabic-speaking countries.
  Zaheer, Zahur, Zayyir

Zahur Arab./Swahili. "Blossom."
  Zahour, Zahoor

Zaki Arab. "Full of virtue, pure." Likely to be mistaken for a variant of the popular **Zachary/Zachariah**.

Zale Gk. "Sea-strength."
  Zayle

Zalman Heb. "Peaceable." The more common form in English is **Solomon**. Author Salman Rushdie.
  Salman, Zalomon

Zan Dim. **Alexander** (Gk. "Man's defender"). A trendy new form of a name that has been quite popular in recent years.
  Zander, Zandro, Zandros, Zann

Zane Derivation and meaning unclear. May be a variation of **John** (Heb. "The Lord is gracious"), or a version of a Scandinavian last name. Made famous by author Zane Grey, who wrote many novels about the Wild West, among them *Riders of the Purple Sage*.
  Zain, Zayne

Zared Heb. "Trap."

Zarek Polish. Var. **Belshazzar** (Babylonian "May Bal watch over the king"). In the Old Testament, the son of Nebuchadnezzar, and the last king of Babylon. At a famous feast held by Belshazzar, handwriting appeared mysteriously on the wall of the banqueting hall. The message was interpreted by Daniel as a warning of the king's doom, hence our saying, "the writing is on the wall." **Balthazar** is a related name.

Zebediah Heb. "Gift of Jehovah." In the New Testament, the father of apostles John and James. The name is all but obsolete today.
  Zeb, Zebedee, Zebediah

Zebulon Heb. "To give honor to." Old Testament name of one of Jacob's sons. Extremely rare.
Zebulen, Zebulun, Zevulon, Zevulun

Zedekiah Heb. "The Lord is just." Name of an Old Testament king of Judah. Mostly 19th-century use.
Zed, Zedechiah, Zedekias

Zeke Heb. "Strength of God." Dim. **Ezekiel**. Ezekiel was an important Old Testament prophet.

Zelig Yiddish. "Blessed, holy." In German, "selig" means holy. Movie buffs will remember a Woody Allen movie in which a character named Zelig turns up at many different historic events.
Selig, Zeligman, Zelik

Zenas Gk. "Hospitable."
Zenios, Zenon

Zeno Name of a Greek philosopher. Derivation unclear.
Zenon, Zino, Zinon

Zenobios Gk. "Life of Zeus."
Zenobius, Zinov, Zinovi

Zephaniah Heb: "Precious to the Lord." A minor Old Testament prophet. Sparing 19th-century use.
Zeph, Zephan

Zephariah Modern name, apparently coined from **Zephaniah** and **Zachariah**.

Zephyr Gk. "West wind." A mythology name that has persisted in variations like **Cefirino** and **Zephirine** (for girls). Laurent de Brunhoff, in his *Babar* books, named the mischievous monkey Zéphir.
Zayfeer, Zayfir, Zayphir, Zefir, Zéphir, Zephiros, Zephirus, Zephyrus

Zerach Heb. "A lamp."
Zerah

Zero Arab. "Void." A rather daunting name for a baby, though actor Zero Mostel seems to have survived it.

Zeus Gk. "Living." The name of the chief of the Olympian gods, who was also father of many gods and goddesses including Athena, Ares, Apollo, and Artemis.

Zikomo Ngono (Malawi). "Thank you."

Zimran Heb. "Holy."

Zindel Yiddish. Var. **Alexander** (Gk. "Defender of mankind").
   Zindil

Zion Heb. "Highest point." In the Christian religion, Zion is a symbolic name for heaven, and is used often in hymns and even the names of some churches.
   Sion

Zipkiyah NAm. Ind. (Kiowa.) "Big bow." As in bow and arrow.

Ziv Heb. "Full of life, glorious, splendid."
   Ziven, Zivon

Zoilo Sp. from Gk. "Life." The most common form of this name is the feminine **Zoe**.

Zoltan Hung. "Life." Composer Zoltan Kodaly.

Zuberi Swahili. "Strong."
   Zooberi, Zubery

Zuhayr Arab. "Small blossoms."
   Zuhair

Zuni Native American tribe: the Zuni live in New Mexico.

Zuriel Heb. "The Lord my rock."

If It's a
GIRL...

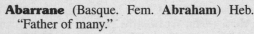

Abarrane (Basque. Fem. **Abraham**) Heb. "Father of many."

Abame

Abebi Nig. "She came after asking."

Abelia (Fem. **Abel**) Fr. from Heb. "Sigh."

Abella, Abelle

Abellona (Fem. **Apollo**) Dan. In Greek mythology, Apollo is the sun god. See **Apolline**.

Aberdeen Scot. Place name: city in northeast Scotland.

Abia Arab. "Great."

Abida Arab. "She who worships" or Heb. "My father knows."

Abiela Heb. "My father is the Lord."

Abigail Heb. "My father is joyful." Biblical name adopted by the Puritans and popular through the 18th century. Abigail was the wife of David, and referred to herself as his "handmaid." Her name became widely used as a term for a ladies' maid by the early nineteenth century, which may have contributed to its fall from favor. After a hundred years of obscurity, it was revived with the trend toward old-fashioned names beginning in the 1970s. Still unusual, but an appealing choice for parents seeking a distinctive but not outlandish name. Abigail Adams, wife of President John Adams; advice columnist Abigail Van Buren.

Abagael, Abagail, Abagale, Abagil, Abaigeal, Abbe, Abbey, Abbi, Abbie, Abbigael, Abbigail, Abbigale, Abby, Abbye, Abbygael, Abbygail, Abbygale, Abegale, Abigael, Abigal, Abigale, Abigall, Abigil, Abigayle, Gael, Gail, Gaila, Gal, Gale, Gayel, Gayle

Abijah Heb. "God is my father."

Abeedja, Abeeja, Abeesha, Abisha, Abishah

Abilene Place name: town in Texas, and also in early Christian times, an area in Lebanon near Damascus.

Abalene, Abalina, Abilena, Abiline

Abina Ghanaian. "Born on Thursday."

Abir Arab. "Scent."
  Abeer

Abital Heb. "My father is dew." Currently popular in Israel.
  Abeetal, Avital

Abra (Fem. **Abraham**) Heb. "Father of many" or Arab. "Example, lesson." King Solomon's favorite concubine was named Abra.
  Abame, Abarrane, Abrahana

Acacia Gk. Name of a blossoming tree that symbolized resurrection. Uncommon even in Greece, though the derivatives like **Casey** occur often in the U.S.
  Cacia, Cacie, Casey, Casha, Casia, Cassie, Cassy, Caysha, Kacey, Kacie, Kasey, Kasi, Kassja, Kassy

Acadia Place name: The French settlers of Nova Scotia called it Acadia after the name of a river there. When the French inhabitants were driven out by the English in the 18th century, many of them settled in Louisiana and became known as "Cajuns."

Accalia Lat. In mythology, the name of the human foster mother of Romulus and Remus, the twins who founded Rome. Legend has it that after their abandonment as infants, they were initially suckled by a she-wolf, whose name is not known. Accalia was her replacement.

Aceline (Fem. **Acelin**) Fr. "Highborn."
  Asceline

Achsah Heb. "Ankle bracelet."
  Achsah

Acima (Fem. **Acim**) Heb. "The Lord will judge."
  Acimah, Achima, Achimah

Acquanetta Invented name related to the particle *aqua*, which is Latin for "water." Possibly derived from the name of the hairspray "AquaNet."
  Acquanette, Aquanette, Aquannette

Ada Ger. "Noble, nobility." Originated as a short form of names like **Adelaide**, and popular in the last quarter of the 19th century, though infrequently used now.
  Adan, Adda, Addi, Addie, Addiah, Addy, Adey, Adi, Adia, Adiah, Adie, Aida, Aidah

Adah Heb. "Ornament, adornment." Biblical name. Unusual, but brought to prominence in the 19th century by American actress Adah Isaacs Mencken. It may also, of course, be considered a variation of **Ada**.

Adair Scot. last name, possibly based on Scots pronunciation of **Edgar**. Attractive, modern-sounding unisex name, currently scarce but appearing more often for girls.
Adare, Adayre

Adalgisa It. from OG. "Noble promise." The name of a priestess in Bellini's popular opera *Norma*, but exceedingly rare.
Adalgise, Adelgise, Adelvice

Adalia Heb. "God is my refuge" or OG. "Noble one." See also **Adelaide**.
Adal, Adala, Adalee, Adali, Adalie, Adalley, Addal, Addala

Adamina (Fem. **Adam**) Heb. "Child of the red earth." In the Bible God created Adam out of the "red earth" and breathed life into him. This unusual feminine version of the name is Scottish in origin.
Ada, Adameena, Adamine, Adaminna, Addie, Ademina, Ademeena, Mina, Minna

Adara Gk. "Beauty" or Arab. "Virgin."
Adra

Addie Dim. **Adelaide, Adeline**, or **Addison**. A nostalgic-sounding nickname.
Addy

Addison OE. "Son of Adam." Transferred surname that is gaining popularity for girls, probably influenced by the top-ten status of soundalike **Madison**.
Addeson, Adison, Adisson

Addula Teut. "Noble cheer."

Adelaide OG. "Noble, nobility." First popular in England after the reign (1830–37) of William IV and Queen Adelaide. She was a German princess who accepted the young prince after he'd been turned down by seven other highborn ladies. The city of Adelaide, Australia, founded in 1836, was named for her.
Adalaide, Adalayde, Addala, Addalla, Addey, Addi,

Addie, Addy, Adel, Adela, Adelaida, Adelais, Adele, Adelheid, Adelina, Adeline, Adelice, Adelicia, Adelis, Adelle, Adey, Adi, Ado, Ady, Aline, Aliosha, Alline, Alyosha, Del, Della, Delle, Delli, Delly, Edeline, Eline, Heidi, Lady, Laidey

Adele OG. "Noble, nobility." See **Adelaide**. Nutritionist Adelle Davis; writer Adela Rogers St. John.

Adelia, Adell, Adella, Adellah, Adelle, Edelle

Adelinda Teut. "Noble, sweet." Comb. form **Adele** and **Linda**.

Adele, Adeline, Adelinde, Linda

Adeline OG. "Noble, nobility." See **Adelaide**. Adelina enjoyed a burst of popularity during the career of operatic soprano Adelina Patti, in the late 19th century, and a well-known song called "Sweet Adeline" also gave the name exposure at the turn of the century. Perhaps too much exposure, for it fell into disuse.

Adalina, Adaline, Adallina, Adelina, Adelind, Adella, Adellah, Ahdella, Aline, Dahlina, Dalina, Daline, Dallina, Delina, Deline, Dellina, Delly, Delyne, Edelie, Lina

Adelpha Gk. "Beloved sister."

Adelfa

Adena Heb. "Decoration."

Adene, Adina, Adinah, Deena, Denah, Dina, Dinah

Adeola Nig. "Crown."

Adola, Dola

Adesina Nig. "She paves the way." Often used to mark a birth if a couple has had trouble conceiving, implying that this will be the first of many children.

Adiba Arab. "Cultured, refined."

Adeeba, Adibah

Adiella Heb. "The Lord's adornment."

Adima Teut. "Noble, renowned."

Adin Heb. Meaning unclear: possibly "Delicate and slender." Appears in the Old Testament as a male name.

Adina, Adeana

Adina Heb. Perhaps "Longing," also possibly "Gentle, delicate." Easily confused by the ear with **Edina**, which is an English name.

Adira Heb. "Noble, powerful."
  Adeera, Edira
Aditi Hindi. "Boundless." In Hindu cosmology, Aditi is the mother of the gods.
Adiva Arab. "Agreeable, gentle."
Adlai Arab./Heb. "Just." More familiar to us as a man's name made famous by U.S. Senator Adlai Stevenson.
Adolpha (Fem. **Adolph**) Ger. "Noble wolf."
  Adolfa, Adollfa
Adoncia Sp. "Sweet."
  Doncia
Adonia (Fem. **Adonis**) Gk. In Greek mythology, Adonis was a young man so beautiful that Aphrodite, goddess of love, became enamored of him. The name Adonis has come to epitomize male beauty.
Adora Lat. "Adored." A rare but appropriate choice for parents who know themseves to be the doting types.
  Adorabelle, Adorae, Adoray, Adoré, Adorée, Adoria, Adorlee, Dora, Dorae, Dori, Dorie, Dorri, Dorrie, Dorry, Dory
Adra Arab. "Virgin."
  Adara
Adrian Lat. Place name: Adria was a North Italian city. First popular in the 1950s in Britain, and more common as a man's name. Hollywood costume designer Adrian (*Queen Christina, The Philadelphia Story*) and 12th-century Pope Adrian IV (the only English pope) both predate its use as a girl's name. Ripe for revival in this era of unisex names. Fashion designer Adrienne Vittadini.
  Adrea, Adreea, Adria, Adriah, Adriana, Adrianah, Adriane, Adrianna, Adriannah, Adrianne, Adrie, Adrien, Adriena, Adrienah, Adrienne, Aydrian, Aydrienne, Hadria, Hadrienne
Aegina In Greek mythology, the name of a nymph (one of many, of course) who was impregnated by Zeus. More familiar to travelers, perhaps, as one of the Greek islands close to the mainland.
  Egina
Afra Arab. "Color of earth" or Heb. "Young deer" or

"Dust." The first female professional writer in England was named Aphra Behn; she was a playwright and a novelist in the latter half of the 17th century.

Affera, Affery, Affra, Aphra

Afraima Arab./Heb. "Fertile."

Africa Place name; the continent. The word also means "pleasant" in Celtic languages, and occurred occasionally as a name in Scotland from the Middle Ages up to the 1700s. In the U.S. it is used among African-American parents to highlight their heritage.

Affrica, Affricah, Affrika, Affrikah, Africah, Afrika, Afrikah, Aifric, Aifrica, Aphria, Aphfrica, Apirka, Apirkah

Afton OE. Place name: a town in southern Scotland. Like so many place names that have become first names, this one was first a name for boys.

Affton

Afua Ghanaian. "Born on Friday."

Agapi Gk. "Love, affection."

Agape, Agappe

Agate OF. A semiprecious stone. Can be considered either one of the jewel names so popular in the 19th century, or a variant of **Agatha**. The agate, though not a particularly beautiful stone, was once believed to have numerous magical and curative powers.

Agatha Gk. "Good." Saint Agatha was a 3rd-century Christian who refused to marry a Roman consul. She was tortured and ultimately martyred. Her breasts were cut off as part of her torture and she is frequently depicted holding them on a plate. Owing to their resemblance to bells, she is the patron saint of bell ringers. Her name was popular in the early years of the Christian Church, but not again until the late 19th century. It now has an unfashionable ring, but some of the international variants are pretty. Writer Agatha Christie.

Ag, Agace, Agacia, Agafia, Agafon, Agapet, Agapit, Agata, Agathe, Agathi, Agatta, Aggi, Aggie, Aggy, Aggye, Agi, Agie, Agota, Agotha, Agueda, Agy, Agye

Agave Gk. "Illustrious, noble."

Aglaia Gk. In Greek mythology, one of the three Graces, epitomizing brilliance. **Thalia** (blossoming) is still sometimes used; Euphrosyne (joy) is obsolete.

Agnes Gk. "Pure, virginal." Another early Christian saint's name. She was a virgin martyr, and her emblem in art is a lamb (the Latin for "lamb" is *agnus*). Very popular in England between the 12th and 16th centuries, Agnes is uncommon now, perhaps because of its connotations of homeliness which were probably magnified by Patrick Dennis's portrait of a a frustrated spinster (Agnes Gooch) in *Auntie Mame*. A French variant, **Anaïs**, is currently very popular in France. Choreographer Agnes De Mille; actress Agnes Moorhead; writer Anaïs Nin; film director Agnieska Holland.

Ag, Agafi, Agafia, Agafon, Aggi, Aggie, Aggye, Aghna, Agi, Agie, Agna, Agnah, Agnella, Agnellah, Agnelle, Agnese, Agnesse, Agneta, Agnetta, Agnettah, Agnola, Agnolah, Agot, Agota, Agote, Agoti, Agy, Agye, Aigneis, Aina, Ainah, Anaïs, Annais, Anneyce, Annis, Annisa, Annisah, Annise, Ina, Inah, Ines, Inessa, Inez, Nessa, Nessah, Nesi, Nessie, Nessy, Nesta, Nestah, Nevsa, Nevesah, Neysa, Oona, Oonagh, Oonah, Senga, Una, Unah, Ynes, Ynez

Agnola It. "Angel." Also a variant of Agnes.

Agnolla, Agnolle

Agraciana Sp. "Forgiving."

Agracianna, Agracyanna

Agrafina Rus. "Born feet first." See **Agrippa**.

Agrippa Lat. "Born feet first." The name of a 1st-century Roman Emperor, the son of Herod. A man's name possibly transferred to female use because of the "-a" ending.

Agrafina, Agrippina, Agrippine

Agrippina Lat. Sister of the corrupt Roman Emperor Caligula and mother of the equally unsavory Roman Emperor Nero, who had her murdered. Not a common name, for obvious reasons.

Ahava Heb. "Loved one."

Ahouva, Ahuva, Ahuda

Aibhlin Ir. Gael. form of **Evelyn** or **Helen**.

Aida Arab. "Reward, present." Name of an immensely popular opera by Giuseppe Verdi.

Aeeda, Ayeeda, Ieeda, Iyeeda

Aidan Ir. Gael. "Fire." Saint Aidan was a 7th-century Irish monk. The name used to be more common for men than for women, but in the last ten years, has become as well used for girls as more familiar names like **Molly** and **Catherine**.

Adan, Aden, Aiden, Aydan, Ayden, Aydenn

Aiko Jap. "Little loved one."

Ailbhe Ir. "Noble, bright."

Alva, Alvy, Elva, Elvy

Aileen Ir. Var. **Helen** (Gk. "Light"). This form has been most popular in Scotland as opposed to the variant **Eileen**, which is more common in the U.S.

Aila, Ailee, Ailene, Ailey, Ailli, Ailie, Aleen, Alene, Aline, Alleen, Allene, Alline, Eileen, Eleen, Elleen, Ellene, Ileana, Ileane, Ileanna, Ilene, Iliana, Iliane, Ilianna, Il-leanne, Illene, Leana, Leanah, Leanna, Leannah, Lena, Lenah, Liana, Lianna, Liannah, Lina, Linah

Ailith OE. "Seasoned warrior."

Aldith, Eilith

Ailsa Scot. The name has two possible sources. As a homonym for **Elsa**, a diminutive of **Elizabeth**, it means "Pledge from God." An alternate source is the tiny Scottish island Ailsa Craig, which has prompted a few homesick Scots to use the name in the U.S.

Ailis, Ailse, Elsa, Elsha, Elshe

Aimée Fr. "Beloved." This form of **Amy** is popular with parents who are looking for a fanciful twist on an old favorite. Evangelist Aimée Semple McPherson.

Aimie, Aimey, Amey, Amie

Aina Scand. "Forever."

Aine Celt. "Happiness."

Ainsley Scot. Gael. Place name: "One's own meadow." A last name converted to a first name, used by both sexes, though never with the frequency of the closely related **Ashley**.

Ainslee, Ainsleigh, Ainslie, Ansley, Aynslee, Aynsley, Aynslie

Airlea Gk. "Ethereal."

Airlia

Aisha Arab. "Woman" or Swahili. "Life." Aisha was the favored wife of Mohammed, hence the name's current popularity among Muslim families. It is also frequently used by African-American families, and just as often respelled or embroidered to make interesting variations.

Aeesha, Aeeshah, Aesha, Aeshah, Aiesha, Aieshah, Aishah, Aisia, Aisiah, Asha, Ashah, Ashia, Ashiah, Asia, Asiah, Ayeesa, Ayeesah, Ayeesha, Ayeeshah, Ayeisa, Ayeisah, Ayeisha, Ayeishah, Ayisa, Ayisah, Ayisha, Ayishah, Ieasha, Ieashah, Ieashia, Ieashiah, Iesha, Ieshah, Ieesha, Ieeshah, Ieeshia, Ieeshiah, Yiesha, Yieshah

Aislinn Ir. Gael. "Dream."

Aisling, Ashling, Isleen

Aithne (Fem. **Aidan**) Ir. Gael. "Fire." Not to be confused, despite its sound, with the name of the Sicilian volcano.

Aine, Aithnea, Eithne, Ena, Ethnah, Ethnea, Ethnee

Aiyana Native American. "Forever flowering."

Aja Hindi. "Goat." Also possibly used as a phonetic variation on Asia.

Azha

Ajua Ghanaian. "Born on Monday."

Akela Haw. "Noble." A form of **Adele**.

Akilina Gk./Rus. "Eagle."

Acquilina, Acuqileena, Aquilina

Akiva Heb. "Protect, shelter."

Akeeva, Keeva, Keevah, Kiba, Kibah, Kiva, Kivah, Kivi

Akosua Ghanaian. "Born on Sunday."

Alaia Arab. "Sublime."

Alaine (Fem. **Alan**) Fr. from Gael. Possibly "Rock" or "Comely." Not actually used in France, where it would be very easily confused with **Hélène**.

Alaina, Alayna, Alayne, Aleine, Alenne, Allaine, Allayne, Alleine, Allene, Alenne, Aleyne

Alala Gk. In Greek mythology, the sister of Ares, the god of war.

Alamea Haw. "Ripe, precious." ·

Alanna (Fem. **Alan**) Gael. "Rock" or "Comely." Also a possible derivative of **Elaine** (OF. "Bright, shining") or **Helen** (Gk. "Light"). Singer Alanis Morrissette; actress Lana Turner.

Alaina, Alaine, Alana, Alane, Alanis, Alannah, Alayne, Alène, Aleyna, Aleyne, Alleen, Allena, Allene, Allyna, Alleynah, Alleyne, Allina, Allinah, Allyn, Lana, Lanah, Lanna, Lannah, Aleyna, Aleynah

Alaqua Native American. "Sweet gum tree."

Alarice (Fem. **Alaric**) OG. "Noble king." Alaric was a king of the Visigoths who sacked Rome.

Alarica, Alaricka, Alarieka

Alastair Scot. Var. **Alexander** (Gk. "Man's defender"). More generally used as a man's name, though the feminizations sometimes crop up in Scotland.

Alasdair, Alastrina, Alastriona

Alaula Haw. "Light of daybreak."

Alba Lat. "White." See **Albinia**. This form is currently very popular in Spain.

Albane, Albina, Albine, Albinia, Albinka, Alva

Alberga Lat. "White" or OG. "Noble." Also closely related to the French and Italian words for "inn."

Alberge, Elberga, Elberge

Alberta OE. "Noble-shining." Rare and old-fashioned now, it was most widely used during the lifetime of Queen Victoria's Prince Consort, Albert. Also the name of a western Canadian province, and a very popular strain of peach.

Alberthine, Albertina, Albertine, Ali, Alli, Allie, Ally, Auberta, Auberte, Aubertha, Auberthe, Aubine, Berrie, Berry, Bert, Berta, Berte, Berti, Bertie, Berty, Elberta, Elbertha, Elberthina, Elberthine, Elbertina, Elbertine

Albinia (Fem. **Alban, Albin**) Lat. "White, fair." From the same root as "albino."

Alba, Albina, Alva, Alvina, Aubine

Albreda (Fem. **Aubrey**) OG. "Counsel from the elves."

Alcestis Gk. In Euripides' play of the same name, Alcestis descends to Hades in place of her husband, and is then rescued by Hercules.

Alcina Gk. In Greek mythology, a sorceress who rules over a magical island. When she tired of her lovers, Alcina turned them into animals, trees, or stones. Despite this startling role model the name occurs from time to time.

Alcine, Alcinia, Allcine, Allcinia, Alseena, Alsina, Alsinia, Alsyna, Alzina

Alcinda Possibly an adaptation of **Lucinda** (Lat. "Light") or a variant of **Alison** (OG. "Noble, nobility").

Alacinda, Alicinda, Alicynthia, Allcinda

Alda (Fem. **Aldo, Otto**) OG. "Old, prosperous."

Aldabella, Aldea, Aldina, Aldine, Aleda, Alida

Aldara Gk. "Winged gift."

Aldis OE. "Battle-seasoned."

Aldith, Ailith

Aldonza Sp. "Sweet."

Aleeza Heb. "Joy."

Aleezah, Alieza, Aliozah, Aliza, Alizah, Alitza

Alegria Sp. "Happiness, joy." For related names, see **Hilary, Felicity, Bliss**. A charming choice for a much-wanted child.

Alagria, Alegrya, Allegria

Alena Rus. Var. **Helen** (Gk. "Light").

Alesia Gk. "Help, aid."

Alessia

Aleta Gk. "Footloose."

Aletta, Alette, Alletta, Allette, Eletta, Elletta, Ellette, Lettee, Lettie, Letty

Alethea Gk. "Truth." Unusual name that first appeared in Britain in the 17th century.

Alathia, Aleethia, Aleta, Aletea, Aletha, Alethia, Aletta, Alette, Alithea, Alithia, Elethea, Elithia

Alexandra (Fem. **Alexander**) Gk. "Man's defender." Became very popular in Britain after the Prince of Wales (later Edward VII) married the Danish Princess Alexandra in 1863. Still used in the English royal family and its many branches. Possibly this aristocratic connection fueled the name's 1990s surge in popularity. Ballet dancer Alexandra Danilova; fashion designer Zandra Rhodes.

Alastrina, Alastriona, Alejanda, Alejandra, Alejandrina, Aleka, Aleki, Alesandare, Alesandere, Alessanda, Alessandra, Alessandre, Alessandrina, Alessandrine, Alessia, Alex, Alexa, Alexanda, Alexandere, Alexanderia, Alexanderina, Alexanderine, Alexandre, Alexandrea, Alexandreana, Alexandrena, Alexandrene, Alexandretta, Alexandria, Alexandrina, Alexandrine, Alexea, Alexena, Alexene, Alexia, Alexina, Alexine, Alexis, Ali, Aliki, Alissandre, Alissandrine, Alista, Alix, Alla, Allejandra, Allejandrina, Allessa, Allessandra, Alle, Allexa, Allexandra, Allexandrina, Allexina, Allexine, Alli, Allie, Allix, Ally, Anda, Cesya, Elena, Ellena, Lesy, Lesya, Lexi, Lexie, Lexine, Lissandre, Lissandrine, Sanda, Sande, Sandi, Sandie, Sandra, Sandrina, Sandrine, Sandy, Sandye, Sanndra, Sasha, Sashenka, Shura, Shurochka, Sohndra, Sondra, Xandra, Zahndra, Zanda, Zanndra, Zohndra, Zondra

Alexis Gk. "Helper." Usually thought of as a short form of **Alexandra**, though it has a different etymological root. Originally a name for both genders, it is now almost exclusively female. Actress Alexis Smith.

Alessa, Alessi, Alexa, Alexi, Alexia, Lexi, Lexie, Lexy

Alfonsine (Fem. **Alfonso**) OG. "Noble and ready for battle."

Alfonsia, Alonza, Alphonsine

Alfreda (Fem. **Alfred**) OE. "Elf power." Actress Alfre Woodard.

Alfi, Alfie, Alfre, Alfredah, Alfredda, Alfreeda, Alfri, Alfried, Alfrieda, Alfryda, Alfy, Allfie, Allfreda, Allfredah, Allfredda, Allfrie, Allfrieda, Allfry, Allfryda, Allfy, Elfie, Elfre, Elfrea, Elfredah, Elfredda, Elfreeda, Elfrida, Elfrieda, Elfryda, Elfrydah, Ellfreda, Ellfredah, Ellfredda, Ellfreeda, Ellfrida, Ellfrieda, Ellfryda, Ellfrydah, Elva, Elvah, Freda, Freddi, Freddie, Freddy, Fredi, Fredy, Freeda, Freedah, Frieda, Friedah, Fryda, Frydah

Alice OG. "Noble, nobility." See **Adelaide**. An old standby name since the Middle Ages that became enormously popular after the 1865 publication of Lewis Carroll's *Alice's Adventures in Wonderland*. Its popularity waned in the 1930s, and it now has a pleasantly old-fashioned air. A good choice for parents seeking an unusual but not startling name. Ballerina Alicia Markova; writers Alice Walker, Alice Sebold; actresses Ali McGraw, Ally Sheedy, Alicia Silverstone; singer Alicia Keys.

Adelice, Ailis, Ala, Aleceea, Alecia, Aleetheea, Aleethia, Ali, Alica, Alicah, Alicea, Alicen, Alicia, Alidée, Alie, Alika, Alikah, Aliki, Alis, Alisa, Alisah, Alisann, Alisanne, Alisha, Alison, Alissa, Alisz, Alitheea, Alitia, Aliz, Alla, Allecia, Alleece, Alleeceea, Alles, Alless, Alli, Allice, Allicea, Allie, Allis, Allison, Allissa, Allisun, Allisunne, Allsun, Ally, Allyce, Allyceea, Allys, Allyse, Allysia, Allysiah, Allyson, Allyssa, Allysson, Alyce, Alyceea, Alys, Alyse, Alysia, Alyson, Alyss, Alyssa, Elissa, Elli, Ellie, Ellissa, Ellsa, Elsa, Illyssa, Ilysa, Ilysah, Ilyssa, Ilysse, Leece, Leese, Licha, Lichah, Lissa, Lyssa

Alida Lat. "Small winged one."

Adela, Adelina, Adelita, Adellyna, Adellyta, Adelyna, Adelyta, Alaida, Alda, Aldina, Aldine, Aldona, Aldonna, Aldyne, Aleda, Aleta, Aletta, Alette, Alidah, Alidia, Alita, Allda, Alldina, Alldine, Alldona, Alldonna, Alldyne, Alleda, Allida, Allidah, Allidia, Allidiah, Allyda, Allydah, Alyda, Alydah, Dela, Della, Dila, Dilla, Elida, Elita, Leda, Ledah, Lida, Lidah, Lita, Lyda, Lydah, Oleda, Oleta, Oletta, Olette

Aliki Var. **Alice** (OG. "Noble, nobility"). Author Aliki.

Alima Arab. "Cultured."

Alina Slavic. Var. **Helen** (Gk. "Light").

Aleen, Aleena, Alena, Alenah, Alene, Aline, Alleen, Allena, Allene, Alline, Allyna, Allynah, Allyne, Alyna, Alynah, Alyne, Leena, Leenah, Lena, Lenah, Lina, Linah, Lyna, Lynah

Alinda Elaboration of **Linda** (Sp. "Pretty").

Alisa Heb. "Great happiness." Easily confused with **Elisa,**

which is a variation of **Elizabeth**. Another similar name, **Alyssa**, is much more popular.

Alisah, Alissa, Alissah, Aliza, Allisa, Allisah, Allissa, Allissah, Allysa, Allysah, Alyssa, Alyssah

Alison Dim. **Alice** (OG. "Noble, nobility"). Actress Allison Janney.

Aili, Alisann, Alisanne, Alisoun, Alisun, Allcen, Allcenne, Allicen, Allicenne, Allie, Allisann, Allisanne, Allison, Allisoun, Allsun, Ally, Allysann, Allysanne, Allyson, Allysoun, Alysan, Alysann, Alysanne, Alyson, Alysoun

Alix OG. "Noble." See **Alexandra**. The ill-fated Alexandra, last Empress of Russia, was known to her family as Alix.

Alex, Alexa, Alexis, Aliki, Alissandre, Alissandrine, Lissandre

Aliya Arab. "Highborn." Pop musician Aaliyah.

Aaliya, Aaliyah, Alia, Aliah, Aliyah, Aliye, Allia, Alliah

Alla Numerous possible origins: a variant of **Ella**, a shortening of any of the myriad "Al-" names, even, possibly, a reference to Allah.

Ala, Alah, Allah

Allegra It. "Joyous." The musical term *allegro* means "quickly, with a happy air." Ballerina Allegra Kent.

Alegra, Allegretta, Alegria, Legra, Leggra

Allena (Fem. **Allen, Alan**) Ir. Possible meaning "Rock" or "Comely." See **Alanna**.

Alana, Alanice, Alanis, Alanna, Alena, Alene, Allene, Alleyne, Allynn, Allynne, Allynn, Alynne

Allura OF. "To entice, attract." Based on the noun, which means "power of attraction."

Alloura, Alura

Allyriane Fr. from Gk. "Lyre." The lyre was a stringed instrument, a predecessor of today's harp or guitar.

Alma Lat. "Giving nurture"; It. "Soul"; Arab. "Learned." Also the name of a river in the Crimea where a famous 19th-century battle was fought, bringing it into prominence as a first name. The more common usage, of course, is "alma mater" for a college or university. Composer's wife Alma Mahler.

Almah, Allma

Almarine OG. "Work ruler."
   Almeria, Almerine

Almeda Lat. "Goal-directed, ambitious."
   **Allmeda, Allmedah, Allmeta, Allmetah, Allmida, Allmi-
   dah, Allmita, Allmitah, Almedah, Almeta, Almetah,
   Almida, Almidah, Almita, Almitah, Maelle**

Almera (Fem. **Elmer**) Arab. "Aristocratic lady."
   **Allmeera, Allmeria, Almeera, Almeeria, Almeria,
   Almire, Almirah, Almyra, Ellmera, Ellmeria, Elmeera,
   Elmeeria, Elmera, Elmeria, Elmira, Elmyra, Elmyrah,
   Mera, Meera, Mira, Mirah, Myra, Myrah**

Almodine Lat. "Precious stone."

Almond Plant name. May refer to skin tone, or to the shape
   of a baby's eyes. The French version, **Amandine**, is currently extremely fashionable there.
   Almandina, Almandine, Almondine, Amande, Amandina

Aloe Plant name. The aloe plant grows in hot climates, and
   its fleshy leaves, though often equipped with thorns, are
   full of sap that is widely considered to have healing qualities.

Aloha Haw. "Love, kindness, affection." The familiar
   Hawaiian greeting.

Aloisia (Fem. **Aloysius**) OG. "Famous fighter."
   Aloysia, Eloisia, Eloysia

Alona Heb. "Oak tree." The many different spellings of
   this name attest to its use all over Europe.
   Allona, Allonia, Alonia, Elona, Ilona, Ilonka

Alonsa (Fem. **Alonso**) Sp./OG. "Ready for battle."
   Alonza

Alouette Fr. "Lark." Bird name. Familiar from the children's song, *"Alouette, gentille alouette, je te plumerai,"*
   which is actually a threat to pluck all the feathers from
   the poor bird.
   Allouette, Alouetta, Alowette

Alpha Gk. First letter of Greek alphabet, corresponding to
   A. Appropriate for a first daughter.
   Alfa

Alphonsine (Fem. **Alphonse**) Fr. from OG. "Ready for
   battle."

Alta Lat. "Elevated."
  Allta
Altagracia Sp. Elaboration of "grace." Also commemorates the feast of "Our Lady of Altagracia."
  Allagracia, Altagrazia
Altair Arab. "Bird." Also the name of the brightest star in the constellation Aquila. It is about ten times as bright as the sun.
Althea Gk. "With healing power." Tennis star Althea Gibson.
  Altha, Althaia, Altheda, Althelia, Althia, Eltha, Elthea, Thea
Altheda Gk. "Like a blossom."
Aludra Gk. "Virgin." Can be used for babies born under the sign of Virgo.
Alufa Heb. "Leader."
Aluma Heb. "Maiden" or "Sheaf" (as in a sheaf of grain at the harvest).
  Alumice, Alumit
Alumina Mineral name: oxygen and aluminium form the substance called "corundum," which is the basis of such gems as ruby, sappphire, and amythest. *Lumina*, the source of the name, is the Latin word for light.
  Allumina
Alura OE. "Godlike adviser." Same sound as **Allura**, but completely different source.
  Alurea, Allura, Ellura
Alva Sp. "Blond, fair-skinned." See **Alba, Albina**. Also Heb. "Foliage." Better-known as a man's name, as in Thomas Alva Edison.
  Alba, Albina, Albine, Albinia, Alvah, Alvit
Alvar OE. "Army of elves." Also used as a man's name, but very unusual.
Alverdine OE. "Counsel from the elves." A rare feminine variant of **Alfred. Alfreda** is more common.
Alvina (Fem. Alvin) OE. "Noble friend" or "Elf-friend."
  Alveena, Alveene, Alveenia, Alvine, Alvineea, Alvinia, Alwinna, Alwyna, Alwyne, Elveena, Elvena, Elvene, Elvenia, Elvina, Elvine, Elvinia, Vina, Vinni, Vinnie, Vinny

Alvita Lat. "Lively."

Alysia Gk. "Entrancing."

Alyssa Gk. "Rational." Also the name of a bright yellow flower, alyssum, and its use may have been influenced by the 19th-century vogue for flower names. Also see the variants of **Alice**. Currently extremely fashionable among American parents.

Alissa, Allissa, Alysa, Ilyssa, Lyssa

Alzena Arab. "Woman."

Alzeena, Alzeina, Alzina, Elzeena, Elzina

Ama Ghanaian. "Born on Saturday."

Amabel Lat. "Lovable, amiable." Somewhat popular in the 19th century.

Ama, Amabelle, Belle, Mab, Mabel

Amada Lat. "Loved one."

Amata

Amadea (Fem. **Amadeus**) Lat. "God's beloved." Amadeus was Mozart's middle name, given great prominence by Peter Shaffer's play and the subsequent film.

Amadée, Amedée

Amadore It. "Gift of love."

Amadora

Amal Arab. "Hope."

Amahl, Amahla, Amala

Amalfi Place name: spectacular Italian town and section of coastline overlooking the Gulf of Salerno.

Amalfey, Malfie

Amalida OG. "Hardworking woman." See **Amelia**.

Amaleeda, Amelida

Amalthea In Greek mythology, the name of the mountain goat that nursed the infant Zeus. Her horns were the basis for the cornucopia, the horn of plenty spilling over with fruits and vegetables.

Amaltheia

Amana Heb. "Loyal, true."

Amanda Lat. "Much-loved." Regularly used since the 17th century, and extremely fashionable in the U.S. during the 1980s and 1990s. Use is dwindling now, however.

Actresses Amanda Plummer, Amanda Peet; pop musician Mandy Moore.

Amandi, Amandie, Amandine, Amandy, Amata, Manda, Mandaline, Mandee, Mandi, Mandie, Mandy

Amapola Sp. from Arab. "Poppy."

Ama, Ammapola, Pola, Poli

Amara Gk. "Lovely forever."

Amargo, Amargoe, Amargot, Amarinda, Amarra, Amarrinda, Mara, Marra

Amarantha Gk. "Deathless." Also the name of both a mythical and a real plant. The mythical one was supposed to be immortal.

Amarande, Amaranta, Amarante, Amaranthe

Amarilla Ger. "Shiny" or Sp. "Yellow." There is a city in Texas called Amarillo.

Amaris Heb. "Pledged by God."

Amariah, Amarit

Amaryllis Gk. "Fresh." Also the name of a flower. Used in 18th-century poetry to refer to an unspoiled rural beauty like an idealized shepherdess.

Amarilis

Amber OF. Name of the gold-brown semiprecious stone. Jewel names were popular in the 19th century, but Amber came to prominence again in the 1960s, prompted by the Kathleen Winsor novel and film, *Forever Amber*. Perhaps because it is a good descriptive name for a golden-skinned baby, Amber is quite well used today. Model Amber Valletta.

Ambar, Amberetta, Amberly, Ambur

Amberly Comb. form **Amber** and **Kimberly**. Or perhaps the popular Amber with the also popular "-ly" ending.

Ambarlie, Amberlea, Amberleight, Amberlie, Amberley

Ambika Hindi. "Mother." Also one of many names for the goddess Devi, wife of Shiva. She has both positive and negative forms, with names for each.

Ambeeka, Ambeika

Ambrosine (Fem. **Ambrose**) Gk. "Ever-living." Like other names with an "-ine" ending, this one has a French air.

Ambrosia, Ambrosina, Ambrosinetta, Ambrosinette, Ambrosiya, Ambrozetta, Ambrozia, Ambrozine

Amelia OG. "Industrious." See **Emily**. An 18th-century Princess Amelia brought the name to Britain, where it was popular in the 19th century. Unusual now, but ripe for a revival. Dress reformer Amelia Bloomer; aviatrix Amelia Earhart.

Aimiliona, Amalea, Amalee, Amaleta, Amalia, Amalie, Amalija, Amalina, Amaline, Amalita, Amaliya, Amalya, Amalyna, Amalyne, Amalyta, Amelie, Amelina, Ameline, Amelita, Ameliya, Amelyna, Amelyne, Amelyta, Amilia, Amy, Em, Emelie, Emelina, Emeline, Emelita, Emma, Emmeline, Emmie, Emmy, Mali, Malia, Malika, Melia, Meline, Millie, Milly

Amelinda Lat./Sp. Comb. form "Beloved" and "Pretty."

Amalinda, Amalynda, Amelindah, Amellinda

Amethyst Gk. "Precious wine-colored jewel." An unusual jewel name, though appropriate for a February baby, since amethyst is that month's birthstone.

Amathyst, Amatista, Amethist, Amethiste

Amica Lat. "Friend." Very unusual. Closely related to Spanish *amiga* or Italian *amica*, the everyday words for "friend" in those languages.

Amicah, Amice, Amika

Amilia Lat. "Amiable." Also possible variant spelling for **Amelia** or **Emilia**, though it comes from a different root than the latter.

Amiliya, Amillia, Amilya

Amina Arab. "Honest, trustworthy." Mother of the prophet Muhammad.

Ameena, Aminah, Amyna

Aminta Lat. "Protector." Aminta was the heroine of a well-known pastoral play of the Renaissance, but her name was not much used in real life.

Amintah, Amynta, Eminta, Minta, Minty

Amira Arab. "Highborn girl." Currently popular in the Arabic-speaking countries.

Ameera, Ameerah, Amera, Amerah, Amirah, Amyra, Amyrah, Meera, Meerah, Mera, Merah, Mira, Mirah

Amisa Heb. "Companion, friend."
   Amissa
Amita Heb. "Truth" or It. "Friendship." See **Amica, Amy**.
Amitola Native American. "Rainbow."
Amity Lat. "Friendship, harmony." Could be promoted to the 21st-century version of the virtue names (Prudence, Charity), so popular with the Puritans.
   Amitie
Amor Sp. "Love."
   Amora, Amore, Amorra
Amorette Fr. "Little love."
   Amoretta
Amy Lat. "Loved." In spite of the prominence given the name by Louisa May Alcott's *Little Women*, and the 1995 film version, it didn't become a favorite until the 1950s. Hugely popular (along with Jennifer) in the 1970s. High-achieving Amys of that generation like Olympic swimmer Amy Van Dyken and actress Amy Madigan are now becoming famous, but today's parents (many named Amy) will probably feel the name is dated. Parents in the British Isles don't seem to have that problem: Amy is a top-ten name in both Scotland and Ireland. Poet Amy Lowell; evangelist Aimée Semple McPherson; singer Amy Grant; actress Amy Sedaris.
   Aimée, Aimie, Amada, Amata, Amé, Amecia, Ami, Amia, Amiah, Amice, Amie, Amii, Amye, Esma, Esmé
Anafa Heb. "Heron."
Analilia Comb. form **Ana** and **Lilia**.
Ananda Hindi. "Bliss."
   Anda
Anastasia Gk. "Resurrection." Indelibly associated with the daughter of Czar Nicholas II who was rumored to have escaped death when her family was assassinated during the Russian Revolution. The 1956 film starring Ingrid Bergman popularized her story, but the name is still something of a mouthful. Short forms like **Stacey** are much more common. Actress Nastassja Kinski.
   Ana, Anastaise, Anastase, Anastasie, Anastasija, Anastasiya, Anastassia, Anastay, Anasztaizia, Anasz-

tasia, Anestassia, Anstass, Anstice, Asia, Nastassia, Nastassiya, Nastassja, Nastassya, Nastya, Stace, Stacey, Stacia, Stacie, Stacy, Stasiya, Stasja, Stasya, Taisie, Tasenka, Tasia, Tasiya, Tasja, Tasya

Anat Heb. "To sing."

Anath

Anatola Gk. "From the east." Anatolia is a region of Turkey, Greece's nearest neighbor to the East. In fact the ancient city of Troy, site of the legendary Trojan War, is actually in Turkey.

Anatolia, Anatolya

Ancelote Fr. Fem. **Lancelot**, the famous knight of the Round Table.

Andrea (Fem. **Andrew**) Gk. "A man's woman." Used very steadily without ever becoming truly fashionable. Actresses Andie MacDowell, Andrea McArdle.

Aindrea, Andee, Andere, Anderea, Andi, Andie, Andra, Andre, Andreana, Andreas, Andrée, Andrel, Andresa, Andrewena, Andrewina, Andri, Andria, Andriana, Andy, Aundrea, Ohndrea, Ohndreea, Ohndria, Ondrea, Ondreea, Ondria, Onndrea, Onndreea, Onndria

Andromeda Gk. In Greek mythology, the beautiful daughter of Cassiopeia (now famous as a constellation), she was chained to a rock as a sacrifice to a sea monster until Perseus rescued her. She, too, became a star. Also the name of a spring-blooming shrub.

Anemone Gk. "Breath." In Greek mythology, Anemone was the name of a nymph who was turned into a flower, which is also called a windflower.

Anemona, Ann-Aymone, Anne-Aymone

Angela Gk. "Messenger from God, angel." **Angel** was originally used as a name for men, and in Latin countries **Angelo** is still popular. Angela came into frequent use in the early 20th century, and is still used often enough to be very familiar. Actresses Angela Lansbury, Angie Dickinson, Angela Bassett, Angelina Jolie, Angie Harmon.

Aingeal, Ange, Angel, Angele, Angeleta, Angelica, Angelika, Angeliki, Angelina, Angeline, Angelique, Angelita, Angelle, Angellina, Angie, Angil, Angiola, Angy,

Angyola, Anjel, Anjela, Anjelica, Anjelika, Anngela, Anngil, Anngilla, Anngiola, Annjela, Annijilla, Gelya

Angelica Lat. "Angelic." See **Angela**. Actress Anjelica Huston.

Angelika, Angelique, Angyalka, Anjelica, Anjelika

Angharad Welsh. "Beloved."

Anice Var. **Agnes**. Also possibly a variant of **Ann**, or even of **Anise**.

Anicka, Annice, Annick, Anis, Annis, Annys

Aniceta Sp. from Ger. "Unconquerable." Saint Anicetus was a 2nd-century pope and a martyr. The name also sounds a great deal like **Anisette**, which has an utterly different source.

Anicetta, Anniceta, Annicetta

Anina Aramaic. "Let my prayer be answered."

Aninna, Annina

Anisah Arab. "Friendly, congenial."

Anisa, Annissa

Anise Plant name. The source of licorice flavoring. This name may also be used as a variant of **Agnes** or **Anne**.

Aneese, Anis, Anisette

Anita Sp. form of **Ann**. Most common in 1950s, possibly because of the popularity of Swedish actress Anita Ekberg. Actress Anita Pallenberg; writers Anita Loos, Anita Brookner.

Anitra, Annita, Annitra, Annitta

Ann Anglicization of **Hannah** (Heb. "Grace"). One of the most frequently used names for girls until the mid-19th century, when it became less popular. When Elizabeth II of England named her daughter Anne in 1950, it became more prominent, but is still more common as a middle name (Betty Ann, etc.). Though the name Ann may seem plain to many, its numerous derivatives offer plenty of variety. The European form **Anna** is now much more fashionable than plain old Ann in the United States, and is a top-ten name in Germany, while **Anya** is popular in Russia. Saint Anne (mother of the Virgin Mary); Anne Boleyn, Queen of England; ballerina Anna Pavlova; Wild West sharpshooter Annie Oakley; actresses Anouk Aimée, Anne

Bancroft, Anne Heche, Anna Paquin; writer Ayn Rand; diarist Anne Frank; tennis player Anna Kournikova; golfer Annika Sorenstam.

Aine, Ana, Anci, Anechka, Anet, Anett, Anette, Ania, Anica, Anika, Aniko, Anissa, Anita, Anitra, Anka, Anke, Anki, Anna, Annabel, Annabella, Annabelle, Annaelle, Annelle, Annelore, Annetta, Annette, Anni, Annice, Annick, Annie, Annimae, Annina, Annis, Annise, Annora, Annus, Annuska, Anny, Anona, Anouche, Anouk, Anoushka, Anouska, Anushka, Anuska, Anya, Anyoushka, Anyshka, Anyu, Asya, Ayn, Hajna, Hana, Hanja, Hanka, Hanna, Hannah, Hanneke, Hannelore, Hanni, Hannie, Hanny, Nam, Nana, Nance, Nancee, Nancey, Nanci, Nancie, Nancy, Nanete, Nanette, Nanice, Nanine, Nanni, Nannie, Nanny, Nanon, Nanor, Neti, Nettia, Nettie, Netty, Nina, Ninette, Ninon, Ninor, Nita, Nona, Nonie

Annabel Possibly comb. form **Anna** and **Belle**: "Graceful" and "Beautiful." Also mutation of **Amabel**. Most famous bearer was Edgar Allan Poe's Annabel Lee, in the poem of the same name.

Anabel, Anabella, Anabelle, Annabal, Annabelinda, Annabell, Annabella, Annabelle

Annamaria Comb. form **Ann** and **Mary**. **Annemarie** is the most popular variation, especially since the 1950s. The reverse form, **Marianne**, is also frequently used. The popularity of the pairing may originate in Roman Catholic veneration of Saint Anne and Saint Mary, mother and daughter.

Annamarie, Annemarie, Annmaria

Annalise Comb. form **Ann** and **Lise**.

Analeisa, Analiesa, Analiese, Analise, Anelisa, Anelise, Annaleisa, Annalie, Annaliesa, Annaliese, Annalise, Annelie, Anneliese, Annelisa, Annelise, Annissa

Annemae Comb. form. **Ann** and **May**.

Annamae, Annamay, Annemie

Annette Dim. **Ann**. Elaborated forms like **Annetta** may also be considered variations of **Agnes**. Actress Annette Bening.

Anet, Anett, Anetta, Annetta

Annis Gk. "Finished, completed." See also variants of **Ann**. Also easily confused by the ear with **Agnes**, a point prospective parents might keep in mind.
Anissa, Annes, Annice, Annys

Annora Lat. "Honor." A phonetic version of **Honora**.
Anora, Anorah, Honor, Honora, Onora, Nora, Norah

Annwyl Welsh. "Loved one."
Annwyll, Anwylle

Anona Lat. from Sp. "Pineapple." A name likely to be used for its pretty sound rather than for its meaning.

Anouska Rus. Var. **Ann**.
Annouska, Annushka, Anusha, Anyoushka

Annunciata Lat. Allusion to the Annunciation, when the Virgin Mary learned she would be Jesus' mother. Sometimes given to a girl born in March, the logical month for such an announcement.
Anonciada, Annunziate, Anunciacion, Anunciata, Anunziata

Annot Heb./Scot. "Light."

Anonna Lat. Name of the Roman goddess of the annual harvest. An appropriate name for an October or November baby.
Anona, Nona

Anselma (Fem. **Anselm**) OG. "Godly helmet." The short forms are much more common.
Selma, Zelma

Ansley OE. Place name: "The awesome one's meadow." Probably not, in spite of the way it sounds, "Ann's meadow" because women so rarely owned property in the days when last names were coming into existence. An alternative to **Ashley**.
Annesleigh, Annslea, Annsleigh, Anslea, Ansleigh, Anslie

Ansonia (Fem. **Anson**). Unclear origin and meaning. Possibly "Son of Ann," though "Son of the divine" seems more likely. It can even be considered a combined form of **Ann** and **Sonia**.
Annesonia, Annsonia, Annsonya, Ansonya

Antalya Rus. from Gk. "From the East." A variant of **Ana-**

tola. Also an anagram of the popular Russian **Natalya**, which means Christmas.

Antaliya

Anthea Gk. "Flowerlike." Used by English 17th-century poets to symbolize spring, but occurring infrequently in real life. Slightly more popular in England, where it has an upper-class aura.

Annthea, Anthe, Antheia, Antheya, Antia, Thia

Anthemia Gk. "In bloom." From the same Greek root as Anthea.

Antheemia, Anthemya, Anthymia

Antje Ger. Var. **Ann** (Heb. "Grace").

Antigone Gk. In mythology, the daughter of Oedipus.

Antoinette (Fem. **Anthony**) Lat. "Beyond price, invaluable." Also a diminutive of **Ann**. Irresistibly associated with the ill-fated French Queen Marie Antoinette. Ballerina Antoinette Sibley.

Antonetta, Antonia, Antonie, Antonietta, Antonina, Antonine, Antwahnette, Antwanetta, Antwinett, Netta, Netti, Nettie, Netty, Toinette, Toni, Tonia, Tonie, Tony, Tonye

Antonia Lat. "Beyond price, invaluable." Also a diminutive of **Ann**. The increasing popularity of dignified Latinate names may bring this one to greater prominence. Willa Cather novel *My Antonía*; English writer Antonia Fraser.

Antoinette, Antonetta, Antonie, Antonietta, Antonija, Antoniya, Antonina, Antonya, Netta, Nettie, Netty, Toinette, Tonechka, Tonette, Toni, Tonia, Tonie, Tony, Tonya

Anwen Welsh. "Very fair."

Anwyn

Anwar Arab. "Rays of light." Most familiar as a man's name borne by Egyptian President Anwar Sadat.

Aphra Heb. "Dust." The English Puritans actually used both Dust and Ashes as first names in the 17th century. Playwright Aphra Behn.

Affera, Affery, Afra

Apolline (Fem. **Apollo**) Gk. The god of the sun in Greek

NAME TRIVIA

- Puritan William Brewster sailed for America on the Mayflower in 1620. With him were his two sons, who had the classic Puritan names of Love and Wrestling.
- *Wall Street Journal* editor Vermont Royster was born in 1914 and named for his grandfather. Grandfather Royster had this unusual name because his father named all of his children for states in the Union.
- American painter Charles Wilson Peale had eleven children, all named after famous painters. Three of them—Raphaelle, Titian, and Rembrandt—actually lived out their father's obvious desires and became painters themselves.
- The first child born in an English colony in North America was Virginia Dare. Born in 1587 in Roanoke, Virginia, she was named after Elizabeth I, England's Virgin Queen.
- The nun known to the world as Mother Teresa was born in Albania and christened Agnes Gonsha Bojaxhiu.
- The Marx Brothers changed their names as they developed their comic act. Harpo was originally known as Arthur, Chico as Leonard, and Groucho as Julius Henry. It's enough to make you wonder if the Seven Dwarves didn't have different names before they met up with Walt Disney.
- Distinguished author Toni Morrison's original name was Chloe Anthony Wofford.
- Boxing champion George Foreman has four sons, all of whom are named George.
- Zane has recently become mildly trendy among urban intellectual types, as a boy's name redolent of the Wild West. Zane Grey was the author of the immensely popular *Riders of the Purple Sage* and dozens of other Western novels. He himself, though, was born in Zanesville, Ohio, with the jokey name of Pearl Grey. It's no wonder he turned tough-guy after that.
- Samuel Clemens, better known to posterity as Mark Twain, had a brother named Orion. He himself took a

while to settle on Mark Twain as his pseudonym: Other names he tried included Sergeant Fathom and W. Apaminondas Adrastus Blab.

- The name Jennifer may be considered the first truly trendy name. In 1960 it was only around 71 on the list of most popular names; by 1970, it was number one.
- Names that are extremely fashionable are also likely to go out of fashion: Betty, a top-five name in 1930, is now almost never used. Other outdated names from the 30s are Dorothy, Doris, and Shirley.
- The best-used boy's names over the last 40 years are James, John, Joseph, Richard, Robert, Thomas, and William. Boys' names that have become fashionable and then faded away are Donald, Ronald, Gary, and Mark.
- On some baby name lists, Tristan is used almost as often as Jason. Other surprises in the middle ranks are Connor, Caleb, Logan, and Dakota.
- The new category of geography names seems to be taking hold for girls: Savannah occurs quite often, with Sierra some distance behind.
- When flower names were first used, in the 19th century, it was home-grown English flowers that became popular, like Violet and Rose. The only popular flower name now is the exotic Jasmine, which may have been boosted to that point by the Walt Disney version of *Aladdin*.
- Football player Deion Sanders, widely acknowledged to be a brilliant athlete, has never been one to hide his light under a bushel. His estimation of himself is clear in the names chosen for his two eldest children: Deion, Jr., and Deiondra.
- Some people just can't resist a pun: There are folks in U.S. phone books with the names Frank N. Stein, Minnie Vann, and M.T. Head.
- Looking for inspiration? Turn to Detroit—or to Japan. Children have recently been given the following car names: Transam, Tercel, Corvette, Neon, Ferrari and Porsche.

mythology. Saint Apollonia was an early Christian martyr. Her teeth were knocked out as part of her martyrdom. In art she is often portrayed with a pair of tongs and an outsized molar.

Abbeline, Abbelina, Appoline, Appolinia, Apollinia, Apollonia, Apollyne, Appolonia

Aponi Native American. "Butterfly."

Aponee

Apple Fruit name. For no very clear reason, fruits are underrepresented among names: **Cherry** is the only one in common usage. Yet we say that a much loved person is "the apple of my eye."

April Lat. "Opening up." First used as a name in the 20th century, and occurs most often for a girl born in that month. Curiously, only the months **April**, **May**, and **June** are used regularly for names, with June the most popular. Pop musician Avril Lavigne.

Aipril, Aprilete, Aprill, Aprille, Averel, Averell, Averil, Averill, Averyl, Averyll, Averylle, Avril, Avrill

Aquilina (Fem. **Aquilino**) Sp. "Like an eagle."

Ara Arab. "Brings rain."

Ari, Aria, Arria

Arabella Lat. "Answered prayer." Unusual name that occurs most frequently in England, where it has an upper-class aura. A ship named the *Arbella* brought a group of Puritan English aristocrats to the Massachusetts Bay Colony in 1630: many socially prominent Boston families are descended from this group.

Ara, Arabel, Arabela, Arabele, Arabelle, Arbela, Arbell, Arbella, Arbelle, Bel, Bella, Belle, Orabel, Orabella, Orabelle, Orbel, Orbella, Orbelle

Araceli Sp. from Lat. "Altar of heaven."

Aracelis, Ariceli, Aricelly

Arachne Gk. In mythology, a young maiden who challenged the goddess Athena to a weaving contest and was turned into a spider for her presumption. Spiders, as a biological group, are known as "arachnids."

Arakne, Archna

Araminta Comb. form **Arabella** and **Aminta**. Invented by an 18th-century English playwright, and very unusual.

Arava Heb. "Willow" or "Arid land." The willow is one of the four kinds of wood used at Sukkoth, the Jewish harvest festival.

Aravah

Arcadia Gk. Originally the place name of a region in Greece which eventually came to stand for the home of simple pastoral happiness, and later still for Paradise itself.

Arcadie

Arcangela Gk. "High-ranking angel." Archangels rank above angels in the celestial hierarchy (which also includes seraphim, cherubim, thrones, principalities, and powers).

Arcangel, Archangela, Archangella

Arcelia Sp. "Treasure chest."

Aricelia, Aricelly

Arda Heb. "Bronze."

Ardah, Ardath

Ardelle Lat. "Burning with enthusiasm." See **Arden**.

Arda, Ardeen, Ardelia, Ardelis, Ardella, Ardene, Ardia, Ardine, Ardis, Ardra

Arden Lat. "Burning with enthusiasm." The Forest of Arden in Shakespeare's *As You Like It* was a magically beautiful place. Most famous in modern times as the surnames of cosmetics queen Elizabeth Arden and actress Eve Arden. Great potential for a 21st-century girls' name.

Ardeen, Ardena, Ardenia, Ardin, Ardis

Arella Heb. "Messenger from God, angel."

Arela, Arelle

Arete Gk. "Woman of virtue." Singer Aretha Franklin has put an indelible stamp on her version of this name.

Areta, Aretha, Arethusa, Aretina, Aretta, Arette, Oreta, Oretha, Oretta, Orette, Retha

Arethusa In Greek mythology, Arethusa was a nymph pursued by a river god, who was changed by Artemis into a stream to avoid a fate worse than death.

Argenta Lat. "Silvery." The country of Argentina is named for the silver its early Spanish settlers hoped to find there—but did not.

Argentia, Argentina

Aria It. "A melody." In the classical operatic form, arias are solos performed by the leading characters.

Ariadne Gk. The mythological daughter of Cretan King Minos, who gave Theseus a thread to guide him out of the mazelike prison known as the Labyrinth. Theseus married, then abandoned, her. Also the subject and title of a Richard Strauss opera.

Arene, Ariadna, Ariana, Ariane, Arianie, Arianna, Arianne, Aryana, Aryane, Aryanie, Aryanna, Aryanne

Ariana Welsh. "Like silver." This is also the Italian version of **Ariadne**. Political commentator Arianna Stassinopolous Huffington.

Ariane, Arianna

Arianwyn Welsh. "Woman of silver."

Ariel Heb. "Lioness of God." In Shakespeare's *The Tempest*, Ariel is a sprite who can disappear at will. The name has the connotation of something otherworldly, and though Shakespeare's Ariel is male, the name is used mostly for girls.

Aeriel, Aeriela, Aeriell, Ariela, Ariella, Arielle, Ariellel

Arista Gk. "The best." The root of our word "aristocrat."

Aristella, Aristelle

Arizona Place name: southwestern U.S. state. The name comes from an Indian word thought to mean "small spring."

Arlene Derivation unclear. Possibly Dim. **Charles** (OE. "Man") or Fem. **Arlen** (related to Gael. "Pledge"). The name first appeared in the mid-19th century, and was popular by the 1930s, though hardly ever used now. Actresses Arlene Francis, Arlene Dahl.

Arla, Arlana, Arlee, Arleen, Arlen, Arlena, Arleta, Arlette, Arleyne, Arlie, Arliene, Arlina, Arlinda, Arline, Arluene, Arly, Arlyn, Arlyne, Arlynn, Lena, Lene, Lina

Arlette Fr. From **Charles** (OE. "Man").

Arlet, Arletta

Arlise (Fem. **Arliss**) Heb. "Pledge."

Arlyse, Arlyss

Armande (Fem. **Armand**) Fr. from OG. "Army man."
   Armanda, Armonde, Ormonde
Armida Lat. "Little armed one."
Armina (Fem. **Armand**) It. from OG. "Army man." **Herman** is another masculine form of the name that both **Armande** and **Armina** are based on.
   Armantine, Armeena, Armine, Arminie, Armyne, Erminia, Erminie, Ermyne
Armona Heb. "Chestnut brown."
   Armonit
Arnalda (Fem. **Arnold**) OG. "Eagle-strength."
   Arnolda
Arnett OE. "Small eagle."
   Arnette, Ornett, Ornetta, Ornette, Orrnett
Arnina (Fem. **Aaron**) Heb. "On high."
   Arna, Arona, Arnice, Arnit
Arsenia (Feb. **Arsenio**) Sp. from Gk. "Manly." This name was little known outside the Spanish-speaking community until comedian Arsenio Hall brought it to notice.
   Arcenia, Arsania, Arsemia
Artemisia Gk./Sp. "Perfect." Also a version of Artemas, a man's name that occurs in the Bible. Better known these days as the name of a shrub fairly common in the U.S., though the colorful life of 17th-century Italian painter Artemisia Gentileschi has recently attracted the attention of novelists and biographers.
   Artemesia
Artha Hindi. "Riches."
Arthuretta (Fem. **Arthur**) Celt. Possibly "Bear" or "Rock." A 19th-century version of the man's name that was very popular until about 1920. The women's forms never really caught on.
   Artheia, Arthelia, Arthene, Arthurene, Arthurette, Arthurina, Arthurine, Artia, Artice, Artina, Artis, Artlette, Artrice
Arza Heb. "Panels of cedar." The walls of Solomon's temple were lined with cedar.
   Ariza, Arzit, Arzice, Arzit
Asención Sp. Literally "ascension," marking Christ's as-

cension into heaven, which is commemorated 40 days after Easter. The capital of Paraguay is Asunción.
Asunción

Ashanti Af. Area in West Africa where many American slaves came from. Used in modern American black families as a link to the African past. The "-i" ending, which is so close to the English diminutives "-ie" or "-y," seems to make it more popular for girls.
Ashanta, Ashantae, Ashantay, Ashante, Ashantee, Ashaunta, Ashaunte, Ashauntee, Ashaunti, Ashuntae, Shantee, Shanti, Shauntae, Shauntee

Ashira Heb. "Rich" or "I will sing."
Asheera, Ashirah

Ashra (Fem. Asher) Heb. "Fortunate, felicitous."
Asheera, Ashirah

Ashby OE. Place name: "Ash tree farm." The definitions of all of these "Ash-" names are virtually irrelevant, since the popularity of **Ashley** has long since eclipsed any meaning the name once had. Related names may gain popularity from it, or the backlash may already have begun, and the tide of fashion may be moving on to distinctly non-Ashley names.
Ashbea, Ashbie

Ashley OE. Place name: "Ash-tree meadow." Originally a surname that migrated to first-name status, possibly helped along by Ashley Wilkes in Margaret Mitchell's *Gone With the Wind*. Though originally used for boys, it is now tremendously popular for girls, having been in the top ten female names for the last dozen years. It is probably the Waspy nature of the name, with its lingering upper-class aura, that continues to make it such a hit. The immense TV exposure of *Full House*'s Ashley Olsen probably doesn't hurt. Actress Ashley Judd.
Ashely, Ashla, Ashlay, Ashlan, Ashlee, Ashleigh, Ashlen, Ashli, Ashlie, Ashly

Ashlynn (Var. Aisling) Ir. Gael. "Dream." Strictly speaking, this name is a Gaelic adaptation, but parents who use it are more likely to be mentally combining **Ashley** and **Lynn**.
Ashelynn, Ashlin, Ashlinne, Ashlynne

Asia Name of the continent. The feminine "-ia" ending lends itself to adaptation as a girl's name, while the pan-global connotations may give it a boost in the next decade.
Aja, Asiah, Azha

Asima Arab. "Guardian."

Asma Arab. "Of high standing." Currently popular in the Arab-speaking community.

Aspasia Gk. "Welcoming." The famous Athenian states-man Pericles had a mistress named Aspasia, who was noted for her beauty and wit. Surprisingly the name enjoyed mild popularity in the straitlaced 19th century. Almost unknown now.

Aspen Tree name: a kind of poplar familiar in the West, with heart-shaped leaves that quiver in the lightest breeze, hence its nickname, the "quaking" or "trembling" aspen. Also a chic ski resort and town in Colorado.

Asphodel Gk. "Lily." Flower name, albeit an unusual one. The asphodel is a member of the lily family.
Asfodel, Asfodelle, Asphodelle

Assunta It. "Raised up." From the Assumption of the Virgin Mary, the day she was raised up to heaven. The feast of the Assumption is celebrated on August 15. **Asunción**, the Spanish term, is also used as a girl's name.

Asta Gk. "Like a star." Also short form of **Anastasia, Astrid, Augusta**, etc. The most famous Asta is probably the terrier owned by Nick and Nora Charles in the famous Thin Man movies of the 1930s.
Astera, Asteria, Asti, Astra, Estella, Esther, Estrella, Etoile, Hadassah, Hester, Stella

Asteria Greek mythology name: Asteria was a woman whom Zeus took a fancy to. She was changed into a quail to escape him.

Astra Lat. "Starlike, of the stars." First appeared in the 1940s, though other "star names," like Estella, have been around longer.
Asta, Astera, Asteria, Asterina, Astraea, Astrea, Astri, Astria

Astraea Gk. The goddess of justice in classical mythology.

When she retired from the earth, according to legend, she became the constellation Virgo. A clever name for a girl born under that sign.

Astraeia

Astrid ONorse. "Beautiful like a god." Unusual in English-speaking countries, but occurs in the royal families of Norway and Belgium. Brazilian singer Astrud Gilberto.

Assi, Astra, Astri, Astride, Astrud, Astryr, Atti

Asunción Sp. Marking the Virgin Mary's ascent into Heaven, which is commemorated on August 15. Also the name of the capital city of Paraguay.

Asención

Atalanta (Fem. **Atlas**) Gk. "Immovable." In Greek mythology, Atalanta was an extremely athletic young maiden who refused to marry any man who couldn't beat her in a foot race. In the end, she was defeated by a ruse involving three golden apples.

Atlanta, Atlante

Atara Heb. "Diadem."

Atera, Ateret

Athalia Heb. "The Lord is exalted." In the Old Testament, Athalia was wife of the King of Judah. She murdered 42 princes to win the throne for herself, and after a reign of six years, was ultimately killed by a mob. A pretty name if you can overlook the history.

Atalee, Atalia, Atalie, Athalee, Athalie, Attalie

Athanasia (Fem. **Athanasius**) Gk. "Immortal."

Atanasia, Atanasya, Athenasia

Athena Gk. The goddess of wisdom in Greek myth. She was a virgin goddess who sprang fully armed from Zeus's head, and Homer, in the *Odyssey*, frequently refers to her as "gray-eyed Athena." A daunting name to live up to.

Athenais, Athene, Athie, Athina, Attie

Atifa Arab. "Empathy, affection."

Ateefa, Ateefah, Atifah

Aubrey OF. "Elf ruler." Originally a man's name that arrived in England with the Norman Conquest. For a girl, the ear will readily confuse it with **Audrey**, which may explain why the name has not caught on as readily as some other previously male names like **Ashley**.

Aubary, Aubery, Aubree, Aubreigh, Aubrette, Aubrie, Aubry, Aubury

Auda OF. "Prosperous."

Aud, Aude

Audrey OE. "Noble strength." Also the root, via Saint Audrey, for the word "tawdry." (In England, cheap and gaudy necklaces used to be sold at Saint Audrey's Fair.) Most popular in the 1920s and 1930s, now out of fashion. Actress Audrey Hepburn.

Audi, Audie, Audra, Audre, Audree, Audreen, Audria, Audrie, Audry, Audrye

Audris OG. "Lucky."

Audriss

Augusta (Fem. **Augustus**) Lat. "Worthy of respect." Imported to England by the German mother of George III. Though common enough in the 18th and 19th centuries, it is little used now. P.G. Wodehouse's foppish hero Bertie Wooster had a terrifying Aunt Augusta, and she may be responsible for the slightly intimidating connotations of the name. It can't help that the most logical diminutive is **Gussie**.

Auguste, Augustia, Augustina, Augustine, Augustyna, Augustyne, Austina, Austine, Austyna, Austyne, Gus, Gussie, Gusta, Tina

Aura Gk. "Soft breeze" or Lat. "Gold." Most familiar now, perhaps, in its psychic sense, meaning the atmosphere surrounding an individual.

Aure, Aurea, Auria, Oria

Aurelia Lat. "Gold." Originally a name used by Roman clans, it resurfaced as a first name in the 19th century, but is seldom seen now.

Aranka, Aural, Auralia, Aurea, Aurel, Aureliana, Aurélie, Aurelina, Aurita, Ora, Oralia, Orel, Orelee, Orelia

Auriel Lat. Dim. "Golden." Not to be confused with **Ariel**. A name used for slaves in the Roman Empire, possibly as a descriptive term. The 19th-century penchant for unusual names brought it back to occasional use, but it is rare now.

Aureola, Aureole, Auriol, Oriel, Oriole

Aurora Lat. "Dawn." Aurora was the Roman goddess of sunrise. Used by 19th-century poets such as Byron and Browning, but never common. In some version of the fairy tale *Sleeping Beauty*, the princess's name is Aurora.

Aurore, Ora, Rora, Rory, Zora, Zorica

Austine (Fem. **Austin** or **Augustine**) Lat. "Worthy of respect."

Autumn Season name, only recently used as a first name.

Ava Lat. "Like a bird." May have originated as a form of **Eva**. Actress Ava Gardner.

Avis

Avalon Celt. "Island of apples." In Celtic mythology, Avalon is an island paradise. In Arthurian legend, it is the island where King Arthur took refuge after his final defeat, and whence he will reappear.

Ave Lat. "Hail."

Avena Lat. "Field of oats."

Avichayil Heb. "Strong father." The Anglicized version is Abigail.

Abichail, Avigail, Avigayil

Aviela Heb. "My father is God."

Aviella

Aviva Heb. "Springlike, fresh, dewy."

Avivah, Avivi, Avivit, Viva, Auvit

Avril A French version of **April**, the month name. Also possibly a version of the name of a 7th-century saint, Everild. Pop musician Avril Lavigne.

Averel, Averell, Averil, Averill, Averyl

Axelle (Fem. **Axel**) OG. "Father of peace."

Axella

Aya Heb. "Bird."

Ayla

Ayanna Recently invented name that may be considered an elaboration of **Anna**, or of the typically feminine "-ana" ending. Probably popular because it sounds pretty.

Aivana, Aivanna, Avana, Avania, Avannia, Iana, Ianna

THEY NAMED THE BABY *WHAT?*

Unless you've been hibernating for the past fifteen years, you know that Bruce Willis and Demi Moore chose, well, *unusual* names for their daughters (Rumer, Scout, and Tallulah). Presumably if your name is Demi you feel perfectly comfortable with startling names. Then again, sometimes it's hard to believe that celebrity parents have spared a thought for their children: Film director Jonathan Demme named a daughter Brooklyn because he liked the way the name sounded—forget the borough, forget the Dodgers, forget the accent. Or do they reason that Chastity Bono and Moon Unit Zappa seem all right, so it's fine to name your child anything? Look at the following remarkable names:

- Kate Capshaw & Steven Spielberg: Destry Allyn
- Kim Basinger & Alec Baldwin: Ireland Eliesse
- Kim Falconer & Robert Downey, Jr.: Indio
- Sting & Trudie Styler: Giacomo Luke
- Robby Benson & Karla DeVito: Zephyr
- John Mellencamp: Speck
- John Travolta & Kelly Preston: Jett
- Cecil Fielder (baseball player): Prince
- Nick Nolte: Brawley
- Sylvester Stallone & Sasha Czack: Sage & Seargeoh
- Brian de Palma & Gale Ann Hurd: Lolita
- David and Victoria Beckham: Brooklyn & Romeo
- Bono: Memphis Eve
- Woody & Soon-Yi Allen: Bechet & Manzie
- Cindy Crawford & Rande Gerber: Presley & Kaia
- Helena Christensen & Norman Reedus: Mingus Lucian
- Alex Kingston: Salome
- Christie Brinkley: Sailor

The winner in the preposterous names stakes, however, seems to be English musician Paula Yates. When married to Bob Geldof, she named one daughter Fifi Trixibelle and another Peaches. With singer Michael Hutchence, she had a baby who rejoices in the name of Heavenly Hiraani Tiger Lily.

Ayesha Per. "Small one."

Aza Arab. "Comfort."

Azalea Lat. "Dry earth." More familiar to us as the name of the shrub that produces brilliant blooms in the spring.
Azalia, Azaleia

Azelia Heb. "Aided by God."

Azhar Arab. "Flowers."

Aziza Heb. "Mighty" or Arab. "Precious."

Azuba Meaning unknown. Biblical name, used occasionally from the 17th through 19th centuries.
Azubah, Zuba, Zubah

Azucena Sp. from Arab. "White lily."
Asucena, Asusena, Ayscena, Azusayna, Azusena, Azuzena

Azura OF. "Azure, sky blue." A good attribute name for a blue-eyed baby.
Azor, Azora, Azure, Azzura, Azzurra

Babe Dim. **Barbara** (Gk. "Foreign"). Also short for "baby," as in "See ya, babe," and a term for an attractive woman. The latter, politically incorrect usage will probably limit the number of Babes on birth certificates for the time being. Socialite Babe Paley.

Babette Fr. Dim. **Barbara** (Gk. "Foreign").

Baila Sp. "Dance."
Beyla, Byla

Bailey OE. "Law enforcer, bailiff." A surname that metamorphosed into a first name in the 19th century, though uncommon. Used more often for boys than for girls.
Bailee, Baily

Baja Geography name: the peninsula attached to the southernmost end of California, which forms part of Mexico. The word comes from the Spanish and means "lower."

Bakura Heb. "A ripe fruit."

Balbina Lat. "Little stutterer."
   Balbine
Ballade Name of a musical or poetic form, usually one that tells a story.
Bambi It. "Child." Short for bambina. Of course, the most famous Bambi is Walt Disney's cartoon deer, who happens to be male.
   Bambalina, Bambie, Bambina, Bamby
Baptista Lat. "One who baptizes."
   Baptiste, Batista, Battista, Bautista
Bara Heb. "To select."
   Barah, Bari, Barra, Barrie
Barbara Gk. "Foreign." The adjective was originally applied to anyone who did not speak Greek; it has the same root as "barbarian." The early Christian martyr Saint Barbara was imprisoned in a tower by her father; she is patroness of engineers and architects. The name had its greatest popularity in the 19th-20th centuries, peaking around 1925, when in the U.S. it was second only to **Mary**. Use since then has dropped off dramatically, and in one 1989 poll it didn't even make the top 100. Many people may associate this name with the popular doll Barbie. Actress Barbara Stanwyck; singer Barbra Streisand; writer Barbara Tuchman; First Lady Barbara Bush.
   Bab, Baba, Babara, Babb, Babbett, Babbette, Babbie, Babe, Babett, Babette, Babita, Babs, Baibin, Bairbre, Barb, Barbary, Barbe, Barbee, Barbette, Barbey, Barbi, Barbie, Barbra, Barbro, Barby, Barra, Basha, Basia, Baubie, Bauby, Beba, Berbera, Berberia, Berberya, Berbya, Bobbe, Bobbee, Bobbi, Bobbie, Bobby, Bonni, Bonnie, Bonny, Varvara, Varina
Barcelona Geography name: the second largest city in Spain, and the site of the 1992 Summer Olympics. It was named for its founder, Carthaginian leader Hamilcar Barca. This is also the name of an influential modern chair designed by Mies van der Rohe in 1929.
Barinda Modern name: probably combined from **Barbara** and **Linda**.

Barra Var. **Barrie**; Dim. **Barbara**.

Barrie A place name (Barry Islands, Wales) turned into a surname turned into a first name used by both sexes. Possibly influenced by the fame of Sir James Barrie, author of *Peter Pan*, since it first appeared as a given name during the height of his renown. It can also be considered a more feminine version of **Barry**.

Bari, Barri

Bartha OG. "Shining, brilliant." Var. **Bertha**.

Barta

Basha Pol. "Stranger." From the same root as **Barbara**.

Basia, Basja

Basilia (Fem. **Basil**) Gk. "Royal, regal." Common in the Middle Ages, but very unusual now.

Baseele, Baseelia, Baseelle, Bazeele, Bazeelia, Bazeelle, Basile, Basilie, Basille, Bazile, Bazille, Bazilia

Basma Arab. "A smile."

Baseema, Basima

Bathilda OG. "Woman warrior." Saint Bathild was a young English girl who became queen of the Franks in the 7th century. She was apparently canonized for opposing the then-flourishing slave trade, and also for founding a convent.

Bathild, Bathilde, Batilda, Batilde, Berthilda, Berthilde, Bertilda, Bertilde

Bathsheba Heb. "Daughter of the oath." Biblical name: Bathsheba was the mistress and later the wife of King David. Surprisingly (given her history), the name was used often by the Puritans. Now rare.

Bathseva, Bathshua, Batsheba, Batsheva, Batshua, Batya, Bethsabee, Sheba, Sheva

Bathshira Arab. "Seventh girl-child." Unlikely to be appropriate in this age of small families.

Batya Heb. "God's daughter."

Bitya, Basha

Bay Geographic name (to describe an indentation of land in a coastline) or plant name. The term "bay" is used for several different kinds of trees, including the bay laurel, whose leaves are used as an herb and were also twined into wreaths by the Greeks, to crown victors. The name is equally unusual for girls or boys, and is usually a family name.

Beata Lat. "Blessed." First word of the Latin version of the famous "beatitudes" section of the biblical Sermon on the Mount: "Blessed are the poor in spirit . . ." A popular name in Northern Europe.

Bea, Beate

Beatrice Lat. "Bringer of gladness." The original form, **Beatrix**, was often found in the Middle Ages in England, then forgotten until its Victorian revival as Beatrice. Its popularity was no doubt boosted by Queen Victoria's naming one of her daughters Beatrice. It fell out of fashion after the 1920s and is very rare today. Heroine of Dante's *Divine Comedy* and of Shakespeare's *Much Ado About Nothing*; entertainer Beatrice Lillie; writer Beatrix Potter; actress Bea Arthur; Queen Beatrix of the Netherlands.

Bea, Beah, Beatrisa, Beatrix, Bebe, Bee, Beea, Beeatrice, Beeatris, Beeatrisa, Beeatriss, Beeatrissa, Beeatrix, Beitris, Beitriss, Trix, Trixi, Trixie, Trixy

Bebba Heb. "God's pledge."

Bechira Heb. "The chosen one."

Becky Dim. **Rebecca** (Heb. "Noose"). Often used as an independent first name. Becky Sharp, heroine of William Thackeray's novel *Vanity Fair*.

Beda OE. "Battle maid."

Bedelia Ir. Var. **Bridget** (Ir. Gael. "Strength, power") by way of **Biddy**. There is a popular series of children's books featuring an excessively literal-minded maid named "Amelia Bedelia." Actress Bonnie Bedelia.

Bedeelia, Bidelia, Delia

Bee Dim. **Beatrice** (Lat. "Bringer of gladness"). Also the name of an obscure 7th-century English saint. There is an English village called Saint Bees.

Begonia Flower name: the showy house plant with fleshy leaves and white, yellow, pink or red blossoms. The plant was named for Michel Begon, an 18th-century governor of Santo Domingo.

Behira Heb. "Shining, bright."

Belinda Unclear origin; possibly comb. form **Belle** and **Linda**. Since the name first occurs in 18th-century English poet Alexander Pope's *The Rape of the Lock*, that derivation seems unlikely. It may be related to the Old German for "dragon." Has upper-class English connotations. Pop singer Belinda Carlisle.

Bel, Belle, Bellinda, Bellynda, Belynda, Linda, Lindie, Lindy

Belita Sp. "Little beauty."

Bellita

Bell Dim. **Isabel** (Heb. "Pledged to God"). Also, surname used as a first name.

Bella Lat. "Beautiful." Or Dim. **Isabella** (Heb. "Pledged to God"). Used as early as the Middle Ages, but not popular until the 18th century. Politician Bella Abzug.

Bell, Belle, Bellette

Bellanca It. "Blond."

Bianca, Blanca

Belle Fr. "Beautiful." Enjoyed a brief fad in the 1870s, but almost unheard-of since then except as the name of one of Disney's most popular heroines. This is probably not a recommendation to parents. Author Belva Plain.

Belinda, Belisse, Bell, Bella, Bellina, Belva, Belvia, Billie, Billy

Bellona Lat. "Goddess of battle." From the same root that gives us the English word "bellicose."

Ballona, Belona

Belva Possibly a variant on Bell, though some sources suggest the name has a Latin root and means "beautiful view." It would be very obscure without the fame of author Belva Plain.

Belva

Bena (Fem. **Ben**) Heb. "Wise."

Benedicta (Fem. **Benedict**) Lat. "Blessed." Extremely rare. **Benita** is the more common form.

Benedetta, Bénédicte, Benedictine, Benedikta, Benetta, Benita, Benoite, Bennie, Dixie

Benicia Sp. "Blessed." A town in Northern California.

Benigna Lat. "Kindly, benevolent."

Benita Sp. Var. **Benedicta**. More common than Benedicta, but very unusual in English-speaking countries. Soprano Benita Valente; writer Benita Eisler.

Bendite, Benedetta, Benedicta, Benedikta, Benetta, Benni, Bennie, Benny, Benoite, Binnie, Binny

Benjamina (Fem. **Benjamin**) Heb. "Son of the right hand." Not one of the more common feminizations, despite the recent popularity of **Benjamin** for boys.

Benyameena, Benyamina

Bentley OE. "Meadow of ben (grass)." Place name become surname become first name, more common for boys. Irresistibly linked in most minds with the luxurious English cars.

Bentlea, Bentlee, Bentleigh, Bently

Bera Teut. "Bear."

Beracha Heb. "A blessing." The male name from the same root is **Baruch**.

Barucha, Berucha, Bracha

Berdine OG. "Bright or glowing maiden."

Berengaria OE. "Maiden of the bear-spear." The wife of English King Richard the Lion-Heart.

Berit Scand. "Gorgeous, splendid, magnificent." Currently popular in Sweden.

Beret

Bernadette (Fem. **Bernard**) Fr. "Bear/courageous." Made famous by Saint Bernadette of Lourdes, a miller's daughter who in 1858 repeatedly saw visions of the Virgin Mary. By the time she was canonized in 1933, Lourdes had become a world-famous destination for pilgrims. The name was popular among Catholic families especially after the 1943 movie *Song of Bernadette*, but is now unusual in English-speaking countries. Actress Bernadette Peters.

Benadette, Bennie, Benny, Berna, Bernadeena, Bernadene, Bernadett, Bernadetta, Bernadina, Bernadine, Bernadyna, Bernardina, Bernardine, Bernee, Berneta, Bernetta, Bernette, Bernie, Bernina, Bernita, Berny

Bernice Gk. "She who brings victory." From the same root as **Veronica**. The name appears in the New Testament and first occurred in Britain in the 16th century, but its only real popularity came at the end of the 19th century. Little used today.

Barri, Barrie, Barry, Beranice, Beraniece, Beranyce, Bereniece, Berenice, Berenyce, Berneece, Bernelle, Bernetta, Bernette, Bernee, Berni, Bernie, Berniece, Berny, Bernyce, Berri, Berrie, Berry, Bunni, Bunnie, Bunny, Nixie, Veronica, Veronika, Veronike, Veronique

Berry Nature name. Also diminutive of **Bernice, Bernadette**, etc. Flower names enjoyed a vogue, especially in Britain, in the 1880s. Berry is also used for men, in that case more often as a transferred surname or a diminutive for **Bernard**. Photographer Berry Berenson.

Berree, Berrie

Bertha OG. "Bright." Also related to the name of a Teutonic goddess. Very popular in the late 19th century, but almost unheard of since 1920. This disuse may be explained by the fact that a German cannon used in World War I was nicknamed "Big Bertha" after Bertha Krupp, daughter of the family that manufactured the weapon. In Spain, **Berta** is currently fashionable.

Berrta, Berrte, Berrti, Berrtina, Berrty, Berta, Berte, Berthe, Berti, Bertie, Bertina, Bertine, Bertuska, Berty, Bird, Birdie, Birdy, Birta, Birtha

Bertilde OG. "Bright warrior maiden."

Bertina Ger. "Bright, shining." Dim. **Bertha**.

Bertrade OE. "Bright adviser."

Bertrice Comb. name, possibly **Bertha** and **Bernice**.

Berura Heb. "Pure."

Beruria Heb. "God-selected."

Beryl Gk. "Pale green gemstone." The beryl was considered a token of good luck. The name first appeared with the fashion for jewel names in the late 19th century. Its popularity peaked in the 1920s, and it is now rare. Author Beryl Markham.

Berri, Berrie, Berry, Beryle, Berylla, Beryn

Beta Gk. Second letter of the Greek alphabet. Also a middle-European variant of **Beth**.

Beth Heb. "House." Dim. **Elizabeth** (Heb. "pledged to God"), **Bethany**. In Louisa May Alcott's **Little Women**, Beth is the sweet, gentle sister who dies young.

Bethany Biblical: the name of the village near Jerusalem where Lazarus lived with his sisters Mary and Martha. Because the New Testament includes some vivid descriptions of life in their house, the name has rather domestic, cozy connotations. In some cases a variant on the combined form **Beth-Ann**. Possibly because it sounds like the phenomenally popular **Brittany**, Bethany is very steadily used.

Bethanee, Bethaney, Bethanie, Bethanne, Bethannie, Bethanny, Betheney, Betheny

Bethell Heb. "House of God." Another biblical place name: the spot where Abraham built an altar. Unusual as a first name.

Bethel, Bethell, Bethelle, Bethuel, Bethuna, Bethune

Bethesda Heb. "House of mercy." Bethesda pool in Jerusalem was supposed to have healing powers after being stirred by an angel.

Bethia Heb. "Daughter of Jehovah." Popular in the eras, such as the 17th century, when Old Testament names have been intensively used.

Betia, Bithia

Betsy Dim. **Elizabeth** (Heb. "Pledged to God"). An old nickname for Elizabeth, made famous by Betsy Ross, who supposedly made the first American flag.

Bets, Betsey, Betsie, Betts

Bettina Dim. **Elizabeth** (Heb. "Pledged to God"). Spanish or Italian in origin, and briefly popular in the sixties. One of photographer William Wegman's canine models was named Battina.

Battina, Betiana, Betina, Bettine

Betty Dim. **Elizabeth** (Heb. "Pledged to God"). A nickname with great popularity in its own right. It first became common in the 18th century, and after a spell of disuse, by the 1920s was one of the top names in every English-speaking country. Now it appears most often in combination with other names: Betty Lou, Betty Ann, etc., and rarely at that. Today's parents seeking a diminutive for Elizabeth are more likely to use **Liza** or possibly **Beth**. Actresses Betty Grable and Bette Davis; singer Bette Midler; First Lady Betty Ford.

Bett, Betta, Bette, Betti, Bettie, Bettina, Bettine

Beulah Heb. "Married." Also used to refer to Israel, and in John Bunyan's *The Pilgrim's Progress*, Beulah is the promised land. It first became a girl's name in the late 16th century. References to "Beulah land" appear in American spirituals.

Beula, Bewlah, Byulah

Beverly OE. Place name: "Beaver-stream." Originally an English place name and a surname, then used for both sexes as a first name. Probably still most famous as a place name, referring to Beverly Hills. The English spelling is usually **Beverley**. Singer Beverly Sills.

Bev, Beverle, Beverlee, Beverley, Beverlie, Beverlye, Bevlyn, Bevverlie, Bevverly, Bevvy, Buffy, Verlee, Verlie, Verly, Verlye

Bevinn Ir. Gael. "Singer." More commonly a man's name, although Ireland's famous 11th-century king Brian Boru had a daughter with the name.

Bevan

Bianca It. "White." The meek younger daughter in Shakespeare's *The Taming of the Shrew*, and subject of a song in the spin-off musical *Kiss Me, Kate*. The most famous Bianca in recent times is former Rolling Stone wife Bianca Jagger. A good name for a fair-haired baby.

Biancha, Bianka, Blanca, Blancha

Bibi Arab. "Lady." Actress Bebe Neuwirth.

Bebe, Beebee

Bibiana Sp. Var. **Vivian** (Lat. "Alive").

Bibiane, Bibianna

Biddy Dim. **Bridget** (Ir. Gael. "Strength, power").

Biddie, Bidou

Bienvenida Sp. "Welcome."

Billie OE. Dim. **Wilhelmina** (OG. "Will-helmet"). Feminine use of what is generally considered a man's name; more popular in the South, though uncommon now. Singer Billie Holliday; actress Billie Burke; tennis player Billie Jean King.

Billa, Billee, Billi, Billina, Billy, Willa

Bina Heb. "Knowledge, perception." Also Dim. **Albina, Sabina**, etc.

Binah, Buna

Bird Eng. Unusual nature name. May also be a nickname for **Bertha**.

Birdey, Birdie, Byrd, Byrdie

Birgit Nor. "Splendid." Var. **Bridget**. The Irish popularity of Bridget is based on the appeal of an Irish saint of that name. There was also a Saint Birgitta, who was the patron saint of Sweden.

Birget, Birgetta, Birgitt, Birgitta, Birgitte, Byrget, Byrgitt

Bithron Heb. "Daughter of song."

Blaine Ir. Gael. "Slender." Surname now used as a first name, more usually for boys. Cropped up as a first name in the 1930s. Socialite Blaine Trump.

Blane, Blayne

Blair Scot. Gael. Place name referring to a plain or flat area. Surname now used as a first name, again more common for boys. Like many similarly transferred names, Blair was used for girls in greater numbers in the 1980s and '90s. Very rare now. Actress Blair Brown.

Blaire, Blayre

Blaise Lat. "One who stutters." Used for both sexes, though more common for men. The alternate spelling of **Blaze** probably refers to fire instead.

Blaize, Blase, Blasia, Blaze

Blake OE. Paradoxically, could mean either "pale-skinned" or "dark." Surname used as a first name for either sex, but more common for boys.

Blakelee, Blakeley, Blakely, Blakenee, Blakeney, Blakeny

Blanche Fr. "White, pale." Very popular in America at the end of the 19th century, but unusual now. Blanche DuBois in Tennessee Williams' *A Streetcar Named Desire* does not provide an encouraging role model.

Bellanca, Bianca, Blanca, Blanch, Blanka, Blinny, Branca

Blanchefleur Fr. "White flower."

Blanda Lat. "Smooth, seductive." Saint Blandina was a 2nd-century martyr, a slave girl who was gored to death by a bull.

Blandina, Blandine

Blasia Var. Blaise (Lat. "One who stutters").

Blaise, Blaisia, Blasya, Blaysia

Blessing OE. "Consecration."

Blimah Heb. "Blossom."

Blimah, Blime

Bliss OE. "Intense happiness."

Blisse, Blyss

Blodwen Welsh. "White flower." Literal translation into Welsh of **Blanchefleur**. Little used outside Wales.

Blodwyn, Blodwynne

Blondelle Fr. "Little pale one."

Blondell, Blondie, Blondy

Blossom OE. "Flowerlike." Generic flower name, used mostly at the turn of the 20th century.

Bluebell Flower name popular in the 19th century, though when it became the typical name for a cow (like Rover for a dog), it dropped out of human use.

Blythe OE. "Happy, carefree." Made famous by the opening lines of Shelley's poem "To a Skylark" ("Hail to thee, blithe spirit!") and Noel Coward's play *Blithe Spirit*. Actress Blythe Danner.

Blithe

Bo Chinese. "Precious." More often used as a masculine diminutive for names like **Robert**. Bo Derek, actress.

Beau

Boadicea Name of a heroic queen of early Britain, who led a massive army against Roman invaders. Has rather intimidating connotations.

Bobbie Dim. **Roberta** (OE. "Bright renown"). Like **Billie**, a feminine version of a man's nickname, often used in combination with a monosyllabic second name, and more common in the South. Also derives from **Barbara** (Gk. "Stranger"). Author Bobbie Ann Mason.

Bogdana Pol. "Gift from God."
Bogna, Bohdana

Bolade Nig. "The coming of honor."

Bolanile Nig. "This house's riches."

Bonfilia It. "Good daughter."

Bonita Sp. "Pretty." Popular in the early 1940s, but unusual now.
Bo, Bonie, Bonnie, Bonny, Nita

Bonnie Scot. "Good, fair of face." The Scots adopted the French word *bonne*, meaning "good." Its most common use as an adjective is the fond nickname "Bonnie Prince Charlie." The old nursery rhyme claims that "the child who is born on the Sabbath Day/Is bonny and blithe and good and gay," which makes this an appropriate name for a Sunday's child. Literary types may also remember that Scarlett O'Hara's daughter by Rhett Butler was named "Bonnie Blue." Actress Bonnie Hunt; Olympic speedskater Bonnie Blair.
Bonne, Bonnebell, Bonnee, Bonni, Bonnibel, Bonnibell, Bonnibelle, Bonny, Bunni, Bunnie, Bunny

Borbala Hung. "Foreigner." Var. **Barbara** (Gk. "Stranger").
Bora, Boriska, Borka, Borsala, Borsca

Bracken Plant name: a large coarse fern. Lovers of English literature are familiar with the word, if not the plant itself.

Bradley OE. Place name: "Broad field." Surname now used as a first name for either sex, though more common for boys. Little seen outside America.
Bradlea, Bradlee, Bradleigh, Bradly

Brandy Name of a liquor. In the early 1980s, one of the most popular names for American girls, reaching the top ten in some surveys. Like most trendy names, it has lost favor rather rapidly. Pop singer Brandy.
Brandais, Brande, Brandea, Brandee, Brandi, Brandice, Brandie, Brandye, Branndais, Brannde, Branndea, Branndi, Branndie

Branice Modern invention: possibly a variation of **Janice** (Heb. "The Lord is gracious").

Braulia Sp. from Ger. "Glowing, one who burns." More familiar in the masculine form, **Braulio**.

Brenda (Fem. **Brendan**) OE. "Burning." One source translates the Irish as "stinking hair," though the origin may also be a Norse word for "sword." Brenda was originally a Scottish name and was particularly fashionable in the 1940s. Actress Brenda Vaccaro; comic strip heroine Brenda Starr.

Bren, Brenn, Brennda, Brenndah

Brenna Ir. Gael. "Raven; black-haired." Also dim. **Brendan**.

Bren, Brenn, Brenne, Brennah, Brinna, Brynna, Brynne

Brett Lat. "From Britain." Surname transferred to first name. Still more common for boys.

Brette, Britt

Brianna (Fem. **Brian**) Ir. Gael. Meaning obscure, possibly "Strong" or "Hill." Substantially popular through the late 1990s.

Brana, Breana, Breanne, Breeann, Breeanna, Breeanne, Breena, Bria, Briana, Brianne, Brina, Briney, Brinn, Brinna, Briny, Bryana, Bryann, Bryanna, Bryanne, Bryn, Bryna, Brynne

Brice Obscure origin, possibly OE. "Noble" or Celt. "Swift." Originally a surname. This is the kind of brisk, unisex name that has been eclipsed in recent years by the multisyllabic and feminine (Jessica, Samantha).

Bryce

Bridget Ir. Gael. "Strength, power." May also derive from the name of a goddess of ancient Ireland. Very popular name in Ireland from the 18th century to the 1950s, so much so that in the late 19th century in the U.S. the stock figure of the Irish housemaid (in plays, cartoons, etc.) was frequently called Bridget. In France, **Brigitte** is currently popular. Saint Brigid of Kildare, patroness of Ireland; opera star Birgit Nilsson; actresses Brigitte Bardot, Brigitte Nielsen, Bridget Fonda; model Bridget Hall.

Beret, Berett, Berget, Bergett, Bergette, Biddie,

Biddy, Birget, Birgett, Birgit, Birgitt, Birgitta, Birgitte, Birkita, Birkitta, Birkitte, Birte, Bitta, Breeda, Bride, Bridee, Bridey, Bridgett, Bridgette, Bridgit, Bridgitt, Bridgitta, Bridgitte, Bridie, Bridy, Brietta, Briget, Brigett, Brighid, Brigid, Brigida, Brigidine, Brigit, Brigitt, Brigitta, Brigitte, Brijet, Brijit, Brijitte, Brita, Britt, Britta, Britte, Brydie, Brydget, Brydgit, Brydgitta, Brydgitte, Brydjette, Brydjitt, Bryget, Brygette, Brygid, Brygit, Brygitte, Bryjet, Bryjit

Brie Fr. Place name for a region in France most famous for the production of its cheese. The name is also sometimes considered a feminine adaptation of **Brian**.
Bree, Briette

Brier Fr. "Heather." Unusual botanical name. Though the personal name derives from the French term for heather, the word in English usually describes a wild rose with small, prickly thorns. In some versions of *Sleeping Beauty*, Prince Charming has to cut through a hedge of briers to reach the princess.
Briar

Brigantia Possibly Celt. "Strength." The name of a legendary goddess of springs. Oddly, the word "brigand," a kind of pirate, comes from the same source.

Brina (Fem. **Brian**) Slavic. "Defender."
Brinn, Bryn, Bryna, Brynn, Brynna, Brynne

Brit Celt. "Spotted, freckled." Also a diminutive of **Brittany**.
Britt

Britannia Lat. "Britain." Personification of Britain or the British Empire. She first appeared on a coin in the 2nd century A.D. For zealous Anglophiles.

Brites Port. "Power."

Brittany Lat. "From England." According to records kept by the U.S. government, this was the sixth most popular girl's name in America in the 1990s, though it has been sliding down the lists since 1990. It may have derived some of its popularity from associations with England, which held tremendous glamor in the 1980s in America, but overexposure has taken its toll. Singer Britney Spears; actress Brittany Murphy.

Brett, Brit, Briteny, Britiney, Britney, Britni, Britny, Britt, Britta, Brittan, Brittaney, Brittani, Britteny, Brittin, Brittiny, Brittnee, Brittney, Brittni, Brittny, Britton

Bronwyn Welsh. "Fair breast." Use of Welsh-language names such as Bronwyn, **Blodwyn**, and the like may be related to periodic surges of separatist or nationalistic feeling in Wales.

Bronnie, Bronny, Bronwen, Bronya

Brooke OE. Place name: "Small stream." Also a surname, and originally more common for boys. But in the last two decades (perhaps influenced by the fame of actress Brooke Shields), this has become a clearly feminine name, used quite steadily. The final "-e" seems to contribute to that perception. Actress Brooke Adams; philanthropist Brooke Astor.

Brook, Brookie, Brooks, Brooky

Brucie (Fem. **Bruce**) OF. "Thicket of brushwood." The man's name was first common in Scotland, after a 14th-century king. The feminine variant is little used.

Brucina, Brucine

Bruna (Fem. **Bruno**) It. "Brown-skinned, brown-haired."

Brunella OF. "Little one with brown hair."

Brunelle, Brunetta, Brunette

Brunhilda OG. "Armor-wearing fighting maid." Heroine of the Siegfried legend popularized in the Ring cycle of operas by Richard Wagner. Brunhilda is one of the Valkyrie, maidens who ride into battle. The name naturally has connotations of great physical strength, slightly comical in nature.

Brinhild, Brinhilda, Brinhilde, Brunhild, Brunhilde, Brunnhilda, Brunnhilde, Brynhild, Brynhilda, Brynhilde, Brynnhild, Brynnhilda, Brynnhilde, Hilda, Hilde, Hildi, Hildie, Hildy

Bryony Botanical name: a vine native to Europe with large leaves and small flowers.

Bryonie, Briony

Bryn Welsh. "Mount." Another place name converted to a Christian name in the 20th century.

Brinna, Brynn, Brynna, Brynne

Buena Sp. "Good, excellent."

Bunny Nickname deriving from a number of "B" names such as **Barbara** or **Bernice**. Has come to be a child's name for a rabbit, of course. Likely to be associated with the famous Playboy Bunnies, the now defunct mid-20th-century emblem of a slightly licentious good time.

Bunnee, Bunni, Bunnie

 Cabalina Sp. from Lat. "Having to do with horses." From the same root as the Spanish word *caballero*.

Cadence Lat. "With rhythm."

Cadena, Cadenza, Kadena, Kadence, Kadenza

Cadette Fr. "Younger." The French word is also the source of the term for students at West Point.

Cady OE. Last name of uncertain meaning. It may have been successfully adopted as a girl's first name because of its resemblance to other popular girls' names like **Katie**. Women's rights pioneer Elizabeth Cady Stanton.

Cade, Cadee, Cadey, Cadi, Cadie, Cadye, Caidie, Kade, Kadee, Kadi, Kadie, Kady, Kadye

Cai Viet. "Feminine."

Caitlin Ir. See **Catherine**. Along with **Megan**, Caitlin has been very popular recently among families with no Irish ties whatsoever, though it is a top-ten name in Ireland. Parents who find the name appealing but want to choose something a little more distinctive tend to opt for one of the many phonetic variations.

Caitilin, Caitlan, Caitlann, Caitlinn, Caitlyn, Caitlynn, Catelan, Catelinn, Catelynn, Catlin, Catlinn, Cayelin, Caylin, Kaitlan, Kaitlann, Kaitlin, Kaitlinn, Kaitlyn, Kaitlynn, Katelan, Katelin, Katelynn, Kayelin, Kayelyn

Cala "Castle, fortress."

Calandra Gk. "Lark."

Cal, Calandre, Calandria, Calendre, Callee, Cailey, Calli, Callie, Cally, Kalandra

Calantha Gk. "Lovely flower."
  Cal, Calanthe, Callee, Calley, Calli, Callie, Cally, Kalantha

Caledonia Lat. "From Scotland." Place name adapted to first name, probably because of its typically feminine "-ia" ending. The Caledonian Canal runs through Northern Scotland, while New Caledonia consists of a group of tiny islands in the South Pacific.

Calida Sp. "Heated, with warmth."
  Calla, Calli, Callida

California Geography name: the state on the West Coast. The original meaning of the name is unclear, but it has distinct connotations in modern American life: palm trees, surfing, the sun setting over the Pacific. . . .

Calla Gk. "Beautiful." Also the name of a flower, though the calla lily, with its smooth, sculptured lines, was not fashionable at the same time as the general vogue for flower names.

Callidora Gk. "Gift of beauty."

Callie Gk. There are many Greek names with the "Cal-" prefix, which means "beautiful" or "lovely." This diminutive (which can also be considered a diminutive of **Caroline** or even **Carol**), being less of a mouthful, is somewhat more accessible. Screenwriter Callie Khoury.
  Callee, Calley, Calli, Kallee, Kalley, Kalli, Kallie

Calligenia Gk. "Daughter of beauty." A subtle compliment to the baby's mother.

Calliope Gk. Muse of epic poetry. See **Clio**. Also the name of a musical instrument typically seen at circuses and carnivals.
  Callia, Callyope, Kalliope

Callista Gk. "Most beautiful." Extremely unusual outside of Greek families, notwithstanding the fame of actress Calista Flockhart.
  Cala, Calesta, Calista, Calla, Callesta, Calli, Callie, Cally, Callysta, Calysta, Kala, Kalesta, Kalista, Kalla, Kallesta, Kalli, Kallie, Kallista, Kally, Kallysta

Callula Lat. "Small beauty."

Calpurnia Lat. Probably from a clan name of uncertain meaning. The name of Julius Caesar's last wife, who appears in Shakespeare's play *Julius Caesar*.

Caltha Lat. "Golden flower."

Calvina (Fem. **Calvin**) Lat. "Hairless." Very unusual.
 Calvine

Calypso Gk. "She who hides." In Greek myth the nymph Calypso held Odysseus captive on an island for seven years. The name is also applied to the lilting music of the West Indies, perhaps because it could make visitors reluctant to leave.
 Calipso, Callypso, Kallypso

Cambria Geography name: a term for Wales and the name of a period of prehistoric time (part of the Paleozoic era, to be precise).
 Cambaria

Camellia Flower name first used in the 1930s, when the rather exotic blooms were quite fashionable. Its root is actually distinct from the more common **Camille**. The confusion arises not from the similarity of the words, but from the fact that Alexandre Dumas' famous 19th-century play *La Dame aux Camélias* was known in America as *Camille*. The heroine (whose name is Marguerite Gauthier) suffers from tuberculosis and the only flowers she can tolerate are camellias, because they have no scent.
 Camellia, Cammelia, Kamelia

Cameo It. from MF. "Skin." A stone or shell (frequently pinkish), carved with a picture, often a tiny portrait. Cameos have been very popular as jewelry at various periods, most recently the Victorian era.
 Cammeo

Cameron Scot. Gael. "Crooked nose." Clan name derived from the facial feature. Little used as a first name, even for boys, until the middle of this century. Now, with the huge push to use previously masculine names for girls, Cameron may well be co-opted. The fame of actress Cameron Diaz may not directly inspire parents, but puts the name in the public eye. Actress Camryn Manheim.

Camaran, Camren, Camron, Camryn, Kameren, Kameron, Kamryn, Kamrynn, Kamrynne

Camille Lat. Meaning unclear, though some sources trace it to the young girls who assisted at pagan religious ceremonies. The heroine of Alexandre Dumas's famous play *Camille* was actually named Marguerite (see **Camellia**). The name has been used consistently since the 19th century, usually in the form **Camilla**. Camille has been more common in the U.S., is a top-ten name in France. Friend of royalty Camilla Parker-Bowles.

Cam, Cama, Camala, Cami, Camila, Camile, Camilla, Cammi, Cammie, Cammilla, Cammille, Cammy, Cammylle, Camyla, Camylla, Camylle, Kamila, Kamilka, Kamilla, Kamille, Kamyla, Milla, Mille, Millee, Milli, Millie, Milly

Canada Geographic name: the large country just to the north of the United States. Its name comes from an Iroquois word meaning "horizon."

Candace Possibly Lat. "Brilliantly white." Historically the name was the ancient title of the queens of Ethiopia before the 4th century. Not much used until the mid-20th century. Actress Candice Bergen; author Candace Bushnell.

Candaice, Candase, Candayce, Candee, Candi, Candie, Candis, Candiss, Candy, Candyce, Dace, Dacee, Dacey, Dacie, Dacy, Kandace, Kandice, Kandiss, Kandy

Candelaria Sp. Relates to the Feast of Candlemass, on February 2, commemorating Christ's presentation at the Temple. The variant **Candela** is currently popular in Spain.

Candelara, Candelarea, Candeloria

Candida Lat. "White." Popular in the early Christian era, then very rare until this century, when it has been used occasionally. Journalist Candida Crewe.

Candi, Candide, Candie, Candy

Candra Lat. "Glowing."

Cantara Arab. "Little bridge."

Caparina Fauna name: like the much more famous **Vanessa**, Caparina is the name of a type of butterfly.
Caprina

Caprice It. "Ruled by whim."
Capreece, Capricia, Caprise

Capucine Fr. "Cowl." French form of an Italian word for a cloak with a deep collar, characteristic of a certain order of Franciscan monks. A French actress who worked in Hollywood in the 1960s gave the name some exposure in the U.S., but it is rare.

Cara Lat. "Darling." Began to be fashionable from the 1970s onward.
Caralie, Caretta, Carina, Carine, Carrie, Carry, Kara, Karina, Karine, Karrie, Karry

Carabelle Comb. form **Cara** and **Belle**. Much more common is **Clarabelle**.
Carabel, Carabell, Carrabelle

Carden ME. "One whom combs wool." Wool must be carded, or combed smooth, before it can be spun. Carding was one of the important occupations in the Middle Ages when the economy of Southern England relied heavily on the wool trade; names like **Fuller** and **Weaver** have survived even when the occupations are virtually defunct. As a name, Carden is rare among both boys and girls.
Cardin, Cardon

Carey Welsh. Place name: "Near the castle." A name used for both men and women. In this form it is a transferred surname, but, especially for women, it may be considered a diminutive of **Caroline**. Actress Carey Lowell.
Carrey, Cary

Carina It. "Dear little one." Dim. **Cara**. Often used in Italy in the exclamation "*Che carina!*" meaning, "How darling!" or even "How cute!"
Careena, Caren, Carena, Carin, Carine, Kareena, Karena, Karina, Karine

Carinthia Place name: an idyllic region of southern Austria.

Carissa Gk. "Grace." See Charis. Also possibly another variation of Cara.
Caresa, Caressa, Carisa, Charissa, Karisa, Karissa, Kharissa

Carita Lat. "Beloved." Also possibly derived from the Latin word for charity, *caritas*. Occasionally used in the last hundred years.
Caritta, Karita

Carla (Fem. **Carl**) Dim. **Caroline** (OG. "Man"). A European-sounding version of the many names that derive from **Charles**.
Carlah, Carlana, Carlette, Carlia, Carlla, Karla, Karlla

Carlie (Fem. **Charles**) Dim. **Caroline, Charlotte** (OG. "Man"). The form **Carleen** (or **Carlene**) was primarily a product of the 1960s; this shorter version is now more popular. Singer Carly Simon.
Carlee, Carleen, Carleigh, Carlene, Carley, Carli, Carline, Carlita, Carly, Carlye, Carlyne, Carlyta, Karlee, Karlene, Karli, Karlie, Karline, Karlita, Karly, Karlyta

Carlin Gael. "Little champion."
Carling

Carmel Heb. "Garden." Biblical place name: Mount Carmel is in Israel, and is often referred to as a kind of paradise. The name has been used by Catholic families for some hundred years, though the form **Carmen** is much more common. Editor Carmel Snow.
Carma, Carman, Carmania, Carmanya, Carmela, Carmeli, Carmelina, Carmelit, Carmelita, Carmia, Carmie, Carmiela, Carmina, Carmine, Carmit, Carmiya, Carmy, Karmel, Karmela, Karmelit, Karmen, Lina, Lita, Melina, Melita, Mina

Carmen Lat. "Song." A derivation of **Carmel**. One of the titles of the Virgin Mary is Santa Maria del Carmen (meaning Saint Mary of Mount Carmel), and this form of the name honors her. The most famous Carmen, of course, is the ill-fated heroine of Bizet's opera. Dancer Carmen Miranda; model Carmen Kass.
Carma, Carmelia, Carmelina, Carmelita, Carmencita, Carmia, Carmie, Carmina, Carmine, Carmita,

Carmyna, Carmyta, Charmaine, Karmen, Karmia, Karmina, Karmita, Lita, Mina

Carna Lat. "Horn." See **Cornelia**.

Carniela, Carniella, Carnyella, Karniela, Karniella, Karnyella

Carnation Lat. "Becoming flesh." Unusual flower name.

Carol (Fem. **Carl, Charles**) OG. "Man." Originally a short form of **Caroline**, not an adoption of "Christmas carol." It first appeared about a hundred years ago, and by mid-20th century was enormously popular, possibly influenced by the career of actress Carole Lombard. It is sometimes paired with a monosyllabic second name, most commonly Ann, as in Carol-Ann. The popularity of the name peaked in the mid-sixties, and it is now out of style. Actresses Carol Burnett, Carol Channing; skater Carol Heiss; playwright Caryl Churchill.

Carel, Carey, Cari, Carla, Carleen, Carlene, Carley, Carlin, Carlina, Carline, Carlita, Carlota, Carlotta, Carly, Carlyn, Carlynn, Carlynne, Caro, Carola, Carole, Carolena, Carolin, Carolina, Carolinda, Caroline, Caroll, Caroly, Carolyn, Carolynn, Carolynne, Carri, Carrie, Carroll, Carrolyn, Carry, Cary, Caryl, Caryll, Charla, Charleen, Charlena, Charlene, Charlotta, Charmain, Charmaine, Charmian, Charmion, Charyl, Cheryl, Cherlyn, Ina, Karel, Kari, Karla, Karleen, Karli, Karlie, Karlina, Karlinka, Karlote, Karlotta, Karole, Karolina, Karyl, Karyll, Karryl, Karryll, Kerril, Kerryl, Keryl, Lola, Loleta, olita, Lotta, Lotte, Lotti, Lottie, Sharleen, Sharlene, Sharline, Sharmain, Sharmian

Caroline (Fem. Dim. **Carl, Charles**) OG. "Man." A rather stately diminutive with royal connotations. The name was brought to England by George II's queen and was popular until the end of the 19th century. It is now enjoying a revival among parents who like its formal, aristocratic, old-fashioned aura. Princess Caroline of Monaco; fashion designers Carolina Herrera, Carolyne Roehm; First Daughter Caroline Kennedy Schlossberg; comedian Caroline Rhea.

Caraleen, Caraleena, Caraline, Caralyn, Caralyne, Caralynn, Carla, Carleen, Carleena, Carlen, Carlene, Carley, Carlin, Carlina, Carlita, Carlota, Carlotta, Carly, Carlyn, Carlyna, Carlyne, Carlynn, Carlynne, Carol, Carola, Carole, Carolin, Carolina, Carolyne, Carolynn, Carolynne, Carri, Carrie, Caroll, Carollyn, Cary, Charla, Charleen, Charleena, Charlena, Charlene, Charline, Charlyne, Ina, Karaleen, Karaleena, Karalina, Karaline, Karalyn, Karalynna, Karalynne, Karla, Karleen, Karlen, Karlena, Karlene, Karli, Karlie, Karlina, Karlinka, Karolina, Karoline, Karolinka, Karolyn, Karolyna, Karolyne, Karolynn, Karolynne, Leena, Lina, Sharla, Sharleen, Sharlena, Sharlene, Sharline, Sharlyne

Caron Var. Karen.

Caren, Carin, Carren, Carron

Carondelet Geography name: street name in New Orleans. The street was named for a Spanish governor of New Orleans from 1791-1807. He was such an inept governor that he almost managed to bring Spain to war with the U.S.

Carondalay, Carondella

Carrington OE. Place name: possibly "Charles's town." Any historical meaning the name might have has been buried by the Carrington family of the popular 1980s TV series *Dynasty*.

Carington

Carys Welsh. "Love." A Welsh name dating from the 1960s.

Casey Ir. Gael. "Watchful." Made famous by the song about the engineer of the Cannon Ball Express, Casey Jones. Used for both boys and girls, though it is increasingly a girl's name. Can be considered a diminutive of **Acacia**.

Cacey, Cacie, Caisee, Caisey, Caisi, Caisie, Casee, Casi, Casie, Caycee, Caycey, Cayci, Caycie, Caysee, Caysey, Caysi, Caysie, Kacey, Kacie, Kacy, Kacyee, Kasey, Kaycee, Kaycey, Kayci, Kaycie, Kaysee, Kaysey, Kaysi, Kaysie, Kaysy, Kaysyee

Casilda Lat. "Dwelling place." Also Spanish from German, "Warlike, a fighter." St. Casilda is the patron saint of Burgos, a town in Spain.
Cassilda

Casiphia Heb. "Gleaming, silvery white." An Old Testament place name.

Cassandra Gk. Perhaps a version of **Alexander**. In Greek mythology, she was the daughter of King Priam of Troy. Apollo gave her the gift of foresight but, because she spurned his advances, decreed that her prophecies would never be believed. In vain she warned the besieged Trojans against accepting the gift of a gigantic wooden horse presented by their Greek enemy; it was full of Greek soldiers, who took the city captive. The name now indicates someone who is always prophesying doom and gloom. Not a cheerful name for a child, unless a beloved relative named Cassandra erases the name's woeful connotations.
Casandera, Casandra, Cass, Cassandre, Cassandry, Cassaundra, Cassi, Cassie, Cassondra, Cassy, Kasandera, Kassandra, Kassi, Kassie, Kassy, Sande, Sandee, Sandera, Sandi, Sandie, Sandy, Saundra, Sohndra, Sondra, Zandra

Cassia Gk. "Cinnamon."

Cassidy Ir. "Clever." Surname transferred to male first name transferred to girl's name. The name was quite trendy in the late '90s, part of the movement toward chosing surnames as first names for girl babies.
Cassady, Cassidey, Kassadey, Kassidy, Kassodey

Cassiopeia In Greek mythology, Cassiopeia was the mother of Andromeda, the maiden who was chained to a rock and rescued by Perseus. Both mother and daughter were placed among the stars after death, according to legend, and there are constellations named after them.
Cassiopia, Kassiopeia, Kassiopia

Castalia Yet another nymph from Greek mythology who met a bad end: Castalia was being pursued by Apollo and fell into a spring on Mt. Parnassus.

Castallia, Kastalia

Catalina Sp. Var. **Catherine**. An island off the coast of southern California is named Catalina.

Catherine Gk. "Pure." One of the oldest recorded names, with roots in Greek antiquity. Almost every Western country has its own form of the name, and phonetic variations are endless. It has been borne by such illustrious women as Saint Catherine of Alexandria, the early martyr who was tortured on a spiked wheel; Empress Catherine the Great of Russia; and three of Henry VIII's six wives. It is currently very popular in England and France, and was one of the top ten American girls' names in the 1980s. It is still a favorite; Social Security records indicate that if you grouped together the most popular spellings of the name (Katherine, Kathryn, and Catherine) as one name, it would have ranked as the eighth most popular girl's name of the 1990s. The fashion in diminutives for Catherine have changed completely in 30 years: if the name is shortened now, it is almost always **Katie** instead of **Cathy**. Actresses Catherine Oxenberg, Catherine Deneuve, Katharine Hepburn, Catherine Zeta-Jones, Cate Blanchett; Australian track star Cathy Freeman.

Cait, Caitey, Caitie, Caitlin, Caitlinn, Caitrin, Caitrine, Caitrinn, Caitriona, Caitrionagh, Caity, Caren, Cari, Carin, Caron, Caronne, Carren, Carri, Carrin, Carron, Caryn, Carynn, Cass, Cassey, Cassi, Cassie, Cassy, Cat, Cataleen, Cataleena, Catalin, Catalina, Cataline, Catarina, Catarine, Cate, Cateline, Caterina, Catey, Catha, Cathaleen, Cathaline, Catharin, Catharina, Catharine, Catharyna, Catharyne, Cathe, Cathee, Cathelin, Cathelina, Cathelle, Catherin, Catherina, Catherinn, Catheryn, Cathi, Cathie, Cathirin, Cathiryn, Cathleen, Cathlene, Cathline, Cathlyne, Cathrine, Cathrinn, Cathryn, Cathrynn, Cathy, Cathye, Cathyleen, Cati, Catia, Catie, Catina, Catlaina, Catreena, Catrin, Catrina, Catrine, Catriona, Catrionagh, Catryna, Caty, Cay,

Caye, Cazzy, Ekaterina, Kait, Kaitey, Kaitie, Kaitlin, Kaitlinne, Kaitrin, Kaitrine, Kaitrinna, Kaitriona, Kaitrionagh, Kaity, Karen, Karena, Kari, Karin, Karon, Karri, Karrin, Karyn, Karynn, Kasia, Kasienka, Kasja, Kaska, Kass, Kassey, Kassia, Kassy, Kasya, Kat, Kata, Kataleen, Katalin, Katalina, Katarina, Katchen, Kate, Katee, Katell, Katelle, Katenka, Katerina, Katerinka, Katey, Katinka, Katha, Katharine, Katharyn, Katharyne, Kathee, Kathelina, Katheline, Katherin, Katherina, Katherine, Katheryn, Katherynn, Kathi, Kathie, Kathileen, Kathiryn, Kathleen, Kathlene, Kathleyn, Kathline, Kathyleen, Kathrine, Kathrinna, Kathryn, Kathryne, Kathy, Kathyrine, Kati, Katica, Katie, Katina, Katka, Katla, Katlaina, Katleen, Katoushka, Katrena, Katrine, Katrina, Katriona, Katrionagh, Katryna, Katushka, Katy, Katya, Kay, Kaye, Kit, Kittee, Kittie, Kitty, Trina, Trine, Trinette, Yekaterin, Yekaterina

Cathleen Ir. Var. **Catherine** (Gk. "Pure"). The "K-" spelling of **Kathleen** is more common, and parents today seem to turn to **Caitlin** as a more fashionable version of **Catherine**.

Cathaleen, Catleen, Catline, Catlin

Cavanaugh ME. "Chubby."

Cavanagh, Kavanagh, Kavanaugh

Cayley Fashionable modern name, probably made up of elements from the trendy **Kayla** and **Ashley**, though a scholar could probably trace the name back to **Catherine** via the hugely popular **Caitlin**. Since this is not a traditional name there is no one "correct" spelling: any one of the many variants will do.

Caileigh, Cailey, Cailie, Caleigh, Caylee, Cayleigh, Caylie, Kaileigh, Kailey, Kailie, Kaleigh, Kaylee, Kayleigh, Kayley

Cecilia (Fem. **Cecil**) Lat. "Blind one." From a Roman clan name. Saint Cecilia is the patroness of music. The name was used in Roman times, then resurfaced in the Victorian era, possibly given a boost by the fame of industrialist (and founder of Rhodesia) Cecil Rhodes. The form **Ce-cily** was briefly popular in the 1920s, but neither name has been used much since. With very feminine names like **Amanda, Jessica,** and **Stephanie** among the top ten nationwide, Cecilia seems a good candidate for rediscovery. Actress Cicely Tyson; soprano Cecilia Bartoli.

Ceceley, Cecely, Cecil, Cecile, Ceciley, Ceciliane, Cecilija, Cecilla, Cecily, Cecilyann, Cecyl, Cecyle, Cecylia, Ceil, Cela, Cele, Celia, Celie, Celli, Cellie, Cesia, Cesya, Cicely, Cicily, Cile, Cilka, Cilia, Cilla, Cilly, Cissie, Kikelia, Kikylia, Sacilia, Sasilia, Sasilie, Seelia, Seelie, Seely, Sesilia, Sessaley, Sesseelya, Sessile, Sessilly, Sessily, Sheila, Sile, Sileas, Sisely, Siselya, Siseel, Sisile, Sisiliya, Sissela, Sissie, Sissy

Celandine Gk. Botanical name: a yellow-blossomed wildflower.

Celadonia, Celida, Cellandine, Selodonia, Zeledonia

Celena Gk. Goddess of the moon, later identified with Artemis. A version of the more common **Selina**, although neither name is frequently used.

Cela, Celeena, Celina, Celinka, Cesia, Cesya, Saleena, Salena, Salina, Selena, Selina

Celeste Lat. "Heavenly." Unusual in any of its forms, and probably most familiar through the fame of actress Celeste Holm. Parents may associate the name with Queen Celeste, wife of Jean and Laurent de Brunhoff's children's book character Babar, the Elephant. Casting agent Celestia Fox.

Cela, Celesta, Celestena, Celestene, Celestia, Celestijna, Celestina, Celestine, Celestyne, Celia, Celie, Celina, Celinda, Celine, Celinka, Celka, Celleste, Celyna, Saleste, Salestia, Seleste, Selestia, Selestina, Selestine, Selestyna, Selestyne, Silesta, Silestena, Silestia, Silestijna, Silestina, Silestyna, Silestyne, Tina, Tinka

Celine Fr. Var. **Celeste.** Singer Celine Dion.

Celinda, Celinde, Salinda, Salinde, Selinda, Selinde, Seline

Celosia Gk. "Aflame."

Cendrine Dim. **Cendrillon**, the French name for Cinderella. Also a phonetic respelling of **Sandrine**, which is derived from **Alexandra** (Gk. "Man's defender").

Cenobia "Power of Zeus." A Spanish form of the slightly more common **Zenobia**.

Cerelia Lat. "Relating to springtime." A nice name for a spring baby.
Cerella, Sarelia, Sarilia

Ceres Roman mythology name: the goddess of the harvest, known in Greek myth as Demeter. She is the mother of Persephone, who was kidnapped by Pluto. Ceres' name is the root of our word "cereal."

Cerise Fr. "Cherry." See **Cherry**.
Cerisse, Charisse, Cherise, Sarese, Sherise

Cesarina (Fem. **Caesar**) Lat. Probably "Hairy, hirsute."
Cesarea, Cesarie, Cesarine, Kesare

Cézanne Name of the French painter Paul Cézanne. Acceptable as a girl's name, perhaps, because of its resemblance to **Suzanne**.

Chamania Heb. "Sunflower."
Chamaniah, Hamania

Chanah Heb. "Grace." See **Hannah**.
Chaanach, Chaanah, Chana, Chanach

Chanina Heb. "Gracious."
Chaninah, Hanina, Haninach, Haninah

Chanya Heb. "Grace of the Lord."
Chania, Chaniach, Chanyah, Hania, Haniah, Hanyah

Chandelle Fr. "Candle." Sounds familiar enough (like **Chantal** and its variants) to seem like a "real" name.
Chantelle, Shandelle, Shantelle

Chandler OE. Occupational name: "Candle maker." In the 1990s, male-sounding last names were fashionable for girls, putting Chandler in the company of old stand-bys like **Priscilla**, **Anne**, and **Susan**. Parental fancy has turned toward more flowery, feminine names, though, so Chandler will probably look less alluring to today's parents.

Chandra Sanskrit. "Like the moon." The greatest Hindu goddess Devi is also known as Chandra.
Candra, Chandi, Shandra

Chanel Fr. Surname of the legendary fashion designer Coco Chanel, and by extension, the name of a number of famous perfumes. Began to be used as a first name in the 1980s, usually in a phonetic variation, probably because of its elegant and luxurious connotations.
Chanelle, Channelle, Shanel, Shanell, Shanelle, Shannel, Shannelle, Shenelle, Shynelle

Chaney Dim. **Chandler**. The "-ey" ending makes for a more girlish-sounding name.
Chainey, Chayney

Chantal Fr. Originally a place name meaning "stony spot," but possibly also derived from the verb *chanter*, "to sing." A top-ten name in France, but unusual in the U.S.
Chantalle, Chantel, Chantelle, Chantele, Shantal, Shantalle, Shantel, Shantell, Shantelle, Shontel, Shontelle

Chappell OE. Place name: "near the chapel." Another place name turned last name, adopted as a girl's first name, but scarce so far.
Chapell, Chappel

Charlesetta Fem. **Charles** (OG. "Man"). The more common feminizations are **Caroline** and **Charlotte**.
Charlesette, Charlesina, Charlice

Charis Gk. "Grace." One term for the mythological Three Graces often depicted in classical art, who embodied charm. Taken individually, the graces were Aglaia (brilliance), Thalia (flowering), and Euphrosyne (joy). Not to be confused with those other legendary female gangs the Fates (also three, who controlled destiny) or the Muses (nine, who inspired the arts and sciences).
Chareesse, Charisse, Charysse, Karas, Karis, Karisse

Charity Lat. "Brotherly love." One of the three cardinal virtues, along with Faith and Hope. They have survived better than many of the other virtue names (Temperance, Fortitude, Humility, Chastity, Mercy, Obedience) popular among the Puritans in the 17th century.

Carissa, Carita, Chareese, Charis, Charissa, Charisse, Charita, Charitee, Charitey, Charitye, Chariza, Charty, Cherri, Cherry, Sharitee, Sharitey, Sharity, Sharitye

Charlotte Fr. "Little and womanly." One of the most popular feminine forms of **Charles**. Like **Caroline**, Charlotte was popularized in England by a queen (George III's wife) and was much used from the 18th century to the beginning of the 20th. In the U.S. its use peaked in the 1870s, but with the recent return to "old-fashioned" names, it has been dusted off for a reappearance. Currently very popular in England. In E. B. White's *Charlotte's Web*, the heroine of the title is a spider. Novelist Charlotte Brontë; actress Charlotte Rampling; singer Charlotte Church.

Carla, Carleen, Carlie, Carline, Carlota, Carlotta, Carly, Carlyne, Char, Chara, Charill, Charla, Charlaine, Charleen, Charlene, Charlet, Charlette, Charline, Charlot, Charlotta, Charly, Charlyne, Charmain, Charmaine, Charmian, Charmion, Charo, Charty, Charyl, Cherlyn, Cheryl, Cheryll, Karla, Karleen, Karlene, Karli, Karlicka, Karlie, Karlika, Karline, Karlota, Karlotta, Karlotte, Karly, Karlyne, Lola, Loleta, Loletta, Lolita, Lolotte, Lotta, Lottchen, Lotte, Lottey, Lotti, Lottie, Lotty, Sharel, Sharil, Sharla, Sharlaine, Sharleen, Sharlene, Sharlet, Sharlette, Sharline, Sharlot, Sharmain, Sharmayne, Sharmian, Sharmion, Sharyl, Sheri, Sherie, Sherrie, Sherry, Sherye, Sheryl

Charmaine From a Latin clan name; also possibly related to **Carmen** and **Caroline**. Enjoyed bursts of popularity in the 1920s and 1950s.

Charmain, Charmane, Charmayne, Charmian, Charmion, Charmyan, Charmyn, Sharmain, Sharman, Sharmane, Sharmayne, Sharmian, Sharmion, Sharmyn

Charmian Gk. "Joy." A distinctly separate name from Charmaine, though they are often confused. Because of its Greek origin, Charmian should be pronounced with a hard *C*, but it rarely is. Actress Charmian Carr.

Charmin, Charmiane, Charmyan, Charmin, Sharmian, Sharmiane, Sharmyan, Sharmyane

Chasidah Heb. "Devout woman." From the same root that gives·its name to the very devout sects of Jews known as the Hasidim.

Chasina Aramaic. "Strong, mighty."

Chastity Lat. "Purity." A virtue name that has, for obvious reasons, fallen out of favor, though Cher used it for her daughter.

Chasaty, Chasity, Chassity, Chastitee, Chastitey

Chava Heb. "Life."

Chabah, Chaya, Chayka, Eva, Hava, Haya, Kaija

Chaviva Heb. "Beloved."

Eva

Chazona Heb. "Oracle, prophetess."

Chazonah, Hazona, Hazonach

Chermona Heb. "Sacred mountain." The mountain referred to is probably Mt. Hermon, in what is now southern Syria.

Chermonah, Hermona, Hermonach, Hermonah

Chelsea OE. "Port or landing place." Place name; possibly owes some of its appeal to British pop culture of the late 1960s and songs like Joni Mitchell's "Chelsea Morning." It seems likely that the name's huge popularity in the early 1990's depended on its aura of English stuffiness rather than Engllish bohemianism. This is by far the most common spelling. First Daughter Chelsea Clinton.

Chelcie, Chelsee, Chelseigh, Chelsey, Chelsie, Chelsy

Chepzibah Heb. "My delight is in her." See **Hepzibah**.

Cher Fr. "Beloved." For most people, inseparable from the singer and actress who uses this name alone, without a surname, though the heroine of the movie and TV series *Clueless* briefly put a new spin on it. Somewhat popular in the late 1960s and early 1970s.

Chere, Cherée, Cherey, Cheri, Cherice, Cherie, Cherise, Cherish, Cherrie, Cherry, Chery, Cherye, Cherylee, Cherylie, Sher, Sherelle, Sherey, Sheri, Sherice, Sherie, Sherry, Sheryll

Cherry OF. "Cherry." The 19th-century vogue for botanical names did not usually extend to fruit, so when Cherry occurs, it is most likely a variant of **Charity** or **Cheryl**.

Chere, Cheree, Cherey, Cherida, Cherise, Cherita, Cherrey, Cherri, Cherrie

Cheryl Familiar form of **Charlotte** or **Cherry**. A 20th-century development that first became popular in the 1940s, and increased in use into the 1960s. Like most 30-year-old fashions, it is now quite dated. Pop musician Sheryl Crow.

Charil, Charyl, Cheriann, Cherianne, Cherryl, Cheryll, Cherylle, Cherilynn, Chryil, Chyrill, Sharil, Sharyl, Sharyll, Sheral, Sherianne, Sheril, Sherill, Sheryl, Shyril, Shyrill

Cherilyn Form of **Cheryl**. Names that are modern developments seem more susceptible to widely variable spellings, as this one is.

Charalin, Charalyn, Charalynne, Charelin, Charelyn, Charelynn, Charilyn, Charilynn, Cheralin, Cheralyn, Cherilin, Cherilynn, Cherilynne, Cherralyn, Cherrilin, Cherrilyn, Cherrylene, Cherrylin, Cherryline, Cherrylyn, Cherylin, Cheryline, Cheryllyn, Cherylyn, Sharalin, Sharalyn, Sharelyn, Sharelynne, Sharilynn, Sheralin, Sheralynne, Sherilin, Sherralin, Sherrilyn, Sherrylene, Sherryline, Sherrylyn, Sherylin, Sherylyn

Chesleigh OE. "Camp on the meadow." Can also be taken as a variation on **Chelsea** and **Ashley**.

Cheslea, Chesley, Cheslie, Chesli, Chesslea, Chessley, Chesslie, Chessli

Chesney OE. Place name referring to a camp. Close enough to **Kelsey** and **Chelsea** to be a reasonable choice.

Chesnea, Chesneigh, Chesnie, Chesni, Chessnea, Chessney, Chessni, Chessnie

Chesna Slavic. "Peaceful."

Chessa, Chessy

Cheyenne Name of a Native American tribe. The Cheyennes originated in what is now Minnesota, and were famous for their courage in battle. They fiercely resisted the Anglo takeover of the Plains. Several features of the Western states were named after the tribe, including the city that is now the capital of Wyoming. Possibly because of the familiar "-enne" ending, this name seems acceptable as a girl's name as another tribal name like Algonquin would not be.

Chayan, Chayanne, Shayan, Shayanne, Chyanne, Shyann, Shyanne

Chiara It. "Light." See **Claire**. Some potential for use in the 21st century by enthusiastic Italophiles.

Chiarra, Kiara, Kiarra

China Geography name. After all, why not name a daughter for the most populous nation on earth?

Chiquita Sp. "Little one." Most parents will probably associate this name with the heavily advertised Chiquita banana.

Chickie, Chicky, Chiqueeta, Chiquin

Chloe Gk. "Young green shoot." Appears in the Bible, and as a name in literature, especially in the tale of Daphnis and Chloe, set to music by Ravel. Enormously popular throughout Great Britain and in France, but only occasionally used in the US. Candice Bergen has a daughter named Chloe. Actresses Chloe Webb, Chloe Sevigny.

Chloe, Clo, Cloe, Cloey, Khloe, Khloey, Kloe

Chloris Gk. "Pale." Another name from Greek mythology, though an obscure one. Actress Cloris Leachman.

Chloress, Cloris, Khloris, Kloris

Cholena Delaware Indian. "Bird."

Christabel Lat./Fr. "Fair Christian." Use has been primarily literary, as in Samuel Taylor Coleridge's poem of the same name, in which the heroine is an example of innocent purity. Used occasionally in Britain.

Christabella, Christabelle, Christobel, Chrystabel, Chrystabelle, Chrystobel, Cristabel, Cristabella, Cristabelle, Crystabel, Crystabella

Christina (Fem. **Christian**) Gk. "Anointed, Christian." **Christian** was used for women in medieval times, but by the 18th century Christina was the more common form. It was superseded in the 1930s by the French form

Christine, which was very popular in the fifties and sixties, but the cycle of fashion has now brought Christina back to solid but not trendy popularity. **Christiane** is currently very popular in Germany. Queen Cristina of Sweden; poet Christina Rossetti; tennis star Chris Evert; model Christie Brinkley; pop singer Christina Aguilera; actress Christina Ricci.

Chris, Chrissie, Chrissy, Chrissta, Chrisstan, Chrissten, Chrissti, Chrisstie, Chrissty, Christa, Christan, Christeen, Christel, Christen, Christi, Christian, Christiana, Christiane, Christianna, Christie, Christin, Christine, Christini, Christinn, Christmar, Christy, Christyna, Chrystal, Chrystalle, Chrystee, Chrystel, Chrystelle, Chrystle, Cris, Crissey, Crissie, Crissy, Crista, Cristal, Cristel, Cristelle, Cristen, Cristena, Cristi, Cristie, Cristin, Cristina, Cristine, Cristiona, Cristy, Crysta, Crystena, Crystene, Crystie, Crystina, Crystine, Crystyna, Khristeen, Khristena, Khristina, Khristine, Khristya, Kirsten, Kirstin, Kit, Kris, Krissy, Krista, Kristeen, Kristel, Kristen, Kristi, Kristijna, Kristin, Kristina, Kristy, Krysta, Krystka, Krystle, Stina, Teena, Teyna, Tina, Tiny

Christmas OE. Name of the holiday, used occasionally through the 19th century for Dec. 25 babies, but now more usually replaced by the French, and somewhat subtler form, **Noel**.

Chryseis Lat. "Golden daughter." A very beautiful young girl named Chryseis appears in Homer's *Iliad*.
Chrysilla

Chuma Aramaic. "Warmth, heat."

Chumani Sioux. "Drops of dew."

Ciara Modern name, created for its sound. Can be traced either to **Chiara** (It. "Light") or to the increasingly popular **Sierra** (Sp. "Saw"). Currently popular in Ireland.
Ceara, Ciarra, Cieara, Searra, Siara

Cilia Scientific term: tiny hairs that project from some cells. The name can also be considered a variation on **Celia**, or a diminutive of **Cecilia**.
Silia, Sillia

Cilicia Biblical: a province mentioned in both Old and New Testaments. It is in southeast Asia Minor.
Cilicea, Salicia

Cimarron Place name: a city in western Kansas and a river that runs 650 miles across the Great Plains from New Mexico to Oklahoma. It was made famous by an Edna Ferber novel that was the basis for movies made in 1933 and 1961.
Cimeron, Simarron, Simeron

Cinderella Fr. "Little ash-girl." The name from the fairy tale. Very rare.
Cendrillon, Cenerentola, Cindie, Cindy, Ella

Cindy Originally a nickname for **Cynthia** (Gk. "Goddess from Mt. Cynthos") or **Lucinda** (Lat. "Light"). Popular for children born in the fifties and sixties, but rarely used since. Singer Cyndi Lauper; model Cindy Crawford.
Cindee, Cindi, Cindie, Cyndee, Cyndi, Cyndie, Cyndy, Sindee, Sindi, Sindie, Sindy, Syndi, Syndie, Syndy

Cinnabar The ore that produces mercury. It is a deep brownish red in color.

Cinnamon Familiar spice that has been grown in tropical climates for thousands of years. It is the inner bark of a small evergreen tree, and has been used by cultures from China to the Netherlands for flavoring food, scenting fabrics and household goods, and for medical purposes.
Cynnamon, Sinemmon, Sinnamon

Cipriana It. "From Cyprus."
Chipriana, Chiprianna, Cipriane, Ciprianna, Cypriana, Cyprienne, Sipriana, Sipriane, Siprianne, Sypriana, Syprianne

Cithara Ancient musical instrument resembling both the lyre and the zither. The name is probably the root of the word "guitar."
Citara, Kitara, Kithara

Claire Lat. "Bright." The original form was **Clare**, as in Saint Clare, 13th-century founder of a Franciscan order of nuns. In the 19th century **Clara** became fashionable, but since the 1960s, the French form Claire has dominated.

Writer Clare Booth Luce; actresses Clara Bow, Claire Bloom, Claire Danes.

Ceara, Cearra, Cheeara, Chiara, Ciara, Ciarra, Clair, Claire, Claireen, Clairene, Claireta, Clairette, Clairey, Clairice, Clairinda, Clairissa, Clairita, Clairy, Clarabel, Clarabelle, Clare, Clarene, Claresta, Clareta, Claretta, Clarey, Clari, Claribel, Claribella, Claribelle, Clarice, Clarie, Clarinda, Clarine, Clarissa, Clarisse, Clarita, Claritza, Clarrie, Clarry, Clary, Claryce, Clayre, Clayrette, Clayrice, Clayrinda, Clayrissa, Clerissa, Cliara, Clorinda, Klaire, Klara, Klaretta, Klarissa, Klaryce, Klayre, Kliara, Klyara, Seara, Searra

Clara Lat. "Bright." Another version of **Claire**, but one that has been very rare for some time. It was at its most popular in the 19th century, but is popular in Spain at the moment.

Clarabelle, Claretha, Claribel, Clarice, Clarie, Clarinda, Clarine, Clarita, Claritza, Clarry, Klara, Klarra

Claramae Eng. A compound form of **Clara**, probably dating from the late 19th century, when **May** was also a popular name.

Claramay

Clarice Var. **Claire**, which enjoyed a flurry of popularity around the turn of the 20th century. **Clarissa** is a Latinized version made famous by Samuel Richardson's 18th-century novel *Clarissa Harlowe*.

Claris, Clarise, Clarisse, Claryce, Clerissa, Clerisse, Cleryce, Clerysse, Klarice, Klarissa, Klaryce

Clarimond Lat./Ger. "Shining defender."

Claramond, Claramonda Claramonde, Clarimunde

Claudia (Fem. **Claude, Claudius**) Lat. Clan name probably meaning "lame." The name has never been very popular in English-speaking countries in any of its forms, in spite of the exposure given it by Colette's novels (*Claudine at School*, etc.) and the career of actress Claudette Colbert. It is currently used quite a bit in Germany. Actress Claudia Cardinale; model Claudia Schiffer.

Claude, Claudella, Claudelle, Claudetta, Claudette,

Claudie, Claudina, Claudine, Claudey, Claudy, Clodia, Klaudia, Klodia

Clea Unknown derivation, but possibly invented by author Lawrence Durrell, for a character in his famous Alexandria Quartet. See also **Cleopatra, Clio**.
Claea, Klea

Clelia Lat. "Glorious." A maiden who figures in the legendary history of Rome. Her story was retold (in 10 volumes!) by the 17th-century French novelist Mlle. de Scudéry.

Clematis Gk. "Vine or brushwood." Flower name, from the blossoming vine with white or purple blooms.
Clematia, Clematice, Clematiss

Clementine Lat. "Mild, giving mercy." **Clemence** and **Clemency** were both Puritan virtue names, but are now unheard-of. **Clementia** was used until the 19th century, when it was replaced by **Clementina**. The well-known song "My Darling Clementine" would make it hard to use that version of the name with a straight face. Winston Churchill's wife was named Clementine.
Clem, Clemence, Clemency, Clementia, Clementina, Clementya, Clementyna, Clementyn, Clemmie, Clemmy, Klementijna, Klementina

Cleopatra Gk. "Her father's renown." There were actually generations of Egyptian princesses of this name, but the most famous is the intriguer who enthralled both Caesar and Antony. Very rare.
Clea, Cleo, Cleona, Cleone, Cleonie, Cleta

Cleva (Fem. **Cleve, Clive**) ME. "Hill-dweller." Place name transferred to a surname and thence to a first name used for men. This feminine form is unusual.

Cliantha Gk. "Glory-flower."
Cleantha, Cleanthe, Clianthe, Kliantha, Klianthe

Clio Greek mythological name of the muse of history. There are nine muses, the daughters of Zeus and Mnemosyne, and each represents an art or science. **Calliope** (epic poetry), **Terpsichore** (choral song and dance), and **Thalia** (comedy) have survived as first names.
Klio

TALK ABOUT TEMPESTUOUS

The National Hurricane Center began assigning names to hurricanes back in 1953. It created six rosters of names in alphabetical order and cycled through them every six years, assigning a name to each storm once wind velocity reached 39 miles per hour. Names were all female until 1979, when they began alternating: girl, boy, girl, boy. There are different lists for the Atlantic and Pacific storms. The names for Atlantic storms are drawn from French, English, and Spanish, while the Pacific possibilities include some Hawaiian names. Every few years the Hurricane Center retires a name if a really fierce storm used it: Hurricane Hugo in 1989, for instance, wrought such havoc that there will never again be another Hugo. The Hurricane Center is apparently just as broad-minded as the American public in its choice of names: Other names that have been retired are Cleo, Fifi, Klaus, and Ione.

Clorinda Lat. Literary name coined by 16th-century Italian poet Tasso. Possibly derived from **Claire** or **Chloe**.
Chlorinda

Clotilda Ger. "Renowned battle." Saint Clothilde was the wife of Frankish King Clovis I in the 6th century, and supposedly went into battle by his side. One of Paris's most fashionable churches is named for her.
Clothilda, Clothilde, Clotilde, Klothilda, Klothilde

Cloudy Weather name. Could be used to describe a baby's delicate coloring, or to refer to the weather on the day of birth.

Clove Name of the spice. It comes from the Latin word for "nail," which whole cloves resemble. Can also be a diminutive for **Clover**.

Clover OE. Flower name. Perhaps because of the modest nature of the flower, the name occurred in the 19th century more commonly as a nickname.

Clymene Gk. "Renowned one." In Greek mythology, most notably the daughter of Oceanus and mother of Atlas and Prometheus, though several other legendary figures also bear this name.

Clytie Gk. "Lovely one." Another mythological figure whose unrequited love for the sun god resulted in her being changed into a heliotrope, or sunflower, which turns to follow the sun's path.

Cochava Heb. "Star."

Cody OE. "Pillow." This is an example of the kind of unisex name that was popular in the '90s. Cody remains more usually masculine.

Codee, Codey, Codi, Codie, Kodee, Kodey, Kodie, Kody

Colette Dim. **Nicole** (Gk./Fr. "People of victory"). Used mostly since the 1940s, though never widespread. Probably made familiar by the French writer Colette, whose last name it was.

Coletta, Collet, Collete, Collette, Nicolette

Coline (Fem. **Colin**, derived from **Nicholas**) Gk. "People of victory."

Colena, Colene, Coletta, Colina, Collina, Colline, Nicoleen, Nicolene, Nicoline, Nicolyne

Colleen Ir. Gael. "Girl." In use since the 1940s in English-speaking countries *except* Ireland. A vogue in the early 1960s faded rapidly. Actress Colleen Dewhurst; writer Colleen McCullough.

Coleen, Collie, Colline, Colly, Kolleen, Kolline

Collis OE. Occupational name: "Coal miner." Scarce for boys and girls.

Collice, Colliss

Columba Lat. "Dove." Saint Columba, 6th-century Irish saint, founded an influential monastery on the Scottish island of Iona, and is supposed to have exorcised the River Ness of a monster. Though the Irish Columba was a man, two other saints of that name were both women. The dove, of course, is a Christian symbol for the Holy Spirit.

Collie, Colly, Colombe, Columbia, Columbine

Columbine Lat. "Dove." Columbine is also a literary character who appears in traditional Italian comedy and English pantomime as Harlequin's beloved. Also a flower name for a delicate two-colored blossom.

Comfort Fr. "To strengthen and comfort." In the Bible the Holy Ghost is referred to as the "Comforter." It was a surname in the Middle Ages, then popular among the Puritans. Almost unused since the 18th century.

Concepción Lat. "Conception." Used mostly in Latin American countries to honor the Immaculate Conception and, by extension, the Virgin Mary.

Cetta, Chiquin, Chita, Concetta, Concha, Concheta, Conchissa, Conchita

Conchita Dim. Concepción.

Conchata, Conchissa

Concordia Lat. "Peace, harmony." In classical myth, Concordia was the goddess of peace succeeding a battle. The concept is memorialized in several place names like Concord, Massachusetts and Paris's Place de la Concorde.

Concord, Concorde

Conradine (Fem. **Conrad**) OG. "Brave counsel."

Connee, Connie, Conny, Conrada, Conradeen, Conradina

Constance Lat. "Steadfastness." Used often in the early Christian and medieval eras, then by the Puritans (usually as **Constant** or **Constancy**). After a brief revival at the beginning of this century, it lapsed back into obscurity. Singer Connie Francis.

Con, Conetta, Connee, Conney, Conni, Connie, Conny, Constancia, Constancy, Constanta, Constantia, Constantija, Constantina, Constantine, Constantya, Constanz, Costanza, Konstance, Konstantija, Konstantina, Konstanze, Kosta, Kostatina, Tina

Consuelo Sp. "Consolation, comfort." Honors Santa Maria del Consuelo. In 1842 George Sand, a popular French author, published an historical novel called *Consuelo*. The heroine, a gypsy, became a successful opera singer.

Chela, Chelo, Consolata, Consuela

Cora Gk. "Maiden." Though some sources trace the name to classical myth, its modern form was probably coined by American writer James Fenimore Cooper in *The Last of the Mohicans* (1826). It grew in popularity through the 19th century, but now its variant forms are more often used. A simple, pretty name with an old-fashioned air. Civil rights activist Coretta Scott King.

Corabel, Corabella, Corabelle, Corabellita, Coree, Corella, Corena, Corene, Coretta, Corey, Cori, Corie, Corilla, Corine, Corinna, Corinne, Corita, Correen, Corrella, Correlle, Correna, Correnda, Correne, Correy, Corri, Corrie, Corrina, Corrine, Corrissa, Corry, Corynna, Corynne, Coryssa, Kora, Korabell, Kore, Koreen, Korella, Koretta, Korey, Korilla, Korina, Korinne, Korry, Koryne, Korynna, Koryssa

Coral Lat. Nature name: first appeared during the Victorian vogue for jewel names, usually in England, though of course coral is not a mineral but the deposits left by tiny aquatic creatures. Actress Coral Browne.

Coralee, Coralena, Coralie, Coraline, Corallina, Coralline, Coraly, Coralyn, Coralyne, Koral, Korall, Koralie, Koralline

Corazón Sp. "Heart." Corazón Aquino, former president of the Philippines.

Cordelia Derivation unclear, but probably related to Latin *cor* or "heart." In Shakespeare's *King Lear,* Cordelia is the youngest and only lovable daughter of the tragic king.

Cordelie, Cordella, Cordelle, Cordey, Cordi, Cordie, Cordy, Delia, Delie, Della, Kordelia, Kordella, Kordelle

Cordis Lat. "Of the heart."

Cordiss

Cordula Ger. from Lat. "Of the heart" or possibly from Welsh, "Sea jewel."

Cordulla, Kordula, Kordulla

Corey Ir. Gael. Place name: "the hollow." Place name transferred to surname. It is still much more popular for boys. Author Corrie ten Boom.

Cory, Cori, Corrie, Corry, Cory, Korie, Korrey, Korri, Korry

Corin Lat. "Spear." The name, which refers both to a male saint and to an early Roman god of war, is more commonly given to boys. As a girl's name, it may even be a variant of **Corinne**.

Coren, Corrin, Cyran, Korin

Corinne French form of **Cora**, used since the 1860s.

Carinna, Carinne, Carine, Carynna, Carynne, Corenne, Corin, Corina, Corinda, Corine, Corinn, Corinna, Correna, Corrianne, Corrienne, Corrinda, Corrine, Corrinn, Corrinna, Karinne, Karynna, Koreen, Korina, Korinne, Korrina

Corinthia Place name: from Corinth, an ancient Greek city that had a very early Christian church. St. Paul wrote two Epistles to the Corinthians that form part of the New Testament.

Korinthia

Corisande Gk. "Chorus-singer." Disraeli used this name for a character in his play *Lothair*.

Corisanda, Corissande, Corrisande

Corliss OE. "Benevolent, cheery."

Corlee, Corless, Corley, Corlie, Corly

Cornelia (Fem. **Cornelius**) Lat. "Like a horn." Comes from a famous Latin clan name, and was often used in the Roman Empire. Modern use is sparing, dating from mid-19th century.

Cornalia, Corneelija, Cornela, Cornelija, Cornelya, Corelie, Cornella, Cornelle, Cornie, Korneelia, Korneelya, Kornelia, Kornelija, Kornelya, Neel, Neely, Nela, Nelia, Nell, Nella, Nellie, Nelly

Corona Sp. "Crown." A spate of English use occurred around the coronation of King Edward VII in 1902, but this sentimental homage to royalty was not repeated at subsequent coronations. Also the name of a very popular Mexican beer, which would seem to limit its further use as a given name.

Coronetta, Coronette, Coronna

Corvina Lat. "Like a raven." A good name for a dark-haired baby.
Corva, Corveena, Corvetta

Cosette Fr. Probably a feminine diminutive of **Nicholas** (Gk. "People of victory"). Given new exposure in recent years by the immensely popular musical *Les Misérables*, whose female romantic lead is named Cosette.
Cosetta

Cosima (Fem. **Cosmo**) Gk. "Order." Very unusual in English-speaking countries. The composer Richard Wagner married (as his second wife) Cosima Liszt, daughter of the composer Franz Liszt. Two of their children were named Siegfried and Isolde, after characters in two of his operas.
Cosma, Cosmé, Kosma

Courtney OE. "Court-dweller." Surname transferred to first name; usually feminine in U.S. Immensely popular in the 1990s, probably owing to upper-class connotations, though when a name or group of names (in this case, **Ashley/Whitney/Brittany** and the like) becomes this fashionable the sheeer glamor of popularity probably eclipses any previous connotations the name may have had. Actresses Courteney Cox, Courtney Love.
Cordney, Cordni, Cortenay, Corteney, Cortland, Cortnee, Cortneigh, Cortney, Cortnie, Cortny, Courtenay, Courteneigh, Courteney, Courtland, Courtnay, Courtnee, Courtnie, Courtny, Kordney, Kortney, Kortni, Kourtenay, Kourtneigh, Kourtney, Kourtnee, Kourtnie

Creola Fr. from Port. "Of American birth but European descent." Used to describe natives of the West Indies and Louisiana who were the offspring of European-born colonists.
Creole, Creolla, Criolla

Crescent OF. "Increasing, growing." Also, by extension, the shape of the crescent moon.
Crescence, Crescenta, Crescentia, Cressant, Cressent, Cressentia, Cressentya

Cressida Gk. Heroine of a tale (*Troilus and Cressida*) that has been told by Boccaccio, Chaucer, and Shakespeare.

Crisanta Sp. from Gk. "Golden flower, chrysanthemum."
Chrisanta, Chrisantha, Chrissanta, Chrissantha, Chryssantha

Crispina (Fem. **Crispin**) Lat. "Curly-haired."

Cristina Lat. "Anointed, Christian." See **Christina**.

Crystal Gk. "Ice." Transferred use of the word, mostly modern, and increasing since the 1950s. The TV series *Dynasty* brought the name to great prominence in the 1980s, though that character spelled it "Krystle." Phonetic variants probably outnumber the original spelling. Curiously enough, Crystal was considered a man's name in Scotland hundreds of years ago, where it was a diminutive of **Christopher**. See **Christina**.
Christal, Christalle, Chrystal, Chrystalle, Chrystel, Chrystle, Cristal, Cristel, Cristle, Crysta, Crystel, Khristalle, Khrystle, Kristle, Krystal, Krystalle, Krystle

Csilla Hung. "Defenses."

Cyanea Gk. "Sky blue."

Cybele Gk. Asian goddess, also known in Greek mythology as Rhea, and in Rome as "Great Mother of the Gods." In legend she was originally bisexual, but made female by the Olympian gods.

Cymbeline Possibly Gk. "Hollow" (which relates to the hollow percussion instrument, the cymbal) or Celt. "Sun lord." The title of one of Shakespeare's lesser-known plays, whose protagonist is a 12th-century king of Britain.
Cymbaline

Cyma Gk. "Flourishing."
Syma

Cynara Gk. "Thistly plant." Made famous by the late-19th-century English poet Ernest Dowson, who is in turn largely remembered by the line "I have been faithful to thee, Cynara! in my fashion."
Zinara

Cynthia Gk. "Goddess from Mount Cynthos," i.e.,

Artemis, the moon goddess, who was supposed to have been born there. Used as a literary name in the 17th century, and by American slave owners in the early 19th century. Enjoyed a period of popularity from the 1920s to 1950s, then was replaced by its nickname, **Cindy**, which is now rare. Although many polysyllabic names ending in "-a" (**Samantha, Jessica, Amanda**) are now extremely fashionable, Cynthia may sound too much like the early 20th century to attract late 20th century interest. Many of the diminutives are also variants of **Lucinda**. Ballerina Cynthia Gregory; actress Cynthia Nixon.

Cinda, Cindee, Cindi, Cindie, Cindy, Cinnie, Cinny, Cinthia, Cintia, Cinzia, Cyn, Cynda, Cyndee, Cyndia, Cyndie, Cyndra, Cyndy, Cynnie, Cynthea, Cynthie, Cynthya, Cytia, Kynthia, Kynthija, Sindee, Sindi, Sindy, Sindya, Sinnie, Sinny, Synda, Syndee, Syndi, Syndy, Syntha, Synthee, Syntheea, Synthia, Synthie, Synthya

Cypris Gk. "From the island of Cyprus."
Cipriana, Cypriane, Ciprienne, Cyprianne, Cyprien, Cyprienne, Sipriana, Siprianne

Cyra (Fem. **Cyrus**) Per. "Sun" or "Throne." Author Cyra McFadden.

Cyrilla (Fem. **Cyril**) Lat. "Lordly."
Ciri, Cirilla, Siri, Sirilla, Syrilla

Cytherea Gk. "From the island of Cythera," i.e., Aphrodite or Venus, who is supposed to have come ashore there after being born of seafoam.

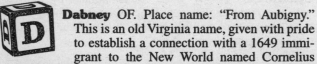 **Dabney** OF. Place name: "From Aubigny." This is an old Virginia name, given with pride to establish a connection with a 1649 immigrant to the New World named Cornelius d'Aubigny. It is used for both boys and girls.
Dabnie, Dabny

Dacey Ir. Gael. "From the south."

Dacee, Dacia, Dacie, Dacy, Daicee, Daicy, Daisey

Dacia Lat. Place name: Dacia was a Roman province which existed where Romania is now.

Dada Nig. "Curly-haired."

Daffodil OF. Flower name for the familiar yellow blossom; an inventive name for a spring baby.

Dagmar OG. Meaning unclear, though possibly "Day's glory." In Denmark Dagmar is a royal name; Tsarina Marie, wife of Tsar Alexander III of Russia, was Princess Dagmar of Denmark. The name appears only rarely in English-speaking countries.

Dagny ONorse. "New day." Probably etymologically related to **Dagmar**.

Dagna, Dagne

Dahlia Scand. Flower name of fairly recent vintage, first used in numbers since the 1920s. The flower itself was named in honor of the 18th-century Swedish botanist Anders Dahl.

Dahiana, Dayha, Daleia, Dalia, Dalla

Dai Jap. "Great."

Daira Sp. from Gk. "Knowing, informed." Extremely rare.

Daeira, Danira, Dayeera

Daisy OE. "Eye of the day." One of the most popular of the 19th-century flower names. It was often used as a nickname for **Margaret**, since in France the flower is called a *marguerite*. It was such a popular name that, when Henry James was writing the story of the typical American girl in Europe, he named her *Daisy Miller*. Little used in the modern era, but this is the kind of name that nostalgia may resurrect. The old song "Bicycle Built for Two" (which begins "Daisy, Daisy, give me your answer, do. . . .") is probably so obscure that it shouldn't prevent parents from selecting the name. Actress Daisy Fuentes.

Daisee, Daisey, Daisie, Dasie

Dakota American place name: the word may be Sioux for "Allies," though another source suggests "forever smiling." Despite its "-a" ending, this is used (perhaps because of the percussive consonants or the ruggedness it evokes) as a name for both boys and girls.

Dakoda, Dakotah

Dale OE. Place name: "Valley." Originally a surname meaning "One who lives in the valley." The term "dale" is still used in parts of England. Most popular as a first name in the 1930s. Actress Dale Evans.

Dael, Dail, Daile, Dalla, Dayle

Dalia Heb. "Slender branch, tendril."

Daliah, Dalit, Daliya, Dalya, Dalyah

Dalila Swahili. "Delicate."

Lila

Dallas Scot. Gael. Place name of a village in northeastern Scotland, used as a first name since the 19th century. Apparently unrelated to Dallas, Texas, which was named for a U.S. Vice President, but few modern Americans will fail to make the connection between the name and the city.

Dalles

Dalmace Lat./Fr. Place name: Dalmatia is a region of northeastern Italy, extending down into coastal Croatia, and the supposed origin of dalmatian dogs, white-haired with black spots.

Dalma, Dalmassa, Dalmatia

Damaris Gk. "Calf" is the most commonly proposed meaning though another source suggests "to tame." A Damaris in the New Testament was converted by Saint Paul, and the Puritans adopted the name with enthusiasm, if not uniformity in spelling. Many variants exist, though the name is very unusual.

Damalas, Damalis, Damalit, Damalla, Damara, Damaress, Dameris, Damerys, Dameryss, Damiris, Damris, Demaras, Demaris, Demarys, Mara, Mari, Maris

Damia Gk. Meaning not clear; possibly "To tame," although the Greek root is also close to the word for "Spirit." The masculine form, **Damian**, is more often seen.

Damian, Damiana, Damiane, Damienne, Damya, Damyan, Damyana, Damyen, Damyenne

Damita Sp. "Little noblewoman." From the root that gives us "dame."

Dama

Dana OE. "From Denmark." Also a surname, used as a boy's first name in the 19th century, but now almost exclusively a girl's name, and a specifically American one. Actress Dana Delany.

Danaca, Danay, Dane, Danet, Dania, Danica, Danna, Danya, Dayna, Donnica

Danae Gk. A character in Greek mythology, whom Zeus visited in the form of a shower of gold (a popular subject for Old Master painters). The child of this union was the heroic Perseus who rescued Andromeda.

Dee, Denae, Dene, Dinae, Dinay, Donnay

Dangelis Modern elaboration of **Angela**, perhaps suggested by the Italian last name, D'Angelo.

Dangela, Dangellis, Deangelis, Diangelis

Danica Lat. "From Denmark." There is a famous (and phenomenally expensive) Royal Copenhagen china pattern known as "Flora Danica," or "Flowers of Denmark." Actress Danica McKellar.

Danaca, Danika, Donika, Donnica

Danielle (Fem. **Daniel**) Heb. "God is my judge." Uncommon until the middle of the 20th century, when, following a revival of Daniel, it became more fashionable. Its popularity peaked in the mid-1990s. Novelist Danielle Steele.

Daanelle, Danee, Danele, Danella, Danelle, Danelly, Danette, Daney, Dani, Dania, Danica, Danice, Danie, Daniela, Daniella, Danijela, Danila, Danit, Danita, Danitza, Danna, Dannette, Danney, Danni, Danniella, Dannielle, Danny, Dannyce, Dany, Danya, Danyell, Danyella, Danyelle

Daphne Gk. "Laurel tree." In Greek mythology, Daphne was a nymph who, attempting to flee an amorous Apollo, was turned into a laurel tree. Though used under the Roman Empire, the name disappeared until the 18th century. It came to the U.S. as a slave name, and enjoyed a brief English vogue between 1900 and 1930. Pretty, unusual, but not trendy, Daphne is ripe for revival. Author Daphne Du Maurier.

Daffi, Daffie, Daffy, Dafna, Dafne, Dafnee, Dafneigh, Dafnie, Danfy, Daphna, Daphney, Daphnie

Dara Heb. "Nugget of wisdom." In the New Testament, a man's name, but its occasional modern use is for girls. Its resemblance to the familiar **Sarah** and **Farrah** probably works in its favor. Olympic swimmer Dara Torres.

Darda, Daria, Darian, Darragh, Darrah, Darya

Daralis OE. "Beloved."

Daralice, Darelis

Darby OE. Place name: "Park with deer." Derived from **Derby**, a surname used as a first name, almost exclusively for boys. Darby is also usually masculine.

Darb, Darbee, Darbey, Darbie, Darrbey, Darrbie, Darrby

Darcie Ir. Gael. "Dark." Also Norman place name, "From Arcy." In Britain, usually a boy's name, but in the U.S., more likely to be feminine. Ballerina Darci Kistler.

D'Arcy, Darcee, Darceigh, Darcey, Darcy, Darice, Darsee, Darseigh, Darsey, Darsie, Darsi

Darenda Invented name, composed of compatible elements to achieve a pretty sound. Though this trend may seem particularly current, parents have been making up names for hundreds of years.

Daria (Fem. **Darius**) Gk. "Rich."

Dari, Darian, Darice, Darien, Darya, Dhariana, Dorian, Doriane

Darice Modern feminization of **Darius**. The "-ice" ending has a real mid-twentieth century flavor.

Dareece, Dareese

Darlene Modern adaptation of "Darling" used for a given name. First used in the late 1930s and extremely fashionable by the 1950s in the U.S. Now out of style, and unlikely to be revived soon.

Dareen, Darelle, Darla, Darleen, Darlenny, Darline, Darlinn, Darlyn, Darlyne, Darrelle, Darryleen, Darrylene, Darryline

Daron (Fem. **Darren**) Modern use. Darren may be a transferred Irish surname, first used widely in the 1950s as a given name. Daron can be considered a feminine form because of its similiarity to **Sharon** (also popular in that era).

Daryl Transferred surname, possibly originated as a French place name, like **Darcy**. Its use was probably influenced by names that were fashionable in the mid 20th century, like **Cheryl**. Actress Daryl Hannah; fashion designer Darryl Kerrigan.

Darel, Darille, Darrel, Darrell, Darrelle, Darrill, Darrille, Darrylene, Darryline, Darryl, Darrylin, Darryline, Darrylyn, Darylin, Daryline, Darylyne, Derrill

Datya Heb. "Belief in God."

Datia, Datiah, Datyah

Davina (Fem. **David**) Heb. "Loved one." The most commonly used feminine variant of the hugely popular masculine name.

Daveen, Daviana, Daviane, Davida, Davidina, Davine, Davinia, Davita, Devina, Divina, Divinia

Dawn OE. "Dawn." Modern use of the word for a name. **Aurora**, the Latin term, dates back some fifteen hundred years, but Dawn first appeared in the late 1920s. Its popularity has waned considerably as taste turns back to the more stately polysyllabic names of the 19th century. Opera singer Dawn Upshaw; comedian Dawn French; basketball player Dawn Staley.

Dawna, Dawnita, Dawnyelle, Dawnysia, Dowan, Duwan, Dwan

Day OE. "Day." Possibly use of the word as a name, like **Dawn**, but more likely to be a transferred surname.

Daya Heb. "Bird of prey." Specifically, a kind of hawk known as a kite.

Dayah

Dea Lat. "Goddess."

Deanna OE. Place name "Valley" or occupational name "Church leader." Feminine of **Dean**, which only came into use as a first name in the 1950s. Could also be considered a version of **Diana**. Actress Deanna Durbin.

Deana, Deann, Deanne, Deeann, Deeanna

Debonnaire Fr. "Urbane, nonchalant." Perhaps a Norman family name: it could have meant "of good lineage." To moderns, debonair is the word you use to describe Fred Astaire.
Debonair, Debonaire

Deborah Heb. "Bee." One of the few significant women's names to figure in the Old Testament; in the Book of Judges, she was an important prophetess and judge. Predictably, the Puritans latched on to the name, but it was not widely used until the 1950s, possibly influenced by the career of actress Deborah Kerr. Like most names popular 60 years ago, it is little used for children now. Actresses Debbie Reynolds, Debra Winger, Debra Messing; Olympic figure skater Debi Thomas; TV journalist Deborah Norville.
Deb, Debb, Debbee, Debbera, Debbey, Debbi, Debbie, Debbra, Debby, Debee, Debera, Deberah, Debi, Debor, Debora, Debra, Debrah, Debs, Devora, Devorah, Dobra

Decca Possibly from the Greek root meaning "ten." Most famous perhaps as the Mitford family nickname for the journalist sister Jessica; and as a defunct American record label.
Decka, Deka

Decembra Month name. A way to refer to the holiday season without using **Noel**.

Decima Lat. "Tenth girl." Unlikely to be used in these days of small families.
Decia

Dee Welsh. "Swarthy." Dim. **Deirdre, Diana, Delia**, etc.
Dede, Dedie, DeeDee, DeeAnn, Didi

Deifilia Lat. "God's daughter."

Deiondra Fem. **Dion**; Dim. **Dionysus**. Dionysus is the Greek god of wine. The name Dion is used occasionally, recently by football player Deion Sanders, who named his daughter Deiondra.
Deionna, Diondra, Dionna

Deirdre Ir. Possible meanings are "Fear" or "Raging woman." In Irish myth, Deirdre was the most beautiful

woman in Ireland, whose tragically complex love life caused several deaths, including her own. The name has only been in use since the 1920s. Actress Deidre Hall.
Dede, Dedra, Dee, DeeDee, Deedre, Deidra, Deidre, Deidrie, Derdre, Didi, Dierdrey

Deja Fr. "Already." As in *déja vu*. Improbably well-used in the U.S.

Delana Adaptation of Delano, Franklin D. Roosevelt's middle name. Usage (it has never been anything but rare) coincided with FDR's presidential career.

Delancey Fr. Place name: Delancey Street in New York City, named for long-ago owners of nearby land.
Delancie, Delancy

Delaney Ir. Gael. "Offspring of the challenger."
DeLaina, Delaine, Delainey, Delainy, Delane, Delanie, Delany, DeLayna

Delia Gk. "From Delos." In Greek mythology, the goddess Artemis was born in Delos, so Delia could be an allusion to her. It may also be a diminutive of **Cordelia** or **Adelaide**. Though it has never had a period of great popularity, it has never faded from sight either. Author Delia Ephron.
Deelia, Delya

Delicia Lat. "Delight." Used in the Roman Empire, and occasionally since then, but never common. Nowadays it might be considered an elaboration of **Alicia**.
Dalicia, Dalise, Dalisha, Dalisse, Dee, DeeDee, Dela, Delice, Delis, Delise, Delisha, Delissa, Deliz, Della, Dellis, Dellise, Delyse, Delysia, Didi

Delight OF. The emotion as a name. Scarce.

Delilah Heb. "Lovelorn, seductive." In the Old Testament, mistress of Samson. The familiar story of how she cuts off his hair to sap his strength probably limits use of her name.
Dalila, Delila, Lila, Lilah

Della Short for **Adelle, Adeline, Adelaide.** Used as an independent name since the 1870s. Singer Della Reese.
Delle, Dellene, Delline

Delores Sp. "Sorrows." Var. **Dolores**.

Delphine Gk. "Dolphin." This is a French form of a name with a complex origin. It alludes to the Greek town of Delphi, home of a famous oracle. The Greeks believed that Delphi was the earth's womb; the dolphin's shape resembles that of a pregnant woman. The larkspur flower, whose center resembles a dolphin, is also known as delphinium, so in some respects this is a flower name. French actress Delphine Seyrig.

Delfa, Delfin, Delfine, Delfyne, Delpha, Delphina, Delphinea, Delphinia

Delta Fourth letter of the Greek alphabet, thus a name for a fourth child. May also be a place name, as in the Mississippi Delta. Actress Delta Burke.

Dellta

Demetria Gk. In Greek mythology, Demeter was goddess of corn, and mother of Persephone, whose abduction to Hades led to the cycle of seasons. Her Roman name is Ceres, from the word root that gives us "cereal."

Demeter, Demetra, Demetria, Demetris, Dimitra, Dimitria

Demelza Cornish. "Fort on the hill." First used as a given name in the 1950s, probably because of its pretty sound.

Demi Fr. "Half." As virtually everyone in America must know, the name of a certain shapely actress who pronounces it the "French" way with the accent on the last syllable.

Demee, Demie

Dena OE. Place name: "Valley." Use of Dena followed the popularity of **Dean** in the 1950s.

Deana, Deane, Deanna, Deena, Dene, Denna, Denni, Dina

Denelle Modern name: perhaps a simplification of the popular **Danielle**, or an elaboration of **Nell**.

Danell, Denell, Dinelle, Donell, Donella, Donelle

Denise (Fem. **Dennis**) Fr. "Follower of Dionysius." Though there is an ancient Latin form of the name (**Dionysia**), this variation dates back only to the 1920s. It was very popular in the 1950s, but since the mid1960s, has been eclipsed. Actress Denise Richards.

Deneigh, Denese, Dennet, Dennette, Deney, Deni, Denice, Deniece, Denisse, Denize, Denni, Dennie, Dennise, Denny, Denyce, Denys, Denyse, Dinnie, Dinny

Deolinda Port. "Beautiful God."

Deora Place name: a tiny town in northeastern Colorado.

Derinda Modern name, probably formed from **Derek** and **Linda**.

Darinda, Dorinda

Derora Heb. "A bird, a swallow."

Derorit, Drora, Drorah, Drorit, Droriya

Deryn Welsh. "Bird." Dates from the 1950s, and its popularity mirrors names like **Karen** and **Sharon**. Unusual after the 1970s.

Derran, Deren, Derhyn, Deron, Derrin, Derrine, Derron, Derrynne

Desdemona Gk. "Wretchedness." In Shakespeare's *Othello,* Desdemona is the beautiful, innocent heroine, wrongly accused of adultery by her husband, who then murders her, and commits suicide in a fit of remorse. Little used, for obvious reasons.

Desmona

Desirée Fr. "Much desired." The Puritans used **Desire** as a given name, though its connotations in the 17th century were religious rather than erotic. The French form is more usual today. An immensely popular novel published in the 1960s traced the biography of the French Desirée Clary from poverty in Marseilles to the throne of Sweden. The name is quite steadily used.

Desarae, Deseray, Desideria, Desir, Desirae, Desirat, Desiray, Desirea, Desiri, Disirae, Dezirae, Deziray

Desma Gk. "Binding oath."

Desmé

Destiny OF. "Fate." Infrequently used.

Desta, Destanay, Destianay, Destinay, Destinee, Destiney, Destinie, Destyni

Detta Dim. **Benedetta** (Lat. "Blessed").

Deva Hindi. "Godlike." In Hindu mythology, Deva is another name for the moon goddess.
Devi

Devin Ir. Gael. "Poet." Also an alternative spelling for **Devvon**.
Deva, Devinne, Devvin, Devyn

Devon OE. Place name: a county in Southern England. More common for girls than for boys. **Devin** may also be considered a variant.
Devan, Deven, Devenne, Devona, Devondra, Devonne, Devvon

Devri Dim. **Devora**; Var. **Deborah** (Heb. "Bee.")

Dextra (Fem. **Dexter**) OE. "Dyer." Lat. "Right-handed." Dexter, like most occupational names, was originally a surname. Dextra could also mean "skillful, dextrous."
Dextera

Deyanira Sp. from Gk. "Devastating, capable of great destruction." In Greco-Roman myth, the wife of Hercules, who managed by trickery to kill him.
Daianira, Dayanira, Deianira, Dellanira, Diyanira, Neera, Nira

Diamond Unusual jewel name, first used in the 1890s but not as common then as **Ruby, Emerald**, etc. In 2001, though, this was by far the most common of the jewel names. The gem is the birthstone for April.
Diamanta, Diamante

Diana "Divine." The Roman goddess of the moon, corresponding to the Greek Artemis. Used steadily since the 16th century, though the French version **Diane** eclipsed it in the mid-20th century. The vogue for Diane faded after the 1960s, and the apotheosis of Lady Diana Spencer as Princess of Wales in 1980 gave Diana new charm for prospective parents, especially in Britain. Even the disillusioning termination of her royal marriage and her tragic death may not deter future parents from naming daughters after this glamorous princess. French courtesan Diana de Poitiers; actresses Diahann Carroll, Dyan Cannon, Diane Keaton, Diane Lane, Dianne Wiest.

Danne, Dayann, Dayanna, Dayanne, Deana, Deane, Deandra, Deanna, Dede, Dee, DeeDee, Deeana, Deeane, Deann, Dena, Di, Diahann, Diahanne, Dian, Diandra, Diane, Diann, Dianna, Dianne, Didi, Dyan, Dyana, Dyane, Dyann, Dyanna, Dyanne

Diandra Possibly an elaboration of **Diana**. Another interpretation goes back to Greek word particles: "di-" means "two" and "-andra" means "male." The name could refer to flowers with two stamens, for instance.
Deandra, Dyandra

Dianthe Gk. "Flower of the gods."
Diandra, Diandre, Diantha

Didi Var. **Diana, Deirdre.** Actress Didi Conn.
DeeDee

Didiane Fr. Fem. **Didier**, which is in turn a form of **Desirée**, through the Latin **Desideratus**. They all mean "Desired." In America this name is likely to be heard as "Didi Ann."
Didiana, Didianna, Didiere

Dido Gk. In Virgil's *Aeneid,* the queen of Carthage who falls in love with the wandering Aeneas, and commits suicide when he leaves her. The name's origins are obscure: Virgil may have coined it. Pop musician Dido.

Didrika (Fem. **Dietrich**) OG. "People's ruler."
Diedericka, Diedricka, Diedrika

Dielle Fr. "God." Probably a female version of the French *dieu.* Unusual.
Diella

Digna Lat. "Worthy."
Deenya, Dinya

Dillian OE. "Idol, god." Pretty and very unusual name.
Diliana, Dilli, Dilliana, Dillianna

Dilys Welsh. "Reliable." Somewhat older than many names now popular in Wales, since it dates from the mid-19th century.
Dillys, Dylis, Dyllis, Dylys

Dimitra (Fem. **Demetrius**) Gk. "Follower of Demeter." Can also be considered a variant of **Demetria**.
Demetra, Demetria, Dimitria

Dimity Name of an unpretentious sheer cotton fabric that is textured with checks or stripes in the weaving.
Dimitee, Dimitey, Dimitie

Dimona Heb. "South."
Demona, Demonah, Dimonah

Dinah Heb. "Justified." Old Testament name. In the U.S., has been popular in the South. Dina may also be considered a diminutive of names like **Claudina**. Actresses Dina Merrill, Dinah Shore.
Dina, Dyna, Dynah

Dinya Heb. "Judgment of the Lord."
Dinia, Diniah, Dinyah

Dionne Two possible sources: Dione, in Greek mythology, is the mother of Aphrodite. The name can also be a feminine version of **Dion** (Gk. "Follower of Dionysus"). It is also a homonym for the French pronunciation of **Diane**. Singer Dionne Warwick.
Deiondra, Deonne, Dion, Diona, Diondra, Dione, Dionetta, Dionis, Dionna

Dionysia Lat. Form of **Denise** (Gk. "Follower of Dionysus").
Deonisia, Deonysia, Dinicia, Dinisha, Dinitia, Dionisia

Dita Var. **Edith** (OE. "Prosperity/battle").

Ditza Heb. "Joy."
Ditzah, Diza

Divina It. "Divine, heavenly." Also Var. **Davina** (Heb. "Loved one").
Divine, Divinia

Dixie Fr. "Tenth." The term "Dixie" for the Southern states, made popular by the song, is mysterious. It might come from the Mason-Dixon line, or from Louisiana dollars printed in French with the word *dix* on them (hence, "the land of 'dixies' "). Actress Dixie Carter.
Dix, Dixee

Docila Lat. "Biddable."

Dodie Heb. "Well loved." Familiar form of **Dora, Dorothy** (Gk. "Gift of God"). Author Dodie Smith.
Doda, Dodee, Dodey, Dodi, Dody

Dolly Familiar form of **Dorothy**. As an independent name, it was most popular at the turn of the century, but never a favorite. First Lady Dolley Madison; country singer Dolly Parton.

Dollee, Dolley, Dollie

Dolores Sp. "Sorrows." An allusion to the Virgin Mary, Santa Maria de los Dolores. During the 1920s and '30s the name crossed over strongly into the Anglo world, possibly sparked by the career of actress Dolores Del Rio.

Dalores, Delora, Delores, Deloria, Deloris, Dolorcita, Dolorcitas, Dolorita, Doloritas, Lola, Lolita

Domina Lat. "Lady."

Dominique (Fem. **Dominic**) Lat. "Lord." French form of a Latin name, rather fashionable in the last 25 years. Could be used for a child born on Sunday, "the Lord's day." Olympic gymnasts Dominique Dawes, Dominique Moceanu.

Domaneke, Domanique, Domenica, Domeniga, Domenique, Dominga, Domineek, Domineke, Domini, Dominica, Dominie, Dominika, Dominizia, Domino, Domitia, Meeka, Mika, Domorique

Domitilla Lat. Clan name: the second-century saint Flavia Domitilla allowed her gardens in Rome to be used as a Christian cemetery.

Domicia, Domitila, Domitilia

Dona Sp. "Lady." Unusual variation on **Donna**.

Donalda Scot. Gael. "World mighty." One of many attempts to form a feminine of **Donald** Scot. Particularly popular in the first half of the 20th century.

Dona, Donaldette, Donaldina, Donaline, Donelda, Donetta, Donia, Donita

Donata Lat. "Given." From the same root that gives us "donate."

Donatila, Donatilia

Donna It. "Lady." The original meaning is closer to "lady of the home." Strictly modern use as a given name, dating from the 1920s. Very popular in the 1950s, but little used now. Actress Donna Reed; swimming champion Donna Devarona; fashion designer Donna Karan; singer Donna Summer.

Dona, Donalie, Donella, Donelle, Donetta, Donia, Donica, Donielle, Donita, Donnell, Donnella, Donnelle, Donni, Donnica, Donnie, Donnisse, Donny, Ladonna

Dora Gk. "Gift." Probably originated as a diminutive of names like **Theodora**, and introduced as an independent name by a character in Charles Dickens's *David Copperfield*. Its heyday in the U.S. came at the turn of the century, but it is currently popular in Greece. Good potential for revival as it is quaint and dignified but not unwieldy for a small child.

Dodee, Dodi, Dodie, Dody, Doralee, Doraleene, Doralia, Doralice, Doralicia, Doralina, Doralisha, Doralyn, Doralynn, Dore, Dorea, Doree, Doreen, Dorelia, Dorelle, Dorena, Dorene, Doretta, Dorette, Doreyda, Dori, Dorie, Dorita, Dorrie, Dory

Dorcas Gk. "Gazelle." New Testament name, Greek version of **Tabitha**. Saint Peter raised her from the dead. Predictably, well used by the Puritans, but uncommon since.

Dorcass, Dorcia, Dorkas

Dorée Fr. "Gilded."

Dorae, Doraie, D'Oray, Dore, Doree, Dorey, Dory

Doreen Several possible origins, including Ir. Gael. "Brooding," Fr. "Gilded," and an elaboration of **Dora**. In the top ten in Britain in the 1920s, now unusual.

Dorene, Doreyn, Dorine, Dorreen, Doryne

Doretta Gk. "Gift from God." Variant of **Dora** or **Theodora**.

Doria Gk. Place name: "From Doris," an area in Greece. Also feminine of **Dorian**; Var. **Dorothy, Theodora** (Gk. "Gift from God").

Dori, Dorian, Doriane, Dorianne, Dorria, Dory

Dorinda Gk./Sp. Var. **Dora**. English poets in the 18th century coined a number of names with the "-inda" suffix. This one has enjoyed a small revival in this century.

Derinda, Dorrinda, Dyrinda

Doris (Fem. **Dorian**) Gk. Place name: "From Doris," an area in Greece. This form is more common than **Doria**, having been hugely popular between 1900 and the 1930s, when it subsided. To most people having children these days, Doris is the name of a much older woman. Actress Doris Day; writer Doris Lessing.

Dori, Doria, Dorice, Dorisa, Dorita, Dorrie, Dorry, Dorrys, Dory, Dorys, Doryse

Dorma Lat. "Sleeping." As in "dormitory." Equally possibly, a variation on the familiar **Norma**.

Dorrma

Dorona Heb. "Gift."

Doran, Dorran

Dorothy Gk. "Gift of God." **Theodora**, never as popular, simply reverses the order of the Greek words. Has had two periods of popularity, around 1500 to 1700, and 1900 to the mid-1920s. The latter vogue may have been inspired by the heroine of Frank Baum's *The Wonderful Wizard of Oz*, published in 1900. The success of the film version (1939) and its perennial popularity ensure that most people, upon first meeting a child named Dorothy, cannot help thinking of Judy Garland. Writers Dorothy Parker, Dorothy Sayers; actresses Dorothy Gish, Dorothy Lamour.

Dasha, Dasya, Dodie, Dody, Doe, Doll, Dolley, Dolli, Dollie, Dolly, Doortje, Dora, Doretta, Dori, Dorika, Dorinda, Dorit, Dorita, Doritha, Dorlisa, Doro, Doronit, Dorota, Dorotea, Doroteya, Dorothea, Dorothée, Dorrit, Dorthea, Dorthy, Dory, Dosha, Dosya, Dot, Dottey, Dottie, Dotty, Tea, Thea

Dorrit Dim. **Dorothy**. Another example of the influence of popular culture on names, as it probably stems from Charles Dickens's novel *Little Dorrit*.

Dorita, Doritt

Dorsey Place name: possibly French, "From Orsay," or related to Dorset, a county on the southern coast of England.

Dorcie, Dorsay, Dorsea, Dorseigh, Dorsie

Dory Fr. "Gilded." Dim. **Dorothy, Isadora**.

Douce Fr. "Sweet."

Dove Bird name. The dove, of course, symbolizes peace, God's covenant with Noah, and the Holy Spirit.

Dova

Doveva Heb. "Graceful."
  Dova, Dovit
Dreama As in what happens when you go to sleep.
Drew Dim. **Andrew** (Gk. "Masculine"). More commonly
  used for boys. When used as a girl's name, it is probably
  a transferred surname, though it has been given new ex-
  posure by the career of actress Drew Barrymore.
Drusilla Lat. Feminine version of a Roman clan name
  which appears in the New Testament. Very unusual nowa-
  days. Philanthropist Drue Heinz.
  **Drewsila, Dru, Drucella, Drucie, Drucilla, Drucy,
  Drue, Druesilla, Druscilla, Drusella, Drusy**
Duane Ir. Gael. "Swarthy." Dates from the 1940s. More
  common for boys. Socialite Duane Hampton.
  Duana, Duna, Dwana, Dwayna, Dwayne
Duena Sp. "Chaperone."
Dulcie Lat. "Sweet." Roman name revived for some years
  at the turn of the 20th century, but extremely unusual
  now. Cervantes used a slightly different form when he
  named the heroine of *Don Quixote* **Dulcinea**.
  **Delcina, Delcine, Delsine, Dulce, Dulcea, Dulci, Dulcia,
  Dulciana, Dulcibella, Dulcibelle, Dulcine, Dulcinea,
  Dulcy, Dulsea, Dulsia, Dulsiana, Dulsibell, Dulsine**
Dumia Heb. "Silent."
  Dumiya
Duscha Rus. "Happy."
  Duschenka, Duschinka, Dusica, Dusa
Dusty (Fem. **Dustin**) An English place name transferred to
  first name. Probably popularized in this century by En-
  glish singer Dusty Springfield. Today's parents are more
  likely to simply use Dustin for a baby of either gender.
  Dustan, Dustee, Dustie, Dustin
Dylana (Fem. **Dylan**) Welsh. "Born from waves." Use of
  Dylan tends to be a tribute to the poet Dylan Thomas.
  Most parents today would not hesitate to use the original,
  masculine name for a girl, though it is markedly popular
  for boys. Entrepreneur Dylan Lauren.
  Dillan, Dillon, Dylane, Dyllan
Dympna Ir. Gael. Saint's name of obscure origin. Many

cures of epilepsy and other mental disturbances were attributed to her, and she became known as patroness of the insane. A medieval mental hospital in Belgium, in the town where her bones were discovered, is still going strong.
Dymphna

Earla (Fem. **Earl**) OE. "Nobleman, leader." Several English aristocratic titles such as Duke, Earl, and Baron have been turned into proper names, a sterling example of wishful thinking. Feminine variants are more uncommon.
Earldena, Earldene, Earldina, Earleen, Earlene, Earletta, Erlette, Earley, Earlie, Earline, Erlene, Erletta, Erlette, Erlina, Erline, Erlinia, Ireleen, Irelene, Irelina, Irelene

Eartha OE. "Earth." Used by the Puritans in the 17th century, but obsolete since then. New Age, environmentally conscious parents may bring this name back to a degree of popularity. Singer Eartha Kitt.
Erda, Ertha, Herta, Hertha

Easter Name of the holiday, transferred to use as a Christian name predominantly in the 19th century. (Some sources trace it to a variation of **Esther**.) A more common Eastertide name is the French **Pascale**.

Ebba OE. "Fortress of riches" or ONorse. "Strength of a boar." There was a 7th-century saint in northern England named Edburga, which was probably contracted to Ebba.
Ebbe

Eberta Teut. "Bright."

Ebony Name of the wood, which is prized for its black color. In use since the 1970s with African-American families, who also favor other descriptive names like **Amber** and **Tawny**. Ebony has dropped dramatically in usage, though, since the mid-1990s.
Ebboney, Ebbony, Ebonee, Eboney, Ebonney, Ebonni, Ebonny, Eboni, Ebonie, Ebonyi

Echo Gk. Name of a mythological nymph who was a disembodied voice. One version of her story holds that she pined away of love for Narcissus until only her voice was left. A pretty choice for lovers of Greek culture, though it might turn out to be a little too appropriate for a chatty child.

Eda OE. "Wealthy, happy." Also possibly a variation of **Edith**.

Ede

Edana (Fem. **Aidan**) Gael. "Fire." Saint Aidan was a 7th-century Irish monk. Although Aidan is still primarily a boy's name (and chugging up the popularity charts at a rapid rate), it is increasingly used for girls as well.

Aidana, Aydana

Edeline OG. "Noble, nobility." Var. **Adeline**.

Edelina

Edelmira Sp. from Ger. "Admired for nobility."

Eden Heb. "Pleasure, delight." It is a short step from the Hebrew meaning of the word to its general association with Paradise. The name is used, infrequently, for boys as well as girls, though its brisk rhythm and alluring meaning could bring it new prominence in the next few years.

Eaden, Eadin, Edenia, Edin

Edina OE. Possibly a form of **Edwina**, or a literary term meaning "From Edinburgh," the capital city of Scotland. One of the characters in the dotty British sitcom "Absolutely Fabulous" is called Edina: she is not what most parents would consider a good role model. Fashion designer Edina Ronay.

Adena, Adina, Edeena, Edyna

Edith OE. "Prosperity/battle." Anglo-Saxon name that continued to be used after the Norman Conquest, and was revived along with other ancient names in the 19th century. By the 1870s it was one of the ten most popular girls' names in Britain, but has been steadily displaced since the 1930s. At the moment associations with characters like Edith Bunker make it seem dated rather than pleasantly old-fashioned. Writer Edith Wharton; singers

Eydie Gorme and Edith Piaf; actresses Dame Edith Evans, Edie Falco.

Dita, Eadie, Eadith, Eda, Ede, Edi, Edie, Edita, Editha, Edithe, Ediva, Edy, Edyth, Edytha, Edythe, Eidith, Eidyth, Eidytha, Eyde, Eydie, Eydith

Edlyn OE. "Small noble one."

Edelynn, Edlin, Edlinn, Edlinna, Edlynn

Edmonda (Fem. **Edmund**) OE. "Wealthy defender." A popular, and sainted, king of the East Angles in the 9th century gave the masculine version of the name enough popularity to survive the Norman Conquest. The feminine variants are unusual.

Edma, Edmée, Edmonde, Edmunda

Edna Heb. "Pleasure, enjoyment." Perhaps arising from the same root as **Eden**. First used in the 18th century, but very popular in the last half of the 19th century, especially in America. Now almost unheard-of. Poet Edna St. Vincent Millay; novelist Edna Ferber.

Eddi, Eddie, Eddna, Eddnah, Eddy, Ednah

Edrea OE. "Wealthy, powerful."

Edra, Eidra, Eydra

Edris (Fem. **Edric**) Anglo-Saxon. "Wealthy, powerful." The masculine version was an Old English name revived slightly in the 19th century; feminine variants are uncommon.

Edrice, Edriss, Edryce, Eidris, Eidriss, Eydris, Edrys, Idrice, Idris, Idrys

Edwardine (Fem. **Edward**) OE. "Wealthy defender." Rare and slightly awkward variant of a steadily well-used masculine name.

Edwarda, Edwardeen, Edwardene, Edwardina, Edwardyne

Edwige Fr. from OG. "Happy battle."

Eduvigis, Edvig, Edvigis, Edwig, Hedvig, Hedwig, Hedwige

Edwina (Fem. **Edwin**) OE. "Wealth/friend." Feminine variant of an Anglo-Saxon name revived in the 19th century, but never hugely popular.

Edina, Edweena, Edwiena, Edwena, Edwine, Edwinna, Edwyna, Edwynne

Effie Gk. "Pleasant speech." Short version of **Euphemia**, used as an independent name starting in the 1860s. Popularity faded after the 1930s.

Efffemie, Effemy Effi, Effy, Efthemia, Ephie, Eppie, Euphemia, Euphemie, Euphie

Efrata Heb. "Fertile, fruitful; honored." An Old Testament name: Efrata was the second wife of Caleb.

Efrat, Ephrata

Egberta (Fem. **Egbert**) OE. "Brilliant sword."

Egbertha, Egbertina, Egbertine, Egbertyna, Ebgertyne

Egeria In Roman mythology, a wise nymph who helped one of the early kings of Rome draft legislation. In more literate times, wise women who advised statesmen were sometimes referred to as "Egeria."

Aegeria, Ejeria, Igeria

Egidia Latinized feminine form of **Giles** (Gk. "Kid, young goat"). Mostly Scottish use.

Aegidia, Egidiana

Egelina OG. from Lat. "Eagle." In the variations on this name you can trace the evolution of the word, from the Latin *aquilina* to the English "eagle."

Agilina, Eaglin, Egilina

Eglantine OF. Poetic-sounding botanical name for the shrub also known as "sweetbrier."

Eglantyne

Eibhlin Ir. Gael. "Shining, brilliant." Form of **Evelyn**, the English phonetic version, or **Helen**. More commonly anglicized as **Eileen** or **Aileen**.

Aibhlin

Eila Dim. **Ilana** (Heb. "Tree, oak tree") or **Eileen** (Ir. "Shining, bright"). Names as short as this are sometimes impossible to trace accurately, because very similar word particles may have different meanings in different languages.

Eilah, Eilona, Ela, Elah, Ila

Eileen Ir. "Shining, brilliant." Form of **Helen**. Irish names were fashionable in England around 1870, when the issue of Irish Home Rule was being hotly debated in Great Britain. By the 1920s (when the Irish Free State was finally formed) Eileen was one of the most popular girls' names in Britain. It has never been quite as fashionable in the U.S. Fashion designer Eileen Fisher; actress Eileen Brennan.

Aileen, Ailene, Alene, Aline, Ayleen, Eila, Eilah, Eilean, Eilleen, Eiley, Eily, Ileana, Ileanna, Ileene, Ilene, Iliana, Ilianna, Leana, Lena, Lianna, Lina

Eilish Ir. Gael. Var. **Elizabeth** (Heb. "Pledged to God").

Eilis, Elis, Elish

Eiluned Welsh. "Idol." Var. **Lynette**.

Eluned

Eir ONorse. "Peacefulness/mercy."

Eira Welsh. "Snow." Mostly 20th-century use; a pretty name for a winter baby.

Eirian Welsh. "Silver." Another modern Welsh name.

Eithne Ir. "Fire." See **Aithne**, feminine version of **Aidan**.

Aine, Aithnea, Eithne, Ena, Ethnah, Ethnea, Ethnee

Ekaterina Slavic. Var. **Catherine** (Gk. "Pure"). Olympic figure skater Ekaterina Gordeeva.

Yekaterina

Elaine OF. "Bright, shining, light." Form of **Helen**. In the King Arthur myths, Elaine is a maiden who desperately loves Lancelot. Tennyson's version of the tale has her dying of this love, but in an earlier telling, she actually has a son—Galahad—by Lancelot. Tennyson's poetry may have contributed to the 19th-century revival of the name. Film director Elaine May.

Alaina, Alayna, Alayne, Allaine, Elaina, Elana, Elane, Elanna, Elaene, Elayne, Ellaina, Ellaine, Ellane, Ellayne, Lainey, Layney

Elata Lat. "Lofty, elevated."

Elba Dim. **Elberta**. Also a place name: the island off the coast of Italy to which Napoleon was first exiled, and from which he escaped. The Elbe, similar in sound, is an important river in Germany and the Czech Republic.

Elbe, Ellba

Elberta (Fem. **Elbert**) OE. "Highborn/shining." Var. **Alberta**.

Elbertha, Elberthe

Eldora Sp. "Covered with gold." The Indian legend about the land of the Golden Man (El Dorado) kept explorers and conquistadores like Coronado and Pizarro combing the South American jungles and mountains through the 16th century.

Eldorada, Eldoree, Eldoria, Eldoris

Eleanor Possibly a form of **Helen** (Gk. "Light") or from a different Greek root meaning "Clemency, mercy." The queen of Henry II of England, Eleanor of Aquitaine, introduced the name to England in the 13th century, and it has been used steadily since, especially in the U.S., under the influence of much-loved First Lady Eleanor Roosevelt. Charles II's mistress Nell Gwynn; Italian actress Eleonora Duse; women's rights activist Eleanor Smeal.

Aleanor, Alenor, Aleonore, Aline, Allinor, Eileen, Elaine, Eleanora, Eleanore, Elen, Elena, Elenor, Elenora, Elenore, Eleonora, Eleonore, Elianora, Elianore, Elienora, Elienore, Elinor, Elinore, Ella, Elladine, Elleanor, Elleanora, Elle, Ellen, Ellene, Ellenora, Ellenore, Elleonor, Elli, Ellie, Ellin, Ellinor, Ellinore, Elly, Ellyn, Elna, Elnora, Elyn, Enora, Heleanor, Heleonor, Helen, Helena, Helene, Helenora, Leanora, Lena, Lenora, Lenore, Leonora, Leonore, Leora, Lina, Nelda, Nell, Nelle, Nelley, Nelli, Nellie, Nelly, Nonnie, Nora, Norah, Norina

Electra Gk. "Shining, bright." Though the name is derived from the same roots as the word "electricity," many people will associate it with the Greek tragedies of the house of Atreus, told by Aeschylus, Euripides, Sophocles, and retold by Eugene O'Neill in the play *Mourning Becomes Electra*. All versions involve incest, murder, and vengeance, themes not usually associated with babies.

Alectra, Elektra, Elettra, Ellectra, Ellektra, Ilectra

Elena Sp. Var. **Helen** (Gk. "Light"). Now used more often than the Anglo version.

Elaina

Eleuthera Gk. "Freedom, liberty." Also a place name: an island in the Bahamas.

Eleftheria, Elefteria, Elesteria, Eleutheria, Eleutherya

Elfrida OE. "Elf/power." See **Alfreda**. Uncommon.

Alfrida, Alfrieda, Elfie, Elfre, Elfredah, Elfredda, Elfreeda, Elfrida, Elfrieda, Elfryda, Elfrydah, Ellfreda, Elva, Elvah, Freda, Freddi, Freddy, Freeda, Frieda, Friedah, Fryda

Elga Slavic. "Sacred." See **Olga**.

Elgiva, Ellga, Helga

Eliane (Fem. **Elias**) Fr. from Heb. "Jehovah is God."

Elia, Eliana, Elianna, Eliette, Elice, Eline, Elyette

Elidi Gk. "Gift of the sun."

Elinda Var. **Belinda**.

Eliora Heb. "The Lord is my light."

Eleora, Eliorah, Elleora, Elliora

Elise Fr. Var. **Elizabeth** (Heb. "Pledged to God").

Eliese, Elisa, Elisee, Elize, Elyce, Elyse, Liese, Liesel, Lieselotte, Liesl, Lise, Lison, Lize

Elisheva Heb. "The Lord is my pledge."

Eliseva, Elisheba

Elissa Form of **Alice** or **Elizabeth**. First appeared around the 1930s, and is now fairly common in all its various spellings, though by far the most popular is **Alyssa**.

Alissa, Allissa, Allyssa, Alyssa, Elissia, Ellissa, Elysa, Elyssa, Elyssia, Ilissa, Ilysa, Ilyssa, Lissa, Lissie, Lissy, Lyssa

Elita Lat. "The elect, chosen."

Elitta, Ellita, Lita

Eliza Dim. **Elizabeth**. Frequently used in its own right from the 18th century onward, and probably most famous as the name of the escaping slave in *Uncle Tom's Cabin* and Cockney flower girl Eliza Dolittle in *My Fair Lady*. Especially popular in the first decade of the 20th century. The recent fondness for nostalgic-sounding names has brought it to some prominence. Actress Eliza Dushku.

Aliza, Alizah, Elizah, Elyza, Elyzza, Liza

Elixyvett Modern name. This combination of elements from **Alexandra** (Gk. "Man's defender") and **Yvette**

(OG. "Yew wood") ends up sounding remarkably like **Elizabeth**. Few portmanteau names end up being as compact and elegant. The variations below are just a few of the ways parents could elect to spell this name.

Alixevette, Alixyvetha, Elixevetta, Elixyvetha, Elixyvette

Elizabeth Heb. "Pledged to God." One of the ten most popular girls' names in the U.S. for the past dozen years; in the top 5 in Australia, Canada, and Great Britain. Used in full, it has a pleasant, old-fashioned ring, though some research attaches a "seductive" connotation to it (perhaps by association with actress Elizabeth Taylor). It is a source of endless diminutives and nicknames which keeps it a perennial favorite. Saint Elizabeth, mother of John the Baptist; poet Elizabeth Barrett Browning; Queens Elizabeth I and II of England; actresses Elizabeth Ashley, Elizabeth Montgomery, Elisabeth Shue, Elizabeth Hurley; politician Elizabeth Dole; suffragette Elizabeth Cady Stanton.

Alixyveth, Babette, Belita, Bell, Bella, Belle, Bess, Bessie, Bessy, Beth, Betsey, Betsie, Betsy, Bett, Betta, Bette, Betti, Bettina, Bettine, Betty, Bettye, Buffy, Elisa, Elisabet, Elisabeth, Elisabetta, Elise, Elissa, Eliza, Elizabet, Elizabetta, Elizabette, Elixyveth, Elle, Elliza, Ellsa, Ellse, Ellsee, Ellsey, Ellsi, Ellspet, Ellyse, Ellyssa, Ellyza, Elsa, Else, Elsee, Elsie, Elspet, Elspeth, Elsy, Elyse, Elyssa, Elyza, Elyzza, Elzbieta, Helsa, Ilsa, Ilse, Isabel, Isabella, Isabelle, Isobel, Leesa, Leeza, Lib, Libbey, Libbi, Libbie, Libby, Libbye, Lilibet, Lisa, Lisabeth, Lisbet, Lisbeth, Lisbett, Lisbetta, Lisbette, Lise, Lisette, Lissa, Lissi, Lissy, Liz, Liza, Lizabeth, Lizbeth, Lizette, Lizzi, Lizzy, Lusa, Lysa, Lysbet, Lysbeth, Lysbette, Lyssa, Lyssie, Lyza, Lyzbet, Lyzbeth, Lyzbette, Lyzette, Ylisabet, Ylisabette, Ysabel, Ysabella, Yzabelle

Elkana Heb. "God has made." More commonly used by men, and a man's name in the Old Testament.

Elkanah, Elkanna

Elke Ger. Var. **Alice** (OG. "Noble, nobility"). Possibly introduced to the English-speaking world by actress Elke Sommer.

Elka, Elike, Ilka

Ella OG. "All, completely." Also possibly derived from **Alice, Eleanor, Ellen**. Common in the Middle Ages and revived in America in the late 19th century, but now unusual. Singer Ella Fitzgerald.

Alla, Ela, Elladine, Elletta, Ellette, Elley, Elli, Ellie, Ellina, Elly

Ellamae Comb. form **Ella** and **May**, two very popular 19th-century names.

Ellamay

Ellen Var. **Helen** (Gk. "Shining, brightness"). Both forms have been popular, but rarely at the same time. In America Ellen has dominated since the 1950s, but neither version is much used now. A diminutive, **Ellie**, is popular in Scotland. English actress Ellen Terry; American actresses Ellyn Burstyn, Ellen Barkin, Ellen DeGeneres.

Elan, Elen, Elena, Elene, Eleni, Elenita, Elenyi, Elin, Ellan, Ellin, Ellene, Ellie, Ellon, Elly, Ellyn, Elon, Elyn

Ellice (Fem. **Elias**) Gk. "The Lord is God." Also possibly variant of **Alice** or **Ellis**.

Elice

Elma Dim. of names like **Wilhelmina** (OG. "Will/helmet") or variant of **Alma** (Lat. "soul").

Ellma

Elmina Dim. **Wilhelmina** (OG. "Will/helmet"). Mildly popular in the 19th century.

Almeena, Almena, Almina, Elmeena, Elmena

Elmira Arab. "Aristocratic lady." See **Almera**. Also possibly a feminization of **Elmer** (OE. "Highborn and renowned").

Allmera, Allmeera, Almeria, Almira, Almyra, Ellmera, Ellmeria, Ellmeera, Elmeeria, Elmera, Elmeria, Elmerya, Elmyrah, Mera, Meera, Mira, Mirah, Myra, Myrah

Elodie Fr. from Gk. "Marsh flower."

Elodea, Elodia, Helodea, Helodia, Helodie

Eloise Fr. form of **Louise** (OG. "Renowned in battle").

Made famous in the 12th century by the love letters between Heloise and Abelard. Modern parents, though, are more likely to think of the madcap six-year-old denizen of New York's Plaza Hotel who stars in Kay Thompson's books for children.

Aloysia, Eloisa, Elouisa, Elouise, Heloise

Elpida Gk. "Hope."

Elrica OG. "Ruler over all."

Elsa Dim. **Elizabeth**. Now rare, in spite of the lingering fame of actress Elsa Lanchester. Nature buffs may remember Joy Adamson's famous lion Elsa in the book and movie called *Born Free*.

Else, Elsie, Elssa, Elsy, Ilsa, Ilse

Elsie Var. **Elizabeth** via its Scottish form, **Elspeth**. Independently used since the 18th century, and extremely popular in the U.S. by the late 19th. After the 1920s, its use faded.

Ellsey, Ellsi, Ellsie, Elsea, Elsee, Elsey, Elsi

Elspeth Scot. Var. **Elizabeth**. Unusual outside Scotland. Author Elspeth Huxley.

Elsbeth, Elsbet, Elspet, Elspie

Eluned Welsh. "Idol, image." Used mostly in Wales. The French version, **Lynette**, is more common in the U.S.

Elined, Eiluned, Lanet, Lanette, Linet, Linette, Luned, Lynette, Lynnette

Elva Ir. "Noble, bright." Phonetic anglicization of the unusual Irish name **Ailbhe**.

Ailbhe, Elfie, Elvia, Elvie

Elvina (Fem. **Elvin**) OE. "Noble friend" or "Elf friend."

Alveena, Alvina, Alvine, Alvinia, Elvena, Elveena, Elvene, Elvenia, Elvine, Elvinia, Vina, Vinni, Vinnie, Vinny

Elvira Sp. Meaning unclear, possibly a place name. An Elvira figures in several versions of the story of Don Juan, as well as other operas. The name seems to be used more in art than in life, however.

Ellvira, Elva, Elveera, Elvera, Elvina, Elvire, Elvyra, Elwira, Lira

Elysia Lat. From "Elysium," the mythical home of the

blessed, also known as the "Elysian fields." Dates from the 1940s. Such modern borrowings from the classical world are unusual, but this name is sufficiently like the familiar **Elise** not to seem peculiar. It also sounds exactly like one pronunciation of the more common **Alicia**.

Aleesyia, Eleese, Eliese, Elise, Elisia, Elyse, Ileesia, Ilise, Ilysa, Ilysia, Ilyse

Emeline OG. Possibly "Industrious." Possibly also a variant of **Emily** or **Amelia**. Norman name revived in the 18th century, now extremely rare despite its numerous variants.

Emaleen, Emalene, Emaline, Emalyn, Embline, Emblyn, Emelen, Emelyn, Emiline, Emlyn, Emmalee, Emmalene, Emmaline, Emmalyn, Emmalynne, Emmeline, Emmiline, Emylin, Emylynn

Emerald Jewel name, less common than **Pearl, Ruby**, or the most popular such name, **Diamond**. Occurs most frequently in its Spanish form, **Esmeralda**. It is the birthstone for May. English socialite Emerald Cunard.

Emeralda, Emeraldina, Emeraude, Esmeralda

Emily Lat. Clan name. In spite of the similarity of form, it has a different root from **Amelia**. Naturally, many of the variants are very close. A hugely popular name in the 19th century, lost status after 1900, and is now in favor again. Emily was the third-most popular name in the United States in the 1990s. It is also very fashionable in Great Britain. Poet Emily Dickinson; novelist Emily Brontë, etiquette maven Emily Post; actress Emily Watson.

Aemiley, Aemilie, Aimil, Amalea, Amalia, Amalie, Amelia, Amelie, Ameline, Amelita, Amy, Eimile, Em, Emalee, Emalia, Emelda, Emelea, Emeli, Emelia, Emelie, Emelina, Emeline, Emelita, Emelly, Emely, Emelyn, Emelyne, Emera, Emila, Emilea, Emilee, Emiley, Emili, Emilia, Emilie, Emiline, Emilla, Emillea, Emilley, Emillie, Emilly, Emlyn, Emlynn, Emlynne, Emmalee, Emmalie, Emmaline, Emmalyn, Emmalynn, Emmalynne, Emmelee, Emmely, Emmey, Emmi, Emmie, Emmilee, Emmilie, Emmily, Emmlee, Emmy, Emmye, Emyle, Emylee, Milka

SPELL THAT, PLEASE

Many parents like to put a twist on their baby's name by spelling it in an unusual way. They may be hoping to add a bit of individuality to the name, or make it memorable. Experts tend to see this as a bad idea: By the time your child reaches school age, the inconvenience of having to spell "Emylee" to every stranger (and correct the ones who get it wrong) tells you why. What's more, you take the chance that their innovative spelling may be seen as pretentious or even illiterate. So think long and hard if you're considering writing "Nickolaus" on the birth certificate. Your child will probably thank you.

Emina Lat. "Eminent."

Emma OG. "Embracing everything." Royal name in medieval England, and hugely popular at the end of the 19th century. Brought back to notice by Emma Peel in the popular TV series *The Avengers,* and is now one of the top girls' names in Ireland and Scotland. Still less common in America, but gaining favor among literate parents, who have a host of historical and artistic Emmas to name their daughters after. Lady Emma Hamilton, Lord Nelson's mistress; Emma Bovary of *Madame Bovary*; Jane Austen's novel *Emma*; actresses Emma Samms, Emma Thompson.

Em, Ema, Emelina, Emeline, Emelyne, Emmaline, Emmalyn, Emmalynn, Emmalynne, Emme, Emmeleia, Emmeline, Emmelyn, Emmelyne, Emmet, Emmett, Emmette, Emmi, Emmie, Emmot, Emmott, Emmy, Emmye

Emmanuelle (Fem. **Emmanuel**) Heb. "God is among us." Fashion designer Emmanuelle Khanh.

Emanuela, Emanuella, Emanuelle, Emmanuella, Emonualle, Emonualle

Empress The title used as name. An empress, of course,

ranks even higher than a queen. Queen Victoria took the
title Empress of India in 1877.

Emperatriz, Imperatrice, Imperatrix

Ena Short for names like **Georgina, Regina,** etc. Queen
Victoria's granddaughter Princess Victoria Eugenie, who
became queen of Spain, was known as Princess Ena.

Eena, Ina

Engracia Sp. from Lat. "Endowed with God's grace."

Enid Welsh. "Life, spirit." Name from the King Arthur
myths revived mildly in the early 19th century and quite
popular in England by the 1920s. Never much used in
America. Author Enid Bagnold.

Eanid, Ened, Enedd, Enidd, Enyd, Enydd

Ennis Ir. Place name: the principal town of County Clare.

Ennish, Innis

Enrica (Fem. **Henry**) It. "Home ruler."

Enricka, Enricketta, Enriqueta, Enriquette

Enya Var. **Eithne** (Ir. Gael. "Fire"). Other sources suggest
"kernel" as a meaning. Enya is the name of an Irish pop
singer.

Aenya, Ennya

Erga Heb. "Yearning, craving."

Erica (Fem. **Eric**) Scand. "Ruler forever." Though a staple in
Scandinavia, it wasn't used in the English-speaking world
until the late 19th century. It still has a strongly European
flair. Writer Erica Jong; singer Rickie Lee Jones; actresses
Ricki Lake, Erika Christensen; singer Erykah Badu.

**Aerica, Aericka, Airica, Airicka, Airika, Enrica, Enrika,
Eraca, Ericka, Erika, Erricka, Errika, Eryca, Erycka,
Eyrica, Rickee, Ricki, Rickie, Ricky, Rikki, Rikky**

Erin Ir. Gael. "From the island to the west." Erin is a literary term for Ireland, hence the name's popularity among
Irish-descended families. Ironically, it is not much used
in Ireland itself, but is currently a favorite in Scotland.

**Aeran, Aerenne, Aerin, Airin, Eire, Eirin, Eirinn, Eiryn,
Eirynn, Erina, Erinn, Eryn, Erynn**

Eris In Greek mythology, the sister of Ares (god of war)
and the goddess of destruction.

Aeress, Eriss, Erys, Eryss

Erlinda Heb. "Spirited."

Erma Var. **Irma** (OG. "Universal, complete"). Enjoyed a brief period of use from around 1890 to 1940; now almost unknown. Humorist Erma Bombeck.

Ermina, Erminia, Erminie, Irma, Irminia, Irminie, Hermia, Hermine, Herminie, Hermione

Ermine OF. "Weasel." Has come to be synonymous with the trappings of royalty, since the robes of royalty are typically trimmed with the fur and tails of ermine, a variety of weasel that turns white in winter.

Ermin, Ermina, Erminia, Erminne

Erna Var. **Ernestine**. Also possibly derived from an Irish root meaning "to know." Modern use.

Ernaline, Ernalynn

Ernestine (Fem. **Ernest**) OE. "Sincere." Use at the end of the 19th century follows **Ernest**'s enormous popularity for boys at that period. A bit dated now.

Erna, Ernaline, Ernesta, Ernestina, Ernestyna

Eroica The name of Beethoven's Third Symphony, the "heroic" symphony which the composer originally intended as a tribute to Napoleon.

Eroiqua, Eroique, Heroica

Ersilia Sp. from Gk. "Delicate." Roman mythology name: the wife of Romulus, Rome's founder, originally one of the famous Sabine women carried off to provide wives for the new citizens of Rome.

Ercilia, Ersila, Erzilia, Hersila, Hersilia

Erwina (Fem. **Erwin**) OE. "Boar/friend."

Irwina

Esma Var. **Esmé**. Possibly short form of **Esmeralda**.

Esmée Fr. "Esteemed." Originally a male name brought to Scotland by a French cousin of James VI. Now used more for girls, though scarce. J. D. Salinger titled a short story "For Esmé with Love and Squalor."

Esmae, Esmay, Esmé, Ismé

Esmeralda Sp. "Emerald." Jewel name first used in the 1880s, and more common than **Emerald**. Now subject to the fame brought by inclusion in a Disney cartoon extravaganza, *The Hunchback of Notre Dame.* Unlike some of the characters in the film, Esmeralda does actually appear in Victor Hugo's original novel.

Em, Emmie, Emerald, Emerant, Emeraude, Esma, Esmaralda, Esmarelda, Esmaria, Esmie, Esmiralda, Esmiralde, Esmirelda, Ezmeralda

Esperanza Sp. "Hope." One of the three cardinal virtues, along with Faith and Charity.

Esperance, Esperantia

Esta Var. Esther.

Estelle OF. "Star." See **Astra, Esther, Stella.** French form of a name apparently coined by Charles Dickens for a character in his 1861 novel *Great Expectations.* Her name is **Estella,** and perhaps because she's such an unhappy creature, Estelle is the more common form of the name. Actresses Estelle Getty, Estelle Parsons.

Essie, Estel, Estele, Estell, Estella, Estrella, Estrellita, Stella, Stelle

Esther Per. "Star." More particularly, the planet Venus. Esther in the Bible was an orphan named Hadassah who became wife of King Ahasuerus under her new name. Her story is told in the Old Testament Book of Esther. In the U.S. the name reached its peak of popularity around 1900, and is now unusual. Swimming actress Esther Williams; cosmetics pioneer Estee Lauder.

Essie, Essy, Esta, Estée, Ester, Ettey, Etti, Ettie, Etty, Hester, Hesther, Hettie, Hetty, Hittie

Etana (Fem. **Ethan**) Heb. "Strength of purpose."

Ethel OE. "Noble." A short form of various old-fashioned names like **Etheldreda.** First appeared on its own in the 1840s, and by the 1870s was very popular. This is one 19th-century name, however, that is unlikely to be revived in the 21st century. For parents who love old sitcoms, "Ethel" will always be Lucy's sidekick from the TV series *I Love Lucy.* Actresses Ethel Barrymore, Ethel Merman.

Ethelda, Ethelin, Ethelinda, Etheline, Ethelyn, Ethelynne, Ethill, Ethille, Ethlin, Ethlyn, Ethlynn, Ethyll

Etheldreda OE. "Noble power." Saint's name from the 7th century, occasionally used in Britain. **Audrey** is the more common modern form.

Ethelinda OG. "Noble serpent." Not a composite, but an old name revived in the 19th century, along with many variants.

Athelina, Ethelenda, Ethelene, Ethelind, Ethelinde, Etheline, Ethlin, Ethlinda, Etholinda, Ethylind

Etta Feminine diminutive suffix (**Georgette, Henriette**) that has attained the status of an independent name.

Ettie, Etty

Eudocia Gk. "Well thought of."

Docia, Docie, Doxie, Doxy, Eudokia, Eudosia, Eudoxia

Eudora Gk. "Generous gift." Unusual name from Greek mythology (Eudora was a minor goddess) that was somewhat popular at the turn of the 20th century. Writer Eudora Welty.

Dora, Dorey, Dorie, Eudore

Eugenia (Fem. **Eugene**) Gk. "Wellborn." The French form, **Eugenie**, was made famous by Napoleon III's beautiful empress, and has persisted in the European royal houses. Recently used in Britain for the second daughter of the Duke and Duchess of York. Actresses Gena Rowlands, Geena Davis.

Eugenie, Evgenia, Geena, Gena, Gene, Genia, Genie, Gina, Janie, Jeena, Jenna, Jennie

Eulalia Gk. "Sweet-speaking."

Eula, Eulalee, Eulalie, Eulaylia, Eulaylie, Lallie, Lally

Eunice Gk. "Victorious." Biblical name: In the New Testament, Eunice is the mother of Timothy. Occasionally used in the modern era. Philanthropist Eunice Kennedy Shriver.

Eunices, Eunike, Euniss, Unice, Uniss

Euphemia Gk. "Favorable speech." Early Christian name borne by a 4th-century virgin martyr, but more common in its short forms like **Effie** through the 19th century. Rare since the 1930s. The word "euphemism" comes from the same roots.

Effam, Effie, Effy, Ephan, Ephie, Eufemia, Euphemie, Euphenia, Euphie, Phemie, Fanny

Eurydice Gk. In mythology, the wife of the musician Orpheus. She was poisoned by a snake, and Orpheus went to the underworld to find her. His music so charmed Hades that he was allowed to bring her back to life, if he could lead her to the upper world without looking at her. He failed, and she returned to Hades. Not surprisingly, the tale is the subject of numerous musical works.
Euridice, Euridiss

Eustacia (Fem. **Eustace**) Lat. "Giving fruit." The male form was used a bit in the 19th century, but the feminine form is rare.
Eustacie, Stacey, Stacia, Stacie, Stacy

Eva Form of **Eve** (Heb. "Life") More common in Europe. Actress Eva Gabor; dictator Eva Peron.
Eeva, Evita

Evadne Gk. Meaning unclear, but may mean something like "Enjoying good fortune" or "Pleasing one."
Evadney, Evadnie, Evanne

Evangeline Gk. "Good news." Derived from "evangel," the term that came to be used for the Gospels, or the four New Testament accounts of Christ's life. First used in English by Alfred Tennyson in his 1847 poem "Evangeline."
Engie, Eva, Evangelia, Evangelina, Evangelista, Evangeliste, Eve, Vangie, Vangy

Evania Gk. "Peaceful."
Evanne, Evannie, Evanny

Evanthe Gk. "Good flower."
Evanthey, Evanthie

Eve Heb. "Life." In the form **Eva**, somewhat popular from the mid-19th century, usually as a shortened version of **Evangeline**. Eve, the French form of the name, is used steadily but not in great numbers. In Ireland the Gaelic form, **Aoife**, is very popular. A clever name for the first girl in a family of boys. Actress Eve Arden; pop musician Eve.
Aoife, Eba, Ebba, Eva, Evaleen, Evelina, Eveline, Evelyn, Evetta, Evette, Evey, Evie, Evita, Evlyn, Evonne, Evvie, Evvy, Evy

Evelina OG. or OF. Possibly "Hazelnut." Norman import to Britain, where it was brought to prominence by Fanny Burney's popular novel *Evelina*, in the 18th century. Gradually overwhelmed by **Evelyn**.

Eveleen, Evelene, Eveline, Evelyne

Evelyn OG. Obscure meaning, from the same root as **Evelina**. Not, as it would seem, a combination of **Eve** and **Lynn**, but originally a surname and later a boy's name. Its greatest popularity came in the first quarter of the 20th century in both Britain and the U.S. Track star Evelyn Ashford.

Aveline, Evaleen, Evalyn, Evalynn, Evalynne, Eveleen, Evelene, Eveline, Evelyne, Evelynn, Evelynne, Evilyn, Evlin, Evline, Evlyn, Evlynn

Evette Fr. Variant form of **Yvette**, in turn a diminutive of **Yvonne**. Also used as a diminutive for **Eve**, though the roots are different.

Eevette, Evetta, Eyvetta, Eyvette

Evonne Fr. Var. **Yvonne**. Tennis star Evonne Goolagong.

Evon, Eyvonne

Fabia (Fem. **Fabian**) Lat. Clan name. Possibly meaning "One who grows beans." Queen Fabiola of Belgium was a Spanish princess.

Fabiana, Fabiane, Fabianna, Fabienne, Fabiola

Fabrizia It. "Works with the hands."

Fabrice, Fabricia, Fabrienne, Fabriqua, Fabritzia

Faida Arab. "Plentiful."

Fayda

Faith ME. "Loyalty." One of the most common of the virtue names used by the Puritans, along with **Hope** and **Charity**. Modern use is sparing. Actress Faith Prince; singer Faith Hill.

Fae, Faithe, Fay, Faye, Fayth, Faythe, Fé

Faline Lat. "Like a cat." Unusual spelling of a familiar term. Second-time parents may recognize this as the name of Bambi's girlfriend in the Disney cartoon.

Faeleen, Fayline, Felina, Feyline

Fallon Ir. Gael. "Descended from a ruler." Surname brought to public notice and some popularity by a character on the TV serial *Dynasty*.

Fallan, Fallen

Fanny (Dim. **Frances**) Lat. "From France." This form became extremely popular in the early 19th century and remained a favorite until around 1910, when its inexplicable adoption as a term for the buttocks extinguished it as a first name. Cookbook author Fannie Farmer; author Fannie Flagg; actress Fanny Ardant.

Fan, Fania, Fannee, Fanney, Fannie

Farica (Dim. **Frederica**) OG. "Peaceful ruler."

Faricka, Fericka, Flicka

Farina Lat. "Flour." Farina is still sometimes available on supermarket shelves.

Fareena

Farrah ME. "Lovely, pleasant." Unknown as a first name until the enormous fame of actress Farrah Fawcett. In the aftermath of her stardom, has a rather dated air.

Fara, Farah, Farra

Fatima Arab. Meaning unclear, though Fatima was Mohammed's favorite daughter. According to the Koran, she was one of only four perfect women in the world, and the name is consequently well used among Muslims. Fatima is also the name of Bluebeard's last wife in some versions of that tale.

Fateema, Fateemah, Fatimah, Fatma, Fatmah

Fauna Roman mythology name: the goddess of nature and animals.

Faune, Fauniel, Fauniella, Fawna

Faustine (Fem. **Faust**) Lat. "Fortunate, enjoying good luck." There is some irony to the name, since the Faust of legend sold his soul to the Devil. Two Roman empresses were called Faustina, and the name was common under the Roman Empire, but little used today.

Fausta, Fauste, Faustina

Fawn OF. "Young deer." Names for girl children have been drawn from various segments of the natural world—flowers, gems, seasons, months—but animal names, for some reason, are rarer. Biographer Fawn Brodie.

Faina, Fanya, Faun, Fauna, Faunia, Fawna, Fawne, Fawnia, Fawnya

Fay OF. "Fairy." Or Dim. **Faith**. First used in significant numbers in the 1920s, probably inspired by the fame of actresses Fay Wray and Fay Compton. Actress Faye Dunaway.

Fae, Fay, Faye, Fee, Fey

Fayette OF. "Little fairy."

Fayetta

Fedora Gr. Var. **Theodora** (Gk. "Gift of God"). In this form, also a kind of soft felt hat with a modest brim, much favored by men until the early 1960s.

Fadora

Felda OG. "From the field."

Felicia (Fem. **Felix**) Lat. "Lucky, fortunate, happy." **Felice** was used in Britain until the early 19th century, when it was replaced by Felicia, which has since been supplanted by **Felicity**. None of them is very common. Actress Phylicia Rashad.

Falecia, Faleece, Falicia, Falisha, Falishia, Felice, Feliciana, Felicidad, Felicie, Felicienne, Félicité, Felicity, Felis, Felisa, Felise, Felisha, Feliss, Felita, Feliz, Feliza, Felysse, Filicia, Filisha, Phalicia, Phalisha, Phelicia, Phylicia, Phyllicia, Phyllisha

Fenella Ir. Gael. "White shoulder." Var. **Fionnula**. This is the anglicized form.

Finella, Fynella

Fenia In Scandinavian mythology, a giantess enslaved by the Danish king Frodi, who reigned peacefully for thirty years.

Fenja, Fenya

Fern OE. "Fern." Dim. **Fernanda**. Unusual botanical name immortalized by E.B. White in *Charlotte's Web*.

Ferna, Ferne

Fernanda (Fem. **Ferdinand**) OG. Possibly "Peace/courage" or "Voyage/courage." Very rare feminine of an equally rare male name.

Anda, Annda, Ferdinanda, Ferdinande, Fern, Fernande, Fernandina, Fernandine, Nan, Nanda

Fernley OE. Place name: "Fern meadow." In Britain, has been used as a first name since the turn of the century for both sexes. Little heard in the U.S.

Fernlea, Fernlee, Fernleigh, Fernlie, Fernly

Fiammetta It. "Little fiery one." The word *fiamma* means flame: it may refer to the flames of the Holy Spirit that descended on the apostles on the day Christians commemorate as Pentecost.

Fiamma

Fiby Sp. Var. **Phoebe** (Gk. "Shining, brilliant").

Fidelity Lat. "Loyalty." Latin form of **Faith**. In the U.S. use of the word for large financial institutions diminishes its appeal as a proper name. The Cuban track star Ana Fidelia Quirot was named in honor of Fidel Castro.

Fedila, Fideila, Fidela, Fidele, Fidelia, Fidelita, Fidella

Fidelma Old Irish name of obscure meaning. A princess named Feidhelm was one of St. Patrick's first converts to Christianity.

Fedelma

Fifi Fr. Dim. **Josephine** (Heb. "Jehovah increases"). The stereotypical name for a French poodle, which would seem to limit its human use.

Fifine

Filia Gk. "Friendship." Currently popular in Greece.

Philia

Filippa Var. **Philippa** (Gk. "Lover of horses").

Filomena It. Var. **Philomena** (Gk. "Loved one").

Filis Sp. Var. **Phyllis** (Gk. "Leafy bough").

Fina Sp. Dim. **Josefina** (Heb. "Jehovah increases").

Fiona Ir. Gael. "Fair, pale." Apparently coined by an English author at the turn of the 20th century, and its popularity in Britain has been growing since the 1930s. The variant **Ffion** is currently very popular in Wales. Rare in the U.S. Musician Fiona Apple.

Fee, Ffion, Ffiona, Ffyona, Fione, Fionna, Fyona

Fionnula Ir. Gael. "White shoulder."
Fenella, Finella, Finola, Fionnuala, Fionnualagh, Nola, Nuala

Flaminia Lat. "Priest."

Flana Ir. Gael. "Russet hair." **Flannery** is probably the most common form of this very unusual name. Author Flannery O'Connor.
Flanagh, Flanna, Flannerey, Flannery

Flavia Lat. "Yellow hair." Originally a Latin clan name, and common enough in the Roman Empire, but never revived in an English-speaking country.
Flavie, Flaviere, Flavyere

Fleur Fr. "Flower." In John Galsworthy's *The Forsyte Saga*, one of the principal characters is called Fleur, which brought the name to some prominence. The BBC TV adaptation also provoked a spate of use.
Fleurette, Fleurine

Flora Lat. "Flower." The name of the Roman goddess of springtime, and of a 9th-century martyred saint. Flora Macdonald was a Scottish heroine who helped Bonnie Prince Charlie escape the English. The name was naturally popular in Scotland, and throughout England in the last half of the 19th century. Now little used, but a good option for parents searching out a quaint, pretty name.
Fiora, Fiordenni, Fiore, Fiorella, Fiori, Fleur, Flo, Flor, Floralia, Flore, Florella, Florelle, Florentia, Florentina, Florenza, Florenzia, Floria, Florida, Florie, Florine, Floris, Florise, Florrie, Florry, Flory

Flordeperla Sp. "Flower of pearl."

Florence Lat. "In bloom." Used for both men and women until the 17th century, when it faded from sight. Modern use is almost entirely inspired by the fame of Florence Nightingale, who was actually named for the Italian city where she was born. (Her less fortunate sister was born in Naples, and given the Greek name of that city: Parthenope.) Like many names popular in the Victorian era, it fell out of fashion by the 1930s. Athlete Florence "Flo Jo" Griffith Joyner; actress Florence Henderson.
Fiorentina, Fiorenza, Flo, Floellen, Flor, Flora, Flo-

rance, Flore, Florenca, Florencia, Florencita, Floren-
tia, Florentina, Florentyna, Florenza, Florenzia, Flori,
Floria, Floriane, Floriana, Florie, Florina, Florincia,
Florinda, Florine, Floris, Florrance, Florrie, Florry,
Florynce, Floss, Flossey, Flossie, Flossy

Flower OF. "Blossom."

Florida Lat. "Flowery." Spanish Var. **Florence**. Spanish
explorer Ponce de Leon dubbed the southern state
"Florida" for the many flowers he found there. Infrequent
current use as a first name probably refers to the state.

Fortney Lat. "Strong." Similar enough to the well-
established **Courtney** to warrant consideration.

Fortnea, Fortnee, Fortneigh, Fortnie, Fortny

Fortune Lat. "Good fate." Garden-variety name in the Roman Empire; Fortuna was the goddess of happiness. Revived somewhat by the Puritans but almost unknown
today.

Fortuna, Fortunata

Forsythia Flower name: the brilliant yellow shrub that is
one of the first signs of spring in a chilly climate. Named
for William Forsythe, the 18th-century botanist who classified it.

Fran (Dim. **Frances**) Lat. "From France." Used as a given
name on its own. Comedienne Fran Drescher; writer Fran
Lebowitz.

Frani, Frannee, Franni, Frannie, Franny

Frances (Fem. **Francis**) Lat. "From France." Until the
17th century, **Francis** was used for both sexes. Spelled
with an "e," it was a very popular choice in the first quarter of the 20th century, but little used since then. A more
elaborate form, **Franziska**, is popular in Germany. Actresses Fanny Brice, Frances McDormand, Franka Po-
tente.

Fan, Fancey, Fanchette, Fancie, Fancy, Fanechka, Fa-
nia, Fanney, Fannie, Fanny, Fanya, Fran, Francee,
Franceline, Francene, Francesca, Francess, Francetta,
Francette, Francey, Franchesca, Franci, Francie,
Francine, Francisca, Franciska, Francoise, Francyne,
Frania, Franie, Frank, Franka, Frankie, Franky,

Franni, Frannie, Franny, Fransabelle, Fransabella, Franzetta, Franzi, Franziska, Fronia

Franisbel Elaboration of **Fran**, influenced by **Isabel** (Sp. from Heb. "Pledged to God").

Franisbella, Franisbelle

Frayda Yiddish. "Joy." The German word *freude* is quite similar.

Frayde, Fraydel, Freyda, Freyde, Freydel

Freda OG. "Peaceful." Dim. **Alfreda, Frederica, Winifred**. Most popular at the end of the 19th century, when Fred was fashionable for men. As **Frida**, currently quite popular in Spain. Artist Frida Kahlo.

Freada, Freeda, Freida, Frida, Frieda, Frydda

Fredella Comb. form **Freda** and **Ella**.

Fredelle

Frederica OG. "Peaceful ruler." Following the popularity of **Frederic**, substantially used in the late 19th century, but now unusual. Opera singer Frederica von Stade.

Farica, Federica, Fred, Fredalena, Freddee, Freddey, Freddi, Freddie, Freddy, Fredericha, Fredericka, Frederickina, Frederine, Frederique, Fredi, Fredia, Fredie, Fredricia, Fredrika, Frerika, Friederike, Rica, Ricki, Rickie, Ricky, Rikki, Rikky

Freya Scand. "Highborn lady." In Norse myth, the goddess of love, corresponding perhaps to the Roman Venus. Friday is named for her. Author Freya Stark.

Fraya

Friedelinde Ger. "Gentle peace." The word particle "Fried-" appears in so many German-based names that peace appears to have been a very lively concern in the era when these names were formed.

Friedalinda

Fritzi (Fem. **Fritz**) OG. "Peaceful ruler." German form of **Frederick**.

Fructuosa Lat. "Fruitful."

Fuensanta Sp. "Holy fountain."

Fuenta

Fulgencia Lat. "Glowing, giving off light."

Fulvia Lat. "Blond one."

Fruma Yiddish. "Pious, deeply religious."

Fuchsia Plant name: the brilliant pink blossoms of this popular plant have given their name to the color. The plant was named for the German botanist Leonhard Fuchs.

Fusha

 Gabrielle (Fem. **Gabriel**) Heb. "Heroine of God." Used in English-speaking countries for the last ninety years, though the Italian form, **Gabriella**, has been popular since the 1950s. Gabriel is an archangel who appears in Christian, Jewish, and Muslim texts. Tennis player Gabriela Sabatini; fashion designer Gabrielle "Coco" Chanel; volleyball player Gabby Reece.

Gabbe, Gabbi, Gabbie, Gabi, Gabriel, Gabriela, Gabriella, Gabriell, Gabriellen, Gabriellia, Gabrila, Gabryel, Gabryelle, Gabryella, Gaby, Gabysia, Gavi, Gavra, Gavraila, Gavrielle, Gavrila, Gavrilla, Gavrina

Gada Heb. "Fortunate."

Gaea Gk. "The earth."

Gaia, Gaiea, Gala

Gaetana It. Place name. Gaeta is a region in southern Italy; the Gulf of Gaeta is just north of Naples.

Gaetane

Gafna Heb. "Vine."

Gail Heb. "My father rejoices." A diminutive of **Abigail** with an unusually strong life of its own, dating from around 1940, with special popularity in the 1950s in the U.S. Authors Gael Greene, Gail Sheehy, Gail Godwin; track star Gail Devers.

Gael, Gahl, Gaila, Gaile, Gaill, Gal, Gale, Gayel, Gayelle, Gayla, Gayle, Gayleen, Gaylene, Gayline, Gayll, Gaylla, Gaylle

Gala OF. "Merrymaking, festivity." More associated with late-night parties than with babies. Salvador Dali's wife was named Gala.
Galla

Galatea Gk. "White as milk." In Greek mythology, the sculptor Pygmalion fell in love with his ivory statue of Aphrodite, and prayed to the goddess to bring the statue to life. When his prayer was answered, he married his creation. The myth, via G. B. Shaw's play *Pygmalion,* is the source of the musical *My Fair Lady.*
Galatée, Galathea

Galiena OG. "High one."
Galiana, Galianna, Galliena, Galyena

Galila Heb. "Rolling hills." The root of this word is the source of the place name Galilee.
Galilah, Gelila, Gelilah, Gelilia, Gelilya, Glila, Glilah

Galina Rus.Var. **Helen** (Gk. "Shining brightly"). Currently very popular in Russia.
Galya

Gallia Lat. "Gaul." The Latin term for the country that would later be known as France; a name used from time to time for French babies.
Gala, Galla

Galya Heb. "The Lord has redeemed."
Galia, Gallia, Gallya

Gambhira Hindi. "Well born, of great dignity."

Gana Heb. "Garden."
Ganah, Ganit

Gardenia Flower name. The powerfully sweet-smelling flower is named for the 18th-century Scottish naturalist Alexander Garden, who first classified it.
Gardeenia

Garland OF. "Garland, wreath."
Garlande, Garldina

Gardner ME. Occupational name: "Gardener." In the eastern U.S., reminiscent of two distinguished families, known as the "blind" Gardners (the name has no *i*) or the "sighted" Gardiners. The former are famous for the Isabella Stewart Gardner Museum in Boston; the latter for

Gardiner's Island on Long Island Sound. Where this occurs as a name for girls, it is usually a family name. Poet Gardner McFall.

Gardener, Gardie, Gardiner

Garnet ME. Jewel name, appropriate for January, since it is the birthstone for that month. Comes from the Old French for "pomegranate," which garnets very closely resemble.

Garnette, Granata, Grenata, Grenatta

Gavrila Var. **Gabrielle** (Heb. "Heroine of God").

Gavrilla, Gavryla, Gavrylla

Gay OF. "Glad, lighthearted." A surname in the Middle Ages, used as a first name very heavily in the mid 20th century. The widespread informal use of the word to mean "homosexual" has limited its current use as a name.

Gae, Gai, Gaye

Gaynor Welsh. "White and smooth, soft." Var. **Guinevere**. Used primarily in Britain.

Gaenor, Gayna, Gayner

Gazella Lat. "Gazelle." Unusual use of the animal name as a given name. Gazelles are traditionally thought of as very graceful creatures.

Gazelle

Geena Var. **Gina**. Made famous by movie star Geena Davis.

Geila Heb. "Joy."

Geela, Geelah, Geelan, Geila, Geiliya, Geiliyah, Gila, Gilah, Gilana

Gelsomina Italian plant name: the plant in question is a kind of jasmine.

Jelsomina

Gemini Gk. "Twin." Appropriate for either a child born under the sign of Gemini, or for one of a pair of twins.

Gemella, Gemelle, Gemina

Gemma It. "Precious stone." Did not, curiously, come into fashion with other jewel names in the late 19th century, but is slightly popular now. Probably helped along by the 1940 canonization of an Italian Saint Gemma, an ordinary young woman whose religious life included manifestations of the stigmata, or the marks of Christ's wounds. In the 1980s this was one of the top ten names in England but has since faded.

Jemma, Jemsa

Gene Dim. **Eugenia** (Gk. "Wellborn") or Var. **Jean** (Heb. "The Lord is gracious"). More common for boys; actress Gene Tierney may have pioneered use of this spelling for girls.

Genie

Genesis The name of the first book of the Bible. In some favor among African-American parents.

Genesies, Genesiss, Gennesis, Gennesiss, Jenesis, Jenesyss, Jennasis

Geneva OF. "Juniper tree." There is considerable confusion about the sources of a constellation of names that include Geneva, **Ginevra**, and **Genevieve**. Use of Geneva may refer to the Swiss city; on the other hand, it may also be reference to the juniper tree, whose old Dutch name was *genever* (hence "gin," which is flavored with juniper berries). Various forms of Genevieve also overlap.

Gena, Genever, Genevia, Genevra, Genevre, Genovefa, Genoveffa, Genoveva, Ginebra, Ginevra, Ginevre, Janeva, Janevra, Jenovefa, Jineeva, Jineva, Joneva, Jonevah

Genevieve A name whose origin is unclear, but sources suggest possibly OG. "White wave" or Celt. "Race of women." Saint Genevieve, the patroness of Paris, was a 5th-century virgin who defended Paris against the depredations of Attila the Hun, among others. Use in English-speaking countries has tended to simmer along at a low level. Actress Genevieve Bujold.

Gena, Genavieve, Geneva, Geneveeve, Genivieve, Gennie, Genny, Genovera, Genoveva, Gina, Janeva, Jenevieve, Jennie, Jenny

Genista Plant name. The Latin name for broom (a shrub like heather) is *planta genista*.

Geneesta, Ginista, Jenista

Georgette Fr. from Lat. "Farmer." The French form of **George**, in mild use since the 1940s. A purposely wrinkled fabric called georgette was named after its French creator. Author Georgette Heyer; socialite Georgette Mosbacher.

Georgetta, Georjetta, Jorjetta, Jorjette

Georgia (Fem. **George**) Lat. "Farmer." The preferred feminine of George in the U.S. and currently quite fashionable in England. A long-ago farmer in Connecticut is reputed to have named each of his ten daughters for a state, and presumably Georgia was one of the eldest, along with **Virginia** and **Carolina**. Painter Georgia O'Keefe.

George, Georgeann, Georgeanne, Georgeina, Georgena, Georgene, Georgetta, Georgette, Georgiana, Georgianna, Georgianne, Georgie, Georgienne, Georgina, Georgine, Georgyann, Georgyanne, Georgyana, Giorgia, Giorgina, Giorgyna, Jorgina

Georgina (Fem. **George**) Lat. "Farmer." A simpler form than **Georgiana**, which has also been used regularly. All of these derivatives are more common in Britain, possibly influenced by Kings George I-IV, who ruled from 1714 to 1830.

Georgeina, Georgena, Georgene, Georgejean, Georgiana, Georgianna, Georgianne, Georgienne, Georgine, Georgyana, Giorgina

Geraldine (Fem. **Gerald**) OG./Fr. "Spear ruler." Though the form was coined in the 16th century, its real popularity followed the fashion for Gerald, in the mid-19th century through the 1950s. Actresses Geraldine Chaplin, Geraldine Fitzgerald; politician Geraldine Ferraro.

Deena, Dina, Dyna, Geralda, Geraldeen, Geraldene, Geraldina, Geralyn, Geralynne, Gerdene, Gerdine, Geri, Gerianna, Gerianne, Gerilynn, Gerri, Gerrilyn, Gerroldine, Gerry, Giralda, Jeraldeen, Jeraldene, Jeraldine, Jeralee, Jere, Jeri, Jerilene, Jerrie, Jerrileen, Jerroldeen, Jerry

Geranium Flower name, though the name of the flower itself derives from the Greek for "crane."

Gerardine (Fem. **Gerard**) OE. "Spear brave."

Gerarda, Gerardina, Gerardyne, Gererdina, Gerrardene

Gerda ONorse. "Shelter."
Garda, Geerda

Germaine Fr. "From Germany." Use today may reflect admiration for the famous author and feminist Germaine Greer.
Germain, Germana, Germane, Germayn, Germayne, Jarmaine, Jermain, Jermaine, Jermane, Jermayn, Jermayne

Gertrude OG. "Strength of a spear." An old name (there was a 7th-century Saint Gertrude) revived to immense popularity with the late 19th-century fashion for the antique. Became so common that it suffered the corresponding fall from favor, and is now resoundingly out of style. Writer Gertrude Stein; actress Gertrude Lawrence.
Geertruide, Geltruda, Geltrudis, Gerda, Gert, Gerta, Gerte, Gerti, Gertie, Gertina, Gertraud, Gertrud, Gertruda, Gertrudis, Gerty, Traudl, Trude, Trudi, Trudie, Trudy

Gerusha Heb. "Sent away."
Jerusha

Geulah Heb. "Redemption."

Gevira Heb. "High ranking lady."

Ghaliya Arab. "Sweet-smelling."

Ghislaine Fr. Unusual name of unclear origin and meaning.
Gillan, Gislaine

Ghita It. Dim. **Margherita** (Gk. "Pearl").
Geeta, Gita

Giacinta It. "Hyacinth."
Giacintha, Jacinta, Jacintha, Jacynth, Jiacintha, Yacinta, Yacintha

Gianina (Fem. **John**) It. from Heb. "God is gracious." The age-old favorite boy's name has spawned endless variants, both masculine and feminine.
Cinetta, Gianetta, Giannina, Giannine, Ginetta, Ginette, Ginnette, Janina, Janine, Jeannine, Jeeanina

Gigi Dim. **Georgina, Virginia**, etc. For a somewhat older generation of parents the name was given a glamorous, *gamine* charm by Audrey Hepburn's performance in the 1951 Broadway production of *Gigi*, based on a short story by Colette. (In the 1958 musical film starring Maurice Chevalier, the ingenue role was taken by Leslie Caron.) Tennis player Gigi Fernandez.

GeeGee, G.G.

Gila Heb. "Joy." See **Geila**.

Gilah, Gilana

Gilia Heb. "Joy of the Lord."

Giliah, Giliya, Giliyah

Gilberte (Fem. **Gilbert**) OG. "Shining pledge." French variant of a Norman name that was fairly popular in the north of Britain.

Berta, Bertie, Berty, Gigi, Gilberta, Gilbertha, Gilberthe, Gilbertina, Gilbertine, Gill, Gillie, Gilly

Gilda OE. "Gilded." More scholarly sources trace Gilda to **Ermengilda**, a now obsolete Anglo-Saxon name, while others propose "God's servant." Actress Gilda Radner.

Gillian Lat. "Youthful." Anglicization of **Juliana**. A standard name in the Middle Ages in England, and revived for about 40 years in this century, but fading since the sixties. Actress Gillian Anderson. Never widespread in the U.S., though its diminutive, **Jill**, had quite a fashionable spell.

Ghilian, Ghiliane, Ghillian, Gilian, Giliana, Gill, Gillan, Gillianna, Gillianne, Gillie, Gillyanne, Jillian, Jillianne, Jillyan, Jyllian

Gina Dim. **Regina, Angelina**, etc. Also could be considered a feminization of **Gene**, or a variant of **Jean**. Independent use dates from the 1920s, concentrated in the 1950s. Currently fashionable in Spain. Actresses Gina Lollobrigida, Geena Davis, Gena Rowlands.

Geena, Geina, Gena, Ginette, Ginna, Jena, Jeena, Jenna

Ginger Lat. "Ginger." Also can be a diminutive of **Virginia** (Lat. "Virgin"). Not to be confused with the usual botanical names, for it depends almost completely on the fame of actress Ginger Rogers, whose given name was Virginia.

Gingee, Gingie, Jinger

Ginny Dim. **Virginia** (Lat. "Virgin").

Ginnee, Ginnie, Jinnee, Jinnie, Jinny

Gioia It. "Joy." Unusual form in this country.

Gioya, Joya

Gioconda It. "Delight." The painting most Americans know as the *Mona Lisa* is also referred to as *La Gioconda*.

Geoconda, Jeoconda

Giovanna (Fem. **John**) It. from Heb. "God is gracious."

Giovana, Jovana, Jovanna, Jovanne

Giselle OG. "Pledge/hostage." Use may reflect a fondness for the famous 19th-century ballet whose tragic heroine is a peasant girl betrayed by a noble suitor. Model Gisele Bundchen.

Ghisele, Ghisella, Gisela, Gisele, Gisella, Giza, Gizela, Gizella

Gita Sanskrit. "Song."

Geeta, Gitika

Gitana Sp. "Gypsy."

Gitane, Gitanna, Jeetanna

Gitta Dim. **Brigitte** (Ir. Gael. "Strength, power").

Gitte

Giulia (Fem. **Giulio**) It. from Lat. "Youthful."

Giula, Giuliana, Giulietta, Giullia, Jiulia, Jiuliana, Jiuliya, Jiyulia, Julia, Juliana, Julie, Juliet, Julietta, Juliette, Jullia, Julliana, Julliane

Giuseppina (Fem. **Giuseppe**) It. from Heb. "The Lord adds."

Giuseppa, Josefina

Giustinia (Fem. **Justin**) It. from Lat. "Just, fair."

Giustina, Justina, Justine, Justiniana

Glade OE Place name: clearing in the woods.

Gladys Welsh. Var. **Claudia** (Lat. "Lame"). Suddenly glamorous in the late 19th century, and used in several Edwardian romantic novels, which further heightened its appeal. The chic way to pronounce it was with a long "a." By the 1930s, beginning to be dated, and now rare. Singer Gladys Knight.

Glad, Gladdis, Gladdys, Gladi, Gladyss, Gwladys, Gwyladyss

Glenda Welsh. "Fair and good." Mildly popular from the 1930s to the 1960s. Actress Glenda Jackson.
Glennda

Glenna (Fem. **Glenn**) Ir. Gael. "Glen." A glen is a narrow valley between hills. Actresses Glenn Close, Glenne Headley.
Gleana, Glenda, Gleneen, Glenene, Glenine, Glen, Glenn, Glenne, lennene, Glennette, Glennie

Glenys Welsh. "Holy." Etymologically unrelated to the similar-sounding **Glynis**.
Glenice, Glenis, Glennice, Glennis, Glennys

Gloria Lat. "Glory." Apparently coined by playwright George Bernard Shaw, in 1898's *You Never Can Tell;* the form **Gloriana** had earlier been used to refer in flattering fashion to Queen Elizabeth I. The exposure given the name by actress Gloria Swanson was probably crucial to its popularity from the 1920s through the 1960s. Now a bit passé. Writers Gloria Steinem, Gloria Naylor; singer Gloria Estefan.
Glaura, Glaurea, Glora, Glorea, Glorcc, Glorey, Gloreya, Glori, Glorie, Gloriana, Gloriane, Glorie, Glorra, Glorria, Glory, Glorya, Gloryan, Gloryanna, Gloryanne

Glynis Welsh. "Small glen." Related to **Glenn** and its variants. Popular in the middle of the 20th century, but mostly in Britain. Actress Glynis Johns.
Glinnis, Glinyce, Glinys, Glinyss, Glynnis

Godfreya (Fem. **Godfrey**) OG. "God-peace."
Godfreyda, Gotfreya

Godiva OE. "God's gift." According to the famous story, the 11th century Lady Godiva rode through the town of Coventry naked, covered only by her long hair. Her motive (generally forgotten) was a pact with her husband, the Earl of Mercia, who relieved the townsfolk of certain taxes after her ride. In this era the name is probably more familiar as a brand of premium chocolates.

Golda OE. "Gold." Use is frequently a tribute to the late Israeli Prime Minister Golda Meir. Actress Goldie Hawn.
Goldarina, Goldarine, Goldee, Goldi, Goldie, Goldina, Goldy, Goldia

Grace Lat. "Grace." Originally had nothing to do with physical grace, but rather with divine favor and mercy. Used in that sense by the Puritans, and taken to America, where it was very fashionable at the turn of the century. Periods of popularity followed in England (in the twenties) and Scotland (through the fifties). Little used now, but ripe for revival. Actress and princess Grace Kelly; singer Grace Jones; choreographer Graciela Daniele.

Engracia, Eugracia, Gracee, Gracey, Gracia, Graciana, Gracie, Graciela, Graciella, Gracija, Gracina, Gracious, Grata, Gratia, Gratiana, Gratiela, Gratiella, Grayce, Grazia, Graziella, Grazina, Graziosa, Grazyna

Grainne Ir. Gael. "Love." Primarily used in Ireland.

Grainnia, Grania

Granada Spanish place name. Granada was a Moorish kingdom in the southwestern part of what is now Spain, from the 700s until 1492, when Ferdinand and Isabella conquered it and drove the Moors definitively out of Europe. The capital city, also called Granada, is home to the famous Moorish fortress the Alhambra.

Granadda, Grenada, Grenadda

Greer Scot. Dim. **Gregory**. (Lat. "Alert, watchful"). Given fame by actress Greer Garson, whose mother's maiden name it was.

Grier

Gregoria (Fem. **Gregory**) Lat. "Alert, watchful."

Gregoriana, Gregorijana, Gregorina, Gregorine, Gregorya, Gregoryna

Greta Ger. Dim. **Margaret** (Gk. "Pearl"). Most used during the 1930s, clearly inspired by Greta Garbo. Marathon runner Greta Waitz.

Greeta, Gretal, Gretchen, Grete, Gretel, Gretha, Grethe, Grethel, Gretna, Gretta, Grette, Grietje, Gryta

Gretchen Ger. Dim. **Margaret** (Gk. "Pearl"). Used on its own in English-speaking countries in this century.

Griselda OG. "Gray fighting maid." In a famous tale told by both Boccaccio and Chaucer, "Patient Griselda" is a meek wife who submits to numerous trials devised by her husband to test her submissiveness. The name has long since been eclipsed by its short form, **Zelda**.

Chriselda, Gricely, Grisel, Griseldis, Griselly, Grishelda, Grishilde, Grissel, Grizel, Grizelda, Gryselde, Gryzelde, Selda, Zelda

Gudrun Scand. "Battle." D.H. Lawrence gave this name to one of the characters in his 1920 novel, *Women in Love,* and Glenda Jackson won an Academy Award for playing her in the 1969 film.

Gudren, Gudrid, Gudrin, Gudrinn, Gudruna, Gudrunn, Gudrunne, Guthrun, Guthrunn, Guthrunne

Guida It. "Guide."

Guinevere Welsh. "White and smooth, soft." The name of King Arthur's ill-fated queen, who betrayed him with his best buddy, Lancelot. The most common form today is **Jennifer**.

Gaenna, Gaynor, Genever, Genevieve, Genevra, Geniffer, Geniver, Genivra, Genna, Gennie, Gennifer, Genny, Ginevra, Guenever, Guenevere, Gueniveer, Guenna, Guennola, Guinever, Guinna, Gwen, Gweniver, Gwenn, Gwennie, Gwennola, Gwennora, Gwennore, Gwenny, Gwenora, Gwenore, Gwyn, Gwynn, Gwynna, Gwynne, Janifer, Jen, Jeni, Jenifer, Jennee, Jenni, Jennie, Jennifer, Jenny, Wendee, Wendie, Wendy, Win, Winne, Winnie, Winny

Gulielma (Fem. **Wilhelm**) It. from OG. "Will-helmet."
Guglielma

Gunhilda ONorse. "Battle-maid."
Gunhilde, Gunilda, Gunilla, Gunna, Gunnel, Gunnhilda

Gustava (Fem. **Gustav**) Swed. "Staff of the gods." Gustav is a royal name in Sweden.
Gustha

Gwen Dim. **Gwendolyn, Guinevere.** Often given as an independent name. Pop singer Gwen Stefani.
Gwenn, Gwyn, Gwynn

Gwenda Welsh. "Fair and good." Rare since the 1960s, even in Wales.
Gwennda, Gwynda

Gwendolyn Welsh. "Fair bow." In some legends, Merlin the magician has a wife named Gwendolyn. The old Welsh name was revived in the late 19th century, and is now rare, though its diminutive, **Wendy**, lingers on.

Guendolen, Guendolin, Guendolinn, Guendolynn, Guenna, Gwen, Gwenda, Gwendaline, Gwendolen, Gwendolene, Gwendolin, Gwendoline, Gwendolynne, Gwenna, Gwenette, Gwenndolen, Gwenni, Gwennie, Gwenny, Gwenyth, Gwyn, Gwyneth, Gwynn, Gwynna, Gwynne, Wendi, Wendie, Wendy, Win, Winne, Wynne

Gwladys Welsh. Var. **Gladys**.

Gwyneth Welsh. "Happiness." Most popular in Wales and Britain in the 1930s and 1940s, but never a strong name in America. Actress Gwyneth Paltrow.

Gweneth, Gwenith, Gwenyth, Gwineth, Gwinneth, Gwinyth, Gwynith, Gwynna, Gwynne, Gwynneth, Winnie, Winny, Wynne, Wynnie

Gwynn Welsh. "Fair, blessed." Also Dim. **Gwendolyn** or **Gwyneth**.

Gwin, Gwinna, Gwinne, Gwyn, Gwynna, Gwynne

Gypsy OE. The tribe of Romany was originally called "gypsy" because it was thought that they had originated in Egypt. Use of the name, as in the case of Gypsy Rose Lee, is more often as a nickname.

Gipsee, Gipsey, Gipsy

Habibah Arab. "Loved one."
  Habiba, Habibi, Haviva, Havivah, Hebiba
Hadar Heb. "Beauty, splendor."
  Hadara, Hadarit, Haduraq

Hadley OE. Place name: "Heather meadow." Has a certain rakish air, perhaps, because one of Ernest Hemingway's four wives was named Hadley.

Hadlea, Hadleigh, Hadly, Hedlea, Hedleigh, Hedley, Hedlie, Hedly

Hadria Lat. Place name. "From Adria." Var. **Adrian**.
Hadriana, Hadriane, Hadrianna, Hadrien, Hadrienne

Hafsa Old Arabic name of unknown meaning or derivation. A 7th-century figure named Hafsa was chosen, after Muhammad's death, to be the keeper of the first written copy of the Koran.
Hafsah, Hafza

Hagar Heb. "Forsaken." In the Old Testament, Hagar is the handmaid of Abraham's barren wife Sarah, and Sarah sends her away when she has a son by Abraham. A similar Muslim name (which also means "forsaken") is **Hajar**, and the same Hagar who was cast out by Sarah is considered the mother of the Arabic race. Though the Puritans tended to scour the Old Testament for feminine names, this was not one they popularized, and its sparing use has dwindled further since early in the 20th century.
Haggar, Hagir, Hajar

Haidée Gk. "Modest." The name was brought to public knowledge by Byron, who used it in his poem "Don Juan." It has never really caught on.
Jaidee, Hadee, Hyday

Hala Arab. "Halo."
Halah

Halcyone Gk. "Kingfisher." In ancient myth, the kingfisher laid its eggs on the sea, and they floated on the water for the two weeks preceding the winter solstice. During this time the waves were always calm, hence the expression "halcyon days" to mean a time of tranquil happiness.
Halcyon, Halcyona

Haldana ONorse. "Half-Danish." The name takes on real significance when you consider that in ancient Britain, the Danes were fierce and frequent invaders.
Haldane, Haldanna

Haley OE. "Hay meadow." Var. **Hailey**. This name and **Hallie**, in their various spellings, have become very popular recently. Haley and Hailey are entered as different names on the Social Security Administration's list of popular names, but combined, they would probably number just below the top ten.

Halea, Haleigh, Hailey, Hayley

Halfrida OG. "Peaceful heroine" or "Peaceful home."

Halimah Arab. "Gentle, soft-spoken."

Haleema, Haleemah, Haleima, Halima, Helima

Halimeda Gk. "Thinking of the sea."

Halameda, Halette, Hali, Hallie, Meda, Medie

Halleli Heb. "Greatly praised." Feminine of Hillel, the name of a great Talmudic scholar. The elaborated version of the name, **Halleliya**, is obviously very close to the Christian expression of praise, "Hallelujah."

Alleluia, Halleliya, Halleluja, Hallelujah, Hilly

Hallie (Fem. **Henry**) OG. "Ruler of the home or estate." Hallie is considered a form of **Harriet**, as **Hal** is a nickname for **Harry**. Parents probably don't differentiate, though, between Hallie and the very similar and fashionable **Hailey**. Actress Halle Berry.

Hali, Halle, Hallee, Halley, Halli

Hamida Arab. "Giving thanks."

Hameedah, Hameida, Hamidah

Hana Jap. "Flower." Fashion designer Hanae Mori.

Hanae, Hanako

Hania Heb. "A place to rest" or Arab. "To be happy."

Chania, Chaniya, Chaniyah, Chanya, Haniya, Haniyah, Hannia, Hanniah, Hanniya, Hanniyah, Hannya, Hannyah

Hanita Hindi. "Grace of the gods."

Hannah Heb. "Grace." In the Old Testament, Hannah is the mother of the prophet Samuel. The name was steadily popular from around 1600 through the 19th century, peaking around 1800. Though the European forms of the name—**Ann, Anne, Anna**, etc.—used to be more common, Hannah has been a top-ten favorite in the U.S. since the mid-nineties. It is also extremely fashionable throughout Britain and, as **Hanne**, in Germany. Anna has been climbing popularity charts in America, possibly on Hannah's coattails. Writer Hannah Arendt; sportscaster Hannah Storm.

Ann, Anna, Anne, Annie, Chana, Chanah, Chanha, Channach, Channah, Hana, Hanna, Hanne, Hannele, Hannelore, Hannie, Hanny, Honna, Nan, Nanney, Nannie, Nanny

Hansika Hindi. "Small swan."

Hansine Dan. Fem. **John** (Heb. "The Lord is gracious") by way of **Hans**.

Hanseen, Hansina

Happy Eng. "Cheerful, lighthearted." Though it was common enough in the 19th century, **Felicity** or **Hilary** are more likely to be used now. Happy does occur as a nickname. The most famous Happy is the late Nelson Rockefeller's wife.

Haralda ONorse. "Army ruler" or "Army power." This form was coined during the great 19th-century popularity of **Harold**, but (as with many feminine variants, like **Arthuretta**) never really caught on.

Halley, Hallie, Hally, Harolda, Haroldene, Haroldina

Harela Heb. "The Lord's mountain."

Charela, Charrela, Harrela, Harrella, Harrellah

Harley OE. Place name. "The long field." Familiar to most people as half of the name of a great motorcycle, the Harley-Davidson. This would have been considered a drawback to any other generation of parents, but 21st-century hipsters may find it appealing.

Arlea, Arlee, Arleigh, Arley, Harlea, Harlee, Harleigh, Harlie, Harly

Harmony Lat. "Harmony." Great name for New Age parents seeking just that. A variant is **Harmonia**, the name of the Greek goddess of order.

Harmonee, Harmoney, Harmonia, Harmonie

Harolyn Variant of **Carolyn** (OG. "Man."). To add some interest to a name, or sometimes to commemorate a beloved relative, families often substitute one consonant for another at the beginning of a name. Singer Harolyn Blackwell.

Harriet (Fem. **Henry**) OG. "Ruler of the home or estate." An informal version of **Henrietta**, very popular in the 18th and 19th centuries, and after nearly 100 years of obscurity, ready for a revival. Older parents may be put off by memories of '50s TV sitcom *Ozzie and Harriet*, however. Avid readers are more likely to associate the name with the children's book *Harriet the Spy*. Author Harriet Beecher Stowe; civil rights leader Harriet Tubman.

Hallee, Halllie, Harrie, Harrietta, Harriett, Harrietta, Harriette, Harriot, Harriott, Harriotte, Hatsee, Hatsey, Hatsie, Hatsy, Hattie, Hatty

Hava Heb. "Life." This is the word that the Anglicized name **Eve** is based on, because of course Eve gave life to the rest of the human race.

Chaba, Chaya, Chayka, Eva, Eve, Hava, Haya, Kaija

Haviva Heb. "Well loved."

Havivah, Havviva, Havvivah

Hayfa Arab. "Slender, well-shaped."

Haifa

Hayley OE. Place name: "Hay meadow." Other sources suggest derivation from a Norse word, *haela*, which means "hero." Probably neither meaning nor history contributes much to the recent popularity of this name, which was made famous by actress Hayley Mills in the 1960s, and 30 years later, was one of the top 50 names given to American girls. Now, along with variant **Haley**, it is extremely popular: in fact the two combined would come close to ranking in the top ten names chosen for American girls.

Haeley, Haelie, Haely, Hailea, Hailee, Haileigh, Haily, Haleigh, Halie, Hally, Haylea, Haylee, Hayleigh, Hayley

Hazel OE. Tree name. The late 19th-century vogue for botanical names tended to concentrate on flowers rather than trees; Hazel is an exception. A long-running comic strip about a maid called Hazel has given it connotations that will be tough to escape. Track star Hazel Clark.

Hazal, Hazell, Hazelle, Hazle

Heather ME. Flower name. Introduced with other botanical names in the late 19th century, but really took off in the late 20th century, especially in the U.S., where its association with Scotland may have endowed it with an upper-class aura. Anglo names like Heather are also em-

blematic of assimilation for families new to the U.S. Now skidding back down the charts. Actress Heather Locklear.
Heath, Hether

Heaven Place name. Use is scarce but may be inspired by a V. C. Andrews novel with that title.

Hebe Gk. "Youth." In Greek legend, Hebe was the goddess of youth and also cupbearer to the gods. Her name was used mostly in the late 19th century.

Hedda OG. "Warfare." The more common anglicized version of **Hedwig**. Mid-20th-century gossip queen Hedda Hopper.
Heda, Heddi, Heddie, Hedi, Hedvig, Hedvige, Hedwig, Hedwiga, Hedy, Hetta

Hedia Heb. "Jehovah's echo."
Hediah, Hedya, Hedyah

Hedwig OG. "Warfare, struggle, strife." Almost unknown in English-speaking countries. Actress Hedy Lamarr was born Hedwig Kiesler.
Hadvig, Hadwig, Hedvig, Hedviga, Hedvige, Hedwiga, Hedwige, Hedy

Hedy Gk. "Delightful, sweet," or Heb. "My echo." Use is more likely to reflect the glamorous Hedy Lamarr's popularity.
Heda, Hedia, Hediah, Hedyla

Heidi Dim. **Adelaide** (OG. "Noble, nobility"). Made popular by Johanna Spyri's famous novel of 1881, first in German-speaking countries, later in the U.S. Its surge of popularity in the 1970s may have been influenced by a highly publicized TV production of the late 1960s. The show went down in sports history as well, since NBC executives chose to begin showing "Heidi" rather than showing the final 50 seconds of a suspenseful football game, known ever since as "the Heidi game." (Two touchdowns were scored in the final minute that sports fans didn't see.)
Heida, Heide, Heidey, Heidy, Hydee

Heladia Sp. from Ger. "Greek." Greece is often known as the land of the Hellenes.
Eladia

Helen Gk. "Light." The most famous Helen is probably Helen of Troy, the daughter of Zeus by Leda. Her phenomenal beauty was, in some versions, the root cause of the Trojan War; hers was "the face that launched a thousand ships." The name has been understandably popular through the ages, and has spawned many variants, of which **Eleanor** is the most common. Still, for a simple, pretty name with many attractive variants and positive associations, it is underused. Writer Helen Keller; actresses Helen Hayes, Helen Hunt, Helen Mirren, Helena Bonham-Carter; publisher Helen Gurley Brown; singer Helen Reddy.

Aileen, Ailene, Aleanor, Alene, Aline, Eileen, Elaina, Elaine, Elana, Elayne, Eleanor, Eleanore, Elena, Eleni, Elenora, Elenore, Eleonora, Elianora, Elinor, Ella, Elladine, Elleanora, Elle, Ellee, Ellen, Ellenora, Ellette, Ellie, Ellin, Elliner, Ellinor, Elly, Ellyn, Galina, Halina, Heleanor, Helenore, Helena, Helenann, Hélène, Helia, Hella, Hellen, Hellena, Hellene, Hellenor, Hellia, Ileana, Ilene, Ilona, Jelena, Lana, Leanora, Lena, Lenore, Leonora, Leonore, Leora, Lienor, Lina, Nelda, Nell, Nellette, Nelliana, Nellie, Nelly, Nonnie, Nora, Yelena

Helga OG. "Holy, sacred." Var. **Olga**.
Helge, Hellga, Hellge

Helice Gk. "Spiral." An unusual name that comes from the same Greek root as helix, or double helix, the shape of the DNA molecule.
Helica, Helike

Helma OG. "Helmet." See **Wilhelmina**.
Hillma, Hilma

Heloise Fr. Var. **Louise** (OG. "Renowned in war"). The 12th-century French philosopher Pierre Abelard fell in love with and seduced his student Heloise. Her uncle and guardian had him emasculated, even though he married Heloise. She became a nun, he a monk. Today the name has housekeeping resonance, however, owing to the reach of the popular *Hints from Heloise* series of books.
Aloysia, Eloisa, Eloise, Heloisa, Lois

Helsa Dan. Var. **Elizabeth** (Heb. "Consecrated to God").
Hellsa

Henrietta (Fem. **Henry**) OG. "Ruler of the house." More
formal version of **Harriet** that briefly became popular at
the turn of the century. A bit of a mouthful for today's
parents.

**Enrichetta, Enrichette, Enriqueta, Etta, Ettie, Etty,
Hatsie, Hatsy, Hattie, Hatty, Hendrika, Henia, Henie,
Henka, Hennie, Henrie, Henrieta, Henriette, Henrika,
Henryetta, Hetti, Hettie, Yetta, Yettie**

Hepzibah Heb. "My delight is in her." Old Testament
name widely used by the Puritans, but by the 20th century it had almost died out, in part because of its lack of
euphony.

**Chepziba, Chepzibah, Eppie, Hefzia, Hefziba, Hephzia,
Hephziba, Hepsie, Hepsibah, Hepzi, Hepzia**

Hera Gk. "Queen." In Greek mythology, Hera was the wife
(and sister) of Zeus, ruler of the gods. She is usually portrayed as a jealous woman who persecutes her husband's
numerous mistresses. Her equivalent in the Roman pantheon is Juno.

Hermia Gk. "Messenger." This is a feminine version of
Hermes, the name of the Greek messenger god (he is often depicted with wings on his heels). One of the characters in Shakespeare's *A Midsummer Night's Dream* is
named Hermia.

Hermia, Hermilda

Hermione Gk. "Earthly." So unusual that readers of the
Harry Potter series of books had no idea how to pronounce it until the first film came out. Still a considerable
mouthful. Actress Hermione Gingold.

Erma, Herma, Hermia, Hermina, Hermine, Herminia

Hermosa Sp. "Beautiful."

Herodias Gk. "To monitor, watch over." In the Bible,
Herodias is the wife of Herod Philip and mother of Salome. She divorced her husband to marry his brother, the
governor of Judea, an act that John the Baptist de-
nounced. When Salome performed her famous dance for
her new stepfather he was so thrilled that he promised her

whatever she wanted: it was Herodias who suggested that John's head on a platter would be an appropriate reward. The story has been retold in a play by Oscar Wilde, an opera by Richard Strauss, and a short story by Gustave Flaubert, among others.

Hersilia Spanish from Gk. "Delicate." Roman myth name: the wife of Romulus, Rome's founder, originally one of the famous Sabine women carried off to provide wives for the new citizens of Rome.
Ercilia, Ersila, Ersilia, Erzilia, Hersila

Hertha OE. "Earth." The name of the German or Scandinavian Earth Mother.
Eartha, Erda, Ertha, Herta

Hesper Gk. "Evening or evening star." The Greeks referred to Italy as Hesperia, since the sun set and the evening star rose there. It is also, fittingly enough, the name of a town in California.
Hespera, Hesperia

Hester Gk. "Star." Var. **Esther**. The most famous Hester is probably the adulteress in Hawthorne's *The Scarlet Letter*, Hester Prynne.
Hesther, Hestia, Hettie, Hetty

Hibernia Lat. Place name for Ireland.

Hibiscus Lat. Botanical name for the plant colloquially known as the marsh mallow.

Hilary Gk. "Cheerful, happy." The name comes from the same root as the word "hilarious." There were a 4th-century saint and a 5th-century pope named Hilary, and the name was used for boys until the 17th century. The late-19th-century revival, though, made it generally a girl's name, which was especially fashionable in the 1950s. Parents can't consider the name now without reference to former First Lady Hillary Clinton. Actress Hilary Swank.
Hilaria, Hilarie, Hillary, Hillery, Hilliary

Hilda OG. "Battle woman." One of the Valkyrie of Teutonic legend was named Hilda. A medieval name with a Victorian revival that lasted through the 1930s. Now unusual.
Hilde, Hildie, Hildy

Hildegarde OG. "Battle stronghold." Rare in English-speaking countries. Saint Hildegarde of Bingen was a learned 12th century abbess who left a considerable body of writing. Opera star Hildegarde Behrens.

Hellee, Hilda, Hildagard, Hildagarde, Hilde, Hildegard, Hildegaard, Hildegunn, Hille

Hildemar OG. "Battle-renowned."

Hildemarr

Hildreth OG. "Battle counselor." Briefly used at the turn of the 20th century in Britain.

Hildred

Hilma Dim. **Wilhelmina** (OG. "Will-helmet").

Halma, Helma

Hinda Heb. "Doe, female deer."

Hynda

Hippolyta Gk. Meaning not entirely clear, but alludes to horses. In Greek legend, she was a queen of the Amazons (a warlike race of women) who was finally bested by Hercules or, depending on the version, by Theseus. She is also a character in Shakespeare's *A Midsummer Night's Dream.*

Hippolita

Holda OG. "Hidden."

Holde, Holle, Hulda

Holiday Originally, "Holy day," which presumably meant some respite from the daily drudgery of pre-industrial Europe to honor the calendar of the Christian church. Now, it has taken on the aura of jollity and mirth.

Holladay, Holliday

Hollis OE. Place name: "Near the holly bushes." The usual transference of a masculine to a feminine name may be accelerated in this case because Hollis sounds like **Holly**.

Hollace, Holles, Holless, Holliss, Holyss

Holly OE. Botanical name. First used at the turn of the 20th century and newly popular in the 1960s, possibly inspired by Truman Capote's novel *Breakfast at Tiffany's,* which was made into a film in 1961. Audrey Hepburn starred as the heroine, Holly Golightly. Obviously a seasonal favorite most intensively used in December. Actress Holly Hunter; singer Holly Near.

Hollee, Holleigh, Holley, Hollie, Hollye

Honey OE. The word used as a name. May be as a diminutive of **Honora**, but is more likely to be a transference of the endearment.

Honeah, Honee

Honora Lat. "Woman of honor." As **Honour**, used by the Puritans (along with other abstract concepts like Constance). **Honoria** was more common in the 18th century. No version of the name is widely used now. Actress Honor Blackman.

Honor, Honorah, Honorata, Honoria, Honorine, Honour, Nora, Norah, Norine, Norry

Hope OE. "Hope." One of the three cardinal virtues, along with Faith and Charity, and probably the one that has survived best as a name, particularly in the U.S.

Actress Hope Lange.

Horatia Lat. Clan name, possibly meaning "timekeeper." The name was coined by the 18th-century admiral Lord Horatio Nelson, for his daughter.

Horacia, Horaisha, Horasha

Hortense Lat. Clan name. A related word means "of the garden." *Hortensia* is the French term for the hydrangea shrub.

Hartencia, Hartinsia, Hortensia, Hortenspa, Hortenxia, Hortinzia, Ortensia

Hosanna Gk. from Heb. "Save now, we pray!" An expression of praise interjected into worship.

Hosana, Osana, Osanna

Huberta (Fem. Hubert) OG. "Brilliant mind."

Hubertina, Hubertine, Uberta, Ubertina

Huette (Fem. Hugh) OG. "Mind, intellect." A feminization of a name that has never had a particular vogue.

Huela, Huella, Huetta, Hugette, Hughette, Hughina, Ugetta

Hulda OG. "Loved one." Or Heb. "Mole." Very unusual, occurs in Scandinavian or English-speaking countries.

Huldah, Huldie

Hyacinth Gk. Flower name. There was a 3rd-century saint of this name, which was used for boys as well as girls. In

Greek legend, Apollo loved a beautiful youth of the name; the hyacinth flower sprang up from his blood when he died.

Cintha, Cinthia, Cinthie, Cinthy, Giacinta, Giacintia, Hyacintha, Hyacinthe, Hyacinthia, Hyacinthie, Hyacintia, Jacenta, Jacinda, Jacinta, Jacintha, Jacinthe, Jackie, Jacky, Jacynth

Hypatia Gk. "Highest."

Hypacia, Hypasia

Iantha Gk. "Purple flower." Popular in the later 19th century, possibly influenced by Romantic poets earlier in the century.

Ianthe, Ianthia, Ianthina, Janthia

Iberia Poetic name for the country of Spain.

Ibeeria

Ida Meaning unclear: possibly OE. "Prosperous, happy" or OG. "Hardworking." Very fashionable at the turn of the 20th century in America, but little used in modern times.

Eida, Eidah, Idaleen, Idalene, Idalia, Idalina, Idaline, Idalya, Idalyne, Ide, Idelfa, Idelfia, Idell, Idella, Idelle, Idetta, Idette

Idina Var. **Edina** (OE. "From Edinburgh, Scotland").

Idona Possiby ONorse. "Renewal," or an elaboration of Ida.

Idonah, Idone, Idonea, Idonie, Idonna, Iduna

Idra Aramaic. "Fig tree." In the parched lands where Aramaic was spoken long ago, a fig tree was a symbol of wealth.

Idris Welsh. "Hotblooded lord." This is a masculine name in Wales.

Edris, Eedris

Iduna ONorse. "Loving one."

Idonia, Idunna

Ieesha Var. **Aisha** (Arab. "Woman"; Swahili. "Life").

Eyeesha, Ieasha, Ieashia, Ieashiah, Ieeshah, Iesha, Yeesha

Ignacia (Fem. **Ignatius**) Meaning unclear, though some sources suggest Lat. "Ardent, burning." Usage tends to commemorate St. Ignatius Loyola, founder of the Society of Jesus, more commonly known as the Jesuits.

Ignatia, Ignazia, Iniga

Ila OF. Place name: "Island."

Eila, Ilanis, Ilanys, Isla

Ilana Heb. "Tree." Several names come from the Hebrew root and are also spelled several different ways.

Elana, Elanit, Eleana, Eleanna, Ileana, Ileanna, Iliana, Ilianna, Ilanit

Ilaria It. Var. **Hilary** (Gk. "Cheerful, happy").

Ilene Modern variant of **Aileen** (Gk. "Light").

Ilean, Ileen, Ileene

Ilesha Hindi. "Earth lord."

Iliana Gk. "Trojan." The poetic name for the ancient city of Troy was "Ilion." **Ileana** has been used by the Greek royal family. Actress Ileanna Douglas.

Ileana, Ileane, Ileanna, Ileanne, Illeanna, Illia, Illiana

Ilka Slavic. "Flattering, hardworking." Writer Ilka Chase.

Ilke, Milka

Ilona Hung. Var. **Helen** (Gk. "Light"). Also carries the connotation of "beautiful," no doubt because of the legendary beauty of Helen of Troy.

Elona, Ellona, Elonna, Illona, Ilone, Ilonka, Ilonna, Ylona, Ylonna

Ilsa Ger. Var. **Elizabeth** (Heb. "Pledged to God"). Mostly limited to Germany, especially in the 19th century.

Ellsa, Elsa, Else, Illsa, Ilsae, Ilsaie, Ilse

Iluminada Sp. "Lit up."

Illuminada, Illuminata, Iluminata, Yluminata

Ima Var. **Emma** (OG. "Embracing everything").

Iman Arab. "Belief, faith." Model Iman.

Eman, Imani

Imelda OG./It. "All-consuming fight." A name occasionally used (especially in Catholic families, after a virgin saint) until the explosive fame of Philippine First Lady Imelda Marcos. Now it seems slated for a long period of neglect. Actress Imelda Staunton.

Amelda, Himalda, Imalda, Ymelda

Immaculada Sp. "Without stain." A reference to the Immaculate Conception, the doctrine that the Virgin Mary, from the moment of her conception, was free of the Original Sin that tainted humankind. It was not proclaimed dogma until 1854.

Imacolata, Imaculada, Immaculata, Immacolata

Imogen Lat. Some sources claim it means "Last-born," while others suggest "Image," while still another traces it back to "Innocent." Despite Shakespeare's use of the name, it was obscure until the 20th century. Still highly unusual. Actresses Imogene Coca, Imogen Stubbs.

Emogen, Emogene, Imogene, Imogenia, Imogine, Imojean, Imojeen

Imperia Lat. "Imperial."

Empress, Imperatrix

Ina Lat. Suffix to make male names feminine, as in **Clementina** or **Edwina**. Used independently since the Victorian era. Cookbook author Ina Garten.

Ena, Yna

Inaya Arab. "Taking care, concerned."

Inayah

India Country name. Like any pretty geographic name, could be used by parents who have a special attachment to the country. Model India Hicks.

Indya

Indiana Lat. "From India." Also the name of a Middle Western state, of course.

Idiana

Indigo A deep blue dye derived from the indigo plant.

Indira Sanskrit. "Beauty." Name of longtime Indian Prime Minister Indira Ghandi.

Indeera

Indu Hindi. "Moon."

Inez Sp. Var. **Agnes** (Lat. "Pure"). Unusual in English-speaking countries, but **Ines** is currently very fashionable in Spain. Designer Inès de la Fressange.

Ines, Inesita, Inessa, Ynes, Ynesita, Ynez

Inga Scand. "Guarded by Ing." Ing, in Norse mythology, was a powerful god of fertility and peace. His name is an element in several modern names like **Ingrid** and **Ingmar**. **Inge** is very popular in Germany. Actress Inger Stevens.

Ingaberg, Ingaborg, Inge, Ingeberg, Ingeborg, Inger, Innga, Inngeborg

Ingrid Scand. "Beautiful." The most popular of the "Ing" names, and the only one to be widely used in non-Scandinavian cultures, doubtless because of the fame of Swedish actress Ingrid Bergman.

Inga, Inge, Inger, Ingmar

Inocencia Sp. "Innocence."

Innocencia, Innocenta, Inocenta, Inocentia, Ynocencia

Io In Greek mythology, Io was yet another maiden who caught Zeus' eye and was transformed to elude him: this time, into a cow.

Eyo

Ioanna Gk. Var. **Hannah** (Heb. "Grace").

Ioana, Ioanah, Ioannah, Joanna, Yohanna

Ionia Place name: the Ionian Sea separates western Greece from Italy, and the Ionian Islands, on the west coast of Greece, include Corfu.

Eionia, Ionija, Ionya

Iola Gk. "Cloud of dawn."

Iole

Iolani Haw. "Hawk of royalty."

Iolanthe Gk. "Violet flower." The more common form is the Spanish variant, **Yolanda**. Gilbert and Sullivan's 1882 operetta *Iolanthe* did little to popularize this form.

Iolanda, Iolanta, Iolantha, Jolantha, Jolanthe, Yolantha, Yolanthe, Yolley, Yollie

Iona Gk. Place name. Island off the coast of Scotland, site of an early monastery. Use as a name is mostly Scottish. Orchestra conductor Iona Brown.

Ione Gk. "Violet." Flower name in an exotic, little-used form. Actress Ione Skye.

Ionia, Ionie

Iphigenia Gk. "Sacrifice." In Greek myth, the daughter of Agamemnon. Her father sacrificed her to gain advantage in the Trojan war, though in most versions of the story, she is saved by Artemis. This savage tale inspired plays by Euripides, Goethe, and Racine.

Efigenia, Ephigenia, Ephigenie, Ifigenia, Iphigeneia, Iphigenie, Genia

Irene Gk. "Peace." Very common under the Roman Empire, but first appeared in English-speaking countries in the mid-19th century. It caught on quickly and was very popular in the first quarter of the 20th century. As **Irina**, fashionable in Russia. Actresses Irene Dunne, Irene Worth.

Arina, Eireen, Eiren, Eirena, Eirene, Erena, Erene, Ira, Ireen, Iren, Irena, Irenea, Irénée, Irenka, Irina, Irine, Iryna, Orina, Oryna, Rena, Rene, Renie, Rina, Yarina

Iris Gk. "Rainbow." Also (and this is probably the source of its popularity) name of a flower. Its use was established and faded with other flower names, from around 1890 to the 1920s. Novelist Iris Murdoch.

Irida, Iridiana, Iridianny, Irisa, Irita

Irit Heb. Plant name: the asphodel.

Irma OG. "Universal, complete." Rare now, but somewhat used in the first part of this century.

Erma, Ermengard, Irmina, Irmine, Irmgard, Irmgarde

Irvette (Fem. **Irving**) OE. "Seafriend." Also Scot. place name. A rather awkward transformation of a name that was never immensely popular.

Earvette, Earvina, Ervette, Ervina, Irvina

Isabel Sp. Var. **Elizabeth** (Heb. "Pledged to God"). Most fashionable in the last quarter of the 19th century, though popularity has increased steadily in the last dozen years with the trend toward old-fashioned feminine names. **Belle** and **Bella** are also independently used, probably because of their own attractive meaning ("beautiful") in

French and Spanish. Henry James named the heroine of his *Portrait of a Lady* Isabel Archer. Actresses Isabella Rossellini, Isabelle Adjani; fashion designer Isabel Toledo.

Bel, Belia, Belicia, Belita, Bell, Bella, Belle, Bellita, Ib, Ibbie, Isa, Isabeau, Isabele, Isabelita, Isabell, Isabella, Isabelle, Ishbel, Isobel, Isobell, Isobella, Isobelle, Issie, Issy, Izabella, Izabelle, Izzie, Izzy, Sabella, Sabelle, Ysabeau, Ysabel, Ysabella, Ysobel, Yzabelle, Yzobel, Yzobelle

Isadora (Fem. **Isidore**) Lat. "Gift of Isis." Isis was the principal goddess of ancient Egypt, and Isidore was a popular name among the ancient Greeks. The most famous Isadora was, of course, modern dance pioneer Isadora Duncan.

Isidora, Ysadora

Isaura Greek place name: Isauria was an ancient country in Asia Minor.

Aura, Isa, Isaure

Ishana Hindi. "Desire."

Ishani

Isis Egypt. The supreme goddess of ancient Egypt, Isis ruled with her brother/husband, Osiris, and her son, Horus.

Isla Name of a Scottish river, used in Britain as a first name.

Islay

Isolde Meaning unclear, though some sources offer Welsh "Fair lady." In legend Isolde is an Irish princess loved by Tristan, but she marries his uncle, King Mark. There are many versions of the tale, the most famous of which is probably Wagner's opera *Tristan und Isolde.* Use of this version of the name probably reflects admiration for the opera.

Iseult, Iseut, Isold, Isolda, Isolt, Isolte, Isota, Isotta, Isotte, Yseult, Yseulte, Yseut, Ysolda, Ysolde, Ysotta, Ysotte

Ita Ir. Gael. "Thirst." Name of a 6th-century Irish saint. Rare outside of Ireland.

Ivana (Fem. **Ivan**) Slavic Var. **John** (Heb. "Jehovah is gracious"). Most recently in the news with Ivana Trump, the ex-wife of Donald Trump.

Iva, Ivanka, Ivanna

Ivory Lat. Word used as name, possibly related to the vogue for jewel names in the late 19th century.

Ivoreen, Ivorine

Ivy OE. Botanical name. Most popular in the first quarter of the 20th century. Author Ivy Compton-Burnett.

Ivee, Ivey, Ivie

 Jacaranda Flower name: a tree with highly scented purple blossoms that flourishes in warm climates.

Jacarannda, Jacarranda, Jakaranda

Jacinda Sp. Var. **Hyacinth** (Gk. Flower name). There was a 3rd-century Saint Hyacinth, and the name was used for boys as well as girls. In Greek legend, Apollo loved a beautiful youth of the name; the hyacinth flower sprang up from his blood when he died.

Giacinda, Giacintha, Giacinthia, Jacenda, Jacenta, Jacey, Jacie, Jacindia, Jacinna, Jacinta, Jacinth, Jacintha, Jacinthe, Jacinthia, Jacy, Jacynth, Jacyntha, Jacynthe, Jacynthia

Jackie Dim., usually of **Jacqueline**. Used as an independent name in the 20th century, most notably by Jacqueline Kennedy Onassis.

Jackee, Jackey, Jacki, Jacky, Jacquey, Jacqui, Jacquie

Jacobina (Fem. **Jacob**) Heb. "He who supplants." **James** is an anglicization of Jacob, and has always been a favorite name in Scotland, which may account for the Scottish use of this feminization. It may also be related to the Scottish Jacobite movement of the 17th and 18th centuries that sought to keep Stuart kings on the throne of England—a lost cause, but a highly romantic one.

Jackee, Jackie, Jackobina, Jacky, Jacoba, Jacobetta, Jacobette, Jacobine, Jacobyna, Jakobina, Jakobine

Jacqueline Fr. Dim. **Jacob** (Heb. "He who supplants"). Existed in Britain as early as the 17th century, but used in numbers only from the beginning of the 20th century. Grew quickly, and was quite a favorite by midcentury. In the U.S., parents may have been inspired by the glamorous First Lady Jacqueline Kennedy, who has put an indelible stamp on the name. It is well enough used to be familiar but not fashionable. Actresses Jaclyn Smith, Jacqueline Bisset.

Jacalin, Jacalyn, Jackalin, Jackalinne, Jackelyn, Jacketta, Jackette, Jacki, Jackie, Jacklin, Jacklyn, Jacklynne, Jackqueline, Jacky, Jaclin, Jaclyn, Jacolyn, Jacqualine, Jacqualyn, Jacquel, Jacquelean, Jacquelin, Jacquella, Jacquelle, Jacquelyn, Jacquelynne, Jacquenetta, Jacquenette, Jacquetta, Jacquette, Jacqui, Jacquine, Jaculine, Jaquelin, Jaqueline, Jaquelyn, Jaquith, Zakelina, Zacqueline, Zhakelina, Zhaqueline

Jade Sp. Jewel name, for the semiprecious green stone. Perhaps because the jewel comes from the Orient, the name has a vaguely exotic air. Mick and Bianca Jagger used this name for their daughter. Quite popular in England. Actress Jada Pinkett.

Jada, Jadra, Jaida, Jayda, Jayde, Jaydra, Zhade

Jadwige Pol. "Safety in battle."

Jadwiga

Jael Heb. "Mountain goat." An Old Testament name: Jael was a heroic woman who killed a Canaanite captain, Sisera, with a tent peg. The name occurred from time to time among the Puritans and again in the 19th century. Now rare.

Jaelle, Jayel, Jayil

Jaffa Heb. "Beautiful." Also a place name: an ancient city that served as the port for Tel Aviv. It was probably most famous for its oranges though it was also the setting for legendary and Old Testament dramas like those of Andromeda and Jonah.

Jafit, Joppa

Jaime Sp. Var. **James** (Heb. "He who supplants"). The use of variations on **Jamie** as a girl's name has increased recently, and parents use this and other creative spellings to indicate the gender of the child. Some parents, however, may prefer to consider it as French for "I love," *J'aime*, in which case they should be prepared to insist on the "Zh-" pronunciation.

Jamee, James, Jamey, Jamie, Jayme, Jaymee

Jaleesa Modern name: **Lisa** with "Ja-" prefix. Probably invented by a TV writer for a character on *A Different World*, and used with some frequency in the early 1990s.

Geleexa, Jaleisa, Jaliza, Jilleesa, Jilleisa, Joleesa, Joleisa

Jamaica Place name: nation in the Caribbean. Its name comes from an Indian word meaning "Isle with many springs." Author Jamaica Kincaid.

Jamaeca, Jamaika, Jemaica, Jemayka

Jamesina (Fem. **James**) Heb. "He who supplants." An old-fashioned form that has been abandoned in favor of the less formal **Jamie**, etc.

Jamesetta, Jamesette

Jamie (Fem. var. **James**) Heb. "He who supplants." Also used as a boy's name, but once a name becomes entrenched as a feminine choice, parents tend to avoid it for their male children. Once Jamie became one of the top fifty girl's names in the U.S., back in the late 1980s, it may have been disqualified for male use. Now considerably less fashionable. Actresses Jamie Lee Curtis, Jami Gertz.

Jaime, Jaimee, Jaimey, Jaimi, Jaimie, Jaimy, Jama, Jamee, Jamei, Jamese, Jami, Jammie, Jayme, Jaymee, Jaymie

Jamila Arab. "Lovely." Currently popular among Moslem families.

Jameela, Jameila, Jamelia, Jamilah, Jamilla, Jamille, Jamillia

Jan (Fem. **John**) Heb. "The Lord is gracious." This version of **Jane** has been completely eclipsed by other feminizations of John. In records kept by the Social Security Administration, it is actually considered a boy's name. Author Jan Morris.

Jana, Janah, Janina, Janine, Jann, Janna, Jannah

Jana (Fem. **John**) Heb. "The Lord is gracious." A Slavic variation of **Jane**. Tennis star Jana Novotna.

Iana, Janaya, Janayah, Janna, Jannah, Yana, Yanna

Janae Modern name probably based on **Jane** or **Jan**.

Janay, Janea, Jenae, Jenay, Jennae, Jennay, Jinae, Jinnea

Jancis Modern name: probably a combination of **Jan** and **Francis** (Lat. "Frenchman").

Jances, Jancess

Jane (Fem. **John**) Heb. "The Lord is gracious." This is the simplest current variant of John (though **Joan** predates it), popular since the 16th century. It has been a tried-and-true standby like **Mary** or **Katherine**, as its number of variants demonstrate. When many women at a time shared the same name, variants sprang up to differentiate them from one another, hence **Janet**, **Janine**, **Janelle**, etc. At the moment, American parents are so hungry for the exotic that "plain Jane" hardly has a chance. Author Jane Austen; actresses Jane Fonda, Jane Seymour, Jayne Mansfield, Jane Wyman, Janeane Garofalo, Jane Kaczmarek; TV newswoman Jane Pauley.

Gene, Gianina, Giovanna, Iva, Ivana, Ivancka, Ivanka, Ivanna, Jaine, Jainee, Jan, Jana, Janaya, Janaye, Jandy, Janeczka, Janeen, Janel, Janela, Janelba, Janella, Janelle, Janean, Janeane, Janene, Janerita, Janessa, Janet, Janeta, Janeth, Janetta, Janette, Janey, Jania, Janica, Janice, Janie, Janina, Janine, Janique, Janis, Janise, Janit, Janka, Janna, Jannel, Jannelle, Janney, Janny, Jany, Jayne, Jaynell, Jean, Jeanette, Jeanie, Jeanne, Jeannette, Jeannine, Jenda, Jenella, Jenelle, Jenica, Jeniece, Jeni, Jenie, Jensina, Jensine, Jess, Jinna, Joana, Joanna, Johanna, Johnetta, Johnna, Johnetta, Jonella, Jonelle, Joni, Jonie, Juana, Juanita, Sheena, Shene, Sinead, Vania, Vanya

Janelle Parents seem to want to use names based in some

way on **John**, but the fashions in these names change widely. Janelle appeared in the middle of this century and is now far more widely used than **Janet**.

Janelba, Janell, Janellie, Janely, Janiella, Janielle, Jenell, Jenelle, Jinella, Jinelle, Johnelle, Jonelle

Janet The most common diminutive form of **Jane** is Janet, but other forms such as **Janeta** and **Jonet** preceded it. Janet was originally mostly Scots, and was very popular in the 1950s. Like most midcentury favorites, it is now out of style. Actresses Janet Leigh, Janet Gaynor; singer Dame Janet Baker; swimmer Janet Evans; figure skater Janet Lynn.

Gianetta, Janeta, Janeth, Janetta, Janette, Jannet, Jannetta, Janit, Janot, Jenetta, Jenette, Jennet, Jennette, Jinnet, Jinnett, Johnetta, Johnette, Jonette

Janice Var. **Jane**. Coined at the turn of the 20th century, in general circulation by the thirties and popular in the fifties. Like **Janet**, now out of favor. Singer **Janis Joplin**.

Janess, Janessa, Janesse, Janessia, Janiece, Janique, Janis, Janiss, Jannice, Janyce, Jency, Jenice, Jeniece, Jenise, Jennice

Janoah Heb. "Quiet, calm." An Old Testament place name. With two familiar names as its components (though they have nothing to do with its meaning), this could be a good choice for parents seeking an unusual but not peculiar name.

Janowa

Jardina Possibly a variant of **Jordan** (Heb. "Descend") or an adaptation from the Spanish word for garden, *jardin*.

Giardeena, Giardena, Giardina, Jardeena, Jardeina, Jardyna

Jarica Modern name made up of two euphonious elements. Since **Jessica** is such a popular name at the moment we can expect to see more names with the "-ica" ending.

Gerrica, Jareeca, Jareika, Jarika, Jarrica, Jerrica

Jasmine Per. "Jasmine flower." Flower name with exotic connotations. The turn-of-the-century vogue for flower names had its source in the English upper class, but was usually confined to temperate-zone specimens. (England's Queen Mother, for instance, had sisters named Rose and Violet Hyacinth.) Jasmine became fashionable a bit later, in the 1930s. It was gaining popularity in the 1990s even before the film *Aladdin* brought Princess Jasmine into millions of households. Now Jasmine is a steady favorite, especially among Hispanic and African American families. Author Jessamyn West; model Yasmeen Ghauri.

Ismenia, Jaslyn, Jaslynn, Jasmin, Jasmina, Jasminda, Jassamayn, Jazan, Jazmin, Jazmon, Jazzmin, Jazzmine, Jazzmon, Jazzmyn, Jazzmynn, Jess, Jessamine, Jessamy, Jessamyn, Jessie, Jessimine, Jessimine, Yasmeen, Yasmin, Yasmina, Yasmine, Yasminia

Jay Lat. "Jaybird." A medieval name that has survived in a small way, especially in the U.S., where it is given to boys and girls alike. Its use may be inspired by a great American jurist, John Jay. It is sometimes used in combination with other names. Gymnast Jaycie Phelps.

Jae, Jaya, Jaycie, Jaye, Jaylene, Jeh, Jey, Jeyla

Jean Var. **Jane**. Scottish origin, unusual elsewhere until the turn of the 20th century; most popular in the 1930s. Now preferred for boys, probably among this country's francophone populations as it is a French version of **John**. Actresses Jean Arthur, Jean Harlow.

Gene, Genie, Jeana, Jeane, Jeanee, Jeaneen, Jeanelle, Jeanene, Jeanette, Jeanie, Jeanine, Jeanique, Jeanna, Jeanne, Jeanneen, Jeannetta, Jeannette, Jeannie, Jeannine, Jeannique, Jenette, Jenica, Jennet, Jennetta, Jennine

Jeannine (Fem. **John**) Var. **Jean** (Heb. "The Lord is gracious"). Modern usage.

Janine, Jeanine, Jenine, Jannine, Jennine

Jearl Modern name: probably Pearl with a "J-." Track star Jearl Miller.

Jerle

Jecolia Heb. "The Lord has prevailed." Old Testament character: the mother of King Uzziah.

Jecholia, Jekolia

Jedida Heb. "Beloved." Another Old Testament person-age, this one the mother of Josiah.

Jeddida, Jedidah

Jelena Rus. Var. **Helen** (Gk. "Light").

Galina, Yelena

Jemima Heb. "Dove." Old Testament name: Jemima was one of the three beautiful daughters of the persecuted Job. The Puritans brought the name to the U.S., where it is now probably most familiar because of the "Aunt Jemima" brand name for pancake mix and syrup, as well as Beatrix Potter's foolish heroine of *Jemima Puddle-duck*. Still, a good candidate for revival with the current interest in old names.

Jamima, Jemimah, Jemmimah, Jemmie, Jemmy, Mima, Mimma

Jena Arab. "Little bird."

Jenna

Jenara Sp. from Lat. "January." A good name for a Janu-ary baby.

Genara, Gennara, Jennara

Jenessa Comb. form **Jennifer** and **Vanessa**. Can also be considered an elaboration of **Janice**, though the current popularity of Vanessa makes it more likely that this is the primary influence.

Gianessa, Janessa, Jinessa

Jenilee Comb. form. **Jenny** and **Lee**.

Jenilea, Jennielee, Jennylee

Jenna Dim. **Jennifer** or Var. **Jean** (Heb. "The Lord is gra-cious"). Made famous by a character on *Dallas*, played by Priscilla Presley. This name is currently quite fashion-able, especially since 2000. First Daughter Jenna Bush; actress Jenna Elfman.

Jena

Jennie Dim. **Janet** or **Jennifer**. Given as an independent name since the 19th century. Swedish soprano Jennie Lind; talk show host Jenny Jones.

Jenee, Jennee, Jenney, Jenni, Jenny

Jennifer Welsh. "White and smooth, soft." The modern and most popular form of **Guinevere**, originally a Cornish variant. Its immense 20th-century popularity began in the 1920s and grew to a 1950s peak in Britain. In the U.S. the name reached the number one spot in the early eighties, and is now slipping down the charts though it is still very heavily used. Actresses Jennifer Gray, Jennifer Jones, Jennifer Jason Leigh, Jennifer O'Neill, Jennifer Aniston, Jennifer Connelly, Jennifer Garner, Jennifer Lopez.

Genna, Genni, Gennie, Gennifer, Geniffer, Genniver, Genny, Jen, Jena, Jenefer, Jeni, Jenifer, Jeniffer, Jenn, Jenna, Jennee, Jenni, Jennica, Jennie, Jenniver, Jenny

---

WHAT WOULD BILL GATES DO?

He's never been cool, that's clear. And all the money in the world isn't going to make him cool either. But Bill Gates doesn't seem to mind. He just goes on his merry way, oblivious to social trends—and when he and bride Melinda French had their first child, they chose the name Jennifer, which has been so popular for so long that it approaches classic stature, like Michael or Matthew. And you know what? Jennifer Gates will never have to spell her name for anybody. (Her brother Rory and sister Phoebe, though, have much trendier names: Could the Gates parents be aware of fashion after all?)

Jeremia (Fem. **Jeremiah**) Heb. "The Lord is exalted."
Jeree, Jeremee, Jeremie, Jeri, Jerri, Jerrie, Jerry
Jerioth Heb. "Curtains." Another Old Testament character.
Jerrie OG./Fr. "Spear ruler." Dim. **Geraldine**.
Jeree, Jeri, Jerree, Jerrey, Jerri, Jerry, Jery
Jerusha Heb. "Married, a possession." In the Old Testa-

ment, the wife of King Uzziah. The name was used by the Puritans and revived slightly in the 19th century. The heroine of James Michener's *Hawaii* is named Jerusha.

Jarusha, Jeruscha, Jerushah

Jessenia A variant spelling of **Yesenia**, a name that's popular in the Hispanic community.

Jesenia, Jesenya, Yesenia, Yessenia, Yessenya

Jessica Heb. "He sees." Coined by Shakespeare from the Old Testament Iscah or Jesca. His Jessica was the daughter of Shylock in *The Merchant of Venice*. Popular in the U.S. in the 1970s, and still one of the top ten names in the nation, well used by every ethnic group. Also very fashionable in England. Curiously for a name with this kind of popularity, there are not many variant spellings, but that may be the next step in its development. Actresses Jessica Lange, Jessica Tandy, Jessica Alba, Jessica Capshaw, Sarah Jessica Parker.

Jess, Jessa, Jessaca, Jessaka, Jessalin, Jessalyn, Jesse, Jesseca, Jessey, Jessie, Jessika, Jessy

Jessie Dim. **Jessica**. Also, in Scotland, a diminutive of **Janet**.

Jess, Jessa, Jesse, Jessey, Jessi, Jessy

Jesusa Sp. Derived from Mary de Jesus, a name for the Virgin Mary.

Jethra Heb. "Plenty, abundance." A feminine form of **Jethro**.

Jeth

Jette Dan. "Black as coal." Mostly used in northern Europe.

Yette

Jewel OF. Word as first name. Though the vogue for jewel names occurred at the turn of the 20th century (along with the flower-name fashion), Jewel came into use a little later, in the 1930s. Pop singer Jewel.

Jewell, Jewella, Jewelle

Jezebel Heb. "Pure, virginal." An Old Testament name that carries strong connotations that contradict its meaning: It was used as a term for a "painted lady" or a brazen hussy as portrayed by Bette Davis in the film *Jezebel*.

Jessabell, Jetzabel, Jezabel, Jezabella, Jezebelle, Jezibel, Jezibelle, Jezybell

Jezreel Heb. "The Lord sows." An Old Testament place name.

Jesreel

Jill Dim. **Gillian**, ultimately of **Juliana** (Lat. "Youthful"). Jill was popular before the 17th century, and revived to widespread use after the 1920s. Now quite scarce. Actresses Jill St. John, Jill Eikenberry, Jill Ireland; English novelist Jilly Cooper; fashion designer Jil Sander.

Jil, Jilian, Jilana, Jillan, Jillana, Jillane, Jillayne, Jilleen, Jillene, Jilli, Jillian, Jillianne, Jillie, Jilly, Jillyan, Jyl, Jyll

Jillian Var. **Gillian**; Dim. **Juliana** (Lat. "Youthful"). In this age of elaboration, now much more popular than blunt, monosyllabic **Jill**.

Jilian, Jiliana, Jilan, Jillana, Jillane, Jilliana, Jillianne, Jillyan, Jillyanna, Jilliyanne

Jimena Sp. "Heard."

Jinny Dim. **Virginia** or Var. **Jenny**. Mostly 19th-century use in this form.

Jinna, Jinnee, Jinni, Jinnie

Jinx Lat. "Spell."

Jinxx, Jynx

Jo Dim. **Joan**, **Josephine**, etc. Often used in combination, as in Jo Ann, Betty Jo. The second daughter in Louisa May Alcott's *Little Women* was called Jo, short for Josephine, and was played by Katharine Hepburn and Winona Ryder in successive film versions of the novel. Still, the usage hasn't caught on widely, and is not likely to do so in an era when the top ten list does not include one monosyllabic girl's name.

Joakima (Fem. **Joachim**) Heb. "God will judge."

Joaquina, Joaquine

Joan (Fem. **John**) Heb. "The Lord is gracious." The medieval feminine version of John; Jeanne d'Arc's first name, for instance, was translated as Joan, **Jeanne**'s popular English equivalent. It was neglected for **Jane** by the

17th century. A brief intense revival occurred early in the
20th century for a score of years, but Joan is again widely
neglected. Actresses Joan Crawford, Joan Collins; singer
Joan Baez; comedienne Joan Rivers; musician Joni
Mitchell; marathon runner Joan Benoit.

Joane, Joanie, Joannie, Jone, Jonee, Joni

Joanna Var. **Jane** or **Joan**. Its 19th-century use increased
with the revival of Joan, and continued to grow until
around 1950 in the U.S. **Joanne**, the French form, was
hugely popular in Britain in the 1970s. Today Joanna is
more heavily used than Joanne in America, just as **Anna**
is much more popular than **Anne**. Actresses Joanna Lum-
ley, Joanne Woodward; author Joanne (J.K.) Rowling.

**Jo, Joana, Joann, Jo Ann, Joanne, Jo Anne, Joeann,
Johanna, Johannah**

Jobeth Comb. form **Jo** and **Beth**. Unusual, found mostly
in the 1950s. Actress JoBeth Williams.

Joby (Fem. **Job**) Heb. "Persecuted." Unusual version of an
Old Testament name widely used by the Puritans and
their descendants well into the 19th century.

Jobey, Jobi, Jobie, Jobina, Jobyna

Jocasta It. "Lighthearted." In spite of its pleasant meaning, the name is little used because of its history. In Greek
mythology, Jocasta is the mother of Oedipus; he later un-
wittingly marries her, unleashing a series of gruesome
tragedies. Interior design writer Jocasta Innes.

Jokasta

Jocelyn Derivation unclear; possibly Old German, possi-
bly Lat. "Cheerful." It was a man's name in the Middle
Ages, revived as a girl's name in the early 20th century.
Cellist Jocelyn DuPré.

**Jocelin, Joceline, Jocelinda, Jocelyne, Josaline,
Joscelin, Josceline, Joscelyn, Joselina, Joseline, Jose-
lyn, Joselyne, Josiline, Josline, Jossline, Josselyn,
Josslyn, Joycelin**

Jocosa Lat. "Joking."

Giocosa

Jody Dim. **Joan, Judith**. Used mostly since the 1950s in

the U.S.; in the Canadian top ten in the 1970s. Actress
Jodie Foster.

Jodee, Jodey, Jodi, Jodie

Joelle (Fem. **Joel**) Heb. "Jehovah is the Lord." Probably
popularized by a vogue for combined forms beginning
with "Jo," like **Joanne** and **Jolene**. Reached its peak in
the 1960s. Actress Joely Richardson.

**Joela, Joelin, Joell, Joella, Joelliane, Joellin, Joelly,
Joely, Joelynn, Joetta, Jowella, Jowelle**

Johanna (Fem. **Johann**) Ger. Var. **John** (Heb. "The Lord is
gracious"). A European-sounding choice among the numerous feminizations of John.

**Giovanna, Joanna, JoeHannah, Johana, Johannah, Jo-
vanna**

Johnna (Fem. **John**) Heb. "The Lord is gracious." May
also be considered a contraction of **Johanna**.

**Giana, Gianna, Giovanna, Jana, Janna, Johna,
Johnetta, Johnette, Jovanna**

Joie Fr. Var. **Joy**. Actress Joie Lee.

Joi

Jolan Gk. "Violet flower." This is a Middle-European form
of **Iolanthe**. The most popular form in the U.S. is
Yolanda.

**Joia, Jolaine, Jolande, Jolanne, Jolanta, Jolantha,
Yolanne**

Jolene Comb. form **Jo** and **-lene**. In the 1940s names ending in "-lene" (**Darlene, Marlene**, etc.) began to be fashionable, and a form beginning with "Jo" was a natural
result. These names are now little used.

**Joeline, Joeleen, Jolean, Joleen, Jolena, Jolina, Jo-
line, Jolyn, Jolyna, Jolyne, Jolynn**

Jolie Fr. "Pretty." Used mainly since the 1960s.

Joely, Jolee, Joley, Joli, Joliet, Jolietta, Joliette, Joly

Jonquil Flower name. Unlike most flower names, this one
did not appear until the 1940s, and its two decades of
popularity were mostly limited to Britain. The jonquil is
a variety of narcissus closely related to a daffodil.

Jordan Heb. "Descend." Named after the River Jordan.
First used in the Middle Ages by Crusaders returning

from the Holy Land. Revived slightly in the 19th century, mostly for boys. It is still very well used for boy babies, and since fashions in female names have moved away from the unisex, it is likely to remain a male name.

Jardena, Johrdan, Jordain, Jordana, Jordane, Jordanka, Jordanna, Jorden, Jordena, Jordenn, Jordie, Jordin, Jordyn, Jorey, Jori, Jorie, Jorrdan, Jorry, Jourdan

Josephine (Fem. **Joseph**) Heb. "Jehovah increases." Napoleon's famous Empress Josephine's real name was Marie Josephe (for the parents of Jesus), but Josephine was used as a diminutive. It did not become fashionable until the mid-19th century, and has never caught on widely in the U.S. Cabaret star Josephine Baker.

Fifi, Fifine, Fina, Finetta, Finette, Guiseppina, Jo, Joette, Joey, Joline, Josana, Josanna, Josanne, Josee, Josefa, Josefena, Josefene, Josefina, Josefine, Josepha, Josephe, Josephene, Josephina, Josephyna, Josephyne, Josetta, Josette, Josey, Josiane, Josianna, Josianne, Josie, Josy, Jozsa

Jovita Lat. "Made glad."
Giovita

Joy Lat. "Joy." Used in the Middle Ages and sparingly by the Puritans, then revived at the turn of the 20th century. Unusual after the height of its popularity in the 1950s.

Gioia, Gioya, Jioia, Jioya, Joi, Joice, Joie, Joya, Joyann, Joye

Joyce Lat. "Joyous." Used in the Middle Ages, but nearly died out until the early years of the 20th century, when it had a spurt of immense popularity, especially in Britain. Advice columnist Dr. Joyce Brothers; writer Joyce Carol Oates.

Joice, Joycelyn, Joyse, Joyous

Juanita Sp. Var. **Joan**.
Janita, Juana, Juniata, Junita, Juwaneeta, Juwanita, Nita, Wahnita, Wahnna, Wanna, Waneeta, Wanita

Jubilee Heb. "Ram's horn." Term for a fiftieth-year celebration, marked in Old Testament times by the blowing of a ram's horn. A great festival was held to mark each fiftieth anniversary of the liberation from Egypt. European monarchs in the 19th century took up the tradition, and Queen Victoria celebrated Silver (twenty-fifth), Golden (fiftieth), and Diamond (sixtieth) Jubilees. A nice name to mark a great celebration.

Jubalee

Judith Heb. "Jewish." Old Testament name overlooked by the Puritans in their quest for girls' names, but fashionable from the 1920s through the 1950s. In the Apocrypha, Judith is a Jewish heroine who decapitates the Assyrian general Holofernes and shows his head to the Hebrew army, inciting them to victory. Actress Dame Judith Anderson; movie critic Judith Crist; chess champion Judit Polgar.

Giuditta, Jodie, Jody, Judee, Judi, Judie, Judit, Judita, Judite, Juditha, Judithe, Judy, Judye, Jutta

Judy Dim. **Judith**. Dates back to the 18th century, but its true popularity follows that of Judith in the 20th century. **Jody** is another frequently used diminutive. Actresses Judy Garland, Judy Holliday, Dame Judi Dench; singer Judy Collins.

Judee, Judey, Judi, Judie, Judye

Julia (Fem. **Julius**) Lat. Clan name. "Youthful." Along with **Juliana**, used among the early Christians, but it was rare in the Middle Ages. Since the 1700s it has gone mildly in and out of fashion without ever being a tremendous favorite. **Julie**, in this century, has been much more popular but in the last ten years the European form with the "-a" ending has soared to very frequent use. Chef Julia Child; opera star Julia Migenes; actresses Julia Ormond, Julia Roberts, Julia Louis-Dreyfus, Julia Stiles.

Giulia, Giuliana, Giulianna, Giulianne, Giulietta, Jiulia, Joleta, Joletta, Jolette, Julee, Juley, Juli, Juliaeta, Juliaetta, Juliana, Juliane, Juliann, Julianne, Julie, Julienne, Juliet, Julieta, Julietta, Juliette, Julina, Juline, Julinka, Juliska, Julissa, Julita, Julitta, Julyana, Julyanna, Julyet, Julyetta, Julyette, Julyne, Yulia, Yuliya

Juliana (Fem. **Julian**) Lat. clan name. "Youthful." Appeared in the early Christian era, and medieval use contracted it to **Gillian** (and from there to **Jill**). Although a royal name in the Netherlands, it is unusual now, possibly seeming too stately. Contracted forms like **Liana** may eclipse it. Actresses Julianne Phillips, Julianne Moore, Julianna Margulies.

Giuliane, Giulianne, Juliane, Julianna, Julianne, Julieanna, Julieanne, Juline, Julinda, Julyana, Julyane, Julyanna, Julyanne

Julie Fr. Dim. **Julia** (Lat. Clan name. "Youthful"). Imported from France in the 1920s and fashionable very quickly, especially in the 1970s. It had earlier taken root on the Continent, as evidenced by Strindberg's 1888 tragedy *Miss Julie.* Actresses Julie Andrews, Julie Harris, Julie Walters, Julie Kavner; cookbook author Julee Rosso; pop singer Julee Cruise.

Jooley, Joolie, Julee, Juley, Julienne, Jullee, Jullie, July, Jully

Juliet Lat. Clan name. "Youthful." Dim. **Julia**. Can scarcely be used without reference to Shakespeare's famous tragic heroine. Girls named Juliet can expect a certain amount of teasing about Romeo. Dancer Juliet Prowse; actresses Juliet Stevenson, Juliette Lewis.

Giulietta, Juliaetta, Julieta, Juliett, Julietta, Juliette, Julyet, Julette

Jumana Arab. "A silver pearl."

Jumanah, Jumanna

Juniata Place name: a county in central Pennsylvania.

June Month used as name, dating from the 20th century but most popular in the 1950s. Scarcely seen today. Actress June Allyson.

Junella, Junelle, Junette, Junia, Juniata, Junieta, Junina, Junine, Junya, Jyune

Juno Lat. "Queen of heaven." Juno was the Roman equivalent of Hera in classical mythology: Jupiter's wife, and the gods' queen. Not widely used in any era; in modern times the adjective "Junoesque" has come to be used for tall women with curvy figures, possibly because of the way Juno is often portrayed in Old Master paintings.

Juneau, Juneaux, Junot

Justice Virtue name for the 21st century. The cardinal

virtues are prudence, fortitude, temperance, and justice, as opposed to the theological virtues of faith, hope, and charity. The last three have been more often used as names.
Justyce, Justiss

Justine Lat. "Fair, righteous." **Justina** was the original form, but the French version took over in the 1960s, probably aided by Lawrence Durrell's famous novel *Justine*. Actress Justine Bateman.
Giustina, Justa, Justeen, Justene, Justie, Justina, Justinn, Justy, Justyna, Justyne

Kadenza Lat. "With rhythm." Modern variant of Cadence.
Cadenza, Kadena, Kadence

Kaitlin Var. **Caitlin**, Irish form of **Catherine** (Gk. "Pure"). A name as popular as Catherine has produced endless variations over the years, and recently Caitlin and its variants have become just as popular as the more familiar form, which is still in the top fifteen or twenty names used in most regions of the U.S.
Caitlin, Caitlyn, Kaitlyn, Katelyn, Katelynn, Katelynne, Kathlin, Kathlinne, Kathlyn

Kala Var. **Kali**.

Kali Sanskrit. "Black one." This is the name of a Hindu goddess in her role as the essence of destruction, which includes a very grisly component (her worshippers, known as "thugs," strangled people to propitiate her).
Kalli

Kalila Arab. "Beloved."
Cailey, Cailie, Caylie, Kailey, Kalie, Kalilah, Kayllie, Kaly, Kaylee, Kylila, Kylilah

Kalliope In Greek mythology, Calliope was the muse of epic poetry. Many of the "C" names that come from the Greek are spelled with a "K" in their original form.
Kallyope

Kallista Gk. "Most beautiful."

Cala, Calesta, Calista, Callie, Cally, Kala, Kalesta, Kalista, Kalli, Kallie, Kally, Kallysta

Kama Sanskrit. "Love"; Heb. "Ripe."

Kamilah Arab. "Perfect."

Kamila, Kamilla, Kamillah

Kamilla European var. **Camilla**. Some sources trace Camilla to the young girls who assisted at pagan religious ceremonies.

Camilla, Cammie, Kamella, Kamila, Kamilka, Kamilla, Kamille, Kamyla, Kemilla, Milla, Millie

Kandace Var. **Candace** (Lat. "Glowing white"). Historically the name was the ancient title of the queens of Ethiopia before the 4th century. Not much used before the middle of the 20th century.

Candie, Candy, Dacie, Kandice, Kandiss, Kandy

Kanara Heb. "Little bird, canary."

Kanarit, Kanarra

Kanga Short for kangaroo: sometimes given as a nickname to an Australian far from home.

Kanisha Very popular invented name, probably an adaptation of the fashionable Tanisha.

Kaneesha, Kanicia, Kenisha, Kinicia, Kinisha, Koneesha

Kara Var. **Cara** (Lat. "Dear one"). Principally used from the 1970s onward. A diminutive form, **Karina**, is currently well-used in Russia.

Cara, Carina, Carita, Karina, Karine, Karita, Karrah, Karrie

Karen Dan. Var. **Katherine** (Gk. "Pure"). Took hold in the 1930s in English-speaking countries, and blossomed to great popularity in the 1950s and 1960s. Unusual today. Writer Karen Blixen (Isaak Dinesen); singer Karen Carpenter; actress Karen Allen.

Caren, Carin, Caron, Caronn, Carren, Carrin, Carron, Carryn, Caryn, Carynn, Carynne, Kari, Karin, Karna, Karon, Karryn, Karyn, Kerran, Kerrin, Kerron, Kerrynn, Keryn, Kerynne, Taran, Taren, Taryn

Karimah Arab. "Giving." Currently popular among Arabic-speaking parents.

Kareema, Kareemah, Kareima, Karima

Karla Var. **Carla** (OG. "Man"). One of the endless names that derive from **Charles**. Fans of John Le Carré's novels will remember that George Smiley's Russian nemesis used the code name Karla.

Karlah, Karlla, Karrla

Karlotta Ger. Var. **Charlotte** (Fr. from OG. "Man").

Karlota, Karlotte, Lotta, Lottee, Lottey, Lottie

Karma Hindi. "Destiny, spiritual force." A New Age name if ever there was one.

Karolina Slavic. Var. **Caroline** (Lat. "Little and womanly").

Karaline, Karalyn, Karalynna, Karalynne, Karla, Karleen, Karlen, Karlena, Karlene, Karli, Karlie, Karlina, Karlinka, Karolina, Karoline, Karolinka, Karolyn, Karolyna, Karolyne, Karolynn, Karolynne, Leena, Lina, Lyna

Kasmira (Fem. **Casimir**) Old Slavic. "Bringing peace." Very unusual.

Kasha Var. **Katherine**. Also, coincidentally, the name of a grain used in Middle European cooking.

Kassandra Var. **Cassandra**. (Gk. Possibly Fem. Alexander).

Kataniya Heb. "Small."

Kate Dim. **Katherine**. Long-standing independent name, especially popular in the late 19th century. Today parents are far more likely to give a child the longer name and use Kate or **Katie** as a nickname. The latter form is very popular in Ireland. Writer Kate Chopin; actresses Kate Capshaw, Kate Jackson, Kate Nelligan, Kate Hudson, Kate Beckinsale, Kate Winslet; German artist Kaethe Kollwitz; designer Kate Spade; model Kate Moss.

Cait, Caitie, Cate, Catee, Catey, Catie, Kaethe, Kait, Kaite, Kaitlin, Katee, Katey, Kathe, Kati, Katie

Katherine Gk. "Pure." One of the oldest recorded names, with roots in Greek antiquity. Almost every Western country has its own form of the name, and phonetic variations are endless. It has been borne by such illustrious women as Saint Catherine of Alexandria, the early martyr who was tortured on a spiked wheel; Empress Catherine the Great of Russia; and three of Henry VIII's six wives. It is currently very popular as **Katharina, Katja** or **Katya** in Northern Europe, albeit displaced by **Caitlin** in England and Scotland. It is still a standard among American girls' names. One of the reasons it is so popular is that parents can name a child the solid, conservative Katherine, and call her anything from **Kathy** to **Katt**. Actresses Catherine Oxenberg, Catherine Deneuve, Katharine Hepburn, Catherine Zeta-Jones; skater Katarina Witt.

Cait, Caitlin, Caitlinn, Caitrin, Caitrine, Caitriona, Caitrionagh, Caity, Caren, Cari, Carin, Caron, Caronne, Carren, Carri, Carrin, Carron, Caryn, Carynn, Cass, Cassey, Cassi, Cassie, Cat, Cataleen, Cataleena, Catalin, Catalina, Cataline, Catarina, Catarine, Cate, Cateline, Caterina, Cathaleen, Cathaline, Catharin, Catharina, Catharine, Catharyna, Catharyne, Cathee, Cathelina, Catherine, Catherina, Catheryn, Cathie, Cathirin, Cathiryn, Cathleen, Cathline, Cathlyne, Cathrine, Cathrinn, Cathryn, Cathrynn, Cathy, Cathye, Cati, Catie, Catina, Catlaina, Catreen, Catreina, Catrin, Catrina, Catrine, Catriona, Catrionagh, Catryna, Caty, Cay, Caye, Ekaterina, Kaatje, Kait, Kaitee, Kaitie, Kaitlin, Kaitlinn, Kaitrin, Kaitrine, Kaitrinn, Kaitrinna, Kaitriona, Kaity, Karen, Karena, Kari, Karin, Karon, Karri, Karrin, Karyn, Karynn, Kasia, Kasienka, Kasja, Kaska, Kasya, Kass, Kassi, Kassia, Kassie, Kas, Kat, Kata, Kataleen, Katalin, Katalina, Katarina, Katchen, Kate, Katee, Katell, Katelle, Katenka, Katerina, Katey, Katha, Katharine, Katharyn, Kathee, Kathelina, Katheline, Katherin, Katherina, Katheryn, Katheryne, Kathi, Kathie, Kathileen, Kathirin, Kathiryn, Kathirynn, Kathleen, Kathlene, Kathleyn, Kathline, Kathlyne, Kathrene, Kathrine, Kathrinna, Kathryn, Kathryne, Kathy, Kathyrine, Kati, Katie, Katica, Katina, Katinka, Katka, Katla, Katlaina, Katleen, Katline, Katoushka,

Katouska, Katrena, Katrien, Katrina, Katrine, Katri-
ona, Katrionagh, Katryna, Katushka, Katuska, Katy,
Katya, Kay, Kaye, Kit, Kittey, Kitti, Kittie, Kitty,
Rina, Trina, Trinchen, Trine, Trinette, Yekaterin,
Yekaterina

Kathleen Ir. Var **Katherine** (Gk. "Pure"). Its use outside
of Ireland began in the 1840s, and may have been influenced by the great wave of Irish emigration sparked by
the potato famines of those years. U.S. popularity peaked
in the 1950s. Actress Kathleen Turner.

Cathaleen, Cathaline, Cathleen, Kaitlin, Kaitlinn,
Katha, Kathaleen, Kathaleya, Kathaleyna, Kathaline,
Kathelina, Katheline, Kathleyn, Kathlin, Kathline,
Kathlyn, Kathlyne, Kathyline, Katleen, Katlin, Katline,
Katlyne

Kathy Diminutive, usually of **Katherine**. Rarely used as a
given name by itself. TV host Kathie Lee Gifford; actress
Kathy Najimy.

Cathie, Cathy, Kathee, Kathey, Kathie

Katrina Var. **Katherine** (Gk. "Pure"). Appealing for its
European sound. Actress Katrin Cartlidge.

Caitrionagh, Catreena, Catreina, Catrina, Catriona,
Catrionagh, Kaitrina, Kaitrona, Katreena, Katreina,
Katriona, Katrionagh, Katryna, Ketreina, Ketrina,
Ketryna, Kotrijna, Kotryna

Kay Dim. **Katherine**. First appeared at the turn of the 20th
century, but widespread in the middle of the century. Actress Kaye Ballard; author Kay Thompson.

Caye, Kai, Kaye

Kayla Modern variant of **Katherine** (Gk. "Pure") or Dim.
Michaela (Heb. "Who is like the Lord?"). Has seen a
huge spurt of usage in recent years, vaulting up to the top
ten girls' names in the U.S. in 1991. It is now losing a bit
of steam, but is still very steadily used.

Cayla, Caylie, Kaela, Kaila, Kaylyn

Kayley Could be considered a combination of perennials
Kay and **Lee**, but is more likely a variant of fashionable
Kayla, with the also popular "-ley" ending. Some

sources even give a Gaelic derivation and meaning: "Slender." Spelling is up to the parents, since there is no traditional form.

Caleigh, Cayleigh, Cayley, Kaeleigh, Kailee, Kaileigh, Kailey, Kaili, Kaleigh, Kaley, Kaylea, Kaylee, Kaylie, Kaylleigh, Kaylley

Kaylin Variant of **Caitlin** or of **Kayla/Kayley**. Often names from different traditions may resemble each other very closely.

Kailyn, Kaylan, Kaylanne, Kaylinn, Kaylyn, Kaylynn, Kaylynne

Keely Ir. Var. **Kelly** ("Battle maid"). Not yet in the **Kayla/Kayley** league, but has all the qualifications. Actress Keeley Shaye Smith.

Kealey, Kealy, Keeley, Keeli, Keelia, Keelie, Keighley, Keighly, Keili, Keilie, Keyley, Keylie, Keylley, Keyllie

Kefira Fem. **Kefir** (Heb. "Young lion").

Kefeera, Kefeira, Kefirah, Kefirra

Keila Heb. "Citadel." Old Testament place name; a town in the kingdom of Judah.

Keilah

Keisha Modern name, possibly formed as a short version of **Lakeisha**, which, in turn, may be a variant of **Aisha** (Arab. "Woman"). Very popular with African-American families.

Keasha, Keesha, Keeshah, Keicia, Keishah, Keshia, Kicia

Keitha Fem. **Keith** (Scot. Gael. "Forest").

Keithana

Kelby OE. Place name: "Farmhouse near the stream."

Kelbea, Kelbeigh, Kelbey, Kellbie

Kelda ONorse. "Spring, fountain."

Kellda

Kelila Heb. "Crowned."

Kayla, Kayle, Kaylee, Kelula, Kelulah, Kelulla, Kyla, Kyle

Kelly Ir. Gael. "Battle maid." Originally a very common Irish last name, and very popular as a girl's first name from about the 1950s, peaking in the 1970s in America. Actresses Kelly McGillis, Kelly Preston, Kelly Ripa.

Kellee, Kelley, Kelli, Kellie, Kellina

Kelsey OE. Place name, incorporating a word particle that means "island." Mostly recent usage, for boys as well as girls. As formerly masculine names like **Ashley**, **Taylor**, and **Schuyler** become first fashionable and then trendy, Kelsey seems likely to follow.

Kelcey, Kelcie, Kelcy, Kellsey, Kellsie, Kelsea, Kelsee, Kelseigh, Kelsi, Kelsy

Kempley ME. "Fighter's meadow."

Kemplea, Kempleigh, Kemplie, Kemply

Kendall OE. Place name: "The valley of the Kent," a river in western England. Some sources also suggest "The bright river valley." In either case, a transferred surname used as a first name since the 19th century, and occasionally adapted for girls.

Kendal, Kendell

Kendra Origin unclear: Some sources suggest OE. "Knowing," while one proposes a modern combination of **Ken** and **Sandra**. Modern, in any case.

Kendrah, Kenna, Kindra, Kinna

Kenna Fem. **Kenneth** (Ir. Gael. "Handsome" or "Sprung from fire").

Kenina, Kennina, Kennette

Kenya Place name used as first name. Since Kenya is a country in eastern Africa this is an especially logical choice for an African American family.

Kenia, Kennya

Kerensa Cornish. "Love." Unusual name that has spread a bit from Cornwall since the 1970s, but still of limited popularity.

Karensa, Karenza, Kerenza

Kerry Ir. Place name: Kerry is a county in southwestern Ireland. Also, according to some sources, Ir. Gael. "Dark-haired." Actress Keri Russell.

Keree, Keri, Kerrey, Kerri, Kerria, Kerridana, Kerrie

Ketura Heb. "Incense." Old Testament name: Keturah was

Abraham's second wife. Revived by the Puritans and used with some steadiness through the 19th century.

Katura, Keturah

Kevyn (Fem. **Kevin**) Ir. Gael. "Handsome."

Kevina, Kevinne, Kevynn, Kevynne

Kezia Heb. "Cassia." Cassia is the generic name for a variety of trees and shrubs, one of which produces cinnamon. One of the three daughters of Job (along with Jemima; though their existance is mentioned in the Old Testament, their names are apocryphal). The name was adopted by the Puritans and brought to the U.S. in the 18th century, when it was popular. Use has declined gradually since then.

Kazia, Kessie, Kessy, Ketzia, Ketziah, Keziah, Kezzie, Kissie, Kizzie, Kizzy

Khadija Arab. "Premature baby." The name of Muhammad's first wife, the mother of his children, and the first convert to Islam. The name is understandably widely used in the Muslim world.

Kadija, Kadiya, Khadiya, Khadyja

Kiana Modern name of unclear origin; one scholarly source links it to **Anna**, but fashion mavens who lived through the 1970s will link it to the then-fashionable synthetic fiber Qiana.

Kia, Kiah, Kianna, Quiana, Quianna

Kiara Var. **Chiara** (It. "Light"). A modern-looking phonetically spelled variation on **Claire**.

Keearra, Kiarra

Kiley More traditional spelling of the popular **Kylie**.

Kyley

Kim Dim. **Kimberly**. Used as an independent name from the mid 20th century, influenced by the careers of actresses Kim Novak and Kim Basinger. Actress Kim Cattrall.

Kimana, Kimm, Kym, Kymme

Kimberly OE. Place name. The "-y" suffix indicates a meadow. *The Facts on File Dictionary of First Names* traces the masculine use of the name to the Boer War, when many English soldiers were fighting in the South African town of Kimberley. It was used for girls after

1940 and became a great favorite in the 1960s and 1970s, now declining but still plenty familiar to nursery school teachers. Judge Kimba Wood.

Kim, Kimba, Kimber, Kimberlee, Kimberleigh, Kimberley, Kimberli, Kimberlie, Kimberlyn, Kimblyn, Kimm, Kimmie, Kimmy, Kym, Kymberleigh, Kymberley, Kymmberly, Kymbra, Kymbrely

Kineta Gk. "Active one." From the same root as "kinetic."
Kinetta

Kinneret Heb. "Harp." Also a place name in Israel.

Kinsey OE. "King's victory." Last name transferred to first name. The immense popularity of **Ashley** has generated interest in a host of Old English names like **Courtney**, **Lindsay**, or **Macy**. The desirable quality these names provide seems to be an aristocratic, anglophile aura, softened by the more feminine vowel ending. Kinsey in particular gets a lot of exposure from Sue Grafton's highly successful series of murder mysteries whose heroine is named Kinsey.

Kinnsee, Kinnsey, Kinnsie, Kinsee, Kinsie, Kinzee

Kinsley OE. "King's meadow." Although parents may waver between **Kinsley** and **Kinsey** as if they were variants of the same name, the derivation is different. This is not likely to matter much in the 9th month of pregnancy.

Kingslea, Kingslee, Kingslie, Kinslea, Kinslee, Kinslie, Kinsly, Kinzlea, Kinzlee, Kinzley, Kinzly

Kira Var. **Kyra** (Gk. "Lady").

Keera, Kiera, Kierra, Kiria, Kiriah, Kirya, Kirra

Kirsten Scand. Var. **Christine** (Gk. "Christian"). Used generally from 1940, though the Scots had adopted this form long ago (possibly because of their geographical proximity to Scandinavia). **Kristen** is the most popular form of the name. Actresses Kirstie Alley, Kirsten Dunst.

Keerstin, Keirstin, Kersten, Kerstin, Kiersten, Kierstin, Kierstynn, Kirsteen, Kirsti, Kirstie, Kirstin, Kirsty, Kirstynn, Kjerstin, Kristyn, Krystin

Kismet Arab. "Fate." Often used in connection with affairs of the heart, so why not for a child?
Kismat

Kitty Dim. **Katherine** (Gk. "Pure"). Used independently before the 16th century and during the 18th and 19th. In the intervening 200 years it was a slang term for a woman of dubious morals. Author Kitty Kelley.
Kit, Kittee, Kittey

Kizzy Var. **Keziah** (Heb. "Cassia"). Adopted enthusiastically by parents after it was publicized in Alex Haley's *Roots* as a traditional African name. Spoilsport scholars, however, point out that **Keziah** and its variants were common slave names as early as the 18th century.
Kissie, Kizzie

Klara Hung. Var. **Clara** (Lat. "Bright").
Klari, Klarice, Klarika, Klarissa, Klarisza, Klaryssa

Klaudia Pol. Var. **Claudia** (Lat. "Lame").

Klementina Var. **Clementia** (Lat. "Mild, giving mercy").
Clemence, Clementine, Klementijna, Klementine, Klementyna

Klotild Hung. Var. **Clothide** (Ger. "Renowned battle").
Klothild, Klothilda, Klothilde, Klotilda, Klotilde

Konstanze Ger. Var. **Constance** (Lat. "Steadfastness").
Constancia, Constantijna, Constantina, Konstance, Konstantia, Konstantijna, Konstantina, Kosta, Kostatina, Kostya, Tina, Stanze

Kora Gk. "Maiden." Though some sources trace the name to classical myth, its modern form was probably coined by American writer James Fenimore Cooper in *The Last of the Mohicans* (1826). It grew in popularity through the 19th century, but now its variant forms are more often used. The "K-"spelling is a particularly modern twist.
Cora, Corabel, Corabella, Corabelle, Corabellita, Corella, Corena, Coretta, Corey, Cori, Corilla, Corrie, Corry, Coryna, Korabell, Koree, Koreen, Korella, Korena, Korenda, Korette, Korey, Korilla, Korina, Korinna, Korinne, Korissa, Korrina, Korrine, Korynna, Koryssa

Kornelia Var. **Cornelia** (Lat. "Like a horn").
Cornelia, Kornelija, Kornelya

Kristen Comb. form **Kirsten** and **Kristina**; Var. **Christine**

(Gk. "Anointed, Christian"). Looks Scandinavian, but isn't. Popular in the last 50 years, along with similar forms like **Kristin** and **Kristine**; this is the most often used spelling. Actresses Kristin Scott Thomas, Kristin Davis.

Khristin, Krissie, Krissy, Krista, Kristan, Kristeen, Kristel, Kristelle, Kristi, Kristijna, Kristin, Kristina, Kristine, Kristyn, Kristyna, Krisztina, Krysia, Krysta, Krystyna

Krystal Var. **Crystal** (Gk. "Ice"). Transferred use of the word, mostly modern, and increasing since the 1950s. The "K" spelling is a recent variation, perhaps prompted by the *Dynasty* character Krystle Carrington.

Cristalle, Cristel, Crysta, Khristalle, Khristel, Khrystle, Khrystalle, Kristle, Krystal, Krystaline, Krystalle, Krystalline, Krystle

Kyle Scot. Place name. "Narrow spit of land." Well-traveled parents may have crossed the Kyle of Lochalsh to reach the Isle of Skye. Traditionally used more often for boys than for girls, and quite popular as a boy's name in the 1990s. For girls, the more elaborate forms like **Kylie** or **Kyla** are more fashionable.

Kyall, Kyel

Kylie Fem. **Kyle.** Also possibly derived from an Irish Gaelic word meaning "Graceful." Well used in Australia in the 1970s and moving up the charts in the U.S. Pop singer Kylie Minogue.

Keyely, Kilea, Kiley, Kylee, Kyley

Kynthia Gk. Var. **Cynthia** (Gk. "From Mount Cynthos").

Kyra Gk. "Lady." A contraction of *Kyria*, the Greek title of respect for a woman. Ballerina Kyra Nichols; actress Kyra Sedgwick.

Kaira, Keera, Keira, Kira, Kyreena, Kyrha, Kyria, Kyrra

Lacey OF. Place name of obscure meaning, used as a boy's name in the 19th century and increasingly for girls today. The fact that the name resembles the adjective "lacy" gives it a feminine connotation missing in many old place names now adopted as first names. Substantially well used. Country singer Lacy J. Dalton.

Lace, Lacee, Laci, Lacie, Lacy, Laicee, Laicey, Laisey

Ladonna Modern elaboration of **Donna** (It. "Lady").

LeDonna

Lady OE. "Bread kneader." By extension, someone in charge of a household; by further extension, a woman of high rank.

Ladey, Laidy

Lainey Dim. **Elaine** (OF. "Bright, shining, light").

Laney

Laila Arab. "Night." See **Leila**. Usually taken to indicate dark hair or a dark complexion. Actress Laila Robbins.

Laela, Lailah, Lailie, Laily, Laleh, Layla, Laylah

Lake Geography name; inland body of water. Single-syllable names are not currently fashionable for girls, so Lake is less likely to become popular than the analogous **Sierra** or **Savannah**.

Laiken, Laken

Lakeisha Popular modern name made up of elements in vogue in the 1980s, the fashionable "La-" prefix attached to **Aisha** (Arab. "Woman"). There are numerous forms, most of them phonetic variations.

Lakeesha, Lakecia, Laketia, Lakeysha, Lakicia, Lakisha, Lakitia, Lekeesha, Lekeisha, Lekisha

Lakshmi Sanskrit. "Good sign, good omen." Lakshmi is the goddess of abundance, plenty, beauty, prosperity, etc.

Laxmi

Lala Slavic. "Tulip."

Lalage Gk. "Babbler, prattler." Extremely unusual, though it occurs in literature.

Lalia

Lalia Lat. "Speaking well."

Lallia, Lalya

Lalika Hindi. "Lovely woman."

Lalla Poetic name. In 1817 poet Thomas Moore published a series of four verse tales called *Lalla Rookh*. The heroine was the daughter of the emperor of Delhi. To a generation of readers, the name Lalla spelled Eastern glamor.

Lallie Dim. **Lalage** (Gk. "Babbler, prattler"). More common than its source, though still rare. Journalist Lally Weymouth.

Lalia, Lally

Lana Var. **Helen** (Gk. "Light") or **Alanna** (Gael. "Rock" or "Comely"). The name also resembles the romance languages' term for wool: *laine* or *lana*. Made famous by actress Lana Turner (whose real name was **Judy**), but not widely used.

Lanae, Lanette, Lanna, Lanny

Lanai Haw. "Porch." Also the name of one of the Hawaiian islands.

Lenai

Lane ME. Place name. More common for boys than for girls, though still unusual for both. This is the kind of name that is likely to be a mother's maiden name transferred to a first name, though parents are increasingly using last names for first names regardless of family precedent.

Laine, Lainey, Laney, Lanie, Layne

Langley OE. Place name: "Long meadow."

Langlea, Langlee, Langleigh

Lani Haw. "Sky."

Lantana Place name: county in Florida. Also the name of a pungent-smelling flower with tiny clusters of orange or purple blossoms.

Lantanna

Lara Unclear origin. Some sources suggest Lat. "Famous"; others trace the name to the Greek **Larissa**. Parents may be reminded of the famous "Lara's Theme" from the 1965 film *Dr. Zhivago*. Actress Lara Flynn Boyle.

Larina, Larra

Laraine Var. **Lorraine** (Fr. "From Lorraine"). Actress Laraine Newman.

Laraene, Larayne, Lareine, Larina, Larine

Lareina Sp. "The queen." Compares to **Leroy** (Fr. "The king"). Uncommon.

Larayna, Larayne, Lareine, Larena, Larrayna, Larreina

Larissa Gk. "Lighthearted." From the same root as **Hilary**. Unusual, even in times like the 18th century, when more elaborate names were the norm. Currently popular in Russia.

Larisa, Laryssa, Lerissa, Lissa, Lorissa, Lyssa

Lark ME. Nature name, used since the 1950s mostly in the U.S. Larks are usually thought of as playful, lighthearted songbirds.

Larkspur Flower name: a kind of delphinium with spur-shaped blue blossoms.

Larsen Scand. "Son of Lars." **Lars** is in turn the Scandinavian version of **Lawrence** (Lat. "From Laurentium"). Even though this is explicitly a boy's name, it has been used for baby girls as part of the fashion for unisex names.

Larson, Larssen, Larsson

Lassie ME. "Little girl." "Lass" is a Scottish and Northern English term for a girl, but the association for most parents is more likely to be a highly intelligent collie as seen on a popular TV series in the 1960s and again in the 1990s.

Lassey

Lata Hindi. "Beautiful vine."

Latanya Modern combined form: the "La-" prefix added to **Tanya**.

Latania, Latanja, Latonia, Latonya

Latifah Arab. "Gentle, pleasant." Singer/actress Queen Latifah.

Lateefa, Lateefah, Lateifa, Lateiffa, Latifa, Latiffa

Latisha Var. **Letitia** (Lat. "Happiness").

Laticia, Latitia, Letisha, Letticia, Lettisha

Latona Myth name: in the Roman pantheon, mother of Apollo and Diana. Closely resembles some of the modern names like **Latoya** and **Latonya**, but predates them by some two thousand years.

Latoya One of the most famous of the modern "La-" names, probably because of Latoya Jackson's renown. Derivation and meaning are mysterious.
Latoyah, Latoia, Latoyla, Letoya

Latrice Modern combined form: **Patricia** (Lat. "Noble") with the "La-" prefix.
Latrecia, Latreece, Latreese, Latreshia, Latricia, Leatrice, Letreece, Letrice

Lauda Lat. "Praise." Also a medieval Italian form of dramatic song.

Laudomia It. "Praise to the house."

Laufeia Norse. "Wooded or leafy island." In Norse myth Laufeia is the mother of Loki, the Norse god of destruction and evil.

Laura Lat. "Laurel." In classical times, a crown made from the leaves of the bay laurel was given to heroes or victors. Two famous Lauras are the unknown woman to whom the poet Petrarch addressed his sonnets, and the heroine of the 1940s film *Laura*. The greatest popularity of the name came at the mid- to late 19th century, and it has remained quite a steady favorite ever since. A series of children's books were written by and about Laura Ingalls Wilder of *Little House on the Prairie* fame. Actresses Laura Dern, Laura Linney; singer Laura Branigan; First Lady Laura Bush.
Laranca, Larea, Lari, Lauralee, Laure, Laureen, Laurel, Laurella, Lauren, Laurena, Laurence, Laurene, Laurentia, Laurentine, Laurestine, Lauretha, Lauretta, Laurette, Lauri, Lauriane, Laurianne, Laurice, Lauricia, Laurie, Laurina, Laurinda, Laurine, Laurnea, Lavra, Lawra, Lollie, Lolly, Lora, Loree, Loreen, Loren, Lorena, Lorene, Lorenza, Loretta, Lorette, Lorey, Lori, Lorie, Lorinda, Lorine, Lorita, Lorna, Lorretta, Lorrette, Lorri, Lorrie, Lorry, Lory

Laurel Lat. "Laurel tree." Nature name whose popularity

has coasted on the coattails of **Laura**, especially in the 20th century.

Laural, Lauralle, Laurell, Loralle, Lorel, Lorelle

Lauren Var. **Laura** or feminization of **Lawrence**. Introduced to the public by Lauren Bacall, and immediately popular probably because the streamlined "modern" character of the name struck a chord in the 1940s. It might be fading from sight by now, but has been given extended popularity by the influential designer Ralph Lauren (né Ralph Lifshitz), who has endowed it with fashionable associations and can probably be credited with keeping the name in the top 20 U.S. girls' names for the last dozen years. It is also extremely fashionable throughout Great Britain. Model Lauren Hutton; First Daughter Lauren Bush; basketball player Lauren Jackson.

Laren, Larentia, Larentina, Larenzina, Larren, Laryn, Larryn, Larrynn, Larsina, Larsine, Laurence, Laurin, Lauryn, Laurynn, Loren, Lorena, Lorene, Lorenn, Lorenza, Lorin, Loryn, Lorne, Lorren, Lorrin, Lorrynn, Lourenca, Lourence, Lowran, Lowrenn, Lowrynn, L'Wren

Laurence Fr. Fem. **Lawrence** (Lat. "From Laurentium"). **Lauren** is the most common feminization in English, but some of the European variants are quite commonly used in their own countries.

Larenzina, Larsina, Larsine, Laurentia, Laurentina, Laurentine, Laurentyna, Laurentyne, Lorenza, Lourenca, Lourence

Laveda Lat. "Cleansed."

Lavella, Lavelle, Laveta, Lavetta, Lavette

Laverne Lat. Classical goddess of minor criminals, though the parents who made this name mildly popular in the 20th century probably didn't know that. It sounds enough like the romance languages' word for "green" (*vert, verde*) to have acquired misplaced connotations of green trees or springtime.

Laverine, Lavern, Laverna, Laverrne, Leverne, Loverna, Verne

Lavinia Lat. "Women of Rome." Classical name. Revived in the Renaissance, again used in the 18th century, rather neglected for the last 200 years but a pretty option for parents seeking a rather feminine name.

Lavena, Lavenia, Lavina, Lavinie, Levenia, Levinia, Livinia, Louvenia, Louvinia, Lovina, Lovinia, Luvena, Luvenia, Luvinia, Vinnie

Lavonne Modern combined form, probably "La-" attached to **Yvonne** (OF. "Yew wood"). Popular somewhat earlier (1950s-1980s) than most of the other "La-" names.

Lavonda, Lavonna, Lahvonne, Levonne, Levonda

Leah Heb. "Weary." Old Testament name: Leah was the wife of Jacob, married to him by a ruse in the place of her sister Rachel. Follows the typical usage pattern of the Old Testament names: revived by the Puritans, and still used with considerable steadiness. The form **Léa** is currently popular in France. Actress Lea Thompson.

Lea, Lee, Leia, Leigh

Leala OF. "Loyal."

Lealia, Lealie

Leandra (Fem. **Leander**) Gk. "Lion man." A spurt of use in the 1960s and 1970s has faded.

Leanda, Leiandra, Leodora, Leoine, Leoline, Leonelle

Leanne Comb. form **Lee** and **Ann**. Singer LeAnn Rimes.

Leana, Leeann, Leanna, Lee-Ann, Leianne, Leyanne, Leigh-Anne, Leighanna, Lianne

Leatrice Comb. form **Lee** and **Beatrice**.

Leda Gk., possibly Dim. **Letitia** (Lat. "Joy, gladness"). In classical mythology, Leda was visited by Jupiter in the form of a swan, and produced four children, among them the beautiful Helen of Troy.

Leida, Leta, Lida

Lee OE. Place name: "Pasture or meadow." One of the few truly unisex names. Usually a name becomes exclusively feminine once it is used for girls, like **Ashley** or **Leslie**. The tenacious masculine hold on Lee may have been helped by tough-guy actor Lee Marvin. U.S. use seems to have been sparked by admiration for Confederate General Robert E. Lee. Peaked in the 1950s. Actress Lee Remick; Princess Lee Radziwill.

Lea, Leigh

Lehava Heb. "Flame."

Lehavit

Leila Arab. "Night." Used by authors in the early 19th century for exotic female characters, and more widely by U.S. parents later in the century. It is in wide use in the Middle East. American pronunciation of the first syllable varies, as the different spellings make clear.

Layla, Leela, Leelah, Leilah, Leilia, Lela, Lelah, Lelia, Leyla, Lila, Lilah

Leilani Haw. "Flower from heaven."

Leith Scot. Gael. "Broad river." An alternative spelling, **Lethe**, is the river of forgetfulness in Greek mythology.

Leithe, Lethe

Leland OE Place name: "Meadow land."

Lelia Lat. Clan name of unknown meaning, used in Britain and the U.S. in the late 19th century.

Leelia, Lilia

Lemuela (Fem. **Lemuel**) Heb. "Devoted to God." Feminization of a name that was mildly popular in the 19th century.

Lemuelah, Lemuella, Lemuellah

Lena Lat. Diminutive of names like **Helena**, **Caroline**, **Marlene**. Independent use dates from the mid-19th century. Actress Lena Olin; singer Lena Horne; director Lina Wertmuller.

Leena, Leina, Lina

Lenis Lat. "Mild, soft, silky." Very rare.

Lene, Leneta, Lenice, Lenita, Lennice, Lenos

Lenna (Fem. **Leonard**) OG. "Lion's strength."

Lenda, Leonarda

Lenore Gk. "Light." Var. **Eleanor**.

Lenor, Lenora, Lenorah, Lenorr, Lenorra, Lenorre, Leonora, Leonore

Leoda OG. "Of the people."

Leota

Leona (Fem. **Leon**) Lat. "Lion." American version; **Léonie** is more popular in Europe. Use since the 1940s has grown, but the notorious Leona Helmsley has probably put a stop to its popularity. Singer Leontyne Price.

Leeona, Leeowna, Leoine, Leola, Leone, Leonelle, Leonia, Leonie, Leontine, Leontyne, Leowna

Leonarda (Fem. **Leonard**) OG. "Lion's strength."

Lenarda, Lenda, Lennarda, Leonarde

Léonie (Fem. **Leon**) Lat. "Lion." The French form of the name, more common in Britain than Leona.

Leoline, Leone, Leoni, Leonine, Leontine

Leonora Gk. "Light." Var. **Eleanor**. Name used for the heroine of three major operas (*Fidelio, Il Trovatore,* and *La Favorita*), but like many literary names, uncommon in real life.

Leanor, Leanora, Leanore, Lenora, Lenore, Leonore, Ora, Norah

Leopoldine (Fem. **Leopold**) OG. "Bold people."

Leopolda, Leopoldina

Leora Gk. "Light." Dim. **Eleanor**.

Leeora, Liora

Leslie Scot. Gael. Place name. Some sources suggest, "The gray castle." Became a last name, then (in the 18th century) a first name used for boys and girls. Boys' use has been tied to admiration for actor Leslie Howard, and is more common in Britain. Not much used now despite the rage for comparable names like **Ashley** or **Kelsey**. Actresses Leslie-Ann Down, Lesley Ann Warren.

Leslea, Leslee, Lesleigh, Lesley, Lesli, Lesly, Lezlee, Lezley, Lezlie

Leta Lat. "Glad, joyful." Classical name mildly revived at the turn of the 20th century.

Leeta, Lita

Letha Gk. "Forgetfulness." In Greek mythology, a river in Hades that causes the dead to forget their lives on earth.

Leitha, Leithia, Lethe, Lethia

Letitia Lat. "Joy, gladness." In medieval England, the form was **Lettice**, which survived into the 20th century. (The name's resemblance to the principal ingredient of salad cannot have promoted its use.) Current use, which is rare, is usually of the Latinized form, Letitia. Etiquette expert Letitia Baldrige.

Laetitia, Laetizia, Latashia, Latia, Latisha, Leda, Leta, Letha, Letice, Leticia, Leticja, Letisha, Letizia, Letta, Lettice, Lettie, Lettitia, Letty, Letycja, Tish, Tisha

Levana Lat. "To rise." In Roman mythology, the goddess of newborn babies, whose fathers accepted them as legitimate in a ceremony involving lifting the infant from the ground.

Levania, Levanna, Levona, Livana, Livanna

Levina Lat. "Lightning bolt."

Levona Heb. "Frankincense."

Lewana Heb. "Shining white one: the moon."

Levana, Levanna, Lewanna, Livana

Lexia Dim. **Alexandra** (Gk. "Defender of mankind").

Lexa, Lexie, Lexina, Lexine, Lexya

Leya Sp. "The law."

Lia It. Dim. **Evangelia** ("Bringer of the gospel"). Used independently in Italy. Writer Lia Matera.

Leeya, Liya

Liana Fr. "To twine around." Liana is the name of a vine common to tropical rain forests. Can also be a diminutive of Italianate names like **Ceciliana** or **Silviana**.

Leana, Leiana, Liahna, Liane, Lianna, Lianne

Liane Diminutive of French variants like **Juliane, Lilliane**. Also a spelling variant of **Lee-Ann**.

Leeanne, Leeahnne, Liahne, Lianne

Libby Dim. **Elizabeth** (Heb. "Pledged to God"). Even if they intend to use a nickname, parents are more likely to put the full name down on a birth certificate, so officially the numbers of names like Libby are very small.

Lib, Libbee, Libbey, Libbie, Libet, Liby, Lilibet, Lilibeth

Liberty ME. "Freedom." Unusual, but occurs in "revolutionary" times like the 1970s.

Licia Dim. **Alicia, Felicia**, etc., used as an independent name.

Leecea, Leecia, Lesia, Lisia

Lida Slavic. "Loved by the people."

Leida, Lidah, Lyda

Lidwina Scand. "Friend of the people."
   Lidweena, Lidweina

Liese Dim. **Elizabeth** (Heb. "Pledged to God"). Mostly
   found in Germany.
   Liesa, Liesel, Liesl

Lieselotte Comb. form **Liese** (Heb. "Pledged to God") and
   Charlotte (Fr. "Little womanly one").

Ligia Gk. "Musical."
   Lygia

Lila Arab. "Night." Can be a diminutive of **Delilah** (Heb.
   "Lovelorn, seductive"). Inching toward trendiness. Phil-
   anthropist Lila Acheson Wallace.
   Layla, Leila, Lilah, Lyla, Lylah

Lilac Flower name. Not very common.
   Lilach

Lilias Scot. Var. **Lillian** (Lat. "Lily").
   Lilas, Lillas, Lillias

Lilibet Dim. **Elizabeth** (Heb. "Pledged to God"). The un-
   likely pet name of Her Majesty Queen Elizabeth II of
   England.
   Lilibeth, Lillibet, Lilybet

Lilith Arab. "Ghost, night demon." One Old Testament
   translation refers to her as "the night hag." She was supposed to descend on sleepers and suck their blood. Connotations of the name are so fearsome that it is rarely
   used.
   Lillis

Lillian Lat. "Lily." Very common variation of the flower
   name, flourishing at the turn of the 20th century. Actress
   Lillian Gish and First Mother Lillian Carter were born
   during the name's peak of fashion, which faded after the
   1930s. Pretty as it is, it carries a rather dated aura. Writer
   Lillian Hellman.
   **Lila, Lili, Lilia, Lilian, Liliana, Liliane, Lilias, Lilli, Lillia,
   Lillianne, Lillie, Lilly, Lillyan, Lillyanne, Lily, Lilyan,
   Lilyann**

Lily Lat. Flower name. Possibly because the lily plays such
   a large part in Christian iconography, this has been one of
   the most popular of the flower names and has produced

DATE THAT NAME

Donald Trump and Marla Maples named their daughter Tiffany because it seemed like the classiest possible name to them: Never mind that its vogue was well past and that young women named Tyffani (or Tiffenie, or Typhanny) are now having their own babies all over the country. There are some names that will always carry with them a whiff of their era. Unfortunately, it's not usually clear what they are until your child reports to nursery school and discovers that he is one of four boys named Josh. The following celebrities may have fallen into the fashionable name trap; in any event, these are names that may very well appear dated in years to come:

- Michael J. Fox & Tracy Pollan: Schuyler (a girl)
- Sheena Easton: Jake, Skylar
- Pam Dawber & Mark Harmon: Ty Christian
  (two trendy names for one child)
- Lee Majors: Dane Luke, Trey Kulley
  (four trendy names for two children)
- Sean Penn & Robin Wright: Dylan (a girl)
- Cheryl Tiegs: Zachary
- Robin Williams: Cody
- Kelly Lynch: Shane
- David Bowie & Iman: Alexandria
- Kate Winslet & Jim Threapleton: Mia
- Téa Leoni & David Duchovny: Madelaine
- Al Roker & Deborah Roberts: Leila
- Kate Moss & Jefferson Hack: Lila
- Elizabeth Hurley: Damian
- Calista Flockhart: Liam
- Pierce Brosnan & Keeley Shaye Smith: Paris
- Johnny Depp & Vanessa Paradis: Lily-Rose
- Angelina Jolie & Billy Bob Thornton: Maddox
- But for real trend overload, check this: David Boreanaz & Jaime Bergman, Will Smith & Jada Pinkett, and Andre Agassi & Steffi Graff all have children named Jaden.

many variants. The "-y" ending, usually thought of as feminine, has probably also boosted its use, though it has not been popular since 1900. Ripe for a revival among parents with a taste for nostalgia, and its use has increased considerably in the last dozen years. **Lilia** is currently well used in Russia. Actresses Lillie Langtry, Lily Taylor, Lily Tomlin, LeeLee Sobieski.

Leelee, Lil, Lila, Lilas, Lili, Lilia, Lilian, Liliana, Liliane, Lilias, Lilie, Lilla, Lilley, Lilli, Lillia, Lillianne, Lillie, Lillika, Lillita, Lilly, Liliosa, Lily, Lilyan, Lilyanne

Limor Heb. "Myrrh."

Leemor

Lina Diminutive of names ending with "-line," like **Caroline**, **Helena**, **Marlene**. Var. **Lena**. Given as an independent name from the 1850s.

Leena, Leina

Linda Sp. "Pretty." Though the name existed as a particle of other English names (**Belinda**, **Melinda**) by the time of its great vogue in the 20th century (late 1930s to 1960s), it was probably interpreted as "pretty." Rather neglected now, since it belongs to the mothers of today's parents. President's daughter Lynda Bird Johnson; actresses Linda Evans, Linda Hunt; singer Linda Ronstadt; journalist Linda Ellerbee; fashion designer Lindka Cierach.

Lin, Lindee, Lindey, Lindi, Lindie, Lindira, Lindka, Lindy, Linn, Lynda, Lynde, Lyndy, Lyn, Lynn, Lynne, Lynnda, Lynndie

Linden Tree name: a tall graceful tree with heart-shaped leaves that grows in temperate climates. Also known in Europe as a lime tree, though unrelated to the tree that produces sour green citrus fruit.

Lindenn, Lindon, Lindynn

Lindsay OE. Place name: "Island of linden trees." Originally a surname, used for boys until the middle of this century, but quite popular as a girl's name in the '80s and '90s. Use has tapered off. Phonetic variants occur frequently. Actress Lindsay Wagner.

Lind, Lindsea, Lindsee, Lindseigh, Lindsey, Lindsy, Lin-

say, Linsey, Linsie, Linzi, Linzy, Linzee, Linzy, Lyndsay, Lyndsey, Lyndsie, Lynnsey, Lynndsie, Lynnzey, Lynsey, Lynzey, Lynzi, Lynzy

Linette Welsh. "Idol" or OF. "Linnet" (a small bird). In historical terms, probably a variant of **Lynette**, which is not, surprisingly enough, a form of **Lynn**. These names and their variations were most popular from the 1940s into the 1960s.

Lenette, Lanette, Linet, Linnet, Linnetta, Lonette, Lynette, Lynnet, Lynnette

Linnea Scand. "Lime or linden tree" is the meaning given by most sources, but an informal network of people named Linnea trace the name to a mountain flower growing in northern climates that botanist Carl Linnaeus named for himself. A popular series of children's books by Christian Bjork featuring a character named Linnea has given the name greater exposure.

Linea, Linnaea, Lynea, Lynnea

Liora Heb. "I have a light."

Leeor, Leeora, Lior, Liorit

Lirit Heb. "Musical."

Leerit, Liri

Lisa Dim. **Elizabeth** (Heb. "Pledged to God"). Used in numbers only since the 1950s, and reached the U.S. top ten in the 1970s. The name is now undergoing that period of disuse that usually follows serious popularity. Actresses Lisa Bonet, Lisa Kudrow; talk show host Leeza Gibbons; basketball player Lisa Leslie.

Leesa, Leeza, Liesa, Liesebet, Lise, Liseta, Lisetta, Lisette, Liszka

Lissa Dim. **Melissa** (Gk. "Bee"). May also be considered a variation of **Lisa**. Unusual.

Lissette, Lyssa

Lissandra Var. **Alexandra** (Gk. "Man's defender").

Liv ONorse. "Defense." Also short for **Olivia**, or even **Lavinia**. Use in this country probably derives from the fame of actress Liv Ullman. Actress Liv Tyler.

Livia Dim. **Olivia** (Lat. "Olive"). Though the historical connotations of Olivia should concern peace and harmony, in the modern era it is hard not to think of the little green morsel at the bottom of a martini glass. Joyce fans, on a higher plane, may use the name to pay homage to the character Anna Livia Plurabelle from *Finnegan's Wake*.

Livija, Livvy, Livy, Livya, Lyvia

Liya Heb. "I am the Lord's."

Leeya

Liz Dim. **Elizabeth** (Heb. "Pledged to God"). Too humdrum for today's parents unless used in one of the elaborated forms. Clothing designer Liz Lange.

Lizanne, Lizette, Lizz, Lyz, Lyzz

Liza Diminutive of **Elizabeth** and more particularly of **Eliza**. The vogue for **Lisa** gave Liza some reflected popularity, but the immense fame of entertainer Liza Minnelli must account for a great deal of its use.

Litsea, Litzea, Liz, Lizette, Lizzie, Lyza

Logan Ir. Gael. Place name: "Small hollow." As Logan is more widely used as a boy's name, parents of girls may cast a favorable eye on it.

Logann

Loelia Var. **Leila** (Arab. "Night"). Unusual form used occasionally at the turn of the 20th century.

Loire Place name: river in France. Travelers know this area as being full of beautiful chateaux and producing pleasant white wine.

Loir, Loirane

Lois Var. **Louise** (OG. "Renowned in battle" though some sources suggest Gk. "Better"). Also, surprisingly enough, a biblical name. Use peaked early in the 20th century. Superman's consort Lois Lane.

Lola Dim. **Dolores** (Sp. "Sorrows"). The most famous Lola has been the 19th-century courtesan Lola Montez, which has given the name a slightly racy aura. It is fairly well used regardless.

Loela, Lolla

Lolita Dim. **Lola** (Sp. "Sorrows"). Made famous by Vladimir Nabokov's 1958 novel about a 12-year-old nymphet and her much older admirer, Humbert Humbert. So famous were the book and the movies adapted from it that the name has become a generic term for a sexually precocious young girl.

Lona Var. **Leona** (Lat. "Lion"). Uncommon. Actress Loni Anderson.

Lonee, Lonie, Lonna, Lonnie

Lora Var. **Laura** (Lat. "Laurel"). Not, as it might seem, a modern phonetic variant, but a throwback to the 14th century, when this was the usual spelling of the name.

Lorabelle, Loree, Lorenna, Lorey, Lori, Loribelle, Lorra, Lorree, Lorrie, Lory, Lowra

Lorelei Ger. Place name. Derives from the name of a dangerous rock jutting into the Rhine. Though popularly supposed to be an old myth, the tale of a siren perched on the rock to lure ships to destruction actually dates from a novel of 1801. The name, however, carries connotations of risky allure. Writer Anita Loos capitalized on this when she created blonde bombshell Lorelei Lee in her novel *Gentlemen Prefer Blondes*. Marilyn Monroe immortalized Lorelei in the 1953 film, virtually sealing the name with her image.

Laurelei, Laurelie, Loralee, Loralie, Loralyn, Lorilee, Lorilyn, Lura, Lurette, Lurleen, Lurlene, Lurline

Lorelle Dim. **Laura** or **Laurel** (Lat. "Laurel tree").

Laurelle, Lorrella, Lowrelle

Lorenza (Fem. **Lorenzo**) Lat. "From Laurentium." Very unusual in English-speaking countries, being primarily an Italian name.

Laurenca, Laurenza

Loretta Dim. **Laura** (Lat. "Laurel"). A name that cropped up with the 19th-century taste for elaboration, and became famous with actress Loretta Young. Country singer Loretta Lynn; actress Loretta Swit.

Laretta, Larretta, Lauretta, Laurette, Leretta, Lorretta, Lowretta

Lori Dim. **Laura** (Lat. "Laurel"). Unlike Lora, this is a modern spelling and was very popular in the 1960s. The rage for the "-i" ending on names has diminished considerably since then, replaced by a fondness for "-ey."

Loree, Lorri

Lorna Scot. Place name converted into a female name for the 19th-century romantic novel *Lorna Doone*. Used occasionally, but to most North Americans, it is probably the name of a cookie. Entertainer Lorna Luft.

Lorrna

Lorraine Fr. "From Lorraine." Lorraine is an area in eastern France, but this is not just your average place name: It was often used for Joan of Arc (who was from Lorraine), and for the style of quiche with bacon and Gruyère cheese. It can also be considered an elaboration of **Lora**. Was well used from the 1930s, and in the U.S. its vogue peaked in the 1940s. Rare now. Actress Laraine Newman.

Laraine, Larayne, Laurraine, Leraine, Lerayne, Lorain, Loraine, Lori, Lorine, Lorrayne

Lottie Dim. **Charlotte** (Fr. "Little, womanly"). Mostly 19th-century use. Singer Lotte Lenya.

Lotta, Lotte, Lotie, Lotti, Lotty

Lotus Gk. "Lotus flower." The name signifies different plants in several different cultures: The Egyptians consider it a kind of water lily, while to the Greeks it is a shrub. It also has great significance in the Indian religions and in Homeric legend, where eating the lotus causes people to forget their homes and families and long for a life of idleness.

Lou Dim. **Louise**. Used mostly in America, and in combined forms such as **Louann, Mary Lou, Louella**, etc.

Louanna, Louanne, Louella, Lu, Loulou

Lourdes French place name: the town where, in 1858, a young girl named Bernadette had visions of the Virgin Mary. Lourdes has since become a major pilgrimage site and a fairly common name among Catholics. Since Madonna named her daughter Lourdes, the name will have an entirely different level of exposure. Ballerina Lourdes Lopez.

Lourdecita, Lourdetta, Lourdette, Lurdes

Louise (Fem. **Louis**) OG. "Renowned in battle." Actually a French (and more euphonious) version of **Ludwig**. **Louisa** was the preferred form in the 18th and 19th centuries, eclipsed by Louise at the turn of the century. Currently very unusual in the U.S. Author Louisa May Alcott; actresses Louise Brooks, Louise Lasser.

Aloisa, Aloise, Aloysia, Eloisa, Eloise, Heloisa, Heloise, Lois, Loise, Lola, Lolita, Lou, Louisa, Louisetta, Louisette, Louisina, Louisiana, Louisiane, Louisine, Louiza, Lovisa, Lowise, Loyise, Lu, Ludovica, Ludovika, Ludwiga, Luisa, Luise, Lujza, Lujzika, Lula, Lulita, Lulu

Love OE. "Love." Unromantically enough, probably not the name of the emotion but a transferred surname. Singer Courtney Love.

Loveday, Lovey

Luana OG. Comb. form **Louise** and **Anne**. One of many possible phonetic versions of the name. Also used in Italy, inspired by a film of the 1930s.

Lewanna, Lou-Ann, Louanna, Louanne, Luane, Luann, Luannah, Luannie, Luwana

Luba Yiddish. "Dear."

Liba, Lubah, Lyuba, Lyubah

Lucerne Lat. "Lamp." Also the name of a city in Switzerland; parents have occasionally named children for the cities where they were born—or, in the modern era of frankness, conceived.

Lucerna

Lucetta Dim. **Lucy** (Lat. "Light"). Mostly 19th century, now very unusual.

Loucetta, Loucette, Lucette

Lucia It. Var. **Lucy** (Lat. "Light"). Uncommon form in English-speaking countries. Ballet patron Lucia Chase.

Lucille Fr. Var. **Lucy** (Lat. "Light"). As **Lucilla**, used by the Romans and revived in the 19th century. Lucille came into use at the turn of the 20th century, and its considerable popularity (roughly 1940-1960) seems to have been inspired by comedienne Lucille Ball. For now, the name has a rather dated air if not a positively ironic one.

Loucille, Luseele, Lusile, Lucila, Lucile, Lucilla, Lucyle

Lucinda Var. **Lucy** (Lat. "Light"). Popular along with the other "-inda" names of the 18th century (**Clarinda, Belinda**), and boosted by the fondness for **Lucille**. In spite of the current craze for longer girls' names (**Amanda**, **Stephanie**, **Jessica**), late 20th century parents have not yet turned to the "-inda" names in significant numbers.

Cindy, Loucinda, Lusinda

Lucita Sp. Dim. **Lucy** (Lat. "Light"). Also an allusion to the Virgin Mary as Santa Maria de Luz.

Lusita, Luzita

Lucretia Lat. Clan name of uncertain meaning, though some sources suggest "wealth." The famous story of the rape of Lucretia concerns a Roman matron who, having been raped, stabbed herself rather than live with her shame.

Loucrecia, Loucresha, Loucretia, Loucrezia, Lucrece, Lucrecia, Lucreecia, Lucreisha, Lucreesha, Lucresha, Lucrezia

Lucy Lat. "Light." The vernacular form of **Lucia**, and more widely used in modern times, peaking in the U.S. at the turn of the century. The 4th-century martyr Saint Lucy, patroness of sight, is often depicted with a pair of eyes in a dish, though her martyrdom did not involve being blinded. The Lucy in Charles Schulz's much-loved "Peanuts" comic strip is the prototypical bossy little girl. For a pretty name with few negative connotations, it is surprisingly little-used in the U.S., though very popular in England. Actress Lucy Liu.

Lou, Loulou, Lu, Luce, Lucetta, Lucette, Luci, Lucia, Luciana, Lucida, Lucie, Lucienne, Lucile, Lucilia, Lucilla, Lucille, Lucina, Lucinda, Lucine, Lucita, Lucyna, Lucyja, Lucza, Lusita, Luz, Luzija

Ludmilla Slavic. "Beloved of the people."

Ludmila, Lyuba, Lyudmila

Luella OE. Comb. form **Louise** (OG. "Renowned in battle") and **Ella** (OG. "All"). Can also be said to come from **Lucy**; it's often not possible to trace a name's roots accurately. Columnist Louella Parsons.

Loella, Lou, Louella, Lu, Luelle, Lula, Lulu

Lulu Dim. **Louise** (OG. "Renowned in battle"). Fashion designer Lulu Guinness.

Luminosa Sp. from Lat. "Brilliant, giving off light."
  Lumina
Luna Lat. "Moon."
  Luneth, Lunetta, Lunette, Lunneta
Lupe Sp. Allusion to the Virgin Mary as she miraculously appeared to a peasant boy in Guadalupe, Mexico.
  Lupelina
Lurleen Modern variant of **Lorelei** (Ger. place name).
  Lura, Lurette, Lurlene, Lurline
Luz Sp. "Light." Another name for the Virgin Mary: Santa Maria de Luz.
Lycia Gk. "From Lycia." A New Testament place name, in southwest Asia Minor.
Lydia Gk. "From Lydia." Lydia was an area of Asia famous for its two rich kings, Midas and Croesus. The name (biblical in origin) was used heavily in the 18th and 19th centuries, less so in the 20th. Cookbook author Lydie Marshall.
  Lidia, Lidie, Lidija, Lyda, Lydie
Lynette Welsh. "Idol." Though it looks like a modern elaboration of **Lynn**, this is actually a French version of the Welsh **Eiluned**, and was popularized by the English poet Tennyson. However, its use (middling, since the 1940s) has certainly depended on the appeal of Lynn.
  Lanette, Linett, Linette, Lynett, Lynetta
Lynn Dim. **Linda** (Sp. "Pretty"). This is one of those names that, along with its variations, is so popular as to virtually swamp its source. Most used in the 20th century. Actress Lynn Redgrave.
  Lin, Linell, Linn, Linnell, Lyn, Lynae, Lyndel, Lyndell, Lynelle, Lynette, Lynna, Lynne, Lynell, Lynnelle, Lynnett, Lynette
Lyris Gk. "Lyre." The lyre is a small stringed intrument that is played by plucking: it is a predecessor of the harp.
  Lyra, Lyria
Lysandra Var. **Alexandra** (Gk. "Man's defender").
  Lisandra, Lisandrina, Lisandrine, Lissandra, Lissandrina, Lissandrine, Lyssandra

Mab Ir. Gael. "Joy, hilarity." Welsh. "Baby." In old English, Welsh, and Irish stories, Queen Mab is monarch of the fairies.

Mave, Mavis, Meave

Mabel Dim. **Amabel** (Lat. "Lovable"). Very popular at the turn of the 20th century, but uncommon now, perhaps because it has the air of being a period artifact. Singer Mabel Mercer.

Amabel, Amable, Amaybel, Amaybelle, Amayble, Mab, Mabelle, Mable, Maible, Maybel, Maybelle, Mayble

Macaria Sp. from Gk. "Blessed."

Macarisa, Macarria, Maccaria, Makaria, Makarria

MacKenna Ir. Gael. "Son of the handsome one." Influenced by the popularity of **Mackenzie**.

Mackendra, McKenna

Mackenzie Ir. Gael. "Son of the wise ruler." A testament to the power of television. This was a last name and occasional male first name but actress Mackenzie Phillips has brought it to prominence at a time when masculine names for girls have been very much in vogue. Now, despite the turn to ultra-feminine names like **Jessica** and **Stephanie**, Mackenzie is still more fashionable every year.

Mackenzey, Makensie, Makenzie, McKenzie, M'Kenzie

Macon Place name: a town in France, and later a town in Georgia.

Macy OF. Place name: "Matthew's estate." Obscure as a name for either sex, but a character on the soap opera *The Bold and the Beautiful* introduced its use for girls. Its similarity to **Lacy**, currently slightly fashionable, will probably help promote it. Pop singer Macy Gray.

Macey, Macie, Maicey, Maicy

Madeline Gk. Place name: Magdala was a town on the Sea of Galilee, the home of Saint Mary Magdalen, whom Jesus healed and who was present at his crucifixion. **Magdalen** was the common form in the Middle Ages, but the "g" was dropped, leaving Madeline as the standard form. The French version, **Madeleine**, became more popular in the 1930s, but the name, pretty as it is, has never been a standard. Many people may be familiar with this name from Ludwig Bemelmans' French schoolgirl Madeline in her wide-brimmed hat, from the children's books. Actresses Madeline Kahn, Madeleine Stowe.

Dalanna, Dalenna, Lena, Lina, Lynn, Mada, Madalaina, Madaleine, Madalena, Madalyn, Maddalena, Maddie, Maddy, Madel, Madelaine, Madelayne, Madeleine, Madelena, Madelene, Madelina, Madella, Madelle, Madelon, Madge, Madlen, Madlin, Madlyn, Mady, Madzia, Magda, Magdala, Magdalen, Magdalena, Magdalene, Magdalina, Magdaline, Magdalini, Magdeleine, Magdelina, Magdolna, Maidel, Maighdlin, Mala, Malena, Malina, Marleah, Marleen, Marlen, Marlena, Marlene, Marline, Marlyne, Maud, Maude

Madeira Place name: a group of volcanic islands in the North Atlantic off Morocco. The principal island, also called Madeira, is famous for the fortified wine made there.

Madera, Madira

Madge Dim. **Madeline, Margaret** (Gk. "Pearl").

Madison OE. "Son of the mighty warrior." Another obscure masculine name that has crossed over into fashionable use for girls, prompted by media exposure. In this case the transfer may have been prompted by the mermaid called "Madison" in Ron Howard's movie *Splash*. But Madison has rocketed up popularity charts lately in a way that only happens when a name somehow matches the mood of the times—it has been in the top ten names for American girls since 1997, but in 1993 was ranked no higher than 78th. Madison may provide the link between the previous naming vogue (WASPy masculine-sounding names) and the current one (multisyllabic feminine names), especially since the nickname, "Maddie," sounds plesantly old-fashioned. The drawback is that names with this kind of rapid ascent to fashion may feel dated in years to come.

Maddison, Madisen, Madisson

Madonna Lat. "My lady." Used mostly by devout Catholic families, like the parents of rock star Madonna Louise Ciccone. Her global fame coupled with some of her more racy public personas make her an unlikely role model for parents.
Madona

Madra Sp. "Mother."

Maeve Ir. Gael. Possibly "Delicate, fragile." Name of a 1st-century queen of Ireland, and used mostly in that country.

Mafalda Sp. Var. **Matilda** (OG. "Battle-mighty"). Also a royal name in Italy.
Maffalda

Magali Var. **Margaret** (Gk. "Pearl").
Magaley, Magalie, Maggali

Magda Ger. Var. **Madeline** (Gk. "From Magdala") or **Maida** (OE. "Maiden").

Maggie Dim. **Margaret** (Gk. "Pearl"). Used as an independent name in the late 19th century. Although babies are more likely to be given the full name these days, Maggie is precisely the kind of nostalgic-sounding nickname that appeals to today's parents. While Margaret is dropping in the charts, Maggie is rising. Dance impresario Maguy Marin; actresses Maggie Smith, Maggie Gyllenhaal.
Magali, Maggey, Maggi, Maggy, Magli, Maguy

Magnilda OG. "Strong in warfare."
Magnhilde

Magnolia Lat. Flower name. The tree was named after 17th-century French botanist Pierre Magnol. Because of the tree's popularity on old southern plantations (the magnolia is the state flower of Mississippi), the name is redolent of Dixie.
Maggie, Maggy, Nola

Mahala Heb. "Tender affection." Old Testament name that was well used in the 19th century. Singer Mahalia Jackson is keeping it alive today.
Mahalah, Mahalath, Mahalia, Mahaliah, Mahalla, Mahelia, Mehalia

Maia Gk. "Mother." In Greek myth, a nymph who became mother of Hermes; also the Roman goddess of the springtime, for whom the month of May is named. Uma Thurman and Ethan Hawke named their daughter Maya. Writer Maya Angelou.

Maaja, Maiah, Maj, Maja, May, Maya, Mayah, Moia, Moja, Moya, Mya

Maida OE. "Maiden." Used with some frequency in the 19th century, often in the diminutive form **Maidie**.

Maddie, Maddy, Mady, Magda, Maidel, Maidie, Mayda, Maydena, Maydey

Maisie Dim. **Margaret** (Gk. "Pearl"). Originally a Scottish variation by way of **Margery**, it became more widespread early in the 20th century. Literary parents may be reminded of Henry James's novel *What Maisie Knew.*

Maisey, Maisy, Maizie, Mazey, Mazie

Majesta Lat. "Majesty."

Majidah Arab. "Splendid."

Majida

Malcolmina Fem. **Malcolm** (Scot. Gael. "Devotee of St. Columba"). Rather clumsy feminization of an uncommon name.

Malcolmeena

Malka Heb. "Queen."

Malcah, Malkah, Malke, Malkia, Malkie, Milcah, Milka, Milke

Mallorca Place name: an island off Spain in the Mediterranean. Mallorca is the larger island: nearby Minorca is smaller.

Majorca

Mallory OF. "Unhappy, unlucky." Literally, *malheureux.* Originally a nickname, transferred to a last name and thus to a first name. Used for boys as well, until some television scriptwriter on *Family Ties* named a girl Mallory and it crept into somewhat fashionable use for female children. Now fading back to obscurity.

Mallary, Mallerey, Malloreigh, Mallorey, Mallorie, Malorey, Malorie, Malory

Malva Gk. "Slender, delicate." Also a flower name, for plants commonly known as mallows.

Melva, Melvina

Malvina Literary name invented by a romantic poet of the 18th century: It may come from the Gaelic words for "smooth brow." Sculptor Malvina Hoffman.

Mal, Malva, Malvie, Maveena, Mavina, Mel, Melva, Melvie, Melvina, Melvine

Mamie Dim. **Margaret** (Gk. "Pearl") or **Mary** (Heb. "Bitter"). The most famous fictional character to bear the name is Patrick Dennis's eccentric *Auntie Mame*, central character of a book, a Broadway musical, and a movie. First Lady Mamie Eisenhower.

Maime, Mame, Mayme

Manda Dim. **Amanda** (Lat. "Much-loved").

Mandee, Mandie, Mandy

Mandisa South African. "Sweet."

Mandoline Name of a stringed instrument in the lute family. The name also sounds like a combination of **Amanda** and **Lynn**.

Mandalin, Mandalyn, Mandalynn, Mandelin, Mandellin, Mandellyn, Mandolin, Mandolyn, Mandolynne

Mandy Dim. **Amanda** (Lat. "Much-loved"). Popular in Great Britain a generation ago. Pop singer Mandy Moore.

Mandee, Mandie

Mansi Hopi. "Plucked flower."

Manuela (Fem. **Emmanuel**) Sp. from Heb. "The Lord is among us."

Manuelita

Mara Heb. "Bitter." In the Old Testament, Naomi says, "Call me Mara, for the Almighty has dealt very bitterly with me." This is widely considered to be the root of that all-time favorite, **Mary**.

Mahra, Marah, Maralina, Maraline, Mari, Marra

Maravilla Sp. from Lat. "Miracle, something to marvel at."

Marvel, Marvella, Marvelle, Marivel, Marivella

Marcella (Fem. **Marcellus**) Lat. "Warlike." First cropped up at the turn of the 20th century. Very unusual.

Marcela, Marcele, Marcelle, Marcellina, Marcelline, Marchella, Marchelle, Marcie, Marcile, Marcilee, Marcille, Marcy, Maricel, Marquita, Marsalina, Marsella, Marselle, Marsellonia, Marshella, Marsiella

Marcene (Fem. **Mark**) Lat. "Warlike." An American variant that occurred in the 1940s and 1950s, following on the popularity of **Marcia**.

Marceen, Marcena, Marcenia, Marceyne, Marcina

Marcia (Fem. **Mark**) Lat. "Warlike." Used in Imperial Rome and not revived until the late 19th century. It gradually became a great favorite in the middle of the 20th century, but was passé by the 1970s. Actress Marsha Mason.

Marcelia, Marcene, Marchita, Marci, Marciane, Marcie, Marcile, Marcille, Marcilyn, Marcilynn, Marcina, Marcita, Marcy, Marquita, Marsha, Marseea, Marsia, Martia

Marcy Dim. **Marcella** (Lat. "Warlike").

Marcee, Marcey, Marci, Marcie, Marsee, Marsey

Mare Ir. Var. **Mary** (Heb. "Bitter"). Actress Mare Winningham.

Mair, Maire

Marelda OG. "Renowned battle maid."

Marilda, Marrelda

Margaret Gk. "Pearl." One of the standard female names of the Western world. In the Middle Ages the virgin martyr Saint Margaret (swallowed by a dragon) was hugely popular, keeping the name current. An 11th-century queen of Scotland was also a saint, and the name is especially common in Scotland. It has been neck and neck with **Mary** from the 17th century until the 1970s, when more novel names have moved to the forefront. Margaret is now less popular than upstart names like **Tara**, **Sierra**, and **Haley**. Britain's Princess Margaret and Prime Minister Margaret Thatcher; actresses Margaret Sullavan, Marg Helgenberger; anthropologist Margaret Mead; writer Margaret Mitchell.

Greta, Gretal, Gretchen, Gretel, Grethel, Gretta, Grette, Gretl, Madge, Mag, Maggi, Maggie, Maggy, Maiga, Maighread, Mairead, Maisie, Maisy, Malgor-

zata, Marcheta, Marchieta, Marga, Margalit, Margalo, Margareta, Margarete, Margaretha, Margarethe, Margaretta, Margarette, Margarida, Margarit, Margarita, Margarite, Margaruite, Marge, Marged, Margeret, Margeretta, Margerie, Margerita, Margery, Marget, Margette, Margey, Marghanita, Margharita, Margherita, Marghretta, Margie, Margies, Margisia, Margit, Margize, Margo, Margot, Margred, Margret, Margreth, Margrett, Margrid, Marguarette, Marguarita, Marguerita, Marguerite, Marguita, Margy, Marjery, Marjey, Marji, Marjie, Marjorey, Marjorie, Marjory, Marketa, Marketta, Markie, Markita, Marquetta, Meg, Megan, Meggi, Meggie, Meggy, Meghan, Meta, Metta, Mette, Meyta, Peg, Pegeen, Peggie, Peggy, Rita

Margery Fr. Dim. **Margaret**. Imported to England in the 12th century and steadily used there until a late-19th-century revival that lasted into the 1930s, usually as **Marjorie**. Because it is unusual but not outlandish, a good candidate for revival. Novelists Margery Allingham, Margery Sharp.

Marchery, Marge, Margeree, Margerey, Margerie, Margey, Margi, Margie, Margy, Marje, Marjerie, Marjery, Marjie, Marjorey, Marjori, Marjorie, Marjory, Marjy

Margo Fr. Dim. **Margaret**. Another import that never matched the popularity of **Margery**. Actress Margaux Hemingway changed the spelling of her name to match that of a famous Bordeaux wine, Chateau Margaux. Ballet star Dame Margot Fonteyn.

Margaux, Margot

Marguerite Fr. Var. **Margaret**. Also botanical, the French name for a daisy, and popular at the same time (late 19th century to mid 20th) as that flower name. French writers Marguerite Duras, Marguerite Yourcenar.

Margarite, Margaruite, Marghanita, Margherita, Margherite, Marguerita, Margurite

Maria Lat. Var. **Mary** (Heb. "Bitter"). Launched in English-speaking countries in the 18th century as a welcome alternative to the all-too-common **Mary**. Faded after some

200 years, but revived in the middle of the 20th century, particularly after the popularity of *West Side Story,* with its famous ballad "Maria." The explosive popularity of singer Mariah Carey has brought her spelling and pronunciation (with a long "-i") of the name to new prominence. However it is pronounced, this version is now slightly more popular than the Anglo Mary. Singer Maria Muldaur; TV journalist Maria Shriver.

Mariah, Marie, Marja, Marya, Mayra, Mayria, Moraiah, Moriah

Marian Fr. Comb. form **Mary** (Heb. "Bitter") and **Ann** (Heb. "Grace"). Var. **Mary**. Actually an anglicization of **Marion**. Common in the Middle Ages, and after a period of neglect, revived in the early Victorian era when medieval history was very popular. Singer Marian Anderson; Robin Hood's love interest Maid Marian; track star Marion Jones.

Mariam, Mariana, Mariane, Marion, Maryann, Maryanne

Marianne Fr. Comb. form **Marie** (Heb. "Bitter") and **Anne** (Heb. "Grace"). Like **Annemarie**, combines the names of the Virgin Mary and her mother, thus appealing powerfully to Catholic families. In English-speaking countries **Mary Ann** is the standard form, though Marianne has had moments of fashion, in the early 19th and mid 20th centuries. Marianne is the name of the official symbol who personifies the spirit of France, while Mary Ann Evans was the real name of Victorian novelist George Eliot.

Mariana, Mariane, Mariann, Marianna, Maryann, Maryanna

Maribel Comb. form **Mary** (Heb. "Bitter") and **Belle** (Fr. "Beautiful"). This is a modern name.

Maribelle, Marybelle, Meribel, Meribella, Meribelle

Marie Fr. Var. **Mary** (Heb. "Bitter"). Also the earliest English spelling of the name, revived in the 19th century, and in the 1970s nearly as popular as Mary. Now much less in vogue. Scientist Marie Curie; singer Marie Osmond.

Maree

Mariel Dutch. Var. **Mary** (Heb. "Bitter"). Actress Mariel Hemingway.

Marella, Marelle, Marial, Marieke, Mariela, Mariele, Mariella, Marielle, Mariet, Marijke, Marilla

Marietta Fr. Dim. **Mary** (Heb. "Bitter") via **Marie**. Current since the mid 19th century. Philanthropist Marietta Tree.

Maretta, Mariet, Mariette, Maryetta

Marigold Flower name. The golden yellow flower, whose name is a combination of **Mary** and "gold." It cropped up in the 20th century, a bit later than the 19th-century craze for flower names.

Maragold, Marrigold

Marika Dutch. Var. **Mary** (Heb. "Bitter").

Marieke, Marijke, Marike, Mariska, Mariske, Maryk, Maryka

Marilyn Dim. **Mary** (Heb. "Bitter"). Possibly also a combination of Mary and **Ellen** (Gk. "Light"). In any case, a modern name promoted by show business, not in the person of Marilyn Monroe (whose career in the 1950s paralleled the name's decline), but by an earlier star, Marilyn Miller. As is often the case with modern names, there are numerous phonetic variations. Author Marilyn French; opera star Marilyn Horne.

Maralin, Maralynn, Marelyn, Marilee, Marilin, Marillyn, Marilynne, Marralynn, Marrilin, Marrilyn, Marylin, Marylyn

Marin Geography name: a bucolic county just north of San Francisco, on the shore of the Pacific Ocean.

Marinn, Marrin

Marina Lat. "From the sea." As in "marine." Also possibly, in the distant mists of time, related to the Latin god of war, Mars. The name was brought into the junior branches of the English royal family in the mid 1930s by Marina, Duchess of Kent, born a Princess of Greece. Currently popular in Russia.

Mareina, Marena, Marine, Marinell, Marinella, Marinna, Marna, Marne, Marnetta, Marnette, Marni, Marnie

Marion Fr. Dim. **Mary** (H...
turned into **Marian** when it arr...
dle Ages, this form was revived as ...
tury and is now just as common. It is o...
for boys as well, and was in fact the given na...
Wayne. Track star Marion Jones.

Marian, Maryon, Maryonn

Mariposa Sp. "Butterfly."

Marriposa

Maris Lat. "Of the sea." Comes from the phrase *stella maris,* or "star of the sea," which refers to the Virgin Mary.

Marisa, Marise, Marissa, Marisse, Marris, Marys, Maryse, Meris

Marisa Var. **Maris, Marissa**. Somewhat eclipsed by Marissa. Actresses Marisa Berenson, Marisa Tomei.

Mareesa, Mareisa, Marysia, Moreisa, Morisa, Morysa

Marisela Comb. form **Mary** (Heb. "Bitter") and "-ela" from **Isabella, Graciela**, etc.

Maresella, Maricella, Marisella, Maryzela

Marisol Comb. form **Mary** (Heb. "Bitter") and *sol* (Sp. "Sun"). A modern name particularly favored in Puerto Rico.

Marissa Var. **Maris** (Lat. "Of the sea"). The "-issa" ending is growing ever more popular, with names like **Melissa** and **Alyssa** quite frequently used.

Maressa, Marisa, Marisse, Marrissa, Merissa, Meryssa, Morissa

Maristela Sp. Comb. form **Mary** (Heb. "Bitter.") and **Estela** (Per. "Star").

Marjolaine Fr. "Marjoram." Unusual botanical nam...

Marjorie Var. **Margery**; Dim. **Margaret** (Gk. ...
Imported to England in the 12th century a...
steadily used there until a late 19th-c...
lasted into the 1930s. This is curr...
form, though the name is inf...
ized in Herman Wouk's n...

Marcharie, Marge, ...
Margery, Marge...

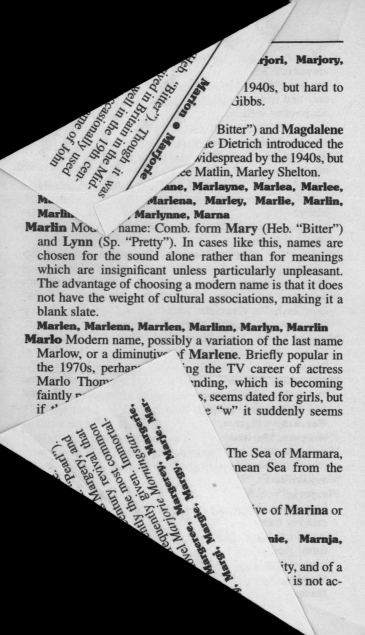

...rjori, Marjory,

1940s, but hard to
...Gibbs.

Bitter") and **Magdalene**
...e Dietrich introduced the
...widespread by the 1940s, but
...ee Matlin, Marley Shelton.

...ane, Marlayne, Marlea, Marlee,
...Marlena, Marley, Marlie, Marlin,
Marli... Marlynne, Marna

Marlin Mo... name: Comb. form **Mary** (Heb. "Bitter")
and **Lynn** (Sp. "Pretty"). In cases like this, names are
chosen for the sound alone rather than for meanings
which are insignificant unless particularly unpleasant.
The advantage of choosing a modern name is that it does
not have the weight of cultural associations, making it a
blank slate.

Marlen, Marlenn, Marrlen, Marlinn, Marlyn, Marrlin
Marlo Modern name, possibly a variation of the last name
Marlow, or a diminutive of **Marlene**. Briefly popular in
the 1970s, perha... ...ng the TV career of actress
Marlo Thom... ...ending, which is becoming
faintly ... ...s, seems dated for girls, but
if ... ...e "w" it suddenly seems

The Sea of Marmara,
...nean Sea from the

...ve of **Marina** or

...nie, Marnja,

...ity, and of a
... is not ac-

Marchesa, Marchessa, Markaisa, Markessa, Marquessa

Marsala Place name: city in Sicily that produces a sweet fortified wine.

Marsalla

Marseilles Place name: city on the Mediterranean coast of France. Marseilles is the second-largest city in France, and the oldest one. The French national anthem is also known as "La Marseillaise."

Marsha Var. **Marcia**. The less common form in America.

Marsia, Marsita, Martia

Martha Aramaic. "Lady." In the New Testament, Martha is the woman who bustles around resentfully getting dinner ready while her sister Mary listens to Jesus. She is patron saint of the helping professions. The name has been very widely used since the Puritans revived it, though it is less common in the last 40 years. Lifestyle maven Martha Stewart has become so famous that she is often known merely as "Martha:" the woman who bustles about getting dinner ready. . . . First Lady Martha Washington; dancer Martha Graham; Martha "Calamity" Jane Burke; actress Martha Plimpton.

Maarva, Marfa, Mariet, Marit, Mart, Marta, Martella, Martelle, Marth, Marthe, Marthena, Marthine, Marthini, Marti, Martie, Martina, Martita, Martta, Marty, Martynne, Martyne, Marva, Mata, Matti, Mattie, Pat, Pattie

Martina (Fem. **Martin**) Lat. "Warlike." Tennis stars Martina Navratilova, Martina Hingis.

Marta, Marteena, Marteina, Martie, Martine, Marty, Tina, Tine

Marvel OF. "Something to marvel at."

Maravilla, Maraville, Marivel, Marivella, Marivelle, Marva, Marvela, Marvele, Marvella, Marvelle

Mary Heb. Though "bitter, bitterness" is the most commonly accepted meaning, the *Facts on File Dictionary of First Names* disputes this. "Rebellious" is also sometimes suggested. Mary is the Greek version of **Miriam**. Although until the Middle Ages it was considered to cred to use, it gradually became the most common female name. The numerous variants, both English and foreign, cropped up as a result of the name's great popularity. In the modern era it is frequently combined with other names (**Mary Jo**, **Mary Lou**, **Mary Beth**). Ironically, the name once thought of as completely commonplace is now quite unusual among young children. This form of the name is used about as frequently as **Maria** while **Marie** lags far, far behind. Actresses Mary Pickford, Mary Martin, Mary Stuart Masterson; Queens Marie Antoinette and Mary of Scots; artist Mary Cassatt; writer Mary Shelley; political strategist Mary Matalin; pop singer Mary J. Blige.

Mair, Marie, Mal, Malia, Mallie, Mame, Mamie, Manette, Manon, Manya, Mara, Marabel, Marabelle, Mare, Maree, Marella, Marelle, Maren, Maretta, Marette, Maria, Mariam, Marian, Mariann, Marianna, Marianne, Marice, Maridel, Marie, Mariel, Mariella, Marielle, Marietta, Mariette, Marilee, Marilin, Marilla, Marilyn, Marin, Marion, Mariquilla, Mariquita, Mariska, Marita, Maritsa, Maritza, Marja, Marje, Marla, Marlo, Marya, Maryann, Maryanne, Marylin, Marysa, Maryse, Marysia, Masha, Maura, Maure, Maureen, Maurene, Maurine, Maurise, Maurita, Maurizia, Mavra, May, Mayme, aymie, Mayra, Mayria, Meridel, Meriel, Mimi, Minette, Minnie, Minny, Miriam, Mitzi, Moira, Moire, Moll, Mollie, Molly, Morag, Moya, Muire, Murial, Muriel, Murielle, Poll, Polly

Maryweld OE. "Mary of the woods."

Masada Heb. "Foundation." Also place name in the Jordan Valley.

Mason OE. Occupational name: "Stoneworker." Transferred from surname status starting in the mid-19th century. Has not yet been widely adapted as a girl's name.
Maison, Maysen

Massima It. from Lat. "The greatest." From the word root that gives us "maximum" and Maximilian.
Maxima

Matana Heb. "Gift."

Matilda OG. "Battle-mighty." William the Conqueror's wife took the name to Britain in the 11th century, when it was pronounced "Maud." It was revived in the 18th century, but faded again in the 19th, and was never a real favorite in the U.S. Even with today's taste for nostalgic-sounding names, Matilda remains neglected, familiar only from the famous Australian song "Waltzing Matilda" and from a novel by Roald Dahl.

Mafalda, Maffalda, Maitilde, Maltilda, Maltilde, Mat, Matelda, Mathilda, Mathilde, Matilde, Matti, Mattie, Matty, Maud, Maude, Maudie, Tilda, Tilde, Tildie, Tildy, Tilli, Tillie, Tilly

Matriona Rus. From Lat. "Married woman, matron."

Matrena, Matresha, Matrina, Matryna, Motreina

Mattea (Fem. Matthew) Heb. "Gift of God."

Mathea, Mathia, Matthea, Matthia, Mattia

Maud Var. Matilda. Although a common enough name after the Middle Ages, its period of real popularity was 1840-1910, especially in Britain. Now rare. Actress Maude Adams.

Maude, Maudie

Maura Ir. Var. Mary (Heb. "Bitter").

Moira, Mora, Morah

Maureen Ir. Var. Mary (Heb. "Bitter"). Popular in the baby boom era, but to today's parents, this is a name for a previous generation. Actresses Maureen O'Sullivan, Maureen O'Hara.

Maura, Maurene, Maurine, Maurise, Maurita, Maurizia, Mavra, Moira, Mora, Moreen, Morena, Morene, Moria, Morine

Mauve Fr. "Mallow plant." The petals of the mallow are purple, hence the use of this word for a color.

Malva

Mavis Fr. "Thrush." Popular mostly in Britain from the turn of the 20th century into the thirties.

Maxine Lat. "Greatest." A modern name that had its moment from the fifties through the seventies, when it con-ferred a cherished air of Continental sophistication on a family.

Massima, Max, Maxeen, Maxena, Maxence, Maxene, Maxie, Maxime, Maxina, Maxy

Maxwelle Fem. **Maxwell** (OE. Place name). In this era, parents are more likely to do without the final "feminine" "-e" and just call a little girl Maxwell.

May Several possible sources: a medieval form of **Matthew** (Mayhew), a nickname form of **Mary**, or an anglicization of **Maia**. It was very fashionable in the U.S. in the 1870s, some 50 years before month names (April and June) became current, and was also tacked onto several names in combination, as in Anna Mae, **Mary May**, etc. This practice has been somewhat more common in the South. Actress Mae West; writer Maya Angelou; poet May Sarton.

Mae, Maia, Maj, Mala, Maya, Mayana, Maye, Mei

Mazarine Fr. Color name: a deep blue. Probably commemorates an influential 17th-century French cleric, Cardinal Mazarin.

Mazine

Mazhira Heb. "Glistening, shining."

Mead OE. Place name: "Meadow." This is more common as a last name, and is a bit stark to join the cavalcade of popular last names turned first names like **Taylor** or **Mackenzie**.

Meade

Meara Ir. Gael. "Jollity."

Mecca Place name: the holiest city of Islam: all Muslims are urged to make a pilgrimage to mecca at least once, and because of its status as a destination in the Near East, the term has since come to stand for a gathering point. Followers of Islam would not use either Mecca or **Medina** (below) as names.

Medea Gk. "Ruling." Since the Medea of Greek mythology was a witch who left a trail of dead bodies behind her (including those of her two children), the name has gruesome connotations and is rarely used.

Madora, Medeia, Media, Medora, Medorah

Medina Arab. "City." The city of Medina in Saudi Arabia

is the site of the tombs of Muhammad and his daughter Fatima.

Mdina

Meg Dim. **Margaret** (Gk. "Pearl"). Rarely given as an independent name. Actresses Meg Tilly, Meg Ryan.

Megan Welsh. Dim. **Margaret** (Gk. "Pearl"). Fairly widespread in the 20th century, and surged into popularity in the early '90s, when it hit the top ten in the U.S. Despite its Gaelic sound and popular opinion, the name has nothing Irish about it. It has been losing popularity recently, replaced in the top ten by more flowery names like **Jessica** and **Samantha**, but is extremely popular in Great Britain. Actress Megan Mullally.

Maegan, Meagan, Meaghan, Meg, Megen, Meggi, Meggie, Meggy, Meghan, Meghann, Meghanne, Meighan

Mehitabel Heb. "Benefited by God." Old Testament name rarely used, except by writer Don Marquis in his tales of the great friends *archy and mehitabel*, a cockroach and a cat.

Mehetabel, Mehitabelle, Hetty, Hitty

Meira Heb. "Light."

Meiriona Welsh name of uncertain meaning and origin. Its use probably depends on its resemblance to the cluster of names derived from **Mary**.

Melanie Gk. "Black, dark-skinned." Uncommon until the publication of *Gone With the Wind*, whose Melanie Wilkes launched it into fashion. Scarlett, though the more memorable character, did not inspire parents in the same way. Actresses Melanie Mayron, Melanie Griffith.

Malaney, Malanie, Mel, Mela, Melaina, Melaine, Melainey, Melaney, Melani, Melania, Melanney, Melannie, Melantha, Melany, Mella, Mellanie, Melli, Mellie, Melloney, Melly, Meloni, Melonie, Melonnie, Melony, Milena

Melantha Gk. "Dark flower."

Mallantha

Melba Name coined in honor of the Australian operatic soprano Nellie Melba (the dessert peach Melba and thin Melba toast was also named after her). She, in turn, took her name from her hometown, Melbourne, having been born Helen Mitchell. Actress Melba Moore.

Malva, Mellba, Melva

Melia Dim. **Amelia** (OG. "Industrious.")

Meelia, Melya

Melina Gk. "Honey." Use was mostly 19th century. Actress Melina Mercouri.

Melibella, Melibelle, Malina, Mallina, Meleana, Meleena, Mellina

Melinda Lat. "Honey." Names ending in "-inda" (**Belinda, Clarinda**) were very fashionable in the 18th century, when this name was coined. It became more widespread in the 19th century, but is still far from common.

Linda, Lindy, Linnie, Lynda, Maillie, Malina, Malinda, Malinde, Mallie, Mally, Malynda, Mandy, Melina, Melinde, Meline, Mellinda, Melynda

Meliora Lat. "Better." Unusual Roman name used by the Puritans, but now rare.

Melisande Fr. Var. **Melissa**.

Lisandra, Malisande, Malissande, Malyssandre, Melesande, Melisandra, Melisandre, Melissande, Melissandre, Mellisande, Melysande, Melyssandre

Melisha Modern name: combination of **Melissa** and any of the "-cia" names like **Alicia** or **Felicia**. Spelling is up to the parental whim.

Malicia, Malisha, Malitia, Melicia, Melitia, Mellicia, Mellisha

Melissa Gk. "Bee." A name that existed in ancient Greece and occurred steadily through the 19th century, but had no real vogue in English-speaking countries until the 1970s. Now somewhat neglected. Singer Melissa Manchester; actress Melissa Gilbert; dancer Molissa Fenley.

Lissa, Malissa, Mallissa, Mel, Melesa, Melessa, Melicent, Melicia, Melisa, Melisande, Melise, Melisenda, Melisent, Melisha, Melisse, Melita, Melitta, Mellicent, Mellie, Mellisa, Melly, Melosa, Milli, Millicent, Millie, Millisent, Millissent, Milly, Missie, Missy

Melita Gk. "honey."

Malita, Malitta, Melida, Melitta, Melyta

Melody Gk. "Song." Though it occurred as early as the 13th century, common usage didn't develop until the 1940s, and didn't endure.

Melodee, Melodey, Melodia, Melodie

Melvina Celt. "Chieftain." A variation of **Malvina**, itself a literary name coined in the 18th century. **Melva** is the most common variant, but all forms are rare.

Malvina, Melva, Melvena

Menemsha Place name: town in Martha's Vineyard, a resort island off the coast of Massachusetts.

Menora Heb. "Candlestick." To most U.S. Jews, the menora is the candelabrum with seven branches used at Hannukah, the Festival of Lights. An appropriate name for a baby born during that season.

Menorah

Mercedes Sp. "Mercies." Refers to Santa Maria de las Mercedes, or Our Lady of the Mercies, rather than to the German luxury car, though the car itself was named for a little girl named Mercedes. Mostly Catholic use. Actresses Mercedes McCambridge, Mercedes Ruehl.

Merced, Mercede, Mercedez

Mercia OE. Place name: Refers to the English Kingdom of Mercia, which comprised much of central England in the 6th through 9th centuries. The name has been used mostly in the 20th century, perhaps under the assumption that it was a variant of **Mercy**.

Mercy ME. "Mercy." One of the names of virtues that were so popular among the Puritans (who, since they were very pious but couldn't use saints' names, were often hard put to find appropriate names for their children).

Mercey, Merci, Mercie, Mersey

Meredith Old Welsh. "Great ruler." Occasionally used for boys, especially in Wales. Elsewhere a girl's name, used with some frequency. Actress Meredith Baxter; newscaster Meredith Vieira.

Meradith, Meredithe, Meredyth, Meridith, Merridie, Merry

Meriel Var. **Muriel** (Ir. Gael. "Sea-bright").

Merial, Merielle, Meriol, Merrill, Meryl

Merle Fr. "Blackbird." Use probably inspired by actress Merle Oberon, whose middle name it was. Little used recently.

Merl, Merla, Merlina, Merline, Merola, Meryl, Myrle, Myrleen, Myrlene, Myrline

Merona Aramaic. "Sheep."

Marona, Merrona

Merrill Var. **Meryl** (Ir. Gael. "Sea-bright"). An anglicized spelling of a name that was popular at the turn of the century. Humorist Merrill Markoe.

Merill, Merrall, Merril, Meryl

Merry OE. "Lighthearted, happy." Also Dim. **Meredith**, **Mercy**. May also be considered a variant of its homonym, **Mary**.

Marrilee, Marylea, Marylee, Merree, Merri, Merrie, Merrielle, Merrile, Merrilee, Merrili, Merrily

Mersera Comb. form. **Mercedes** and **Sara** (Heb. "Princess").

Meryl Var. **Muriel** via **Meriel**. Strictly a 20th-century name, which in the U.S. is strongly associated with actress Meryl Streep (who was actually christened Mary Louise).

Meral, Merel, Merrall, Merrell, Merril, Merrill, Merryl, Meryle, Meryll

Mesa Geographic name: flat-topped hill found in the southwestern United States. The word *mesa* means "table" in Spanish. The popularity of **Savanna** and **Sierra** as names, and the legendary beauty of America's southwest, have opened the door to the use of geographic features as proper names.

Maisa, Maysa

Messina Lat. "Middle." Also a place name: Messina is a town in Sicily.

Massina, Mussina

Meta Ger. Dim. **Margaret** (Gk. "Pearl"). Use is mostly German.

Mia It. "Mine." Also a Scandinavian variant of **Mary**. Probably owes much of its use to the career of actress Mia Farrow. Soccer player Mia Hamm, model Mia Tyler.

Mea, Meya

Mica Heb. var. **Michael**.

    Meeca, Melca, Mika, Myka, Mykah

Michaela (Fem. **Michael**) Heb. "Who is like the Lord?" The most common feminine form of Michael is the French **Michelle**, but Michaela gained ground briefly in the 1990s. It is an example of a name that may seem clumsy to one generation but intriguing to another. Probably the late 90s affinity for three-syllable names adds to its appeal. Phonetic variants are legion, and the derivative **Kayla** is very well used. Actress Michael Learned.

    Macaela, MacKayla, Makayla, Makyla, Mechaela, Meeskaela, Mekea, Micaela, Michal, Michael, Michaelina, Michaeline, Michaila, Michalin, Michele, Michelina, Micheline, Michelle, Mickee, Mickie, Miguela, Miguelina, Miguelita, Mahalya, Mihaila, Mihalia, Mihaliya, Mikaela, Mikhaila, Mikhayla, Mishaela, Mishaila, Miskaela

Michelle (Fem. **Michael**) Fr. var. Heb. "Who is like the Lord?" Spelled with one or two *l*s, fashionable right from its 1940s appearance in English-speaking countries. The Beatles' famous song "Michelle" gave the name even more of a boost, putting it on some top-ten lists in the 1970s. Now past its prime but still steadily chosen by parents. Very popular in Germany. Actresses Michelle Pfeiffer, Sara Michelle Gellar; figure skater Michelle Kwan.

    Chelle, Machelle, Mashelle, M'chelle, Mechelle, Meechelle, Meshella, Mia, Micaela, Michaela, Michaelina, Michaeline, Michaella, Michal, Michele, Michelina, Micheline, Michell, Micki, Mickie, Midge, Miguela, Miguelita, Mikaela, Miquela, Misha, Mishaelle, Mishelle, M'shell, Mychelle, Myshell, Myshella

Michiko Jap. "The righteous way." The name of the first commoner ever to become empress of Japan.

    Michee, Michi

Migdalia Possibly variant of **Madeline** (Gk. "From Magdala").

    Magdala, Migdalla

Mignon Fr. "Cute." First used as a name by the German

poet Goethe, and has spread from literary to real-life use, but not with great frequency. Opera singer Mignon Dunne.

Mignonette, Mignonne, Mingnon, Minyonne, Minyonette

Milada Czech. "My love."

Milagros Sp. "Miracles," another name actually referring to the Virgin Mary as Santa Maria de los Milagros.

Mila, Milagritos, Miligrosa

Mildred OE. "Gentle strength." An Anglo-Saxon name that was revived in the 17th century, but its real popularity came in the U.S. from 1900–1930. By the time of the 1945 film *Mildred Pierce,* it was already slightly dated.

Mildrid, Millie, Milly

Milena Czech "Love, warmth, grace." Popular in the Czech Republic: also used elsewhere in Europe perhaps because it can be considered a combination of **Milagros** (Sp. "Miracles") and **Elena** (Gk. "Light"). Costume designer Milena Canonero.

Milada, Milana, Miladena, Milanka, Mlada, Mladena

Milka Heb. "Queen, counselor."

Malka, Malke, Malkia, Malkiela, Malkit, Malkiya

Millicent OG. "Highborn power." Norman name that has been used mostly in Britain, at its most fashionable around 1900, but never a standard. U.S. Congresswoman Millicent Fenwick.

Lissa, Mel, Melicent, Melisande, Melisenda, Mellicent, Mellie, Mellisent, Melly, Milicent, Milissent, Millie, Millisent, Milly, Milzie, Missie

Mimi Dim. **Mary**, **Miriam**, etc. First used by parents after the appearance of Puccini's famous opera *La Bohème* whose tragic heroine is named Mimi. Actress Mimi Rogers.

Meemee, Mim

Min Dim. **Araminta**, **Wilhelmina**, **Mignon**. Magazine editor Min Hogg.

Mina

Mindy Dim. **Melinda** (Lat. "Honey").

Mindee, Mindie

Minerva The name of the Roman goddess of wisdom. Those great revivalists the Victorians brought it back for their daughters, but by the Jazz Age it was obsolete.
Min, Minette, Minnie, Myna

Minna Dim. **Wilhelmina** (OG. "Will-helmet"). Most common at the turn of the 20th century. **Mina** is currently well-used in Germany.
Min, Mina, Minetta, Minette, Minne, Minnie, Minny

Minnie Dim. **Mary, Wilhelmina**. Enjoyed a great vogue as an independent name around the 1870s for no very clear reason. Most parents now will associate it with Mickey Mouse's girlfriend. Actress Minnie Driver.
Minnee

Minorca Place name: island off Spain in the Mediterranean. Mallorca is the larger, Minorca the smaller in a trio known as the Balearic Islands, the third of which is tiny Ibiza.
Menorca

Minta Dim. **Araminta**. An 18th-century literary name.
Minty

Minuit Fr. "Midnight." Also the last name of the Dutch explorer who purchased Manhattan Island from the Canarsee Indians in the 17th century.

Mira Lat. "Admirable." Dim. **Miranda** or Var. **Myra**, although it is usually pronounced with a short *i*. In Spanish *mira* spelled this way means, "Look!" The name was most used in the 19th century. Fashion designer Myrène de Premonville.
Mireille, Mirella, Mirelle, Mireya, Mirielle, Mirilla, Mirra, Myra, Myrella, Myréne, Myrilla

Mirabel Lat. "Wonderful." In this case the "-bel" ending does not mean "beautiful," though the variations often spell it "-belle." In fact, it was at one period a man's name. Very rare.
Meribel, Meribelle, Mira, Mirabella, Mirabelle

Miranda Lat. "Admirable." Another name contributed to us by Shakespeare, this time directly from the Latin: He used it for the heroine of *The Tempest*. Use has been steadily slight until the early '90s when it had a brief flare of popularity, since extinguished. Actress Miranda Richardson.

Maranda, Meranda, Mira, Miran, Mirandah, Mireille, Mirella, Mirra, Mirranda, Myra, Myranda, Myrella, Myrilla, Myrrilla, Randa, Randi, Randie, Randy

Mireio Provencal. Var. **Miriam** (Heb. "Bitter"). More frequently seen in the form **Mireille**. Singer Mireille Mathieu.
Mireilla, Mireille, Mireya

FAMOUS INVENTED NAMES

Sometimes it seems that today's parents are awfully quick to invent names for their children. Conservative observers might wonder, "Why not just use a *real* name?" So it can be surprising to learn that many of what we consider *real* names (names that are somewhat familiar) have been made up, too—by some of the top wordsmiths of all time. They appeared in plays or books, and caught on. So the next time somebody objects to your choice because it's too innovative, trot out a couple of the following:

- Cora, 1826, in James Fenimore Cooper's *Last of the Mohicans*
- Dora, 1850, in Charles Dickens' *David Copperfield*
- Estelle, 1861, in Charles Dickens' *Great Expectations*
- Evangeline, 1847, in Alfred Tennyson's *Evangeline*
- Gloria, 1898, in G.B. Shaw's *You Never Can Tell*
- Jessica, 1595, in Shakespeare's *Merchant of Venice*
- Lorna, 1869, in R.D. Blackmore's *Lorna Doone*
- Miranda, 1887, in Shakespeare's *The Tempest*
- Pamela, 1590, in Philip Sidney's *Arcadia*
- Thelma, 1887, in Marie Corelli's *Thelma*
- Vanessa, ca. 1700, in Jonathan Swift's *Cadenus and Vanessa*
- Wendy, 1904, in J.M. Barrie's *Peter Pan*

Mireya Sp. From Lat. "Admired."
Maraya, Mirella

Miriam Heb. Possibly "Bitter" or "Rebellious." This is the source of **Mary**, which is its Latin form, and its translation is not quite clear, though "bitter" is very widely accepted. Overlooked by the Puritan fervor for Old Testament names, but revived in the 18th century and quite common for some 250 years, peaking around 1900 in the U.S. Now unusual. Singer Miriam Makeba.
Mariam, Maryam, Meriam, Meryam, Mimi, Mirham, Mirjam, Mirjana, Mirriam, Miryam, Mitzi, Mitzie, Miyana, Miyanna

Mirta Sp. From Gk. "Crown of thorns."
Meerta, Meertha, Mirtha, Mitra

Missy Dim. **Melissa** or **Millicent**. Pop singer Missy Elliott.
Missie

Misty OE. "Mist." Briefly popular in the U.S. in the middle of the 20th century.
Mysti

Mitzi Ger. Var. **Mary** (Heb. "Bitter"). Actress Mitzi Gaynor.
Mitzee, Mitzie

Modesty Lat. "Modesty." As **Modesta**, used by the Romans, but very rare ever since, even during the Puritan craze for virtue names.
Modesta, Modestia, Modestina, Modestine

Moira Ir. Var. **Mary** (Heb. "Bitter"). Dancer Moira Shearer.
Moire, Moyra

Molly Dim. **Mary** (Heb. "Bitter"). Not Irish, in spite of the famous song "Cockles and Mussels" about Dublin's "sweet Molly Malone." Since a "moll" has meant, at various times, a prostitute or a gangster's girlfriend, the name has had long periods of disuse, but now that these slang terms are obsolete, only the pleasantly nostalgic aura remains, and the name has found its way into the top 100 in the U.S. Actress Molly Ringwald; author Mollie Hardwick.
Moll, Mollee, Molley, Mollie, Molly

Mona Ir. Gael. "Aristocratic." Spread from Ireland in the mid 19th century. Never widespread, but common enough not to be outlandish.

Moina, Monah, Monna, Moyna

Monet Adaptation of the last name of Impressionist painter Claude Monet. Also a brand of costume jewelry. Actress Monet Mazur.

Monay, Moné

Monica Possibly Lat. "Adviser" or "Nun." Established by Saint Monica, the mother of Saint Augustine, and favored by Catholic families.

Mona, Monca, Monicka, Monika, Monike, Moniqua, Monique, Monnica

Montana Sp. "Mountainous." Geographic name: the northernmost western state that the Rocky Mountains run through.

Montanna

Morela Pol. "Apricot."

Morgan Different sources give different meanings, including Welsh "Great and bright" and OE. "Bright or white sea dweller." Morgan is most common in Wales as both a first and a last name, for both sexes. The current trend toward unisex names suggests that the feminizations are in for a spell of disuse, and that any Morgan encountered in a nursery school—and there will be some, for the name is rather well used—is likely to be a girl. Actress Morgan Fairchild.

Morgana, Morgance, Morgane, Morganica, Morganne, Morgen, Morgin

Moriah Heb. "The Lord is my teacher." May also be arrived at as a variant of **Mariah/Maria/Mary**.

Moraia, Moraiah

Morwenna Welsh. Perhaps "Maiden," perhaps "White seas."

Morwena, Morwina, Morwinna, Morwyn, Morwynna

Moselle (Fem. **Moses**) Heb. Possibly "Savior." Also a variety of delicately sweet white wine.

Mosella, Mosette, Moiselle, Moisella

Mouna Arab. "Wish, desire."

Mounia, Muna, Munira

Moya Nor. Var. **Maia** (Gk. "Mother").
Moja

Muriel Ir. Gael. "Sea-bright." Some names, like this one, seem rooted in a certain period (in this case the first half of the 20th century), but Muriel actually dates back to the Middle Ages. Perhaps the children of the 21st century will eventually find it nostalgic enough to use for *their* children. Novelist Muriel Spark.
Merial, Meriel, Merrill, Muireall, Murial, Muriella, Murielle

Musetta "Little bagpipe." "Musette" came to be the term for a dance tune that employed the musette, an instrument fashionable in the 18th century.
Musette

Musidora Gk. "Gift of the Muses."

Myra (Fem. **Myron**) Lat. "Scented oil." Literary name coined in the early 17th century, but real-life use dates from the 19th century. Harpsichordist Dame Myra Hess; author Maira Kalman.
Maira, Mira, Myree

Myrna Ir. Gael. "Tender, beloved." The era of the name's popularity, the 1930s and 1940s, spans the career of actress Myrna Loy.
Meirna, Merna, Mirna, Moina, Morna, Moyna, Muirna

Myrtle Botanical name. The myrtle is a dark green shrub with pink or white blossoms. The name first appeared in the 1850s, before the true vogue for flower names, but it became more popular along with those other names in the 1880s. Now dated.
Mertice, Mertis, Mertle, Mirtle, Myrta, Myrtia, Myrtice, Myrtie, Myrtis

Mystique The air of mystery surrounding someone.
Mistique

Naavah Heb. "Lovely."

  Nava, Navit

Nabila Arab. "Highborn."

  Nabeela, Nabilah

Nadette OG. "Bear/courageous." Dim. **Bernadette**.

Nadia Rus. "Hope." **Nada** appeared in English-speaking countries at the turn of the 20th century, but Nadia had taken root by the 1960s. Though not outlandish, it has a pleasantly foreign sound. Currently fashionable in Russia. Gymnast Nadia Comaneci; poet Nadezhda Mandelstam.

  Nada, Nadege, Nadejda, Nadezhda, Nadie, Nadija, Nadiya, Nadja, Nady, Nadya, Nadyenka, Nadzia, Nata, Natka

Nadine Fr. Var. **Nadia**. Author Nadine Gordimer.

  Nadeen, Nadena, Nadene, Nadie, Nadina, Nadyna, Nadyne, Naydeen

Nadira Arab. "Precious, scarce."

  Nadirah, Nadra

Nagida Heb. "Wealthy."

  Negida

Nahara Aramaic. "Light."

Naida Gk. "Water nymph."

  Naia, Naiad, Naiada, Nayad, Niada, Nyad, Nyada

Naima Arab. "Satisfied, contented."

  Naeema, Naimah

Nairobi Place name: capital of Kenya, in east Africa. Occasionally used by African American parents.

Nalani Haw. "Serenity of the skies."

  Nalanee

Nan Var. **Ann** (Heb. "Grace"). At its most common in the 18th century, but now occurs most often as a nickname for Ann. Its diminutives (**Nana, Nanny**) have come to mean "grandmother" or "person who looks after children."

  Nana, Nance, Nanci, Nancie, Nancy, Nanella, Nanelle,

Nanette, Nania, Nanine, Nanna, Nannette, Nannie, Nanny, Nanon, Nettie, Ninon

Nancy Var. **Ann** (Heb. "Grace"). Also originally a nickname whose use as a given name began at roughly the same time as **Nan**, in the 18th century. Nancy, however, took root more firmly (perhaps because it had not acquired any other meanings) and was very popular in the U.S. in the middle of the 20th century. First Lady Nancy Reagan; skater Nancy Kerrigan; writer Nancy Mitford.

Nainsey, Nainsi, Nance, Nancee, Nanci, Nancie, Nancsi, Nanice, Nanncey, Nanncy, Nannie, Nanny, Nansee, Nansey

Nanette Fr. Dim. Nan.

Nannette, Nettie, Netty, Ninon

Naomi Heb: "Pleasant." Old Testament name; the mother-in-law of Ruth, who, after her sons died, said, "Do not call me Naomi, call me Mara, for the Almighty has dealt very bitterly with me." Naomi came into English-speaking use not with the Puritan revival of biblical names, but in the 18th century. Actress Naomi Watts.

Naoma, Naomia, Naomie, Nayomi, Navit, Noami, Noémi, Noémie

Narcissa Gk. "Daffodil." Not actually a flower name, but the unusual feminine version of the masculine (and equally unusual) **Narcisse**, which comes from the legend of the beautiful Greek youth who became enamored of his own reflection—hence "narcissism."

Narcisa, Narcisse, Narcyssa, Narkissa, Narsissa

Narda Lat. "Scented ointment."

Nastasia Gk. "Resurrection." Dim. **Anastasia**. Actress Nastassja Kinski.

Nastassia, Nastassija, Nastassja, Nastassiya, Nastassya

Nasya Heb. "The Lord's miracle."

Nasia

Nata Lat. "Swimmer."

Natalie Lat. "Birth day." More specifically, the Lord's birthday, or Christmas. This is probably the most common of all the Christmas names, and certainly the only one that is used for babies born at other times of the year (unlike **Noel**). Though there was a 4th-century Saint Natalia, this Frenchified form did not crop up until the late 19th century. Actresses Natalie Wood, Natalie Portman; singer Natalie Cole.

Nat, Nata, Natala, Natalee, Natalene, Natalia, Natalja, Natalina, Nataline, Nataly, Nataliya, Natalya, Natasha, Natelie, Nately, Nathalia, Nathalie, Nathaliely, Nathalija, Natilie, Natividad, Nattilie, Nattie, Nettie, Talia, Talya, Tasha

Natana Heb. "He gave." A feminine form of **Nathan**.

Nataniela

Natasha Rus. Var. **Natalie**. Actress Natasha Richardson.

Nastaliya, Nastalya, Natacha, Natascha, Natashenka, Natosha, Natucha

Nathania (Fem. **Nathan**) Heb. "A gift or given of God."

Natania, Nataniella, Nataniya, Natanya, Natanyah, Nathaniella, Nathanielle, Netanella, Netania, Netanya, Nethania

Nathifa Arab. "Immaculate, pure."

Nathifah, Natifa, Natifah

Natividad Sp. "Christmas." See **Natalie**.

Natura Sp. "Nature."

Nausicaa Character from *The Odyssey*: a princess who treats the shipwrecked Odysseus with courtesy and consideration, unlike most of the women he meets on his voyage.

Nausikaa

Neala (Fem. **Neal**) Gael. "Champion." Unusual feminization of the male name that was quite popular in the middle of the 20th century.

Neale, Nealla, Neila, Neile, Neilla, Neille

Nebraska Place name. The name of the state comes from a Sioux Indian word meaning "flat water."

Nebula Lat. "Mist." Used by astronomers to describe hazy masses around stars.

Nechama Heb. "Comfort, solace." The most common masculine version of the name is **Nachum**, one of the minor prophets in the Bible. **Nehemiah** is also related.

Nachmanit, Nachuma, Nechamah, Nechamit, Nehamah

Neda (Fem. **Edward**) OE. "Wealthy defender" via the nickname **Ned**, or Rus. "Born on Sunday." In any case, very unusual.

Nedda, Neddie, Nedi

Nedra OE. "Underground."

Neddra, Needra

Nefertiti Queen of Egypt around 1350 B.C. She has an aura of glamor because several portrait sculptures of her have survived, and she is strikingly beautiful, even by the standards of a world some 2,400 years later than hers.

Nehara Heb. "Light of day."

Nehira, Nehora, Nehura

Neila Heb. "Closing, locking." The final service on Yom Kippur is called Neila.

Neilla

Neilina Scot. Feminization of **Neil** (Ir. Gael. "Champion").

Neala, Neale, Neel, Neelle, Neille

Neima Heb. "A melody."

Neka Native American. "Goose, wild goose."

Nelia Dim. **Cornelia** (Lat. "Horn").

Neelia, Neelie, Neelya, Nela, Nila

Nell Dim. **Helen, Eleanor** (Gk. "Light"). Used sparingly as an independent name, though some of its variants like **Nellie** have had periods of popularity. Charles II's mistress Nell Gwynn; opera star Nellie Melba.

Nel, Nella, Nellene, Nellie, Nellwen, Nellwin, Nellwyn, Nelly

Nelsey Modern name: the popular **Kelsey/Chelsea** with an "-N." Also reminiscent of **Nell**.

Nellsea, Nellseigh, Nellsey, Nellsie, Nelsea, Nelseigh, Nelsie, Nelsy

Nemera Heb. "Leopard."

Neneca Sp. Var. **Amelia** (OG. "Industrious").

Nenica, Nenneca, Nennica

Neola Gk. "Young one." Comes from the same root as the widely used prefix "neo-."

Neoma Gk. "New moon."

Neomah, Nioma

Nera Heb. "Light of a candle." An appropriate name for a daughter born during Hannukah.
Nerit, Neriya

Nereida Sp. from Gk. "Sea nymph."
Nireida

Nerine Gk. "Sea nymph."
Narine, Narice, Narissa, Nerice, Nerida, Nerina, Nerissa, Neryssa

Nerissa Unusual name possibly derived from "nereid," the Greek term for a sea nymph. Shakespeare wrote a character named Nerissa into *The Merchant of Venice*. The name is just as likely, though, to be a modification of the popular **Marisa/Marissa**.
Narissa, Naryssa, Neryssa

Nerola It. "Orange flower."
Nerolia, Nerolie, Neroly

Nerys Welsh. "Master, lord."
Neris, Neriss, Neryss

Nessie Dim. **Agnes** (Gk. "Lamb"). Also the name of the Loch Ness Monster, which might limit its appeal.
Nesha, Nessa, Nessia, Nessya, Nesta, Neta, Netia

Nesta Dim. **Ernesta, Agnes**.
Nest

Nettie Diminutive of "-ette" names like **Henrietta** or **Nanette**. Use as an independent name mostly around the turn of the 20th century.
Netta, Netty

Neva Sp. "Snowy." Nevada, which means "covered with snow," is one of the American state names (like Florida) that adapts nicely to use as a girl's name. Actress Neve Campbell.
Nevada, Nevara, Neve, Nieves

Nia Swahili. "Goal, purpose." Actress Nia Vardalos.
Nea, Nya

Niagara Place name: home of the famous Falls. Niagara Falls used to be a premier honeymooning destination. The Falls are 186 feet high.

Nichele Modern name: Comb. form **Michele** and **Nicole**.
Nichelle, Nishell, Nishelle, N'Shell

Nicia Dim. of "-nice" names such as **Eunice** and **Berenice**.
Neecia, Nicija

Nicole (Fem. **Nicholas**) Gk. "Victory of the people."
Nicola, the Italian form, is more common in Britain
(though its vogue peaked there in the 1970s). This French
version has been more popular in other English-speaking
countries, reaching the top ten in the U.S. in the 1980s.
Still quite widely used, but it has lost its trendiness. The
diminutive **Nicolette** is very popular in France. Singer
Nicolette Larson; actress Nicole Kidman.
**Cola, Colette, Cosetta, Cosette, Nichelle, Nichola,
Nicholassa, Nichole, Nicholette, Nicholl, Nicholle,
Nicia, Nicki, Nickola, Nickole, Nicky, Nico, Nicola, Nico-
lasa, Nicolea, Nicolene, Nicoleen, Nicolette, Nicolie,
Nicolina, Nicoline, Nicolla, Nicolle, Nika, Niki, Nikita,
Nikki, Nikky, Niko, Nikola, Nikole, Nikoleta, Nikoletta,
Nikolia, Niquole, Niquolle, Nychole, Nycholl, Nykia,
Nycole, Nykole, Nykolia, Nyquole, Nyquolle**

Nicosia Capital city of Cyprus. Similar enough to **Nicole**
and other derivatives of **Nicholas** to be considered one of
them.
Nicotia

Nidia Sp. from Gk. "Graceful, sweet."
Nibia, Nydia

Nikita Gk. "Unconquered." Those who remember Nikita
Khruschev may think of this as a masculine name, but it
is often used as a variant of **Nicole**.
Nakeeta, Nikeeta, Niquita

Nigella (Fem. **Nigel**) Ir. Gael. "Champion." Very unusual
form of a name found mostly in England. Cookbook author Nigella Lawson.

Nike Gk. "Victory." Also, and more commonly to most
Americans, the name of a very popular athletic shoe.
Nika

Nikki Var. **Nicole**. Used mostly in the 1960s.
Nickie, Nicky, Niki, Nikkey, Nikky

Nila Geography name, based on the river Nile. Logical
choice for Egyptophiles.
Naila, Nyla

Nilda Dim. **Brunhilda** (OG. "Battle woman.") A surprising proportion of Spanish names are directly adapted from the German, possibly going back to the days when Spain and Germany were alllied as part of the Holy Roman Empire. Nilda is often used as an independent name.

Nillda

Nilsine Scand. Fem. **Nils** or **Neil** (Ir. Gael. "Champion").

Nilsa, Nilsina

Nina Sp. "Girl." Dim. **Ann** (Heb. "Grace"). History buffs will remember that Nina was the name of one of Christopher Columbus's three ships. The name is rather uncommon. Ballerina Dame Ninette de Valois.

Neena, Neina, Nenna, Neneh, Ninacska, Nineta, Ninete, Ninetta, Ninette, Ninnette, Ninon, Ninochka, Ninoska, Ninotchka, Nyna

Ninfa Sp. from Gk. "Nymph."

Ninon Fr. Dim. **Ann** (Heb. "Grace"). A famous 17th century Parisian belle was named Anne de Lenclos, better known as Ninon de Lenclos.

Ninette

Niobe Gk. "Fern." In mythology, Niobe was a boastful queen of Thebes whose children were all killed as a reprimand for her arrogance. In her resulting misery she asked Zeus to turn her to stone. In art she is usually depicted weeping.

Nira Heb. "Plowed field."

Niran, Nirela, Nirit

Nissa Two possible sources, Heb. "Sign" or Scand. "Elf." May also be independently arrived at as an attractive-sounding pair of syllables, vaguely reminiscent of **Vanessa**.

Nissana, Nissanit, Nyssa

Nita Sp. Dim. **Juanita**, **Anita**, etc. Unusual.

Nitsa Ger. Dim. **Irene** (Gk. "Peace").

Nituna Native American. "My daughter."

Nitza Heb. "Bud."

Nitzana, Nitzaniya

Nixie OG. "Water sprite." Usually beautiful and antagonistic to men, unlike pixies, which, though mischievous, are content to share the world with humans.

Noel Fr. "Christmas." Though used since the Middle Ages for both boys and girls, it is more common for the latter.

Noela, Noeleen, Noelene, Noeline, Noeliz, Noella, Noelle, Noelleen, Noelynn, Nowel, Noweleen, Nowell

Nokomis NAm. Indian. "Daughter of the moon." The source is Longfellow's famous poem *The Song of Hiawatha.*

Nola Dim. **Finola** (Gael. "White shoulder"). Related to **Nuala** but not, as many parents think, to **Nolan**.

Nowla

Nolan Ir. Gael. "Renowned." A last name transferred to first name and generally used for boys.

Noland, Nolanda, Nolen, Nolin, Nolynn, Nollan

Noleta Lat. "Unwilling."

Nolita

Nona Lat. "Ninth." Although it was originally used for a family's ninth baby, it would hardly have survived to this day if parents had not been willing to overlook its meaning.

Nonah, Noni, Nonie, Nonna, Nonnah

Nora Dim. **Eleanor** (Gk. "Light") or **Honora** (Lat. "Woman of honor"). Used independently, especially for the half century around 1900. Well-read parents will remember Nora as the heroine of Ibsen's *A Doll's House;* she sets a discouraging precedent, however. Writer Nora Ephron; pop singer Norah Jones.

Norah, Norella, Norelle

Norberta (fem. **Norbert**) OG. "Renowned northerner." Occurs in Germany.

Nordica Lat. "From the North." Familiar to skiers as a manufacturer of ski equipment, and to opera fans as the last name of turn-of-the-century soprano Lillian Nordica, who was actually born Lillian Norton in Farmington, Maine. In those days, a plain Anglo-Saxon name was insufficiently exotic for an opera star.

Norda

Noreen Ir. Dim. **Nora**. Originated in Ireland.
  Norene, Norina, Norine
Norma Lat. "Pattern." From the same root that gave us "normal" or "the norm." Launched by Bellini's 1831 opera of the same name, and boosted in the 1920s by popular actress Norma Shearer. Out of fashion for the last couple of generations. Fashion designer Norma Kamali.
  Norm, Normie, Normina
Normandie Place name: the province of Normandy in northeastern France. Famous as the area that launched the Norman Invasion of England in the 11th century, and the Allied invasion of German-dominated Europe, in 1944. Sometimes used as a girl's name, especially to compliment a relative named **Norman**, if **Norma** seems too out of date. After all, if Brittany (another French province) can reach the top ten. . . .
  Normandee, Normandey, Normandy
Norna Scand. Mythology name: the goddess of time.
  Norne
Novia Lat. "New"; Sp. "Girlfriend."
  Nova
Nova An exploding star that becomes temporarily extraordinarily bright. Typically a nova loses only a tiny part of its matter in the explosion. Chevrolet used to make a small car called a "Nova," which might dissuade parents who owned one from using this name for a baby.
Nuala Dim. **Fionnula** (Ir. Gael. "White shoulder"). Irish writer Nuala O'Faolain.
  Nola, Noola, Nualla, Nula
Nubia Place name: a region in ancient Africa, in part of what is now Sudan.
Nunzia It. "Messenger." See **Annunciata**.
  Nunciata
Nur Arab. "Light." The Arabic name adopted by the former Queen of Jordan, an American woman known as Lisa Halaby until she married the King.
  Noor, Nour, Noura, Nureen, Nurine
Nurit Heb. "Buttercup."

Nydia Lat. "Nest." Also Sp. from Gk. "Graceful."
   Nidia, Needia
Nysa Gk. "Goal, ambition." Currently used in Greece.
   Nyssa
Nyx Gk. "Night."
   Nix, Nixe

Oba Nigerian, the name of a goddess of rivers.
Ocarina A small simple wind instrument shaped like a jug with a spout.
   Oceana Gk. "Ocean." In Greek mythology, Oceanus was a river that flowed around the earth. Oceania is a collective name for the islands in the Pacific.
Oceania
Octavia Lat. "Eighth." Used most often in the Victorian era of large families.
   Octaviana, Octavianne, Octavie, Octiana, Octoviana, Ottavia, Tavia, Tavie, Tavy
Odele Derivation disputed. Some sources relate it to either German "Rich" or Greek "Song," but *The Facts on File Dictionary of First Names* claims that it derives from an Old English place name: "Woad hill." Woad is a blue dye reputedly used by the ancient Druids in their religious rites. Yet another possibility is that it is a variation of **Adele**.
   Odela, Odelet, Odelette, Odelina, Odeline, Odell, Odella, Odelle, Udele, Udelia, Udilia
Odelia Heb. "I will praise the Lord." Possibly also related to **Odele**.
   Oda, Odeelia, Odele, Odelinda, Odella, Odellia, Odilia, Udele, Udelia, Udilia
Odessa Gk. "Long voyage." As in "odyssey," more specifically Homer's epic poem about the wandering Odysseus. The Russian port of Odessa was supposedly named to honor *The Odyssey*.
   Odissa, Odyssa, Odyssia

Odette Fr. from Ger. "Wealthy." In the famous ballet *Swan Lake,* the same ballerina usually dances as both Odette, the good swan, and Odile, the evil black swan. Folk singer Odetta.

Odetta

Odile Fr. Var. **Otthild** (OG. "Prospers in battle"). Related to **Odette** and also to **Odelia**. For balletomanes, the malevolent alter ego of Odette.

Odila, Odilia, Odolia, Udelia, Udile, Udilia

Ofra Heb. "Fawn." Another form of the name that is most famous as **Oprah**. See **Orpah**.

Ofrat, Ofrit, Ophra

Ogenya Heb. "God is my help."

Oksana Rus. From Heb. "Praise to God". Well used in what used to be the USSR, and made familiar world-wide by Ukrainian figure-skating champion Oksana Baiul.

Oksanna

Ola Var. **Olesia** (Gk. "Man's defender").

Olla

Olathe Native American. "Lovely."

Oleisa Var. **Elise**, Fr. Var. **Elizabeth** (Heb. "Pledged to God").

Oleesa, Olisa

Olena Rus. Var. **Helen** (Gk. "Light").

Alena, Elena, Lena, Lenya, Olinia, Olinija, Olenya, Olina, Olinia, Olinija

Olesia Gk. "Man's defender."

Ola

Olethea Var. **Alethea** (Gk. "Truth").

Oleta

Olga Rus. "Holy." The Russian form of **Helga**, and perhaps more common than Helga in English-speaking countries. The Russian Saint Olga was a princess from Kiev and a 10th-century Christian convert; the name was favored in the ill-fated Russian imperial family. Gymnast Olga Korbut.

Elga, Helga, Ola, Olenka, Olia

Oliana Polynesian. "Oleander."

Oleana, Olianna

Olinda Lat. "Scented."

Olivia Lat. "Olive tree." The most common form of the name today, though **Olive** had a flurry of popularity with other nature names at the turn of the 20th century. It would be hard to use Olive today given the fame of Popeye's scrawny girlfriend, Olive Oyl. This form, though, is speeding up popularity charts. According to the U.S. Social Security Administration, in 2001 Olivia was the 11th most popular name for girls. Its ascent into fashion is probably influenced by our current fondness for three-syllable girls' names. Also very popular in England. Actresses Olivia de Havilland, Olivia Hussey; singer Olivia Newton-John.

Liv, Liva, Livia, Livvie, Livvy, Olia, Oliff, Oliffe, Oliva, Olive, Oliveea, Olivet, Olivette, Olivija, Olivine, Olivya, Ollie, Olva

Olwen Welsh. "White footprint." Along with **Bronwen**, one of the best-known Welsh-language first names. Nevertheless, it is very unusual outside Wales.

Olwenn, Olwin, Olwyn, Olwynne

Olympia Gk. "From Mount Olympus," the home of the gods. Slightly more common in Europe, where it may avoid the faintly commercial connotation of the Olympic Games. Actress Olympia Dukakis; Senator Olympia Snowe.

Olimpe, Olimpia, Olimpiada, Olimpiana, Olypme, Olympie

Oma Arab. "Leader." Infrequent use.

Omega Gk. "Last." It would seem to be tempting fate to use this name for a youngest child.

Omyra Var. **Myra** (Lat. "Scented oil").

Omeira

Ondine Lat. "Little wave." In mythology, Undine is the spirit of the waters. Edith Wharton created a heroine in *The Custom of the Country* who was named Undine for the haircurling tonic that had made her father rich.

Ondina, Ondyne, Undine

Oneida Native American. "Long awaited." In the U.S. probably most familiar as a brand of silverware, which

was originally manufactured by a utopian colony that was
disbanded in the 19th century because its residents prac-
ticed polygamy.

Onida, Onyda

Onella Gk. "Light."

Oneonta Place name: town in Central New York State.

Onnjel Var. **Angela** (Lat. "Angel").

Onjella

Onora Var. **Honoria** (Lat. "Honor").

Onnora, Onoria, Onorine, Ornora

Oona Ir. Var. **Una** (Lat. "Unity").

Oonagh, Una

Opal Sanskrit. "Gem." One of the less common of the
jewel names, but a logical choice for an October baby.

Opalina, Opaline, Opall

Ophelia Gk. "Help." Most famously, the young girl in
Hamlet who goes mad. Mostly used in the late 19th century, but its connotations are far from happy.

**Availia, Filia, Ofelia, Ofilia, Ophélie, Ophelya, Ophilia,
Ovalia, Ovelia, Phelia, Ubelia, Uvelia**

Ophira Fem. **Ophir**, Biblical place name. In the Old Testament, Ophir is frequently mentioned as an exceptionally rich source of gold, sandalwood, precious stones and
other luxuries. Its actual location is a moot point: scholars can narrow it down no further than India, Africa, or
Arabia. In the late 19th century one of the most productive mines in California's Comstock Lode was called
"Ophir."

Ofeera, Ofira

Ora Lat. "Prayer." Homonym for **Aura**, which means
"Gold" or "Breeze."

Orabel, Orabelle, Orareeana, Orarariana, Orra

Oracia Sp. Fem. **Horace** (Lat. clan name). This name may
also be taken as something to do with prayer or with gold,
since the latinate roots are all very similar.

Orasia, Oratia, Orazia

Oralee Heb. "My light."

Orali, Oralit, Orlee

Oralie Fr. Var. **Aurelia** (Lat. "Golden").

Aurelie, Oralee, Oralia, Orelie, Oriel, Orielda, Orielle, Orlena, Orlene

Orane Fr. "Rising." From the same Latin source as **Oriana**.

Orania, Oriane

Orange Name of the fruit.

Orangetta, Orangia, Orangina

Orela Lat. "Announcement from the gods." Related to "oracle."

Orelda, Orella, Orilla

Orfea Fem. **Orpheus**. In Greek mythology, Orpheus was a brilliant musician. He married a dryad, Eurydice, who was fatally poisoned by a snake, and he descended into the underworld to find her. His music so charmed Hades that he was allowed to bring her back to life, if he could lead her to the upper world without looking at her. He failed, and she returned to Hades.

Orfeya, Orfia, Orphea, Orpheya, Orphia

Oriana Lat. "Dawning." From the same root as **Aurora**. Italian journalist Orianna Falacci.

Oria, Oriane, Orianna

Oriel Lat. Dim. of "Golden." The more usual spelling for these "gold" names is "Au-." An oriel is also an architectural feature, an elaborate bay window.

Auriel, Auriella, Aurielle, Oriella, Orielle

Orinda Place name: town in California. Possibly related to the Spanish for gold (*oro*) or a variant of the Spanish for pretty (*linda*).

Orinthia Fem. **Oren** (Heb. "Pine tree" or Ir. Gael. "Fair-skinned").

Orenthia, Orna, Ornina, Orrinthia

Oriole Lat. "Golden." Most commonly the name of a bird with golden markings, or the name of the Baltimore baseball team.

Auriel, Oreolle, Oriel, Oriella, Oriola, Oriolle

Orit Heb. "Light."

Ora, Orah, Orya

Orla Ir. Gael. "Golden lady."

Orlagh, Orrla

Orlanda Fem. **Orlando**; Sp. Var. **Roland** (OG. "Famous land"). Very unusual.

Orpah Heb. "A fawn." Old Testament name rarely used. Talk show star Oprah Winfrey's unusual name is the result of a misspelling of this name.

Afra, Aphra, Ofrit, Ophrah, Oprah, Orpa

Orquidea Sp. "Orchid."

Orsa Var. **Ursula** (Lat. "Bear").

Orsalina, Orsaline, Orsel, Orselina, Orseline, Orsola, Orssa, Ursa

Osaka Place name: Japanese city known as both a commercial and cultural center.

Orszebet Hung. Var. **Elizabeth** (Heb. "Devoted to God").

Ortensia It. Var. **Hortense** (Lat. clan name).

Ortensa, Ortensija, Ortensya

Osma Fem. **Osmond** (OE. "Divine protector"). Avid readers of the entire series of Oz books by Frank Baum will remember Ozma of Oz.

Ozma

Ostia Place name: the original port for the city of Rome, now some distance inland because of silt deposited by the Tiber.

Otamisia Var. **Artemisia** (Gk/Sp. "Perfect").

Otameesia, Ottamisia

Otthild OG. "Prospers in battle." **Odile** is perhaps the most common form.

Otthilda Ottila, Ottilia, Ottilie, Ottiline, Ottoline, Otylia

Ottilie Fr. Var. **Otthild**.

Ottalia, Ottilia, Ottilie, Ottolie

Otzara Heb. "Treasure, wealth."

Otzarah, Ozara

Ouida Pen name of a Victorian romantic novelist named Marie Louise de la Ramée. It originated as a childish version of **Louisa**.

Pacifica Sp. "Peaceful." Geography name, for the ocean bounding the West Coast of the USA. Good choice for surfers and peaceniks.
Pasifica

Padma Hindi. "Lotus."

Page Fr. A young boy in training as a personal assistant to a knight. Usually a transferred surname, possibly indicating an ancestor who was a page. Use as a girl's name is quite recent, going back to the mid-twentieth century. Monosyllables are little-used today, though, so Page is scarce.
Padget, Padgett, Paget, Pagett, Paige, Payge

Pallas Gk. "Wisdom." Another name for the Greek deity Athena, goddess of wisdom.
Paladia, Palladia, Palles

Palma Lat. "Palm tree." Also a place name used in several countries, no doubt to indicate locales where palm trees grew.
Pallma, Pallmirah, Pallmyra, Palmeda, Palmeeda, Palmer, Palmira, Palmyra

Paloma Sp. "Dove." Little known until the recent fame of designer Paloma Picasso, daughter of the artist.
Palloma, Palometa, Palomita, Peloma

Pamela Gk. "All honey." Literary name coined at the end of the 16th century, growing gradually more common until a distinct vogue in the 1950s and 1960s. Likely to be neglected by the current generation of parents, precisely because it was popular among their elders. Actresses Pam Dawber, Pamela Reed, Pamela Anderson; tennis star Pam Shriver.
Pam, Pama, Pamala, Pamalla, Pamelia, Pamelina, Pamelin, Pamelina, Pamella, Pamelyn, Pamelynne, Pamilla, Pammela, Pammie, Pammy, Permelia

Pamina Name of Italian origin, meaning unknown: a character in Mozart's famous opera, *The Magic Flute*.

Pandora Gk. "All gifted." In Greek mythology, Pandora was the first woman, endowed with gifts by all the gods. She is famous for the box that was her dowry; it contained all the world's evils, which flew out when the box was opened. One of the more common of the Greek names in English-speaking countries, but still highly unusual.
Dora, Doura, Panndora, Pandorra, Pandoura

Pangiota Gk. "All is holy."

Pania Dim. **Stepania** (Gk. "Crowned"). The most familiar version of this name right now is **Stephanie**, which is hugely popular in the U.S.
Paniya, Panya

Panphila Gk. "All loving." A pleasant notion, though the name might require a lot of explanation.
Panfila, Panfyla, Panphyla

Pansy Flower name from the late 19th century: the name of the flower originally came from the French word for thought, *pensée*, possibly because the petals of the flower are thought to resemble wise little faces.
Pansey, Pansie

Panthea Gk. "All the gods." An early Middle Eastern queen was named Panthea, but the name is more familiar from its close relative "pantheon," which means a temple to all gods.
Pantheia, Pantheya, Panthia

Paquita Sp. Dim. **Frances** (Lat. "From France") via **Paco**.

Paradisa Gk. "Garden, orchard." Paradise is the ancient name of the home of the blessed. In the Old Testament "paradise" refers to the Garden of Eden, while in the New Testament it refers to heaven.

Paris Place name: the capital city of France. Also the name of a character in Greek myth who was Helen of Troy's lover, but most modern parents using this name are likely to be thinking of the French City of Light.
Parris, Parrish

Parker OE. "Park keeper." Occupational name turned last name, borrowed for a girl's first name. Rare, but possibly appealing to parents looking for a WASPy first name. Actress Parker Posey.

Parmenia Sp. "Intelligent, stuidous."
Parmenya, Permenia

Parrish OF. "Ecclesiastical locality." A parish is the area under the care of one pastor or priest. The name would originally have been a last name based on a place name. Used primarily for boys.
Parish

Parthenia Gk. "Virginal." Used most often at the turn of the 20th century, when the attributes of the virgin were particularly highly valued.
Partheenia, Parthenie, Parthinia, Pathina, Pathinia

Parthenope Name from Greek mythology: she was one of the Sirens, who threw herself into the sea when she failed to lure Odysseus to his death. Also the original name for the Italian city of Naples. Florence Nightingale's sister was named Parthenope.

Pascale (Fem. **Pascal**) Fr. "Easter." Despite some English-speaking use in the last 30 years, still primarily a French name.
Pascalotte, Pascaline, Pascalle, Pascha, Paschale, Pashelle, Pascua, Pascuala

Pat Dim. **Patricia**. Used as an independent name, but neglected with the recent leaning toward the nostalgic and elaborate.

Patches Occurs rarely as a family name. Scholars consider it a distant derivative of **Peter**.
Patch

Patience Virtue name. One of the more popular of the 16th century names, though eclipsed in the 20th century by **Hope**. Patience, after all, is not a very modern virtue.
Paciencia, Patient, Patienzia, Pazienza

Patricia (Fem. **Patrick**) Lat. "Noble, patrician." Obscure until it was used for one of Queen Victoria's granddaughters, which launched its enormous popularity for close to fifty years. It has now returned to near-neglect. In Spain, however, it is a favorite. Singers Patti LaBelle, Patsy Cline, Pat Benatar; choreographer Trisha Brown; actresses Patty Duke, Patricia Neal, Patricia Arquette; First Lady Pat Nixon; Congresswoman Pat Schroeder.

Pat, Patreece, Patreice, Patrica, Patrice, Patricka, Patrizia, Patsy, Patte, Pattee, Pattey, Patti, Pattie, Patty, Tricia, Trish, Trisha

Paula (Fem. **Paul**) Lat. "Small." Roman name that cropped up in English-speaking countries in this century and was rather well used in the Baby Boom era. Actress Paulette Godard; singer Paula Abdul.

Paola, Paolina, Paule, Pauletta, Paulette, Paulie, Paulina, Pauline, Paulita, Paulla, Paullette, Pauly, Pavia, Pavla, Pola, Polina, Pollie, Polly

Pauline (Fem. **Paul**) Fr. from Lat. "Small." Popular earlier than **Paula**, having peaked at the turn of the 20th century in the U.S. Model Paulina Porizkova.

Pauleen, Paulina, Polline, Paulyne

Paxton Lat./OE. "Peace town." A place name.

Paxten

Payne Lat. "Countryman." The Spanish word is *paisano*. the French word *paysan*. "Peasant" is probably the closest English cognate.

Paine

Paz Sp. "Peace."

Pazia Heb. "Golden."

Paza, Pazit

Peace ME. Word used as a name. Though not strictly a virtue name, this is the kind of abstract quality celebrated by the Puritans in their choice of names.

Peachy From the fruit. Very much a modern name, used perhaps to describe an infant's complexion or temperament.

Peach

Peale Unusual former last name. May refer to a landmark like a "peel tower," a stronghold common in Northern Britain, or may be related to the Latin word *pax,* which means "peace."

Peall, Pealle, Peele

Pearl Lat. "Pearl." Probably the most common of the jewel names, though of course it is not a gemstone. The Greek form, **Margaret**, is far more widespread and has been used for centuries, while Pearl only appeared in the late Victorian era. Writer Pearl S. Buck; singer Pearl Bailey.

Pearla, Pearle, Pearleen, Pearlette, Pearline, Perl, Perla, Perle, Perlette, Perley, Perline, Perlline

Peggy Dim. **Margaret** (Gk. "Pearl.") Used as an independent name since the 18th century, and parents who choose it today probably do so without thinking of Margaret. Its greatest vogue came in the first third of the 20th century. Skater Peggy Fleming; singer Peggy Lee; actress Peggy Lipton.

Peg, Pegeen, Pegg, Peggie

Pelagia Gk. "Ocean, sea."

Palasha, Pasha, Pelage, Pelageia, Pelageya, Pelagie, Pellagia

Pelia Heb. "Marvel of God."

Peliah

Penelope Gk. "Bobbin worker." The bobbin probably refers to part of the equipment for weaving, since the Penelope of Greek myth was the wife of Odysseus. To put off the many suitors who courted her when it seemed that the wandering Odysseus must be dead, she told them she couldn't marry until she finished the tapestry she was weaving. She would work all day and unravel her work at night, hoping that her husband would come home. The name was most popular in the middle of the 20th century, in Britain. Model Penelope Tree; parenting expert Penelope Leach; actresses Penelope Ann Miller, Penelope Cruz.

Pen, Penelopa, Penina, Penna, Pennelope, Penney, Pennie, Penny

Peninah Heb. "Pearl."

Pnina

Penny Dim. **Penelope** (Gk. "Bobbin worker"). Given as an independent name mostly in the 20th century.

Penee, Pennee, Penney, Pennie

Penthea Gk. "Fifth." Related to "Pentagon."

Peony Unusual flower name.

Pepita Sp. Dim. **Joseph** (Heb. "Jehovah increases") via Pepe.

Pepa, Peppie, Peppy, Peta

Pepper Plant name. Because of the spicy nature of its

namesake plant, children with spunky temperaments sometimes end up with Pepper as a nickname. Used very infrequently, for both boys and girls.

Perdita Lat. "Lost." Coined by Shakespeare, and rarely used since his day.

Perfecta Sp. "Perfect, flawless." A daunting name to give any child.

Peri Heb. "Outcome, result."

Pernella (Fem. **Peter**) Fr. from Gk. "Rock."
Parnella, Pernelle, Pernilla, Pernille

Perpetua Lat. "Forever, perpetual." Saint Perpetua, whose feast day is March 6, was one of the early Christian martyrs.

Perrin Fem. Var. **Peter** (Gk. "Rock") or **Peregrine** (Lat. "Voyager"). Names with "-in" or "-en" endings were quite fashionable in the late '90s.
Perran, Perren, Perrine, Perryn

Perry Fr. "Pear tree." Or Dim. **Peregrine** (Lat. "Voyager"). Originally a boy's name and common as a last name, but also used in America as a girl's name. The masculine names with "-y" or "-ie" endings (**Leslie**, for instance) seem more susceptible to feminine appropriation, which is irreversible. Author Perri Klass.
Perrey, Perri, Perrie

Persia Place name: the Middle Eastern country now known as Iran.

Persis Lat. "From Persia."
Perssis, Persys

Petaluma Place name: town in Northern California.

Petra (Fem. **Peter**) Gk. "Rock." The simplest feminization of a name that seems to resist being feminized: but not for want of trying, as the variants below demonstrate.
Pella, Pernilla, Pernille, Perrine, Pet, Peta, Peterina, Peternella, Petria, Petrina, Petrine, Petronela, Petronella, Petronelle, Petronia, Petronija, Petronilla, Petronille, Petrova, Petrovna, Piera, Pierette, Pierrette, Pietra

Petula Derivation unclear: may be a version of **Peter**, may come from a Latin word meaning "to seek." The name

might even be an adaptation of the flower name **Petunia**. Its use is based entirely on the fame of singer Petula Clark.
Petulah

Petunia Flower name, for the rather humble trumpet-shaped flower with white or bright pink blossoms.

Phaedra Gk. "Bright." In Greek mythology, the daughter of King Minos, who was married to the hero Theseus and fell in love with her stepson Hippolytus. When he spurned her advances, she committed suicide. One of those pretty Greek names with a not-so-pretty history.
Faydra, Phaedre, Phaidra, Phedra, Phèdre

Phemia Gk. "Language." **Euphemia**, while still rare, is the most common name containing this particle.
Femia, Femie, Phemie

Pheodora (Fem. **Theodore**) Rus. from Gk. "Gift of God."
Fedora, Feodora, Fyedora

Phila Gk. "Loving." This particle is the basis for many more common names.
Fila

Philadelphia Gk. "Loving people." The City of Brotherly Love was founded by Quakers with very high ideals: it was tradition among the Friends (as they were known) to name the eldest daughter in each family after the city. Possibly a little difficult to pull off in the 21st century.

Philana Gk. "Loving mankind."
Filania, Filanna, Phila, Philena, Philene, Philina, Philine, Phillane, Phillina

Philantha Gk. "Lover of flowers."
Filanthia, Philanthia, Philanthie

Philiberta OE. "Very brilliant." Feminine of **Filbert**, which is the unusual modern form of **Philibert**, an Anglo-Saxon saint's name.
Filberta, Filiberta, Philberta, Philberthe

Philippa (Fem. **Philip**) Gk. "Horse lover." Another unusual feminization, though it was used somewhat in the 19th century. Something of a curiosity today.
Felipa, Filipa, Filipina, Filippa, Flip, Pelipa, Pelippa, Phil, Philipa, Philippe, Philippine, Phillie, Phillipa, Phillipina, Philly, Pippa, Pippie, Pippie, Pippy

Philomela Gk. "Lover of song." In Greek mythology, Philomela is a princess who, after becoming entangled in a bloody and vengeful love triangle with her sister and brother-in-law, is turned into a nightingale, a bird renowned for its musical call.

Philomella

Philomena Gk. "Loved one." Name of a saint worshiped enthusiastically, especially in Italy, in the 19th and 20th centuries. However, her cult was based on nothing more than a set of bones discovered in Rome in 1802, which linked up very vaguely with a Roman inscription. It was assumed that she was a virgin martyr, and many miracles were attributed to Saint Philomena after a shrine was established to her. But in 1961, after archaeologists proved the bones in the shrine could not have been those of a young girl, her veneration was forbidden by Rome.

Filimena, Filomena, Filomene, Filumena, Philomène, Philomina

Philopena Fem. Var. **Philip** (Gk. "Lover of horses").

Felipina, Filipina, Filippina, Filippine, Philippina

Philothea Gk. "Lover of God." The elements are the same as in **Theophilus**, but reversed.

Filothea, Filotheya, Phillothea, Philotheia

Philyra Gk. "Lover of music."

Fillira, Phillira, Phillyra

Phoebe Gk. "Shining, brilliant." One of the epithets of Apollo, the sun god, was Phoebus Apollo, referring to the fact that he brought light. A Phoebe appears in the New Testament, but the name didn't gain ground until the 18th century. Reached a peak in the last part of the 19th century, now pleasantly old-fashioned and ripe for revival. Singers Phoebe Legere, Phoebe Snow.

Febe, Pheabe, Phebe, Pheby, Phoebey, Phoeboe

Phoenix Gk. "Red as blood." The name of the mythical bird that, after a long life, set itself aflame and arose recreated from its own ashes. A common symbol of renewal or immortality.

Feenix, Fenix, Phenice

Phyllida Var. **Phyllis** (Gk. "Leafy bough"). Rare name that appeared in the 16th century; mostly literary use. Actress Phyllida Law.

Fillida, Phillida, Phillyda

Phyllis Gk. "Leafy bough." Name of a mythological woman, taken up by generations of poets to stand for the idealized country lass. Parents applied it to babies increasingly through the 19th century, but it died out after the 1930s. Poet Phyllis McGinley; comedienne Phyllis Diller.

Filis, Fillis, Fillys, Fyllis, Philis, Phillis, Philys, Phylis, Phyllida, Phyllie, Phylliss, Phyllys

Pia Lat. "Pious." More common in Europe than in English-speaking countries. Singer/actress Pia Zadora.

Picabo Place name: small town in Idaho that gave its name to one of America's top female skiers, Picabo Street. She pronounces it "Peekaboo."

Piedad Sp. "Piety, devotion."

Pierette Fr. Dim. **Peter** (Gk. "Rock"). Quite a few of Peter's feminizations come from the Continental form **Pierre/Piero/Piers**.

Piera, Pierina, Pietra

Pilar Sp. "Pillar." An allusion to the Virgin Mary, in her role as a "pillar" of the Church. Used mostly by Spanish-speaking parents.

Pima Place name: county in Arizona.

Piper OE. Occupational name: "Pipe player." Transferred to last name, and occasionally used as a first name, probably inspired, however indirectly, by actress Piper Laurie.

Pippa Dim. **Philippa** (Gk. "Lover of horses"). Almost exclusively British use.

Pippy

Placidia Lat. "Calm, tranquil." From the word that gives us "placid." It seems a bit dangerous, however, to make predictions about a baby's temperament at birth.

Placida, Plasida

Pleasant Fr. "Agreeable to the senses." Unusual, but occurs now and then for men as well. Entrepreneur Pleasant Rowland.

Pleasance

Pléiade Gk. The group of stars called the "Seven Sisters." They are named after seven sisters in Greek mythology, the daughters of Atlas and Pleione.

Pocahontas Native American. "Playful." The real Pocahontas' given name was Matoaka: Pocahontas was a nickname. Pocahontas was the daughter of a Native American chief in Virginia, who is said to have rescued the English settler John Smith from hostile tribesmen. She married Englishman John Rolfe, and later visited England, where she became something of a celebrity.

Polly Var. **Molly**; Dim. **Mary** (Heb. "Bitter"). Independent name, used especially in the 19th century. Never as common as Molly, for no discernible reason. Actress Polly Bergen.
Poll, Pollee, Polley, Polli, Pollie

Pomona Lat. "Apple." The Roman goddess of fruit trees.

Poppy Lat. Flower name that reached its peak in the 1920s.

Porsha Possibly a phonetic variation of **Portia**, but more likely a feminization of Porsche, the glamorous German sports car.
Porscha

Portia Lat. Clan name, obscure meaning. The heroine of Shakespeare's *Merchant of Venice*, an enterprising woman who disguises herself as a lawyer to save her husband's life. In spite of this worthy prototype, the name is uncommon. Actress Portia de Rossi.

Prairie Geography name, for that unique American feature, miles of fertile rolling grassland.

Precious Lat. "Of great worth, expensive." Adjective used as name.

Priela Heb. "Fruit of God."
Priella

Prima Lat. "First."
Primalia, Primetta, Primina, Priminia

Primavera It. "Spring." Pretty name for a spring baby.

Primrose ME. "First rose." The primrose does not actually belong to the rose family, but it is one of the flowers that blooms early in spring. A 19th century flower name.
Primarosa, Primorosa, Primula

Princess Word as a name. Every little girl has the potential to live up to this name.
Princella, Princessa, Princesse, Principessa

Priscilla Lat. "Ancient." New Testament name and common in the early Christian era, then revived strongly by the Puritans. After generations of neglect, it was taken up in the 19th century, but has been scarce since the last half of the 20th century, possibly because the most natural nickname is "Prissy." Actress Priscilla Presley.
Cilla, Pris, Prisca, Priscella, Prisilla, Prissie, Prissy, Prysilla

Provence Place name: a picturesque area in southeastern France, brought special attention in the 1990s by Peter Mayle's books.

Prudence Lat. "Caution, discretion." Virtue name most common in the 19th century after its first popularity in the 16th and 17th centuries. Use now is mostly British.
Pru, Prudencia, Prudie, Prudy, Prue

Prunella Lat. "Small plum." Actress Prunella Scales.
Prunelle

Psyche Gk. "Breath" and, by extension, life or soul. In mythology, Psyche was a mortal girl whom Cupid loved. In post-Freudian times someone's psyche is his innermost soul or mind.

Purity ME. The word as name; a virtue name comparable to **Chastity**.
Pureza

Qiturah Arab. "Incense, scent." The name is more familiar in its Hebrew cognate form, **Keturah**.
Qeturah, Quetura, Queturah

Queen OE. "Queen."
Quanda, Queena, Queenette, Queenie

Quenby OE. Place name: "Queen's settlement."
Quenbie, Quinbie, Quinby

Querida Sp. "Dear, beloved."

Questa Fr. "One who seeks."

Quiana Possibly a variant of **Hannah**, but more often, a variation on **Ayanna**. A synthetic fabric very popular in the 1970s was called Qiana.

Qiana, Qianna, Quianna, Quiyanna

Quilla ME. "Feather." As in a quill pen.

Quylla

Quinn Ir. Gael. Meaning unknown. Very common Irish last name, occasionally transferred to first-name status, though less often for girls. Actress Quinn Cummings.

Quin

Quincey OF. Place name: "Estate of the fifth son." Last name of a prominent Massachusetts family whose name is borne by a town and by the 6th U.S. President, John Quincy Adams.

Quinci, Quincie, Quincy, Quinsy

Quintana Place name: Quintana Roo is a state on the east coast of Mexico.

Quintina Lat. "Fifth."

Quentina, Quintana, Quintessa, Quintona, Quintonette, Quintonice

Quirina Lat. "Warrior." In Roman mythology, Romulus (one of the founders of Rome) was deified as Quirino.

Rabab Arab. "Pale cloud."

Rabiah

Rabiah Arab. "Gentle wind."

Rachel Heb. "Ewe, female sheep." In the Old Testament Rachel is the wife of the patriarch Jacob. Like many Old Testament names, this one was taken up by the Puritans in the 17th century and remained current but not fashionable until parents of the late sixties and seventies used it in great numbers. Curiously enough, that usage didn't date the name, which was still very popular into the 1990s, reaching a peak of top-ten usage in the middle of the decade. It is now less of a favorite in the U.S. but extremely fashionable in Scotland and Ireland and, as **Raquel**, in Spain. The popularity of the TV show *Friends,* in which Jennifer Aniston played a character named Rachel, may have contributed to an American perception that the name is overexposed. Actresses Raquel Welch, Rachel Ward, Rachel Griffiths; author Rachel Carson.

Rachael, Racheal, Rachelce, Rachele, Racheli, Rachelle, Rachil, Rae, Raechell, Rahel, Rahil, Rakel, Raquel, Raquela, Raquella, Raquelle, Ray, Raychel, Raychelle, Rashell, Rashelle, Rechell, Shell, Shelley, Shellie, Shelly

Radha Sanskrit. "Success." In Hindu religion, the name of one of Krishna's consorts.

Radmilla Slavic. "Industrious for the people."

Radilla, Radinka, Radmila, Redmilla

Rae Dim. **Rachel** (Heb. "Ewe"). Used independently in modern times. Actress Rae Dawn Chong.

Raeann, Raelaine, Raeleen, Raelene, Ray, Raye, Rayette, Raylene, Raylina, Rayma, Rayna, Raynelle, Rayona

Rafa Arab. "Well-being, prosperity."

Rafah

Ragnild Teut. "All-knowing power."

Ragnhild, Ragnhilda, Ragnhilde, Ragnilda, Ranillda, Reinheld, Renilda, Renilde, Reynilda, Reynilde

Raina Var. **Regina** (Lat. "Queen") or Fem. **Ray** (OG. "Wise guardian"). Modern name of several possible origins, including allusion to the wet stuff that falls out of the sky. Like many names that have appeared in this century, it has numerous variations, none of which is clearly a favorite.

Raenah, Raene, Rainah, Raine, Rainey, Rainelle, Rainy, Raleine, Raya, Rayann, Rayette, Rayleine, Raylene, Raylina, Rayline, Rayna, Rayne, Rayney, Raynelle, Raynetta, Reyna, Reyney

Rainbow The phenomenon as a name. The rainbow, in Old Testament terms, is a symbol of the convenant between God and Noah, that God will sustain his people. Loosely, it is also seen as a symbol of hope and (more recently) of ethnic and gender-preference tolerance.

Raissa Yid. "Rose."

Raisa, Raisabel, Raisse, Raizel, Rayzel

Raja Arab. "Hope."

Raleigh OE. Place name: "Meadow of roe deer." Commemorates Sir Walter Raleigh, explorer and court favorite of Queen Elizabeth I, who is supposed to have spread his cape over a puddle so she could cross with dry feet. The city in North Carolina was named for him. Usually a name for boys, but the two-syllable "-leigh" form popularized by **Ashley** is prompting parents to look at many formerly masculine names as potential girls' names.

Raileigh, Railey, Raley, Rawleigh, Rawley

Ralphina Fem. **Ralph** (OE. "Wolf-counsel").

Ralphine

Rama Heb. "On high, exalted." The Hindu deity Vishnu (a kindly god in the pantheon) appears in two forms as Rama.

Ramona (Fem. **Raymond**) Sp. "Wise guardian." A 19th-century historical novel of the same title was immensely successful, and brought the name to wide attention, but it is scarce now. Character in a very popular series of children's books of the same name by Beverly Cleary.

Mona, Ramoena, Ramohna, Ramonda, Ramonde, Ramonna, Ramowna, Romona, Romonda, Romonde

Ramsay OE Place name: "Raven island" or "Ram island." Originally a last name common in Scotland, only rarely used as a first name for boys.

Ramsey

Randy Dim. **Miranda** (Lat. "Admirable"). Mostly U.S. use, and infrequent at that.

Randa, Randee, Randelle, Randene, Randi, Randie

Rana Arab. "Beautiful thing, eye-catching."

Rani Sanskrit. "Queen."
 Raine, Rana, Ranee, Rania, Ranice, Ranique, Ranit, Rayna, Raynell
Ranielle Modern name: Danielle with an "R."
Ranita Heb. "Song."
 Ranice, Ranit, Ranite, Ranith, Ranitra, Ranitta
Raoule Fem. **Raoul** (Fr. Var. **Ralph**, OE. "Wolf-counsel").
 Raoula, Raula
Raphaela (Fem. **Raphael**) Heb. "God heals." The feminization is very unusual in English-speaking countries, though Italian parents use it with some frequency. Author Raffaella Barker.
 Rafa, Rafaela, Rafaelia, Rafaella, Raffaela, Raffaele, Raffaella, Rafella, Rafelle, Raphaella, Raphaelle, Raphayella, Raphella, Refaella, Refella, Rephaela, Rephayelle
Rashida (Fem. **Rashid**) Turkish. "Righteous, rightly advised."
 Rasheda, Rasheeda, Rasheida, Rashidah, Rashyda
Raven Name of the large black bird that is closely related to the crow. A fanciful name for a black-haired or dark-skinned baby. Actress Raven Symone.
 Ravenne, Rayven, Rayvinn
Ravenna Place name: city in Italy renowned for its Byzantine mosaics. Does not actually have anything to do with ravens, despite the sound.
 Ravena, Ravinia, Ravinna
Rawnie Romany. "Lady." This is an English Gypsy term.
Raziah Aramaic. "The Lord's secret."
 Razi, Raziela, Raziella, Razili
Ray Variant spelling of **Rae**, thus Dim. **Rachel** (Heb. "Ewe"). This spelling may look a little more "masculine," but short names like this are out of style anyway.
 Raye, Rayla, Raylene
Reba Dim. **Rebecca**. Singer Reba McEntire.
 Reyba, Rheba
Rebecca Heb. "Joined." A prominent Old Testament name; Rebecca is the wife of Isaac and mother of Jacob and

Esau. Predictably, the name was taken up by the Puritans and remained fairly common through the 19th century. Subsequent revivals (in the thirties in the U.S., in the late sixties in Britain) may have been prompted by literary and cinematic use of the name, especially in the novel and film *Rebecca*. It is still used very steadily, as a familiar name in the currently fashionable three-syllable category. Very popular in Ireland. Philanthropist Rebekah Harkness; author Rebecca West; actress Rebecca De Mornay.

Becca, Becka, Beckee, Beckey, Beckie, Becky, Bekka, Bekki, Bekkie, Reba, Rebeca, Rebecka, Rebeka, Rebekah, Rebekkah, Rebeque, Ree, Reeba, Rheba, Revekka, Ribecca, Riva, Rivah, Rivalee, Reveka, Revekah, Rivekka, Rivi, Rivka, Rivkah, Rivy

Reed OE. "Red-haired." This is the most common spelling for masculine use of this name, which rarely crosses over to girls. The slightly less conventional spellings, however, may seem more feminine.

Read, Reade, Reid, Reida

Reese Var. **Rhys** (Welsh. "Fiery, zealous"). Actress Reese Witherspoon.

Reece

Regan Ir. Celt. "Son of the small ruler." Use for girls may hark back to Shakespeare's play *King Lear,* but the king's daughter of that name is so cruel that this seems unlikely. Where Regan occurs it is more likely to be a family name adapted to a girl's name.

Reghan

Regina Lat. "Queen." Cropped up at the end of the Victorian era, possibly encouraged by the fact that Her Majesty was often known as Victoria Regina. It may also be used as an allusion to the Virgin Mary, Regina Coelis ("Queen of the Heavens"). Nightclub founder Régine; track star Regina Jacobs.

Gina, Raina, Raina, Raine, Regan, Reggi, Reggie, Régine, Reginette, Reginia, Reginna, Reina, Reine, Reinetta, Reinette, Reyna, Rina, Riona, Rionagh

Reina Sp. "Queen." See also **Raina**, for other spellings.

Reinella, Reinelle, Reinette, Reyna, Reynelle

Rella Var. **Ella** (OG. "All, completely").

Remedios Sp. "Help, remedy." Currently popular in South America.

Remy Fr. "From Rheims." Champagne, and the fine brandies made from champagne, are the principal product of Rheims, a town in central France.
Remi, Remie, Remmy, Rhemy

Rena Heb. "Melody" or Dim. **Irene** (Gk. "Peace").
Reena, Rina

Renata Lat. "Reborn." The Latin (and less popular) form of **Renée**. It was used in this guise by the Puritans. Author Renata Adler.
Ranae, Ranay, Renae, Renate, René, Renée, Renelle, Renetta, Renette, Renie, Renisa, Renita, Renise, Rennae, Rennay, Rennie

Rene Dim. **Irene** (Gk. "Peace"). Used on its own, primarily around the turn of the 20th century.
Reney, Renie, Rennie

Renée Fr. "Reborn." The French form of **Renata**, more common (though not really widespread) in modern times. Tennis star Renee Richards; actresses Renee Russo, Renée Zellwegger.
Ranae, Ranay, Ranée, Renae, René, Renell, Renelle, Renie, Rennie, Renny, Rhinaye, Rrenae

Renita Lat. "Resistant." Has come into use since the 1980s.
Reneeta, Renyta

Reseda Latin term for a flower more commonly known as mignonette.

Reta Var. **Rita**; Dim. **Margaret** (Gk. "Pearl").
Reda, Reeda, Reeta, Rheta, Rhetta

Rexana It is possible to translate this name by its parts, *rex* being Latin for "king," and *anna* a variant of the Hebrew word for "grace." Or it may be a feminization of **Rex**, or a variant of **Roxane**.
Rexanne, Rexanna, Rexalla, Rexella, Rexetta, Rexina, Rexine

Reza Hung. Dim. **Teresa** (Gk. "Harvest").
Rezi, Rezka, Riza

Rhea Gk. "Earth." In Greek mythology, Rhea was an

earth-mother who bore Zeus, Demeter, Hera, and Poseidon, among other gods. Actress Rhea Perlman.
Rea, Rhia, Ria

Rheta Gk. "A speaker, eloquent." From the same root as the word "rhetoric."

Rhiannon Welsh. "Witch, goddess."
Rhianna, Rhianon, Rianon, Riannon

Rhoda Gk. "Rose"; Lat. "From Rhodes." Rhodes is a Greek island originally named for its roses. The name is found in the New Testament, and was used mostly in the 18th and 19th centuries.
Rhodeia, Rhodia, Rhodie, Rhody, Roda, Rodi, Rodie, Rodina

Rhodanthe Gk. "Rose blossom."
Rhodante

Rhona ONorse. "Rough island." A form of **Rona** more common in Britain.
Rhona, Roana

Rhonda Welsh place name: The Rhondda Valley is a significant landmark in southern Wales, named for the river that runs through it. (In Welsh, the name means "noisy.") The most likely cultural association in the U.S. is with the Beach Boys's song, "Help Me, Rhonda!"
Rhonnda, Ronda

Ria Dim. **Victoria** (Lat. "Victor"). Used occasionally as an independent name.
Rea

Riane (Fem. **Ryan**) Ir. Last name. Uncommon, but analogous to the more widely used **Briana**.
Rhiane, Rhianna, Riana, Rianna, Rianne, Ryann, Ryanne

Rica Familiar form of **Erica** (Scand. "Ruler forever") or **Frederica** (OG. "Peaceful ruler") or possibly Sp. "Rich."
Rhica, Ricca, Ricki, Rickie, Ricky, Rieca, Riecka, Rieka, Riki, Rikki, Riqua, Rycca

Ricarda (Fem. **Richard**) OG. "Powerful ruler." One of many feminine forms of a very popular man's name, none of which has been adopted in large numbers.

Richanda, Richarda, Richardella, Richardene, Richard-ette, Richardina, Richardyne, Richel, Richela, Richele, Richella, Richelle, Richenda, Richenza, Richette, Richia, Richilene, Richina, Richmal, Richmalle

Rickie Dim. **Frederica** (OG. "Peaceful ruler"). Also possibly a feminine version of Richard, and certainly more popular than the longer forms. Occurred most often in the middle of the 20th century. Singer Rickie Lee Jones; actress Ricki Lake.

Rickie, Ricki, Ricky, Ricquie, Rika, Riki, Rikki, Rikky, Ryckie

Rihana Arab. Plant name: "Basil."

Riley Ir. Gael. "Courageous." Irish last name used as a first name for the last 150 years. Occasionally occurs as a girl's name.

Reilley, Reilly, Ryley

Rilla Middle German. "Small brook."

Rella, Rilletta, Rillette

Rima Arab. "Antelope."

Rimona Heb. "Pomegranate."

Riona Ir. Gael. "Like a queen."

Rionach, Rionagh, Rionna, Rionnagh

Risa Lat. "Laughter." A pretty name, but very unusual in English-speaking countries. Opera singer Rise Stevens.

Riesa, Rise, Rysa

Rita Dim. **Margaret** (Gk. "Pearl"). Comes via the Spanish form, **Margarita**. First used on its own some hundred years ago, and quite popular for 50 years. Actresses Rita Hayworth, Rita Moreno; authors Rita Mae Brown, Rita Dove.

Reeta, Reita, Rheeta, Rida, Riet, Rieta, Ritta

Ritsa Gk. Dim. **Alexander** (Gk. "Man's defender").

Riva Var. **Rebecca** (Heb. "Joined"). Also possibly from the French for "shore," but the Jewish families who use it most often probably have the Old Testament associations in mind.

Reba, Ree, Reeva, Reevabel, Reva, Rifka, Rivalee, Rivi, Rivka, Rivke, Rivkah, Rivy

Roanna Var. **Rosanne.**
Ranna, Roanne, Ronni, Ronnie, Ronny

Roberta (Fem. **Robert**) OE. "Bright fame." While **Ricarda**, another simple feminization of an Old German name, never caught on, Roberta was rather widespread between its introduction in the late 19th century and its fall from favor some eighty years later. The name's similarity to the familiar **Alberta** probably promoted its acceptability. Singers Roberta Peters, Roberta Flack.
Berta, Bertie, Berty, Bobbe, Bobbee, Bobbette, Bobbie, Bobby, Bobbye, Bobette, Bobi, Bobina, Bobine, Bobinette, Reberta, Roba, Robbee, Robbey, Robbi, Robbie, Robby, Robeena, Robella, Robelle, Robena, Robenia, Robertena, Robertene, Robertha, Robertina, Robetta, Robette, Robettina, Robin, Robina, Robinett, Robinette, Robinia, Robyn, Robyna, Robynna, Ruperta, Rupetta

Robin Dim. **Robert** (OE. "Bright fame"). Originally a boy's nickname (as in Winnie the Pooh's friend Christopher Robin), but appropriated for girls in increasing numbers starting in the middle of the 20th century. Now out of fashion for both sexes. Actresses Robin Givens, Robin Wright Penn.
Robee, Robbey, Robbi, Robbie, Robbin, Robby, Robbyn, Robena, Robene, Robenia, Robi, Robina, Robine, Robinet, Robinett, Robinette, Robinia, Robyn, Robyna, Robynette

Rochelle Fr. Place name: "Little rock." Enthusiastically used as a first name starting in the 1940s, but rare now.
Roch, Rochell, Rochella, Rochette, Roschella, Roschelle, Roshelle, Shell, Shelley, Shelly

Roderica (Fem. **Roderick**) OG. "Renowned ruler."
Rica, Roddie, Roderiga, Roderiqua, Roderique, Rodriga

Rohana Sanskrit. "Sandalwood."
Rohanna

Rolanda (Fem. **Roland**) OG. "Famous land."
Orlanda, Orlande, Rolande, Rollande

Roline Dim. **Caroline** (OG. "Man"). Unusual diminutive that appears from time to time in the South. It may also be a feminization of **Roland**.

Roelene, Roeline, Rolene, Rollene, Rolleen, Rollina, Rolline, Rolyne

Roma It. Place name: the capital city, Rome. Rather widely used since it first appeared in the late 19th century, though of course, it never approached the popularity of **Florence**. Actress Roma Downey.

Romelle, Romilda, Romina, Romma

Romaine (Fem. **Romain**) Fr. "From Rome." A pretty name that might be associated with a common variety of lettuce. **Romane** is popular in France at the moment.

Romane, Romayne, Romeine, Romene

Romola Lat. "Roman woman." Actress Romola Garai.

Romala, Romella, Romelle, Rommola, Romolla, Romula

Romney Old Welsh. Place name: "Winding river."

Romy Dim. **Rosemary** (Lat. "Dew of the sea") or related to **Roma**. Actress Romy Schneider.

Rona ONorse. "Rough island." In Britain, used interchangeably with **Rhona**. Both versions cropped up at the turn of the century and have occurred steadily without ever being fashionable. Gossip columnist Rona Barrett.

Rhona, Ronella, Ronelle, Ronna

Ronni (Fem. **Ronald**) OE. "Strong counsel" or Dim. **Veronica** (Lat. "Image").

Ronalda, Ronee, Ronette, Roni, Ronna, Ronnee, Ronnelle, Ronnella, Ronney, Ronnie, Ronny

Rosabel Comb. form **Rose** and **Belle**. A combination that appeared in the mid 19th century. Its meaning ("beautiful rose") probably appealed as much to parents of the era as the name itself, which lost favor in the unsentimental 20th century. If **Isabel** becomes more popular, though, Rosabel may seem more appealing.

Rosabella, Rosabelle

Rosae Modern name: Rose with the innovative "-ae" ending. Also sounds like rosé wine: this spelling guarantees the right pronunciation.

Rosai, Rosay, Rose, Rosee, Rosey

Rosalba Lat. "White rose." Artist Rosalba Carriera.

Rosalie Fr. Var. It. **Rosalia**. Possibly "rose garden." Mostly 19th-century use.

Rosalee, Rosaleen, Rosaley, Rosalia, Rosalina, Rosaline, Rosalyne, Roselia, Rosella, Roselle, Rozalia, Rozalie, Rozele, Rozelie, Rozely, Rozella, Rozelle, Rozellia

Rosalind Sp. "Pretty rose" is the most common interpretation, though the name was actually coined in 16th-century Britain. A German form also existed, formed of words that meant "horse" or "renown" and "shield" or "snake." It has been used since the mid-19th century, with a surge in the middle of the 20th century. Today's parents considering the name may be haunted by the memory of Rosalynn Carter, a worthy but not exactly glamorous personage. Actress Rosalind Russell.

Ros, Rosalen, Rosalin, Rosalina, Rosalinda, Rosalinde, Rosaline, Rosalinn, Rosalyn, Rosalynd, Rosalynda, Rosanie, Roselin, Roselina, Roselind, Roselinda, Roselinde, Roseline, Roselinn, Roselyn, Roselynda, Roselynde, Rosina, Roslyn, Roslynn, Roslynne, Roz, Rozali, Rozalia, Rozalin, Rozalind, Rozalinda, Rozalynn, Rozalynne, Rozelin, Rozelind, Rozelinda, Rozelyn, Rozelynda

Rosalyn Comb. form. **Rose** and **Lynn** (Sp. "Pretty"). The most common of the modern variants of **Rosalind**. First Lady Rosalynn Carter.

Rosalin, Rosalynn, Roselynn, Roslyn, Rozlynn

Rosamond OG. "Renowned protector." Also translatable (from the Latin) as "rose of the world." More popular in the 19th century than it is today. Author Rosamond Bernier; actress Rosamund Pike.

Ros, Rosamonde, Rosamund, Rosamunda, Rosemond, Rosemonda, Rosmund, Rosmunda, Roz, Rozamond

Rose Lat. Flower name. Scholars actually trace the name (which the Normans imported to Britain in the 11th century) to an Old German name meaning something like "renown," but the flower meaning has had much more currency, particularly given the Christian symbolic meaning of the rose. (The "rosa mystica" is the Virgin Mary.) It reached its peak use at the turn of the 20th century, along with other flower names. An elaboration, **Rosario**, is currently popular in Spain. Actress Rosario Dawson; talk-show host Rosie O'Donnell.

Rasia, Rasine, Rasja, Rasya, Rhoda, Rhodea, Rhodia, Rhody, Rosa, Rosaleen, Rosalia, Rosalie, Rosalin, Rosalina, Rosalind, Rosaline, Rosalinn, Rosalynn, Rosanie, Roselia, Roselina, Roseline, Rosella, Roselle, Rosena, Rosenah, Rosene, Rosetta, Rosette, Rosey, Rosheen, Rosie, Rosina, Rosita, Roslyn, Rosy, Roza, Rozalie, Rozaline, Rozalyne, Roze, Rozele, Rozella, Rozene, Rozina, Rozsa, Rozsi, Rozsika, Rozy, Ruza, Ruzena, Ruzenka, Ruzha, Ruzsa, Zita

Roseanne Comb. form. **Rose** and **Anne**. The pairing of the two names appeared in the 18th century, and various forms have drifted in and out of popularity. In our era, the name will inevitably summon associations with outspoken actress Roseanne Barr. Actress Rosanna Arquette.

Ranna, Roanna, Roanne, Rosanagh, Rosanna, Rosannah, Rosanne, Roseann, Roseanna, Rosehannah, Rozanna, Rozanne, Rozeanna

Rosemary Lat. "Dew of the sea" is the correct meaning, though the name gained great currency with the flower name fad of the late 19th century. The fact that most parents read it as a combination of **Rose** and **Mary** (both already popular, and with strong religious resonance for Catholics) can't have hurt. Singer Rosemary Clooney.

Rosemaree, Rosemarey, Rosemaria, Rosemarie, Rosmarie, Rozmary, Romy

Ross Scot. Gael. "Headland." A place name in Scotland. The name (like so many of the "R" names) may also come from the Gaelic word for "red."

Rosse

Rowena Welsh. "Slender and fair." This meaning is an approximation. The name was actually brought to public notice by novelist Sir Walter Scott with his immensely popular *Ivanhoe*, in the early 19th century.

Roweena, Roweina, Rowina

Roxanne Per. "Dawn." In history, the wife of Alexander the Great was named Roxane, but 20th-century parents may be more familiar with the Roxane who is the heroine of Rostand's play *Cyrano de Bergerac,* or the character played by Daryl Hannah in Ron Howard's film adaptation.

Oksana, Oksanna, Roksanne, Roxana, Roxane, Roxann, Roxanna, Roxene, Roxey, Roxiane, Roxianne, Roxie, Roxine, Roxy, Roxyanna, Ruksana, Ruksane, Ruksanna

Royale OF. "Regal one." Something of a curiosity in the democratic United States.

Royalla, Royalene, Royalina, Royall, Royalle, Royalyn, Royalynne

Royce Meaning and origin unclear: Some sources offer OF./OE. "Son of the king"; others suggest OG. "Kind fame." The most famous Royce is the man who, along with Mr. Rolls, began turning out England's foremost luxury car. Very scanty use for girls.

Roice

Rubena Fem. Reuben. Heb. "Behold, a son."

Reubena, Reubina, Rubina, Rubine

Ruby Jewel name. Launched in the 1870s with other jewel names, but passé by the mid-20th century. Dancer Ruby Keeler.

Rubee, Rubetta, Rubey, Rubi, Rubia, Rubie, Rubina, Rubinia, Rubyna

Rudelle OG. "Renowned." From the same root that produces the male name **Rudolph**.

Rudella

Rufina Lat. "Red haired." Can be considered a feminine version of **Rufus**, which is given to boys regardless of their hair color.

Rufeena, Rufeine, Ruffina, Ruphyna

Ruta Lith. "Rue." The name of a plant.

Ruth Heb. "Friend, companion." The Old Testament Book of Ruth is about the widowed Moabite woman who refuses to leave her Hebrew mother-in-law, Naomi, and says, "Whither thou goest, I will go." Her sentiments appealed greatly to Victorian poets. The name has been consistently used ever since the 17th century, peaking at the turn of the century. Actresses Ruth Gordon, Ruth Buzzi; author Ruth Rendell.

Ruthe, Ruthelle, Ruthetta, Ruthi, Ruthie, Ruthina, Ruthine

Ruthann Comb. form. **Ruth** and **Ann**.

Ruthanna, Ruthanne

Ryan Irish last name. Meaning is unclear, though some sources connect it with "king." It has been very popular as a boy's name in recent years (well into the top 20 names on some lists) and is beginning to cross over as a girl's name. Actress Ryan Haddon.

Rian, Ryen, Ryenne

Saba Gk. "From Sheba"; Arab. "Morning." The queen of Sheba is mentioned in the Old Testament as having been hugely rich and very ostentatious.

Sabah, Sheba, Shebah

Sabina Lat. "Sabine." The Sabines were a tribe living in central Italy around the time Romulus and Remus established the city of Rome. In an effort to provide wives for the citizens of Rome, Romulus arranged the mass kidnapping of the Sabine women, which came to be known (and frequently portrayed in art and literature) as the "Rape of the Sabines." The name was used among the ancient Romans and in English-speaking countries after the 17th century, but has been very rare lately.

Bina, Byna, Sabine, Sabinna, Sabiny, Sabyna, Sahbina, Savina, Savine, Sebina, Sebinah

Sabra Origin disputed: may be Heb. "To rest," or possibly "Cactus." Is now used as a term for a native-born Israeli.

Sabrah, Sebra, Sabrette

Sabrina Lat. Place name: the Latin term for the Severn River in England. Though Milton (among others) writes about a Sabrina, she appeared most vividly in modern culture as *Sabrina Fair* in the play and movie. The name was used in the 19th century and cropped up again in the last part of the 20th century. Though it resembles many currently popular names it may not be familiar enough to most parents to seem an appealing choice.
Brina, Sabreena, Sabrinna, Sabryna, Sebreena, Sebrina, Zabrina

Sachi Jap. "Child of joy."
Sachiko

Sadie Dim. **Sarah** (Heb. "Princess"). Use as an independent name occurred mostly at the turn of the 20th century. The trend toward folksy old-fashioned names may turn parents toward Sadie, though it is not as typically feminine as blockbusters like **Amanda** and **Jessica**. Actress Sada Thompson.
Sada, Sadah, Sadelle, Saida, Saidee, Saidey, Saidie, Saydie, Sydell, Sydella, Sydelle

Sadira Pers. "Lotus tree." The lotus has great significance in several of the Eastern religions.

Saffron Flower name: Saffron refers to a substance (the dried stamens of saffron crocuses) used as a spice in Mediterranean and other Southern cuisines. It produces a bright orange-yellow color, and is sometimes used as a dye. Monks of some Eastern religions wear saffron robes, which may explain why the name was used occasionally in the 1960s, an era when saffron robes and Eastern religions went mainstream. This usage was mocked in the comic TV series *Absolutely Fabulous*. Actress Saffron Aldridge.
Saffran, Saffren, Saffronia, Saphron

Sagara Indo-Pakistani. "The sea."

Sage Lat. "Wise, healthy." More likely to be a boy's name, perhaps via associations with sagebrush, cowboys, and the Wild West. Highly unusual, but this is the kind of allusive, genderless name that was popular in the 1990s.
Saige, Sayge

Sahara Arabic. "Desert." Place name: desert in North Africa. The Sahara is the legendary desert, exceedingly inhospitable to mankind.
Saharra

Sakura Jap. "Cherry blossom."

Salena Var. **Selina** (Gk. "Moon goddess").
Salina

Salama Arab. "Peace." Related to **Solomon**, which is Hebrew for "peace" or "peaceful." Also related to **Salome**, but without the racy connotations. Actress Salma Hayek.
Sallama, Salma, Saloma, Soloma

Salamanca Place name: city in Western Spain, seat of an ancient university. It has been occupied by Hannibal, the Goths, the Moors, the French, and the English.

Salimah Arab. "Healthy, sound." Currently popular in Arabic countries. This was the name adopted by one of the English wives of the current Aga Khan when she married him; appropriate, since her English name was Sally.
Salima, Selima

Sally Dim. **Sarah** (Heb. "Princess"). A popular independent name in the 18th century and again in the 20th. Although Sarah has been hugely popular for more than ten years, this nickname is barely used at all as a given name. Talk-show host Sally Jessy Raphael; actress Sally Field; astronaut Sally K. Ride.
Sal, Salcia, Saletta, Sallee, Salletta, Sallette, Salley, Sallianne, Sallie, Sallyann

Salome Heb. "Peace." Possibly from the same root that gives us the greeting "Shalom." The most famous biblical Salome is the woman who danced for King Herod and demanded, as her reward, the head of John the Baptist on a platter. In spite of this unsavory antecedent, the name was used somewhat in the 19th century, but its connotations make it an unlikely choice.
Sahlma, Salima, Salma, Salmah, Saloma, Salomea, Salomey, Salomi, Selima, Selma, Selmah, Solome, Solomea

Salvadora Sp. "Savior." Referring, of course, to Jesus Christ.

Salvia Lat. "Whole, healthy." The Latin name for the herb known as sage, which has mild healing powers as well as being an aromatic used in cooking.
Sallvia, Salvina

Samala Heb. "Requested of God."
Samale, Sammala

Samantha (Fem. **Samuel**) Heb. "Told by God." Also contains the Greek form "-antha," which means flower. Occasionally used in the 17th-19th centuries, but truly popular in the 1960s and 1970s, possibly triggered by the TV series *Bewitched*. Unlike many names that were current a scant thirty years ago, Samantha is also popular now, having been a top-ten choice for the last decade. Actress Samantha Eggar.
Sam, Samey, Sami, Samentha, Sammantha, Sammee, Sammey, Sammie, Semantha, Semanntha, Simantha, Symantha

Samara Heb. "Under God's rule."
Samaria, Samarie, Sammara, Semara

Samuela (Fem. **Samuel**) Heb. "Told by God." Very scarce, particularly compared with Samantha.
Samella, Samelle, Samuella, Samuelle

Sancia Lat. "Sacred."
Sancha, Sanchia, Santsia, Sanzia

Sandra Dim. **Alexandra** (Gk. "Defender of mankind") via It. **Alessandra**. Popular in the middle of the 20th century, but today's parents are more inclined to prefer the full four syllables of the original name. Comedienne Sandra Bernhard; actresses Sandrine Bonnaire, Sondra Locke, Sandra Dee, Sandra Bullock; Supreme Court Justice Sandra Day O'Connor.
Sahndra, Sanda, Sandee, Sandie, Sandreea, Sandrella, Sandrelle, Sandretta, Sandrette, Sandria, Sandrina, Sandrine, Sandy, Sanndra, Sanndria, Sauhndra, Saundra, Sohndra, Sondra, Sonndra, Wysandria, Zandra

Sandy Dim. **Sandra**. Mostly used post-1950.
Sandee, Sandi, Sandie, Sanndi

Sanna Dim. **Susanna** (Heb. "Lily"). Used as an independent name in Scandinavia.
Sana, Zanna

Santana Sp. "Holy." May remind prospective parents more of a rock band that was famous in the '60 and '70.
Santa

Santuzza It. "Holy." This is a diminutive form.

Sapphire Heb. Jewel name. Unusual biblical name, and the birthstone for September. One of the least used of the jewel names.
Safira, Saphira, Sapphira, Sephira

Sarah Heb. "Princess." In the Old Testament, the wife of the patriarch Abraham. Came into vogue with other biblical names in the 16th century and was enough of a staple for 400 years to have spawned a variety of nicknames (though not as many as the multisyllabic **Elizabeth**, for instance). Sarah was the fourth most popular girls' name in the 1990s and is still in the top ten. It is also very well used in Ireland and Scotland, though not as popular in England. As **Sara**, it's fashionable in Germany. Actresses Sarah Bernhardt, Sarah Siddons, Sarah Jessica Parker, Sarah Michelle Gellar; singer Sarah Vaughan; poet Sara Teasdale; Sarah Ferguson, Duchess of York; figure skater Sarah Hughes.
Sadee, Sadella, Sadelle, Sadellia, Sadie, Sadye, Saidee, Sal, Sallee, Salley, Sallie, Sally, Sara, Sarai, Saraia, Sareen, Sarely, Sarena, Sarette, Sari, Sarika, Sarina, Sarine, Sarita, Saritia, Sarka, Sarolta, Sarotta, Sarotte, Saroya, Sarra, Sarrah, Sasa, Sera, Serach, Serah, Serita, Shara, Sorcha, Sydel, Sydelle, Zahra, Zara, Zarah, Zaria, Zarita

Sardinia Place name: mountainous island off the west coast of Italy. Sardines probably take their name from this island.
Sardegna

Saril Turkish. "Noise of flowing water."

Sasha Rus. Fem. and Dim. **Alexander** (Gk. "Man's defender"). The "-sha" ending is not necessarily feminine

NICE NORMAL NAMES

Not all celebrities choose unusual names. Some of them seem to be swayed by the very same winds of fashion as the rest of us. For the children below, it's not their first names that are going to attract attention—it's the last names of their very famous parents:

- Annette Bening & Warren Beatty: Kathlyn, Benjamin
- Isabelle Adjani & Daniel Day-Lewis: Gabriel
- Marlee Matlin: Sarah
- Jamie Lee Curtis & Christopher Guest: Annie, Thomas
- Kevin Costner: Annie, Joseph
- Vanna White: Nicholas
- Natasha Richardson & Liam Neeson: Michael, Daniel
- Katie Couric: Caroline, Elinor
- Dorothea & Jon Bon Jovi: Jacob
- Bradley Whitford & Jane Kaczmarek: Mary
- Cynthia Nixon & Danny Mozes: Charles
- Sarah Jessica Parker & Matthew Broderick: James

Rob Lowe and Sheryl Berkoff, as well as Michelle Pfeiffer and David Kelley, should get extra "common sense" points for naming sons the old standby, John.

in Russia, and Sasha is more commonly a male nickname there. In the U.S., though, it is considered a girl's name. **Sacha, Sasa, Sascha, Saschenka, Zsazsa**

Saskia Dutch name of unknown meaning. It would probably have been forgotten, but it was the name of Rembrandt's wife, who is depicted in some of his finest canvases. Actress Saskia Reeves.

Sato Jap. "Sugar."

Savannah Sp. "Treeless." Originally familiar as a place

name, as in the city in Georgia, or name of a geographical feature: a wide, treeless plain. But its pretty sound and fashionable 3-syllable, "-a" ending form have made it increasingly fashionable among sophisticated parents. With the current trend acceptance of geography names, this popularity will probably continue.

Savana, Savanna, Sevanna

Scarlett ME. "Scarlet." Given its fame by the inimitable Scarlett O'Hara, heroine of *Gone With the Wind*. Not hugely popular, possibly because the young lady in the novel is so headstrong. She probably came by the name from the family tree, but it does carry connotations of "the scarlet woman," a lady of easy virtue. It is nevertheless the middle name of one of Mick Jagger's children with Jerry Hall.

Scarlet, Scarletta, Scarlette

Scirocco It. from Arab. "Warm wind." The word originally described the wind that blew over Italy from the Libyan deserts.

Cirocco, Sirocco

Scotia Latin term for Scotland. Before the Irish invaded the country in 258 A.D., it was known as Caledonia.

Scout OF. "To listen." Occupational name: someone who scouts, gathers information quietly. When Bruce Willis and Demi Moore named their daughter Scout after a character in *To Kill a Mockingbird*, they gave the name a new credibility.

Scoutt

Season Lat. "Time of sowing." The word used as a name. Cropped up in the 1970s (along with **Spring** and **Summer**), when children were given counterculture names, but seems unlikely to endure. Actress Season Hubley.

Sedona Place name: city in Arizona much cherished for its natural beauty and tranquil ambiance.

Sadona, Sedonah, Sedonia

Seema Heb. "Precious thing, treasure."

Cima, Cyma, Seemah, Sima, Simah, Sina

Sebastiane (Fem. **Sebastian**) Lat. "From Sebastia." Unusual feminization of a name that is very infrequent in America.

Bastia, Bastiana, Sebastiana, Sebastienne

Secunda Lat. "Second."

Sefarina Sp. from Gk. "Gentle wind." This is the Spanish form of **Zephyr.**

Sefirina, Sepharina, Zefarina, Zepharina, Zephirina

Segovia Place name: province and city in central Spain. The name is most familiar to Americans through the fame of guitar player Andrés Segovia.

Selby OE. Place name. "Manor village."

Selbea, Selbee, Selbeigh, Selbey, Selbie

Selena Gk. "Moon goddess." Most popular in the 19th century, though the immense fame of the late Tejana pop star of this name may promote its use.

Celene, Celie, Celina, Celinda, Celine, Cellina, Celyna, Saleena, Salena, Salina, Sela, Selene, Selia, Selie, Selina, Selinda, Seline, Sena

Selima Heb. "Tranquil." Another version of **Salome.**

Saleema, Saleemah, Selimah

Selma (Fem. **Anselm** by way of **Anselma**) OG. "Godly helmet." Selma is the more common form, though it is far from an everyday choice. Actress Selma Blair.

Anselma, Sellma, Selmah, Zelma

Semele Gk. In Greek mythology, the mother of Dionysus by Zeus. Her name may come from the name of a very early Greek earth goddess. English composer G.F. Handel composed a secular oratorio about her.

Samelle, Semelle

Semiramis Heb. "Highest heaven." Semiramis was an Assyrian queen who, myth has it, built Babylon and turned into a dove after death. Her legend inspired both Voltaire and Rossini.

Semira

Senalda Sp. "A sign."

Seneca Name with both Native American and ancient Roman resonance. The Seneca tribe of Iroquis lived in the Finger Lakes region of Western New York state and gave their name to a lake, a river, and a town. Entirely coincidentally, Seneca was also the name of an important Roman philosopher and tragedian, who was the emperor Nero's tutor.

Senecca, Seneka, Senneca

Senga Var. **Agnes** (Gk. "Pure"). A rare Scottish name; it is **Agnes** spelled backward.

September Month name. Much less common than **April, May,** or **June**.

Septima Lat. "Seventh." If one has a seventh child, why not celebrate with her name?

Sequoia Tree name. The great sequoia is an ancient and immense tree native to northern California. The tree was named for a Cherokee Indian of the early 19th century who invented a system for writing down the Cherokee language.

Sacoya, Secoya, Saquoia, Saquoya, Sequoya

Seraphina Heb. "Ardent." The seraphim are the highest-ranking angels in Heaven (above angels, archangels, cherubim, etc.). They have six wings and are noted for their zealous love.

Sarafina, Serafina, Serafine, Seraphe, Seraphine, Serofina, Serophine

Serena Lat. "Tranquil, serene." Used by Roman Christians, and periodically popular since, though never in a big way. Tennis player Serena Williams.

Cerena, Reena, Sarina, Saryna, Serene, Serenna, Serina, Serenity, Seryna

Serilda OG. "Armed warrior woman."

Sarilda, Serhilda, Serhilde, Serrilda

Sesame The seed and flavoring agent.

Sesamey, Sessame, Sessamee

Sesheta Name from Egyptian mythology: Sesheta was the goddess of the stars and the patroness of writing and literature.

Sevilla Sp. Var. **Sibyl** (Gk. "Seer, oracle"). Also the name of an ancient Spanish city, home of painter Diego Velazquez and the setting of Bizet's famous opera *Carmen*.

Shadow OE. "Shade."

Shadoe

Shandy Derivation unknown. Name of a drink popular in Britain, half beer and half lemonade or ginger ale. Possibly adapted as a girl's name because it sounds so much like the familiar **Sandy** and **Mandy**.

Shandea, Shandee, Shandeigh, Shandey, Shandie

Shaina Heb. "Beautiful."

Shaine, Shana, Shanee, Shani, Shanie, Shayna, Shayne

Shaka Modern name: "Sha-," like "La-," is a very fashionable prefix, attached to any number of other particles to form names that have no specific meaning but sound attractive.

Shakeela, Shakeita, Shakeera, Shakette, Shakila, Shakina, Shakira, Shakitra, Shaquina, Shaquita

Shalimar Name of a Guerlain perfume, which in turn was named for the famous Shalimar Gardens, 80 acres of gardens near what is now Lahore, Pakistan. The gardens were laid out by Shah Jahan, who also had the Taj Mahal built.

Shalamar, Shalemar, Shallimar

Shalom Heb. "Peace." Not a name but a greeting to speakers of Hebrew. Nevertheless adapted by some parents for its meaning. Model Shalom Harlow.

Shalome, Shalva, Shalvah, Shelom, Shilom, Sholome

Shamira Heb. "He who defends."

Shamirah, Shameera, Shemira

Shana Dim. **Shannon**, or anglicization of **Shaina**, or diminutive of **Shoshana**. Uncommon, but kept in the public eye by journalist and biographer Shana Alexander. Singer Shania Twain.

Shanah, Shania, Shanna, Shannah

Shaneika Modern U.S. Another elaboration of the popular "Sha-" prefix. Some of the more common of these names are the ones that sound like **Ashanti**, the name of an area in Western Africa that was the original home of many American slaves. Other "Sha-" names, like the "La-" names, are limited in form only by parental imagination.

Shandee, Shandeigh, Shandey, Shandeya, Shanecka, Shaneese, Shaneikah, Shanequa, Shaneyka, Shaniece, Shanika, Shanique, Shanisse, Shanneice, Shanta,

Shantee, Shanteigh, Shantella, Shantelle, Shantey, Sheniece, Shenika, Sheniqua, Shonyce

Shanelle Modern U.S. name which is a phonetic spelling of "Chanel," the name of the great French couturier. It has double-barreled appeal, since it combines the "Sha-" prefix with an evocation of great feminine elegance.

Shanel, Shanella, Shanelly, Shannel, Shaney, Shanilly, Shanisse, Shanita, Shenell, Shenelle, Shinella, Shonelle, Shynelle

Shani Heb. "Scarlet." Refers to a metaphorical "scarlet thread" or theme of a story.

Shanit

Shannon Ir. Gael. "Old, ancient." The name of an important river, county, and airport in Ireland, used as a first name in this century. Most popular among families with Irish roots, but little found in Ireland. Actresses Shannen Doherty, Shannyn Sossamon; gymnast Shannon Miller.·

Channa, Shana, Shandy, Shane, Shani, Shanna, Shannae, Shannen, Shannin, Shanon

Shantal Var. **Chantal** (Fr. place name). Its popularity may be associated with both Shanelle and the other "Sha-" names, rather than with the rather obscure French first name.

Shanta, Shantahl, Shantay, Shantalle, Shante, Shantella, Shantelle, Shontal, Shontalle, Shontelle

Sharlene (Fem and Dim. **Charles**) OG. "Man." Var. **Caroline**. One of the numerous variations that were popular in the 1950s and 1960s.

Sharleen, Sharleyne, Sharlina, Sharline, Sharlyne

Sharon Heb. Place name: "A plain." In the Old Testament, refers to flat land at the foot of Mount Carmel. Not picked up by the 16th-century Puritans, probably since it wasn't a personal name, but by mid 20th century it was quite popular in America. Now much less common. Actresses Sharon Gless, Sharon Stone.

Charin, Cheron, Shara, Sharan, Sharen, Sharene, Shari, Sharie, Sharla, Sharolyn, Sharona, Sharonda, Sharren, Sharrin, Sharronne, Sheran, Sheron, Sherri, Sherry, Sheryn, Sherynn

Shashi Hindi. "Moonbeam."

Shasta Oregon mountain of some 14,000 feet that rises from nearly sea level. It is at the southernmost end of the Cascade Mountain range. Also the name of a brand of soda, though parents using this name are more likely to be evoking America's natural beauty.
Shahsta, Shastah

Shavonne Phonetic var. **Siobhan** (Ir. Gael. Var. **Joan**; Fem. **John**). Heb. "The Lord is gracious."
Shevon, Shevonne, Shivonne, Shyvon, Shyvonne

Shawn (Fem. Var. **Sean**; Ir. Var. **John**) Heb. "The Lord is gracious." Use of Sean and its variants peaked in the 1970s, but they are still used quite substantially for boys. Girls with this name are a rarity. Actress Sean Young.
Sean, Seana, Seanna, Shana, Shanna, Shaun, Shauna, Shaunee, Shaunie, Shawna, Shawnee, Shawneen, Shawnette, Sianna

Shawnee Name of a Native American tribe that originated in the eastern forests of the U.S. and gradually migrated westward. Shawnee Mission is the name of a town in Kansas. Also, possibly, a variant of **Shawn**.
Shawney, Shawnie

Shayla Var. **Sheila** (Ir. From Lat., "Blind") or Dim. **Michaela** (Fem. **Michael**, Heb. "Who is like the Lord?").
Shaela, Shae-Lynn, Shaila, Shailagh, Shaylah

Shayna Var. **Shaina** (Heb. "Beautiful").
Shaina, Sheina

Shea Ir. Gael. "From the fairy fort." More commonly an Irish last name. Basketball player Shea Ralph.
Shae, Shay, Shaye, Shayla, Shaylyn

Sheba Heb. "From Sheba." Also a short version of **Bathsheba** (Heb. "Daughter of the oath"). The queen of Sheba is mentioned in the Old Testament as having been hugely rich and very ostentatious.
Saba, Sabah, Scheba, Shebah, Sheeba, Shieba

Sheena Ir. Var. **Jane** (Heb. "The Lord is gracious"). Many of the "Sh" names are Gaelic versions of **Jane, Jean**, and **Joan**, which are in turn variations on that old staple, **John**. Rock star Sheena Easton.

Sheenagh, Sheenah, Sheina, Shena, Shiona, Shionagh, Sina, Sine

Sheherezade Arab. "Dweller in cities." Sheherezade was the famous teller of tales, married to a sultan who had resolved to marry a woman a day and strangle her at dawn. For 1001 nights, Sheherezade told him stories with cliffhanger endings and each dawn he let her live so that she could finish the tale that evening. Finally he relented, and gave up his resolve to kill her.

Scheherezade, Sharazad, Sharizad

Sheila Ir. Var. **Cecilia** (Lat. "Blind"). Popular mid-20th century in Britain and the Commonwealth; in Australian slang, a "sheila" is a woman.

Seila, Selia, Shayla, Shaylah, Sheela, Sheelagh, Sheelah, Sheilagh, Sheilah, Shela, Shelagh, Shelia, Shiela

Shelby OE. Place name: "Estate on the ledge." Used to occur infrequently as a man's name, but it has recently been taken up by parents, reaching into the top 40 U.S. girls' names by 1991. Use since then has tapered off.

Sholbea, Shelbee, Shelbeigh, Shelbey, Shelbie, Shellby

Shell Several possible sources: diminutive for **Michelle** or **Shelley**, or use of the object as a name.

Choll, Chella, Chelle, Shella, Shelle

Shelley OE. Place name: "Meadow on the ledge." Last name made famous by the poet Percy Bysshe Shelley. Use as a feminine first name seems to have been related to **Shirley**. Actresses Shelley Winters, Shelley Duvall, Shelley Long.

Schelley, Shellee, Shellie, Shelly

Shera Aramaic. "Brightness."

Sheridan Ir. Gael. Unclear meaning, possibly "wild man." Used mostly in Britain as a male name, but the "Sher-" element sounds enough like **Cheryl** or **Sharon** to make use for girls possible.

Sheredon, Sheridan, Sheridawn, Sheriden, Sheridon, Sherridan, Sherriden, Sherrydan

Sherrerd Unknown origin. Possibly related to **Sheridan**. Familiar-sounding enough, owing to the "Sher-" component, to be used occasionally as a girl's name. There is no definitive spelling.

Sherard, Sherrard, Sherrod

Sherry Var. **Cher** (Fr. "Dear"), **Sharon** (Heb. "The plain"), or **Cheryl** (Var. **Charlotte**, OG. "Man"). In the 1950s and 1960s these three names and their variants were all popular, giving rise to a parade of further forms, spellings, and elaborations. Tracing the exact origin of any of them is difficult. Puppeteer Shari Lewis.

Cheray, Sharee, Shari, Sharie, Sharrie, Sherae, Sheraie, Sheray, Sheree, Sherey, Sheri, Sherice, Shericia, Sherie, Sherina, Sherissa, Sherita, Sherree, Sherrey, Sherri, Sherryn, Sherye, Sh'rae

Sheryl Var. **Cheryl** (Var. **Charlotte**, OG. "Man"). Actress Sherilyn Fenn; singer Sheryl Crow; basketball player Sheryl Swoopes.

Cheralin, Cheralyn, Cheralynne, Cherilynn, Sheralyn, Sheralin, Sherileen, Sherill, Sherilyn, Sherilynne, Sherrell, Sherrill, Sherryl, Sheryll

Shiloh Biblical place name. Also the name of a Civil War battle in Tennessee.

Shilo, Shylo

Shifra Heb. "Lovely."

Schifra, Shifrah

Shiri Heb. "My song."

Shira, Shirah, Shirit

Shirley OE. Place name: "Bright meadow." Originally a last name, brought to immense fame and popularity as a girl's name with the career of child star Shirley Temple. Now widely neglected. At the moment, almost any name with an "-ley" ending is considered suitable for girls. The popularity of first Shirley, then **Ashley** and **Kelly**, paved the way for this fashion. Actress Shirley MacLaine; politician Shirley Chisholm; novelist Shirley Hazzard.

Sherlee, Sherli, Sherlie, Sherrlie, Sheryl, Shirely, Shirl, Shirlea, Shirlee, Shirleen, Shirleigh, Shirlene, Shirlinda, Shirline, Shirlley, Shirly, Shirlyn, Shurlee

Shona Ir. Gael. Var. **John**. While **Sinead** is a Gaelic form of **Janet**, Shona is the equivalent form of **Joan**.

Shonagh, Shonah, Shone, Shuna, Shunagh

Shoshana Heb. "Lily." The more common form is the anglicized **Susan** or **Susanna**. Fashion designer Shoshana Lonstein.

Shosha, Shoshanah, Sosanna, Sosannah

Shoshone Native American tribe, indigenous to eastern Nevada, southern Idaho, and western Utah. These nomads were also known as the Snake Indians. Sacajawea, Lewis and Clark's guide on their Western explorations, was a Shoshone.

Shoshoni

Shulamith Heb. "Peace." Composer Shulamit Ran; writer Shulamith Firestone.

Shula, Shulamit, Sula, Sulamith

Shura Rus. Dim. **Alexander** (Gk. "Man's defender"). Used in Russia as a nickname for a man.

Shurka

Sian Welsh Var. **John** (Heb. "The Lord is gracious"). Actress Sian Phillips.

Sibyl Gk. "Seer, oracle." In ancient myth, sibyls interpreted the messages from oracles devoted to particular Gods, but their legend was also taken up and Christianized, and the name was common in the Middle Ages. Use dropped off and was revived at the turn of the 20th century, but the name now has a slightly dated aura. Actress Cybill Shepherd.

Cybele, Cybil, Cybill, Cybilla, Sabilla, Sabylla, Sib, Sibbell, Sibel, Sibell, Sibella, Sibelle, Sibilla, Sibyll, Sibylla, Sybel, Sybella, Sybelle, Sybill, Sybilla, Sybille

Sicily Place name: large island off the tip of Italy's "boot." Many Italian immigrants to the United States have roots in Sicily.

Sicilia, Sicillia, Sicilly

Sidney OE. "From St. Denis." Famous English last name turned first name in the 18th century, very fashionable in the late 19th century, now little used for boys but beginning to be fashionable for girls in the **Kelly/Ashley** mold.

Siddeny, Sideny, Sidneigh, Sidni, Sidnie

Sidonie Lat. "From Sidonia." Sidon was an area in the Middle East. Not uncommon in France, but easily confused with **Sidney** in the U.S.

Sidaine, Sidonia, Sidony, Sydona, Sydonah, Sydonia, Syndonia

Sidra Lat. "Of the stars."

Siena Place name: town in Tuscany not far from Florence, home of many art treasures. The town gave its name to a reddish shade of brown.

Sienna

Sierra Place name. Sierra is Spanish for "saw," and was the name Spanish settlers gave to the sharp, irregular peaks of some of the Western mountains like the Sierra Nevada (literally, "snowy saw"). Now used from time to time as a proper name, along with other geographical features like **Savannah** and **Mesa**.

Ciera, Cierra, Siera

Sigfreda OG. "Peaceful victory."

Sigfreida, Sigfrida, Sigfrieda, Sigfryda

Sigismonda It. from OG. "Victorious shield."

Sigismunda, Sigmonda, Sigmunda

Signa Unknown Scandinavian meaning: "Victory" is a possibility. The name is very unusual.

Signe, Signild, Signilda, Signilde, Signy

Sigourney Origin unclear, and made familiar almost single-handedly by actress Sigourney Weaver, who was christened **Susan**.

Sigornee, Sigournie

Sigrid ONorse. "Fair victory." Little used outside of Scandinavian countries. Novelist Sigrid Undset.

Sigred

Silence Puritan virtue name. No longer considered a virtue.

Silken Modern name, adapted from the fabric. Rower Silken Laumann.

Silkie, Silkya

Silja Scand. Dim. **Cecilia** (Lat. "Blind").

   Silia, Silija, Siliya, Sillia, Sillija, Silliya, Silya

Silver Name of the precious metal. Could describe a baby's pale coloring, perhaps.

   Silverey, Silverie

Silvia Var. **Sylvia** (Lat. "From the woods"). This was the original form of the name, eclipsed by the "-y-" spelling in the 19th century.

   Silva, Silvana, Silvanna, Silvie, Silvija, Sirvana, Sirvanna, Silvy, Silvya, Sylvia, Sylvie

Simcha Heb. "Joy."

Simla Place name: hill town in northern India where, in the days of the Raj, the British spent the hot summers.

Simone (Fem. **Simon**) Heb. "Listening intently." Used outside of France from the middle of the 20th century. Actress Simone Signoret; writer Simone de Beauvoir; gymnast Simona Amanar.

   Shimona, Shimonah, Simeona, Simmina, Simona, Simonetta, Simonette, Simonia, Simonina, Simonna, Simonne, Symona, Symone

Sinead Ir. Var. **Janet** (Fem. **John**, Heb. "The Lord is gracious"). This name and **Siobhan** are a little more common than most Gaelic names, possibly influenced by actresses Sinead Cusack and Siobhan McKenna. **Sheena** is a short version of Sinead. Singer Sinead O'Connor.

   Shinead, Seonaid, Sina, Sine

Siobhan Ir. Var. **Joan** (Fem. **John**, Heb. "The Lord is gracious"). Many of the phonetic forms of this name are probably intended as a combination of the "Sha-" prefix and **Yvonne**. Actress Siobhan McKenna.

   Chavonne, Chevonne, Chivon, Chyvonne, Shavaun, Shavon, Shervan, Shevon, Shevonne, Shirvaun, Shivahn, Shivaun, Shovonne, Shyvonne, Sh'vonne, Sioban, Siobahn, Siobhian, Syvonne

Sintra Place name: town in Portugal. Because it sounds so much like **Cynthia**, Sintra has more plausibility as a first name than some place names.

   Cintra

Sirena Gk. "Entangler." In Greek mythology, sirens were creatures that were half-woman, half-bird. They sang so sweetly that men dropped everything to listen, and starved to death. Odysseus outwitted them in his travels. Easily confused with **Serena**, which has very different connotations.
Sireena, Sirene, Syrena

Siria Sp. from Persian. "Sun-bright, glowing." Sirius, the Dog Star, is the brightest star in the heavens.
Seeria, Syria

Sissy Dim. **Cecilia** (Lat. "Blind"). Also a common nickname for a sister, since this is the way a younger sibling may say that word. Actress Sissy Spacek.
Cissee, Cissey, Cissi, Cissie, Cissy, Sissee, Sissey, Sissie

Sitka Place name: city in western Alaska. It is the second oldest city in Alaska, having been founded as a fur-trading post by Russians in 1799.

Sivney Ir. Gael. "Well-going." Rare Irish last name.
Sivneigh, Sivnie

Skye Scot. Place name: the name of a spectacular island off the west coast of Scotland. With the current trend toward nature and geography names, it may also refer to the big blue bowl overhead.
Skie, Sky

Skyler Dutch. "Giving shelter." Most probably an adaptation of the Dutch last name of **Schuyler**, which was brought to New York by 17th-century settlers. Used a bit for both boys and girls now, possibly prompted by the 1990s fondness for **Kyle/Kyla**.
Schyler, Schuyler, Skyla, Skylar, Skyllar

Sloane Ir. Gael. "Man of arms." An Irish last name that has become well entrenched in Britain and the U.S. Sometimes makes the leap to first-name status, perhaps as a maternal maiden name. Given extra prominence by the fact that Britain's preppy cousins are known as "Sloane Rangers," for the area in London where they congregate.
Sloan

Snowdrop Flower name. The snowdrop, a modest white flower, blooms very early in the spring.

Socorro Sp. "Aid, help." Currently well used in Spain. Most likely refers to the aid or help provided by the Almighty.

Secorra, Socaria, Socorra, Sucorra

Soki Possibly var. **Sukey**; Dim. **Susan** (Heb. "Lily").

Sokey, Sukie

Solana Sp. "Sunlight."

Solenne, Solina, Soline, Souline, Soulle

Solange Fr. "With dignity." A classic name in France.

Souline, Zeline

Soledad Sp. "Solitude."

Soleil Fr. "Sun." Actress Soleil Moon Frye.

Solveig Scand. "Woman of the house."

Solvag, Solvej

Soma Indo-Pakistani. "Moon."

Somers Probably short for an Old English place name having to do with summer, like "Somerset."

Sommer, Sommers

Sondra Var. **Sandra** (Dim. **Alexandra**, Gk. "Defender of mankind"). Actress Sondra Locke.

Saundra, Sohndra, Sonndra, Zohndra, Zondra

Sonia Var. **Sophia** (Gk. "Wisdom"). Used since early in the 20th century. The current Queen of Norway is named Sonja. Skater/actress Sonja Henie; painter Sonia Delaunay.

Sohnia, Sohnnja, Sondja, Sondya, Sonja, Sonje, Sonnja, Sonya

Sonoma Place name: an extremely picturesque county in Nothern California.

Senoma, Sonohma

Sonora Place name: state in northwestern Mexico.

Sophia Gk. "Wisdom." Used in English-speaking countries since the 17th century, though the French form, **Sophie**, has given it much competition in Britain. The famous Istanbul mosque Hagia Sofia was once a Christian church, but it was dedicated, not to Saint Sophia (an obscure and possibly nonexistent martyr), but to the Holy

Wisdom, i.e., the Word of God. The name is becoming increasingly fashionable, both in the U.S. and in Europe. It is in the top ten names in England and Scotland (as **Sophie**) and Germany (Sophia), and in the top twenty in Ireland (Sophie). Actresses Sophia Loren, Sophie Dahl.

Saffi, Sofia, Sofie, Soficita, Sofka, Sofy, Sofya, Sonia, Sonja, Sonnie, Sonya, Sophey, Sophie, Sophy, Zofia, Zofi, Zofya, Zosia

Sophronia Gk. "Sensible, prudent."

Soffrona, Sofronia

Soraya Persian name of unknown meaning, brought to prominence by the last Empress of Iran.

Sorcha Ir. Gael. "Bright, shining." Used almost exclusively in Ireland. Actress Sorcha Cusack.

Sorrel Botanical name. Sorrel is a wild herb. Much less common than **Laurel** or **Rosemary**, but the herb itself is delicate and not widely found.

Sorel, Sorelle, Sorrell, Sorrelle

Soubrette Dramatic term: the traditional part of a coquettish ladies' maid in 18th and 19th century plays.

Spencer ME. Occupational name: "Provider." Used for the person in a large household who dispensed food and drink. Usually a last name, but occurs as a first name, more commonly in Britain.

Spenser

Speranza It. "Hope."

Esperance, Esperanza, Speranca

Spring OE. "Springtime." Use as a given name dates from (and is almost exclusive to) the 1970s.

Stacy Gk. "Resurrection." Dim. **Anastasia**. Most popular since the 1970s, and has long since outstripped its source. It was substantially popular for a while, but has dropped out of the top 100 U.S. names.

Stace, Stacee, Stacey, Staci, Stacia, Stacie, Stasa, Stasee, Stasey, Stasia, Stasie, Stasey, Stasha, Staska, Stasy, Staycee, Staycey, Staysie, Staysy, Tacy, Taisie

Star Word as name. Translations, such as **Stella** (Greek) and **Esther** (Persian), are far more common.

Starla, Starlene, Starletta, Starlette, Starr

Starling Bird name. The starling is a fairly common bird with drab plumage, so the name's appeal may reside in its resemblance to the word "star."

Stella Lat. "Star." Use was mostly literary until the 19th century, when the name became fashionable. For a generation of parents brought up on classic movies, it is hard to dissociate from Marlon Brando bellowing "Stella!" in *A Streetcar Named Desire.*

Estelle, Estella, Estrella, Stela, Stelle

Stephanie (Fem. **Stephen**) Gk. "Crowned." Cropped up in the 1920s and current since then. Use peaked in the top ten in the 1990s, and has since dwindled. Tennis star Steffi Graff; actresses Stefanie Powers, Stephanie Zimbalist; poet Stevie Smith.

Fania, Fanya, Phanie, Phanya, Stefa, Stefania, Stefanie, Stefenney, Stefcia, Steffa, Steffaney, Steffanie, Steffenie, Steffie, Stefinney, Stefka, Stefya, Stepa, Stepania, Stepanida, Stepanyda, Stepahnie, Stepfanie, Stepha, Stephana, Stephania, Stephanina, Stephanino, Stephannie, Stephene, Stepheney, Stephine, Stephney, Stephoney, Stesha, Steshka, Stevana, Stevena, Stevie, Stevey, Stevonna, Stevonne

Stetson Probably Old English surname meaning "Stephen's son." Extremely unusual, and more likely to be used for boys, though it has a certain rakish air for girls, probably conveyed by the associations of the famous Stetson "ten-gallon" hat, worn by cowboys in the late 19th century.

Stetcyn, Stettson

Stina Dim. **Christina** (Gk. "Anointed, Christian").

Stine

Stockard Probably an Old English place name referring to a tree stump (the "stock-" particle). Used as a first name and brought to public attention by actress Stockard Channing, whose given first name, like Sigourney Weaver's, was **Susan**.

Storm OE. Use of the word as a name: may be a last name transferred. The adjective "stormy" is occasionally used to describe temperament.

Stormee, Stormie, Stormy

Sukey Dim. **Susan** (Heb. "Lily"). Appeared in the 18th century and revived in the 20th, following the popularity of Susan itself.

Soki, Sokie, Sukee, Sukie, Suky

Summer OE. Name of the season. Like **Spring** and **Season**, a phenomenon of the 1970s. Swimmer Summer Sanders.

Somer, Sommers, Summers

Sunny Eng. Word as name: most likely to be a nickname characterizing a child's temperament.

Sunnee, Sunnie, Sunshine

Surya Hindi. Name of the sun god. Figure skater Surya Bonaly.

Susan Heb. "Lily." After 18th-century use, neglected until a huge surge of popularity made it a top choice in the middle years of the 20th century, thus a name to overlook in the 21st. The huge range of variations attest to the popularity of this name throughout Europe and the United States. Suffragette Susan B. Anthony; authors Susan Cheever, Susan Isaacs; actresses Susan Hampshire, Susan Dey, Susan Sarandon; basketball player Sue Bird.

Sanna, Shoshana, Shoshanah, Shoshanna, Shushana, Shu Shu, Sioux, Siouxsie, Siusan, Soosan, Soosanna, Sosanna, Suanny, Sue, Suesann, Suesonne, Suezanne, Sukee, Sukey, Sukie, Sonel, Sunel, Susana, Susanetta, Susanka, Susann, Susanna, Susannagh, Susannah, Susanne, Suse, Susee, Susette, Susi, Susie, Susy, Suzan, Suzana, Suzane, Suzanna, Suzanne, Suze, Suzee, Suzetta, Suzette, Suzie, Suzon, Suzy, Suzzanne, Zanna, Zanne, Zannie

Susannah Heb. "Lily." The original version of the name, and ripe for revival, combining as it does the nostalgic and the unusual (like **Molly** and **Emma**). Actress Susannah York.

Sanna, Sannah, Shoshanna, Shanna, Shu Shu, Suesanna, Susana, Susanna, Susannagh, Suzanna, Zanna, Zannie

Suzanne Fr. Var. **Susan**. It has more or less followed Susan into and out of fashion. Ballerina Suzanne Farrell; actresses Suzanne Pleshette, Suzanne Sommers.

Suesana, Susanna, Susanne, Suzane, Suzannah, Suzette, Suzzanne, Zanne, Zannie

Svetlana Rus. Meaning unclear, though some sources suggest "Star." The name is currently very popular in Russia. Author Svetlana Stalin.

Svetlanna, Svjetlana, Swetlana

Swanhild Saxon. "Battle swan."

Swanild, Swanilda, Swanilde, Swanhilda, Swanhilde, Swannie, Swanny

Sybil Var. Sibyl. The most common spelling of the name, though it only became prevalent in the last century. Actress Cybill Shepherd.

Cybele, Cybill, Sibell, Sibilla, Sibyl, Sibylla, Sybel, Sybella, Sybelle, Sybill, Sybilla

Sydney OF. Place name: "Saint Denis." Originally Saint Denis would have been the name of a village, and the name Sydney would have indicated a resident there. The name used to be almost exclusively male, but was given prominence as a woman's name in the 1980s by madam/celebrity Sydney Biddle Barrows. Though many of today's parents like flowery old-fashioned names, there is also a strong trend toward formerly male names like this one, which is steadily climbing popularity charts. The alternate spelling, **Sidney**, is less common but also increasingly fashionable.

Cydney, Cydnie, Sidnee, Sidney, Sidnie, Sydel, Sydelle, Sydnie

Sylvia Lat. "From the forest." The Latin form, **Silvia**, predominated for centuries, but when the name was at its most popular (from the 19th century into the 1940s), Sylvia was the spelling of choice. Poet Sylvia Plath; actress Silvana Mangano.

Silva, Silvaine, Silvana, Silvania, Silvanna, Silvia, Silviana, Silvianne, Silvie, Sylva, Sylvana, Sylvanna, Sylvee, Sylvette, Sylviana, Sylvianne, Sylvie, Sylvine, Sylwia, Zilvia, Zylvia

Tabina Arab. "Muhammad's follower."

Tabitha Aramaic. "Gazelle." New Testament name reintroduced in the 17th century passion for biblical names. Neglected in this century until a minor revival in the 1960s. Possibly too unfamiliar to gain much from the current old-name trend, but its Old New England aura may make it appealing to some parents. Journalist Tabitha Soren.

Tabatha, Tabbee, Tabbey, Tabbi, Tabbie, Tabbitha, Tabby, Tabatha, Tabetha, Tabita, Tabotha, Tabytha

Tacita Lat. "Silence." Never a standard, but somewhat more common in eras when a woman's role was to be quiet.

Tace, Tacey, Tacia, Tacie, Tacye

Taffy Welsh. "Loved one."

Tahira Arab. "Virginal, pure."

Tahnee Name of actress Tahnee Welch, Raquel Welch's daughter. The name may be a variant spelling of **Tawny**.

Taima Native American. "Peal of thunder."

Taimah, Taoimah

Taisie Meaning and origin uncertain: possibly **Maisie** spelled with a "T," or a variation of **Tacey**. May even be a derivation of **Stacey**, with the initial "S" left off. Another possibility is a shortening of the Russian **Taisiya**, derived from the Greek **Thaïs**.

Tayzie

Taisiya Russian. Meaning uncertain: possibly "Bond," or an adaptation of **Thaïs**, which itself is an old name of uncertain meaning.

Taisia, Taisie, Tasia, Tasiya, Tasya, Taya

Talbot Meaning unknown. An aristocratic last name in England, used as a first name since the 19th century. The women's clothing store Talbots sells very conservative, preppy apparel.

Talbert, Talbott, Tallbot, Tallbot

Talia Heb. "Heaven's dew." May also be a variant of **Thalia**, or a derivative of **Natalie**. A pretty name, but infrequently used. Actress Talia Shire.

Talicia Modern name: **Alicia** with an initial "T" added. Ballet superstars Peter Martins and Darci Kistler used this name for their first child.

Tal, Tali, Talie, Talija, Talley, Tallia, Tallie, Tally, Tallya, Talora, Talya

Taliesin Welsh. "Shining brow." Also the name of a Welsh bard of the 6th century, who is mentioned in Tennyson's *Idylls of the King*. More famous in the U.S. as the name of architect Frank Lloyd Wright's houses in Wisconsin and Arizona.

Taliessin, Talliesin

Talise NAm. Ind. "Lovely water."

Talitha Aramaic. "Young girl." Actress Talitha Soto.

Taleetha, Taletha, Talicia, Talisha, Talita

Tallulah Choctaw Indian. "Leaping water." Not, as one might expect, an invented name, nor even one assumed by its most famous bearer, actress Tallulah Bankhead. It was a Bankhead family name, and is also a place name in Georgia. Could not now be used without reference to the actress, however.

Talley, Tallie, Tallula, Tally, Talula

Tally Dim. **Talia** (Heb. "Heaven's dew") or creative respelling of **Sally**.

Tallee, Talley, Tallie

Talma Heb. "Hillock, mound."

Talmah, Talmit

Tamara Heb. "Palm tree." Old Testament name with a hint of the picturesque. **Tamar** was the more common version until this century, when Tamara, the Russian form, overtook it. Quite fashionable in the 1970s. Skiing champion Tamara McKinney; author Tama Janowitz.

Tama, Tamar, Tamarah, Tamarra, Tamary, Tamera, Tamma, Tammara, Tammi, Tammy, Tamora, Tamra, Tamrah, Thamar, Thamara, Thamarra, Thamera

Tamika Modern U.S. name of unknown origin. Some sources suggest a Japanese root meaning "people," but this seems farfetched since the name is not used in the Japanese community. More likely to be a variant of the popular **Tanisha**. Basketball player Tamika Catchings.

Tameka, Tameeka, Tameika, Tamiecka, Tamieka, Tamike, Tamiko, Taminique, Tamiqua, Temeequa, Temika, Timeeka, Tomika, Tonica, Tonique, Tymmeeka, Tymmiecka

Tammy Dim. **Tamara** (or other "Tam-" names). A nickname that took on a life of its own in the 1950s and 1960s, and was probably used without much interest in its source or meaning. Now out of fashion. Actress Tammy Grimes; singer Tammy Wynette; evangelist Tammy Faye Bakker.

Tami, Tamie, Tammee, Tammey, Tammie

Tamsin Var. **Thomasina** (Heb. "Twin"). Very old name that was revived by British parents in the middle of the 20th century, but did not spread widely to the U.S.

Tamasin, Tamasine, Tamsine, Tamsinne, Tamsyn, Tamzen, Tamzin

Tandy Origin unclear: probably a modern name created by substituting "T" for the initial letter "S" or "M" of **Sandy** or **Mandy**. Parents seeking novelty often switch initial letters on an old favorite, and for some reason the initial "T" is especially popular as in **Taryn** (probably from **Karen**) and **Tally** (a variant of **Sally**). Actress Thandie Newton.

Tandee, Tandie, Thandee, Thandey, Thandie, Thandy

Tanga Modern name, possibly a combination of the informal **Kanga** and the sultry Latin dance, the tango.

Tangela Modern name: **Angela** (Gk. "Angel") with an initial "T."

Tanjela, Tanjella, Tanngela

Tanisha Modern name of unclear meaning, though several sources propose an African origin. Its popularity may stem from a contemporary fondness for 3-syllable names ending in "-a." And while the "Ta-" prefix doesn't approach the popularity of "La-" or "Sha-," the similarity of sound probably contributes to Tanisha's widespread use. This is probably a combination of "Ta-" and the much-favored **Aisha**.

Taneesha, Taniesha, Tanitia, Tannicia, Tanniece, Tannisha, Teinicia, Teneesha, Tinecia, Tiniesha, Tynisha

Tansy Gk. "Everlasting life." Also the name of a fairly unusual herb. Used mostly since the 1960s, by parents whose acquaintance with herbs goes beyond the supermarket shelf.

Tanazia, Tandie, Tandy, Tansee, Tansey, Tansia, Tanzey, Tanzia

Tanya Dim. **Tatiana**, an ancient Italian name. This diminutive has been more popular than the full name, especially in the 1970s. Notorious figure skater Tonya Harding has probably given the name bad connotations for years to come. Photographer Tana Hoban; country singer Tanya Tucker.

Tana, Tanazia, Tahnee, Tahnya, Taneea, Tania, Tanita, Tanja, Tarnya, Tawnya, Tonnya, Tonya, Tonyah

Tara Ir. Gael. "Rocky hill." Though Irish legends mention a place called Tara, its real prominence came in the 1940s when most Americans knew that Scarlett O'Hara's plantation home was called Tara. This seems to have launched the use of the name, which is now quite steadily used. Actress Tara Reid.

Tarah, Tarra, Tarrah

Tarleton OE. "Thor's settlement." Margaret Mitchell fans will remember the Tarleton twins, admirers of Scarlett O'Hara, in the early pages of *Gone With the Wind*. This name is unusual even for boys.

Tarlton

Taryn Var. **Tara**, or respelling of a group of names that was popular in the 1950s and '60s, **Karen, Sharon**, and **Darren**.

Taran, Tarin, Tarina, Tarnia, Tarren, Tarryn, Taryna, Teryn

Tasha Dim. **Natasha** (Rus. "Christmas"). Author Tasha Tudor.

Tahsha, Tashey, Tashina, Tasia, Tasenka, Taska, Tasya

Tasmine Possibly a variant of **Tamsin**, or the highly popular **Jasmine** with a new initial consonant.

Tasmeen, Tasmeena, Tasmin, Tasmina, Tasmyne

Tate ME. "Happy, cheerful."

Tait, Taitt, Tayte

Tatiana Rus. Var. of an ancient Italian name. Has penetrated the U.S. somewhat in recent years; Caroline Kennedy Schlossberg named her second daughter Tatiana. Opera star Tatiana Troyannos.

Tania, Tanya, Tati, Tatianna, Tatie, Tatijana, Tatiyana, Tatjana, Tatyana, Tatyanna, Tonya

Tatum Possibly ME. "Light-hearted." Made famous by actress Tatum O'Neal, but not generally used.

Tawny OE. "Golden brown." A descriptive name first used in the mid-twentieth century.

Tahnee, Taney, Tauney, Tawnee, Tawney, Tawni, Tawnie

Taylor ME. Occupational name: "Tailor." The "last name as first name" trend brought Taylor streaking into the nation's top ten names for girls during the mid-nineties, but it has since begun to fade almost as fast as it became popular.

Tahlor, Tailor, Tayler

Tea Var. **Thea** (Gk. "Goddess"). Or possibly diminutive of **Dorotea** (Gk. "Gift of God"). Actress Téa Leoni.

Teague Ir. Gael. "Bard, poet."

Teage, Teigue

Teal Bird name: a kind of duck noted for its dark greenish blue feathers. Also, by extension, a shade of blue.

Teali, Tealle, Teil, Teill, Teille

Tecla Gk. "Fame of God." Traditionally Saint Thecla, converted by Saint Paul, was the first female Christian martyr, but her legend seems to be largely fantastic. The name has been most popular in Greece.

Teccla, Tekla, Tekli, Telca, Telka, Thecla, Thekla

Tehila Heb. "Praise song."

Tehilla

Temira Heb. "Tall."

Temora, Timora

Temperance Puritan virtue name. Temperance is moderate consumption of food and drink: the temperance movement of the late 19th and early 20th centuries went a step further and attempted to ban liquor entirely.

Tempest OF. "Storm." Rare usage is probably a matter of a family name transposed, since few parents wish for a child with a stormy temperament. Actress Tempestt Bledsoe.

Tempesta, Tempeste, Tempestt

Terena (Fem. **Terence**) Roman clan name. Used mostly in the middle of the 20th century.

Tareena, Tarena, Tarina, Tereena, Terenia, Terenne, Terriell, Terriella, Terina, Terrena, Terrene, Terrin, Terrina, Teryl, Teryll, Teryna, Therena

Teresa Popular alternate spelling of **Theresa**. Actress Teresa Wright; basketball player Teresa Weatherspoon.

Techa, Terasa, Terasina, Terasita, Terecena, Teresia, Teresina, Teresita, Tereska, Teresse, Tereza, Terezilya, Terezita, Terosina, Terrie, Terrosina, Terry, Tersa, Tersia, Terushka, Teruska, Tesa, Tesia, Teskia, Tess, Tessa, Tessie, Tessy

Terra May be used as a derivation of the female **Terence** names, or short for **Teresa**, or even as a reference to the earth, which is *terra* in Latin.

Tera, Terah, Terrah, Tiera, Tierra

Terry Dim. **Theresa**. This and other nicknames for Theresa were at their most popular in the middle of the 20th century. Actresses Theresa Russell, Teri Garr.

Terall, Terea, Teree, Tereigh, Terell, Terella, Terelynn, Terelynn, Teri, Terie, Terree, Terreigh, Terrey, Terri, Terrye

Teryl Modern name, either a variant of **Teresa** or combination of **Terry** and **Cheryl**.

Terelyn, Terrall, Terrell, Terrena, Terrene, Terrill, Terryl

Tertia Lat. "Third." Unusual, as most of these number names (**Prima, Secunda**) are. Curiously, **Octavia** (which means "eighth") is the only one that has taken on a life of its own.

Tercia, Tersia, Tersha

Tesla Name of a rock band, and before that, of a pioneer electrical engineer named Nikolai Tesla.
Tessla

Tessa Dim. **Theresa**. Some sources also suggest Gk. "Fourth child." Pretty, simple, and uncommon. Thomas Hardy's famous novel, *Tess of the d'Urbervilles,* is widely read in English literature classes.
Tess, Tessie, Tessy, Teza

Texana Modern name, possibly respelling of **Rexana** or homage to the state of Texas.
Texanna

Thaddea (Fem. **Thaddeus**) Gk., meaning unsure: "Brave" is one possibility.
Tada, Tadda, Taddie, Thada, Thadda, Thadée, Thaddie

Thaïs Ancient Greek name, meaning unknown. There was a famous Athenian courtesan named Thaĩs who traveled with Alexander the Great. Some stories add that she then went to Egypt and became the mistress of the reigning Ptolemy. Massénet based an 1894 opera on her story.
Tais, Taisa, Taisse, Thaisa

Thalassa Gk. "Sea, ocean."
Talassa

Thalia Gk. "Blooming, in flower." In Greek legend Thalia is one of the Three Graces (along with Aglaia and Euphosyne); she is also one of the nine Muses, daughters of Zeus and Mnemosyne, each of whom represents an art or a science. Thalia represents Comedy.
Talia, Talie, Talley, Tally, Thaleia, Thalie, Thalya

Thana Arab. "Thanksgiving."

Thea Gk. "Goddess." Also Dim. **Dorothea** (Gk. "Gift of God"). Actress Téa Leoni.
Tea, Theia, Thia

Theda Possibly diminutive of **Theodosia**, or derived from Old German, "People." Reminiscent of exotic silent film star Theda Bara.
Theida, Thida, Theta

Thelma Gk. "Will." Literary name coined in the late 19th century, at its peak in the first third of this century. It has the aura of a bygone era, but not so bygone that it is attractive to modern parents. Even the great success of the film "Thelma and Louise" didn't do much to make it popular.

Telma, Thellma

Themis Greek mythology name: Themis is the goddess of justice who is so often depicted on our civic buildings as a majestic female with a pair of scales to weigh the fate of mortals.

Temis, Temiss, Themiss

Theodora Gk. "Gift of God." Much less common than its synonym, **Dorothy**. At its peak in the middle third of the 20th century, but never a standard. Actress/vamp Theda Bara.

Dora, Fedora, Feodora, Fyodora, Teddey, Teddie, Tedra, Teodora, Teodory, Theadora, Theda, Theo, Theodosia, Todora

Theodosia Gk. "Gift of God." Little-used variant given some prominence by Anya Seton's 1941 historical novel *My Theodosia,* about Aaron Burr's daughter.

Docia, Dosia, Feodosia, Theda, Teodosia, Tossa, Tossia

Theone Gk. "Name of God." Costume designer Theoni V. Aldredge.

Teone, Teoni, Theoni

Theophania Gk. "God's appearance." Immensely popular in its contracted modern form, **Tiffany**, but almost unheard of in this full version.

Theofania, Theophanie, Teofanie, Teophania, Teophanie

Theophila Gk. "God-loving." The masculine form, **Theophilus**, is slightly less rare.

Teofila, Teophile, Teophila, Theofila

Theresa Gk. "Harvest." May also stem from a Greek place name. The name owes its popularity to two important Catholic saints, the astringent, intellectual mystic St.Teresa of Avila, and the humble young nun, St.Thérèse of Lisieux. It seems to have spread from Catholic families to wider acceptance, and was especially common in the 1960s. Actresses Theresa Russell, Teresa Wright, Teri

Garr; humanitarian Mother Teresa; basketball player Theresa Edwards.

Resi, Rezi, Rezka, Taresa, Tera, Terasa, Teresa, Terese, Teresia, Teresina, Teresita, Teressa, Tereza, Terezinha, Terezsa, Teri, Terrasa, Terresa, Terresia, Terri, Terrosina, Terry, Terrya, Tersa, Tersina, Tersita, Terza, Tess, Tessa, Tessey, Tessi, Tessie, Tessy, Thérèse, Theresina, Theresita, Theressa, Tracey, Tracie, Tracy, Treesa, Tresa, Tressa, Trescha, Treza, Zita

Therma Possibly a compound name, combining the first syllable of **Theresa** with the end of **Irma**. May also refer to warmth, since *therme* is the Greek word for heat.

Thermia

Thisbe Greek name from mythology. Ovid's *Metamorphoses* tells the tragic tale of the lovers Pyramus and Thisbe, which is reprised in Shakespeare's *A Midsummer Night's Dream.*

Thomasina (Fem. **Thomas**) Heb. "Twin." **Thomasin** was the earliest form, replaced by Thomasina in the Victorian era, and **Tamsin** a hundred years later. Now quite scarce.

Tammi, Tammie, Thomasa, Thomasin, Thomasine, Thomazine, Toma, Tomasina, Tomasine, Tomina, Tommie, Tommy

Thora Scand. "Thor's struggle." Thor is the Norse god of thunder. Actress Thora Birch.

Thordia, Thordis, Thyra, Tyra

Thurayya Arab. "Star." Actually refers to the Pleiades.

Soraya, Surayya, Surayyah, Thuraia

Tia Sp. "Aunt." Probably used as a first name with little reference to its actual meaning, but fondness for its sound. Actress Tia Carrere.

Thia, Tiana, Tiara

Tiara Lat. "Coronet, jeweled headband." Pretty-sounding name for a very attractive object. A small, potently scented gardenia known as "tiaré" grows in the Pacific islands.

Teara, Tiarra

Tiberia Lat. Place name: The river Tiber flows through Rome, and Tiberius was a Roman clan name.

Tibbie, Tibby, Tyberia

Tierney Ir. Gael. "Lord." Unusual as a last name, though Gene Tierney's fame has made it familiar. Has potential as a girl's first name, if the unisex trend continues.
Tiernan, Tierneigh, Tiernie

Tierra Sp. "Land." In keeping with the current trend toward geography names, and rhyming with the rather more popular **Sierra**, this name is unusual but not outlandish.

Tifara Heb. "Splendor, brilliance, beauty."
Tiferet

Tiffany Gk. "God's appearance." Literally, **Theophania**. Traditionally used for babies born on Epiphany, the day when the Three Kings first saw the Christ Child. Now associated with Tiffany & Co., the New York City jeweler. The name has become shorthand for upper-class luxury, and was hugely popular in the 1980s. By 1990 it was sliding down the list of popularity, out of the top 20, but Donald Trump still named his baby with Marla Maples Tiffany. Likely to fade even further as the bulk of Tiffanys reach childbearing age themselves. Actress Tiffani Thiessen.
Theophanie, Tifara, Tifonnie, Tiffaney, Tiffani, Tiffanie, Tiffeny, Tiffenie, Tiffie, Tiffney, Tiffy, Tiphanie, Tiphara, Tiphenie, Tipheny, Tyffany, Tyffenie

Tigris Ir. Gael. From Lat. "Tiger." According to legend, St. Patrick had a sister named Tigris. It is also the name of a significant river that runs through Iraq.

Tikva Heb. "Hope."
Tikvah

Tilda Dim. **Matilda** (OG. "Battle-mighty"). Actress Tilda Swinton.
Thilda, Thilde, Tildie, Tildy, Tilley, Tillie, Tilly

Timothea (Fem. **Timothy**) Gk. "Honoring God." Uncommon feminization of a well-established boy's name.
Thea, Timaula, Timmey, Timmi, Timmie, Timotheya

Tina Dim. **Christina**, etc. Used in the 20th century, but especially popular in the 1960s. Rock star Tina Turner; actress Tina Louise; playwright Tina Howe; basketball player Tina Thompson.
Teena, Teenie, Teina, Tena, Tine, Tiny

Tirion Welsh "Kindly, gentle."

Tirian, Tirien, Tirrian, Tirrien, Tiryan, Tiryon

Tirza Heb. "Pleasantness." Although many versions of the name exist, it is rarely used in modern times. It is one of the few Old Testament female names that was not used widely in the Puritan era.

Thersa, Thirsa, Thirza, Thirzah, Thursa, Thurza, Tierza, Tirzah, Tyrzah

Tisa Invented name: probably **Lisa** with an initial "T."

Tita Probably derived from Spanish diminutives like **Martita**; may be considered a feminization of **Titus** (or **Tito**).

Teeta, Tyta

Titania Gk. "Giant." The Titans in Greek myth were a race of giants. A more familiar use of the name, though, is the Queen of the Fairies in Shakespeare's *A Midsummer Night's Dream*. Easily confused with the more familiar **Tatiana**.

Tania, Tita, Titaniya, Titanya, Tiziana

Tivian Invented name: **Vivian** with a "T." Unusual.

Tivyan, Tyvyan

Toby Heb. "God is good." More commonly a boy's name, used from time to time for girls.

Taube, Taubey, Taubie, Thobey, Thobie, Thoby, Tobe, Tobee, Tobey, Tobi, Tobiah, Tova, Tovah, Tove

Toni Dim. **Antoinette** (Lat. "Beyond price, invaluable"). Unusual in this era of full-length first names. Author Toni Morrison; actress Toni Colette.

Toinette, Toinon, Tola, Tona, Tonee, Toney, Tonia, Tonie, Tonina, Tony, Tonya, Twanette

Topaz Lat. Jewel name. Less common than **Ruby** or **Pearl**, but a good candidate for a November baby (it is that month's birthstone) or for a baby with topaz (golden) coloring.

Tori Dim. **Victoria** (Lat. "Victory"). Actresses Tori Spelling, Tori Amos.

Torey, Toria, Torie, Torrey, Torrye, Tory

Tosca It. "From Tuscany."

Tosha Slavic. Var. **Antoinette** (Lat. "Beyond price, invaluable").

Toshka, Tosia, Tosiya, Toskia

Tossa Dim. **Theodosia** (Gk. "Gift of God").

Tova Heb. "Good." Actress Tovah Feldshuh.

Tovah

Toya Modern U.S. name, perhaps a diminutive of **Latoya**, one of the most popular "La-" names. It has no particular meaning.

Toia

Tracy Dim. **Theresa** (Gk. "Harvest"). First used in numbers in the 1940s, probably in response to the film *The Philadelphia Story* whose main character is named Tracy Lord. This touched off a long period of popularity that is now distinctly fading. Actress Tracey Ullman; tennis player Tracy Austin; singer Tracy Chapman; swimmer Tracy Caulkins.

Trace, Tracee, Tracey, Traci, Tracie, Trasey, Treacy, Treasa, Treasey, Treasa

Tranquilina Sp. from Lat. "Calm, peaceful."

Tranquila, Tranquilinia

Traviata It. "One who goes astray." As in the great Verdi opera, *La Truviata*.

Trea Modern name possibly related to the Latin term for "third" (*tertia*). The name **Trey** is scantily used for boys.

Treia, Treya

Treasure The word as name, of the same school of thought as **Precious**. What all doting parents feel their babies to be.

Tesora, Trésor

Trelane Possibly an invented name, following the pattern of **Delaney** (Ir. Gael., "Offspring of the challenger").

Tralaine, Trelaine, Trelaney

Treva Fem. **Trevor** (Welsh. "Large homestead").

Trevia, Trevina

Tricia Dim. **Patricia** (Lat. "Aristocratic"). Choreographer Trisha Brown.

Treasha, Trichia, Tris, Trisa, Trish, Trisha, Trisia, Trissina

Trilby Literary name coined at the turn of the 20th century. Trilby, the central character of the eponymous novel and play, became a great singer. (The name may refer to vocal trills.) A trilby hat, worn by the character in the 1895 stage production, is a soft felt hat with a dented crown.

Trilbea, Trilbee, Trilbeigh, Trilbey, Trilbie, Trillby

Trina Dim. **Katrina** (Gk. "Pure").

Treena, Treina, Trine, Trinette, Trinnette

Trinity Lat. "Triad." Refers to the Holy Trinity, the three forms of God in the Christian faith. Used mostly among Spanish-speaking families. Actress Trini Alvarado.

Trini, Trinidad, Trinidade, Trinita, Trinitee, Trinitey

Trista Lat. "Sad." An inauspicious name for a baby, however pretty it sounds. A 2002 reality show called "The Bachelorette" featured a woman named Trista Rehn.

Tristana Fem. **Tristan** (Welsh. Meaning unknown). In the medieval legends Tristan is a knight, in love with Isolde, the wife of his uncle. The tale has been told in many forms, including an epic poem by Tennyson and an opera by Wagner.

Tristen, Tristenna

Trixie Dim. **Beatrice** (Lat. "Bringer of gladness").

Trix, Trixee, Trixy

Trudy Dim. **Gertrude** (OG. "Strength of a spear"). Cropped up in the middle of the 20th century, but little heard now.

Truda, Trude, Trudey, Trudi, Trudie, Trudye

Truth Concept as name. Akin to the Puritan virtue names but quite scantily used.

Truly, a variant, turns up occasionally as a first or last name. Civil rights activist Sojourner Truth.

Truley, Truly

Tryphena Gk. "Delicacy." Mentioned in one of Paul's epistles to the Romans. Very scarce.

Trifena, Triphena, Tryphana, Tryphaena, Tryphenia

Tsifira Heb. "Crown, diadem."

Tsila Heb. "Shade."

Tzelya, Tsilah, Tzila, Tzilah, Tzili

Tuesday OE. Day of the week. Given exposure by actress Tuesday Weld, but not in general use.

Tuesdee

MR. SMITH AND MR. LI

Over one-third of the immense population of China shares five last names: Wang, Chen, Liu, Zhang, and Li. Nearly half of the people in South Korea share three names: Lee, Kim, and Park. In Scandinavia, so many citizens share names ending in "-sen" or "-son" that the government encourages them to choose new last names to minimize confusion.

In the United States, things are very different. A 1990 Census listed close to 89,000 last names, as unusual as Abigantus, Malafronte, and Turtle. But one cliche turns out to be accurate: The most common last name is still Smith. (Followed by Johnson, Williams, Jones, and Brown.)

Tully Ir. Gael. "Powerful people."

Tulia Sp. from Lat. "Bound for glory."
   Toolia, Toulia, Toolya, Toulya, Tula, Tulla, Tulya

Tundra Geography name: an arctic plain with permanently frozen subsoil. Most likely to be used by well-traveled parents who have actually seen the tundra—or by parents who simply like the way the name sounds.
   Tunndra

Turkessa Modern name, probably related to the color turquoise. That word is French for "from Turkey," and the color originally got its name from the opaque blue-green stones mined in Turkestan and Persia.
   Turquessa, Turkissa, Turkwessa, Turquissa

Twyla Modern name of uncertain meaning and derivation. Some sources suggest it may be related to twilight, others to the French word for star, *étoile,* while others still suggest a relationship to the manufacture of twill, a kind of fabric. Choreographer Twyla Tharp.
   Tuwyla, Twila, Twilla

Tyler Occupational name: "Maker of tiles." The name of one of the country's less memorable president's (John

Tyler, 1841–1845). Very unusual as a girl's name, but one of the country's top ten for boys in the mid-1990s.

Tyller

Tyra Var. **Thora** (Scand. "Thor's struggle.") Model Tyra Banks.

Thyra, Tyria

Tzefira Var. **Zephyr** (Gk. "West wind").

Zefira

Tzipporah Var. **Zippora** (Heb. "Bird"). Zipporah was the wife of Moses. Despite its Biblical prominence, the name is not popular.

Tzipora, Tzippora, Zipporah

Tzigane Hung. "Gypsy."

Tsigana, Tsigane

Uberta It. Var. **Huberta** (OG. "Bright or shining intellect").

Uberrta, Ubertha, Yuberta

Udele OE. "Wealthy."

Uda, Udella, Udelle, Yewdelle, Yudella, Yudelle

Ula Celt. "Gem of the sea."

Eula, Ulla, Ulli, Yulla

Ulani Haw. "Cheerful."

Ulima Arab. "Astute, wise."

Uleema, Ulima, Ullima

Ulla ONorse. "Will, determination." Also possibly short for Ulrica.

Oula, Ula

Ulrica (Fem. **Ulric**) OG. "Power of the wolf" or "Power of the home." Very unusual outside of Germany.

Rieka, Rica, Ricka, Uhlrike, Ulka, Ullrica, Ullricka, Ulrika, Ulrike, Uulrica

Ultima Lat. "End, farthest point." In English, hard to dissociate from "ultimate."

Ulltima, Ultimata

Ulva OG. "Wolf."

Uma Sanskrit. "Flax or turmeric." Uma is also the name of the Indian goddess Sakti, in her guise as light, and is a Hebrew name meaning "nation." For all the fame of actress Uma Thurman, the name may be too exotic for widespread use.
Ooma

Umnia Arab. "Desire, longing."
Umniah, Umniya, Umniyah

Una Lat. "One." The origin of the name may be Irish, though its Celtic meaning is lost. Very unusual. In Edmund Spenser's 16th century epic poem *The Faerie Queen*, the heroine of the first book is Una. She is the personification of truth and unity.
Euna, Oona, Oonagh, Unah

Undine Lat. "Little wave." In myth, Undine is the spirit of the waters. Edith Wharton created a character in *The Custom of the Country* who was named Undine for the hair-curling (or "waving") tonic that had made her father rich.
Ondina, Ondine, Undeen, Undone, Undina

Unice Var. **Eunice** (Gk. "Victorious").
Uniss

Unique Adjective used as first name. Every child is, of course, unique, and perhaps no one feels that more intensely than parents of a newborn.
Uniqua

Unity ME. "Oneness." Used by the Puritans and extremely uncommon. Most people have heard of it only in connection with Unity Mitford, one of the famous English Mitford sisters.
Unita, Unite, Unitey

Urania Gk. "Heavenly." Urania was one of the Greek Muses, the nine daughters of Zeus and Mnemosyne identified with particular arts and sciences. Urania was in charge of astronomy. The seventh planet away from the sun, discovered in 1781, is called "Uranus" after the Greek sky god, however, not after the muse.
Ourania, Ouranie, Urainia, Uraniya, Uranya

Urbana Lat. "Of the city." The male form, **Urban**, is a bit more familiar, having been used by eight popes. In the U.S. the name is likely to be associated with the town where the University of Illinois is located.

Urbanna

Uriela Heb. "God's light." An appropriate name for girls born during Hannukah.

Uriella, Uriyella

Urit Heb. "Brightness."

Urena, Urina, Uriya, Urith

Ursula Lat. "Little female bear." Saint Ursula was a much-venerated virgin martyr, allegedly executed by Attila the Hun, though her story has little basis in fact. The name was most popular in the 17th century. Fans of Disney cartoons will be bound to associate it with the overweight octopus sea-witch in *The Little Mermaid*. Author Ursula K. Le Guin; actress Ursula Andress.

Orsa, Orsala, Orsola, Orsolla, Seula, Sula, Ulla, Ursa, Ursala, Urselina, Ursella, Ursie, Ursley, Ursola, Ursule, Ursulette, Ursulina, Ursuline, Ursy, Urszula, Urszuli

Uta Origin unclear: possibly Dim. **Otthild** (OG. "Prospers in battle"). Actress Uta Hagen.

Ute, Utte, Yuta

Val Dim. **Valentina, Valerie**. Occasionally an independent name.
Vala OG. "Singled out."
Valla

Valda (Fem. **Waldemar**) OG. "Renowned ruler." Occurs in some Northern European countries, and from time to time in Britain, but very scarce in the U.S.

Vallda, Velda

Valencia Place name: city on the Mediterranean coast of Spain, noted for its oranges.

Valentina Lat. "Strong." This name and **Valerie** come from the same Latin root. **Valentia** was the earliest form, but it entered the modern age as Valentina. **Valentine** is used for both boys and girls (the former more frequently in Britain), and the early Christian martyr for whom the holiday is named was male. Cosmonaut Valentina Tereshkova.

Teena, Teina, Tena, Tina, Val, Vale, Valeda, Valena, Valencia, Valenteen, Valenteena, Valentia, Valentijn, Valentine, Valenzia, Valera, Valida, Valina, Valja, Vallatina, Valli, Vallie, Vally, Velora

Valera Name of a famous Irish statesman, Eamon de Valera, who was born in New York of a Spanish father and an Irish mother. He was very active in the process that ultimately ended in the formation of the Irish Republic.

Valerie Lat. "Strong." The French form of an early Christian name (**Valeria**) that was revived at the turn of the 20th century. It was very popular in the middle of the 20th century, less so now. Actresses Valerie Harper, Valerie Bertinelli, Valerie Perrine.

Val, Valaree, Valarey, Valaria, Valarie, Vale, Valeree, Valeria, Valeriana, Valory, Valerye, Valka, Vallarie, Valleree, Vallerie, Vallery, Vallie, Vallorey, Vallorie, Vallory, Valorie, Vallrie, Valry, Valka

Valeska (Fem. **Vladislav**) Old Slavic. "Splendid leader."

Valetta Place name: principal city on the Mediterranean island of Malta. Also, and more likely, a modern name made up of the popular "Val-" element with the feminine diminutive "-etta" ending.

Valeda, Valeta, Valletta

Valkyrie Scandinavian mythology figures: the attendants of Odin, who conduct the heroes slain in battle to the feasting hall in Valhalla. The Valkyrie fight with each other for pleasure, but their wounds magically heal each day.

Valkyria, Valkyrria, Vallkyrie

Valley Geography name: a low spot in a landscape. Well adapted to first name use because of the "-ey" ending which is usually interpreted as feminine. Could also be construed as a diminute for **Valerie**.

Vallee, Vallia, Vallie

Vallombrosa It. "Shady valley." The name of a forest resort southeast of Florence in Italy, famous for the Benedictine monastery sited there. A name for Italophile parents.

Valombrosa

Valonia Lat. Place name: "Shallow valley."

Vallonia, Valonya

Valora Lat. "Courageous." From the same root that gives us "valor."

Vallora, Valoria, Valorie, Valory, Valorya, Valoura, Valouria

Vanda Var. **Wanda**. OG. Tribal name. Mostly used at the turn of the century.

Vahnda, Vannda, Vohnda, Vonda

Vanessa Literary name, invented by *Gulliver's Travels* author Jonathan Swift. Suddenly leapt into everyday use in the middle years of the 20th century, achieving some popularity in the 1970s, and quite considerable use recently. It is also the name of a genus of butterflies that includes the Red Admiral and the Painted Lady. Actresses Vanessa Redgrave, Vanessa Williams; celebrity Vanna White.

Nessa, Nessie, Nessy, Van, Vanesa, Vanesse, Vanetta, Vannessa, Vannetta, Vania, Vanija, Vanna, Vannie, Vanya, Venesa, Venessa, Venetta, Vinessa, Vonessa, Vonesse, Vonnessa

Vanora Old Welsh. "White wave."

Vannora

Varda Heb. "Rose."

Vardia, Vardice, Vardina, Vardis, Vardit, Vardith

Varina Name of unknown origin, though it may be a respelling of **Verena**. It has strong emotional resonance for Southerners, and Virginians in particular. Varina was the name of one of the earliest Virginia plantations, and also of the wife of Jefferson Davis, hero of the Confederacy.

Verina

Varvara Var. **Barbara** (Gk. "Stranger"). In Greek pronunciation the "V" and "B" sounds are quite close, hence the ties between these names.

Varenka, Varina, Varinka, Varka, Varya, Vava, Vavka

Vashti Per. "Lovely." In the Old Testament, the wife of the proud King Ahasuerus of Persia. Passed over by the Puritans (perhaps because she became a divorcée), but revived very slightly in the 19th century.
Vashtee

Vasilia Fem. **Basil** (Gk. "Royal, kingly"). In languages like Greek and Russian, the "B" and "V" sounds are very similar. This name with the initial "B" was quite common in the Middle Ages.
Vaseelia, Vasilija, Vasiliya, Vasillia, Vasilliya, Vazeelia, Vazeeliya, Vaseelia

Veda Sanskrit. "Knowledge, wisdom." The Vedas are the four sacred books of the Hindus.
Vedis, Veeda, Veida, Veta, Vida

Vedette It. "Sentry, scout." By extension, because a sentry or a scout is often singled out or separated from the group, the French term *vedette* means something (like a headline) that is singled out graphically. And by further extension, in everyday usage, *vedette* is the French word for a movie star.
Vedetta

Vega Arab. "Falling," Swedish from Latin, "Star." Vega is the name of one of the largest and brightest stars.
Vaga, Vaiga, Vayga

Velda Var. Valda.
Vellda

Velika Old Slavic. "Great, wondrous."

Velma Origin disputed. Possibly Dim. **Wilhelmina** (OG. "Will-helmet"), possibly a late 19th-century invention. In general use since the 1920s, but not fashionable.
Vehlma, Vellma

Velvet OF. "Shaggy." The name of the fabric, which has connotations of great luxury and sensuousness.
Vellva, Velva, Velvetta, Velvette, Velveina, Velvina

Venerada Sp. "Venerated."

Venetia Place name. Never reached the stature of that other great Italian tourist mecca, **Florence**. Cropped up from the 17th century onward; use increased in the 19th century, but the name would still be considered a bit fanciful. The English form, **Venice**, is also used occasionally.

Vanecia, Vanetia, Venecia, Venetta, Venezia, Venice, Venise, Venita, Venize, Venitia, Vennice, Vinetia, Vonitia, Vonizia

Venus Name of the Roman goddess of love and beauty. Used in Britain in the 16th century through the 19th, but very scarce now. It creates a lot of expectations for a female baby. Tennis star Venus Williams has endowed the name with some of her own powerful glamor, however.

Venusa, Venusette, Venusina, Venusita

Vera Slavic. "Faith"; Lat. "Truth." Use by two popular novelists in the late 19th century promoted the name to high fashion, but it is hardly found now. Actress Vera Miles; fashion designer Vera Wang.

Veradis, Verasha, Veera, Veira, Vere, Verena, Verene, Verina, Verine, Verinka, Verka, Verla, Verochka, Veroshka, Veruschka, Verushka

Verbena Lat. "Holy plants." Originally referred to olive, laurel, and myrtle, plants with spiritual significance to the Romans. In modern times, a class of plants with medicinal properties and, frequently, pleasant scents.

Verbeena, Verbeina, Verbina, Verbyna

Verdad Sp. "Truth."

Verde Sp. "Green." A descriptive name to commemorate spring, perhaps.

Verda

Verena Lat. "True." Derives from the same root as **Vera.** Primarily English use.

Varena, Varina, Vereena, Verina, Veruchka, Veruschka, Veryna

Verity Lat. "Truth." Puritan virtue name, much less common than **Constance, Prudence, Hope,** etc. Still occurs from time to time in Britain, however.

Veretie, Verety, Verita, Veritie

Verna Lat. "Springtime." Use spans the late years of the 19th century to the middle of the 20th, but the name has a dated air and is rare today. Actress Virna Lisi.

Verda, Verne, Verneta, Vernetta, Vernette, Vernice, Vernie, Vernis, Vernise, Vernisse, Vernlta, Virna

Verona Dim. **Veronica**. Also the name of a northern Italian city well-known to tourists, so it may be used by reminiscent parents.

Varona, Veron, Verone, Verowna

Veronica Lat. "True image." Or Var. **Bernice** (Gk. "She who brings victory"). According to a legend that sprang up in the Middle Ages, a young girl wiped Jesus' sweating brow on his way to Calvary. The handkerchief she used later showed a perfect image of his face. (Three separate Italian churches now claim to own this holy relic.) The name first appeared in Britain in the 17th century, spread beyond Catholic families in the 19th century, and became popular in the 1950s. Possibly reminiscent of the Archie and Veronica comic books. Also, in an age that avoids nicknames, four syllables is awfully long. Actress Veronica Lake.

Rana, Ranna, Roni, Ronica, Ronika, Ronna, Ronnee, Ronni, Ronnica, Ronnie, Ronny, Veera, Veira, Vera, Veranica, Veranique, Verinique, Vernice, Vernicka, Vernika, Verohnica, Verohnicca, Veronice, Veronicka, Veronika, Veronike, Veroniqua, Véronique, Veronka, Veronqua, Vonnie

Vespera Lat. "Evening star." The source of the term "vespers" for an early evening church service.

Vesperina, Vespers

Vesta Lat. The Roman household goddess. Her altar was tended by six virgins (the "vestal virgins"), who were kept under severe discipline. They were buried alive if they lost their virginity. Most common late 19th to early 20th century, when these things still mattered a great deal.

Vevina Ir. Gael. "Sweet lady." This is an anglicization of the Gaelic word that produces the name **Bevan** or **Bevin**.

Vica Hung. from Heb. "Life."

Vicenza Place name: Italian city famous for several architectural features, notably buildings designed by the great Renaissance architect Palladio.

Vicensa, Vicenzia, Vichensa, Vichensia, Vichenza

Vicky Dim. **Victoria**. Author Vicki Baum; actress Vicki Lawrence.

Vicci, Vickee, Vickey, Vicki, Vicky, Vicqui, Vikkey, Vikki, Vikky, Viqui

Victoria (Fem. **Victor**) Lat. "Victory." Extremely common in Christian Rome, but curiously not fashionable during the reign (1837–1901) of the woman who gave her name to the Victorian age. Most recently popular in the 1950s and 1960s, but daughters in those days were probably called "Vicky." Parents who use it now are more likely to insist on the whole mouthful, or **Tori** in a pinch. For the past dozen years, Victoria has hovered in the top 20 percent of American girls' names. Actress Victoria Principal.

Tori, Toria, Torie, Tory, Toya, Vic, Vicci, Vickee, Vickey, Vicki, Vickie, Vicky, Victoriana, Victorie, Victorina, Victorine, Victory, Vika, Vikkey, Vikki, Vikky, Viktoria, Viktorija, Viktorina, Viktorine, Viktorka, Viqui, Vitoria, Vittoria

Vida Dim. **Davita** (Heb. "Loved one") or Sp. "Life."

Veda, Veeda, Vidette, Vieda, Vita, Vitia

Vidonia Port. "Branch of a vine."

Veedonia, Vidonya

Vienna Place name: the capital of Austria, a city known for its music and culture.

Vienne, Viennia

Vigilia Lat. "Wakefulness."

Vigdis Nor. "War goddess."

Vigdess

Vilhelmina Var. **Wilhelmina** (OG. "Will-helmet").

Vilhelmine, Villhelmina, Wilhelmina

Villette Fr. "Small town." The name of one of Charlotte Brontë's lesser-known novels.

Vilma Rus. Dim. **Vilhelmina**.

Wilma

Vina Dim. **Davina, Lavinia**, etc., or Sp. "Vineyard." In either case, probably a name whose use was promoted by the feminine ending "-a." A name parents may choose simply because they like the way it sounds.

Veena, Vena, Veina, Vinetta, Vinette, Vinia, Vinica, Vinita, Vinya, Vyna, Vynetta, Vynette

Vincentia (Fem. **Vincent**) Lat. "Conquering." An unusual feminization of a name that has not been very common in America.

Vicenta, Vicentia, Vincenta, Vincentena, Vincentina, Vincentine, Vincenza, Vincenzia, Vincetta, Vinetta

Vinia Dim. **Lavinia** (Lat. "Woman of Rome"). Used as an independent name.

Veenia, Veenya, Venia, Vinya

Violante Gk./Lat. "Purple flower." This may be considered the root of **Yolanda**.

Violanthe

Violet Lat. "Purple." A flower name in longer use than most. Occurred first in the 1830s and lasted nearly a hundred years, but always more popular in Britain (whose cool, damp climate is more hospitable to the spring flowers). **Viola** has been a less-used choice. Ballerina Violette Verdy.

Eolande, Iolande, Iolanthe, Jolanda, Jolande, Jolanta, Jolantha, Jolanthe, Vi, Viola, Violaine, Violanta, Violante, Violanthe, Viole, Violeine, Violetta, Violette, Viollet, Violletta, Viollette, Vyolet, Vyoletta, Vyolette, Yolanda, Yolande, Yolane, Yolantha, Yolanthe

Virginia Lat. "Virgin." The name probably derives from a Roman clan name, but the current meaning has been assumed for hundreds of years. A great favorite in the U.S. from the mid 19th century to the mid 20th; the first child born in the U.S. was Virginia Dare, in 1597. The state of Virginia was named in compliment to the Virgin Queen, Elizabeth I. A good candidate for 21st century revival, though it is currently quite scarce. Author Virginia Woolf; tennis player Virginia Wade.

Geena, Geenia, Geenya, Genia, Genya, Gigi, Gina, Ginella, Ginelle, Ginger, Gingia, Ginia, Ginnee, Ginni, Ginnie, Ginny, Ginya, Jenell, Jenella, Jenelle, Jinia, Jinjer, Jinnie, Jinny, Verginia, Verginya, Virge, Virgenya, Virgie, Virgine, Virginie, Virginnia, Virgy

Viridis Lat. "Green."

Virdis, Viridia, Viridian, Viridiana, Viridianna, Viridi-anne

Virtue Lat. "Strength." The original virtue name. In this case, virtue means strength to resist sin, though originally there was probably some connotation of manliness (the Latin *vir* means "man").

Visitacion Sp. From Lat. "Visitation." Refers to the visit the pregnant Mary paid to her cousin Elizabeth on July 2, according to the New Testament.

Vita Lat. "Life." Also occasionally a nickname for **Victoria**, as in the case of English writer Vita Sackville-West.
Veeta, Vitel, Vitella, Vitka

Viveca Scan. "Alive." Var. **Viva.** Actresses Viveca Lindfors, Vivica Fox.
Vivecka, Viveka, Vivica, Vivika

Viva Lat. "Alive." Most familiar from the expression meaning "Long live . . ." as in *"Viva l'Espana"* or *"Vive la France."* Actress Viva.
Veeva, Viveca, Vivva

Vivian Lat. "Full of life." Used for boys in Britain (although infrequently), generally for girls in the U.S. In spite of the early martyr Saint Vivian, the name has been current only since the 19th century, and has never been a real favorite. Actresses Vivien Leigh, Vivian Vance.
Bibi, Bibiana, Bibiane, Bibianna, Bibianne, Bibyana, Vevay, Vi, Vibiana, Viv, Vivee, Vivi, Vivia, Viviana, Viviane, Vivianna, Vivianne, Vivie, Vivien, Vivienne, Vivyan, Vivyana, Vivyanne, Vyvyan, Vyvyana, Vyvyanne

Volusia Place name: county in Florida.

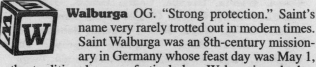

Walburga OG. "Strong protection." Saint's name very rarely trotted out in modern times. Saint Walburga was an 8th-century missionary in Germany whose feast day was May 1, the traditional pagan festival day. Walpurgisnacht has come down in legend as the night of the witches' sabbath.

Walberga, Wallburga, Walpurgis

Walda (Fem. **Waldo**) OG. "Ruler." Extremely unusual feminization of a name that is also unusual for boys.

Waldena, Waldette, Waldina, Wallda, Welda, Wellda

Walker OE. Occupational name: "Cloth-walker." The era that saw the rise of last names was also the great English era of the wool trade, giving us such cloth-manufacturing names as **Fuller, Tailor**, and **Weaver**. In that medieval era, workers trod on the wool to clean it. This name is very unusual for girls.

Wallker

Walkiria Var. **Valkyrie**, German mythological name.

Wallis Var. **Wallace** (OE. "From Wales"). Famous as a feminine name because of Wallis Simpson, the woman who very badly wanted to be queen of England, but became Duchess of Windsor instead.

Walless, Wallie, Walliss, Wally, Wallys

Waltrina Fem. **Walter** (OG. "People of power").

Walteena, Walterine, Waltina

Wanda Probably a Slavic tribal name, though some sources suggest OG. "Wanderer." Use has been pretty well confined to the middle of the 20th century. Harpsichordist Wanda Landowska.

Vanda, Walnnda, Wandah, Wandie, Wandis, Wandy, Wannda, Wenda, Wendaline, Wendall, Wendeline, Wendy, Wohnda, Wonda, Wonnda

Wanetta OE. "Pale-skinned." From the same root that gives us "wan," which is not exactly a complimentary term. In the U.S. this name is more likely a phonetic spelling or variant of **Juanita**.

Waneta, Wanette, Wanita

Warda (Fem. **Ward**) OG. "Guardian."

Wardia, Wardine

Warna (Fem. **Warner**) OG. "Fighting defender."

Waverly OE. Place name: "Meadow of quivering aspens." Pretty sound, pretty meaning; good potential for a crossover boy/girl name.

Waverley

Wendell OG. "Wanderer." Probably acceptable as a girl's

name because of its resemblance to the familiar **Wendy**.

Wendaline, Wendall, Wendelle

Wendy Literary name: coined by James Barrie for the human heroine of *Peter Pan*. The parents who used it in great numbers in the middle of the 20th century may have been inspired by either the musical play or the animated movie. Some, wishing to call a daughter Wendy, no doubt named her **Gwendolyn**, but the names aren't actually related. It is very rarely used today. Ballerina Wendy Whelan; playwright Wendy Wasserstein; actress Dame Wendy Hiller.

Wenda, Wendaline, Wendee, Wendeline, Wendey, Wendi, Wendie, Wendye, Windy

Weslia Fem. **Wesley** (OE. "Western meadow"). Usually used in honor of John and Charles Wesley, who founded the Methodist church in the 18th century.

Wesleya, Weslie

Whitley OE Place name: "White meadow." Related to other "-ley" names like **Ashley**, as well as to **Whitney**.

Whitelea, Whitlea, Whittley

Whitney OE. Place name: "White island." Boy's name that became hugely popular for girls in the early 1980s, possibly because of its connotations of old wealth. It was sliding out of the top 100 names by the early 1990s and is now almost an oddity. Singer Whitney Houston.

Whitnea, Whitneigh, Whiteney, Whitnee, Whitni, Whitnie, Whitny, Whittaney, Whittany, Whittney, Whittnie

Wibeke Ger. Var. **Viveca** (Scand. "Alive").

Vibeke, Wiebke, Wiweca

Wilda OE. "Willow" or OG. "Untamed."

Willda, Wylda

Wilfreda Fem. **Wilfred** (OE. "Purposeful peace"). Unusual feminization of a rarely used name.

Wilfridda, Wilfrieda

Wilhelmina OG. "Will-helmet." Despite the number of variants spawned by the name, it hasn't been very popular in any form. Probably used more often to honor a beloved relative named **William** rather than on its own merits. Actress Billie Burke; author Willa Cather.

Billa, Billee, Billey, Billie, Billy, Ellma, Elma, Guglielma, Guillelmina, Guillelmine, Guillema, Guillemette, Guillemine, Helma, Helmina, Helmine, Helminette, Min, Mina, Minna, Minnie, Minny, Valma, Velma, Vilhelmina, Villhelmina, Villhelmine, Vilma, Wileen, Wilene, Wilhelmine, Willa, Willabella, Willabelle, Willamina, Willamine, Willeen, Willene, Willemina, Willetta, Willette, Williamina, Willie, Williebelle, Wilmette, Willmina, Willmine, Willy, Willybella, Wilma, Wilmette, Wilmina, Wilna, Wylma

Willow Tree name. A phenomenon of the 1970s. TV reporter Willow Bay.

Wilma Dim. **Wilhelmina**. Less of a mouthful than its source, but reminiscent of the dizzy Stone Age housewife Wilma Flintstone in the TV cartoon show *The Flintstones*. Track star Wilma Rudolph.

Valma, Vilma, Willma, Wilmina, Wylma

Wilmot OE. Last or diminutive name related to **William**, **Wilhelmina**, etc.

Wilmotina, Wilmott

Wilona OE. "Longed-for."

Wilone

Winifred Welsh. "Holy peacemaking." Also often explained as Old German "Friend of peace." Popular in Britain for fifty years around the turn of the 20th century, but little used otherwise.

Fred, Freddie, Freddy, Fredi, Fredy, Wina, Winafred, Winefred, Winefride, Winefried, Winfreda, Winfrieda, Winifryd, Winne, Winnie, Winnifred, Wynafred, Wynifred, Wynn, Wynne, Wynnifred

Winola OG. "Charming friend."

Winona Sioux Indian. "Firstborn daughter." This is one of the very few Native American names that has achieved wide usage among European-American families, probably because it was popularized by poets such as Henry Wadsworth Longfellow. Actress Winona Ryder; country singer Wynonna Judd.

Wenona, Wenonah, Winnie, Winnona, Winoena, Winonah, Wynnona, Wynona, Wynnona

Winsome OE. "Agreeable, light-hearted."
 Wynsome

Winter OE. Season name. Like **Summer**, used mostly in the 1970s.
 Wintar

Wisdom English: virtue name. Exceedingly rare.

Wistar Ger. last name of uncertain meaning. Used with pride as a first name among Philadelphia families: Caspar Wistar was a very prominent doctor in late 18th century Philadelphia, and taught at what became the University of Pennsylvania. An earlier Caspar Wistar (in all likelihood the doctor's father) founded a thriving glass factory in Southern New Jersey in the 1740s.
 Wistarr, Wister

Wisteria Flower name: vine with cascading purple-blue blossoms. Named for the 18th-century Philadelphia physician, Caspar Wistar.
 Wistaria

Wren OE. Bird name: A wren is a small brown songbird.

Wyanet Native American. "Beautiful."
 Wyanetta, Wyonet, Wyonetta

Wyetta Fem. **Wyatt** (OF. "Small fighter").
 Wyette

Wynne Welsh. "Fair, pure." Uncommon, simple, but distinctive in a way that may appeal to today's parents.
 Win, Winne, Winnie, Winny, Wyn, Wynn

Wyome Native American. "Wide plain." The name of the state of Wyoming comes from this word. Track star Wyomia Tyus.
 Wyomia, Wyomie

Wynstelle Comb. form **Wynne** (Welsh. "Fair, pure") and **Stella** (Lat. "Star").
 Winstella, Winstelle, Wynstella

Wysandra Comb. form **Wynne** (Welsh. "Fair, pure") and **Sandra** (Gk. "Defender of mankind").
 Wysandria

Xanthe Gk. "Yellow." A description of someone's coloring. Almost unknown.
    Xantha, Xanthia, Zanthe

Xaviera (Fem. **Xavier**) Basque. "New house." Given some exposure by Xaviera Hollander, the author of a book that caused some stir in the early 1970s. It was called *The Happy Hooker*.
    Exaviera, Exavyera, Xavienna, Xavyera, Zaveeyera, Zaviera

Xenia Gk. "Welcoming." Occasionally spelled with the "X"; occurs once in a while with a "Z."
    Xeenia, Xena, Xiomara, Zeena, Zena, Zenia, Zina, Zyna

Ximena Possibly a variant of **Xenia**, or an archaic Spanish form of **Simone**.

Xylia Gk. "Wood-dweller." Related to the far more common **Sylvia**.
    Xylina, Xylona, Zylina

Yaffa Heb. "Lovely."
    Jaffa, Yaffah

Yahaloma Heb. "Diamond."

Yaira Heb. "To illuminate."
    Yeira

Yakira Heb. "Costly, precious."
    Yekara

Yalena Rus. Var. **Helen** (Gk. "Light").
    Yelena, Lenuschka, Lenushka, Lenya, Lenyushka

Yaminah Arab. "Suitable, proper."
    Yamina, Yemina

Yancey Name of unclear origin: possibly a Native American word that, misunderstood by its hearers, resulted in the term "Yankee." Carries a whiff of the West about it courtesy

of Edna Ferber's novel *Cimarron*, whose hero was named Yancey. Rare for boys or girls. Actress Yancey Butler.
Yancee, Yancie, Yancy

Yannick Fr. Var. **John** (Heb. "The Lord is gracious"). This form originates in Brittany, and is used more for boys than for girls in France.
Yanick, Yann, Yannic

Yarina Rus. Var. **Irene** (Gk. "Peace").
Yaryna, Yerina

Yarmilla Slavic. "Trader."

Yarona Heb. "She will rejoice."

Yasmin Arab. "Jasmine." A variation of a flower name that was quite popular in the late eighties and early nineties. Princess Yasmin Aga Khan; model Yasmin Le Bon.
Yasamin, Yasiman, Yasmeen, Yasmeena, Yasmena, Yasmene, Yasmina, Yasminda, Yasmine

Yekaterina Rus. Var. **Katherine** (Gk. "Pure"). Figure skater Yekaterina Gordeeva.
Ekaterina

Yelisabeta Rus. Var. **Elizabeth** (Heb. "Pledged to God").
Yelisabetta, Yelizabet, Yelizavetha

Yerusha Var. **Jerusha** (Heb. "Married, belonging to someone").
Yeruscha

Yesenia Form of **Jesenia**, a popular name in the Hispanic community. Its origin is unclear but its popularity stems from that of a character in a Spanish-language soap opera.
Yasenia, Yazenia, Yesemia, Yessenia, Yessenya

Yessica Var. **Jessica** (Heb. "He sees"). In the early and mid-1990s, Jessica was the most popular American name for girls. This kind of heavy usage often prompts variations in spelling and pronunciation as parents seek a name that is fashionable but a little bit different.
Yesseca, Yessika

Yetta OE. Dim. **Henrietta** (OG. "Ruler of the house"). Used at the turn of the 20th century, but virtually unheard-of now.
Yette

Yeva Rus. Var. **Eve** (Heb. "Life").
Yevka

Ynez Sp. Var. **Agnes** (Gk. "Pure").
Ines, Inez, Ynes, Ynesita

Yoana Var. **Joanna**; Fem. **John** (Heb. "The Lord is gracious").
Yana, Yanna, Yoanah, Yoanna, Yoannah

Yoconda Sp. Var. **Gioconda** (It. "Delight").

Yoko Jap. "Good, positive." Would probably be unknown outside Japanese families without the fame of Beatle wife Yoko Ono.

Yolanda Gk. "Violet flower." The Spanish version of **Violet**. Used in English-speaking countries in the 20th century, particularly during the 1960s.
Eolande, Eolantha, Iola, Iolanda, Iolande, Iolantha, Iolanthe, Jolan, Jolanna, Jolanne, Jolanta, Jolantha, Jolanthe, Yalinda, Yalonda, Yola, Yolaiza, Yoland, Yolande, Yollande, Yolantha, Yolanthe, Yolette, Yolie, Yulanda

Yonina Heb. "Dove."
Jona, Jonati, Jonina, Yona, Yonah, Yonina, Yoninah, Yonit, Yonita

Yordan Var. **Jordan** (Heb. "Descend"). The substitution of "Y" for "J" at the beginning of a name is particularly comfortable for speakers of Spanish, in which the two letters are pronounced similarly.
Yordana, Yordanna

Yoslene Var. **Jocelyn**, derivation unclear. This is an unusual and inventive modern adaptation of a very old name.
Yosleen, Yoslina, Yosline

Yosepha (Fem. **Joseph**) Heb. "Jehovah increases." A possibility for parents who don't like **Josephine**.
Josefa, Josepha, Yosefa, Yuseffa

Ysabel Var. **Elizabeth** (Heb. "Pledged to God") via **Isabel**.
Yabell, Yabella, Yabelle, Ysabell, Ysabella, Ysabelle, Ysbel, Ysbella, Ysobel

Ysanne Modern name, combination of **Ysabel** and **Anne**. Found in Britain.
Ysande, Ysanna

Yudit Heb. "Praise."

   Yehudit, Yudelka, Yudif, Judit, Judith, Yudita, Yuta

Yuliya Rus. Var. **Julia** (Lat. "Youthful").

   Youliya, Yula, Yulenka, Yulinka, Yulka

Yuma Place name: desert and city in Southwestern Arizona.

Yuridiana Probably an invented name, related to the Russian **Yuri** (cognate of **George**).

Yvette Dim. **Yvonne**. Actress Yvette Mimieux.

   Ivett, Ivetta, Ivette, Yevette, Yvedt, Yvetta

Yvonne (Fem. **Ivo**) Fr. from OG. "Yew wood." Since yew wood was used for bows, Ivo may have been an occupational name meaning "archer." The most common male form is probably **Yves**, but Yvonne is more widespread in English-speaking countries. It was particularly popular in Britain in the 1970s. Tennis star Evonne Goolagong; actress Yvonne DeCarlo.

   Eevonne, Evonne, Ivonne, Yevette, Yvetta, Yvette

Zada Arab. "Fortunate, prosperous." Author Zadie Smith.

   Zadie, Zaida, Zayeeda, Zayda

Zahavah Heb. "Gilded."

   Zachava, Zachavah, Zahava, Zechava, Zehavah, Zehavit

Zahira Arab. "Brilliant, shining."

   Zaheera, Zahirah

Zahra Arab. "White," or "Flower." Currently popular in Arabic-speaking countries.

   Zahrah

Zandra Var. **Sandra**; Dim. **Alexandra** (Gk. "Defender of mankind"). Fashion designer Zandra Rhodes.

   Zahndra, Zandie, Zandy, Zanndra, Zohndra, Zondra

Zanna Dim. **Susanna** (Heb. "Lily").

   Zana, Zanne, Zannie

Zara Heb. "Eastern brightness, dawn." May also be a form of **Sarah** (Heb. "Princess"). Literary name used often over the centuries for exotic characters. Taken up in the 1960s in Britain (Princess Anne's daughter is named Zara), but unusual in the U.S.

Zaira, Zarah, Zaria, Zarina, Zarinda, Zayeera

Zarya In Slavic mythology, Zarya is a water priestess and protector of warriors.

Zaria

Zea Lat. "Grain."

Zefira Heb. "Morning."

Zifira

Zelda Dim. **Griselda** (OG. "Gray fighting maid"). The original name has long been eclipsed by this nickname, which was made famous by F. Scott Fitzgerald's glamorous but unstable wife.

Selda, Zelde, Zellda

Zelenia Var. **Selena** (Gk. "Moon goddess").

Zelaina, Zelenya

Zelia Origin unclear; perhaps Gk. "Zeal" or Fr. "Solemn," from a saint's name. Also possibly a variant of **Cecilia** (Lat. "Blind"). Rare.

Zalia, Zailie, Zaylia, Zele, Zelene, Zelie, Zelina, Zeline

Zelma Dim. **Anselma** (OG. "God-helmet"). A less common form than **Selma**.

Zellma

Zena Var. **Xenia** (Gk. "Welcoming"). This is the slightly more common form of the name. Tennis player Zina Garrison.

Zeena, Zeenia, Zeenya, Zenia, Zenya, Zina

Zénaïde Var. **Zenobia**.

Zenaida

Zenobia Gk. "Power of Zeus." A 3rd-century empress of Palmyra, whose name was revived in the 19th century but has a rather quaint sound today.

Cenobia, Cenobie, Zeba, Zeena, Zena, Zenaida, Zénaide, Zenayda, Zenda, Zenina, Zenobie, Zenna

Zephyr Gk. "West wind."

Cefirina, Sefira, Sefarina, Sephira, Tzefira, Tzephira, Tzephyra, Tzifira, Zefeera, Zefir, Zefiryn, Zephira, Zephirine, Zephyra, Zephyrine

Zerlinda Heb./Sp. "Beautiful dawn."
Zerlina
Zetta Heb. "Olive."
Zeta, Zetana
Zia Lat. "Grain."
Zea
Zigana Hung. "Gypsy."
Tsigana, Tsigane, Tzigana, Tzigane, Ziganna
Zilla Heb. "Shadow." Old Testament name revived by the Puritans and again in the 19th century, when it was more popular than one might suppose, given its current obscurity.
Zila, Zillah, Zylla
Zilpha Heb. Meaning unclear. Old Testament name revived in the 18th century and gradually fading ever since. Children's author Zilpha Keatley Snyder.
Zilpah, Zillpha, Zylpha
Zinaida Rus. From Gk. "Belonging to Zeus."
Zena, Zenaida, Zenaide, Zinaide
Zinnia Lat. Flower name. In this case the flower itself was named for its classifier, 18th-century German botanist Johann Zinn.
Zinia, Zinnya, Zinya
Zippora Heb. "Bird." Another Old Testament name; Zipporah was the wife of Moses. This biblical prominence has not translated into great popularity for the name, which sounds to some people like a way to do up a skirt.
Zipora, Ziporah, Zipporah
Zita Gk. "Seeker." Also Dim. **Teresita, Rosita,** etc. The name of the last Hapsburg empress, who was given the name when it was at its most popular, at the turn of the century.
Zeeta, Zyta
Zitomira Slavic. "Renowned life."
Ziva Heb. "Brilliance, brightness."
Zeeva, Ziv
Zivanka Slavic. "Full of life."
Zivka
Zizi Hung. Dim. **Elizabeth** (Heb. "Pledged to God"). Anal-

ogous to the Hungarian diminutive for **Susan, Zsa Zsa**. French singer Zizi Jeanmaire.
ZsiZsi

Zlata Czech/Slavic. "Golden."
Zlatina, Alatinka, Zlatka

Zoe Gk. "Life." Currently popular in Greece, and catching on strongly in English-speaking countries, especially in Britain. Although most people pronounce the final "-e" as a separate syllable, it is occasionally pronounced to rhyme with "toe." A variant, **Zooey**, comes from J.D. Salinger's novel entitled *Frannie and Zooey*—although the character Zooey is actually a young man named Zachery. Actresses Zoe Caldwell, Zooey Deschanel.
Zoee, Zoelie, Zoeline, Zoelle, Zoey, Zoie, Zoya

Zohara Heb. "Light, splendor."
Zahara, Zaharira

Zoila Sp. From Gk. "Full of vigor."
Soila, Soilina, Soilla, Soyla, Zoilina, Zolla, Zoyla

Zola It. "Lump of earth." Like **Zona**, probably used more for its sound than for its meaning. Runner Zola Budd.
Zoela

Zona Lat. "Belt, girdle." The name given to the constellation in Orion's belt. Generally U.S. use.
Zonia

Zora Slavic. "Dawn's light." Author Zora Neale Hurston.
Zorah, Zorana, Zorina, Zorine, Zorra, Zorrah, Zorya

Zoya Rus. Var. **Zoe**.
Zoia, Zoyenka, Zoyya

ZsaZsa Hung. Dim. **Susan** (Heb. "Lily"). Made famous by actress and celebrity Zsa Zsa Gabor.
Zsuzsa, Zsuzsanna

Zsofia Hung. Var. **Sofia** (Gk. "Wisdom").

Zuleika Arab. "Brilliant and lovely." Inseparable from Max Beerbohm's comic heroine in the eponymous novel *Zuleika Dobson*, for the sake of whose love all the undergraduates of Oxford University drown themselves. Not, perhaps, an inspiring example for parents.
Zulaica, Zuleica

Zulma Arab. "Healthy, full of life."
   Zulema, Zuma
Zuni Native American tribe: the Zuni Indians live in New
   Mexico and are known for their beautiful pottery, weav-
   ing, and basketmaking.
Zureidy Sp. From Arab. "Well-spoken, articulate."
   Zoraida, Zuraide, Zureida